ARTIST OF WONDERLAND

Victorian Literature and Culture Series

Jerome J. McGann and Herbert F. Tucker, Editors

ARTIST OF WONDERLAND

THE LIFE, POLITICAL CARTOONS, AND ILLUSTRATIONS OF TENNIEL

FRANKIE MORRIS

UNIVERSITY OF VIRGINIA PRESS
CHARLOTTESVILLE

In memory of my father, Joseph Chaikin (1901–1957)

University of Virginia Press
© 2005 by the Rector and Visitors of the University of Virginia
All rights reserved
Printed in the United States of America on acid-free paper

First published 2005

1 3 5 7 9 8 6 4 2

LIBRARY OF CONGRESS CATALOGING-IN-PUBLICATION DATA

Morris, Frankie.
  Artist of Wonderland : the life, political cartoons, and illustrations of Tenniel /
Frankie Morris.
    p.   cm. — (Victorian literature and culture series)
  Includes bibliographical references and index.
  ISBN 0-8139-2343-3 (cloth : alk. paper)
  1. Tenniel, John, Sir, 1820–1914. 2. Artists—Great Britain—Biography. 3. Wit and
humor, Pictorial. 4. Tenniel, John, Sir, 1820–1914—Criticism and interpretation.
I. Tenniel, John, Sir, 1820–1914. II. Title. III. Series.
N6797.T44M67 2005
741.6'092—dc22

                                                                                2004030406

Illustration credits follow index

Contents

Illustrations

Preface

This work began at a time long past when, banished to the "land of counterpane" by a childhood illness, I received from class and teacher the combined *Alice* books. How elegant the little volume seemed to me with its gold-embossed ivory cover, coated pages, and pale blue ribbon to mark my place. It would be years before I realized that its ninety-two illustrations by John Tenniel might have been better reproduced.

But at that time there was so much to wonder at: the impossibly slender legs of Father William's son and the way his mouth formed a tiny *o*, the grim profile of the Duchess's cook, the way the mask-faced King of the frontispiece came alive in the forty-first picture, and the contrast of the stiff wooden skirts of the chess people with their lively little feet. The strangeness of those books was like a private place to which I returned again and again to imbibe its odd flavor.

Passing over the years, how exciting to learn that the maker of these pictures was not only a political artist but also the chief cartoonist of his age. At first the twenty-three hundred cartoons were enigmas to me, except that here and there I caught glimpses of Queens—both Red and White, swains, and country louts reminiscent of the *Alice*s. But soon certain drawings seemed to form distinct sets. Two of these—my incipient studies of Tenniel's handling of Irish and of working-class issues—eventually appeared in a single chapter of my 1985 dissertation. Other embryonic studies, now incorporated into the last part of this book, were written for the 1991 *Punch* conference in London and the 1994 international Lewis Carroll conference in Winston-Salem. Then an added chapter—the nineteenth—seemed needed to clarify the politics of Tenniel and *Punch*. In these propaganda studies I have tried to present both sides on issues, but it will be no secret that Tenniel's social philosophy is not my own.

The *Alice* chapters evolved separately. Having long avoided the topic (expecting that everything about these books would have been said many times over), I came upon an 1865 engraving in which actors disguised as chess pieces played upon a giant board. Once aware of the everyday Victorian world behind the creatures and scenes of Wonderland, I was assailed by a string of new insights. Ian Anstruther's book on the Eglinton tournament, a Carroll

Society talk on movable books, a chance remark on magic lanterns and dissolving views, a giant advertisement in a London tube station picturing Tenniel's blue Caterpillar—these all played their part.

Like my other investigations, the biographical search yielded discoveries. For example, Tenniel was of a higher social class, was more active in society, and had British roots going further back than many had supposed. Still, this being perfectly compatible with the personality that spoke so clearly from some forty-seven hundred drawings, there were no real surprises.

Finally, there was a last chapter to be written—not the one that appears last in this book, but the fifteenth, "The Grotesque Alice." It is the one most personal to me, for it explores the fascination that began with a happy childhood gift.

I am grateful to the Swann Foundation for Caricature and Cartoon for the financial means to conduct research in London in 1986–87 and to the Ludwig Vogelstein Foundation for making possible my biographical search in England in 1993. Among the many to whom I am indebted are the descendants of Tenniel's relatives and friends, who were generous in sharing with me their collections, letters, and reminiscences. These are Derek Stanley Green and Sally Green, Robert Riviere Calkin, Ian Calkin, Maurice Calkin, David B. Calkin, Ann Richardson, Hineira Amy, Paula Ashton King, W. Tenniel Evans, John Hemming, Jeremy Hemming, and Jeanne Wilkins. Others who have furthered my work by making their collections available to me are the Earl of Eglinton and Winton, Robin de Beaumont, Selwyn H. Goodacre, Simon Houfe, and Catherine and Mark Richards.

First among the many who sent materials, furnished valuable suggestions and information, or eased my access to important depositories is Draper Hill, who has been a loyal supporter and friend from the start. I am also thankful to Richard Bienvenu, Sandor Burstein, Patricia Crown, Canon Ivor Davies, Mark Girouard, Michael Hancher, David Kunzle, Charlie Lovett, Peter Mellini, Lady Delia Millar, Shirley Nicholson, Selma Landen Odom, Leonée Ormond, Charles Press, Alice Prochaska, Peter Stansky, Robert Stewart, Edward Wakeling, John Wilson, Betsy Windisch, Marjana Winterbottom, Christopher Wood, and the late R. G. G. Price. Help in securing and preparing the final artwork was provided by Bob Parson, archivist at Utah State University, and by my friend Mary Donahue.

I am obliged to the many libraries, public record offices, and organizations that aided my research. Special mention must be made of the assistance given by Amanda-Jane Doran, *Punch* archivist; Richard Bowden, archivist of the Marylebone Library; Malcolm Hay, curator of works of art at the Houses of Parliament; and Nigel Roche, St. Bride's Printing Library. And a great debt is owed to those workers at the Logan library, Utah, who have cheerfully borne with my interlibrary loan requests.

Also I am grateful to those who helped with housing during my research—the Penn Club, London; Courtney Cazden, who gave me the freedom of her apartment in Cambridge, Massachusetts; and Teresa Bailey, who provided a home base during my final London research.

Last, my thanks go to my daughter Rachel Morris for her unflagging patience with my computer questions, and to my friends for their faith that this project would one day see completion.

ARTIST OF WONDERLAND

Introduction

In the spring of 1901 an unprecedented event took place in London—an elaborate banquet initiated and attended by Britain's most eminent men to mark the retirement of their loved political artist (see chapter 1). For as far back as most of those present could recall, John Tenniel's weekly cartoons in *Punch* had embodied the thoughts, beliefs, and prejudices of the classes of which they were the elite representatives. Although it had not spurred this occasion, he had also done the delightful pictures for Lewis Carroll's *Alice* books.

Reading the toasts made on that gala evening, the praises and the cheers, one cannot help but think that in celebrating his long career the participants also celebrated his paper, the reign that had ended less than four months earlier, their society, and, in a sense, themselves. Those present had little doubt that the cartoonist's name would be held forever in "honor and esteem."[1] Yet the power that Tenniel exercised has largely vanished from memory; his cartoons are reproduced anonymously, his history is mythicized by a century's accumulation of guesswork, and even his *Alice* contribution is played down.

I have attempted to redress these shortcomings with a biographical sketch and selective essays on Tenniel's drawings. The biography presents those things in Tenniel's life that most affected his work: the social milieus in which he moved, his preferences in literature, his lifelong fascination with all forms of Victorian theater, his love for children. If the narrative after 1850 centers mainly on his friendships with *Punch* colleagues this is because most of the information about those years comes from them. There was a part of Tenniel's life that took place between the completion of his cartoon each Friday evening and the *Punch* dinner on the following Wednesday that is unknown to us, mainly because he wished it so. Surely we should not begrudge his privacy to one who gave so much of himself in his drawings. In the essays on Tenniel's book illustrations the *Alice* pictures take pride of place as they are tours de force and endlessly revelatory about the period. The final essays are studies in propaganda through the political cartoon and focus on some key issues of the period.

Before embarking on these things it may be helpful to consider what it was in his circumstances, his art, and in himself that allowed Tenniel to become so leading a representative of his age to those celebrants of 1901.

A Bully Pulpit

Without *Punch* Tenniel might never have attained such prominence. Founded in 1841, its clever blend of political commentary and domestic humor lent the paper a sort of gemütlichkeit that struck just the right note with its largely middle-class readers. As Richard Altick has pointed out, these classes, then coming into prominence, were eager to see themselves—their biases, foibles, and everyday lives—portrayed in word and picture.[2] Mirroring and sometimes leading public opinion, *Punch* became a decided force, its articles, and particularly its full-page political drawing (the cartoon), studied by ordinary readers and statesmen alike.

The paper was recognized as a national institution, one writer declaring that it was "an acknowledged power in the state," another that it had "made itself a necessity to the people of these islands."[3] It is telling that the statesman Arthur J. Balfour, chairman for the Tenniel dinner, specified early in his toast, "this banquet is to the man who for more than 50 years has been connected with our great comic journal." At times *Punch* seemed almost an arm of government itself.

At Odds with the Very Medium

How great a role did artistry play in Tenniel's success? Surely the main virtue of his sixteenth-century hatching, cross-hatching, outlining—a treatment so conventional that we hardly notice it—is that it does not compete with the message. The only distinctive thing about it is the absolute control with which it was employed, for Tenniel had learned early to draw precisely with sharply pointed pencil and with scarcely an erasure. In this he was like the German artists the Nazarenes, with whom he later studied.

More likely to attract readers was Tenniel's unerring sense of design—that indefinable rightness that makes a drawing satisfying or graceful. Of course, a number of cartoons, as they required only two facing figures, gave little scope for this genius. But countless others were masterfully designed and drew the admiration of such notable critics as John Ruskin and Cosmo Monkhouse.

Most characteristic of Tenniel is the intense particularity of his drawings (see also chapters 11 and 15), something that may have stemmed from the early fencing accident that cost the sight of his right eye. For example, in a 1986 study of vision deficits in artists one sculptor attested that his own narrowed visual field had "created an energy" that enhanced his seeing. The "wonderful memory of observation" to which Tenniel owned was probably related to his monocularism or dependency on the sight of one eye. This is suggested by the experience of two vision-impaired artists, one finding that his narrowed field seemed to activate his inner vision, thus enhancing his visual and spatial memory; and the other—who experienced difficulty in spatial processing—discovering that he had "a photographic memory for things that are flat."[4] While little is known about the effects of vision impairments, and still less about photographic memory, the evidence is suggestive.

Additionally, Tenniel's enhanced recall may have heightened his "view invariant" memory, a type of memory that enables us to recognize persons from angles at which we have not previously seen them. As Tenniel had often to draw a subject from a single photographic source—to "'judge' the full face [from a profile], and *vice versâ*"[5]—this would have been an important ability.

Some find his precise line unsympathetic although singularly apt to its purpose. In 1859 the French writer Hippolyte Taine wrote that *Punch*'s cartoons were as hard and exact as if "drawn by John Bull himself," and in 1914 the *New York World* observed, "There his [Tenniel's] cartoons are, just as England was, a little heavy, but exceedingly reliable, strong and competent." There were cartoonists more aesthetically enterprising, but Tenniel's almost styleless line, "intensely deliberate," proved the more potent weapon.[6]

Others find Tenniel's exactitude disturbing. In Taylor Stoehr's book on Dickens's imagery we read: "The strange impression one gets in looking at the work of Cruikshank or Tenniel, that somehow realism and fantasy have been clamped together in a single style without being integrated, comes from their elaborate use of detail, their strict definition of line, light, shadow, and their careful filling in of background" so that what is conveyed is "strangely at odds with the very medium." While Stoehr had the *Alice* books in mind, some may find Tenniel's political work surreal as well. I don't find it so, perhaps because cartoons so often incarnate things that would be highly grotesque if they were not seen as metaphors. Still, the dignified Earl of Derby as an acrobat in baggy trunks flying head over heels in a cartoon of 1860 or the whiskered statesman John Bright, his plump bare shoulders rising above an elaborate ball gown in one of 1865, may be weird images to today's viewers.[7] This is because they are drawn with Tenniel's usual exactness instead of the comic techniques to which we are now accustomed. From all indications, Victorians—much more inured to the grotesque than we—simply saw these things as amusing. More importantly, Tenniel's precise delineation lent a sort of corporeality to his images, and this allowed them to be reified.

A Great Gentleman

How do we explain Tenniel's ability to inspire the love of his compeers? Here we should cite the chairman's concluding words at the Tenniel banquet: "to us he is the great artist and the great gentleman." When Balfour said this he assuredly knew that the word "gentleman" would be understood in the nineteenth-century sense of a chivalrous gentleman with all that this implied of "simple faith and of high honour."[8] Tenniel had the prescribed traits: courage, modesty, generosity, love of vigorous sport, a cavalier attitude toward money, loyalty, honesty, and simplicity. The last two were key.

Like Thackeray's Colonel Newcome, with whom he was often compared, Tenniel had "got the obstinate habit of telling the truth." This was soon discovered by correspondents who might seek his appraisal of an artist friend's portfolio or send him a badly reproduced "Alice calendar." Honesty permeates his work; after his death the *Athenaeum* remarked, "What made his drawing notable was not its accomplishment, but its extraordinary sincerity." Straightforward himself, he disliked redundancy, pretence, silliness. For example, the overblown national thanksgiving for the Prince of Wales's recovery from typhoid in 1872 irked him, and his obligatory cartoon on this occasion was one of his worst. When, seven years later, the country excessively feted and celebrated the returning soldiers of the Zulu Wars, his cartoon cautioning "Don't Overdo It!" was probably more to his liking.[9]

Often one reads of Tenniel's "sweet and simple nature," his "strong simplicity." For the chivalrous gentleman, character was held to be above intellect (which might be mistrusted as mere cleverness). Although Tenniel was certainly not as simple as Colonel Newcome, neither was he an intellectual. That much may be ascertained from the contents of his library, which held little of a speculative nature. He was inclined to see issues in terms of black and white. This tendency, found by recent psychological studies to be more characteristic of those on the political right, stems from a somewhat low tolerance for ambiguity and complexity.[10] Tenniel's political philosophy, formed early and adhered to all his life, is expressed in his cartoons with an assurance that must have been comforting to readers wanting clear-cut answers. It was one of his great strengths.

The *Athenaeum*, although sparing in its praise, could not help but admire the strong conviction in his work. An 1895 article reads, "we *do* recognize in Sir John's designs prodigious *verve,* a stern and upright purpose . . . and a strong sense of the dignity of his office as a sort of artistic prophet."[11] The desire for unambiguous answers, as the studies also find, may lead to stereotyping and to punitiveness toward outsiders or those who seem to violate cultural norms. This too is found in Tenniel's cartoons.

The Britannia Family

Finally, Tenniel's cartoons provided reassurance. Victorian society lived in fear of a lower-class insurrection and of revolution imported from abroad; its proneness to panic was demonstrated several times during the century. On these fears Tenniel's cartoons would have exerted an ameliorating influence, largely through certain protector figures that appear in about 30 percent of the drawings. Let us call these figures the "Britannia family," to borrow from the cartoonist David Low.[12]

Tenniel did not invent John Bull, Britannia, and the British Lion, although some believed he had. He personated them and, with his view-invariant facility, created them three-dimensionally. This was in marked contrast, say, to the cartoons in *Fun,* where John Bull's face might change from issue to issue.

They watched over the country's welfare, these guardians, aided by their surrogates: Mr. Punch and, less often, Peace or Justice. Quick to recognize valor, spy injustice, exact retribution, extend sympathy, demand a strong defense, they advised statesmen and spoke for the paper's readers. Tenniel recognized their import; on his deathbed—imagining he was looking at other men's drawings—his repeated protest was, *"That's* not Britannia! no lion ever looked like *that!*"[13]

What confidence they exuded. Seaman John Bull steers the wave-washed ship *Britannia* and assures Mr. Punch, "She's threshed through worse!!" Britannia (ironically dubbed "The Unprotected Female") grips the sword of patriotism after having laid waste to all about her. Ever watchful, the Lion leaps at the Bengal Tiger or snarls at the Afghan wolves.[14]

Still, rigorous cartoons alone would have palled. These fierce protectors had variants: a plump and matronly Britannia, her helmet's crest suggested by a row of ruffles; a comic Lion, his tail poking out of a pair of Union Jack swimming trunks. John Bull was shown in many moods. In 1859 Tenniel portrayed him as the symbol of England's volunteer movement, smiling fatuously and guarding the immense national pudding. Some twenty years later Ruskin was still remonstrating, "Is this the final myth of English heroism, into which King Arthur, and St. George, and Britannia, and the British Lion are all collated . . . like four whale cubs combined by boiling?"[15] But what the art critic had missed and what Tenniel well understood was that this ability to treat hallowed institutions lightly showed a confidence more profound than would any number of patriotic tableaux.

Sometimes the guardians voiced the reader's thoughts—his puzzlement, his disapproval—asking "What Next?" during the eastern crisis or rebuking the Liberal and Conservative leaders, "a plague on both your houses."[16] They supported his biases and sustained his righteous pride. But mainly—whether benevolent or stern, comic or lofty—they reassured. Mingling comfortably with Britain's statesmen and drawn as if from life, they might easily be confused with real persons. Who was John Bull? Was he the government? the nation? the reader?—did anyone stop to ask? After a time he was simply himself: bluff, stout hearted, tenacious, choleric at perceived injustice, unintellectual, and somewhat lovable.

Nothing Like It Will Be Seen Again

The leverage exerted by Tenniel's work is attested to by his contemporaries. Worldwide it was felt that his cartoons, "swaying parties and peoples too," had "exercised great influence" on the men and events of his period.[17] This is Tenniel's chief import.

He did not appreciably change the art of cartooning despite some last-century nonsense about his having tamed political art; *Punch*'s cartoons already had a recognizable tone in the forties. Nor was he a markedly Victorian artist in the way that Linley Sambourne or C. H. Bennett was; his "Düreresque pencillings" might belong to several periods. There were copyists in his own time, of course. The closest was John Proctor, who aped Tenniel's types. But no one could mistake another's work for Tenniel's. The spirit would invariably be missing.

Never was an artist more revealed in his work. To painter William Powell Frith he was *"sui generis,"* his style unique. "Nothing like it has ever been seen before," Frith wrote, and "nothing so quaint, so humorous, so completely appreciative of the subject suggested will be seen again." Today, removed from Victorian life by more than a century, we may miss much of Tenniel's humor. But to Britons faced with rising meat prices, the Demon Butcher (a pantomime character) terrifying the little customer with his roar, "Beef? Fourteen Pence a Pound. Ha Ha!" must have seemed funny indeed; and to a public skeptical about Disraeli's Royal Titles Bill, so would Tenniel's picture of the premier, an *Arabian Nights* magician smoothly offering the crown of India to Victoria.[18]

Tenniel did not outlive his fame. He died just months before the start of World War I. After that slaughter the symbols that had glorified its opening days—the goddesses and armored knights that he more than any other had vivified—began to fade from the vocabulary of political cartoons. The world did not want to look back. The "perfunctory" cartoons—the scenes of royal pageantry that Tenniel least enjoyed doing[19]—were held up as typifying his work. In this there is an irony—that Tenniel, a master of the stereotype, should have himself been stereotyped.

The *Athenaeum,* always Tenniel's most penetrating critic, foresaw that he would be remembered "above all, by his illustrations to Lewis Carroll's two famous books"[20]—a prospect that would probably have not pleased Tenniel, for whom book illustrating ran second to his primary career. Still, it was Carroll's stories that most brought out his inventiveness, his puckish humor, his delight in the things of the Victorian world. Here, too, his style—despite the inevitable copyists—was too much his own to be counterfeited or passed on. His pictures, like Carroll's texts, are simply a perpetual gift.

BIOGRAPHICAL SKETCH

Fig. 1. Banquet to Tenniel. (Private collection, U.S.A.)

Toast of the Evening

1901

*I think that if there was any incident in his life that
he would gladly have forgotten, it was that Banquet.*
—F. ANSTEY, *A Long Retrospect*

The Guest

The guest of the evening rises to face the company. It is 12 June 1901,
and the place is the Hôtel Métropole in London. Opened some fifteen years
before, this much-touted establishment lies just north of the government
offices for which its main dining room is named. This Wednesday night in
the Whitehall Rooms long tables traverse the great space from wall to mir-
rored wall. It is a dark room for all its display of tinted glass and crystal and
the gilding that highlights the carved beams and brackets, the pilasters, and
the capitals of the tall flanking columns. Looking down from the high table
where, on his left, sits the first lord of the Treasury and, on his right, the
American ambassador, the guest of honor sees table backing table and the
unrelieved pattern of white shirtfront against black (fig. 1). Finally—could he
see to the far back—beneath the balcony where earlier there had played
M. Carl Heubert's Viennese band he might make out the single row of ladies.
And atop all the shirtfronts and white ties are the faces—kindly, expectant—
of some two hundred of the nation's "chiefest men."[1]

Tenniel may have hoped to retire quietly. His eyesight had been wors-
ening for some years, and six months ago he had confided to longtime colleague Linley Sambourne that he would soon draw his final cartoon for
Punch. He had mustered all his remaining strength for that last and powerful political drawing and, on the day it appeared, had gone through a touching farewell with his co-workers at their weekly dinner in Bouverie Street.[2]

Through much of January the world's press had run articles on John Tenniel's fifty-year tenure at *Punch,* although on the 22nd all news was preempted by the queen's death. By March Tenniel was again in the news, it having been determined that his retirement was too important an event to be
passed over without the suitable honor of a public dinner. The *Times* of 18

Fig. 2. Bernard Partridge, "So Say All of Us!" cartoon, *Punch*, 12 June 1901

April had given further details, listing an organizing committee of some sixty-five eminent persons—a list that read like a roll call of first names in the nobility, government, law, science, and the arts. The date was set, and in the interim two months he had composed and committed to memory the "beautiful speech" that he would surely be required to give.[3]

The evening had begun with an excellent feast. From the first course (clear turtle soup) to the petits fours and dessert the dinner had been served with a noble selection of wines and liqueurs. Not quite the number of entrées, entremets, and removes that a grand dinner of the Victorian heyday would have had but still very fine. Writing in their diaries that night, Sambourne (who appreciated the pleasures of the table) judged it "a remarkably good dinner," and Thomas Anstey Guthrie (playwright and likewise a *Punch* colleague) commented on the numerous waltzes and operatic selections that had accompanied it, "Good orchestra, playing well."[4]

The dinner over, there had followed the loyal toasts to king, queen, and royal family. Then the toastmaster called, "My Lord Duke, Your Excellency, my Lords and gentlemen. Pr-r-ray silence for the Chair,"[5] and Arthur Balfour, first lord of the Treasury and nephew of the prime minister, rose to speak.

Balfour had figured in Tenniel's cartoons since becoming Irish secretary in Salisbury's cabinet in 1887. Aside from the Liberal hiatus in 1892–95 he had held posts continually in Conservative governments, and soon he would be prime minister. Toward the end of his first tenure of office Balfour had been awarded *Punch*'s seal of approval in two of Tenniel's cartoons: one depicting him as Hogarth's Industrious Apprentice (in contrast to Randolph Churchill's Tom Idle), the other celebrating his accession to the House of Commons. Over the years he had appeared in the typically varied run of parts assigned to statesmen in *Punch* cartoons: ringmaster (three times), schoolboy, cricketer, pugilist, Trojan soldier, headsman, coster, hairdresser, oarsman, and groom. About two years earlier Tenniel had even pictured him as Lewis Carroll's Alice, pince-nez in place, examining the new Local Government Act.[6]

Moments before, in characteristic attitude—hands clutching the lapels of his coat—Balfour had proposed Tenniel's health in what journalist Henry W.

Lucy was to consider one of his most charming speeches.[7] Humorously referring to himself as one of the "predestined victims" of Tenniel and his colleagues, he saw himself as the "proverbial lamb" proposing "the toast of the wolf on his retirement after a long and honourable career of destruction." Abundantly lauding Tenniel's "more than two thousand cartoons for *Punch*," he found none "in which the great cause of peace, humanity, and civilization was not furthered by his efforts" and prophesied that they would be "for the historian of the future one of the great sources from which to judge of the trend and character of English thought and life in the latter half of the 19th century." Concluding, the statesman said, "But we have little concern with them, to us he is the great artist and the great gentleman; and it is as the great artist and the great gentleman that I now ask you with full glasses to drink his health."

The moment had already been portrayed in Bernard Partridge's cartoon published in that day's *Punch*—Tenniel, cigar in hand, turning toward Balfour, and behind them, John Bull (toastmaster) calling out, "My lords and gentlemen, pray charge your glasses. Bumpers! The toast is 'Sir John Tenniel!'" (fig. 2). Now, from the real Balfour, came the toast, "Ladies and gentlemen, 'The Guest of the Evening.'" The company, having over a dozen times punctuated the chairman's speech with cheers, now burst into a storm of acclaim that one attendee would recall as "one of the most striking demonstrations" he had ever seen. Then, the real toastmaster announced, "My Lord Duke, Your Excellency, My Lords and Gentlemen—Pr-r-ray silence for 'Our Guest.'"[8]

The Hosts

Are there any in the assembly he now addresses who do not represent some facet of the guest's long and busy life? The duke of the toast is Lord Devonshire, who sits on Tenniel's left between Balfour and Lord Rothschild. It was fifty years ago that Tenniel, a young amateur actor, performed with Charles Dickens's company at Devonshire House before an earlier duke. Devonshire's long face, with its prominent lips and beard, had been caricatured in Tenniel's cartoons since at least 1875 (when he was Lord Hartington). The earliest of that year showed him straining to bend the "Bow of Ulysses" (the Liberal leadership) after that party's general election defeat. The assassination in early 1882 of Hartington's brother Lord Frederick Cavendish, the newly appointed chief secretary of Ireland, had brought forth the angriest of Tenniel's Irish cartoons (fig. 181). A leading opponent of Gladstone's Irish home-rule policy, Hartington is shown attacking Actaeon-Gladstone in "Actaeon and His Hounds," and, in Tenniel's takeoff on Thackeray's poem "Little Billee," he and Lord Salisbury, two knife-wielding sailors, threaten the little home-rule bill, "Oh, Bill-ee! We're going to kill and eat you / So undo the button of your chemie."[9]

Also at the high table is the noted animal painter Briton Riviere, who will respond to the toast to art. He is there in lieu of the president of the Royal Academy, Sir Edward Poynter, who is too ill to attend. In his years of struggle before becoming a royal academician Riviere had briefly drawn for *Punch*. Like the Tenniels, the Rivieres were among the early Huguenot residents of Marylebone, and in 1857 their families were connected by the marriage of Tenniel's cousin George Calkin to Riviere's cousin Emily Mary Riviere.[10]

Among the diners is Harry Baird Hemming, reporter to the House of Lords and son of George Wirgman Hemming, queen's counsel and brilliant mathematician. About sixty years ago Tenniel had adopted the Hemmings of Eltham Place, Kennington, as almost a second family. The sons closest to his age—Henry Jr. (living these past forty-nine years in Quebec) and George Wirgman—had been his dearest friends.

Present, too, at one of the long tables, is Henry Fielding Dickens, bencher of the Inner Temple and son of the novelist. The elder Dickens had in 1848 engaged Tenniel to help illustrate his last Christmas book and soon opened his home to him. How many years had passed since he last heard Dickens's merry laughter or rowed the Thames down from Oxford with the writer's son young Charlie?

Scattered among the company are Tenniel's recent *Punch* colleagues; he could see writer Anstey Guthrie's open countenance close by to the right. Here, too, are the paper's editor, Frank Burnand, and proprietor, Sir William Agnew—both close friends—and Marion H. Spielmann, art writer and *Punch* historian, to whom Tenniel had in 1889 granted his sole interview. In this sea of faces is Sir Edward Reed, one of the promoters of knighthood for Tenniel in 1893 and father of *Punch*'s E. T. Reed;[11] and Sir John Robinson of the *Daily News,* who had journeyed to Osborne along with Tenniel to be knighted.

Here, too, are Sir Edward Levy-Lawson, owner of the *Daily Telegraph;* criminal lawyer Charles ("Willie") Mathews; and actor-manager John Hare—all cronies from his old riding club, the Two Pins. With these, and several others, Tenniel had met for Sunday morning rides to Richmond Park, Hampton Court, or Epsom. Some had taken their last ride on earth since those idyllic jaunts—the cheerful solicitor general Sir Frank Lockwood and, more recently, Lord Chief Justice Charles Russell. Now, Russell's son, another Charles, sits in the crowded room. Both father and son played leading roles in the arbitration of the Bering Sea sealing industry dispute in 1893, the success of which was celebrated in a Tenniel cartoon.[12]

There is John Fletcher Moulton, jurist and member of Parliament in whose social circle Tenniel was a familiar figure. Tenniel had become friends with Moulton's stepdaughter when she was still Elspeth Thomson, and their mock April-September flirtation still continued after her marriage to writer

Kenneth Grahame in 1899. Grahame is also present, while Elspeth is probably among the ladies at the back.[13]

What field is not represented? There are several royal academicians, including Tenniel's friend Luke Fildes. Sir James Linton, past president of Tenniel's own artistic fraternity, the Royal Institute of Painters in Watercolours, is here, as is the present incumbent, E. J. Gregory. Present is F. Carruthers Gould, who would make a specialty of politicizing Tenniel's "Alice in Wonderland" designs for the *Westminster Gazette*. Here, too, representing the publishers of the *Alice* books, the reissuance of which had involved Tenniel for over three decades, is Frederick Macmillan.[14] Appropriately for the stage-loving Tenniel, there is a large contingent of actors and theatrical writers, managers, critics—among them James M. Barrie, Arthur Wing Pinero, William S. Gilbert, William Archer, Sir Squire Bancroft, George Grossmith; the list is long. And the presence of Disraeli's biographer George Buckle, and Herbert Gladstone, son of the late statesman, reminds us of Tenniel's many cartoons featuring the great rivals.

Not least, among the ladies at the back table who were so cavalierly ignored by the toastmaster sits Tenniel's sister Lydia Victoire (or Victoire Lydia as she prefers to sign herself), friend and companion. Victoire had shared his widower's home since the death, twenty-five years ago, of his mother-in-law, Eve Giani.

As he begins, it is as if, on this night, all those whose lives have touched his own—the living and the ghosts—have crowded into this great hall to hear him speak.

2

A Pretty Place
1776–1840

We abroad to Marrowbone and there walked in the garden,
the first time I ever there, and a pretty place it is.
—SAMUEL PEPYS, *Diary*, 7 May 1668

As well as I can remember—my chief "youthful aspiration" was to be a clown in a Circus.
—TENNIEL, to the editor of the *Captain*, 11 February 1899

Noel Tenniel

Let us take Tenniel's story back to a time preceding his own—to a marriage in Marylebone Village when the boundary of London was still almost a mile away. Imagine that it is an autumn day in 1776 and we are on the north side of Oxford Street, or Tyburn Road as its western half was then called. A half mile to the west is the turnpike, where a gallows is still raised from time to time. Some three-quarters of a mile in the opposite direction another tollgate marks where Tottenham Court Road meets the east end of Oxford Street. From our starting point we turn northward onto Marylebone Lane, passing the row of buildings that line the main road and following the meandering course of the Tyburn River through open fields where cattle graze and, in spring, honeysuckle blooms.

Soon the lane jogs left and widens into the high street. Less than a quarter mile off on our right is the Basin (or "Bason," as it is called in old maps and prints), a large circular pond that holds the district's water supply. In an eighteenth-century engraving well-dressed families promenade its edge, swimmers paddle nearby, and in the distance among Gainsborough trees one can see the manors and country houses of affluent Marylebone.[1]

Continuing up the high street we soon see buildings backed by gardens and then fields. On our left we pass Paddington Street where, a short distance westward, lie two burial grounds, one dating from 1731, the other new, their monumental inscriptions bearing many French names.[2] North of that is a workhouse and an infirmary.

On the opposite side of the Marylebone high street are the old Rose of Normandy Tavern and small French chapel, testifying further to Marylebone's Huguenot community. Immediately north of that lies Marylebone (or Marybone) Gardens, a large and popular pleasure ground with handsome pavilions and great tree-lined avenues where one can enjoy fireworks, theatricals, and other entertainments.[3] Should we choose to go further we would pass the Manor House school, a great Tudor pile that was originally a country palace for Henry VIII, and come to the still-unfinished New Road—the Marylebone Road of today.

Instead, we shall stop before the northern boundary of Marylebone Gardens where, looking to the west side of the high street, we see the parish church of St. Mary le Bone, its modest flat front continued by high churchyard walls. An earlier church had occupied the site from 1400 to 1740, its interior known to us from the *Rake's Marriage* in Hogarth's 1735 series. The church that we now

Fig. 3. *Noel Tenniel,* miniature

approach is a "little dingy building, with its high-backed pews and gallery running round three sides." Here, on 31 October 1776, the thirty-one-year-old Noel Tenniel marries Margaret Parker, spinster of the same parish. Present at the ceremony is Louis Tenniel, possibly Noel's brother as he would name his second son Noé and Noel's youngest daughter would be named Louisa.[4]

Noel and Margaret Tenniel soon settle in Westminster, a "center of French fashion, cuisine, and high society." There, five more daughters will be born to them (a first daughter was born in the previous March), their baptisms recorded at St. James, Westminster. Then, on 25 August 1792, the parish clerk would record the baptism of a son, John Baptist, the future father of John Tenniel.[5]

Fig. 4. Tenniel's tankard

A miniature of Noel Tenniel shows him at, perhaps, forty—a slender man with the worldly look one often finds in eighteenth-century portraits (fig. 3). His hair (lightly powdered?) is tied back with a small ribbon. It is a clever face—the nose aquiline, the lips hinting of humor. He was probably in the arts—perhaps a dancing master, as this seems to have been a frequent family occupation; Noel's daughter Victoire would marry James Calkin, whose largely musical family included several dancing masters, and his grandson John Tenniel would one day marry a dancing master's daughter. In France the family may have belonged to the lesser nobility, for on Tenniel's pewter tankard there appears a crest—a pair of wings surmounting a torse or crest wreath, which one doubts he would have adopted had he not credited it with some legitimacy (fig. 4).[6]

John Baptist and Eliza Maria

We next locate John Baptist in the Marylebone of 1816. Even before the turn of the century this was no longer a separate village, for a grid of Georgian houses and squares had spread from Oxford Street to the New Road and as far west as Baker Street and beyond. Gone are the pleasure grounds, the French chapel, the Rose of Normandy Tavern, and the Manor House. And where the wealthy once lingered beside the picturesque Bason they now take their evening walks in exclusive Portland Place.

Beyond the New Road the farms of Marylebone Park stretch northward to Primrose Hill, where the occasional duel is still fought. In 1808 the six-year-old future animal painter Edwin Landseer walked among its streams and osier beds sketching sheep, goats, and donkeys. Others whose childhood fell in the 1820s would recall the area's charms.[7] But as this formerly leased land had reverted to the crown in 1811, time was fast running out for its pasturelands and fields of wheat.

It is in this partially rural Marylebone that John Baptist Tenniel has settled. He has given an engagement ring of mixed stones to the Scottish-born beauty Eliza Maria Foster, currently of the parish of Portsea, and he now journeys to Southampton to wed her and bring her home.[8]

Fig. 5. *(Left)* Robinson, *Eliza Maria Tenniel,* watercolor, 1819. Fig. 6. *(Right)* Robinson, *John Baptist Tenniel,* watercolor, 1819

They will have twelve children.[9] The first two are Bernard and Eliza Margaret. Twin watercolor portraits show Eliza Maria and John Baptist in 1819, the year before their second son, John, was born (fig. 5 and fig. 6). The portraitist, a Robinson of Suffolk Street, has included, beyond the conventional draperies and columns, some attractive countryside suggestive of landed status. There is the misty softness of youth, the assurance of affluence about the pair. Eliza Maria wears a high-waisted riding habit of deep blue with a collar of ruffled lawn. Her face is a sweet oval, fine featured, and her hair, combed flat from the center part, spreads into bouffant curls intruding charmingly on each side of the smooth forehead and accenting the dark eyes. Her gloved hands, resting in her lap, lightly hold a black top hat. John Baptist seems younger than his twenty-seven years. Above the high collar and stock, soft curls frame a smooth face.

At Allsop's Buildings

The area where they live is prosperous and peaceful, far removed from the marches, riots, and machine wrecking of the midlands and northern counties that had punctuated the years since Waterloo. Still, even in Marylebone, the hard times in trade and agriculture have their repercussions. On 23 February 1820 revolutionaries, allegedly plotting to kill the Tory ministers, are apprehended in a loft in Cato Street (subsequently renamed Horace Street) within the district's western boundary.[10] Five days later Tenniel is born—probably not a half mile distant.

In January of Tenniel's birth year George III had died at Windsor. Contrasting with the still-uncrowned George IV's libertinism, the country is in the midst of an evangelical revival, prelude to the reign of the future queen (at this time still an infant.) In 1818 Thomas Bowdler had published his expurgated family Shakespeare, and while Corinthians (the dandies of the time) might affect elaborate neckwear, wasp waists, and flowered vests, dress for most is increasingly sober.

Those who grew up in this period would recall such premodern vestiges as tinder boxes, "brimstone matches," and folded letters sealed with wax or wafers, the writing crossed and recrossed to cut down on the high postage rates. They would remember when Kensington was a villagelike suburb; Belgravia, a stretch of lonely fields; Russell Square, the site of a gravel pit; and Green Park, a place where cows grazed. Even in the heart of London ruddy-faced farmers might still haggle over the price of hay in the Haymarket or exchange wives at the Smithfield cattle market.[11]

North of the New Road the work of creating a landscaped park ringed by expensive terraces has begun. By 1817 the project was sufficiently underway for the Regent's Park, at least its southern boundary, to be enclosed by a handsome iron railing, as was the Park Crescent Gardens. A painting

Fig. 7. Allsop's Buildings.
(City of Westminster Archives
Centre)

of the period shows the prospect looking south from the York Gate, with "a party of haymakers sketched from life" and "only three houses dotted about the new parish church of St. Marylebone."[12]

This church, designed by Thomas Hardwick, has replaced the old parish church to the south and dominates the New Road. Its multiply staged tower is as tall again as the nave, its dome held by brilliantly gilded caryatids. The interior, said to accommodate three to four thousand parishioners, is equally lavish. The altarpiece, an eight-by-seventeen-foot annunciation, is by Royal Academy president Benjamin West, a longtime householder in Newman Street in the district's older section, and around double galleries are molded swags of fruit hung from winged cherub heads.[13] Years later, Tenniel may have recalled these cherubim when designing his House of Lords fresco and when depicting "a great many boy's heads" taking "their flight" in a scene for *The Ingoldsby Legends*.

By 24 March 1820, when Tenniel is baptized under the gaze of these many boys' heads, the five Tenniels and their two female servants are, in all probability, already ensconced at Allsop's Buildings on the north side of the New Road where the next year's census will find them. Allsop's Buildings is a row of some forty-three homes divided midway by Baker Street's course northward to the park. The Tenniels are at number 25—the third house west of the Baker Street corner.[14]

Further west by five doors is the family of the painter John Martin. Around 1817 Martin (a rising artist of about twenty-eight), advised by friends that he must make "a little show in the world," had borrowed the money to pay the first year's rent on number 30. His son Leopold would later describe it as an address of "considerable consequence," the buildings opposite (the York Buildings to the south) being "chiefly occupied by persons of some mark. . . . Leigh Hunt, Lord Erskine, William Beckford." This "superior house," as John Martin calls it, rents for seventy pounds whereas number 25 goes for sixty.[15]

A photograph shows the homes shortly before their demolition in the 1920s (fig. 7). Their brickwork, height, and surmounting parapet are late eighteenth century, but the stone facing of the lower stories and graceful wrought-iron work may be regency additions. While the 1756 act that created the New Road had required that all buildings be set back by at least fifty feet, this would be set aside during the later widening of the road. But in the Tenniels' and Martins' time the lots are deep—about seven times their width. Martin is able to build in his back garden "a substantial private painting establishment and convenient painting room, attached to the house by a long gallery." At the back of the Tenniels' house, which originally opened onto the unenclosed fields of the Portman estate and later onto Allsop's Mews, is their stable.[16]

Artistic Families

Was the affluence suggested by this and subsequent Tenniel homes derived solely from John Baptist's teaching? This was possible. Masters' earnings varied considerably. The *Boarding-School and London Masters' Directory* for 1828 speaks of rates as high as a guinea for every forty minutes of instruction. While some, like Prince Turveydrop in Dickens's *Bleak House,* might work desperately hard for much less, John Baptist probably charged fees equivalent to those of drawing master Daniel Valentine Riviere, later to be related by marriage. Riviere, head of a large household near fashionable Fitzroy Square to the east, taught at a ladies' school in Kensington. Recalling the dearness of drawing materials at this school, his daughter Fanny observed, "His remuneration must have been 'dear' also, I suspect, as he earned *all* the money to keep and educate us."[17]

By all indications, the Tenniels were tonish. Entries for John Baptist surface regularly in such fashionable directories as the *Royal Blue Book* and *Boyle's Court Guide.*[18] In 1859, the wedding of his fifth son, Adolphus, would appear in the *Gentleman's Magazine,* long a source for "Marriages of Remarkable Persons."

John Baptist's occupation is less clear, changing from decade to decade, as did that of his third son, William Rickards, who seems to have assisted his father in all his pursuits. Pigot's 1832 London directory lists John Baptist as a professor of drawing. In successive censuses from 1841 to 1871 John Baptist described himself as "artist," "teacher of personal exercise," "teacher of drawing," and "teacher of dancing." Since his pupils would recall him as a "first rate" and "celebrated" dancing master, an "indefatigable teacher," this was probably his prime calling. Concurrently, he taught deportment, fencing, and calisthenics.[19] John Baptist's dancing-master's fiddle (or kit, as it was called),

Fig. 8. John Baptist Tenniel's kit

measuring fourteen and a half inches in its entirety, remains in family possession (fig. 8).

John Baptist's incursion into drawing seems consistent with the broad involvement in the arts that characterized certain Marylebone families. For example, his sister Victoire's 1808 marriage to the musician and composer James Calkin produced several prominent instrumentalists, singers, and composers. Eventually Victoire's son George would marry a granddaughter of Daniel Valentine Riviere. Riviere, who after his day's labors in Kensington liked to relax by playing the flute, had fathered several painters, a celebrated soprano, and a binder of fine books. Close by the Rivieres, in Norton Street (now Bolsover Street), lived the dancing master Julius Giani, father of Tenniel's future bride. Related to Julius (perhaps his father, as they had the same address in 1821) is Lorenzo Giani, artist, whose daughter Georgiana would be a professor of music. Lastly, the 1844 marriage of Tenniel's sister Eliza Margaret to Leopold Martin would also create distant ties with the Corbould dynasty of artists as well as with Tenniel's friend the artist Charles Keene.[20] One suspects that this pattern was one of long standing.

Did the Martin friendship predate the Allsop's period? We learn from Leopold that in the years of Tenniel's childhood "the families were one." There were, indeed, some affinities between the neighbors. Like John Baptist, Martin was a fencer, his father Fenwick Martin having taught sword and singlestick in their native Northumberland. Furthermore, the diminutive Martin—somewhat of a dandy with his tight pantaloons and pumps, his curled and oiled hair—may have struck a responsive chord in the elegant John Baptist.[21]

By the New Road

Around them the district changed rapidly. On the park's northern boundary the Regent's Canal opened in 1820 with a procession of gaily decorated boats, their passengers raising wine-filled glasses to toast the occasion. In the same year, Martin exhibited at the Royal Academy two watercolor views of a proposed triumphal arch, in commemoration of Waterloo, bridging the New Road from Portland Place to Regent's Park. One, taken from inside the railing, shows the park at this time—barren with great excavations, evoking the sort of romantic desolation that Martin was partial to.[22]

What a rich succession of sounds, rising from the various menders, carriers, buskers, and traders who came and went from breakfast until dusk, must have reached the youngest Tenniel from his nursery windows. Then, once the lamplighter had departed with his ladder, the night sounds would begin: the watchmen with their wooden rattles calling the hour and half hour, the solemn tolling of the Marylebone parish church clock, and the clatter of the night coaches. Finally came the morning carts, the "dust-ho!" of the dustman, and it would all start over again.[23]

Along the New Road there would pass within the next few years the funeral cortege of Queen Caroline to mixed jeers and signs of mourning and, to greater mourning, that of Byron. Benjamin West died, and Sir Thomas Lawrence headed the Royal Academy in his place. The third census was taken, and the regent, wearing star-studded robes and a great plume of ostrich feathers in his hat, went to Westminster Abbey to be crowned George IV.[24] As the decade progressed, cheap literature was made more available to the working classes, Catholic emancipation passed, and London gained its first police force. This period of relative calm would close in 1829 with the agricultural riots of "Captain Swing."

A boy growing up at Allsop's Buildings in those years would have found life sufficiently entertaining. In the time before he was "breeched," or put into trousers (for little boys wore petticoats up to school age), the number of young Tenniels would grow to five, William Rickards coming along in late 1821 and Lydia Victoire two years after. When the children were old enough they might have been walked along the New Road, past the Park Crescent Gardens ("tastefully laid out as a shrubbery") with its bronze statue of the Duke of Kent, to Daguerre and Bouton's Diorama. There, from an auditorium that revolved "like a snap table with all its spectators," bright day turned to moonlight, and calm followed storm in painted scenes that merged before one's startled eyes.[25]

Work on the Regent's Park and its ring of stately terraces advanced rapidly, the first buildings composing Cornwall Terrace directly north of Allsop's. Close by, the York Gate opened onto an idyllic landscape of "groves, gardens, sheets of water . . . lodges, airy bridges." Passing the lake on the left, and Jenkins Nursery in the inner circle, and traversing a large stretch of ground to the north, one came to the zoological gardens (opened in 1828). There, one might watch the sleek otter chase round his pool, peer into the dens of the great cats, see the brown bear climb a post to reach for the buns that visitors extended to him on long sticks, admire the gaily colored parrots, laugh at the lumbering birds of prey and the agile monkeys, and feed ginger nuts to the elephant. Here Tenniel's British Lion, Bengal Tiger, Russian Bear, and Imperial Eagles performed long years before we meet them again in his *Punch* cartoons. In the year following there opened, not far from the Diorama, Decimus Burton's 112–foot-high Colosseum. From within its dome visitors might look down on Thomas Horner's panorama of London as seen from the top of St. Paul's or climb further to see the real panorama of London from the building's crowning parapet.[26]

Besides these wonders there was the constant sideshow of the district's streets. The milk women making their rounds with pails suspended from the wooden yokes across their shoulders, crossing sweepers, dustmen with leather flaps at the back of their caps, the barrel-organ man, the muffin man, the peep show man, the Punch-and-Judy man, and the man wheeling a "happy family" cage of small animals. On May Day one might see a Jack-in-the-Green in his bower of green leaves and flowers coming slowly down Baker Street, accompanied by mummers and sweeps just as he appears in Benjamin Haydon's painting. And in the Marylebone high street one might spot the charity school girls in their eighteenth-century dress and mushroom-shaped caps much as Tenniel would depict them when they visited the Crystal Palace in 1851.[27]

Childhood

It is probable, as his older brother Bernard attended the school near Kensington Gravel Pits where John Baptist taught dance and fencing, that Tenniel went there too; future colleagues would place his first tuition in Kensington. In all likelihood he studied under the reputed headmaster, Edward Slater, had his early games on the school's elm-bordered playground, and enjoyed the beefsteak pies that made the Friday dinners memorable. He would now have advanced to trousers, perhaps buttoned to the close-fitting jacket of a shell or skeleton suit such as he gave Tweedledum and Tweedledee.[28]

The school had both regular and day boarders, and since John Baptist traveled there daily he would have taken his sons with him as day boarders. While Prince Turveydrop might "put his little kit in his pocket" and walk to "his school at Kensington," one imagines that John Baptist, whose homes were always backed by his own stables, arrived in a gig like Dickens's own dancing master, or with a child sharing his saddle.[29]

Outside of school hours there was no lack of companionship. The Martins had six children; the second son Leopold was about two years older than Tenniel, and Charles was his own age. The painter delighted in games of skill, and days when the light was poor for painting he and his boys might be found kneeling on the studio floor engrossed in a game of "knuckle down." Was Tenniel there with his own favorite marble? Or did he throw the "javelin" at the target chalked on a tree, perhaps to be rewarded with a lollipop, brandy ball, or bull's eye by the sweets-loving Martin?[30]

On other days he might visit his Aunt Victoire and his eight Calkin cousins at Edwards Street east of the Regent's Park. He was probably closest with Joseph, four years older than he, for he would maintain lifelong ties with this cousin's children. This member of the musical Calkins would later, as a tenor, adopt the professional name of Tennielli, testifying to the popularity of Italian singers in this period.[31]

In the early thirties a new reign, a change of government in France, agitation for parliamentary reform, would probably be far less momentous to the future rider and huntsman than the opening of the Horse Bazaar in King Street, just four streets south of Allsop's. Formerly a life-guard barracks, this complex within a spacious block off Baker Street housed stabling and galleries for some three hundred horses, five hundred carriages, and a large riding school. It also had a ladies' bazaar and handsomely arranged rooms for the sale and display of furniture, jewelry, and works of art.[32] One imagines the scene—the color and excitement, the air filled with stable dust, and, stepping between stalls of saddlery and fancy articles, the ringletted ladies in the immense bonnets and balloon sleeves of the period, with their silk-hatted escorts. Soon the site would house Madame Tussaud's large collection of life-size wax effigies, a bazaar feature for fifty years before their final move to Marylebone Road.

Leopold Martin's reminiscences seem to suggest this period, or one earlier, for the accident that blinded Tenniel's right eye rather than the age of twenty that is sometimes given. In Leopold's account of the practice session in question, Tenniel "when quite young" was touched on the right eye when the button came off John Baptist's foil, both fencers being maskless. One wonders, masks being then in use, why this precaution was not taken. In two of Robert Cruikshank's etchings to Pierce Egan's *Life in London* (1821) fencers are shown protecting themselves with small wire masks, and in 1827 the noted fencing master P. G. Hamon prescribed the mask as an "indispensable" part of the fencer's dress. The story has it that John Baptist never learned of his son's impairment, something that seems incomprehensible today and may be a reflection of the formal relations that often prevailed between fathers and their children in those times.[33]

Early Pencilings

We learn from Leopold Martin's recollections that Tenniel, when "little more than a child," had joined the Martin children in their art studies at the "the Print Room, Reading Room, or Townley Gallery of the British Museum . . . receiving all the advantages of joint instruction and suggestions." This would have begun after 16 November 1832 when Martin, who wanted his sons to study the museum's works on costumes of various times and countries, wrote to keeper of prints and drawings John Thomas Smith to ask his assistance. Eventually this would result in Charles and Leopold Martin's two volumes on English costume. Although Smith, an antiquarian and an able draftsman, would have been an excellent guide, he was dead in less than four months after Martin's letter. At some point Sir Frederic Madden of the Manuscripts Department, no poor artist himself, reportedly became Tenniel's mentor.[34]

By 1832 work was in progress to expand the museum's original home, the old Montague House. At this time, the Townley Galleries housed the Greek, Roman, and Egyptian antiquities, and two rooms in the recently constructed east wing temporarily served as the fifth set of reading rooms since the museum's opening in 1759. To reach them, readers ascended the steep and narrow exterior stone steps, left their umbrellas and walking sticks in the small and chilly lobby, and entered the first of the two rooms, which had high windows over grated bookshelves. It was best to come early as the tables, with chairs for 112 readers, were quite insufficient. Perhaps our young researchers were too engrossed in their copying to note the smell when the badly ventilated rooms became full, or to suffer from "museum headache" or the infamous "museum flea." We picture them—Leopold and Tenniel assiduously at work, and Charles sketching desultorily when not distracted by the entrance of a fashionable patron.[35]

In two great scrapbooks containing drawings from every phase of Tenniel's career, and probably dating from this time, are numerous tiny studies of costume, armor, saddlery, weaponry, and such miscellany as a thumbscrew, firedog, spanner, and touch box. Most are of exquisitely penciled figures, from one and one-half to four inches high, in costumes of various reigns and times. One or two have notes on sources: a Monsieur Chery's *Studies of Costumes and Theaters of All Nations* (1790) and Meyrick's *Ancient Arms and Armour* (1830). Superimposed on one Tenniel sketch (a head of a fourteenth-century lady in a wimple) and penciled in a childish hand, probably of a younger sibling, are the words "J Tenniel is an ass/oh Yes he is/ Very"—a delightful reminder that in any period youngsters are much the same.[36]

A smaller scrapbook, compiled by Tenniel himself, contains some 170 similarly tiny drawings. They are undated but range from 1835 to about 1847 or later and depict actors observed from the pits of various London theaters. These lively pencil studies of costume, expression, and gesture he subsequently finished with sparing watercolor touches. The "Pencillings in the Pit. 1835—," its title probably adopted from the name of a journal that ran briefly from 1838 to 1839, represents some thirty performances, with opera and Shakespeare predominating. These are interspersed with extravaganza, melodrama, comedy, burlesque, and equestrian spectacle.[37]

While preferable to the gallery, the pit could not have provided the happiest environment for the sketcher. Two or three shillings secured a place in this province of the lower middle classes. This was followed by a rush for front seats, often reached by climbing over the backless wooden benches accessible by no central aisle. Around half-past six or seven a rousing overture would begin the (usually) triple bill that might go for five hours or more before the final black curtain. The young artist would have had to handle carefully the badly printed programs that blackened one's fingers and to block from his consciousness the stomping, kicking, hissing, and shouting, so tumultuous that actors might resort to playing in dumb show. He would have had to put up with the inevitable second rush for seats when the half-price ticket holders came in at nine o'clock.[38]

But these years also held advantages for the artist in the pit. From start to finish the house was bathed in light—gaslight in most cases. And when an actor met audience expectations by playing up to certain climactic "points" in a piece, the protracted pause during the applause that followed made it easier to observe players who might otherwise be in motion.

Some of the sketches can be traced to particular offerings of the thirties and forties. Of course, there was Shakespeare, with the tragic Mary Warner or the enchanting Pricilla Horton by William Macready's side. Tenniel would have seen the "metaphysical" actor cast himself "with a hoarse cry . . . on the ground like a maddened bull" before Banquo's ghost, or seen him turning up the whites of his eyes as the soliloquizing Hamlet.[39] Also treading the green carpet of tragedy were Samuel Phelps, James Wallack, George Vanderhoff, and the young Charles Kean, all portrayed in Tenniel's pencilings.

Shakespearean "travestie" was not excluded, and Tenniel saw a famous one: Maurice G. Dowling's *Othello, According to Act of Parliament*. It was described in 1837 by theatrical diarist Charles Rice as the "best burlesque that has ever appeared," which tells us something about the others. Othello's address to the senate—"Potent, grave and rev'rend sir, / Very noble massa"—recalled the black impersonations that Charles Mathews had introduced to Londoners in 1824 and tied in with the country's new craze for blackface minstrelsy.[40] Indeed, Tenniel's sketch of one Sweeny as an "Ethiopian delineator" forecast his depiction of these popular entertainers in several *Punch* cartoons.

From this period, too, comes Tenniel's sketch of Isaac Van Amburgh with one of his lions. In the late thirties the American lion tamer thrilled audiences at Astley's Amphitheatre and later at Drury Lane where the new queen saw his act six times.[41] Scarcely less intrigued was the future limner of the British Lion.

High Art

What art instruction was available to Tenniel in those years? There was most likely some from John Baptist and perhaps from Martin. But, as the first was a probable dabbler, the second a landscape painter and a weak figure draftsman, we can safely assume what is ultimately true of most artists—that he taught himself to draw.[42] Still, the groundwork that Martin encouraged in costume and armor was invaluable for Tenniel's future work.

Since Martin was an instigator, subscriber, and regular exhibitor of the Society of British Artists, it was here, in the society's gallery in Suffolk Street, that Tenniel and Charles Martin began showing their work in 1835. Tenniel would exhibit here regularly through 1841, with sixteen pieces that showed a predilection for watercolor and for scenes from Scott's *Waverley Novels*. It was an oil, however, *The Stirrup Cup* of 1837, that marked his first known sale, its purchaser the popular stage Irishman Tyrone Power. The same year saw his first successful entry at the Royal Academy's summer exhibition where he would exhibit regularly through 1843 and later intermittently. Here,

Fig. 9. John Martin, *Coronation of Queen Victoria*, oil painting, 1839. (© Tate, London 2004)

too, he favored period subjects. His 1839 and 1840 entries at the society—designs based on the seventeenth-century song about the old English courtier who "kept a brave old house at a bountiful rate / And an old porter to relieve the poor at his gate"—might be taken as early indications of his Tory leanings.[43]

The Martin friendship may have been Tenniel's entry to the first of a succession of brilliant social circles. In his years of prosperity (1825 to 1835) John Martin brought together at his weekly "evenings at home" many leading personalities in literature, art, and the sciences, among them William Godwin, the Landseers (John and his sons Charles and Edwin), Sir Charles Wheatstone, Tom Moore, Samuel Lover, Tom Hood, Harrison Ainsworth, and Allan Cunningham. Tenniel may also have seen at Martin's several who would figure in his later life: George Cruikshank, Samuel Carter Hall, Douglas Jerrold, and Charles Dickens. Here, in Martin's drawing room, furnished in rosewood and crimson damask, coffee served in lilac and gold Sevres china accompanied the most stimulating conversation. Leopold Martin would recall one June night in 1832 when Tom Moore sat at Martin's grand piano and "warbled melody after melody," while present was "the lovely sister of . . . John Tenniel," later to become Leopold's wife.[44] As Eliza Margaret would have then been a bit short of her fourteenth birthday, it is probable that Tenniel, too, reached an age when he might be included before the "evenings" ended with Martin's change in fortunes.

By 1837 the painter was heavily in debt. His schemes for metropolitan improvements, his generous loans to friends such as the artist Benjamin R. Haydon, had drained his funds. In addition, his sales had dropped off and he lacked the advantages that academician status might have given. For fourteen years he had shown nothing at the Royal Academy, probably for the reasons that he and Haydon gave in 1836 when, before a select committee on the arts, they protested their treatment at that institution.[45] Then, in early 1838, he suffered a nervous collapse. Growing up in the heady atmosphere of "high art," Tenniel could thus witness the disparities between high aspirations (possibly megalomania in the case of Haydon) and the capricious art market and entrenched authority.

By August of 1838 Martin had recovered and was again painting. Queen

Victoria's coronation at Westminster earlier that summer had inspirited him with the notion of a coronation scene in which many of the most distinguished attendees would be painted from life.[46] Having been rebuffed in his application for the post of historical painter to the new monarch, he may have hoped to reverse that decision. In any case he proceeded with gusto, drawing at the abbey and inviting some one hundred persons of note to sit for portraits. The latter revived his fortunes, for they came—among them Prince Albert, Earl Grey, Lord Howick, and the Duke of Sutherland—and bought and commissioned paintings. Martin, with Charles assisting with the portraits, worked tirelessly through 1839 and finally the 73 × 93 inch canvas was submitted to Buckingham Palace, where it was not bought. It did, however, find a purchaser for the good sum of two thousand guineas. Martin's view of the abbey, caught after a burst of sunlight had illuminated the central dais, would find an ironic transmutation some twenty years later in one of Tenniel's designs for Moore's *Lalla Rookh* (fig. 9 and fig. 10).

Fig. 10. Tenniel, "There on that throne," illustration for "The Veiled Prophet," Thomas Moore, *Lalla Rookh*, 1861

The Eglinton Rehearsals

While Martin was "going on in glory" with his *Coronation,* a little more than a mile away some thirty-five young aristocrats were rehearsing for the medieval revival event of the century.[47] By this time, Tenniel, through his study of costume and armor and his reading of Scott, was himself something of a medievalist. He had probably seen the tournaments staged at Astley's and may have seen Lord Burghersh's opera *The Tournament* in which the Queen of Beauty was sung by Anna (née Riviere) Bishop, a daughter of the drawing master Daniel Riviere.

The Eglinton Tournament grew out of Tory dissatisfaction with the economical excision of certain ancient ceremonies from the coronation festivities. The eagerness of certain noblemen to compensate for this and the story of how the thirteenth earl of Eglinton was swayed by press and public into staging a full-scale tournament at his castle in Ayrshire, Scotland, is well documented. In June and July of 1839 the "Eglinton Knights" practiced for the August event in the gardens behind the Eyre Arms Tavern in the St. John's Wood area of northern Marylebone. A popular location for athletic sports, the gardens of this handsome Georgian place of entertainment housed assembly rooms, a ballroom and theater, and offered band concerts and fireworks displays.[48]

Here the "knights" met twice weekly to practice tilting against mounted dummies in true medieval fashion. The sessions were touted in the press, and admission tickets, emblazoned with a device of crossed lances and a crown, were granted by the participants themselves—at least for the crowded final Saturdays. But it appears that on other days one might just walk in. One gentleman who happened to be passing the Eyre Arms that summer, "struck by the blast of trumpet and the clash of arms," simply entered and "beheld a sight . . . sufficient to cause the canonized bones of the author of *Ivanhoe* 'to burst their cerements.'" It is hard to believe that the young Tenniels and Martins did not take the short jog up the Park Road and then the Wellington Road, which led directly to the lists. Martin himself may have had some interest in the sessions, having painted the tournament from *Ivanhoe* some nine years before.[49]

Of some hundred thousand spectators at Eglinton Park in Ayrshire on 28 August, most are unrecorded. We cannot say if Tenniel joined the artists and reporters in their special stand. Several of the artists there may have been known to him through Martin. Edwin Landseer was an old friend of the painter; Edward Henry Corbould, who illustrated an 1840 volume on the tournament, would marry Martin's niece; and James Henry Nixon, illustrator of John Richardson's lavish *Eglinton Tournament* (1843), is believed to have studied with Martin.[50]

As to the downpour that turned the most extravagant spectacle of the age into a rout, the only surprise is that anyone should have been surprised as Ayrshire summers are notoriously wet. Two weeks before the event the *Times* quoted a Cheltenham paper's prediction of a very splendid pageant, "if it happens to be fine weather," and its further comment: "but if it should rain, an enterprising spectator might realize something handsome by forwarding a good supply of umbrellas and mackintoshes, for the use of the knights and squires." Judging by the quantity of umbrellas that snapped into sight like "a growth of green mushrooms," or "the backsides of thousands of elephants," many came prepared. But who could foresee the flooding of the stands? One spectator, Miss Jeanie Boswell, wrote to her brother Patrick of the rain that "like a water spout . . . completely drenched the whole party, destroying the splendid equipments and making the feathers hang like cocks on a wet day."[51]

Satirists soon personified the event by a knight with an umbrella. The symbol—first seen in *Cleave's Penny Gazette*—appeared in drawings by Richard Doyle and "Alfred Crowquill" (Alfred Henry Forrester) and as late as the sixties in designs by Charles H. Bennett and "Bab" (William Schwenck Gilbert).[52] No one revived it more often than Tenniel.

"Jan"

1840–1850

"O, the merry days—the merry days when we were young!"—Old song
—TENNIEL, *"Bouts-Rimés* (and other *nonsense)"*

With Hooke of Steel

It was a time when a missed engagement might inspire effusive verses
from the disappointed comrade, or a private theatrical receive the care that
one might expect at London's patent houses. From two letters, an old playbill, some scraps of writing, we learn of the effort Tenniel expended on such
social frivolities.

In 1840 Tenniel's carefully crafted rhymes, to which he signed himself
"Jan," twice reproved his good friend Henry Hemming Jr. for failing to show
for a morning dip in the Serpentine, the body of water between Hyde Park
and Kensington Gardens. As their first tryst was arranged for shortly past
sunrise, Tenniel set their next meeting for a bit later, only to swim alone a
second time.[1]

While the distance to the Serpentine from 22 Gloucester Place on the
New Road (the costly terrace that the Tenniels had taken around Michaelmas
1834) was less than two miles, from the Hemmings at Eltham Place in Kennington it was twice that—a possible disincentive. Tenniel went on foot (he
describes himself as going "at a dooce of a pace"), probably a safe enough
walk thanks to the police force that Sir Robert Peel had instituted some ten
years before. As he approached Oxford Street near the Cumberland Gate
he would have seen the shop boys sprinkling dust on the walks with watering
cans or taking down the shutters. In early summer he probably passed the
crowds of strawberry girls on their way to town from the fields of Ham-
mersmith, gracefully balancing on their heads the large baskets of tender
fruit.[2]

At the stream he would not be alone; indeed his verses describe "A scene
arcadian!!" with "Here and there . . . fauns and satyrs, sporting of themselves / Or on the grass—or in the fresh'ning wave." These were people of

the working classes, swimming nude in the fashion of the time. So would they be when sighted here in 1860, "veiled by the pearly mists of the early hours."[3]

The rhymester already gives promise of a lifelong passion for vigorous sport. He plunges into the stream "with antilopic [sic] bound," cleaves the waters "with brave defiant heart," and, traversing his route, returns "Triumphant, as if with every stroke / A new supply of health was pump-*ed* in!!" He also reveals a hardy constitution, for the Serpentine was then highly polluted. In 1828 Martin had called it "a receptacle of all the filth and drainage" of the northern suburbs. In ten years time the problem would, reportedly, become so severe that "an evening stroll by the waters sometimes ended in sudden fever, collapse, and death."[4] Perhaps it was just as well for Henry Hemming that he did not join in Tenniel's morning dips.

From the verses we learn that the friends have a shared fondness for Shakespeare. In the first letter alone, Tenniel deplores that he had no friend to accompany him to "yonder point," perhaps to save him as Cassius did Caesar, and then, parodying the famous lines of Henry V at Agincourt, predicts that his "faithless friend," then "snug in bed," when learning of his "merry sport" shall "hold himself but *cheap* he was not *there*."[5] We catch a bit of medieval speech in his gentlemanly sneer at the cited nymphs and satyrs whose "garments dingy—cast aside" prove "Sad tell-tale of a race y'clept unwashed." We learn, too, of Tenniel's sunny and positive nature, his wholehearted capacity for fun.

The second letter seems almost modern. The writer, having checked his watch, "is '*up*'—like a bottle of ginger-pop!!" He is "into his 'Flannels'— he's into his socks," and with "jaunty air" and "cheerful face" he is on his way.

Finally we learn from the letters that Tenniel nurtured his intimate friendships. Hemming likewise placed great value on friendship and expressed this, some sixty years later, in Shakespearean terms to a young granddaughter. Writing from Canada—his adopted home since 1852—he trusted that she would soon find friends "worthy to be grappled with hooke of steel" (a slightly altered version of the advice given Laertes by Polonius).[6] It was with "hooke of steel" that Tenniel bound to himself his new friends, the Hemmings.

He first met the Henry Keene Hemmings in early 1840 (there seems to have been a Corbould-Keene-Hemming family connection) and soon became a frequent and intimate visitor at Eltham Place. Theirs was a sparkling world of fancy dress, theatricals, art, and sports. He called Mrs. Hemming (Sophia Wirgman) "Aunt Hemming." They called him "Jan," and of the five Hemming children he was closest to Henry Jr., two years older than he. With George Wirgman, his junior by one year, he was also friends. In 1840 he painted Sophia in her costume for a fancy-dress ball as an Egyptian priestess (or Cleopatra) and Henry Sr. as Henry VIII.[7]

Fig. 11. Tenniel, Henry
Hemming Jr. as Hamlet,
watercolor, 1842

In another sketch, two years later, he showed young Henry as Hamlet—a slender, somewhat sharp-featured young man with dagger in hand and a distant gaze. Below are the cryptic initials. S. G. C. B. (fig. 11). It was an apt impersonation for the family's traditions hint of a line of descent from the Danish king Hemming, who in 811 made peace with Charlemagne, and from John Hemming or Heminge, who was Shakespeare's associate. These beliefs were discounted by Henry Jr., who concluded his account of Hemming history for his son Christopher with "It's a fine old story at any rate!"[8]

At the start of 1841 Eltham Place was the scene of a dramatic entertainment for which the preparations must have begun months before. In the double bill for 5 January Tenniel embarked on his avocation as an amateur actor by taking a supporting role in the Charles Dance comedy *Naval Engagements*. Playing a stage Irishman, a type he would adapt to his Irish nationalist images for *Punch,* he had such characteristic lines as "Sure the young gentlemen that dined upstairs yesterday never went home to their mammies this morning, and it's the devil a bit of bed I've had."

On the same bill, Tenniel played the romantic lead in J. M. Morton's *Chaos Is Come Again*. The part had been taken two years before at Covent Garden by James Vining, a well-known portrayer of fops and lovers. In 1848 and in 1852 Tenniel would again play roles introduced by this actor. Other leads on this evening were taken by Henry Jr. and George Hemming and their friends and relations, the latter filling the supporting parts as well. In *Chaos* the Hemmings' brother Edward had a minor role, while leading the dancers was Tenniel's younger brother William Rickards, who, being John Baptist's assistant, was well qualified in that department.[9]

In these, as in several other comedies, farces, and dramas in which Tenniel would appear over the years, the action depended upon such Gilbertian devices as mistaken identities, disguises, and impersonations. It is perhaps indicative of the level of writing in this period that three of the plots feature characters, thought to be defunct, who "return from the dead" to effect a happy ending.[10]

So popular were private theatricals among the upper classes in this century that by 1895 French's Acting Editions, noting "the great difficulty experienced by Amateurs . . . in obtaining Scenery, &c.," offered a series of mounted or unmounted colored scenes, a proscenium, and various architectural features that might be set up in the drawing rooms of country houses.[11] The Eltham Place players had no such requirement, for the program (professionally done by a Hemmings relation, the printer Coe of Cheapside) announced that the scenery was "painted expressly for the occasion by Mr. John Tenniel."

Royal Academy Schools and Sketching Clubs

By this time, although still without formal schooling, Tenniel had acquired considerable finesse in portraiture. This is seen in the pendant watercolors of his parents (fig. 12 and fig. 13). In this census year of 1841, in which her twelfth and last child was born, Eliza Maria was still a beauty. Auburn ringlets, somewhat less profuse than formerly, border the alert wide-set eyes, and the charming lines of her satin ball gown, cut to expose her neck and shoulders, show a slender figure. John Baptist, in his portrait, looks younger than his forty-nine years.

In that year, Tenniel and Charles Martin submitted their work for the last time to the Society of British Artists. This may have resulted from the society's new rules prohibiting exhibition by nonmembers, as membership might have been prejudicial to their standing with the academy.[12]

Fig. 12. *(Left)* Tenniel, *Eliza Maria Tenniel,* watercolor, 1841. Fig. 13. *(Right)* Tenniel, *John Baptist Tenniel,* watercolor, 1841

From the start of 1842 Tenniel was a probationer at the Royal Academy Schools, admission requiring the applicant to submit an acceptable chalk drawing (or drawings) from the antique and a testimonial from a person of eminent respectability as to his moral character. He should have needed no introduction for, starting in 1837, Tenniel had shown work in each of the academy's annual exhibitions. This was no small achievement when many older artists queued up at the porter's station only to learn that their year's "performances" had once again been "chucked." Generally, students did not show their work until one or more years had elapsed following acceptance in the schools—a notable exception being Edwin Landseer, whose first exhibited work predated his admission at fourteen by one year.[13] Tenniel's five years as an exhibitor prior to his probationership may well have been unprecedented.

The academy was then in Trafalgar Square, about two miles from Gloucester Place and made more inconvenient by the two-to-three hour gap between day and evening classes. In the three-month probation period it was Tenniel's task to prepare a set of drawings to be judged by the school's council. He cleared these hurdles to duly receive his reward—the "ivory ticket" or "bone," a small disk inscribed on one side, "Royal Academy / Antique School / 1768," and on the other, "John Tenniel / admitted 15 April 1842."[14]

Due to the academy's all-important annual summer exhibition, which took up all its space, school was suspended through August, students using the interim to make copies from sculpture at the British Museum or paintings in the National Gallery. It was probably in this period that Tenniel studied the Elgin Marbles and other sculptures at the museum with academy hopefuls James Clarke Hook and Henry Le Jeune. It may have been in this year, too, that John Baptist (teaching deportment at the Misses Cahusac's school in Highgate) brought in a portfolio of Tenniel's designs for Bunyan's *Pilgrim's Progress,* which had won a prize at the Society of Arts. Annie Gilchrist, then a pupil at the school, when recalling the "great pride" with which John Baptist displayed his son's work to Miss Cahusac, thought that Tenniel had been a student at the time.[15]

But even for a rising young artist, summer must have its lighter pleasures. One dawn found Tenniel and three companions asleep aboard the yacht *Amethyst,* moored in Portsmouth Harbor, when "a tremendous *crash* was heard, and out of bed they scuffled / Then Wadham shriek'd, and Tenniel roar'd, The Skipper join'd the hustle."[16] In further extravagant lines, transcribed by Tenniel many years later, his shipmate George Cockburn Hyde relates how a "Night Alarm" disturbed what was doubtless a jolly voyage.

In September classes resumed. From the benches on the curved side of the semicircular gallery that served for the antique school, students were set to work copying the casts that were ranged against the opposite wall—the *Fighting Gladiator,* the *Apollo Belvedere,* the *Dancing Faun,* and so on.

Henry Holiday—a student shortly after Tenniel's time—would struggle with this routine for two or three years, finally deciding, there being no teaching "worthy of the name," to conduct most of his studies at home. Tenniel, older and less patient with merely "being allowed to teach" himself, "soon left in utter disgust."[17]

As a knowledge of anatomy was his most pressing need, sometime after this he began work at the Artists' Society's life-drawing sessions at 29 Clipstone Street, less than a mile east of his home. Here, on one side of the spacious premises acquired for his work for the National Gallery, the architectural sculptor C. H. Smith (husband of Fanny Riviere) had built two large studios for the society. The fifteen members and seventy subscribers were mostly professional artists who came to draw from models who were posed draped or nude on alternate weeks. Although the sessions themselves were instructorless, occasional lecturers were brought in—a Dr. Rogers, who spoke on anatomy, and Smith himself, expert in perspective.[18]

It may have been at Clipstone Street that Tenniel first met Charles Keene, his junior by over three years, and, until 1847, serving a five-year apprenticeship at the wood-engraving firm of Whympers. Like Tenniel, the tall, shy, and grave young man was an assiduous worker with a great love of old costumes, old ballads, seventeenth-century romances, Shakespeare, and Italian opera. He shared, too, Tenniel's conservative politics and dislike of interviews. But, unlike Tenniel, who tended toward the elegant in dress and order in surroundings, the casualness of Keene's dress, the welter of his workplace, were notorious. His association with the Artists' Society would outlast Tenniel's as he later became a member and, in the late fifties, was still one of its most constant workers.[19]

The sketching club, which met on Friday evenings, had been a society institution since 1838. Participation was limited to those proposed and elected by its members. After completing their two-hour memory sketches, based on given titles, the artists discussed the results and enjoyed a late supper. This practice may well have sparked the convivial evenings of the mid-forties that Tenniel and Keene spent sketching with their friend Thomas Barrett. Such informal sketching clubs were not uncommon; the artist Clarkston Stanfield was in a similar group in the late thirties, and Holiday would initiate one with artists Marcus Stone and Simeon Solomon around 1856.[20]

At the Barretts', after dinner their host would produce lamp, paper, and colored chalks, and he and the two artists would set to, producing series of drawings that burlesqued lines from Shakespeare, Plutarch, *Percy's Reliques,* history, and so forth.[21] The resulting folio of drawings they entitled "The Book of Beauty" after one of the steel-engraved annuals that had been fashionable in the 1820s and 1830s.

It is in these drawings that Tenniel first emerges as a satirical draftsman. In fact, one of his Shakespearean burlesques, "My lord; 'tis I. The early village cock" (*Richard III,* act 5, scene 3), resurfaces again in an 1855 *Punch* drawing in which the speaker of the line likewise wears a helmet resembling a cock's head.[22] As in the "Book of Beauty" sketch, Tenniel's depiction of Richard III displays his fondness for caricaturing the actor Charles Kean.

Pierian Draughts

While Tenniel amused himself with comic sketches, momentous events were agitating the world of high art. The first of the Westminster competitions to determine the decoration of the newly rebuilt Houses of Parliament was held in 1843. Both Martin and Haydon had submitted cartoons, or full-size preparatory drawings for frescoes. To enable himself to paint the life-size figures required, Martin had "bought bones and figures, and set to work with heart and soul to study anatomy." Luckily, there had been a general upturn in Martin's fortunes that year, so that the adverse verdict of the Fine Arts Commission, followed by some scathing reviews in the papers, were not as crushing as they might have been. This was not so for Haydon. Having long urged the government to invest in public art, he exultantly thought in 1834 as he watched the parliamentary buildings burning, "There is now a better prospect of painting a House of Lords," and in that year he successfully petitioned for the government to set aside areas of wall in the new buildings for this purpose.[23] Now, the rejection of his cartoon barred him from further competition.

In that summer of 1843, while all the cartoons were on view at Westminster Hall, artist John Leech slyly changed the title of his large engraving in *Punch* from "Pencillings" to "Cartoon," thus giving a new meaning to that word. Meanwhile, Tenniel, for the "Book of Beauty," drew a mock entry for the competition of that year entitled "Chivalry—Parmilientary [*sic*] Cartoon," replete with knights on toy horses.[24]

Around this time Tenniel was involved in another, smaller contest. In the previous year the London Art Union had announced the first of its annual outline competitions, a premium being offered for a series of ten designs suggesting the simplicity, calm, purity of drawing, and "severe beauty of form" found in ancient vases and in the outlines of John Flaxman and certain Germans. As subjects were to be drawn from British history or the work of British authors, Tenniel chose Chaucer's telling of the story of the patient Griselda from the "Clerk's Tale." The first premium went to H. C. Selous, a former pupil of Martin. Tenniel, F. R. Pickersgill, and Noël Paton each received honorary premiums of twenty pounds. The award, monetarily negligible, was probably instrumental in bringing Tenniel's talents to the attention of S. C. Hall, editor of the *Art-Union Monthly Journal.* Soon Tenniel would be contributing to the second series of Hall's *Book of British Ballads* (1844) along with his fellow winners of the Art Union's outline competition and a number of others whose work accorded with the popular Germanic trend in illustration.[25]

The artists, many of them in the early stage of their careers, met at Hall's cottage in Old Brompton to receive their assigned ballads and the wood blocks for their border designs.[26] For Tenniel, as for some of the others, it was a first experience in drawing on wood for engraving. He was assigned ten small illustrations for "King Estmere"—a piece from *Percy's Reliques* with such familiar balladic walk-ons as the boy messenger who travels at successively greater speeds and a proud porter at the gate.

Tenniel, like some others on the project, drew in "shaded outlines," a technique popularized by the German followers of Flaxman (particularly Friedrich Retzsch) in which the lines on one side of figures or objects are given extra thickness or are drawn as double lines in order to suggest shading or volume.[27] Tenniel must not have been working at Clipstone Street long, for the anatomy is weak. But there is promise of the future illustrator in the expressiveness of face and gesture.

Forty years later Hall wrote of the planning meetings, "I can not doubt that these 'Evenings' have prominent places in the recollections of some who may, perhaps, associate with them the earliest draughts they drank of the Pierian spring, of which they have since quaffed so liberally." For the artists, however, it was not Pierian draughts that stayed in memory, but the lack of draughts and of food, too, more nourishing than the coffee and biscuits that Hall served, and once the meeting was over they procured an excellent supper at an inn, " some partying till daybreak."[28]

A Great Idea of High Art

Early in 1845, with little accomplished since the first Westminster competition, the fine arts commissioners opened a new contest. For the chamber of the House of Lords they chose three allegorical subjects—Justice, Religion, and Chivalry—and three historical subjects, inviting six artists to submit. The competition was additionally open to all others not previously disqualified. Tenniel now entered a design.[29]

Unlike the 1843 notice, which had specified that the cartoons be "not less than ten or more than fifteen feet in their longest dimension," the new rules, which called for a color sketch and fresco specimen as well, required cartoons the size of the chamber's compartments—over nine feet wide by sixteen feet high. Both times the satirists responded to these extraordinary dimensions. In "Guy Fawkes treated classically," an etching for his 1844 *Comic Almanac,* George Cruikshank showed what happens when an artist "forgets the prescribed size and carries the grand classical to such a height" that it cannot be gotten through the doorway to Westminster Hall. Then, an 1847 issue of *Punch* showed Mr. Punch having a nightmarish "Dream of the House of Lords" in which high art prevailed, "not only from the top

of the wall, but even down to the lowest depth of the skirting-board." Two months later, Richard Doyle's cut of Mr. Punch, painter, accompanied the declaration that "England will never know what High Art really is till it has seen *Punch*'s own historical picture, thirty five feet by ten, painted with the aid of a ladder" (fig. 14). Tenniel made a similar pun when he told Spielmann in 1889, "I had a great idea of High Art; in fact, in 1845 I sent in a sixteen-foot high cartoon for Westminster Palace."[30]

To accommodate this scale, Tenniel rented studio space. The biographer of painter Ford Madox Brown noted that at Tudor Lodge (a "nest of studios" near Mornington Crescent in the Albert Road) Tenniel worked next door to Brown, likewise engaged on a "Spirit of Justice," as were Tudor Lodge workers William Cave Thomas (one of the six invited to compete) and John Marshall. Tenniel was in good company, for in this complex there labored others who would win premiums in the cartoon and oil categories.[31]

While occupied in this stimulating milieu, Tenniel still lived in the family household at 22 Gloucester Place, as shown by his letter of submission to Secretary of the Commission Charles Eastlake. Its message was brief: "According to the requisition . . . I beg to send herewith a color'd sketch of the Allegory of *Justice* together with a specimen in Fresco—and a cartoon—which last I regret to say, owing to illness, is but a sketch." Was this fortuitous, or did Tenniel recall from the 1842 notice that the judges would favor "precision of drawing" and "effective arrangement" over tonal rendering or "chiaroscuro"? As it was, the *Times* critic declared that Tenniel's cartoon reminded him of "Retzsch's happiest creations."[32]

By 28 June, before the official opening of the 1845 Westminster Hall exhibition, the word was out. Edward Armitage, Paton, and Tenniel had each won a premium of two hundred pounds. Two weeks later the *Illustrated London News* reproduced Tenniel's outline cartoon (fig. 15), and, in 1848, from his carefully finished watercolor "sketch" (which had been purchased by the Art Union), a lithograph version was produced.[33]

In Tenniel's cartoon, Justice, who vaguely resembles the young queen, forms the apex of a circular grouping of figures arranged on a flight of steps. There are overtones of a North Renaissance Last Judgment, except that in

Fig. 14. Richard Doyle, "Punch's Own Picture," illustration, *Punch,* 17 July 1847, 19

place of the archangel Michael (usually shown with a sword and a balance) is Justice. Her right hand grasps a sword; an angel dangles a balance above her head. But where convention calls for the worthy to rise on stage right (the viewer's left), the damned to be cast down on stage left, Tenniel has reversed the scheme—something he would repeat in two subsequent Last Judgment arrangements. The "terrified Boy" (as the *Athenaeum*'s critic called him) who clings to Justice's gown is a motif that would reappear in two later Tenniel designs. About two dozen other figures—sitting, kneeling, lying, falling—are representative of all humanity, its virtues and its defects. Following the precepts of Sir Joshua Reynolds, Tenniel draped them in the most generalized clothing so that they cannot be identified as to time, class, or type, except for the Knight Templar or Red-Cross Knight, distinguishable by his robe of white with the large cross on its front, and the shadowed executioner to his left.[34] Since it was the knightly ideal to defend the weak and the oppressed against injustice, the Templar—a twelfth-century militant "Knight of Christ"—was an apt symbol.

Fig. 15. Engraving of Tenniel's "Allegory of Justice," *Illustrated London News,* 12 July 1845, 25

The extensive press coverage during the two-month-long showing of the entries was generally favorable. The *Illustrated London News* declared that Tenniel's was "a name . . . no more to remain unknown in art," and several other leading papers thought he showed "the highest promise," "was destined to high positions," and would be expected "to excel." These more than offset the *Athenaeum*'s review, which found the expression in some cases "pushed to exaggeration," the drawing faulty," and thought that the circular composition left "a considerable amount of central space entirely 'to let.'"[35]

Tenniel's fellow "Germanists" of Tudor Lodge fared less well than he. The *Times* judged Thomas's *Justice* "hard and stiff" and Brown's "crowded and exaggerated in expression," while the *Literary Gazette* said of the latter, "high German and grotesque (far beyond the Retzsch-like #85 of Tenniel) . . . the whole is a mistake."[36]

By August Tenniel was one of the five who, having "distinguished themselves as designers or as fresco-painters," were chosen to do one of the eight frescoes in the Upper Waiting Hall (the Hall of Poets). In early November he was in Munich studying the art of fresco painting, although his specimen in this technique had been judged, at least by the *Illustrated London News,* as "one of the most successful in the Hall."[37] But two years would pass before the artists were invited to select their subjects.

Pit and Stage

Meanwhile, Tenniel was happily occupied. Through much of the decade he added to his sketches in the pit. Some from 1841 depict the original cast of Dion Boucicault's *London Assurance*—William Farren, Ben Webster, and Mrs. Nesbitt of the "silvery laugh." The next year there was Rossini's *Semiramide* featuring Adelaide Kemble in her last year on the stage, and Handel's *Acis and Galatea* with the exquisite contralto Priscilla Horton. Donizetti's *Linda di Chamouni,* with its obligatory pursued heroine and disguised nobleman, we trace to 1843, when Tenniel saw it with Fornasari, the celebrated tenor Mario, and Lablache of the immense voice and girth. In 1843, too, he saw Michael Balfe's *Bohemian Girl* in which another distraught maiden and camouflaged nobleman sang to the sentimental strains of "When other lips and other hearts" and "I dreamed I dwelt in marble halls." For tragedy there was William Macready in the title role in *Athelwold* with Samuel Phelps and the admirable Helen Faucit; for extravaganza, J. R. Planché's *Fortunio, or the Seven Gifted Servants;* and, for spectacle, the Easter opening of the new Astley's Amphitheatre with comic favorite Henry Widdicombe.[38]

From another extravaganza, Charles Dance's *Magic Horn,* comes the sketch of a woeful Robert Keeley beating a drum marked "native," his squat body in American Indian dress. Elsewhere we see Keeley as Dickens's Sairy Gamp and as Clown in *The Winter's Tale.* The jack-tar incarnate "in blue jacket and loose white ducks," T. P. Cooke, is shown as William in Jerrold's *Black-Eyed Susan;* and Charles Mathews and the still fetching Madame Vestris (who had charmed audiences at Drury Lane the week that Tenniel was born) are depicted in *Little Devil.* In one sketch, General Tom Thumb stoutly thumbs his nose at the comedian Mr. Emery, and in another, F. Matthews wears a crown of straw as the mad emperor Babashaw—the last to be redrawn in 1851 as a *Punch* initial.[39]

By 1846 Tenniel himself would attract some critical notice for his portrayal of Frederick in Thomas Morton's comedy *The School of Reform; or, How to Rule a Husband.* The triple bill (there were two farces as well) was a benefit put on by the Artists' General Benevolent Institution, which had been founded in 1814 to help needy artists and their dependents. Possibly inspired by Martin, who had been active on the institution's behalf, Tenniel would become a lifelong supporter.[40]

In the romantic lead, originally played by the handsome Charles Kemble in 1805, Tenniel spoke such ardent lines as "but oh, this heart. This grateful heart was bursting!" Supporting the male members of the cast—artists by occupation and actors by avocation—were professional actresses with at least one, Miss Arden, familiar from Tenniel's pencilings. The *Art-Union Monthly Journal* judged the performances at the St. James's Theatre to be entirely professional, and along with the artist F. W. Topham, who played the outlaw Tyke, Tenniel was singled out for the highest acclaim, the critic declaring that he "had the advantage over the class of actors who, in these our days, personate young gentlemen . . . he looked and spoke as gentlemen really do in private life." Playing the title role in the closing farce, W. B. Rhodes's *Bombastes Furioso,* was Tenniel's long-time acquaintance George Cruikshank, always ready to "throw down his tools and stroll about the country with a theatrical company," or to improvise a cape and sing the "Loving Ballad of Lord Bateman."[41]

Before Tenniel would appear again at the St. James's, he played a bit part in a real-life drama. The year 1848 saw revolutions on the continent and, at the same time, the third presentation to Parliament of the People's Charter—a document outlining reforms conceived in the interests of the working classes. On the morning of 10 April a procession was to bring the giant charter with its millions of signatures from Kennington Common to the House of Commons. Fearing a lower-class insurrection, the government had dispersed troops and artillery around the city, fortified and garrisoned the Bank of England and all public offices, and sworn in about 150,000 special constables. On 9 April diarist Charles Greville described the preparations as so extensive "that it is either very sublime or very ridiculous." It was not sublime. The affair fizzled out when the leaders were dissuaded from taking the procession to Westminster, and the petition was peacefully delivered by coach.[42]

Tenniel, sworn in as a constable and supplied with a truncheon and an armband that said "Special," had walked up and down his assigned beat "hoping" he "shouldn't have to fight anybody." Not far north of him, near Euston Square, Henry Thompson, a first-year medical student (later a noted surgeon and a friend of Tenniel's), was going his rounds too, baton in hand; and, in another part of the city, Tenniel's future *Punch* colleagues, editor Mark Lemon and artist John Leech, were on patrol together, as Leech recalled, "trying the area gates, etc., Mark continually finding excuses for taking a small glass of ale or brandy and water."[43]

The alarms of 10 April over, on the 27th the St. James's saw the second of the Artist's General Benevolent Institution performances. Six of the original artist-actors had returned. Some of the cast, including Tenniel—handsome in a skirted long coat, lace cravat, high boots, and shoulder-length wig—are pictured in the *Illustrated London News* of 6 May (fig. 16). In the title role of George Coleman's comedy *The Heir at Law* Tenniel again had lines that seem more appropriate to melodrama: "Disappointment!—'tis torture—

it racks me—Caroline fled, none knows wither—unprotected! Perhaps exposed to want too!"[44]

A farce followed—Charles Kemble's *Plot and Counterplot; or, the Portrait of Cervantes*—with Tenniel as the lover, Don Leon, gorgeous in a purple and silver tunic and white silk pantaloons. Although he had lines of firm resolve ("Whatever be the consequence, I will discover myself") and of passion ("let me behold your charming mistress, adore her, and expire at her feet"), the main kudos of the *Illustrated London News* went to Cruikshank, "irresistibly droll" as the don's valet Pedrillo.[45]

The Illustrator

The year was mainly remarkable for Tenniel's introduction to Dickens, to whose Christmas book *The Haunted Man* he contributed five designs. Tenniel had received several commissions since *The Book of British Ballads,* perhaps as result of his Westminster Hall fame. In 1845 he executed a design for the third volume of *The Book of Nursery Tales* and did the eleven illustrations for an edition of F. H. C. de la

Fig. 16. "Artists' Amateur Performance," *Illustrated London News,* 6 May 1848, 299 (detail)

Motte Fouqué's *Undine,* both published by James Burns and noteworthy for Tenniel's exuberantly grotesque border designs in the German manner. His next contribution was to Burns's *Poems and Pictures* (1846), along with many others whose names are familiar from the Westminster Hall competitions. Continuing in this vein for *Sharpe's London Magazine,* he pictured a knight's vigil in 1846 and, in the next year, the story of Griseldis, probably based on his Art Union outlines.[46]

Around this time, a letter to a client to arrange a portrait sitting shows that Tenniel had moved from the family home to lodgings in 53 Berners Street in the heart of east Marylebone's artists' colony. This would have provided a less distracting working environment than the house in Gloucester Place, which, although spacious, held up to nine other Tenniel children and two to three servants. Furthermore, there were his father's students; John Baptist's small treatise of March 1845 announced that "Mr. Tenniel's exercises can be seen by applying at his residence . . . and they are taught by Himself and his Sons [Tenniel's younger brothers William Rickards and James]."[47]

It was probably at Berners Street that Tenniel completed his major commission of this period, more than one hundred illustrations for Rev. Thomas James's version of *Aesop's Fables.* The introduction to the *Aesop*'s publisher, John Murray of the long-established firm in Albemarle Street, came through Leopold Martin, who was also responsible for the wood engraving of Tenniel's designs. These, in the judgment of the *Art-Union Monthly Journal,* were engraved "with a degree of skill which Bewick himself might have claimed."[48]

It may be that the recommendation that Tenniel join John Leech, Clarkston Stanfield, and Frank Stone as illustrator for *The Haunted Man* came from Dickens's publishers, Bradbury and Evans, who had printed the *Aesop.* By late October, Tenniel and Dickens had met and discussed the project, for the novelist wrote to Leech, "He seems a very agreeable fellow, and modest; we must arrange a dinner here, very shortly, when you and he may meet." On 3 January 1849, at Devonshire Terrace just east of the Marylebone parish church, Dickens held a "christening dinner" for *The Haunted Man.* Besides the book's illustrators, the guests included Mark Lemon and *Punch* proprietors William Bradbury and Frederick Mullett Evans. This commission introduced Tenniel to the *Punch* team, as well as providing an entrée to the social circle of Dickens.[49]

Saint Cecilia

All this time the fresco project was in abeyance. The previous September the commissioners had committed to Tenniel the subject of his choice, "Alexander's Feast," John Dryden's ode on Saint Cecilia's Day. This tribute to the invention of organ music may have been Tenniel's salute to his own musical family, for his uncle James Calkin was the noted organist of the Regent Square Church in St. Pancras; James's brother William was organist for the county of Sussex; and James's son John Baptiste, now twenty-one, had held the post of organist and choirmaster at St. Columba's College near Dublin since 1846.[50]

Because the English dampness, cold, and fog would prevent the proper drying of the fresco, the artists could only paint in the months of June through September. This gave the commissioners enough time to change Tenniel's subject after his design "had been decided on and worked out." John Callcott Horsley, assigned the compartment next to Tenniel's, had also suffered a change of subject. The painting that Tenniel commenced in that summer of 1849 was based on another and simpler poem on the patroness of music—Dryden's "Song for Saint Cecilia's Day" (fig. 17).[51]

Tenniel's design illustrates the poem's sixth stanza:

> But oh! what art can teach
>   What human voice can reach,
> The sacred organ's praise?
> Notes inspiring holy love,
> Notes that wing their heavenly ways
>   To mend the choirs above.

Fig. 17. Engraving of Tenniel's "St. Cecilia," *Illustrated London News,* 14 Apr. 1855, 353

The saint, her hands over the fingerboard of a small organ, kneels in a brilliant light. The "choirs above," unlike the airborne angel-songsters in representations of the saint by Raphael and Reynolds, are symbolized by cherub heads ornamenting the framing Roman arch, their wings suggesting a Norman zigzag pattern. With the surrounding figures, Tenniel had approximated another circular composition—although not as pronounced as in his *Justice.* The attitudes of the kneeling knight, the woman with hands crossed over her breast, the brooding king, are evocative of another of the poem's lines: "What passion cannot Music raise and quell?"[52]

By the time the commissioners authorized the work in the Hall of Poets it was already clear that conditions at Westminster constituted a painters' nightmare. As fresco required that the water-soluble paints be laid on the still-damp plaster, the work had to be broken down into small manageable sections, the plasterer and painter working together. There was no opportunity for correction or for the gradual building up that one does in oil painting, and once the plaster was laid the painter had to continue laboring without rest until the area begun was completed. It required the most careful planning to avoid visible joinings between one day's work and the next, and to match tints that dried lighter than when they were applied.[53]

In addition to these challenges, fresco demanded certain atmospheric conditions for proper drying and preservation of the work. At Westminster, in the space between the laths that held the plastering and the outer stone wall, the damp accumulated with no way of escape. Thus the preparatory layer was not always sufficiently dry before the finishing plaster was laid. Effacing the work even while it was in progress were the contaminants in the air: coal gas from the vast workshop on the building's terrace and sulfur dioxide from the gasoliers that, condensing, formed sulfuric acid.[54]

Worst of all were the sewer gases from the Thames, so strong that passengers crossing Westminster Bridge were forced to hold their noses. *Punch,* campaigning for action, cried, "Dirty City, dirty City!" and ran pictures showing "Dirty Father Thames" and the streams of putrefying materials that flowed into the river. Testimony from the first group of artists working in the Chamber of the House of Lords—William Dyce, Charles Cope, and Horsley—tells a story of "cracks in the plaster preparation," "deposits of London dirt on the surface, of a yellow brown colour," of days when "the wet ran down the surface in streams," and of "foul and most destructive gases," causing decay at one end of a painting while they were "painfully working at the other."[55]

These conditions would have confronted Tenniel as well, in a summer that coincided with a severe cholera epidemic in London. They were mitigated only by the smaller dimensions of the frescoes in the Waiting Hall—about one third the size of those in the Lords' Chamber. Fortunately, Tenniel was a watercolorist. Whereas most had submitted their color studies for the competition in the form of oil sketches, he had not. Unlike the painters in oils, he was used to paints that dried lighter than when applied, that did not lend themselves to blending or reworking. Thus, the *Art Journal* of 1852 would find "in the execution and finish" of his *Saint Cecilia* "a taste and novelty which appear to reduce fresco to the facility of water-colour drawing in the hands of this artist." His fresco, "painted thinly with very fluid washes," was still in relatively good preservation in 1895 when the adjoining works, which had been painted more heavily, had blistered and peeled to the point where they had to be covered over.[56] Tenniel had the advantage, too, of being an extremely methodical worker. One pictures him, starting out each morning for his daily six- or seven-hour stint at Westminster with his usual "jaunty air" and positive attitude. The fresco was duly finished and signed and dated 1849.

From start to finish the project had lasted over four years. The Fine Arts Commission, for all its ostensible care, had in its misguided course produced a failure and caused years of wasted labor for some of the artists. All in all Tenniel benefited, not so much monetarily—although the two-hundred-pound premium and four-hundred-pound commission were fair sums in those days—as in prestige at a time when this was most welcome for his career. In addition to the frequent press coverage, a lithograph of his design had been issued for private circulation, even while the work was in progress.[57]

Still, these years provided lessons in the drawbacks of high art sufficient to daunt a well-adjusted young man. There was Martin in the late thirties, in conflict with the academy and losing money through the pirating of his prints; there was Haydon, "suddenly changed to an old man" at the rejection of his Westminster cartoon and a suicide three years later.[58] But just as persuasive, perhaps, was Tenniel's own irrepressible tendency to see the absurdities that might accompany lofty aspirations.

"Jackides"
1850–1862

No longer Jack, henceforth Jackides call.
—MARK LEMON, speaking of Tenniel at the *Punch* table

A Kindly Destiny

A November day in 1850 found Tenniel on his way to the editorial office of *Punch* close by the bustling newspaper center of Fleet Street. Then, as today, this busy thoroughfare juxtaposed old and new with cool impartiality. Near its western end he would have passed Christopher Wren's Temple Bar, a huge gateway of Portland stone that would continue to impede traffic for another twenty-eight years. Other landmarks seem eternal: St. Dunstan's in the West, its two carved giants poised to strike the hour; and the Temple with its landscaped quadrangles, fine old halls, barrister's chambers, and twelfth-century Temple Church. Further on, past unobtrusive entryways leading from the traffic-filled street into centuries-old passageways and courts, lies Bouverie Street. Sloping southward toward the river, it occupies land once held by a Whitefriars monastery. There, by the second turn on the right at number 11 was the firm of Bradbury and Evans, publishers of the comic weekly *Punch*. Number 6, once a residence, housed the workshop of the firm's engraver, Joseph Swain, and nearby were the press buildings where great rolls of paper were hoisted by rope and pulley onto landing stages just as they would be through much of the next century.

Tenniel came to Bouverie Street this day by invitation, for Mark Lemon was hard-pressed for an artist experienced in drawing on wood to complete the decorative work for the paper's nineteenth half-yearly volume.[1] This entailed doing the title page, headings and tailpieces for the preface and index, a border for the 1851 almanac (which might contain as many as fifty tiny figures), and thirteen initial letters—all work that needed to be begun straightway.

Despite its frothy tone, the nine-year-old weekly was already a formidable organ of political and social commentary. With a large readership including many in government itself, it was well on its way to becoming what a foreign observer would later call "a national epitome." It was its anti-papal language regarding the conferring of certain ecclesiastical titles in England by the Church of Rome that had caused the paper's leading decorative artist, the Catholic Richard "Dicky" Doyle, to relinquish his enviably secure berth. That sensitive young man, whose sprightly lilliputian figures were largely responsible for the appeal of *Punch*'s volumes of the forties, had left the paper in a situation that was inconvenient, if not as desperate as is sometimes implied. Since proprietor Frederick Mullett "Pater" Evans drafted his reply to Doyle's initial notice on 15 November, this would have left a month until the almanac went to press. The firm moved quickly to engage Tenniel. His first contribution, an initial *L* showing a seventeenth-century gentleman preparing to mount a horse, was probably drawn on the block by 22 November for it to appear in the 30 November issue.[2]

The choice of Tenniel seems natural enough, as his 1848 *Aesop* had shown skills appropriate to *Punch*. But also, important for the staff's close-knit social fellowship, he was known to several of the Punchites. Writer Douglas Jerrold, at whose instance the invitation came, had been a habitué of Tudor Lodge and Devonshire Terrace and might thus have already been an acquaintance. Leech, Lemon, Bradbury, and Evans had met Tenniel at the 1849 "christening" for *The Haunted Man*, if not earlier.[3]

Tenniel's acceptance of Lemon's offer is just as unsurprising. Since the summer of 1849, when he painted his signature into the still-wet fresco at Westminster, Tenniel does not appear to have had any notable commissions. In fact, our sole knowledge of him at this time comes from Amy Evans, the wife of Pater Evans's son Fred, who retained a childhood memory of Tenniel as a "good-looking, dapper, bright, well-set-up young artist, about twenty-nine," engaged by her father, publisher and engraver Richard Lloyd, to paint some figures into a historical scene. The staff position on *Punch* was a most desirable situation, secure and well paid (by the sixties Tenniel would realize over twice as much as his counterpart on the comic paper *Fun*). It was attractive enough that in the early sixties artist George du Maurier confided to his mother that he had made "a dead set at that paper," wearing out a pair of boots "running after this Mark Lemon." "Let them once get me to one of the Punch dinners, that's all!" he wrote—an ambition that took him four years to realize. Despite Spielmann's assertion that Tenniel hesitated, "struggling against a kindly destiny," he could hardly have been other than pleased at the paper's invitation. His reported reaction—"Do they suppose, . . . that there is anything funny about *me*?"—was typical of his playacting, as Tenniel was well aware that he was a humorist.[4]

Work and Play at *Punch*

The *Punch* dinner to which du Maurier had aspired was the regular Wednesday feast at which the literary and artistic staff broached, debated, and settled upon the subject of the next political engraving. This full- or, occasionally, double-page "large cut" ("cut" meaning an impression from a cut or engraved design) was the paper's central feature, both in location and importance.

The large cut was not yet called the cartoon. While Leech had applied the word facetiously to his full-page political drawings in 1843 when the competing fresco cartoons were displayed at Westminster Hall, this usage lapsed until the late 1860s, the word "cartoonist" coming after. As late as 1868 an article in the *Mask* called Tenniel the "cartooner and principle artist of *Punch*."[5] Like Doyle, Tenniel did the occasional large cut, his cartoon contributions for the two 1851 volumes totaling seven. But "big cutting" was for the most part left to Leech in Tenniel's first seven or eight years on the paper.

Mainly, Tenniel did the fixed chores—titles, headings, tailpieces—for each half-yearly volume, plus a vast amount of initial letters and miscellaneous illustrations; in his first full year on *Punch* he designed 177 cuts. By early 1853 he ceased monogramming his work entirely (before then his device had appeared sporadically), so that by late 1862, when he began to monogram all his pieces, he had done about fifteen hundred unidentified drawings (see the appendix). As the literature on Tenniel rarely reproduces an unmonogrammed cut, it seems that most of this output is not credited to him at all—a particularly unfortunate outcome since his skills as a humorist (most evident in this early period) are often unacknowledged. For example, the preface to an anthology of *Punch* says of Tenniel (while incidentally reproducing, with no artist identification, three of his playful pieces), "His humorous captioned drawings possess little visual wit and he had no gift for fooling."[6]

His almost nine hundred decorated initials, being autonomous, may best show Tenniel's seemingly endless capacity for invention, his puckish humor. In chivalric subjects he was a worthy successor to Doyle, the "Professor of Medieval Design." An infidel hangs from a crusader's grasp by the seat of his pants, his nose serving as the crossbar of the letter *A* formed by his dangling limbs. A knight is lashed by his middle to a tree trunk with which his extended upper and lower body create a *K*. An *H* is formed by two Romanesque figures in chain mail, carrying between them a spear over which a third is limply draped (fig. 18, fig. 19, and fig. 20). Several knights carry umbrellas in memory of the Scottish tournament. Folk from earlier centuries do everyday things: a boy dangles a tidbit just out of reach of a chained dog—another chalks words on a hoarding, a lover holds taut a skein of yarn that his lady winds; a knight plays cricket. In other subjects, a botanist stretches himself over a crevasse to pluck a flower, a scalp hunter snatches a wig off a military officer, a lawyer pursues a sprite in a judge's wig, a stout woman recoils from a fortune-teller; the variety seems endless.[7]

In larger cuts he might mimic his serious designs. The Last Judgment scheme of his *Justice* was reborn in *Punch*'s title page for late 1850, the space "to let" now occupied by such lettering as the title required (fig. 21). Here the central figure is King's champion Punch, his gauntlet flung down to the wicked. Nations and classes ascend, while tumbling down on the other side are the sinful—figures representative of *Punch*'s favorite butts: the Smithfield Market, "pampered" footmen, dishonest tradesmen, and so on. One, holding a placard that reads "Noses and Son"—a slur on the slop-goods merchants Moses and Son—almost repeats a figure from Tenniel's Westminster car-

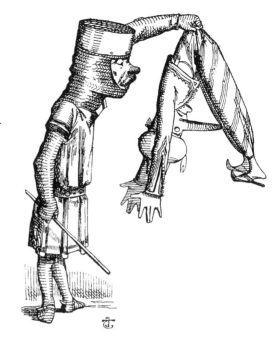

Fig. 18. Tenniel, initial *A, Punch,* July–Dec. 1851, 138

toon. Soon his Great Exhibition cartoon, "May Day, Eighteen Hundred and Fifty-One," would duplicate the general composition of Tenniel's allegory "The Great Industrial Meeting of All Nations" (then on view at the Royal Academy), even incorporating (in reverse) the figures of two litter bearers from the original.[8]

Fig. 19. Tenniel, initial *K, Punch,* July–Dec. 1851, 196

Fig. 20. Tenniel, initial *H, Punch,* Jan.–June 1851, 141

Fig. 21. Tenniel, title page, *Punch* vol. 19, July–Dec. 1850

From the start Tenniel grappled the proprietors to him with "hooke of steel." This was aided, certainly, by his graceful handling of money matters. Payments to the staff were handled by Evans, who with round form and eyes smiling benignly behind his spectacles was regarded affectionately by the *Punch* men. On 24 December 1850 Tenniel had sent Evans a list of his first drawings for *Punch,* stating that he would leave the amount of payment entirely up to him. But, as Evans then requested a scale of charges, this was supplied. Then, a third letter—a model of gentlemanliness—thanks Evans for not reducing his account, which he is "very sorry should have been above the rate of charges," adding, "I think the best plan in future will be for me to send you a list of my work leaving the amount entirely up to you, for I do assure you my wish is to fall in with your views to the fullest extent of my power, and I would not for the world appear exorbitant where I know that liberality is the order of the day." His further letters to the proprietors were usually social; an early one thanks Evans for another addition to a "long list of kindnesses"—a gift set of Dickens's *Household Words*. Although his earnings at *Punch* would rise from about £360 to £1,200 per annum over his fifty-year tenure, the files of the firm (later Bradbury and Agnew) reveal no further correspondence from Tenniel about payments, other than his acknowledgments of checks received. This is in marked contrast to the other artists.[9]

Pater Evans would remark at one of the paper's celebratory dinners, "Sociability is the seat of the success of Punch." It was generally agreed that this was owing to Lemon, who had fostered staff cohesion from the first, the weekly large-cut dinners being somewhat of a ploy to that end. *Punch*'s corpulent editor was a resourceful man. He could act quickly to best a perceived rival or squelch any proprietary attempt to interfere with his autonomy. The journalist and engraver Henry Vizetelly recalled him as "one of the most accomplished humbugs of his time." But to Dickens he was "a most affectionate and true-hearted fellow," and to *Punch*'s Shirley Brooks he was "the oldest and dearest friend" he "had in the world." It testifies to Lemon's adroitness that he was able to keep the "machinery" of *Punch* "oiled by good feeling and humour" in the paper's first years, a time when Jerrold's radical articles contrasted sharply with the often-bigoted pieces appearing in the same issues. Further strengthening the bonds between editor and staff were Lemon's Thursday morning visits to the homes of his artists and writers to ensure that there were no problems with the work for the coming issue.[10]

Punch camaraderie did not begin and end with the somewhat elaborate feasts at Bouverie Street, sometimes followed by a late evening at Evans's Song and Supper Rooms on the Piazza at Covent Garden. Other dinners were held at the Bedford Hotel at Covent Garden and the Albion Tavern in Aldersgate Street. Then there were home dinner parties and outings to Richmond, Hampton Court, Greenwich, Dulwich, and, each spring, the derby at Epsom Downs.[11]

In two early drawings for *Punch,* Tenniel showed his happiness in his new situation. His large cut for the derby issue of 1852, "The Epsom Marbles," is a spoof on the Elgin Marbles, on view at the British Museum since 1817 (fig. 22). In Tenniel's version of the Parthenon frieze (depicted in five bands) Punch leads the procession, followed by the proprietors, editor, and staff. Closing the *Punch* ranks, after Leech and William Thackeray, a beaming Tenniel rides at the start of band two. He and Leech grasp their graphite hold-

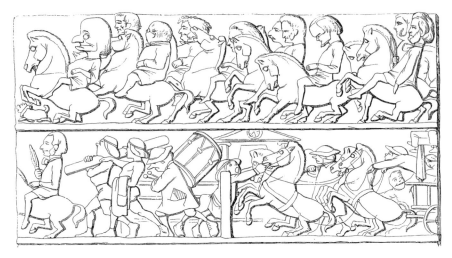

Fig. 22. Tenniel, "The Epsom Marbles," cartoon, *Punch,* 29 May 1852 (detail)

Fig. 23. Tenniel, half title, *Punch*
vol. 27, July–Dec. 1854

ers like thyrsi, suggesting that this is, after all, more of a bacchic procession than a Panathenaic one. After Tenniel come the acrobats, their assistant with "reedy pipes and drum," and a motley train comprising "every kind of carriage, van and wain" bound for "Epsom's verdant plain." Similarly, Tenniel's half-title for the late 1854 volume is the embodiment of conviviality (fig. 23). Under the surveillance of Mr. Punch, William Bradbury, and Evans, the staff are shown as schoolboys at play. Young Master Shirley Brooks (newly recruited) pitches a ball to batsman Thackeray, Tom Taylor vaults over Horace "Ponny" Mayhew, and Gilbert Abbot à Beckett (or is this Percival Leigh?) is about to send a shuttlecock to a gracefully tripping Lemon. The waspish Jerrold takes aim at some skittles that have human faces, and a smiling Leech rides his hobby horse over a little fence (perhaps Tenniel's sly dig at Leech's timid riding). In the background, an equally pleased Master Tenniel chalks a childish portrait of Mr. Punch on a nearby wall.[12]

Theatricals with Dickens

Tenniel had not completed his first six months on *Punch* when he was involved, along with Jerrold and Lemon, in the most ambitious of Dickens's theatricals. These performances, begun in 1845 with a cast drawn largely from the *Punch* staff, were to culminate in the formation of the Guild of Literature and Art, founded by Dickens and the writer Edward Bulwer Lytton. Like the Artists' General Benevolent Institution, the guild was created to aid artists and their dependents. But it planned for broader and longer-lasting benefits, which would be limited to its members and their widows. A three-by-five-inch booklet, put out after the guild was incorporated in June 1854, shows Tenniel to have been on its first council along with Lemon, à Beckett, and a collection of well-known writers, artists, and other notables.[13]

To help launch the guild, its president, Lytton, had written a five-act comedy, *Not So Bad as We Seem: or, Many Sides to a Character*. The Duke of Devonshire had granted the use of his town house in Picadilly for two performances, and no effort was spared in the production. A movable theater was erected; seven painters, two of them royal academicians, did the sets; and the program design (depicting the privations that had been suffered in the previous century by writer Daniel Defoe and artist Richard Wilson) was by E. M. Ward.[14] On 16 May 1851 the amateurs played triumphantly before the queen, the prince consort, and as many as could be gotten into the duke's great drawing room.

With action revolving around a Jacobite plot and counterplot, conspiring lovers, and a visored lady of mystery who surreptitiously flings bouquets at her estranged spouse, one doubts that it would appeal today. Leading roles were taken by Dickens, Jerrold, and Lemon, other parts falling to several noted artists and writers, among them Martin's son-in-law, the writer Peter Cunningham.

Tenniel played the stage rustic Hodge, a type he was to satirize in cartoons, his lines of broad dialect interspersed with such exclamations as "Fegs" and "Zooks." His role may not have been as miniscule as shown in the printed play; one of the players, R. H. Horne, wrote that "the minor parts . . . have all been reduced to mere shreds in the acting copies since published." Tenniel himself wrote that Hodge was, for him, "quite a good little part," although not as important as the one he was to later receive. The second performance, at Devonshire House on 29 May, was to be followed by other showings that year at the Queen's Rooms in Hanover Square, and in Reading and Bristol.[15]

In 1852 the company toured several northern counties, Tenniel doing his part in touching up and arranging the scenery. February found them in Liverpool, May in Birmingham, August in Sunderland, and September again in Liverpool. By May, with the illness of Dickens's friend John Forster, who had filled the "very important" role of the cynical Hardman, Dickens assigned the part to Tenniel.[16]

However, it may have been a performance of Boucicault's *Used Up* that prompted Dickens to write to Forster from Liverpool, "you have no idea how good Tenniel, [F. W.] Topham, and [Wilkie] Collins have been in what they had to do." The comedy headed the bill on 3 September 1852 in the group's final appearance at Liverpool's Philharmonic Hall with Tenniel as the rogue Tom Saville, crony of the bored or "used up" nobleman to whom the title refers. Also in the repertory was Planché's historical drama *Charles XII*. Might a real-life predicament during one of its performances have inspired Tenniel's small cut in *Punch*'s 1866 almanac? In "Private Theatricals— Jones's Dressing-Room," the excited Jones, whose boots have not been provided by the costumer, protests to Brown: "I can't play Charles XII in patent leather boots with green tops! I must have yours." Presumably, as Gustavus de Mervelt (another J. Vining role), Tenniel suffered no such inconvenience and appeared splendidly arrayed in gold-trimmed surtout, leather breeches, large boots, and cocked hat trimmed with yellow fringe and ostrich feathers. As the lover he had such feverish lines as "Distraction! I shall go mad immediately" and "Fortune, thou hast done thy worst."[17]

While on tour, the company made it a rule to "dine and sup together." Usually this was followed by a bit of rough play, leapfrog around the dinner table being a favorite. The athletic Tenniel could clear the "high back" that Dickens invariably presented, but Lemon's bulk might be another matter. Tenniel recalled the ludicrous image of a player who "landed on Lemon's back and stuck there until pushed off by his successor in the round," and of another whose "vigorous run" at Dickens's back "sent both leaper and 'frog' flying under the table."[18]

Julia

Recalling some of the happy pastimes of those years is an album bound in red morocco and cloth, compiled by Tenniel in his retirement years and entitled "*Bouts-Rimés* (and other *nonsense*)." Bouts-rimés or rhymed endings, a word game popular since the eighteenth century, has been described as follows: "A number of slips of paper are distributed, and each person is invited to write two words that rhyme. The slips are then collected and read aloud, and each player is then required to write a stanza introducing all the rhymes in question." The authors of the fifteen poems in Tenniel's album are "Julia," "A. B.," "E. H. W.," and Tenniel, who also illustrated them all, later reusing some of the designs in the 1850 and 1851 *Punch* volumes.[19]

As in his work for *Punch,* medieval subjects predominate. The drawings have the facetiousness and anomalousness characteristic of R. H. Barham's then-popular *Ingoldsby Legends* (1837). A Spanish knight, named Widdicomez after the principle comic of Astley's Amphitheatre, Henry Widdicombe, and resembling him in Tenniel's drawing, is slain by four Victorian footmen. Crusaders smoke cigars, sport umbrellas and mufflers, and are accompanied by "boys in buttons" (page boys). One poem, "Count Robert," is clearly a version of "The Loving Ballad of Lord Bateman," and in Tenniel's drawing the Saracen's daughter is a close sister to Sophia the Turk's daughter in George Cruikshank's 1839 etchings to the ballad.[20]

The player Julia is Julia Giani whose mockingly plaintive poems display a fondness for knight errantry matching Tenniel's own. Her family, like his, had roots in the artistic community of Marylebone, where we find the surname recorded as early as 1806. But of direct interest for Julia is a double wedding performed in the parish church in the New Road on Boxing Day (26 December) 1821, two of the principals sharing the surname Berry. There, the eighteen-year-old Eve, a minor, on this day and with the consent of her father, Henry Berry, married the young dancing master Julius Giani. The marriage was sufficiently fashionable to have been noted in the *Times,* which gave the groom's address as Charles Street, Middlesex Hospital, the same as for one Lorenzo Giani, artist.[21]

The Gianis were people of means. Three years earlier, a Giani marriage at St. Marylebone had been mentioned in the exclusive *Gentleman's Magazine.* On 3 August 1824 Eve and Julius brought the month-old Julia to be baptized in the parish church, perhaps from 66 Norton Street, Fitzroy Square, where the *Boarding School and London Masters' Directory* locates "Mr. Julius Gioni [*sic*], Dancing Master" in 1828.[22]

It was a large home, renting for well over the cost of 25 Allsop's Buildings (or Allsop's Terrace, as it was later called) and by the 1831 census occupied by two families of Gianis and their three servants. The homes on the east side of Norton Street backed onto the houses on Cirencester Place, where the drawing master Riviere lived with his family. His daughter Fanny, residing in that neighborhood of "artists, musicians, and engravers" until her marriage in 1834, recalled the houses as "good, well-built, commodious" but "with most unsanitary *backs,*" noting that "consumption was very prevalent, but no one attributed it to unhealthy dwellings." Perhaps it was this, or that other nineteenth-century scourge, cholera, but by the Quarter Day (one of the four annual days when dwelling rates were due) of midsummer 1834 the house on Norton Street stood vacant. As reported in the *Times,* Julius Giani had died "in his 38th year, much and deservedly regretted by his numerous friends. He had made his will two months before Julia's birth, leaving to his "lawful wife Eve everything" that he possessed, "being of whatsoever nature it may." The genuineness of the writing was attested to by two occupants of the home on Norton Street. One was Ann Berry, "spinster," Eve's sister and most probably the "A. B." of the bouts-rimés.[23]

Eve was thirty-one, Julia ten. For a time little is recorded of them. Eve's name is listed in the *Royal Blue Book Fashionable Directory* for 1841 and in *Boyle's Fashionable Court and Country Guide* for 1843, books in which Tenniels also appear. Her address given in these guides, 28 Oxford Terrace, Hyde Park, would in 1851 be that of the thirty-six-year-old solicitor William James Giani.[24]

The year 1853 found Julia in Upper Chelsea, and it is in the church of that parish, on 1 September, that she and Tenniel marry. Witnessing the ceremony were Tenniel's brother William Rickards and sister Caroline, William Berry, Ann Berry, and Tenniel's old friend Thomas Barrett. Tenniel, who had been living in Newman Street (London's "Latin Quarter") in a house shared with three other artists, a chemical color manufacturer, and a hatter, now moved with Julia to Maida Vale.[25]

The house at Portsdown Road, where Tenniel would spend the next fifty-five years, belonged to Eve. It was on a wide street running parallel to and west of the Edgeware Road (the dividing line between Marylebone and Paddington). Until recently, most of this northeastern part of Paddington had been open country.[26] Number 3 stood on the east side of Portsdown, a short distance from the Regent's Canal. As the street filled in, it would be redesignated number 5 and then number 10.

With its ample streets and italianate villas and terraces, Maida Vale conveyed a sense of affluence. Attractive, too, were the canals that met two blocks west of Portsdown in the triangular water today known as Little Venice. The waterways with their narrow boats and tree-shaded towpaths gave relief to the heavy stuccoed buildings. Some, like the fictional Dr. Phillips in an 1887 novel of that name, might have found the architecture more pretentious than graceful. We read in this *Maida Vale Idyll*, "The house in Portsdown Road began to haunt him with its dullness, its four stories of windows, out of which looked no face; the lack of beauty it had always had."[27]

Fig. 24. Number 10 Portsdown Road. (City of Westminster Archives Centre)

Tenniel's home, the southernmost of three attached villas, showed only three stories of windows, the first being a raised ground floor. Below, concealed from the front by the shrubbery that backed a substantial stone balustrade, one no doubt found the usual Victorian basement with its kitchen, larder, scullery, and, probably, servants quarters. Tenniel's studio was on the first floor, many years later to be described as "a comfortable room with well-filled bookshelves, old armour, carved oak cabinets." In the sixties there was a billiard table and a billiard room to house it.[28]

Stuccoed buildings show neglect more readily than most, and pictures taken before its demolition around 1959 prove that Tenniel's house was no exception (fig. 24). In its days of prosperity, perhaps with trees to soften the heavy cornices, quoins, window surrounds, and columned entry porch, and tended by a succession of servants, it would have had warmth and charm. Presumably

Fig. 25. Tenniel, *Julia Tenniel,* watercolor, 1856

Eve lived there too, and as families then shared their large homes with unmarried and widowed female relatives, the household may have included Ann Berry, who was indeed living there in 1879.[29]

The marriage was to be brief as Julia was already consumptive. According to Tenniel's last editor, Francis C. Burnand, the couple, "hoping for the best," had married in the face of Julia's uncertain health. At Portsdown Road on 23 January 1856, after little more than two years of marriage, Julia Tenniel died. Her aunt Ann Berry was by her bedside. On 26 January Tenniel purchased a plot at Kensal Green Cemetery where Julia was interred on the 29th. Then, from memory, he painted a portrait of Julia, a small watercolor (now in family possession) showing a three-quarter length figure of a slender girl in a white dress, with long dark ringlets (fig. 25).[30]

Miscellaneous Work

Roughly, the marriage had paralleled the time of the Crimean War, Julia's death occurring less than two months before its end. This conflict, which saw a rise in Tenniel's political work for *Punch,* brought a quite different assignment as well. During the war the queen had visited military hospitals in England and had received veterans at Buckingham Palace. To have these events recorded in photographs and paintings she engaged a number of artists, Tenniel among them. "At the command of Her Majesty" Tenniel executed four works in all. The last—which showed the unveiling of a monument honoring Florence Nightingale—came after the war. These neatly stippled watercolors, with their rows of tiny figures and precisely rendered architecture, are sufficiently dull. Meanwhile, for *Punch*, Tenniel drew the queen far more imaginatively—as a cross between Britannia and Joan of Arc, dedicating her sword to God.[31]

At this time, too, after a lapse of five or six years, Tenniel resumed his illustrating of books. Many years later he would admit to Spielmann, "In looking back, it strikes me rather forcibly that from *1850* I must have perpetrated—apart from Punch—a very considerable amount of miscellaneous work, conjointly with others—in the illustration of certain books, magazines, &c. &c. now completely and absolutely out of date." But aside from his illustrations for the 1854 edition of Martin Tupper's long-popular *Proverbial Philosophy*, which Tenniel probably began before his marriage, most of this output dates from the midfifties. Many of the texts published or reissued at that time reflected the Victorian preoccupation with death, loss, and mutability, and this is seen in the eleven books to which Tenniel contributed drawings. Again, in two of his designs for Tupper, he reverted to the Westminster style of composition. One, "Of Compensation," recalls Daniel Maclise's *Spirit of Chivalry* in the House of Lords, a work that Tenniel must have admired as there is an exact outline copy of it among his drawings.[32]

Tenniel's *Punch* connection brought new commissions in the late fifties with Shirley Brooks's second novel, *The Gordian Knot*, and Bradbury and Evans's new periodical, *Once a Week*. Shirley (baptized Charles William Shirley), considered by Jerrold to be "the most rising journalist of the day" and by Lemon to have "the gracefullest pen in London," had contributed parliamentary summaries and light prose and verse to a number of publications before joining *Punch* in 1854. Bearded and plump, "Rosy cheeked, fresh looking," with a "ready smile" and equally ready wit, he would be recalled by Burnand as "handsome, gay, toujours debonnaire Shirley Brooks." He had "the faculty of holding people close to him," and women friends seemed to want to mother him—to paint sentimental little pictures or to make slippers for him. Despite his sometimes risqué humor at the *Punch* dinners and his not altogether happy marriage, from all indications Brooks was a faithful and conscientious family man. A compulsive worker, once, after he and Tenniel had decided on the cuts for two issues so that Tenniel might do them early and get away, Shirley asked in his diary, "What can men want holidays for?"[33]

Encouraged by the success of his first novel in 1857, Shirley made an agreement with the publisher Richard Bentley, with Dickens as witness, to write a second, which would appear in monthly illustrated parts commencing that December. The twenty-two illustrations were done as etchings on steel, perhaps as a cost-saving measure. Although Bentley's imprints on Tenniel's plates say "1858," some must have been done later as Shirley did not complete his novel until late 1859, the Punchites meanwhile calling it "The

Gordian Not Yet" and "The Gordian Perhaps." As would later be the case with Lewis Carroll's books, author and illustrator proceeded together. For one scene, Tenniel lightheartedly asked Shirley to write in "just one gleam of moonlight," depicting for him what the picture would otherwise resemble— a totally inked-in area, "very easy to draw."[34]

Brooks, in *The Gordian Knot,* affirmed his warm friendship for certain colleagues. The work's dedication was to his closest friend, Mark Lemon, and to Lemon's wife Helen. Jerrold, who had died in June of 1857, is resurrected in the story as the admirable Jasper Beryl. As to Tenniel, Brooks broke into a commentary on one of the story's events to say, "My friend, Mr. Tenniel has revealed that fact in the masterly series of medallions [ornaments] which he has carved [etched] in my aid, and which are now in the reader's hand."[35]

A more intimate token of friendship came in an earlier chapter when Shirley used the nickname for one of his principals that he himself had given Tenniel at the *Punch* table. This was "Jackides," a grecianized version of Jack, for Brooks was very fond of making classical allusions. In *The Gordian Knot* he drew parallels between key characters and such figures as Demosthenes, Ajax, Teucer, and Andromeda. Tenniel's nickname occurs in chapter 8 where the major character, Philip Arundel, first refers to his close friend Jack Claxton as "Johannes Claxtonius" and then as "Jackides."[36] The last was already in use for Tenniel; the letter in which Tenniel requests that Shirley incorporate a "gleam of moonlight" in the text is signed "J. Tenniel / Jackides / [monogram]—X his mark."

Tenniel would do forty-three illustrations for another of Shirley's soap operas, *The Silver Cord,* which appeared in *Once a Week* from 10 November 1860 through 31 August 1861. But between these commissions for Brooks, Tenniel created what was in his opinion his finest work, sixty-nine designs for a deluxe edition of Thomas Moore's *Lalla Rookh.* Despite their occasional theatricality, Tenniel's illustrations to Moore's oriental romance contain some of his most stunning designs. Sam Lucas, in the *Times,* wrote glowingly of the book, as did the reviewer for the *Art Journal.*[37]

Curiously, one of the *Lalla Rookh* illustrations evokes John Martin's *Coronation of Queen Victoria.* Martin's piece was notable for its expansive view of the interior of Westminster Abbey and the shafts of sunlight coming down from the right. While those present at the actual event were said to witness "the sudden burst of sunshine, almost at the moment when the crown was placed on the head of the Queen," what Martin portrayed occurred slightly after the crowning—the queen rising to assist a lord who had tripped on the throne steps.[38]

Tenniel must have been familiar with this painting, which stood for a year or more in Martin's painting room, for he borrowed the composition outright for the opening illustration to Lalla Rookh's first story, "The Veiled Prophet of Khorassan" (fig. 9 and fig. 10). The abbey's transept (viewed from the right of center), the framing pillars, ribs arching over the rose window, vaulted galleries, rows of attentive peers, crowded platform, are translated to the exotic vernacular of Egyptianized columns, oriental dome, keyhole and round arches, kneeling worshippers, and dais. And the scattered rays that brightened the coronation are, in Tenniel's scene, a great spotlight beam holding within it the dread prophet of Moore's story.[39]

Handsome Jack

Tenniel's great friend during these early years on *Punch* was Leech. Until 1860, when Charles Keene was elevated from the rank of outside contributor to a place at the Punch table, Leech and Tenniel constituted between them the major part of the artistic staff.[40]

The two were tall, well built, quietly elegant in their dress, and gentlemanly. To Tupper they were "a pair well-matched in kindliness, cleverness, and good looks." Leech, who was Tenniel's senior by two years, had wide-set thoughtful eyes, a sensitive mouth. From John Everett Millais's striking portrait of him at age thirty-seven one can see why writers Albert Smith and Edmund Yates referred to Leech as "Handsome Jack." He had considerable personal charm and was said to be a brilliant storyteller and mimic. But he also had a certain languidness and melancholy, and many would recall how at parties he would sing in his deep bass voice,

> King Death was a rare old fellow!
>   He sate where no sun could shine;
> And he lifted his hand so yellow,
>   And poured out his coal-black wine
>   Hurrah! for the coal-black wine![41]

Unlike Tenniel, Leech had a nervous temperament, doubtless intensified when, at seventeen or eighteen, his father's bankruptcy ended the security of his early years and his medical studies at St. Bartholomew's Hospital.[42] He turned to illustrating, but henceforth seems to have been a driven man. He held prejudices against Jews (as a result of an early confinement in a sponging house—a place of preliminary detention for debtors—where the keeper was a Jew), Irishmen, minorities, "pampered menials," and those outside his definition of a gentleman.

He could be sharply critical of other artists and satirists (he was not on friendly terms with either Doyle or Cruikshank), and at one Punch dinner the writer Ponny Mayhew was provoked into saying, "Ah, you never admit the talent of anyone but yourself, Leech." Still, Leech was realistic about his own abilities. He laughed off the suggestion of the painter William Powell Frith that he (Leech) was the "backbone of *Punch*," and once remarked to Frith, "Talk of drawing, my dear fellow, what is my drawing compared to Tenniel's?"[43]

Leech and Tenniel had much in common. Being of the old school of illustrators, they relied almost entirely on memory drawing, although with different results. They both held strong opinions as to which subjects would constitute a good cut; Keene recalled Leech as a "Juggernaut" during large-cut discussions. Both could be generous in helping novice writers and artists in whom they had taken an interest.[44] They disliked personal publicity, were keen theatergoers and Shakespeareans, and shared a love of horses.

Sometimes they would go together to Barkway, in the heart of Hertfordshire's hunting country. There, while visiting Leech's old friend Charley Adams, they would savor the joys of the "field." Adams would later recall the "happy times" his dining room had seen, "when Leech, Millais, Lemon . . . Tenniel, and others, found themselves round" his table.[45]

At other times the two hunted with novelist Anthony Trollope, the most daring and avid of the three. Although Trollope much preferred *hunting* (used only when the game was fox) to shooting, the burly and bushy-bearded Brown in Tenniel's 1870 social cut (a small nonpolitical cut), who nearly shoots Jones while bagging Jones's bird, looks suspiciously Trollopeian. From Trollope's book on British sports one learns of such satisfactions of the hunt as owning one's own mount and the chance to see the country "in many of its most charming aspects." Then there were the shaking off of one's friends, the strong scent of the fox, the glorious straight run, the kill in the open. Conversely, there were the miseries: days with cold wind and rain, or a glut of other hunters, or days that were simply "blank days" when there was no fox.[46] These, they also endured, Leech turning them to advantage in his series on that undaunted sportsman Mr. Briggs.

They went regularly on Saturdays while the hounds were running. Not for them the newer subscription packs; they rode with the old aristocratic hunts—the Puckeridge and the Berkeley. For Leech, besides providing endless material for his drawings, hunting symbolized the aristocratic life to which he aspired. "I'm a man of simple tastes," he said, "Give me my claret and my hunter, and I ask not for more."[47]

Tenniel, a lifelong rider who was said to sit a horse as easily as the Duke of Wellington, may have hunted to ride as much as he rode to hunt. He, too, would draw on his outings for his social cuts, a favorite theme being novice riders and their mounts. In one early drawing the rider, his hat fallen over his eyes, responds to the query, "Well, Charley, How do you like the old horse?" with "Be-be-beau-ti-ful,-a-ea-sy as a ch-a-ir."[48]

Big Cutting

From the first Tenniel's *Punch* contributions had been partly political, although this had begun modestly. In addition to two cartoons, he did three small political cuts for the early 1851 volume. The next year saw several political initials, as did the subsequent years. Since the articles they adorn have no political connotations, they would have been done on Tenniel's own initiative.[49] This becomes more telling when we find that *Punch*'s outside contributors did not generally politicize their initial letters. Then, in January 1855, Shirley, who had spent five sessions in the reporters' gallery of the House of Commons, began "Punch's Essence of Parliament," a highly successful series that provided satirical coverage of the week's happenings in Parliament whenever that body was in session. More often than not, the "Essence" began with a political decorated initial, most of the early ones done by Tenniel.

Six months later, Tenniel began a very different series, probably devised by him, as is suggested by some trial quotations in an 1855 sketchbook. "Punch's Illustrations to Shakspeare" [sic] depended for its humor on visual puns on Shakespeare's lines and on the resemblance of some of its caricatures to actors from the contemporary stage—Cardinal Wolsey to Charles Kean, Macbeth to William Macready, and Trunculo to the actor John Pritt Harley. Then, in the 29 September cut, Hermione's lines, "The Emperor of Russia was my father:/ O, that he were alive, and here beholding," were illustrated by a portrayal of Czar Alexander II weeping over the ruins of Sebastopol. After this, eleven more references to topical events appeared intermittently in the series. The Prussian emperor (a tipsy Oberon) eavesdrops in Paris—"I am invisible; and I will overhear the conference"; a furious British Lion roars lines from *Henry VI*—"Is all our travail [the Crimean War] turned to this effect?"; Punch smiles approvingly while a British Portia tells Shylock that the Jewish Disabilities Bill "must not" and "cannot" be; and so on.[50]

The number of Tenniel's large cuts had been gradually rising, in 1854

Fig. 26. Tenniel, "Turkey in Danger," cartoon, *Punch*, 9 Apr. 1853

equaling those of Leech. The Crimean War inspired Tenniel's first great animal cartoons—the panicked Turkey receiving a huge bear hug from Russia's Bruin (fig. 26), the Bear attacked by the bees (the armies of various nations), the Bear at bay, and, finally, the British Lion "smelling a rat" at the Paris Conference that ended the war. Russophobia and impatience with the Earl of Aberdeen's unwarlike government had spawned the earliest of Tenniel's humorous cartoons—Czar Nicholas learning his future from a shell—a cannon ball held to his ear (fig. 27); Aberdeen asleep at the wheel of the yawing ship *Government;* Aberdeen as an old woman shipping out to the Crimea; and Austria playing the "scotch fiddle" (used here as a metaphor for both the Scottish Aberdeen and the itch).[51]

After a drop in 1855 and 1856 (as one

might expect with Julia's sickness and death) the steady increase in Tenniel's portion of large cutting resumed. This occurred mainly in the latter half of each year (possibly Leech wanted more freedom during hunting season). Then, in August 1857, Tenniel drew the cartoon that marked him as a powerful political artist. With the country shocked over a rebellion of native troops in India against their British officers and the consequent massacre of women and children at Cawnpore, his double-spread cut, "The British Lion's Vengeance on the Bengal Tiger," demonstrated that while some Tenniel drawings might amuse, others could rouse national passions (fig. 28). Despite the flawed anatomy of the victim, and the fact of the Tiger being "most ill-placed to receive the impact" of the Lion's leap, there was something iconic about the springing beast. The cut was taken up as a symbol of retribution, was reproduced on banners (as shown in Tenniel's double-page cut of the week following), and was so effec-

Fig. 27. Tenniel, "What Nicholas Heard in the Shell," cartoon, *Punch,* 10 June 1854

tive that, according to Spielmann, the authorities feared that public opinion might force them into measures more extreme than those they were prepared to take. The design had great impact on the popular imagination. It was duplicated in the Standard Theatre's pantomime that December in which, as the *Times* noted, in "the concluding scene but one in the harlequinade . . . all parties are entrapped in Punch's picture of 'The British Lion attacking the Bengal Tiger,' headed 'Caught at Last.'" Early the next year the *Illustrated London News* review of *The Gordian Knot* declared, "Mr. Tenniel's reputation stands too high to need eulogy, and the noble engraving which he supplied to Punch a few months ago, depicting the 'British Lion's Vengeance,' is in every household."[52]

By 1860 Tenniel was drawing about four-fifths of the paper's large cuts, Leech being ready to relinquish political work in favor of the social drawings in which he excelled. In 1859 writer Henry Silver recorded in his diary of the *Punch* dinners, "John [Leech] says he . . . hates politics and never thinks of them when walking out. Detests big cutting." On one hand, this sounds simply like Leech's characteristic peevishness, for he held very definite political opinions; Silver's coverage of large-cut discussions shows Leech to have been as prolific a suggester of cartoons as any. But cartoon drawing presented problems for Leech. He had trouble catching likenesses, and the above state-

Fig. 28. Tenniel, "The British Lion's Vengeance on the Bengal Tiger," cartoon, *Punch*, 22 Aug. 1857

ment had followed his vain request to Lemon for more photographic portraits for guidance.[53] Easier for him the anonymous pretty girls and stout patresfamilias of his social cuts. On the other hand, Tenniel had already undertaken most of the political work, while his playful initial letters dwindled from over forty in volume 34 (1858) to almost none after 1860.

In 1860 Tenniel did one of his last nonpolitical assignments for the paper—123 drawings for the weekly series "Punch's Book of British Costumes." Silver's facetious survey of British dress from the Celts to the Tudors owed its humor largely to Tenniel's delightful drawings and captions, which claimed such origins as "very scarce" engravings, "rude" drawings, and "ever so many" manuscripts of the period in question. This project more or less marked the close of Tenniel's small cutting, aside from some almanac socials (through 1873), his rare political small cuts, and his designs for the separately issued *Pocket Book*. In 1862 he became *Punch*'s chief political artist.[54]

5

On Gen'l Punch's "Staff"
1862–1874

"I don't know a happy man" says Shirley. Jackides looks one.
—HENRY SILVER, Diary, 11 August 1869

A Very Keen Sense of Humor

At this high point in his career Tenniel posed for a photograph of the kind then used for calling cards (fig. 29). Relaxed, he rests one hand against his waist; the other holds his silk hat and riding crop. As in all his pictures he is faultlessly groomed, stylish enough to have drawn attention at the *Punch* table by his "first appearance in a black choker!"[1] His hair, thinning on top, is brushed forward at the sides so that it curls above his ears in the fashion of the time. The face, clean shaven except for the Dundreary side whiskers, is a strong one, capable of humor. The aquiline nose he inherits from his grandfather Noel Tenniel. The mouth is broad and generous, the chin determined.

His playfulness, no longer vented in light-hearted initials and other small cutting for *Punch,* finds an outlet now in the cartoons. These show a sharp rise in the number of statesmen and other dignitaries portrayed as women and as small children, a favorite in this category being the diminutive Earl Russell. Also in for considerable ribbing was Pope Pius IX, and during the struggle for Italian unification endless variations (usually related to feminine attire) were devised on the tiara. It is the period of the American Civil War, and a series of comic blacks shuffle through the war years grinning at the rift between the states, greeting each other with great shouts of joy on the battlefield. Years later Tenniel would tell Spielmann, "Now, I believe that I have a very keen sense of humor, and that my drawings are sometimes really funny."[2]

He could also be counted on for the occasional stagy dialect or inebriate speech needed for the legend or "cackle." To Lemon's suggestion of statesmen John Bright and Robert Lowe under the mistletoe, he added, "Letsh shewem 'ternal friendship. Been boshe in the wrong." When a reader ob-

Fig. 29. Tenniel's Carte-de-visite photograph. (By permission of Jeremy Maas)

Fig. 30. Tenniel, "The State," illustration, *Punch's Pocket Book,* 1863

jected that the lines given Disraeli (portrayed as an Irish pig drover)—"O'd loike to *zee* any o' *you* droive un!"—was a mixture from three counties, Tenniel had to own that he'd adopted the dialect from the stage. One of his more inspired efforts in legend writing would be for an 1871 social cut in which a choleric major shouts at columns of mounted hussars, "When I d'saye draa-a—, mind thee *be-ant* to draa-a—; but when I d'saye souards,—whip 'em out smeart and 'dress up' t'gutter."[3]

Punch's yearly *Pocket Book*s continued to foster some of Tenniel's most delicate and playful work. These little leather-bound volumes, comprising business ledger, memorandum book, and diary, began with pages of useful information on government, the military, the post, amusements, and so forth, followed by some light fiction.[4] The opening section had been illustrated by Tenniel since 1852, and every year followed a different theme. In 1855 Assyrian and Egyptian sculptures from the British Museum danced jigs and reels in the "Amusements" section, in 1857 the character was rococo with a shepherdess Britannia among Gainsborough trees, and in 1862 chivalric subjects prevailed with Mr. Punch riding forth as a valiant knight. Following the showing of Japanese art at the 1862 International Exhibition, the 1863 theme was more or less Japanese, with delightful pastiches on Hokusai and others, including a British Lion all curlicued in the "Chinese lion" mode (fig. 30). Tenniel was probably the first comic artist to imitate oriental styles, the next being William S. Brunton in the 1868 calendar page of *Fun.*

Despite his extensive experience as an illustrator of books and periodicals, all of Tenniel's extra-*Punch* subjects, with the exception of his friend H. Cholmondeley-

Pennell's *Puck on Pegasus* (1861) and an *Arabian Nights* spoof in the 1862 *Once a Week,* had been serious if not downright depressing. Now, his commission to do thirty-one illustrations for a twenty-seventh edition of R. H. Barham's *Ingoldsby Legends; or, Mirth and Marvels* (1864) was exactly in the spirit of the burlesque, anomalous, medievalizing humor that had characterized many of Tenniel's private verses and drawings. Although *Ingoldsby* did not achieve the "immortality" that the *Illustrated London News* projected for a book illustrated by Cruikshank, Leech, and Tenniel, his work for it was a fitting prelude to a project that would indeed gain immortality.[5] Already in 1862 a tutor at Christ Church College, Oxford, named Charles Dodgson had devised the story of *Alice* for three little girls during a now-famous journey up the Thames to Godstow. At the time that the new *Ingoldsby* came out, Dodgson (or "Lewis Carroll") was exploring the possibility of enlisting Tenniel to illustrate his little book. To discuss the resulting pictures will require a section in itself.

His Friends Mustered in Troops

Except for the half-yearly title page and the annual almanac cartoon and *Pocket Book* cuts, Tenniel's *Punch* work now consisted solely of the weekly political cartoon. Thus, the part of the week spent working for *Punch* spanned a relatively short time, including the Wednesday dinner, which began at six. During the next two days he worked steadily, finishing at half-past six or seven on Friday evening, when the block with the completed drawing had to be handed over to the engraver's messenger. Aside from any illustration work he may have arranged for, the remainder of his time was his own, to be used for riding, rowing, and other outdoor pursuits as well as a full social calendar.

He was one of the oldest, but not the least active, members of several artists' clubs that flourished from the mid-fifties to sixties, where the average age was about thirty. A great sponsor of such fellowships was the amateur artist, etcher, and much-lauded host Arthur J. Lewis. Lewis, a wealthy linen draper, had been a regular evening sketcher at the Artists' Society at Clipstone Street where he may have met Tenniel, and he continued his attendance after the society's move to Langham Chambers, All Souls Place, around 1856. Lewis seems to have been the chief promoter of the Junior Etching Club, which counted several of the Langhamites in its membership. The club produced two fine books of illustrated poems, each with a handsome contribution from Tenniel.[6] It was probably no coincidence that 1858, the date of the club's first volume, was the year in which Tenniel also illustrated *The Gordian Knot* with etchings on steel, a medium new to him. At Lewis's chambers in Jermyn Street, the etchers—among them Keene, Millais, James McNeill Whistler, Henry Stacy Marks—met and compared proofs, exchanging shoptalk and anecdotes.

Soon the Jermyn Street chambers provided the venue for still more festive gatherings—meetings of singers who called themselves the "Jermyn Band." Their all-male "smoking concerts" seem to have been arranged somewhat on the order of the entertainment at the song and supper rooms of the time. That is, first came the serious part of the concert—part songs, glees, and madrigals. Then, after supper (which at Lewis's was a feast of oysters) there came the comic songs and recitations lasting till midnight. Tenniel, unlike Keene, did not sing with the Jermyn Band or with the Moray Minstrels, as they renamed themselves in 1863 when Lewis acquired his "bachelor's paradise," Moray Lodge at Campden Hill. But he and the Punchites, along with other leading artists from Lewis's wide circle of friends, were regular habitués. At Moray Lodge the bachelor parties became even grander, so that one might see there the Prince of Wales and a selection of peers. As Brooks noted after returning from one of these in 1865, "good music . . . excellent supper, fine pictures, everybody there and do as you like." When, in late 1867, Lewis married Kate Terry, Henry Silver would mourn, "No more Moray Minstrelsy," and du Maurier would regret that the marriage had robbed them of "a nice actress and some jolly evenings." Lewis was one of the three originators of the Arts Club as well, a club to which Tenniel is said to have belonged, and which included artists, writers, and other professionals, among them Keene (an original member) and du Maurier.[7]

Around 1860 a group more bohemian than the Jermyn Street coterie met regularly at a large studio in Newman Street that was rented by the artist Matt Morgan. Here, in an atmosphere quite as blue with smoke as at Lewis's, artists and their friends engaged in bouts of boxing, wrestling, "cock fighting" (between competitors bound hand and foot), single stick, and fencing. Tenniel was recalled as always watching the last with great amusement. Although authoritative in the sport, after the injury to his eye he never again touched a foil. Following dinner, which consisted of sandwiches and the beer that had flowed freely all along, the evenings concluded with a variety of impromptu turns—"Songs, recitations, imitations, conjuring."[8]

Some picture of the gregarious Tenniel can be gleaned from the recollections of friends. The writer Henry Lucy said, "His friends mustered in troops," and spoke of Tenniel's withdrawal in his last years "from the social life in which as far back as the time of Charles Dickens he was accustomed to take a leading part," and Gladys Storey, daughter of the painter George Adolphus "Dolly" Storey, remembered how Tenniel, "always full of fun . . . enlivened many a party." His enjoyment of parties is affirmed by Brooks, who recorded in 1870, when Tenniel had to devise a second cartoon in view of the declaration of war between Germany and France, "He is a most loyal fellow, and threw over a pleasant garden-party to-morrow that he might work. He likes these things, therefore be it noted to his praise." Tenniel himself, when a similar situation occurred in 1872, wrote disgustedly about having to miss "what was safe to be a jolly evening" at his friend

Dolly Storey's, "all along of a grand (!) double-page, dratted, detestable, allegorical, national, historical, sentimental subject" that required his time.[9]

Carroll's diaries, too, reinforce the picture. One June he catches sight of Tenniel at a garden party at Moray Lodge. It is "a gay and striking scene—350 guests or more, wandering about the beautiful grounds, a band of music playing, and all manner of good things to eat and drink" (one thinks of the tantalizing garden beyond the little door in Wonderland). Then, it is March 1870, and following a talk with Tenniel, who is now working "with a will" on *Through the Looking-Glass, and What Alice Found There* (1872), Carroll again goes to Camden Hill, where he will be an overnight guest of the Arthur Lewises. Tenniel joins them for dinner, and evening finds them in the large billiard room where, a few short years before, the Moray Minstrels had gathered. The walls are decorated with trophies of arms and hand-colored prints of Leech's sporting subjects from *Punch*. And there, on the table that had once, protected by a heavy cover, been laden with pipes, cigars, tobacco jars, tankards, and liquid refreshments for Lewis's bachelor evenings, the hosts along with Carroll and Tenniel have "a game of billiards for four."[10]

But mainly we rely on clues: gift drawings made for friends, presentation copies of books given him, parties at which he was sighted by Brooks (and later by Sambourne). These show a wide acquaintance, not only with artists, but with jurists, diplomatists, medical men, linguists, philanthropists, and writers in diverse fields.[11]

In late summer he vacationed at the seaside—Bognor, Ramsgate, Eastbourne—returning late (in three successive years) to join his colleagues at the *Punch* table. Probably Eve, who continued to reside with him after Julia's death, accompanied him as she did in 1872 when their time at Bognor overlapped with Carroll's. Then there were trips to the country—to Charley Adams's home at Barkway and to Tenniel's sister Mary's family up north. In 1862 this younger sister had married Thomas Goodwin Green, who soon bought a pottery employing fifty men at Church Gresley in what is now South Derbyshire and proceeded to expand it considerably. Tenniel seems to have had close ties with the Greens, and occasional references to visits to that vicinity occur.[12]

Certainly these years were not trouble free. Both a younger and older brother had died at the start of the sixties. Then, in late 1864, two losses followed close upon one another. Leech, long suffering from angina, had in October followed King Death to "where no sun could shine." Eliza Maria, too, had been ill but seemed by September to have recovered. This proved deceptive, for on 16 December Tenniel lost his mother. But his was too robust a nature for him to dwell on his bereavements. His positive outlook comes through in a debate recorded at the *Punch* table the next May. The subject was suicide, some claiming that it was justified in certain cases. Tenniel took an opposing view, arguing that hope should be "a preventative"—that even in "apparently incurable disease a remedy may be invented."[13]

Punch Jollities

His *Punch* colleagues formed Tenniel's chief social fraternity. Late 1865 finds them all at the Albion Tavern feasting on turtle and partridge in celebration of the new firm of Bradbury, Evans and Co., the Co. denoting the firm of Agnew, wealthy art dealers. Speeches and toasts are followed by cigars and singing—a lively French song from du Maurier and a sentimental popular one from William H. Bradbury (possibly the son of William Bradbury). Charles Keene sings an ancient ballad about a slain knight whose hawks and hounds, aided by a supernatural doe, protect his body from the beaks of three ravens. One pictures Keene with his mournful face singing in a deep tremolo,

> She lift up his bloudy hed
> And kist his wounds that were so red.
> With a downe derrie, derrie, derrie,
>   downe, downe.

Tenniel's choice is the sixteenth-century patriotic ballad of "The Spanish Lady" and "How She woo'd an English Man." Presumably he rendered the lady's Gilbertian plea with appropriate fervor:

> Leave me not unto a SPANIARD
>   Thou alone enjoy'st my heart;
> I am loving, young and tender,
>   Love is likewise my Desert.
> Still to serve thee Day and Night
>   My mind is prest;
> The Wife of every ENGLISHMAN
>   Is surely blest.[14]

Memorable in the paper's annals was the year 1867, when the sudden death of the clever but impecunious *Punch* artist Charles H. Bennett involved his colleagues in two benefit performances in aid of his large family. Since the bill included Francis C. Burnand's and Arthur Sullivan's *Cox and Box,* Tom Taylor's *Sheep in Wolf's Clothing* (a domestic drama of the time of James II), songs by the Moray Minstrels, plus some smaller pieces, not only the Punchites but several of their friends were drawn into the venture. Arthur Lewis was involved as were Sullivan and the professionals, Ellen and Kate Terry and Arthur Cecil (Blunt), who played alongside the amateurs.[15]

Henry Lucy would one day recall that Tenniel had "greatly cherished some photographs, 'two pence coloured,' in which he was almost unrecognisable in theatrical dress." We see one reproduced in Spielmann's *History*—the whole company assembled, and Tenniel in the back row eclipsed by a great ringlet wig and a hat with many feathers. He played Colonel Lord Churchill in Taylor's drama—a small but noble part with such brave lines as, "Before you abuse your men for not obeying orders, Colonel [Kirke], best be sure you have the right." On the entrance of the "celebrated cartoonist" a "whirlwind of enthusiastic welcome" seemed to last for several minutes, drowning out the voice of Burnand (cast as Kester, a servant) and delaying further action. Successfully suppressing his emotion, Tenniel courteously bowed his acknowledgment to the house and delivered his lines with true professional aplomb. This was duplicated in July when the group played at the Theatre Royal in Manchester and seems to have occurred independent of Tenniel's histrionic skills.[16]

Probably the most extravagant celebration attended by *Punch* was the "grand 'do'" at proprietor William Agnew's home near Manchester early in the next decade to mark the coming of age of Agnew's eldest son. At the *Punch* dinner the week before, the cuts for two weeks were decided in advance so Tenniel could get away. To Dolly Storey he writes, "Air you going to Manchester? Agnew says you're a sweep if you don't, and tells me to convey the message to you." They meet at Euston Station, and joining them is the painter Henry Stacy Marks who, like Storey, is a member of the St. John's Wood Clique, a brotherhood of seven artists living in northwest Marylebone. No sooner do they arrive when they must dress to join the "dinner parties, dancing parties, luncheon parties, garden parties" that follow "in close order." The next day they are taken to the depot where, fortified with sausages and champagne, they merrily greet more arrivals including Shirley and du Maurier. Eventually most of the clique and a goodly *Punch* contingent will arrive, along with others well known in the various arts. The journey home is festive too, for their host has provided a saloon carriage (the ladies are in another car) and, for a "railway-picnic" lunch, a hamper of delicacies. As they ride southward through a landscape whitened by spring snow— now lit by sunshine, now obscured by a short storm—the singer Charles Santley entertains them with many a delightful song.[17]

Between 1865 and 1872 a smaller coterie exists within the larger one of *Punch*. This consists of Shirley, Fred Evans (a proprietor since 1865 when his father, "Pater" Evans, relinquished his place in Fred's favor) and his wife Amy, and Tenniel. Sometimes this small group is joined by a Laura Vigers, of whom we learn little except that her father is "a man of business and of wealth." On Christmas Eves Fred and Amy host a party, the guests including Shirley and Tenniel. Then on 31 December it is as always the Brookses' "Eve," with Tenniel usually the last to leave, staying "as afore times for a final cigar."[18]

They meet at the homes of others. In April 1867 they dine with the newly married Silver and his French wife, who have leased Leech's old house in Kensington. Shirley writes, "The furniture is Mrs. Leech's and it was like a theatrical scene—old properties, but a change of actors." That August they are fishing at Henley. Shirley draws a diagram of their lines as they float in the stream, Amy's next to his, and then Tenniel's and Lloyd's (probably Amy's father, Richard). Shirley gets skunked. On Christmas Eve they are at the Fred Evanses'—a party of about twenty to which Tenniel comes with Eve Giani. Shirley records: "Charade—'Inn-spectre' by M. M.," adding, "Tenniel, Bradbury, du Maurier, Louis Evans and Brooks, and Mrs. Orridge, who looked very pretty as a landlady." The next week Shirley writes, "Our party . . . Lady Thompson [wife of the surgeon Sir Henry Thompson] good naturedly took, and capitally played the landlady in Tenniel's charade." One suspects that this charade, too, was based on *inspector* as there were then published lists of words suitable for acting.[19]

Seaside and River

A bright and breezy fall day in 1871 finds them vacationing at Folkestone on the Dover Strait. Making up the party are Shirley and his wife Emily, Fred and Amy, Lloyd, and Tenniel. For Tenniel, this holiday may mark the completion of his work on *Through the Looking-Glass,* soon to be "printing off rapidly." They fish from two boats, and Brooks, finding little sport in his catch of a conger eel and "some few whiting," returns with Emily and Lloyd to their hotel. Tenniel and the Evanses stay out for some time. When they land, Fred, whose dog is attacked by one larger, strikes the other animal with his stick and is promptly floored by its owner. Soon Shirley comes on the scene to find Fred "flat on his back, bleeding at the nose, Amy kneeling near him," and his assailant, a Mr. King, scowling nearby. Shirley learns that Tenniel had "laid hold of" Fred's attacker, but that King's "women clung to Jackides, and begged him to do nothing." Eventually an apology was made, and King's offer to pay five pounds to any charity accepted. That night Brooks reflects, "So much for that day's part of a blackguard business. I said not that King was represented as very excitable, and liable to fits, for which reason only I am glad Tenniel did not wop him." On the next day, "A lovely day, Wind S. E.," he records, "E[mily], I, Tenniel and Fred (with such black eyes) out for a sail, which was delightful."[20]

It is in this period that Tenniel celebrates in verse a trip "From Oxford to Henley," one of his annual rowing holidays. We follow the excursionists on this journey from their boarding at Salter's Yard in Oxford to their arrival at the Red Lion Inn at Henley. The party consists of

> Mistress Fred-rick E-e-vans
> And Miss Laura Vigers too—
> And her brother and young Fred-e-rick

who with Tenniel "compose the 'Crew.'" With Amy at the rudder lines and Laura by her side, both looking "quite sweet and plea-a-sant," they head downriver past eyots (small islands) and meadows sweet with flowering grasses.

Easily they pass through Sandford Lock, "Tho' other folks might feel alarm." Soon there is a wood, and a railway bridge, the river now curving eastward, and presently they will be gliding under the medieval bridge of Abingdon where, "if the coast is all serene," they will "go ashore to make some pur-cha-ses—/ Which the plan has always been."

After shopping in the market square in the shadow of Abingdon's great town hall, they reboard their craft. By the time they reach the deep lock at Culham, as the verses tell us,

> Very hungry we shall be—
> So we spread out the refre-esh-ments
> Beneath a nice umbrageous tree.

There is no shortage of lovely picnic sites. They might choose to go down by the river at Sutton Courtenay with its picturesque eyots and old wooden weirs, or by the small brook that runs past an ancient manor house and joins the river.

After lunch, there is a long straight run before the river curves northward to Clifton, then to Burcot before turning south again. By twists and turns they pass Shillingford; then Benson, where, over immense volumes of water, they go through Benson Lock; then past the ruins of Wallingford Castle, and under the seventeen-arched bridge. There, having reached their night's haven, they

> go up straightway to the "Lamb"!
> Where *Miss Katie* [the landlord's daughter] caters fo-or us
> The mutton chops and the eggs-and-ham!

The poet continues

> The next morning after bre-ak-fast
> We assemble at the boat—
> And we pack up the "imped-i-ments"
> And are once again afloat—
> Then away for "Happy Henley!"

Here Tenniel omits the greater part of the journey that lies ahead, "tho' the work will be *hard* and *wa-arm*." Let us fill in the missing part. Leaving Wallingford, they skim past hills dotted with sheep, an osier farm, fields of potatoes and lettuces, snug little houseboats with curtained windows, cottages and stately homes, ancient abbey ruins, chalk cliffs, and woods dropping sharply to the water. Accompanied by the sounds of river life—of rooks and wood pigeons—they glide past banks fragrant with flowers and over water so clear that they can see far down to the river weeds swirling beneath them. They pass a marsh where kingfishers and herons shelter among the reeds, and shallows where gudgeon feed on the gravelly bottom. Finally they negotiate one last lock, pass banks covered with meadowsweet, loose-strife, and comfrey, and find themselves in the gentle currents of Henley. There they pull into a landing space by the balustered stone bridge, debark, and make for the inn where, the poet concludes,

> they take us in—
> All the crew, and the brave Jeunes-dames—and
> At the Inn they take us in—at the Inn they give us gin
> Ger-*beer* for the brave Jeunes-dames.[21]

Shirley

The early seventies saw two significant changes at *Punch:* the change of editorship, as that post had fallen to Shirley on Lemon's death, and the last of Bradbury and Evans, Fred having been induced to "walk" (to use Shirley's expression). In November 1872 there was announced the new firm of Brad-bury, Agnew and Co.[22]

Shirley had been Tenniel's closest friend at *Punch,* at least since the death of Leech and perhaps before then. The warmth of their relationship comes through in Tenniel's sportive letters in which he addresses him as "My dear Chawles" and "Dear Mr. Editor," signing off with calligraphic embellish-ments. Shirley's diary of 9 April 1873 shows that Tenniel had asked him to "put him down at the 'G' [Garrick Club]." Shirley acted quickly, for three days later Tenniel's name was proposed by Millais (Shirley believing that this should be done by a "great man in art") and seconded by Shirley. The "Com-mittee 'G'" met on 3 May, and that night Shirley wrote, "When Tenniel's name was read, there was a general cry that we 'did not need to hear any-thing about him.' He was, of course, unanimously elected" (which is borne out by one of the most signature-filled pages in the Garrick's candidate book).[23]

In this year, two other legacies proceeded from Shirley. One was initi-ated on the last day of October when Shirley wrote to Tenniel about "some-thing important which it is desired he should do for the almanac." They conferred, Shirley being "strong for a chariot in the sky, and a rushing pro-cession of everybody and everything." This was adopted, and Shirley pre-dicted that December that Tenniel's big picture "ought to make a sensa-tion." It was the first of Tenniel's double-spread almanac cartoons—drawings that might later contain as many as fifty or more figures (the suggesters at the "Almanac dinners" delighting in "piling on the agony")—and it set a precedent that Tenniel would follow through the rest of the century.[24]

It was probably through Shirley, who seems to have provided his intro-duction to the surgeon Henry Thompson, that Tenniel became involved in the struggle to legalize cremation. Thompson was Tenniel's age and, like him, slender, handsome, mustached. Outside of his profession, in which he had achieved great eminence, his many interests included painting (he was an exhibitor at the Royal Academy), writing, and cookery. In 1872 he instituted his famous "Octaves"—eight-course dinners for eight male guests representing different professions—a number not too large for all to participate in the discussion of a single topic. Although the name "octave" probably relates to the fact that Thompson's wife was the well-known pianist Kate Loder, her gender disqualified her from attendance.[25]

Shirley recorded a dinner in 1867—a pre-octave gathering, although presumably not much different from the later affairs. The service was rare blue and white Nankin china (Thompson being a collector), and the courses were prepared under his personal supervision, each accompanied by its own wine. On this occasion there were eleven guests including Tenniel, Shirley, Arthur Lewis, and others prominent in their various fields. The main subject of discussion turned out to be a homosexual enclave in Maida Creek about which Shirley would commit some angry words to his diary later that night.[26]

In late 1873 Thompson was sufficiently aroused by a revival of interest in cremation, occurring in Italy, and by experimental work there on cremating apparatuses to write a paper in support of this movement for the *Contemporary Review*. Shirley had noted in December that Thompson was "going to resume his idea about cremation," adding, "I am with him in this—we spoke of it years ago." London's graveyards had long been a scandal; according to S. C. Hall, they were "appalling to the sight, offensive to the nostrils, creating disease and spreading it—the terrible allies of Death." It is to such a place (believed to have been based on the churchyard of St. Martin-in-the-Fields) that Jo takes Lady Dedlock in Dickens's *Bleak House*. In 1853, the year the novel was published, a *Punch* article claiming that decomposing matter from the "Graveyards of London" was polluting the water and air was accompanied by a Tenniel drawing of Mr. Punch as Hamlet wrathfully confronting a gravedigger. Now, at the start of the new year, Shirley wrote to *Punch*'s Percival Leigh, "I am going to dine with Sir H. Thompson on Wednesday [7 January], and talk *Cremation*. . . . It is not a topic we can *often* touch in P. [*Punch*] but it might be well to have one profession of faith thereanent." Soon after, the paper published a short paragraph on cremation, and *Punch*, being *Punch*, trusted that the first crematory "would be in Berner's Street."[27]

At a second meeting at Thompson's, on 13 January 1874, the following declaration was proposed, penned by Shirley, and signed by the sixteen present: "We, the undersigned, disapprove the present custom of burying the dead, and we desire to substitute some mode which shall rapidly resolve the body into its component elements, by a process which cannot offend the living, and shall render the remains perfectly innocuous. Until some better method is devised we desire to adopt that usually known as cremation." The signers represented various professions, Tenniel's name appearing boldly between those of Millais and Trollope.[28] Thus was born the Cremation Society of England, although it would be ten more years before cremation was legalized.

By now, Shirley's lifestyle, which combined years of overwork and an overly rich Victorian diet, was telling on him. Although his 1873 "Eve" sounds a jolly affair—Mark Twain giving a "funny little speech" to honor his hosts, du Maurier singing French songs "exquisitely," and Tenniel, "who always waits to the end, per agreement," not getting off until 2:30 in the morning—Shirley wrote: "It may be that it was only my fancy that made me think our supper less effective than our other gatherings have been."[29] Perhaps he guessed it would be his last. On 23 February, writing for *Punch* even on his deathbed, Shirley Brooks expired. Five days later, on Tenniel's fifty-fourth birthday, his friend was buried at Kensal Green.

Good Sir John!
1874–1893

It is always delightful to receive the congratulations of old friends,
and I have heaps *of them!!*
—TENNIEL, in a letter to Lewis Carroll, 4 July 1893

The Real Enjoyment of Painting

With Shirley's death, the erudite Tom Taylor became the third editor of *Punch*. Although half of his seventy-five or more plays were light in tone, Taylor was a serious man. He was honest, strong willed, and, according to Burnand, "all-impatience" and inclined to heavy-handedness.[1] His "Essence of Parliament," as opposed to Shirley's clever if frothy coverage, was often straight political commentary.

Taylor was also art critic of the *Times* and the *Graphic*. He appraised paintings from a literary viewpoint and in 1865 declared at a *Punch* dinner that Whistler had "no poetry in him" and preferred "mean and groveling subjects." Thus, in 1878 when Whistler sued the art critic John Ruskin for charging him with flinging "a pot of paint in the public's face," Taylor testified for the defense at the court hearing and spoke in favor of identifiable subject matter in painting. He greatly admired Tenniel's work, and in an 1863 article calling for state-supported public art, Taylor wrote of the "great power for vigorous historical work on a large scale" that was "lying dormant in men like Tenniel" as well as several other illustrators and watercolorists.[2]

Now, with Tenniel's return to painting and exhibiting, Taylor's support was most fortuitous. Already, in 1871, Tenniel had declined a commission from the publisher George Bentley, explaining, "I am completely weary of drawing on wood; perfectly sick of wood engraving; and I have more work on hand than I know what to do with. I am building a new roof to my studio, and I am again 'going in' for the real enjoyment of painting." Tenniel's reluctance to relinquish his earlier ambitions is shown in the occupational entries in successive censuses. They begin with "Historical painter" in 1861 and move to "artist painter, etc. etc."; it was only in 1891 that he unbent enough to enter, "Artist, Oil, Watercolour and Punch."[3]

Since his last exhibited work in 1853 Tenniel had done the occasional watercolor. Now, after a lapse of twenty years, he entered his work at the Royal Academy and would be an intermittent exhibitor there through 1880. More importantly, he was elected an associate member of the Institute of Painters in Water-Colours (later the Royal Institute), that organization breaking with precedent by omitting the usual candidate's applications for Tenniel and five others. In that year, too, he was elected to full membership. This was the appropriate organization for a figural artist as the other exhibiting group in his medium, the Old Watercolour Society, favored landscape subjects.[4]

Since Tenniel employed a slow method of delicate stippling, incorporating gouache into his highly finished paintings, his production was relatively small—about fifteen works between 1873 and 1888. Still, when he did exhibit this was noted in the review columns, for Taylor could be counted on to applaud Tenniel's execution and spirited subject matter in both his papers. It is remarkable how Taylor's fairly short reviews of exhibitions, representing close to one hundred artists from the institute and perhaps fifteen hundred contributors to the academy, contrived to bring Tenniel's (and thus *Punch*'s) name to public notice, even when Tenniel was not among the exhibitors. In 1876 Taylor regretted that the exhibition at the Dudley Gallery "does not include the original drawings of John Tenniel, so that *Punch*'s Political Cartoon's might have been represented"; and in the opening of his 1887 institute review he noted, "Nor are Herkomer and Tenniel represented among the exhibiting members."[5]

One doubts that Tenniel paid great attention to these puffs, or to the equally flattering ones in S. C. Hall's *Art Journal*. Twice the Punchites (in Taylor's absence) had argued a question that art reviewers have debated for decades—"whether the critic's training should be artistic or literary"—with Tenniel taking the position that writers had "no right to criticise a picture."[6]

Not all the reviews were favorable. The *Athenaeum* critic (probably F. G. Stephens) gave a terrific drubbing to Tenniel's *Lighting the Beacon* (1875), which pictured a Saxon warrior, his side pierced by Danish arrows, giving the signal that will bring reinforcements. The review declares, "Why the man's mouth is opened in such an appalling way, or why his form is so contorted, his hair so strangely wild, his action so frantic, above all, why his figure is so badly drawn, and what was Mr. Tenniel's object in painting thus flimsily, are questions we cannot answer." Despite this not undeserved judgment, one version of the work would become the institute's gift to the queen in the jubilee year of 1887.[7]

Also bringing mixed reviews was his *Pygmalion and the Statue* of 1878. The subject was very popular around this time, with the revival of W. S. Gilbert's comedy *Pygmalion and Galatea* at the Haymarket; W. Calder Marshall's statue of Galatea, *From Stone to Life;* Edward Burne-Jones's four canvases on the theme; and one by Edward Armitage, similar in concept to Tenniel's. Ten-

Fig. 32. Tenniel, portrait believed to be of Roger Thorpe
Green, watercolor, 1876

Fig. 31. Tenniel, *A Sheep in Wolf's Clothing* (*The
Misfits*), based on Sir Walter Scott, *Old Mortality,* watercolor, 1876

niel showed his interpretation of the story at the institute. Although a charming work, with the rosy glow of life beginning to spread downward through
Galatea's form as she is clasped by the ardent sculptor, there is a clumsi-
ness about her figure that even the *Art Journal* could not help noting.[8]

Of Tenniel's other watercolors, two were based on Sir Walter Scott, and
these are among the most pleasing. One, Tenniel's 1876 institute entry, picturing Guse Gibbie from Scott's *Old Mortality* (fig. 31) has the general phys-
iognomy and innocent expression of the delightful little watercolor portrait
of 1876 in family possession, believed to be of his seven-year-old nephew
Roger Thorpe Green (fig. 32). A subject from Cervantes bears the same title
as Tenniel's 1838 submission to the Society of British Artists and may be a
revamp of it.[9] Most, however, are watercolor versions of his book illustrations
and his *Punch* cartoons. In all of these he seems to have savored the joy of
delicate brush manipulation.

New Arrangements and *Punch* in the Great Depression of 1873–1896

At 10 Portsdown Road the domestic scene was serene. In 1881 the cook
and housemaid were the same as those shown in the census for 1871. This

may have been unusual if the Thomas Carlyles's experience of thirty-four maids in thirty-two years at Cheyne Row was anything like the norm.[10]

At the start of 1879 Tenniel lost his companion of twenty-three years, Eve Giani, possibly through a recurrence of the cancer that had attacked her six years earlier. Living now at 10 Portsdown Road, at least since 1877, was Eve's sister Ann, perhaps there to care for her in her last illness. Eve's will, made two years before, simply says, "I give and bequeath unto my dear son in law John Tenniel my house situated at 10 Portsdown Road . . . and I also bequeath to my dear sister Ann Berry all and everything else I may die possessed of."[11]

By now, there remained of Eliza Maria's and John Baptist's twelve children only Tenniel, his brother Adolphus (long an accountant living in London), and three sisters: Eliza Margaret Martin, Lydia Victoire Tenniel, and Mary Green. John Baptist, who had at last settled on his primary profession as a teacher of dancing, was living with the forty-eight-year-old Victoire and their one servant at Lanark Villas, Clifton Road, about two streets away from Tenniel. In March, while visiting his daughter Mary's family at Hartshorne, near Burton-on-Trent, John Baptist died at eighty-seven.[12] The most notable thing about his will is its opening, with the specific bequest to his sons of all his "musical instruments music and books"—

evidently things that he much treasured. Generally, the will, which includes some choice Marylebone property, reveals the estate of a man of affairs and a gentleman. Now Victoire took Eve's place at Portsdown Road, and this seems to have been as happy an arrangement as the former one.

At *Punch*, the year 1880 inaugurated a new era with Taylor's sudden death in July. Frank Burnand, a very funny man, became editor. He was handsome and sturdy looking with his curling mustaches and his already graying and neatly pointed beard sharply contrasted by eyebrows so broad and black as to look pasted on. Under these, his blue eyes were full of humor. He was twenty-seven when he joined the table in 1863 and fresh from the comic paper *Fun*. Already, some fifteen of his theatrical pieces had been produced on the London stage. Eventually his total would exceed, by his own reckoning, one hundred and fifty, one-third being in the burlesque mode—a form influential for Tenniel's cartoons (see chapter 18). He was a

Fig. 33. Tenniel, E. Danvers as Dame Hatley in F. C. Burnand, *The Latest Edition of Black-Eyed Susan*, 1875. (By permission of Francis Burnand's Estate)

compulsive punster, as some of his play titles reveal: *Ixion Rewheeled, Faust and Loose, The Moor the Merrier, Fowl Play, The Frightful Hair*.[13]

Burnand succeeded Brooks as Tenniel's closest friend at *Punch;* they had long enjoyed one another's wit. On the 1875 revival of Burnand's burlesque takeoff on Jerrold's *Black-Eyed Susan* Tenniel was sufficiently delighted with the swift-footed E. Danvers as Dame Hatley to present Burnand with a sketch in which the dancer appears to have eight feet (fig. 33), a device seen, perhaps, only once before—in Wilhelm Busch's drawing of a seven-fingered pianist. Tenniel and Burnand were both enthusiastic horsemen, and together they frequently rode to Epping Forest, or to the country northwest of London around Harrow, or south of the river through open commons and secluded valleys to Richmond Park, or farther still to Hampton Court or Epsom.[14]

Meanwhile, Shirley's place as suggester-in-chief of Tenniel's large cut had fallen to Edwin J. Milliken, a newcomer to *Punch* and an outside contributor for two years before being called to the table in 1877. Milliken was a quiet and modest man, teeming with ideas for cartoons and almanac cuts. The fondness with which he was held by the staff comes through in a letter from Tenniel to Millais (who in 1883 was a member of the Garrick Committee) asking for his "vote and interest" on behalf of "Our Mr. Milliken."[15]

With Milliken's input Tenniel's almanac cartoons of the eighties showed the country eagerly pursuing the heady promise of technology, various reforms, and imperialism. Things actual or desired fill these double-page spreads—electrical power as "The Coming Force," progress in sanitation and education, the equipping of the navy with ironclads and torpedoes, electoral and governmental reform, Sunday opening of museums, coffee taverns as replacements for gin palaces. Again and again these drive before them the wrongs of a passing age: smog and sickness, roughs (ruffians), "Bumbledom"—the bungling of beadles (minor parish officials), jerry-building, and jobbery. Dirty Father Thames gets a good scrubbing, and the Duke of "Mud Salad [Covent Garden] Market" is ousted in disgrace.

We see imperialism exultant in the 1883 cut "Io Triumphe!"—a lord mayor's procession with drum major Gladstone (the erstwhile anti-imperialist), his chest swelling with pride as he leads the colonial troops in review before Britannia and Mr. Punch. The country had recently crushed an Egyptian nationalist revolt, and a banner plays on the words of an 1878 music hall song: "We didn't want to fight, but by jingo when we did." Succeeding cuts celebrate the golden jubilee of Queen Victoria's reign. Colonial loyalty to the monarch is their theme.[16]

Less confident are the weekly cartoons. Violence in Ireland runs through this decade, and the depression in trade, unemployment, and a rise in English socialism brings such cartoons as "The Two Voices"—the "real" unemployed workman unable to make himself heard above the din of demagogues and rowdies, and "The Great Unemployed"—the commissioner of police sleeping heavily at his desk while rioters from an unemployment meeting in Trafalgar Square throw brickbats outside his window.[17]

These decades have their share of comic cartoons: Lord Hartington, a shepherd offered the crook of the liberal leadership on Gladstone's resignation, who scratches his head in bafflement and asks, "Hey, but Measter!—where be the sheep?"; trainer Gladstone sadly observing his "Non-Performing Dogs" (Lords Granville and Derby of the Foreign and Colonial Offices)—"One of 'em does it all wrong, and t'other don't do it at all!"; Randolph Churchill ("Churchillius"), having suddenly resigned from the exchequer, leaping à la Marcus Curtius into the gulf. Both Martin and Haydon had painted the sacrifice of the Roman hero, and it is Martin's Curtius, with sword and shield upraised, that is recalled in Tenniel's cartoon.[18]

To the theatrical themes, music hall has been added. The "Irrepressible Chinee" who violates the terms of the Burmese Convention dances to the tune of the popular American ditty "Little Ah Sid." Gladstone makes three appearances as a lead comedian of the halls and, in another, "knocks 'em" in the "West-min-is-ter Road" in imitation of the Albert Chevalier number "Wot Cher!"[19]

A Dapper Equestrian

Old *Punch* photographs show Tenniel in these years—slim, mustached, and wearing a derby hat. We see him out for a day's ride with *Punch* artist Linley "Sammy" Sambourne, peering from among the Punchites assembled behind the wheel of what seems to be a canal boat, and leaning against the shaft of his umbrella in a woodsy setting. Aside from his rides and his river outings, he stays fairly close to home and likes to say "London is good enough for me." His only known trip abroad is a jaunt to Venice in 1878, and when the staff visit the Paris exposition in 1889, he, Keene, and Henry Lucy stay behind to "hold the fort."[20]

His greatest recreation now is his riding, to which he attributes "his wonderful health." Frequently Tenniel is seen in Rotten Row, the one-mile stretch westward from Hyde Park Corner to Kensington Gardens. He is a "well-dressed, well-mounted figure . . . mustachioed, whiskered and ruddy complexioned" and, according to Burnand, "a dapper equestrian, with an equable hand, cool head, and unshakable grip." One imagines that he avoids the Row in the height of the London season (Easter to midsummer), or at least during hours when it presents a "glittering pageant" of riders in frock coats and silk hats, carriages, and fashionable onlookers on the adjoining gravel paths. But earlier in the day he might see familiar faces there—members of Parliament and perhaps Gladstone, who is a regular morning rider.[21]

Sometimes Tenniel accompanies Burnand on his Sunday morning rides with Sambourne, lawyers Frank Lockwood and Willie Mathews, and occasionally others. On one outing in 1890 they form a riding club—the Two Pins

Club, named for the fictional rider John Gilpin and the real highwayman Dick Turpin. Tenniel, at seventy, is the oldest of the group; he will ride with them for only two or three more years. It is a remarkable company. Two members, aside from Punchites Burnand, Sambourne, and the artist Harry Furniss, are probably known to Tenniel from earlier days: the comedian-producer John Hare was one of his seconders at the Garrick Club, and newspaper magnate Edward Levy-Lawson had been a friend of Shirley's. Lockwood and Mathews are celebrated trial lawyers, and member Charles Russell is an MP and a former attorney general. They are all men of wit and talent, and their friendship corroborates Henry Lucy's assertion about English political life—that the "rancour of partisanship is not habitually carried into the social circle."[22] While Russell is an active fighter for home rule for Ireland, and Lockwood and Mathews are likewise Gladstonians, Levy-Lawson and his powerful paper support the Unionist position, as do the Punchites.

High honors would soon accrue to the riders. Two will be raised to the peerage as barons, one will become a baronet, and four will be knighted. It is another instance of Tenniel's propensity to move in such distinguished circles as had surrounded Martin, the Hemmings, Dickens, Arthur Lewis, and Henry Thompson.

These years bring two more illustrious friends. Tenniel became acquainted with the American writer James Russell Lowell when Lowell was minister to England in the early eighties, and the friendship was renewed when Lowell revisited England in 1886. Then, by 1892, Tenniel was in the social circle of famous patent lawyer John Fletcher Moulton—one that included many well-known painters, scientists, and literary men.[23]

The Black-and-White Knight

Tenniel had now been a celebrity for some time. It was he who was asked to respond to the toast to "Periodical Art" at the 1876 Mansion House banquet for the representatives of art. While the "whole of the brilliant company cheered to the echo," Tenniel made his first public speech:

> I am called upon in the most sudden and unexpected manner to return thanks for the toast which you have so kindly received of "Periodical Art." I am naturally of the most modest and retiring disposition in the world (laughter); and when I tell you I have never made a speech in my life, you will readily understand my feelings at this present moment. Periodical art is a term, I think, of perhaps rather wide interpretation; and as it might take some little time to tell you what I think upon the subject, I think, perhaps, I had better only thank you in a very simple and commonplace kind of way for the honour, my Lord Mayor, you have done to periodical art in proposing the toast, and next for the honour you have conferred upon me in associating my name with the toast (cheers).[24]

Fig. 34. *Sir John Tenniel,* oil painting by Frank Holl, 1883. (National Portrait Gallery, London)

By the early eighties, *Punch*'s famous cartoonist had become the subject of several portraits and of various writings both biographical and critical. In 1879 he had been caricatured in *Vanity Fair* by "Spy" (Leslie Ward), and in William Powell Frith's 1882 canvas *The Private View at the Royal Academy, 1881* he is seen behind a group of aesthetes. When confirming his sitting for the painting, Tenniel had written to Frith, "I have cut off those ridiculous whiskers." Although in Frith's picture he is without the "Picadilly weepers," we see the enormously long side whiskers in the 1883 *Graphic,* in a group portrait (apparently made earlier) where he is among the members of the Institute of Painters in Water-Colours. The most interesting of his portraits is by Frank Holl, displayed in the Grosvenor Gallery in 1883 and judged by the *Magazine of Art* to be Holl's best (fig. 34). Holl caught two aspects of his subject. First there is the soldierly quality that many had noted; with his intent look, "his long moustaches, his healthy complexion," his erect posture, Tenniel gave more than one observer the impression of being a retired colonel or general. But at the same time, the portrait has a certain quaintness. One thinks of Mary Gladstone's letter to a friend in 1884: "Supper at Santley's, next Tenniel, the *Punch* cartoon man, dear old thing with hair brushed straight from the back of his head toward his cheeks, don't you know."[25]

He is discussed in several books: Ruskin's *Art of England* (1884), Robert Walker's *Toiler's in Art* (before 1889), Frith's *Victorian Canvas* (1886), and Graham Everitt's *English Caricaturists and Graphic Humourists of the Nineteenth Century* (1886). In 1892 Tenniel was one of the twenty-five "People in the Front Rank" to rate an article in *Wit and Wisdom*—a selection beginning with the queen.[26]

Already, inspired by *Punch*'s fifty-year anniversary in 1891, Tenniel's colleague Henry Lucy had written confidentially to Akers Douglas, chief whip of the majority party, urging knighthood for Tenniel and noting that Tenniel had several friends in the ministry. There were precedents for this honor; artists Landseer, John Gilbert, Millais, and the sculptor Edgar Boëhm had been likewise elevated. As Douglas was unable to approach Lord Salisbury on the subject before the Liberals were returned to power, Lucy passed their correspondence on to the chancellor of the exchequer, Sir William Harcourt, who replied, "les beaux esprit se recontre" (brilliant minds agree), and saw that it was arranged. Apparently Lucy had been joined in this project by Tenniel's erstwhile riding companion Sir Frank Lockwood, who wrote to his daughter Lucy in 1893, "I am trying to get Mr. G[ladstone] to make John Tenniel a knight." As Gladstone had previously expressed warm admiration for *Punch*'s cartoons, this was not difficult. Lockwood soon reported in triumph that Tenniel would be knighted on the queen's birthday.[27]

Tenniel accepted the knighthood, it was said, mainly in the interest of his paper. It would be the first time that the accolade was bestowed primarily for a career in black-and-white art (Gilbert, for example, had also been president of the Old Watercolour Society), and thus it was a compliment to *Punch*. Anticipation there was high; already in January Burnand had hinted to Sambourne that he should look in the papers for something to the advantage of *Punch*.[28]

On 3 June the press announcement was made, and on that day Tenniel wrote to Spielmann that he was receiving "shoals of letters and telegrams." To Carroll, he wrote thanking the author for recognizing his "new 'dignity'(!)" adding, "How true it is that 'some have *greatness thrust* upon them!'—and you may be quite sure that it was none of *my* seeking." Plainly, he was surprised and gratified to learn how many well-wishers he had, and as late as December, in a letter to William Agnew, he still spoke of his pride in his "pretty considerable number of good friends."[29]

The ceremony itself was less fulfilling. On 11 August 1893, the day that Tenniel was knighted at Osborne (the queen's mansion on the Isle of Wight), journeying there with him to be similarly honored was the manager of the *Daily News,* John Richard Robinson. Robinson was particularly anxious that the queen should say something to Tenniel (later observing, "she does not see a Tenniel every day at her Court"), and they had decided on his reply if she should. To Robinson's eager query when Tenniel returned, the answer was simply, "No, she didn't say a word." Although Tenniel "had deprecated the idea of special notice," it was clear to Robinson that he was disappointed.[30]

Punch had already begun celebrating. Back in June a poem to "Good Sir John!" exulted, "They've dubbed him Knight at last, who ne'er was aught but Knightly," the accompanying cut by Sambourne picturing him as the "Black-and-White Knight" with pencil lance and palette shield. Now the festivities included a banquet at the Arts Club and another at the Mitre at Hampton Court. And the paper, taking advantage of his glorification, put out a two-volume set of his cartoons.[31] For Tenniel's later image the knighthood proved to be less happy, the "Sir John" tending to sound a bit stiff—something that Tenniel never was.

Exeunt
1893–1901

*The time is drawing very near when I must—with a sore heart—
resign my "Commission" on Gen'l Punch's "Staff."*
—TENNIEL, in a letter to Philip L. Agnew, 28 May 1900

Vision Loss and the "Furious Flycycle"

While all these honors accrued to Tenniel, his vision was gradually weakening. He had always borne the inconvenience of his one sightless eye with little complaint. But drawing on wood must have caused additional strain since the white preparation that was applied to the drawing surface of the block did not wholly conceal the wood grain. Presumably, he anticipated deadlines so that he might avoid working by lamplight, a practice claimed by Briton Riviere (who drew for *Punch* for a short while in the sixties) to have permanently injured his left eye. Two other one-eyed Victorian illustrators worked, like Tenniel, on wood: Arthur Boyd Houghton, who suffered greatly from headaches, and du Maurier, who was constantly fearful that his other eye might fail.[1]

Like others of the visually impaired who unconsciously adopt certain compensatory skills, Tenniel may not have realized just how much loss there was.[2] The limitation to his depth perception and peripheral vision had always been offset by an excellent visual memory. In fact, the "intense scanning" said to accompany such disabilities may have something to do with the curiously superreal quality in some of his work, especially in the *Alice* drawings. By mid-1889 even Tenniel's corrective mechanisms did not prevent some intermittent distortion, specifically in the drawing of heads. From 1894 on there is a gradual loss in linear elegance; hatching lines that are too close result in black splotches. An occasional figure is out of drawing or a limb does not foreshorten properly.

Yet, from time to time, he was capable of a striking cartoon. His 1890 "Dropping the Pilot" (one of Tenniel's two most famous cartoons), depicting the dismissed chancellor Bismarck descending the gangway of the German ship of state under the gaze of the young kaiser, shows that he could still, on his better days, execute a powerful drawing (fig. 35). Even as late as 1899 there is the occasional clean and sure work of former times, as in such cartoons as "Diogenes Morley" and "Harcourt's Pastoral."[3]

Already by the late eighties, Tenniel started to withdraw from certain activities that might tax his eyes or require a swift response. The year 1888 marked the last time that he exhibited one of his finely stippled watercolors with the (now "Royal") institute, and after 1891 he no longer rode. However, a believer in vigorous exercise, he still walked the four to five miles from Maida Vale to Bouverie Street, although he took a cab back.[4]

In the nineties, even before the appearance of the motorcar at mid-decade, London's streets—congested with four-wheelers, hansom cabs, horse-drawn omnibuses, railway buses, and a variety of other vehicles—presented dangers for the one-eyed pedestrian. At least there was warning of their approach in the clattering of iron-tired wheels and the clopping of hooves. For Tenniel, with his narrowed vision, the relatively noiseless pneumatic-tired bicycles were an added hazard. He had always considered bi-

Fig. 35. Tenniel, "Dropping the Pilot," cartoon, *Punch*, 29 Mar. 1890

cycles a poor substitute for the horse, and when his colleagues took to riding them in the midnineties he commented on the "beastly things" in comic disgust.[5]

With amused skepticism Tenniel's almanac cartoons greeted the modern age. His cuts for 1879 and 1882 had celebrated the march of science by depicting the god Mercury perched (unhappily) atop a unicycle and airborne balloons more evocative of Hieronymus Bosch than of the Montgolfiers. Now, with the proliferation of aerial experiments, Tenniel satirized both flying machines and bicycles. His title illustration for the late 1896 volume shows an airborne Mr. Punch, his arms strapped to Icarus-like wings, guiding a windmill-fitted bicycle frame by means of cables going from his shoes to the handlebars (fig. 36). Two years later he improved on this with the "Furious Flycycle," a device that he drew for Moulton's stepdaughter, Elspeth Thomson. His accompanying letter tells her that it, too, is steered by the "*Handlebar* of the common or vulgar bicycle." He flatters himself that this

Fig. 36. Tenniel, Title page, *Punch* vol. III (July–Dec. 1896)

"newest thing in 'Flying Machines'" is "for perfect *simplicity*, absolute *practicability*, and amazing *cheapness*," far beyond any other. In this decade of daring parachute descents by balloonists and glider flights of birdmen (reported in the sports pages alongside items generated by the current bicycle craze), Tenniel's invention was not so far off the mark.[6]

Uncle John

Aside from stresses associated with aging, Tenniel's life in the nineties went on as pleasantly as before. "Known as 'Uncle John' to all relatives and many friends," he enjoyed the company of children and "young persons" and, as confirmed by the census, his home was open to these when they come to London.[7] A Catherine M. Metcalfe, eighteen and born in Madras, India, is listed at 10 Portsdown Road in the census for 1881, and Tenniel's nephew Bernard C. Green, twenty-four and a medical student, is shown to have been there in 1891.

One youngster, a grandnephew attending school at Epsom, often spent his holidays with his Uncle John. The boy's sister, Alice Julia Tenniel King, who had been brought up in Australia, stayed with her Uncle John and Aunt Victoire when at age twelve she was returned to England for schooling. A half century later she would remember Tenniel as a "tall slight man with a long drooping moustache and a sense of humour," adding, "Owing to his disability, he would never allow a *cat* or footstool in his house as he was afraid of tripping over them. He owned a dog, I believe it was a poodle, named Toby, he trained it to ring one of those old fashioned bells (with a curved handle by the fire place) for the maid etc. in such a way that the bell only gave one 'ring' in the basement kitchen, as he hated the sound of a jangling bell. . . . he was very fond of children and I know he was always very kind to me."[8]

The picture of Victoire is less clear. Alice King recalled that she "was stone deaf and used an ear trumpet." And while the writer Anstey Guthrie described her as "portly and handsome," Marion Sambourne (Mrs. Linley Sambourne) wrote after one visit, "dear little old lady, so pretty and neat." As was customary for ladies in this period, Victoire had her weekly "at home" day when friends might call unannounced for tea, hers being Wednesday—the day when Tenniel conveniently dined at *Punch*. Like Tenniel, she was fond of young people. To her nephew Thomas Stanley Green on his eleventh birthday she gave a small Church of England book of common prayer bound in tan leather with brass corners and clasps and inscribed "from his loving Aunt L. Victoire Tenniel." Then, when he was twenty-three (perhaps when Green lived with his Uncle John and Aunt Victoire while working in a London office), she presented him with the miniature portrait of his great-grandfather Noel Tenniel. From the recollections of Gladys Storey, who as a youngster was "regaled" by Victoire with cake and milk while her father reminisced with Tenniel, one gathers that Portsdown Road was indeed a pleasant place to visit.[9]

We find a small trail of gifts and letters from Tenniel to children. An 1866 copy of *Alice's Adventures in Wonderland* is inscribed "Maj. Colville, Oct 27 / 66 From Uncle John"; a letter informs Thomas Agnew that Tenniel is "'cooking up' a little Punch drawing" that he "promised Willie on his birthday"; and a letter to an Alice White is followed by two valentines, both sent to her on the same day.[10]

He was active on behalf of children in need and in 1892 sought information in connection with a widows' and orphans' fund that he hoped could be applied to the sons of an old friend. More than once his efforts had supported children's hospitals. From the "Manchester tales" supplied by the Agnews comes the following: "When £22,000 was raised for the Children's Hospital, Tenniel, then 63, danced the hornpipe with Miss Kate Terry [Mrs. Arthur Lewis], and finished after a quarter of an hour as fresh as a 'skipping ram.' Nor was this all he suffered for sweet charity's sake, for, hiding behind a screen he permitted his extended hand to be kissed by all and sundry at the ridiculously low charge of half-a-crown a time!" In 1898, for Carroll's memorial, he raised funds to endow a permanent cot at the Great Ormond Street Hospital for Sick Children. To this end he wrote to an old acquaintance, A. W. Mackenzie, himself a founder of the Hospital Saturday Fund—a project in which he had in 1877 involved Tenniel. Then, in 1900, Tenniel contributed a drawing to the souvenir book for *Punch*'s matinee performance at the Palace Theatre to raise money for the same hospital—a jolly scene showing Pied Piper Punch leading a train of children. Among the many "pretty and charming actresses who sold programmes at the matinee," was Tenniel's niece, Miss Irene Rickards (daughter of William Rickards?).[11]

Young in spirit, he enjoyed the friendship of those who, while not exactly young persons, were still less than half his age. By 1892 he was friends with the vivacious Elspeth Thomson, then around thirty and also a friend of Sambourne's. Her portrait by Frank Dicksee shows a gamine face, arresting rather than beautiful, with longish nose and upper lip, and large eyes. Tenniel wrote to her in a self-mocking histrionic manner, elaborately seeking forgiveness for minor transgressions and receiving her pardon with "unbounded thanks." Small things were "calamities," he claimed to be "breaking up altogether," and in three instances he wrote that melancholy had "marked him for her own." She sent him a cigar cutter, some "Invincibles" (cigars?), and a statuette. He sent her drawings, and they exchanged Valentine Day verses through 1907.[12]

In early 1900 he wrote to Elspeth (by then married to writer Kenneth Grahame) that just before Christmas he had broken down badly "owing to extreme pressure of overwork" and that he was, luckily, able to take a week's holiday at his brother-in-law's place in the country. It was perhaps this visit that inspired him to write the "Verses written by Jack Tenniel and sent to me after staying with me at the Cottage on the Works at Church Gresley" that were entered into the scrapbook of Thomas Stanley Green. This nephew, besides his energetic management of the pottery ("He taught the British Workman in a most surprising way / The art of making 'Jellies' out of common Garden Clay"), apparently won Tenniel's heart as a sportsman, for "when he wasn't half the night, engaged on Wages lists, / He'd show the budding Champion how he ought to use his fists."[13]

The Fellowship Knight

The end of the year had always been a stressful time for Tenniel with the usual added chores—the title page for the newly completed volume and the almanac cut for the year following. On 7 January 1901 he confessed to the *Punch* historian, "During the last two months I was considerably worried in many ways and overdone with work." Furthermore, he could not accept Spielmann's (dinner?) invitation, explaining, "I have just recovered from the severest cold I ever had, I am told to be very careful, and I dread to be out o' nights."[14] It was not only work that had brought Tenniel to this state of exhaustion. It was the wrenching experience of parting with *Punch*.

Fig. 37. Tenniel, "Our Enthusiastic Artist Is Quite Prepared for the French Invasion," small cut, *Punch*, Jan.–June 1852, 83

It will be recalled that when Tenniel was knighted, *Punch* pictured him as a medieval knight. This had been echoed in the adjoining poem, which said, "Forty year, and more, at the Table Round, we've boasted / England's later LAUNCELOT in JOHN TEN-NI-EL!" In this period when the chivalrous ideal was the desideratum for an English gentleman, Tenniel was often spoken of in these terms. Between the two varieties of knights (and chivalrous gentlemen) identified by historian Mark Girouard, Tenniel was clearly a fellowship knight. Not for him the solitary quest or bravado of the knight-errant. In fact, he laughed at the thought of himself in a heroic role (as when describing his patrol duty as a special constable in 1848), and in 1852 he depicted in a small cut for *Punch* "Our Enthusiastic Artist" at the easel, ludicrously loaded down with weaponry in preparation "for the French Invasion" (fig. 37).[15]

As Tenniel was a true fellowship knight, adherence to a group, a cause, a leader, was more his style, and for fifty years his great allegiance had been to *Punch*. Nor was he a mere hireling. His gentlemanly stance on remuneration had put him on a quite different footing with the paper's owners. Assistant editor Arthur William à Beckett would later write of Tenniel, "He was on the most intimate terms of friendship with the proprietors, the Bradburys and the Evans[es] of the past." This continued through the paper's changes of ownership, as indicated by his letters to W. H. Bradbury and William Agnew. Most tellingly, when a new editor had to be named, Tenniel was one of the small inner circle to whom this decision fell. In 1870, on the day of Lemon's death the regular dinner was postponed, and Shirley, Tenniel, Bradbury, and Evans dined that night in a private room at the Rainbow—assuredly to decide more than the large cut. And on Taylor's sudden death ten years later, Tenniel was again one of the small group—the others being à Beckett, Leigh, and Burnand—to dine at the Bedford, "the editorship of *Punch*" being "in commission." With his editors, as Shirley commented in 1872, Tenniel was "loyalty itself."[16] Although the time had surely come for him to leave *Punch*, in doing so Tenniel gave up the major part of his life.

The first hint of the end had occurred in his letter to proprietor Phil Agnew the previous May, for he wrote apropos of his objection to adapting to new methods of reproduction, "The infirmities of age are creeping on—I am in my *81*st year—and seeing, moreover, that the time is drawing

Fig. 38. Silver tobacco box, presented by the *Punch* staff to Tenniel on 5 Dec. 1900

very near when I must—with a sore heart—resign my 'Commission' on Gen'l Punch's 'Staff'—I am particularly anxious to *close my career* in a graceful and dignified manner—whilst my work is—well—not much worse than it is at the present time."[17]

The last year told on him. He left the *Punch* dinner early on 21 March and did so again on 26 September, Sambourne recording that night in his diary, "Tenniel nervy and crotchety." In early October, when he was not present, the diners talked of a "presentation to Tenniel" to mark his long service on the paper. They decided on a tobacco box (fig. 38). On 7 November, the firm sent a letter marked *"Extra Special"* to each staff member (except Tenniel) as a reminder of the presentation to be made at the Wednesday dinner on 5 December. The day came, and the tobacco box was on the table. Designed by Sambourne, it was a handsome piece wrought in solid silver and topped by the figure of Mr. Punch. On the base was duplicated the frieze from Doyle's famous *Punch*-wrapper design, and on three faces of the box were reproduced the signatures of staff and proprietors. The fourth face showed Dog Toby holding up a placard on which was inscribed:

To
Sir John Tenniel,
our "Jackides,"
on completing fifty years of work
on the staff of "Mr. Punch."

Presented to him
by
his friends & fellow workers
round the "Table"
Wednesday, Dec. 5th 1900.

But there was no Tenniel, for he was unwell, and a deputation had to carry the box to him from Bouverie Street.[18]

The week before, following his usual custom, Tenniel had shared a cab with Sambourne on the journey home from *Punch*. That night he confided to Sammy his intention of resigning at the end of the year, adding that he was "no good."[19]

Dropping the First Mate

At the *Punch* meeting of 17 December Tenniel suggested the subject for his last cartoon, which, with some amendments, was adopted (fig. 39). On the way home he told Sambourne of "his determination not to do another cut and also that he wanted means." His double-spread cartoon, "Time's Appeal," appeared in the 2 January 1901 issue. It depicted the Roman goddess of war, Bellona (representative of Britain's embroilment in the Boer War), reining in her chargers at the signal of Father Time, who holds in his arm an infant (the dawning year). Accompanying him is Peace, who clasps her hands

Fig. 39. Tenniel, "Time's Appeal," cartoon, *Punch,* 2 Jan. 1901

Fig. 40. F. Carruthers
Gould, "Dropping the
First Mate," cartoon, *Fun*,
19 Jan. 1901

together in mute entreaty—a somewhat hollow
display of humanity as *Punch* had run a line of
jingo cartoons from the outset of the war. Gar-
nering the last of his failing powers, Tenniel had
produced a cartoon far stronger than many a one
preceding it, and he could say with some satisfaction, "This is my last, but not, I think, my
worst." In the same issue there was published
Burnand's tribute to Tenniel, which inquires,
"*His last appearance*! Can it be possible? Is it per-
missible?"[20]

Also on 2 January, Tenniel dined with *Punch*
for the last time as a member. That night Anstey
Guthrie recorded, "Wm. Agnew making a speech
—Tenniel saying he supposed he must reply—
'But you haven't drunk my health yet!' getting up,
saying it was better to retire before he was
obliged—occasionally halting—w. evident emotion—'Well, we won't prolong the agony'—and
talking of the banner of my dear old comrade
Frank [Burnand] under which he had served so
long. Curious mistake at beginning of '30 yrs
ago' when he evidently meant '50 yrs.' F. C. B.
[Burnand] invited to reply by Wm A. [Agnew] but
saying that after T's anything he cd say wd be
an anti-climax."[21]

Sambourne, too, wrote in his diary that night,
entering, "Affective evening" and "very touching." It was a difficult time for
Sammy as all the publicity over Tenniel's retirement had quite eclipsed his
own advancement to the first cartoonist slot. On the previous night he had
noted, "Nothing in any letters. No congratulations no nothing," reiterating
the last statement in red ink. This night he wrote, "No sort of reference whatever to me."

The excitement over Tenniel continued. The *Punch* office was besieged
with requests from papers nationwide that wanted to reproduce his last cartoon, his first, and his portrait. On 19 January, *Fun* published F. Carruthers
Gould's "Dropping the First Mate"—a takeoff on Tenniel's "Dropping the
Pilot"—in which Mr. Punch leans dejectedly over the bulwarks, Dog Toby
sets up a howl of anguish, and Tenniel himself descends the companion
ladder (fig. 40). The next week the queen's death brought a letter from Elspeth, apparently beseeching him to draw one last obituary cartoon. Tenniel informed her of the "absolute impossibility" of carrying out her suggestion, writing, "I really could not think of it for a moment.—*my 'long day's*

task is done!'—Sambourne is duly installed in my place—he had his 'subject' on the *previous Monday*—and was—of course, hard at work upon it when I received your letter." That March, *Punch,* determined to get full mileage from his popularity, put out another volume of Tenniel's cartoons, an ebullient puff announcing, "The Cartoons of Sir Jackides the Inimitable." The poet and art critic Cosmo Monkhouse prepared a monograph on Tenniel for an Easter annual for the *Art Journal,* and finally, although Tenniel had gratefully made what he considered to be his conclusive exit, his admirers felt they must have one more show of appreciation in the form of a public dinner. In March the papers announced that the scheme to do "suitable honour" to Tenniel had originated with the former premier Lord Rosebery, who was joined in this venture by several prominent lords, and that the event would probably take place in June.[22]

That April Tenniel attended the *Punch* table for the first time since leaving. Returning again in May, "looking older," he confided to Sambourne that he was "breaking up." He came again to the 5 June dinner, at which they arranged for Bernard Partridge's cartoon celebrating the public banquet, and Sammy recorded that Tenniel was "querulous."[23]

Now it is the 12th. The dinner, the toasts to the king and the royal family, the speech from the chair, have gone by as if in a dream. The chair concludes, "And it is as the great artist and the great gentleman that I now ask you with full glasses to drink his health. (Cheers.) Ladies and gentlemen, 'the Guest of the Evening.'" The toast is drunk. Three cheers are given, and the toastmaster calls, "Silence for 'Our Guest.'" As Tenniel rises there is a demonstration of applause that for its loudness, enthusiasm, length is sufficient to "literally" break "him down." Guthrie would later recall that Tenniel looked "as he always did anywhere, the most gallant and distinguished person present, and he began in his clear and beautifully modulated voice." He starts confidently enough: "If any answer were needed or example, I should say, to prove the truth of the old adage that some have greatness thrust upon them, none I think could be more convincing than that which my presence at this particular time affords, and which the tremendous reception which has just been accorded me so unmistakeably confirms. (Cheers.) What I have done that this amazing honour should be thrust upon me, and why I should be here at all, altogether passes my feeble imagination to discover. Unhappily I have no gift of words; I have never addressed, or attempted to address ——." He stops, meanwhile "exhibiting signs of strong emotion." The cheering begins anew, and Tenniel resumes ("his heavy gray moustache twitching nervously"), "Anything I might attempt to say would not in the least degree express my feelings, and I am afraid I can only express my very heartfelt thanks. (Loud cheers.)" Then, the audience, rising, again gives "three enthusiastic cheers for their guest," and sings, "For he's a jolly good fellow."[24]

Out of the *"Show"* Altogether

1901–1914

As it is—dear boy—my day is done! *I have made* my bow!
I am quite content to subside again into my original obscurity!
—TENNIEL, in a letter to Philip L. Agnew, 11 April 1902

I Have Not Given Up Drawing

A large oil portrait by his cousin Lance Calkin shows Tenniel at the start of his retirement (fig. 41).[1] Clean shaven, except for his moustache, still slender and soldierly, ruddy complexioned—at first glance he seems as keen as ever and ten years younger than his eighty-plus years. But then one sees that the expression is not so much intense as frowning, that there is, in fact, a jaded look about the eyes—the look of a man who is quite done up.

The thirteen years of Tenniel's retirement were blighted by his increasing loss of sight. It would not be particularly illuminating to treat of them in great detail. Until sometime in 1907, when the deterioration of his vision accelerated, Tenniel could see well enough to read, write, and, for short periods in the day, work in watercolors for his own amusement. But by his eighty-eighth birthday he was obliged to respond to a reporter's query, "No, I have not given up drawing. Drawing has given me up."[2] By 1913 he was stone blind.

In these years, he declined to contribute his work to exhibitions (with the exception of one *Punch* show in 1911) on the grounds that it would be tasteless for him to thrust himself into popular notice so soon after the "tremendous public recognition" upon his retirement. He felt, too, that his drawings would be overpowered if surrounded by pieces in the bolder and blacker styles then favored. In one demurral he wrote, "In self defense, I am bound to put myself—not only as the French Artists say—'Hors Concours'—but out of the 'Show' altogether."[3]

His memories of the public banquet were marred by the fact that he had broken down in his prepared speech, although most agreed that the emotion revealed was far more eloquent than any words could have been. More than thirty years later, Sir Henry Dickens wrote, "The whole incident was one which deeply affected all who had the good fortune to be present at this almost unique gathering. I have never forgotten it." The fact is that John Martin, in 1821, and Sir Leslie Ward, in 1921, had been similarly affected when facing such "appallingly respectable" assemblies.[4]

Beside his painting, Tenniel occupied himself with various small projects: disposing of the original designs for his book illustrations, making up albums of his verses and theatrical sketches, doing the occasional gift drawing for a friend. But the undertaking that may have given him the greatest satisfaction was his contribution to the Royal Drawing Society, an organization founded to encourage the visual arts in school curricula, with emphasis on "preserving and developing the Spontaneous Pictorial Memory Drawing, Painting, and Modelling by Children." From 1890 the society held annual exhibitions at the Guildhall Art Gallery, featuring original illustrations and "snap shot" (memory) drawings by artists aged two to twenty. Distinguished artists donated their time and money, annual prizes being given by Lord Leighton, Millais, George Frederic Watts, Linton, and Tenniel. Others spoke at meetings. The society's papers show that the "Tenniel Prize" was offered for the years 1906–1907 through 1909–1910. Through 1913 Tenniel would remain one of the society's thirty-five vice presidents.[5]

Fig. 41. *Sir John Tenniel*, oil painting by Lance Calkin, 1902 (detail)

Outside of 10 Portsdown Road, where he led a comfortable if somewhat entrenched existence, the city changed alarmingly. To Tenniel—in whose boyhood years sedan chairs could still be hired in St. James's Street—motorcars must have seemed outlandish indeed. Preceded by petrol buses and motorized cabs, by 1904 they numbered about eight thousand in London alone.[6] The hustle and bustle of the new age would have penetrated even to Maida Vale, and when Guthrie called on him in 1907, Tenniel indicated he had not been out of the house for months due, apparently, to the traffic menace.

Meanwhile, at *Punch* his seat at the table was kept for him, as was the long clay pipe with his monogram on the bowl. On a snowy day in 1907 he wrote to Henry Lucy, expressing his hope to visit the table and meet "all the dear clever boys again." But by June, six years to the day after the public dinner in his honor, he wrote again, "I am wonderfully well in health, 'I give Heaven praise,' the great trouble being steadily increasing blindness, the mere thought of which fills me with terror and dismay."[7]

If Only I Could See!

The year 1908 was made doubly difficult by the move to a ground-floor flat in Kensington, Victoire being lame and no longer able to negotiate the stairs at Portsdown Road. In his now circumscribed life, he who had always shunned reporters began to welcome their visits. On his eighty-eighth birthday he was boyishly pleased when a representative of the *Express* called, although he protested, "I have been having birthdays every year. Surely nobody is interested in me?" His ninetieth birthday turned out to be a gala occasion with "shoals of telegrams and messages of congratulation," and when the floral tributes threatened to overwhelm his small drawing room, Tenniel exclaimed, "It looks as if you'll have to put me outside." To one caller he boasted of his fitness—his biceps and fencing forearm—saying, "Once muscular, always muscular," and he spoke of his long-past days in the old St. George's rowing club.[8]

As in former days, *Punch* was sent to him every Monday night. Victoire read it to him, describing the drawings minutely. After Victoire's death in 1911, Tenniel's employed companion, Inez Juster, read to him for many hours daily—always the political articles in the papers, as well as sports and other news. Sometimes Tenniel's hand would describe the outlines of a cartoon in the air, and he would say, "If only I could see—if only I could see! I could draw it now!"[9]

The papers spoke of great changes. England had moved closer to her old competitors France and Russia, joining the Triple Entente. The naval buildup that Tenniel's cartoons had constantly advocated intensified as the country strove to keep ahead of the kaiser's program. The Liberals, now in office, were busily enacting the social legislation that Tenniel had ridiculed in the 1890s when he depicted Joseph Chamberlain as the "Tricksy Spirit" for sponsoring the only significant social reform of the Conservative era. Now, an eight-hour day was a reality (at least for miners), and the old-age pension, scorned in 1899 as "only another dole," in 1908 passed into law.[10] Ireland, despite a succession of land ownership acts, had gained neither independence nor internal peace. At home, union membership and strikes were on the increase, and the suffragist movement—a target of *Punch* and of Tenniel long years before it acquired that name—assumed a new militancy. Listening to his companion read the papers in rooms now grown shadowy for him, it must have seemed to Tenniel as if the old enemy Anarchy was just barely held in check.

By the end of 1911, Tenniel's almost-extinguished vision was subjecting him to vertigo and strange optical distortions—furniture looking as if "covered with snow after a heavy storm" and walls on each side of him "rising to high red cliffs." This he told Guthrie (who was a regular visitor), describing how, when sitting alone, he imagined vivid pictures on the opposite wall.

One—"a troop of cavalry riding by" in which he saw "every man and horse distinctly" even hearing "the clinking of their bits"—accords strangely with the sense that many had on meeting Tenniel—that "In some other life he must have set a squadron in the field."[11]

In July of 1913, down with the flu and not expecting to leave his bed again, Tenniel quoted to Guthrie (with slight alteration) the farewell to Brutus made by Shakespeare's Cassius—"If we do meet again, why we shall smile; / If not, why, then, this parting was well made." He later rallied, but by the end of the year it was evident that he was breaking down. In the final weeks Tenniel alternated between a wandering state—in which he smoked an imaginary cigar or delivered, in ringing tones, long passages from Hamlet and Macbeth—and short periods of awareness. In his lucid intervals his old humor surfaced; he responded, when asked by the nurse to put out his tongue, "Yes—and look like a fool!" and protested when being turned over to be washed, "Damn it—I can't stand being exhibited to this publicity!"[12]

Guthrie's pathetic letter to Partridge described Tenniel's last days: "Happily he does not suffer at all, but he is seldom, if ever, completely conscious, and no one who loves him could wish his life prolonged, especially when one remembers him, as we do, still in his prime. When he is awake he rambles on for hours—generally, I was told, imagining that he is looking at other men's drawings of Britannia, lions and tigers (curiously characteristic this!). . . . When he is asked—and I think you will like to know this—if it is a drawing of *yours,* he replies indignantly, 'No, no. *He*'s a draughtsman! *He*'d never draw a thing like this!'"[13]

Despite successive rallies, death found him on the evening of 25 February. It was a Wednesday, and unknowing, the *Punch* staff were at their dinner planning the next week's cartoon. For hours, intermittently, Tenniel's hand had been holding an imaginary pencil and describing figures in the air.[14] And so he died, a smile on his face, dreaming that he was still drawing for *Punch.*

Postscript

These cartoons of Punch may hereafter be as valuable as even Kaulbach's Inks,
at least in telling future generations, in noble form, of the great events which
we have passed through.
—CHARLES KINGSLEY, in a letter to Shirley Brooks, 31 December 1872

He *Was* England

No sooner was news of Tenniel's death made known when the *Punch*
office was flooded with requests from papers wishing to reproduce his cartoons in eulogistic articles. General (later Field Marshall) William Riddell
Birdwood wrote, urging that Tenniel be buried in Westminster Abbey. But,
according to Tenniel's wishes, the small casket containing his ashes was
interred in a family grave at Kensal Green, where he joined the three women
who had been closest to him: Julia, Eve, and Victoire.[1] Today the grave is
marked by no memorial more solemn than the chance primrose.

Newspapers worldwide observed Tenniel's passing as if it were but yesterday, and not thirteen years before, that he had retired. Tributes in the *Daily
Telegraph*—the paper of his friend Levy-Lawson (later Baron Burnham)—
ran to several columns in each of two successive issues, one describing the
cessation of Tenniel's weekly cartoon in *Punch* as "something like the suspension of a Law of Nature." The *Times* recalled that his "retirement from
active service on *Punch* was felt to be a national event," predicting that Tenniel's works would be "read as long as humanity takes an interest in pictures."[2] Others repeated Balfour's closing words at the public dinner—that
Tenniel had been "a great artist and a great gentleman."

The continental obituaries were scarcely less laudatory. In Nancy, *L'Est
Republicain* claimed that Tenniel's cartoons had more than once averted international conflicts, declaring that the 1886 drawing "What of the Night"—
an armed Europa at the ramparts, contemplating the heavens where Ursa
Major (the Russian Bear) treads menacingly—had precipitated Russia's withdrawal from Bulgaria. *L'Eclair* of Paris commented on Tenniel's "humour
de la qualité la plus rare," the *Journal de Genève* on his service to both public and state, and the *Kölnische Zeitung* on his power and modesty.[3]

In America, encomium mingled with some still-rankling memories of his Civil War cartoons satirizing Lincoln. A memorable tribute came from the *New York World,* which held, "As the power of a cartoonist is gauged by his ability to interpret his time and his country, then Tenniel is much greater than his more sophisticated rivals on the Continent. He *was* England—the embodiment of the mid and late Victorian epoch."[4]

The only discordant note that February came from former *Punch* artist Harry Furniss, who hastened to tell the *Evening News* that Tenniel "was a man without ideas." A few months later Furniss wrote a series of articles for *Tit-Bits* in which he maligned all the artists who had been on *Punch*'s staff during his time.[5]

The next month, *Punch* published its homage to Tenniel. More than seventeen years before, Burnand (then editor) had written to Spielmann, "May the King of Cartoonists live forever! But as *that* is impossible I should like to have *ready at hand* a well considered *page* of a résumé of his life and work on Punch for publication in *Punch.*" He then proposed that the piece display one or two portraits of Tenniel, stressing that he would like to give him *"all the tribute possible,"* and concluded, "maybe it will be my turn to disappear before *him.* Anyway my successor will be glad to have the legacy of such a provision."[6]

Thanks to Burnand's forethought the unprecedented sixteen-page supplement to the 4 March 1914 issue contains statements taken from Sambourne and Silver, both of whom predeceased Tenniel. Other colleagues recalled Tenniel as the "youngest of the staff" in spirit, one who might occasionally break his reserve to reveal rare "flashes of fun." They spoke of his "simple straightforward dignity," and more than one attested to the "reverence and affection" that he inspired. The briefest statement, but perhaps the most telling, came from Sambourne. Ambitious, inclined to privately nurse his resentments, he might have found cause for embitterment at his long years in second place at *Punch.* Instead, he simply said, "For nearly forty years not the slightest shadow crossed our friendship."[7]

More honors were to come. At the annual Royal Academy dinner that May, Poynter, speaking of the academy's losses of the year, added, "While on this melancholy theme, I cannot omit the name of John Tenniel." Following the cries of "Hear, hear," the president went on to speak of Tenniel's skill, his fame, and his "delightful sense of humour which appealed to everybody." Then, in April, the National Portrait Gallery waived its rule that a painting could not be hung in less than ten years following the subject's death, to hang Frank Holl's portrait of Tenniel. "Any objection," said the *Pall Mall Gazette,* "in the case of such men as Scott [Robert Falcon Scott, the Antarctic explorer?] and Tenniel is, of course, out of the question."[8]

The final public business to be transacted was the sale in December 1915 of Tenniel's library, a collection of some 350 books, among which were 24 presentation volumes. The largest category consisted of poems, ballads, plays, including 18 volumes of Shakespeare. One huge book, probably a legacy from John Baptist, provided a chilling reminder of Tenniel's eye injury. It was Girard Thibault d'Anvers's 1628 *Académie de l'Espée,* a sumptuously produced work financed by Louis XIII of France and nine German princes. Several of its surreal twenty-seven-by-nineteen-inch engravings portray vast marble halls in which pairs of fencers demonstrate how to run a blade through an opponent's chest or his right eye.[9]

A belated recognition of Tenniel's importance came in 1930 when the London County Council affixed a plaque to the house at Portsdown Road—a medallion of light green glazed ware that read "Sir John Tenniel (1820–1914) artist and cartoonist lived here." Although the street (renamed Randolph Avenue in 1939) suffered some bombing damage during the Second World War, Tenniel's house stood until 1959, when it and plaque were demolished.[10]

One of the Great Sources

Many, especially in Britain, may have greater familiarity with Tenniel's work than they realize. Visitors to London in 1981 would have seen his drawing of Mark Lemon as Falstaff boldly displayed on the backs of the city's buses to publicize the forthcoming opera season at Sadler's Wells.[11] A tube traveler six years later would have seen giant blowups of Tenniel's Blue Caterpillar advertising the construction of Bellway Homes.

Of all Tenniel's creations, the one that seemed most likely to be slated for annihilation was his *St. Cecilia.* The Lords' Committee had observed in 1907 that although Tenniel's was the only one of the eight frescoes to survive, it was "not well seen, for a telephone box of huge dimensions and portentous ugliness" had "been placed immediately in front of it." By 1956 all the frescoes were covered over, but they have recently been restored.[12]

As for most of Tenniel's book illustrations, being wedded to outdated texts, they are sought out mainly by collectors. His *Lalla Rookh* was republished until 1880, and the volume of *Ingoldsby Legends* that contains his drawings, until 1930. The great exceptions, of course, are the *Alice* books, which are continually reissued. Although many reillustrated *Alice*s have appeared since the forty-two-year copyright expired in 1907 (and two in America before then), they have not supplanted Tenniel's pictures. In that year England saw eleven reillustrated *Wonderland*s. Then, in December of 1907, E. T. Reed's *Punch* cartoon "Tenniel's Alice Reigns Supreme" showed the original Alice and some of her dream acquaintances gazing dubiously at their counterparts by W. H. Walker, Charles Robinson, Millicent Sowerby, and Arthur Rackham.[13] According to those who worked at the "Alice Shop" in Oxford (famed as the original of the little shop in *Looking-Glass* and specializing in "Alice" gifts) when I visited there in 1987, items using the designs of other illustrators had failed because customers wanted only those based on Tenniel's pictures.

Almost from the first, his *Alice* designs had embellished calendars, wallpapers, biscuit tins. From playing cards to tarot cards, tea towels to T-shirts, figures from the giant bronzes in New York's Central Park to those molded in soap for gift packages, the Tenniel version predominates.[14] His pictures illustrate texts on such diverse topics as the Hubble telescope, money management, oysters, hares, and drugs. A boon to advertisers, the Tenniel cuts have helped sell British railcards, houses, computers, and brassieres.

Tenniel had burlesqued his *Alice* drawings in several cartoons, and others soon did the same. From 1904 to 1905 Francis Carruthers Gould's political adaptations of Tenniel's Alice were a regular feature of the *Westminster Gazette*. A set of *Alice* takeoffs by W. Tell illustrated Horace Wyatt's World War I article "Malice in Kulturland"; a series was done for the 1916 *Passing Show* by E. T. Reed, and another by Leslie Illingworth appeared in the 1950 *Punch*.[15] But examples are countless and will probably proliferate for as long as cartoons themselves do.

The cartoons, too, continually return to new roles. In little more than five months after Tenniel's death, Austria, with German backing, found a pretext to declare war on Serbia, a move that would bring into the conflict Russia, France, and, finally, Britain. Young Britons, brought up on such chivalric views of warfare as had been fostered by Tenniel's cartoons, would soon respond to Lord Kitchener's call for one hundred thousand recruits. Aeronautics, which in Tenniel's youth was represented by the daring ascents of Charles Green's red and yellow silk balloon from Vauxhall Gardens, had by 1912 culminated in the Royal Flying Corps. Soon British "knights" of the air would be flying World War I reconnaissance missions over the continent.[16]

Tenniel's cartoons could now be used to inculcate hatred of England's enemies. In four special supplements, all appearing in the first year of the conflict, Tenniel's cartoons were reprinted along with those of other *Punch* artists. This was not the first time the paper did this, as Tenniel's work had already been reissued in the memorial supplements for Queen Victoria and Edward VII. The first war supplement, "The New Rake's Progress," drew lightly on his cuts on the kaiser, but a second, which followed a London exhibition of *Punch* cartoons illustrative of the rise of Germany, had ten of his portrayals of the "Prussian Bully." Turkey's entrance into the conflict on the side of the Triple Alliance called for ten more of his cartoons, this time showing the "Unspeakable Turk." And the early 1915 supplement, "Our Volunteer Army," used an 1860 Tenniel cartoon as its title illustration.[17]

Punch often received requests from applicants eager to reproduce its cartoons in articles, pamphlets, books, slide lectures, and school texts and to re-create them as theatrical tableaux. In 1915 a London Hippodrome review

with a wartime theme featured a series of tableaux based on *Punch* cartoons. One of the "living pictures" was Tenniel's "Dropping the Pilot," the
1890 cartoon that had noted Bismarck's dismissal, subsequently inspiring
countless takeoffs. This was a signal year for "Dropping the Pilot": the *Sidney Bulletin's* David Low pictured John Bull dropping the kaiser, *Punch*
showed Bismarck's ghost reboarding the "Haunted Ship," and in the *New
York Evening Sun* Civilization herself was "dropped."[18]

Also reproducing Tenniel cartoons at this time were pro-German propagandists in New York. Designed to discourage American entry into the war,
their pseudo-*Punch* issue, entitled "As England sees U. S.: Some Famous and
Forgotten Cartoons That the Present Generation of Americans Should See,"
featured fifteen *Punch* cartoons, nine of them selections from Tenniel's Civil
War satires.[19]

A century has passed since Tenniel made his last drawing for *Punch*—
sufficient time to gauge their durability. When Balfour said at the public
dinner that Tenniel's cartoons were destined to be "one of the great sources"
for future historians, he was merely expressing what had been said for years.
This belief was asserted continent-wide at Tenniel's death. One reads again
and again that they provide "a panorama of history," "the best political history of the Victorian era," "a graphic history of a half-century.[20]

One confirmation of this belief is in their reproduction in school texts.
In the last month of Tenniel's tenure the McDougall Education Company
of Edinburgh received permission from *Punch* to reproduce Tenniel's cartoons in a schoolbook. Between the wars Tenniel's cartoons were familiar
to a generation of British schoolchildren through Dennis Richards's standard text *The Illustrated History of Modern Europe*. This book, with twenty-
three Tenniel cartoons, was in its fifth edition in 1950 when a sister volume by Richards and J. W. Hunt came out, *The Illustrated History of Modern
Britain*, making use of eight more Tenniel cartoons and reissued the following year.[21]

It was said during Tenniel's *Punch* tenure, "The world awaited the advent of his cartoon at the judgment seat." His drawings epitomized middle-class thinking at a time before the burgeoning of daily cartoons in mass-
circulation papers would make the individual cut less weighty. Identified
solely as cartoons from *Punch,* they are continually republished in studies
of Victorian social and political history; in *History Today* hardly a volume
appears without two or more of Tenniel's cartoons.[22] Thus they fulfill the predictions of his contemporaries and remain an unceasing source for political and social historians.

METHODS AND MODES

10

Drawing on Wood

O woodman, spare that block,
  O gash not anyhow:
It took ten days by clock;
  I'd fain protect it now.
—Dante Gabriel Rossetti, to the Dalziels, February 1857

The Schools

Of all artists who drew on wood for facsimile engraving, none was more accomplished in the art than Tenniel. His half-century production at *Punch,* supplemented by close to six hundred wood-engraved book and magazine illustrations, places his productivity, if not on a level with that of John Gilbert, William Harvey, and Gustave Doré, at least in the next echelon.[1] However, it was not this, but his meticulous draftsmanship, close monitoring of the engravers' work, and uncompromising standards that brought facsimile to the peak of what might be achieved by such means. Since Tenniel's adherence to older working methods in the face of late-nineteenth-century innovations in line reproduction is often brought into question, his reasons for doing so will be examined here.

By the 1840s, when Tenniel produced his first illustrations, wood engraving was the preferred means of reproduction. It was a simple relief process, best imagined if one keeps in mind the words of artist Henry Holiday: "On wood the engraver starts with pure black."[2] That is, if one inked the flat surface of the uncut woodblock and printed it, the impression would be a solid black rectangle. Every cut that the engraver makes with his burin results in a lowered portion, one that will not receive the ink, be it applied with roller or dabber. Only the uncut, or relief, portions of the block can hold the ink and thus transfer the artist's design (that is, its mirror image) to paper. Any child who has printed from the cut half of a potato understands the principle.

The method used by the late-eighteenth-century school of Thomas Bewick is called white-line engraving. Its practitioners thought in terms of creating the image with strokes of white cut from a black ground. However, by the 1830s black-line or facsimile engraving had overtaken the earlier school. Here, the aim was to emulate a drawing done with a black line (say by pen and ink) on white paper by cutting away all but the lines—the outlines and the lines of hatching or crosshatching alike. Victorian wood engraving is mostly facsimile, and this was the method used for all of Tenniel's wood-engraved work.

As the name "facsimile" indicates, the artist's drawn lines were exactly preserved by the engraver. This is made clear by engraving manuals of the period and was affirmed most emphatically by George du Maurier who wrote in 1890, "It is more than his [the facsimile engraver's] place is worth to add a line of his own, or leave out one of the artist's."[3] The only lines that an engraver might add were for areas of flat tone such as skies or shadows where the artist had brushed in an india ink wash showing the degree of darkness desired. This the engraver translated by a series of parallel lines cut with a tint tool. Through the forties and early fifties Tenniel employed tint tool work, but by the time of his 1854 designs for Tupper he began producing some of his darks by the far livelier method of hand-drawn cross hatching. Mechanical lines seldom appeared in Tenniel's cuts after 1860.

A third method was initiated by the *Graphic* in the seventies, and used also by the *Illustrated London News*. The artist painted his picture in black, white, and gray tones for the engraver to photograph onto the block and to interpret as he saw fit by means of white line, black line, dots, and hatchings.[4] This "laid on" technique was relatively coarse (Ruskin dubbed it "blottesque"), and it was never used by Tenniel, who left nothing to chance.

From Sketch to Block

The standard procedure, before it became possible to photograph a design onto the block, was for the artist to make his sketch on drawing paper or board and then, by means of tracing paper, to transfer the main contours of his design to the prepared surface of the woodblock. He would then work on the block itself, strengthening and improving the faintly indicated outlines and adding the details and shading lines. This is what is meant when one speaks of "drawing directly [or "straight"] on the woodblock," to differentiate it from the later method in which the designer worked up his drawing in full detail on paper so that it might be photographed onto the block.

The expression, however, has caused much confusion as some take it to mean designing directly on the block—a practice that would have been beyond the capabilities of all but a very few artists. To be certain, apocryphal accounts of artists designing on wood exist. For example, Henry Silver wrote of Leech, "Sure of hand, he drew the figure ["The French Porcupine"] on the wood block, without making any sketch for it, as he had before done for Mr. Punch's Fancy Ball, which was far more elaborate, but the dozen or so of figures were drawn within three hours." Yet, describing a gala *Punch* evening in 1867, Silver did not neglect to mention the wall "over the fireplace—where hangeth the first sketch of Mr. Punch's Fancy Ball." John Gilbert could design on the block. Tenniel seems to have done so in the fifties before the use of bolted blocks (see below) allowed the artist more time; to an applicant for the first sketch of his "British Lion's Vengeance" Tenniel replied, "I have no sketch—the drawing in question, like all my drawings for Punch, was made at once upon the wood." Yet, one or two designs for cartoons—merely small-scale suggestions—do appear in some of his pocket-sized sketchbooks of the midfifties. For his later cartoons, Tenniel did make a rough sketch that he then traced and transferred to the block.[5]

As Tenniel's illustrations for books did not have the short press deadlines of his work for *Punch,* he could make both rough and finished drawings before going onto the block. Thus the *Alice* originals include both preliminary and finished versions, plus intermediary tracing-paper overlays on which he worked out modifications to his designs. Arthur Boyd Houghton is reported to have also made a rough and then a more finished sketch before going onto the block, and Millais was said to have made as many studies before transferring his design as he would for a painting.[6] The fact is that while adroitness and speed may excite admiration in themselves, they are, in the final analysis, irrelevant to the excellence of the work or of the artist.

The Art of Drawing on Wood

Drawing on wood demanded certain skills. Earlier in the century artists might apprentice themselves to well-known engravers in order to acquire these skills. Those who did include Harvey, George Cruikshank, Hablôt K. Browne [Phiz, pseud.], Leech, Keene, Fred Walker, and Birket Foster. Probably an equal or greater number simply gained the training through experience, as did Tenniel. Later, Tenniel helped instruct *Punch* novices Captain H. R. Howard [Trident, pseud.], and R. T. Pritchett in the art.[7]

Certain cautions had to be observed when designing for the block. For example, delicate lines that were unsupported by neighboring ones of "greater strength or closeness" might be damaged by the force exerted during press runs; "The designer," warns treatise writer William A. Chatto, "should always bear in mind that he is *working for the press.*" There was also the problem of joined sections. Since usable cuts of boxwood were not very large, blocks needing to exceed five square inches were usually made up of two or more pieces joined by iron pins or screws. Later (estimates of their first use range from the early forties to 1860) there were bolted blocks of four, six, or eight pieces that could be dismantled so that several engravers might work at the same time on one illustration. *Punch*'s single-page cartoons took six pieces, and its double-page cartoons took eight. For obvious reasons the designer would want to avoid locating heads and hands, and other details requiring precision, where the joins occurred.[8]

But the thing most needful for the draftsman on wood was clean and unambiguous delineation so that the engraver could read each line accurately. The ability to execute highly detailed drawings in small scale, as both George Cruikshank and Richard Doyle had been trained to do in their youth, was essential. Tenniel also had this skill. His earliest studies of costume and armor at the British Museum and of actors in London's theaters are exquisitely drawn with sure and sensitive pencil lines on small slips of paper, some figures being less than two inches high. His sketchbooks too (really memorandum books of perhaps four by five or six inches) sometimes have several drawings to the page. And his pencil sketches for *Punch*'s calendar pages are marvels of readability with myriad tiny figures, each about one-half to three-quarters of an inch high.[9]

Even those champions of the white-line school who thought black-line a perversion of true wood engraving regarded Tenniel's work highly. In his 1872 diatribe against facsimile, Ruskin gave Tenniel's cartoon "Astraea Redux" as an example of this method. Although deploring the labor required to cut the block, he wrote, "Here is a woodcut of Tenniel's which I think contains as high qualities as it is possible to find in modern art." Seven years later, Henry Holiday similarly contrasted the best of facsimile with the white-line technique that he favored (and which he had used when illustrating Carroll's *Hunting of the Snark*). Holiday reproduced three one-inch-square examples of foliage, identifying the first—a white-line specimen from Thomas Bewick's *Aesop*—and adding, "Figs. 2 and 3 are from fac-simile cuts of drawings by artists of deservedly high reputation, who have drawn perhaps more for wood than any others in the country." His unidentified figure 2 was from Tenniel's illustration of the Cheshire Cat in a tree.[10]

Not everyone could work on the block. S. C. Hall, for whose *British Ballads* Tenniel had first essayed the art, wrote of "the difficulty of getting British artists to draw on wood." The master engraver W. J. Linton also spoke of artists who, "not drawing easily or well, disliked the trouble." Engraver and publisher Henry Vizetelly noted that "Clarkson Stanfield . . . like many other painters, found the difficulty of drawing on the boxwood block with the necessary neatness and precision almost insurmountable"; and the Dalziel brothers (engravers for many of Tenniel's book illustrations) reproduce in their memoirs a letter from the painter and (by 1860) royal academician J. C. Hook declining to draw for them as he did not "manage wood-drawing well at all."[11]

Some had their designs put on the block for them. Vizetelly records that in the forties Thackeray either had his drawings on wood touched up or drawn on the block entirely by an engraver's assistant. Knowing himself to be an indifferent draftsman, Thackeray once enlisted Tenniel's help with an initial letter, his note (accompanied by his own sketch) pleading, "Do do draw an eagle (on a wood block) for me with a broken wing covering over half a sheet of stars and stripes—and oblige Your faithful W M T." To this he appended, "If ever you want any *boots* done or anythink of that sort, shall be appy to elp you. A Punch boy will probbbbly be with you ere long send eagle by him to Swain [the engraver] please."[12]

The Pencils

While uncut Victorian blocks display a variety of techniques, including fine linework done with brush and black ink, or Chinese white lines over a black or gray wash, or white lines scratched into a wash with a sharp tool (most of these combined with pencil work), the method of choice for facsimile was pencil drawing alone. Critical to the success of a drawing on wood was the hardness of the lead. When apprenticed to Linton, Walter Crane was taught "to get the lines as clear and sharp as possible for the engravers" with a 4H pencil. Richard Doyle, who had been supplied with his pencils (reportedly 6H) by *Punch*'s engravers, agonized over finding sufficiently hard leads after he had left *Punch*. One time he excused his failure to meet a publishing deadline with "Er—er—the fact is, I had not got any pencils." Another time he asked the Dalziels for extra blocks as he had "got into a mess with rubbing out," and yet another time he wrote that several drawings on wood, packed into a portmanteau for a return journey to London, had "got so rubbed as to be quite spoiled." Tenniel, who used a 6H lead, was also wary of this danger. After testing three different preparations on woodblocks sent to him by Swain, he reported to the engraver, "Two won't do at all—too soft and the pencilling rubs off." Others used pencil leads of the same grade as Tenniel; in an 1862 letter to a friend du Maurier rhapsodized, "I dream of creamy whites and silks and satins expressed with the 6H point."[13]

Lines made with a hard lead, besides being less susceptible to smudging and to being misread by the engraver, would be less easily effaced during the engraving process. This last was no small problem. To protect the drawing, the entire block, except for the small area on which the engraver was then employed, was tightly covered with paper. In damp or frosty weather engravers wore nose-and-mouth masks lest the lines be obliterated by the action of their breath. In the face of all this, why did Spielmann write the following in the 1895 article that became the basis of the section on Tenniel in his *Punch* history: "Tenniel, indeed, always drew with a specially manufactured six-H pencil (which appears more impressive with its proper style of 'HHHHHH'), and so light was the drawing that it looked as if you could blow it off the wood. The result is that Swain has always *interpreted* Sir John Tenniel's work, not simply facsimilied it, aiming rather at producing what the artist intended or desired to have, than what he actually provided in his exquisite grey drawings. . . . Doubtless the artists might deplore the 'spoiling' of their lines; but pencil greys are not to be reproduced in printer's ink; they must inevitably be 'rendered'"?[14]

The fact is that this writer on art knew very little about wood engraving and consequently relied on his friend Harry Furniss, a self-proclaimed expert in the art. In the previous year, Furniss had resigned from *Punch,* complaining of the "harassing treatment" he "had received at the hands of" his "editor and proprietors during the last twelve months." While on the paper he had associated familiarly with Swain's assistants, who dubbed him "Furnace, a hot 'un." One of them, J. B. Groves, recalled, "One thing, he always stood up on behalf of the engravers" (against the other artists?). In Furniss's retaliatory articles on *Punch* (see chapter 9) he wrote, "Poor Swain, the woodengraver, responsible for the cutting of Tenniel's and all other 'Punch' work for many years; how he was misrepresented!" Then follows a discussion of Tenniel's pencil work on wood from which can be recognized the source of Spielmann's, no doubt well-meaning, defense of Swain (who needed no defending). Spielmann's suggestions that work done with a hard lead might be especially fugitive and, furthermore, that *Punch*'s artists were unaware that black printer's ink printed black rather than gray make little sense. At the start of 1895, with Spielmann at work on the history, Burnand (then editor) had written him, "Tenniel will correct your errors: *would* do so *if he would only take the trouble.* But 'laissez faire' is his motto—and when I say he '*will*' I mean he can: as he has told me to." Burnand offers no specifics but concludes his remarks with "H. F.'s [Furniss's] statements as to Punch must be taken 'cum multo grano' [along with many grains—of salt?]."[15]

Spielmann's 1895 article was included in his history of *Punch,* published later that year. He first sent the article for comment to Tenniel who, regretting that he had not seen it before publication, observed that "certain passages" appeared to be "rather unnecessary, and, here and there, not altogether so accurate as you might desire." Tenniel returned the text, marked with a fair number of changes, but—probably hesitant to appear overly critical— made only two in the long paragraph on wood engraving. Deleted was a fictitious description of Tenniel's tutelage in drawing on wood under Swain (Spielmann, who had already alluded to Tenniel's book and magazine illustrations of the forties, should have known that those were on wood), and "firm and solid as were the lines" was inserted before "it looked as if you could blow it off the wood." The rest stood, so that Monkhouse, in his 1901 monograph, felt obliged to write that Tenniel "of course thoroughly understood how his pencil lines would be reproduced by the engraver."[16]

Furniss's charge in *Tit-Bits* that Tenniel's work lacked "colour" (dark and light contrast) and that this was added by the engraver is not borne out by the uncut blocks in family possession that I was able to examine in 1993 (fig. 42). These show no lack of depth, nor is there a lack of color in Tenniel's drawings on prepared paper, done in the late nineties for photographing onto the wood. The quality of his blocks is also attested to by E. J. Milliken, who wrote for the catalog of Tenniel's exhibition at the Fine Art Society's galleries in 1895, "Anyone who has seen, as the present writer has been privileged to do, many of Tenniel's cartoons in their pristine state of strong yet

Fig. 42. Tenniel, drawing on woodblock of cartoon intended for *Punch* issue 23 July 1870

delicate pencil-drawings on the box-wood block, must keenly regret the un-avoidable loss of such a mass of masterly artistic achievement."[17]

Proofs and Pangs

Once the entire block was cut, the engraver, or his "proof taker," could pull the proofs. The finest were taken on India paper with a specially made ink. The paper was laid on the inked block, and the design was transferred by "rubbing all over with a burnisher pressing through a card." A proof might also be taken with a hand press. Groves said of Tenniel's *Punch* proofs (presumably for his title, almanac, and pocket-book cuts, as he received no prior proofs for the cartoons), "He would never have India proofs of his drawings, but always had rough pulls taken by the printer on a hand press." This would, of course, have given a closer approximation of how the cut would look in the printed edition.[18] The proof was then sent to the artist for comment and correction ("touching").

The cartoon block with its drawing went to Swain on Friday evening. Within twenty-four hours it was cut and delivered to the printers, who began work directly on the Monday morning edition. It was different for Tenniel's other work for periodicals and for his book illustrations. The proofs that Tenniel returned to the Dalziels, with the tiniest touches of the brush in white or light red where something needed cleaning up (say the corner of a mouth or eyelid) and with neatly penciled explanatory notes, left no ambiguity. Especially he was concerned about the dark-light contrasts that gave depth to his work. Sometimes a figure would need lines split and shadows lightened to make it softer, more "radiant." Or a figure would need to be "grayer" (less contrasty) to set it behind the foreground figures. Less easily rectified was any excessive cutting away of his blacks. Once Tenniel objected, "All the colour has been cut out of this. It must be printed as *dark as possible.*" This could be done selectively as the printer might increase the pressure on specific parts of the block by means of paper "overlays"—thus printing them blacker than the rest. For the opposite effect the engraver could, before it received the final drawing, slightly lower certain portions of the block that were required to be printed lighter than the rest.[19]

Despite all precautions, disappointments occurred. According to William Chatto, artists on wood were generally of the opinion that there were always "alterations or omissions made by engravers, and invariably for the worse." Some forty years later the veteran comic artist J. F. Sullivan said in the *Magazine of Art,* "The artist's constant wail is that the engravers *will* 'improve' instead of reproducing their work, i. e. changing a pug to Roman nose. The artists loath the printer too; he is always using ink that is a dirty brown, or too thin, or too thick, or otherwise spoiling their work." The lamentations of the *Punch* artists support Sullivan's assertion. Leech, du Maurier, Sambourne all at one time or another expressed their unhappiness, most often with the cutting of their designs, but only Tenniel has been censured for this. Although Tenniel told Spielmann in 1889 that on viewing his published cartoon each Monday night he received his "weekly pang," this was hardly strange as he could neither monitor the cutting nor the printing, either of which might spoil his effects. In 1868, when his lovely Hibernia appeared in a cartoon with unpleasing darks in her face, Tenniel alerted the proprietors that he had sent a "strong protest" to Swain. But the next day he wrote the proprietors again to correct his error, having since learned that the problem lay in the printing, which had been done with excessive pressure.[20]

Once he reproved Swain for having made a change in a drawing, writing, "I wish you would not make alterations without at least—consulting *me*." But generally, his surviving twenty or so letters to Joseph Swain and to his son and successor J. B. Swain were cordial, one saying, "The engraving of last week's cut is very good and spirited." After Tenniel's retirement J. B. Swain recalled the artist's last letter to him, attesting that Swain's engraving of his cartoons, for more years than he cared to remember, had invariably given him "the greatest satisfaction." His letters to the Dalziels were likewise appreciative, commenting that he liked the proofs they sent "very much," or that they are "everything" he could wish. On the proofs themselves his corrections are balanced by such compliments as, "In most respects capital" and, "very good indeed," the one of "The Death of Zelica" from *Lalla Rookh,* one of Tenniel's best designs, simply saying, "very beautifully engraved."[21]

Photographing onto the Wood

Sometime in the sixties a means was found of transferring the image from a photographic negative, taken from an ink drawing done on paper, to the light-sensitized surface of a woodblock. The method must have been slow at first or still imperfect, for it was not adopted until the seventies or early eighties by either Swain or the Dalziels. It was not until late 1889 that it seems to have been sufficiently advanced for Sambourne (always alert to the latest innovations) to enter in his diary, "This is the last cartoon I draw on the wood."[22]

The advantages were several. The artist retained his original drawing—otherwise lost in the cutting—which he might later sell; he could work in a larger scale if he wished, since the design could be photographically reduced; and it was not necessary to reverse his drawing, making it a mirror image of what was desired, since this could be done photographically as well. Also, drawing on paper must have been easier on the eyes as there was not the wood grain (never entirely masked by the preparation) to contend with.

But the drawbacks were impressive too. Linton observed in 1876 that photographed blocks were never correct—that "even in the clearest photographs, *the details are lost.*" That left two options. Either the engraver had constantly to shift his gaze between the block he was cutting and the original drawing beside him—a practice that caused considerable eyestrain, or the artist had to first touch up the image on the block. When working on *The Nursery Alice,* Tenniel wrote to the color engraver and printer Edmund Evans, "I must see all photographed blocks, before engraving, as they will probably require re-touching." Furthermore, drawing on the smooth block with a hard lead allowed a degree of finesse that was difficult to otherwise attain. On receiving Arthur Burdett Frost's drawings for *A Tangled Tale,* a disappointed Carroll wrote that he didn't think pen and ink work could possibly equal Tenniel's results. He observed, "The ink lines run into each other, and the roughness of the paper makes it impossible to get such clear true lines as can be drawn with a pencil on wood," and proposed that Frost redraw some of the designs directly on the block.[23]

Because of the short cartoon deadline, Tenniel continued to draw directly on the wood well after he began doing his almanac and *Pocket Book* drawings on paper in pen and ink. His reluctance to change entirely to pen and ink may be explained by Partridge's recollection that Tenniel found pen and ink work "irksome, though he used it with mastery." I can attest to Tenniel's skill in this medium, having personally cleaned a century's grime from Tenniel's beautifully inked 1887 almanac drawing when researching at the *Punch* archives in 1987. But ink rendering is slow compared with pencil, and meeting the engraver's schedule would have been a strain. Still, early in 1891 Tenniel wrote Swain, "I propose to make my drawings in future—as every one else does—on paper—in pen and ink, so don't be surprised if you receive a Cartoon made in that way. I think I can manage to let you have the drawing much earlier than usual on the Friday—I believe it will be an immense advantage to me in every respect. In fact I ought to have done it long ago." Apparently he tried this method for a time, for the Searight collection at the National Art Library has the pen and ink drawing for Tenniel's 21 November 1891 cartoon "The Egyptian Pet." However, it soon became possible to photograph pencil work onto the wood, and according to Spielmann, by 1892 Tenniel was drawing his cartoons in pencil on the "chinese whitened surface of cardboard" to be photographically transferred. The Searight collection has two cartoons in pencil on prepared paper (one for 1894 and another for 1897) that exactly match the published versions.[24]

Why was it advantageous for Tenniel to draw in pencil on paper rather than wood? He still worked at the same scale, and, as the paper was washed with white to simulate the texture of the prepared block, the drawing would not have had great salability; while adequate for reproduction, it did not have the beauty of work on untreated paper. The change was probably to avoid further eyestrain, a real problem for Tenniel by the 1890s.

Process

Around the time that Tenniel began drawing his cartoons on paper, *Punch* published its first cut to be reproduced by photoengraving. Zincography, or "process" as it was then called, was a method whereby a line drawing could be photographed and transferred (or directly photographed) onto a metal plate, etched so that the lines were in relief, and then printed like a wood engraving, along with the type. Although the method was invented in France around midcentury, it was not until the late eighties that it was sufficiently improved to gain a foothold in English journals.[25]

Its advocates could point to some very real advantages, as did illustrator Joseph Pennell in his *Modern Illustration* (1895). Pennell wrote, "As many days will be given to the production of a good wood-engraving, as hours are needed to produce a good process block. . . . besides, there is as much difference in the cost as in the methods themselves, a process block being worth about as many shillings as the wood engraving is pounds." Spielmann—not a great admirer of process—admitted the cost to be one quarter that of engraving. The speed of process work was a great advantage to an artist like Sambourne. His "Cartoon Junior" (*Punch*'s second cartoon, which began around 1884) was subject to the same time constrictions as Tenniel's cartoons. Unlike Tenniel, he worked painstakingly from models, often made two or three sketches preliminary to his design, worked late on Fridays or even through the night, and, by his own admission, kept down the number of his crosshatching lines due to the shortness of engraving time remaining.[26]

For a time, the debate over process raged, its supporters arguing that no one could tell the difference between a cut printed from an etched metal surface or from the woodblock; and its detractors maintaining that wood gave a fuller range of tones, and that process cuts were coarse and mechanical looking. They were both right and both wrong, depending on the quality of the work.[27]

Photoengraving changed considerably from the 1880s to the early years of the new century. An earlier and cruder method, involving transfer paper, was being supplanted by a method in which the image could be photographed directly onto the zinc. But, undoubtedly, for a while both methods were in use. And process had other variables, just as wood engraving did. Pennell wrote about the prevalence of "Bad cheap process" in England, and Partridge—one of the first to adapt to the new method on *Punch*—lamented the press's failure to "grapple with the difficulties of modern 'process,'" maintaining that there was no inducement to do his best work while the paper was "so abominably printed."[28]

Tenniel never did work for process. In April of 1893, when *Punch* informed Swain that they would be employing another firm to do their process work, they added, "This will not apply to the work of Mr. Tenniel or Mr. G. du Maurier whose Drawings you will be good enough to send for as usual."[29]

Several months before his retirement, at the suggestion of proprietor Phil Agnew, Tenniel consented to have some process proofs taken for what may have been the title page for the 118th volume of *Punch*. Then, in a tactful but firm letter of rejection he wrote, "Even granting the process reproduction to be an absolute fac-simile of the drawing it should still be too *weak* and *pale,* and *utterly wanting in the striking effect* which I take to be—and has ever been—a most important feature in the opening page of Punch."[30] That he was not pressed further is shown by his ensuing work, which, to the last, bears the familiar engraver's signature "Swain sc."

The rightness of Tenniel's decision can be seen by comparing Sambourne's work in the 1892 Christmas number (cut by Swain in that year and bound into the start of *Punch* volume 104 for early 1893) with the process reproductions of Sambourne's drawings in the rest of the 1893 volume. The difference is evident. The process cuts have an overall flat grayness. Furthermore, the etch has undercut the lines, resulting in jagged edges that contrast unfavorably with the clean sharp lines cut by the engraver's burin in the earlier reproduction.[31] The same differences can be seen in the volumes for 1900, where Tenniel's cartoons print cleaner, sharper, blacker than the paper's other cuts.

Tenniel and the Engravers

Tenniel was esteemed by engravers, both as an artist and as a technician. Linton, considered by some the "first wood engraver" of the somewhat earlier white-line school, admitted that "the mechanics in *Punch*" had "improved, in a great measure owing to the careful drawings of Tenniel." George and Edward Dalziel wrote in 1901 that Tenniel's pencil drawings on wood "were fine examples of his varied powers of design and delicate manipulation" such as gave them "great pleasure in the rendering." In 1902 Edward Dalziel rejected collector Harold Hartley's bid for Tenniel's touched proofs, explaining, "His remarks on them are not only complimentary to my craft but are so purely technical in an Art Educational way as to make them invaluable to the Board of Education South Kensington. Therefore I have forwarded them to that Institution." Five years before, a selection of their *Looking-Glass* proofs had secured for the Dalziels a silver medal in the fine art section of the Victorian Era Exhibition in London. Testifying to the cordiality of their quarter-century association, two presentation volumes in Tenniel's library were inscribed to him with the "kind regards" (1856) and the "high appreciation and esteem" (1901) of the brothers Dalziel.[32]

With the Swains it was the same. In 1915, J. B. Swain had declared himself to be "justly proud" of Tenniel's 1901 letter of appreciation to the firm. In the previous year he and "some of his old staff associated with Tenniel's famous wood blocks" had been "among those whose attendance [at Tenniel's funeral services] attested the devotion of his old colleagues on 'Punch.'"[33]

Tenniel had drawn some four thousand designs directly on the wood and close to five hundred more on paper for photographing. Leaving as little as possible to human fallibility, his woodblocks, drawings, and touched proofs were models of clarity for the facsimile engraver. His rejection of new and still imperfect processes, regardless of their possible convenience to himself, shows his constant and unerring craftsmanship.

Before Alice

Then came "Lalla Rookh" which—"under correction of bragging" I take to be the best,
as I hold the "Gordian Knot" to be the worst *of my performances.*
—TENNIEL, in a letter to M. H. Spielmann, 24 August 1900

By the time of his first meeting with Lewis Carroll, Tenniel was an illustrator of some twenty years' standing. His stylistic development in those years
(1844–64), and the distinct strains that formed his art, have yet to receive
sufficient study. This is probably due to the ambivalent assessments of Tenniel's work by the editor Gleeson White and the novelist and literary critic
Forrest Reid who, in 1897 and 1928, respectively, published what are regarded
by some as the authoritative texts on the illustrators of the "sixties."[1] As the
biases of these men were in favor of "a literal imitation of nature"—something Tenniel had not the slightest interest in achieving—their judgments
tend to be beside the mark. They are also curiously retrograde, even for the
times in which White and Reid wrote. Thus we acknowledge that Tenniel
does not rate highly with advocates of the realist school.

In two important respects Tenniel adhered to methods that (in the words
of his colleague George du Maurier) characterized "the old school—the good
old school." First, he worked entirely from imagination. What Baudelaire had
said of Daumier could as easily have been written of Tenniel: "He draws as
the great masters draw. He has a wonderful, an almost divine memory which
for him takes the place of the model." This ability was cultivated by the early
nineteenth-century illustrators, probably to encourage creativity. For example,
Richard Doyle was trained to work entirely from memory by his father, the
artist John Doyle (HB, pseud.); and several of the older school, like John
Gilbert, continued to do "chic work," as memory work was called, into the
sixties and beyond, as did some of the newer men like Houghton. But the
general trend was toward pictures that appeared to have been drawn from
life. In 1862 du Maurier commented to his mother, "I never touch a block

(unless it be an initial letter or something of the sort) but what I take a model—expensive but must be done." Years later he would wonder, "Perhaps we of the new school are too much the slaves of the model."[2]

The realistic emphasis was no isolated phenomenon in Britain. One finds it from the fifties on in Frith's modern-life paintings and in the novels of the period; soon it would make inroads in drama.[3] It was a trend that accompanied the growth of the middle classes, who delighted in seeing themselves portrayed at home or abroad at their various occupations and amusements.

A further identification with the old school was Tenniel's sympathetic interpretation of his texts—this, at a time when many books were embellished with more or less static and neutral scenes that might apply as easily to one story as to another. Tenniel expressed his dislike of bland texts that might be thus illustrated in a letter of around 1857 to the Dalziels, who, as publishers as well as engravers and printers, supplied his commissions at the time. Of "*Love subjects,*" he complained, "they admit of so little variety of treatment." He then asked them for "something with more action and incident."[4]

While most regard Tenniel as an essentially humorous or satirical artist, only 22 percent of his roughly six hundred illustrations for books and magazines (aside from *Punch*) fall in that class. The other 78 percent are either idealistic with a strong flavor of knight errantry or melodramatic. This may well have reflected a personal choice, as several of Tenniel's letters to writers and publishers show him to have either chosen the books or the subjects that he illustrated.[5] With the Gothic revival in the ascendant, and melodrama still retaining its hold on theater audiences, Tenniel was no less in tune with his times than were the realists.

As Tenniel drew about 468 illustrations before 1864, only a selected portion can be chosen to trace his stylistic growth. These selections show the worst and the best of his designs.

Germanism and the 1848 *Aesop*

Some maintain that Tenniel's style never changed.[6] Yet, after the mid-fifties, his fundamental approach to drawing altered radically. If we compare Tenniel's original designs for the Reverend Thomas James's *Aesop's Fables* (1848) with the revised version of 1858 this becomes clear.

Monkhouse wrote of Tenniel's 108 designs for the first *Aesop* edition, "They possess, certainly, the hard clear outline, the dignity of figure and composition, the reticence in expression, and the paleness of tone, which are characteristic of the German woodcuts of the time." He may have had in mind the richly illustrated *Nibelungenlied* that was produced in Germany in 1840. This monument to German Romanticism is said to have inspired *Art-Union Monthly Journal* editor S. C. Hall to produce *The Book of British Ballads*

Fig. 43. Tenniel, "The Bundle of Sticks,"
illustration for *Aesop's Fables*, 1848 ed.

Fig. 44. Tenniel, "The Old
Woman and Her Maids,"
illustration for *Aesop's Fables*,
1848 ed.

(1842–44) to which Tenniel contributed ten drawings on wood. Tenniel's advocacy of what *Punch* derisively dubbed the "Classico-German Style" is reflected in all his illustrative work at this time. There is, however, a hint of his later inventiveness in the fantastic borders that Tenniel produced in 1845 for the frontispiece to *Undine* and for the opening page of the nursery tale "The Children in the Wood."[7]

Hall's *Art-Union Monthly Journal* commended Tenniel's *Aesop* illustrations, as it had his *Undine* pictures, for their "exceeding taste and elegance"; reproducing seven of the cuts, it declared that they possessed "that classic character which so befits the writings of the Greek." In fact, Tenniel seems to have followed the academic precepts set forth in the previous century by Sir Joshua Reynolds, namely that the artist who wishes to "raise" his subject, "approaches it to a general idea," leaving out "all the minute breaks and peculiarities in the face" and portraying garments specific to no country or time.[8] What could be more inimical to Tenniel's later style?

Despite a good deal of fine design, the *Aesop* suffers from sparsity of detail and occasional anatomical lapses. But worst of all is the weak stage direction. The archer's arrow aims at a point some feet above the one-eyed doe, the husbandman's gaze falls well to the side of the youth who strives to bend the bundle of sticks (fig. 43), and the interest in "The Countryman and the Snake" is split between the two adversaries and the group formed by the man's family. A like division causes our attention to waver in the scene depicting "The Old Woman and Her Maids" (fig. 44).[9]

Fig. 45. Tenniel, "The Bundle of Sticks," illustration for *Aesop's Fables*, 1858 ed.

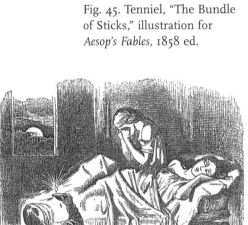

Fig. 46. Tenniel, "The Old Woman and Her Maids," illustration for *Aesop's Fables*, 1858 ed.

These faults also plague Tenniel's early work at *Punch*. Figures in cartoons seem unfocused, fail to make eye contact, and point or look offstage entirely. In 1898 Tenniel would say of his first cartoon—in which the gaze of Lord Jack (Russell) the giant killer falls considerably wide of the advancing giant (Cardinal Wiseman)—"And awfully bad it is; in fact, all my work, at that particular time, now seems to me about as bad as bad could be, and fills me with wonder and amazement!!"[10]

The *Aesop* Revised

For the 1858 edition of *Aesop*, Tenniel revised eighteen of his original pictures, doing an added design for a scene he had not previously illustrated, while sixty-two cuts were reprinted from his old blocks. Also for this book, twenty-five subjects were newly interpreted by animal artist Josef Wolf.

Tenniel's revised designs correct the weaknesses in staging. The one-eyed doe now stands grazing high on a cliff where the lines of various features in the landscape and the trajectory of the archer's arrow converge. Importantly, the increased backward slant of the archer's body adds to the tension of both his bow and the design. The husbandman points to the bundle of sticks, now curved by the youth's efforts, while further attention is drawn to the action by an inquisitive onlooker (fig. 45). The countryman's contest with the snake is brought to center stage, with the family group placed behind the action. The straightening of the countryman's weight-bearing leg, the readjustment of his fingers on the handle of the axe, will ensure that the blade will come down forcibly on the viper. And the old woman—whose candle in the first drawing had merely lit the ladder she was preparing to ascend—now stands on a middle rung so that her figure connects the two parts of the design, her raised lamp illuminating the sleeping maids (fig. 46).[11]

The pictures are modernized; the mechanical horizontal lines of the tint tool are replaced by vigorous hand-drawn hatching that intensifies the darker areas. Once-generalized scenes acquire a new energy through details specific to time, locale, and individual character.

Most telling for Tenniel's development is the new interest in human types and expression. While the original scene for "The Mountain in Labour" displayed a back view of the bystanders observing the distant mouse, now the positions are reversed so that beyond the silhouetted animal in the foreground one can see the spectator's amusement. This arrangement would carry over into Tenniel's *Wonderland* scene "queer-looking party," with the mouse well downstage so that we can observe the expressions of the animals around him—alert, bored, sleepy, disgusted, etc.[12]

Fig. 47. *(Left)* Tenniel, "The Old Woman and the Wine-Jar," illustration for *Aesop's Fables,* 1848 ed. Fig. 48. *(Right)* Tenniel, "The Old Woman and the Wine-Jar," illustration for *Aesop's Fables,* 1858 ed.

The protagonists of the fables are individualized. In "The Bundle of Sticks," the husbandman, who in the first version resembles a Greek philosopher with his refined face, trim beard, and long robes, now has the rugged features, unkempt hair, and rough clothing appropriate to a farmer. The intense curiosity of the man who leans over the youth with the sticks lends humor to the scene. In "The Old Woman and Her Maids," one of the maids—originally resembling the classical sculpture of the sleeping Ariadne—now, more aptly, exhibits the open-mouthed slumber of the exhausted. And in a small vignette for "The Old Woman and the Wine-Jar," the original refined dame is now a commoner who sniffs ecstatically with eyes closed at the mouth of the jar that she embraces as if it were a lover (fig. 47 and fig. 48).[13]

What induced this change in style? Certainly, the late-fifties impulse toward realism cannot be discounted. But more importantly, Tenniel had been on *Punch* for seven years—years in which he had been required to present in each of the 110 cartoons he drew before 1858 a single compelling idea that was lively, forceful, and instantly readable. Already, in late 1853 and early 1854, his satires on the Russian Bear and on the unwarlike British premier had shown a new assurance.

Punch brought out Tenniel's latent talent for caricature. Years later, when he asserted, "Caricature is always ugly and often vulgar, and I do not like it," Tenniel was doubtless thinking of gross caricature—the carbuncled noses, squinting eyes, and gouty legs favored in early century prints—and not the subtler exaggerations that he adopted. In these first years on *Punch* Tenniel developed a caricaturist's intense interest in the uniqueness of persons and

Fig. 49. *(Left)* John Everett Millais, illustration for "Sweet Story of Old," Henry Leslie, *Little Songs for Me to Sing,* c. 1865.   Fig. 50. *(Right)* Tenniel, illustration for" Alice in Arm-Chair," Lewis Carroll, *Through the Looking-Glass,* 1872

things, supplying an almost human personality to the very objects in the environment. The insistent singularity that Tenniel eventually imparted to even inanimate things is seen if one places Millais's picture of a child in an armchair next to a comparable one from *Looking-Glass* (fig. 49 and fig. 50).[14] Whereas Millais's chair is a casual prop, the one that holds Alice has a presence; it is almost menacing. This particularity would become a hallmark of Tenniel's style.

The Haunted Man and Miscellany

The year of the first *Aesop* ended with what Tenniel would call his "poor little contributions" to Dickens's Christmas book *The Haunted Man.*[15] Replacing Richard Doyle (as he would soon do on *Punch*), Tenniel joined three fellow artists on this project. His five designs included a many-figured fantastic border (another Last Judgment scheme) that rings the circular frontispiece illustration.

But it is an illustration for the second chapter that points to a new direction, for here is the staginess that enters much of Tenniel's later work—a characteristic that can no doubt be traced to his own acting experiences. In this case, it was a perfect reading of Dickens's own theatricalism. The facing illustrations, which can be read as a single scene, show on the left-hand page a plump round-eyed matron, her frightened children clinging to her skirts, and high on the next page, shielding the candle that lights his way upstairs, the "haunted man" (fig. 51). Here is the "piercing eye," the "half-crazed look," the "stealthy step" of the stock melodrama villain. In fact, it seems to be a portrait of a particular stage villain, the "uncanny" O. Smith, who for close to thirty years chilled audiences at the Adelphi Theatre with his "deep, almost sepulchral voice" and "taunting" laugh. That December, when the dramatized version played at the Adelphi with Smith as the haunted man's ghostly double, *Bell's New Weekly Messenger* observed that the actor seemed to have been in the author's mind when he conceived the "Phantom."[16]

By this time Tenniel's was a known name. The *Examiner* appeared predisposed to praise his designs for the book; the *Morning Post* spoke of "the catching names of Stanfield, Leech, Stone, Tenniel"; and *Bell's,* while considering the illustrations "not above mediocrity," noted that "honoured names are attached to them."[17]

Tenniel's illustrations of the fifties show that his abandonment of his earlier style was only gradual. Seventeen designs for the 1854 edition of Martin Tupper's best-selling *Proverbial Philosophy* (he had declined Tupper's suggestion that he illustrate the entire work) are still Germanic. One is put off by such mannered personifications as the rapt Religion and by the coldly mechanical lines of the tint tool. When Tenniel does break away from "reticence in expression," it is to fly to the opposite extreme, as

Fig. 51. Tenniel, Redlaw on staircase, illustration for Charles Dickens, *The Haunted Man,* 1848 (detail)

with the wild-eyed rider in the essay "Of Thinking." Still, there are touches of real observation, as shown in the seated pilgrim who cranes his neck toward Religion in the book's half title, or the gently snoring guard in the tailpiece to "Of Estimating Character." Tenniel reused some of his more expressive figures in later drawings. The woman with her dead lover from "The Dream of Ambition" reappears (reversed) in his etching for the 1862 *Passages from Modern English Poets,* and the prisoner in the "Estimating Character" section serves, in part, for the madman in Robert Pollok's *Course of Time* (1857). The pose (although not the orientation) of the despairing man in "The Dream of Ambition," who sits with elbows on knees, hands clasped over his head, would become a Tenniel standby; seen from the side, it appears in his cuts to Robert Blair's *Grave* (1858), Brooks's *Silver Cord* (1860), and W. Haigh Miller's *Mirage of Life* (1867).[18]

By 1857, Tenniel's work hovered between two manners. In Barry Cornwall's *Dramatic Scenes* the theatrical "Ludovico Sforza" illustrations contrast with the somewhat Teutonic ones for "The Falcon." Poe's "Raven" would in 1858 again quicken Tenniel's theatricalism and incidentally inspire a most

Fig. 52. Tenniel, tavern scene, illustration for Robert Blair, *The Grave,* 1858 ed.

handsome tailpiece design showing the prophetic bird on the bust of Pallas. And a new edition of Blair's mid-eighteenth-century poem *The Grave* would display his emerging skills as a caricaturist—the drawing of the publican and his customers (fig. 52), the official departing the cottage, and the chemist in his laboratory showing an eye for character that would bring us the memorable Hatter, Duchess, and chess queens of the *Alices.*[19]

At this time, Tenniel contributed to a number of books initiated by the Dalziels, whose productions appeared under the imprint of various publishers. These often involved period subjects, some evoking the apocalyptic mood that had been favored by Tenniel's old friend John Martin. But where Martin's drama was scenic, Tenniel's emphasis was invariably figural. He developed a specialty in scenes showing the aftermath of great battles, the ground strewn with the bodies of warriors and horses. This theme occurs in six books of the mid-to-late fifties, resurfacing later in *Passages from Modern English Poets* and *Lalla Rookh.*[20]

In 1859, the new periodical *Once a Week,* published by *Punch* proprietors Bradbury and Evans, brought a fresh source of work. Its prospectus, which came out that May, listed Tenniel's name directly after that of its chief illustrator, John Leech. It is here that Tenniel's Germanism soon took its final bow—in a knightly subject (a poem by George Meredith) and, appropriately, in an illustration to Goethe's poem "Eckart the Trusty." In the magazine's first few years, Tenniel would contribute seventy illustrations, forty-three of them for Brooks's novel *The Silver Cord.* Other cuts portrayed battle scenes, scenes from history and legend, fairy lore, and in one case an *Arabian Nights*–type spoof. Several are macabre. A traveler gapes at the spectral companion of his railway journey; a madman, chained to a dead woman, clutches at his hair; a scowling black man is about to fling his bound and terrified victim overboard (fig. 53). But before charging Tenniel with undue melodrama, let us look at the stories themselves. The beautiful railway ghost is a murderess, the madman will cannibalize his dead sweetheart, and the text for the third scene reads: "We saw his white teeth glisten again as he grinned in his revenge, and the metallic shine of agony on the Portingallo's face, and the sweat pouring down him, and the wrinkled anguish of his brow, and the bristling of his hair in the extremity of his terror; and then, last of all, we heard the gentle plashing of the boat swayed with their movement, and the fretting of the rope, and each touch of their naked limbs, and the gurgle in the victim's throat, and the breathing of the avenged and doomed."[21] Tenniel was merely following his author's words.

Domestic Melodrama I: *The Gordian Knot*

Even before *Once a Week,* Tenniel was immersed in melodrama thanks to his friend and colleague Shirley Brooks. Shirley, a long-time contributor to the London stage, had, besides several comedies and farces, a melodrama and two dramas to his credit. The title of his new book, *The Gordian Knot: A Story of Good and of Evil,* divulges its melodramatic character. This was a time when the public still expected, and oversized theaters encouraged, the broadest acting styles. *The Gordian Knot,* essentially the story of a marriage that manages to survive in the face of the bride's impecuniosity, her "wicked and ill-fated parents," and the plotting of her deranged admirer, fulfills the requirements of the form. That is, it has an absurd plot, teeming with obstacles for the innocent pair and ending with villainy exposed and virtue rewarded. To emphasize the undercurrent of evil, in one scene Shirley introduces a casual bystander, a man in a stage devil's costume; he would use the same device in *The Silver Cord.* So theatrical is Shirley's thinking that in his final chapter he confides, "And now we will clear the stage of all rascaldom. I wish I might do this in the summary way in which I once saw a terrible melodrama concluded."[22]

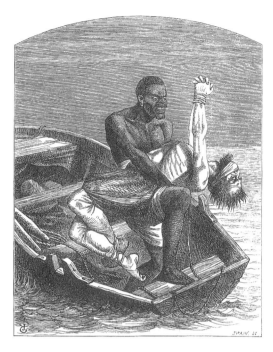

Fig. 53. Tenniel, illustration for Alfred B. Richards, "The Negro's Revenge," *Once a Week,* 7 July 1860, 52

While Shirley was pleased with the illustrations, Tenniel would years later condemn them. One suspects that he undertook the work more to help his friend than from any attraction to this soap opera; it was only in the previous year that he had expressed his disinterest in love subjects to the Dalziels. The etchings impress the viewer with the labor they must have entailed. Unessential details and extraneous figures impart a peculiarly Victorian cast to the cuts, as, for example, in the fourth plate (fig. 54). Like the furnishings and fashions of the time, they tend to be vaguely oppressive and a bit ludicrous. In his subsequent work Tenniel would more effectively separate the stars from the supernumeraries, and figures would be larger, backgrounds lighter in tone, with a few details serving to suggest many. Certain

Fig. 54. Tenniel, "Telemachus and Mentor," illustration for Shirley Brooks, *The Gordian Knot,* 1860

scenes—a workingmen's pub, a railway platform, a penny gaff (or theater)—show an emerging interest in social types. A seaside picture of the young couple is charming. But there is some downright bad drawing, as in the villain's head in the nineteenth plate, or in the plaid pattern of the hero's clothing in the fifteenth—which is laid on flat in disregard of the man's form.[23]

Yet proponents of realism have maintained that this was Tenniel's best work. Perhaps so much conspicuous labor suggests that Tenniel was taking his art "seriously," seriousness being a requisite for admirers of the "sixties school."[24] Furthermore, the drama is interspersed with some fairly static scenes, which lend the book a faint "sixties" flavor.

Tenniel's recently elevated fame on *Punch* helped to publicize the novel. After a few parts had come out, the *Illustrated London News* ran an early review (actually a tremendous puff) of Shirley's book.[25] This is no surprise as *Punch*'s editor Mark Lemon was closely associated with the *Illustrated*'s owner, Herbert Ingram, both in the paper's founding and as editor of its Christmas supplement, and Shirley had been a contributor for years.

Domestic Melodrama 2: *The Silver Cord*

The Gordian Knot appeared in book form in 1860, and in November of that year Shirley began another domestic drama in serial parts, this time in the journal *Once a Week*. Running until late summer in 1861, each of *The Silver Cord*'s forty-three installments was headed by a half-page illustration by Tenniel. Reid would declare of this venture, "What the subject of that romance in ninety-seven chapters may be I have lacked courage to discover, but Tenniel seems to have seized on all its more stormy moments for the purposes of illustration." Had he bothered to read the book, Reid would have found few moments that were not stormy. Shirley acknowledged later that his plan had been to keep the story "devoid as far as possible of description, either moral or physical, and resting its claims to attention on action and dialogue, after the manner of the French novels of the day."[26] The impossibly intricate plot—involving scandal, blackmail, spying servants, and compromising letters by misidentified writers—leaps from intrigue to intrigue. It must have succeeded with his readers, for while it ran Shirley was deluged with suggestions as to how he might best achieve the moral denouement with which such dramas must end.

Acknowledging the book's debt to the stage, he owned that the virtuous sentiments proclaimed by one of his characters were the same as those "uttered by many a melodrama." Later, in a final aside, Shirley regretted that the heroine's morally reprehensible sister, who "ought to have made a sorrowful end, upon which (to preserve the theatrical image) the rose-coloured light of a sentimental repentance should have been thrown," is too weak even "to offer an example of poetic justice" and instead winds up remarried and distributing religious tracts.[27]

Working along with Shirley from week to week, Tenniel kept to a simple formula. Consisting mainly of two- or three-person compositions, which fill the framed area, the cuts offer little scenic relief (fig. 55). The

Fig. 55. Tenniel, illustration for Shirley Brooks, *The Silver Cord*, in *Once a Week*, 11 May 1861, 533

drama—moving between Lipthwaite in Surrey, and London, Boulogne, and Versailles—carries with it the same constricted and airless space. Foliage, drapery, and furnishings (sometimes densely shaded), provide a minimal setting for the actors as they move from one agonizing encounter to another. It is all as two dimensional as the text itself—and as theatrical. The principals might be following stage directions given in a nineteenth-century actor's handbook. The scoundrel Adair portrays villainy "with folded arms and somber scowls." In two cuts the errant wife, Bertha, throws herself "vehemently on her knees." In one illustration, M. Silvain (the benevolent helper) shows his rage with "mouth open, and drawn on each side towards the ears, showing the teeth in a gnashing posture," the right arm "thrown out and menacing, with clenched fist."[28]

The most that can be said of the pictures is that they were adequate for their purpose. The one heading the eighteenth chapter (a picture of two men struggling) is of slightly greater interest, as it somewhat resembles the conflict of the American twins, North and South, in a Tenniel cartoon published later that year.[29]

The Greatest Illustrative Achievement

Moore's *Lalla Rookh* was a subject after Tenniel's own heart. Three of its four parts are full of "action and incident." Among art gift books it was a commission to be coveted. Longman, its original publisher, had twice had it embellished with steel engravings—in 1817 when it first appeared and again with new pictures in 1838. Additionally, in 1837 a volume of lithographic portraits of the type known as "keepsake beauties" had claimed Moore's oriental romance as its inspiration.[30]

From the late fifties, probably due to the expiration of Longman's copyright, *Lalla Rookh* was a prime source for the gift-book market. In 1857 and in 1859 two more publishers brought out books based on selections from its stories, each with several metal engravings. The year 1860 saw a gorgeous edition of the story "Paradise and the Peri" illumined with chromolithographs by Owen Jones and Henry Warren, and also in that year the complete book with forty-one wood-engraved illustrations after ten "eminent artists" was put out by Routledge. Then, in 1861, Longman published a new edition with sixty-nine illustrations by Tenniel. The *Times*'s comment, that this edition, "so long projected by the Messrs. Longman, has appeared at last" and its reference to "the deferred date of its publication" suggest that Longman may have hoped to precede Routledge's edition. The *Times* reviewer Samuel Lucas declared, "We have never seen a more splendid giftbook in respect of paper, type, binding, ornamentation of introductory pages." His other assertion, that Tenniel's cuts represented "the greatest illustrative achievement of any single hand," may have shown some partiality, as Lucas was editor of *Once a Week* and was also one of the few outsiders to occasionally appear at the *Punch* table. In a market where most illustrated gift books ranged from twenty-one shillings to thirty-one shillings sixpence, Longman's new edition at five guineas was indeed a costly book.[31]

Even in the years of *Lalla Rookh*'s popularity, some found its sentiments excessive. Hinda's lament to Hafed in "The Fire Worshippers"—

> I never nurs'd a dear gazelle
>   To glad me with its soft black eye
> But when it came to know me well,
>   And love me, it was sure to die!—

was satirized by Dickens in Dick Swiveller's lament in *The Old Curiosity Shop*, "But when it came to know me well, and love me, it was sure to marry a market-gardener"; and later by Carroll, whose poem "The Dear Gazelle" is a word game based on the four lines.[32]

Indeed, the two chief stories ("The Veiled Prophet of Khorassan" and "The Fire Worshippers") have several of melodrama's components: villains are villainy incarnate, lovers suffer with commendable intensity, and plots turn on idealism, betrayal, and vengeance. Separating the two is a shorter piece with Christian overtones. Another brief episode—a romantic confection—ends the set.[33]

Unlike the book's previous editions, which included a large proportion

of scenic views and the occasional keepsake beauty, Tenniel's version misses
none of the pivotal moments of conflict,
terror, heroism, which involve about half
the pictures. The dramatic scenes are
somewhat weakened by Tenniel's dis-
concerting proneness to portray great
depth of feeling by turning up the whites
of his actor's eyes or by showing them
wildly staring. In no less than eight pictures our attention is diverted from an
otherwise fine design by these histrion-
ics, and it helps little to learn that in at
least three cases the upturned eyes are
specified in the text. Tenniel's some-
times-stagy interpretation was picked up
by Lucas, who found "something affected" in the play of Zelica's hands in the
picture of the fiend Mokanna unveiling,
recalling that he had seen "something
like it . . . at the Adelphi from Madame
Celeste," an actress famed for the subtlety
of her movements (fig. 56). Nor did Lucas
care any better for Hafed in "The Fire
Worshippers," in whom he recognized the
influence of the actor Macready. Azim, in
"The Veiled Prophet of Khorassan," was
likewise modeled on Macready. Years
later, after Tenniel borrowed Azim's pose
from the illustration "Oh! curse me not
she cried, as wild he toss'd / His desperate hand tow'rds Heaven" for Britannia in
"Too Late" (the cartoon that announced
General Gordon's death at Khartoum),
the *Athenaeum*'s critic declared, "He
never designed anything worse."[34]

But these mannerisms aside, Tenniel's work on *Lalla Rookh* was a tour de
force. The staging is faultless. In two designs Tenniel used his old *Aesop* device,
placing the unveiled Mokanna downstage
and in back view, so that we witness the
reactions of Zelica or of his horrified sol-

Fig. 56. Tenniel, "He raised his
veil," illustration for "The Veiled
Prophet," Thomas Moore, *Lalla
Rookh,* 1861 ed.

Fig. 57. Tenniel, "All, all are
there," illustration for "The Veiled
Prophet," Thomas Moore, *Lalla
Rookh,* 1861 ed.

diers. The attention to details is exquisite, as in the two symbolic vignettes—the one for the "Veiled Prophet" (an antelope in the toils of a serpent, taken from an analogy in the text), and the other for the "Fire Worshippers" (an ancient Persian fire altar). The horrors of the "Veiled Prophet" are relieved by harem scenes of considerable loveliness (fig. 57), and the drama of the "Fire Worshippers" by two of Tenniel's rare landscapes.[35] Overall, the figural density, richness of ornament, relatively shallow stage, and network of fine crosshatching within an often-limited value range lend the drawings a surface intricacy that suits the Eastern subject.

It was said that in *Lalla Rookh* Moore had hinted at his native Ireland's national aspirations. Tenniel, too, had a personal theme, for beneath his orientalism there lies a chivalric spirit that evokes an almost-Arthurian mood. In fact, Mokanna's clenched fists above the water as he sinks (the verse merely says, "He sprung and sunk") recalls several Victorian pic-

Fig. 58. Tenniel, "He sprang and sunk," illustration for "The Veiled Prophet," Thomas Moore, *Lalla Rookh*, 1861 ed.

Fig. 59. *(Left)* Tenniel, "And pray that He may pardon her," illustration for "The Veiled Prophet," Thomas Moore, *Lalla Rookh*, 1861 ed.   Fig. 60. *(Right)* Tenniel, "As mute they passed," illustration for "The Fire Worshippers," Thomas Moore, *Lalla Rookh*, 1861 ed.

tures showing the fairy hand risen from the lake to grasp Arthur's sword Excalibur (fig. 58). There is more a flavor of Western chivalry than of the East in such scenes as depict the death of Zelica in the "Veiled Prophet" (fig. 59), or the Persians taking vows of vengeance, or the chiefs passing in silent file before the Mithraic altar in the "Fire Worshippers" (fig. 60).[36] In these beautiful and somber designs, there is something so deeply felt that they well deserve to survive their outmoded text.

Mirth and Marvels

Lalla Rookh had brought out Tenniel's romantic tendencies. His next important commission, thirty-one designs for the 1864 edition of the Reverend Richard Barham's *Ingoldsby Legends; or, Mirth and Marvels,* called up his sense of fun. Until now (outside of his *Punch* work) he had done few lighthearted illustrations.[37]

Barham's jocular retelling of these hoary stories, brimful of superstition, murder, witchcraft, revenge, had seen many editions since the first collected version of 1840 with its etched plates by Leech and George Cruikshank. On being asked to contribute to a new volume (refurbished with wood engravings by the original artists to run alongside many of the old plates), Tenniel chose seventeen subjects.[38] But later, given more time, he added fourteen others. Three illustrated a piece called "The Cynotaph," a rambling discussion about where to bury a favorite dog—chosen, no doubt, for its lines on the Eglinton tournament.

It is easy to see how Tenniel—who for *Punch* had drawn cigar-smoking armored knights in mufflers and pea jackets, with their ubiquitous umbrellas—would have enjoyed Barham's anomaly-filled verses. Furthermore, like Tenniel, Barham delighted in the stage. As required in Victorian theaters, "pretty pink silken hose" cover the "ankles and toes" of his water nymph Lurline, this story appropriately inspiring two burlesques on the London stage. In "The Lay of St. Romwald," a knight's blaspheming causes the sky to flash with blue, red, and green fire (obligatory for theatrical sensation scenes), which would have unhorsed that gentleman had he not "recovered his seat" with a spring worthy of "our great Widdicombe," the famous ringmaster at Astley's whom Tenniel had extolled in his bouts-rimés verses, "Widdicomez". And, the hellish horseman who abducts the witch before she is burned at the stake is a "sort of infernal Ducrow" (recalling another of Astley's great equestrians), appropriately depicted by Tenniel as a stage devil.[39]

These are the most richly worked of Tenniel's drawings. Night scenes are boldly lit against areas of dense hatching that blend to velvety blacks, keeping them in line with the heavily shaded work of the other contributors. But contrasting with the alternately bulbous and spidery forms of Cruikshank and the hardly more exact drawing of Leech, Tenniel's detailing is as fine as any he has done; the carvings on a pope's throne, the floral pat-

Fig. 61. Tenniel, 2nd illustration for "The Smuggler's Leap," R. H. Barham, *The Ingoldsby Legends,* 1864 ed.

Fig. 62. Tenniel, 4th illustration for "The Tragedy," R. H. Barham, *The Ingoldsby Legends,* 1864 ed.

tern on a courtier's trunk hose, the ornament on a crosier, are exquisite. The designs, too, are among his strongest, particularly the two for "The Smuggler's Leap." Both depict the pursuit of a smuggler by an exciseman mounted on a steed from hell—a spectral animal in the "sublime" tradition of George Stubbs, Henry Fuseli, and Benjamin West. These are among the most exciting of Tenniel's works, particularly the second scene, with its modern geometric forms (fig. 61). Tenniel himself thought well enough of them to re-accomplish the two pictures as enlarged chalk and charcoal drawings.[40]

Just as his style contrasts with that of his predecessors, so do his demons, murderers, and spooks differ from theirs. Tenniel's are a touch less jovial, and while open-mouthed astonishment is still the most favored facial reaction, other, more subtle expressions occur. A false lover tilts his head ingratiatingly toward his lady, a bored courtier toys thoughtfully with his beard, a husband registers suspicion as he lifts an incriminating scarf with his cane.[41]

Most characteristic are such supertextual jokes as the architectural carving that smirks at Lurline's revenge, the bodyless head of the Saracen that grins from ear to ear, the ornamental rainspout that screams silently at the sight of a drowned page's rosetted pumps protruding from a water butt (fig. 62), or the repetition of the blasphemous knight's posture in the vacated clothing of his dame. Drawings of saints are playfully medieval. In a med-

ley of styles the Romanesque St. Ermengarde, standing in a circle of baroque
cherub heads (one sailing upside down),
glares down at some soldiers from a
North Renaissance resurrection (fig. 63).
In a few instances one is reminded of
Punch. A standardized rustic (Hodge)
gapes at the devil horseman, dog Tray is
pursued by a rawboned bluestocking
(Sarah Suffrage), and Old Nick is a Jewish
stereotype.[42] It is a short step to the humanized imposts, Anglo-Saxon attitudes,
and social caricatures of *Alice*.

While most of the literature for these
works is dated—even the *Ingoldsby Legends,* which was projected by one reviewer
to "live as long as the English language"[43]
—many of the artist's finest designs belong to this pre-*Alice* period. Close attention to his texts (even to their implied
messages) and the particularity acquired
on *Punch* were to characterize Tenniel's illustrations from the late fifties. These di-

Fig. 63. Tenniel, 3rd illustration for "The Lay of
St. Odile," R. H. Barham, *The Ingoldsby Legends,*
1864 ed.

vide between subjects that brought out his innate idealism and those in which
the prevailing tone was theatrical or comic. By the midsixties, his eye for
the singular, his insistently precise delineation, had gained a power that
would seduce and fascinate generations of *Alice* readers.

ENCHANTING ALICE

Enchanting ALICE! Black-and-white
Has made your deeds perennial;
And naught save "Chaos and old Night"
Can part you now from TENNIEL.
—Austin Dobson

12

The Draftsman and the Don

What I tell you three times is true.
—THE BELLMAN

I Should Prefer Mr. Tenniel

When Lewis Carroll inquired, in 1863, if Tenniel would consider illustrating a children's book for him, the artist was at the top of two professions. His elevation to cartoonist-in-chief at *Punch* had followed closely upon the issuing of a deluxe edition of *Lalla Rookh* with sixty-nine of his designs. Although the *Times*'s glorification of this work as "the greatest illustrative achievement of a single hand" may have been a bit overblown, Tenniel's was a respected name.

Carroll, a little-known Oxford tutor with some small publication experience, had a manuscript entitled "Alice's Adventures Under Ground," which he had begun to illustrate with his own drawings. In a letter in late 1863 he asked *Punch* writer Tom Taylor to see if the famed cartoonist would be open to drawing "a dozen wood-cuts" for him, acknowledging, "Of all artists on wood I should prefer Mr. Tenniel."[1]

This was no lightly considered choice. Carroll had been a *Punch* reader since his teens, and his small collection of cuttings, taken from 1856 to 1862 for the purpose of convincing the Christ Church Common Room to keep a special volume of extracts from *Punch*, shows a preponderance of drawings by Tenniel. Of the seven books containing Tenniel's illustrations in Carroll's library, the three that were published before 1863 may well have been acquired before his letter to Taylor.[2]

On 5 April 1864, Tenniel, who had asked to see Carroll's manuscript before deciding, gave his consent. As reported by Carroll's friend Robinson Duckworth, Tenniel declared that he "would feel it a pleasure to illustrate so delightful a story."[3]

The two seemed designed to work together. While Tenniel was Carroll's senior by twelve years and more urbane than the author, their similarities far outweighed their differences. Of the same social class, politically conservative, single (one a bachelor and the other a childless widower), they were matched in their honesty, their scrupulousness in their creative work (about which they tolerated no compromise), and in the things that they both loved: absurdity, incongruity, visual surprises (they would both experiment with mirror writing), animals, old ballads, Shakespeare, medievalism, magic-lantern shows, word games, circuses, Christmas pantomimes, blackface minstrel shows, and most forms of Victorian theater and entertainment.[4] Most importantly, they delighted in children. Coming, both, from large families, each had shared his boyhood home with eight younger siblings. Later, as "Uncle Dodgson" and "Uncle John," they would show many kindnesses to the children of family and friends.

The Problematic Bits

One well-bred prejudice that they both held would work to their disadvantage. This was their abhorrence of personal publicity. They were gentlemen—unostentatious, jealous of their privacy, and ready to protect the privacy of a friend. Carroll's hatred of publicity and of the "whole tribe of autograph hunters and of celebrity hunters" is well known; and Tenniel, when declining to give an interview to *Cassell's Saturday Journal* in 1891, stated his "decided and positive objection—personally and on principle—to being 'interviewed.'" Eight years later he would inform one applicant that he had no "*reminiscences* whatever of either Lewis Carroll—or in connection with 'Alice' to give." This uncommunicativeness could backfire. One would-be biographer who had gone directly to Carroll for data felt so rebuffed that he later retaliated with a vengeful obituary of the writer in the *Daily Chronicle*. But despite the reticence of their subjects, biographies and studies will appear, and where there is a void any allegations that are offered are eagerly taken up. In this case, practically all the testimony regarding the Carroll-Tenniel relationship comes from one who was seventeen and living in Ireland when *Looking-Glass* was published, and who later harbored considerable animus toward both men. He was, furthermore, an inveterate self-publicist.[5]

The striking thing about all of artist Harry Furniss's alleged quotations from Tenniel is how closely they express his own feelings toward Carroll. Their almost nine-year association over the *Sylvie and Bruno* books had often been strained, and Carroll was driven, on more than one occasion, to write sarcastically to Furniss. In his *Strand Magazine* article of 1908, Furniss reiterated his earlier claim that Tenniel had described Carroll to him as "Impossible," adding, "Tenniel could not tolerate 'that conceited old Don' any more." Even setting aside the fact that Furniss was no confidant of Tenniel—who would not, in any case, have disparaged a friend, and who is not known to have referred to Carroll as a don—is it likely that he would have spoken of someone twelve years younger than himself as "that conceited old Don"? But Furniss, who was Carroll's junior by twenty-two years, speaks in the same article of "Dodgson the Don" and in his memoirs complained that Carroll was "in some respects a typical Oxford Don," treating "grown-up men of the world as if they were children."[6]

Accounts of Tenniel's work with Carroll rely heavily on the following observation in Stuart Dodgson Collingwood's biography of the writer: "Mr. Dodgson was no easy man to work with; no detail was too small for his exact criticism. 'Don't give Alice so much crinoline,' he would write, or 'The White Knight must not have whiskers, he must not be made to look old'— such were the directions he was constantly giving." Did Collingwood, born in the year that Tenniel began working on *Looking-Glass,* get this information from copies of Carroll's letters, or had it been told to him by one of his correspondents? Carroll himself informed Macmillan in 1896, "I don't keep *copies* of my letters, but only précis of them in a Register." Perhaps this was not always so, as Collingwood reportedly told an interviewer that Carroll "kept copies of many of the letters he dispatched." Tenniel kept no letters at all and would not in any case have given out such information. We note that Collingwood, who usually introduces his informants with such phrases as "The following account is from the pen of" or "some reminiscences . . . have been kindly sent me by," makes no mention of any correspondence with Tenniel. Unlike Furniss, whose helpfulness seems to have impressed the young biographer, it is probable that Tenniel sent him nothing more than the photographic portrait of himself, very dignified in frock coat, that appears on page 128 of Collingwood's book. The statement itself doesn't agree with the facts. The abandonment of Alice's puffed horsehair crinoline (shown in the first *Looking-Glass* proofs) for a party skirt with overskirts was a change in concept rather than style (the revised skirt is almost as bouffant); and from preliminary to final, Tenniel's drawings of the White Knight show no "whiskers"—whiskers in Victorian times meaning a growth of hair on the sides of the face. On the other hand, Carroll had forewarned Furniss regarding Sylvie's costume, "I hate the crinoline fashion," and had complained of Furniss's portrayal of two male characters that one appeared far too old and that he did not like the other's hair.[7] In any case the Collingwood statement, even if true, would not in itself affirm that there had been a contentious relationship between the two men. It only seems to do so when quoted in support of that allegation.

These questions dealt with, there is sufficient material directly traceable to Carroll and Tenniel to reconstruct their thirty-four-year association. From their letters, Carroll's diary entries, and the recollections of others, it appears to have been satisfactory in every way. They coordinated closely on all aspects of the work, Carroll benefiting from Tenniel's long experience with authors, publishers, and engravers, and they adjusted amicably to one another's wishes. After Tenniel, for reasons having nothing to do with Carroll, curtailed his illustrating of books, they remained friends and associates until the end of Carroll's life.

The Working Arrangement

At first Carroll, whose amateur drawings showed some talent for the grotesque, had planned to publish his children's book with his own illustrations. To that end in July 1863 he brought a trial drawing on wood to be engraved by a Mr. Jewitt, who had agreed to "improving on it a little"— probably with respect to some faulty anatomy pointed out to Carroll several days before by the sculptor Thomas Woolner. By December Carroll concluded that the result "would not be satisfactory after all."[8]

In his letter to Taylor, Carroll had proposed sending Tenniel his manuscript "to look over, not that he should at all follow my pictures, but simply to give him an idea of the sort of thing I want." Tenniel would have seen the manuscript before giving Carroll his consent on 5 April 1864. As Carroll did not complete his pictures until September of that year, the manuscript Tenniel saw would have been only partially illustrated. This may account for the two main compositional parallels between his pictures and Carroll's—the scenes that Carroll identified as "Splash" and "Cucumber Frame"—falling in the first third of the book. Of course, Carroll may have brought his fully illustrated manuscript with him when they met again on 12 October, the day on which they agreed to "about thirty-four pictures." In any case, the correlation between the subjects themselves (about 75 percent) is certainly not remarkable for so densely illustrated a book.[9]

As shown in his letters to writers Tupper and Cholmondeley-Pennell and to publishers George Bentley and the Dalziels, it had been Tenniel's practice to select subjects from the texts and to determine the treatment, sizes, and placement of his cuts. His letter to Carroll on 8 March 1865 shows that the same method applied here:

> Dear Mr. Dodgson,
>
> I cannot see your objection to the page as at present arranged, but if you think it would be better to place the picture further on in the text, do it by all means. The "two Footmen" picture is certainly too large to head a chapter. Could you manage to let me have the text of "A Mad Tea-party" for a day or two? There is much more in it than my copy contains. The subjects I have selected from it are—The Hatter asking the riddle; which will do equally well for any other question that he may ask: and can go anywhere:—and—the March Hare and the Hatter, putting the Dormouse into the tea-pot.

We now want an intermediate one, but I don't think "Twinkle twinkle" will do, as it comes close upon the first subject, ie, in *my copy*.

In great haste—

Yours very sincerely,

J. Tenniel

P.S. I am very glad you like the new pictures.

From Carroll's correspondence with later illustrators this seems, in fact, to have been the standard way of choosing subjects.[10] Surely it was the most sensible way, as the artist was the one to best visualize where he might make a good picture.

Of course there had to be mutual consent and accommodation. Carroll prevailed on "Twinkle twinkle," which appears as the second illustration in "A Mad Tea-Party." And in the second book, it was at Carroll's request that the chessboard landscape was recut to remove the figure of Alice.[11]

The tasks were split logically between them. Tenniel supplied sketches for Carroll's approval; he engaged the Dalziels and told them the size blocks he required, and after he had completed his drawings on the wood, he returned them for cutting. On receiving the engraver's proofs he sent them to Carroll for comment, himself "touching" them by brush with his minute corrections, which he explained in marginal notes. After the improvements were made Tenniel inspected the new proofs before he gave approval for the block to be sent on to Macmillan's for electrotyping and printing.[12]

The Dalziels' statement (made thirty-seven years later) that "During the process of completing the illustrations a great deal of correspondence, always of a most agreeable nature, took place with the Rev. Mr. Dodgson, as to their execution and finish" should be discounted as so much amiable twaddle as there would have been untold confusion had the Dalziels received instructions from two sources. Later, it would be necessary for Carroll himself to deal directly with the firm regarding the blocks for *Rhyme, and Reason* and *A Tangled Tale* as the artist, Arthur Burdett Frost, was then in America.[13]

Carroll made one known visit to the Dalziel shop when they were working on *Wonderland* (on 28 October 1864), afterward recording in his diary, "Mr. Dalziel showed me proofs of several of the pictures . . . and decidedly advised my printing from the wood-blocks." As the practice of printing from electrotypes (duplicate plates made by a process discovered in 1839) was fairly standard from around midcentury, it is probable that Carroll, meaning to write "decidedly advised [against] my printing from the wood-blocks," inadvertently left out the key word.[14]

It was Carroll's responsibility to deal directly with the publisher Alexander Macmillan on such matters as paper, page size, type, layout, printing, binding—some of these things being arranged first with Tenniel. In order to communicate with both publisher and artist on chapter and page layout, Carroll would have needed the pagination guides that were, indeed, found among his papers—one for each of the books. In the case of the *Alices* these would have been especially needful as some pictures were planned to register on successive pages—for example, "cat in tree" and "cat's grin." Tenniel probably had a similar system of accounting for the placement of his cuts. His letter of 8 March 1865 (above) and another of 4 April [1870] in which he appends, "You shall have some more sizes in a few days,"[15] show that he furnished some of the information for Carroll's guides. The suggestion that is often made by Carrollians that Carroll used these lists to impose his own ideas on Tenniel hardly seems flattering to the author, who was far too intelligent and too aware of his own inexperience to engage a seasoned professional only to dictate to him.

Drawing for Carroll

Far from being "no easy man to work with," his correspondence with illustrators shows Carroll to have encouraged their input, even with respect to his texts, and to have softened his own artistic proposals with such qualifiers as, "All these are merely suggestions: *you* will be a far better judge of the matter than I can be, and perhaps may think of some quite different, and better design"; "Don't adopt any of it if you don't like it"; "If you think you can find a better subject, I shall be quite disposed to defer to your judgment"; and "If you don't think the proportions . . . pretty, you can alter them." Contrast this with Dickens's precise laying out of scenes for Hablôt K. Browne and the detailed changes he required.[16] Yet Dickens has no similar reputation for dictatorialness or overfastidiousness.

Carroll praised generously. To Holiday he pronounced the head of Hope (a personification originated in this instance by the artist) to be "a great success." His early letters to Frost were interspersed with compliments such as "This is very charming"; "This is a *great* success, I think"; and "With such pictures the book will be famous at once." He declared himself "charmed" with Furniss's idea of dressing Sylvie in white and wrote, "If pictures could sell a book, *Sylvie and Bruno Concluded* would sell like wild-fire!" Of course, Carroll had to object to pictures that ignored his texts or were deficient in humor when that was required, or that failed to portray a character consistently from drawing to drawing.[17]

Still, it would be a mistake to take Carroll's dealings with his later illustrators as the model for his working arrangement with Tenniel. Besides Tenniel's greater experience and reputation there was their difference in age. Holiday, born seven years after Carroll, came next, and Frost, E. Gertrude Thomson, and Furniss ranged from eighteen to twenty-two years younger than the author. This was bound to have affected the relationship.[18]

While Carroll might call for modifications in Tenniel's work (in one case in "the face of the heroine" and in another in the chessboard landscape) these seem to have been infrequent. His delight in the *Alice* drawings is well documented: his invitations to Duckworth and others, as new sketches arrived from Tenniel, to come to his rooms and "feast . . . on the pictures"; his anxiety to procure Tenniel's services for the second book; his displaying of the yet-unpublished *Looking-Glass* designs to the family of Lord Salisbury and the aristocratic company at Hatfield House; and, after *Looking-Glass,* his renewed search for "any artist worthy of succeeding to Tenniel's place." Later years would find him "chortling" to the young readers of *The Nursery Alice* over Tenniel's animals, "Isn't it a little *pet?* and "Isn't it a little *darling?*" and telling the historical painter Mrs. E. M. Ward that the success of *Alice* had been due "entirely to its beautiful illustrations."[19]

Carroll's subsequent illustrators were to be assessed by the standard set by Tenniel. Of Holiday, Carroll wrote in his 1874 diary, "If *only* he can draw grotesques . . . the grace and beauty of his pictures would quite rival Tenniel, I think." From Frost, he required pictures with "the same amount of finish as Tenniel's drawings usually have," later telling him to consider himself engaged for the yet-unnamed *Sylvie and Bruno* "now that Tenniel is past hoping for." When the quality of Frost's work deteriorated with *A Tangled Tale,* Carroll suggested that he examine his pictures in juxtaposition with either the *Wonderland* or *Looking-Glass* cuts. Furniss would be similarly enjoined.[20]

If there was a drawback to working with Carroll it was his habit of starting his artists when he himself had not completed or, sometimes, not begun writing; giving them bits of text out of order; making frequent changes to his manuscripts; and exhibiting his perennial tendency to be behind his own optimistic schedules. In later years, referring to the "chaotic mass of fragments" from which *Sylvie and Bruno* had evolved, he would confess, "I *can't* write a story straight on!"[21]

Although in 1863 and early 1864 Carroll had the Clarendon Press in Oxford supply him with trial pages in type for "Alice's Adventures," these would have represented writing that was still in flux. At first progress was slow. Carroll noted in May 1864 that he "sent to press a batch of manuscript from the first chapter." A few days before, he had supplied Tenniel with the "first piece of slip set up" from the beginning of chapter three, but it would not be until August that he sent this chapter to Mr. Combe of Clarendon Press, possibly with the addition of the caucus race, which did not appear in his original manuscript. Before 12 October Carroll seems to have had a shorter book in mind, more on the order of the first version, as may be shown by the trial title pages for 1864, which announced only twenty illustrations. In mid-December Carroll wrote Macmillan that he had sent him "the whole" of his "little book in slip." But he was to have been further inspired, for next March he had a more complete version of "A Mad Tea-Party" than did Tenniel (see above), which implies that he had recently worked on this chapter. From Carroll's notation, "20 June 1865,—sent last portion marked press," it appears that he revised and expanded the text right up to the printing deadline, increasing the final version by two entirely new chapters. This would have entailed considerable revision as the new characters—the Cheshire Cat, Duchess, Hatter—reappear in later chapters. As for the expanded length, the collector Justin Schiller places the final word count at 26,708 as opposed to 12,715 in the original manuscript.[22]

Looking-Glass saw the same disparity between wish and actuality. With his usual enthusiasm, Carroll first projected a publication date of Christmas 1867. But he did not complete the manuscript until 4 January 1871.[23] Tenniel's letter of the previous April reveals the still-fluid state of the plot:

> My dear Dodgson,
>
> I should have written sooner but I have been a good deal worried in various ways.
>
> I would infinitely rather give no opinion as to what would be best left out in the book—but since you put the question point-blank, I am bound to say—supposing excision somewhere to be absolutely necessary—that the Railway scene never *did* strike me as being *very* strong, and that I think it might be sacrificed without much repining—besides—there is no subject down in illustration of it in the condensed list.
>
> Please let me know to what extent you have used—or intend using—the *pruning knife*—my great fear is that all this indecision and revision will interfere fatally with the progress of the book.
>
> In haste to even post
>
> Yours sincerely
J Tenniel
>
> You shall have some more sizes in a few days.[24]

Carroll was still struggling with his plot in June of 1870, as shown in Tenniel's better-known letter of the first, in which he recommended that Carroll have Alice lay hold of the Goat's beard when the railway carriage rises up in the air, and that he excise the "wasp chapter"—suggestions that were both taken up. This writing pattern would be repeated for Carroll's later books.

A Curious Fact

After *Looking-Glass*, Tenniel terminated his illustrating of books, with the exception of *Punch's Pocket Book* (which appeared annually through 1881), two drawings that he contributed gratis to S. C. Hall's temperance books, and a few designs for a projected Shakespeare. In response to Carroll's proposal that he illustrate another of his books, Tenniel responded, "It is a curious fact that with Through the Looking-Glass the faculty of making drawings for book illustration departed from me, and, notwithstanding all sorts of tempting inducements, I have done nothing in that direction since." Certainly, much has been made of this, although Tenniel gave no indication that he had ceased illustrating *because* of *Looking-Glass*. His continued good relations with Carroll are shown by Tenniel's consent in 1875 to draw a frontispiece for "Alice's Puzzle-Book" (a project that failed to materialize) and his work on *The Nursery Alice* in the 1880s.[25]

Actually, Tenniel had greatly curtailed his work (outside of *Punch*) after *Wonderland,* doing only thirty-one illustrations in the five years between the two *Alices*. Five days after Carroll recorded that *Looking-Glass* was "now printing off rapidly," Tenniel turned down a "very flattering proposal" from the publisher George Bentley on the grounds that painting would henceforth occupy his free time. True to his word, Tenniel (who as early as 1863 had confided his wish to resume painting to his *Punch* colleagues) returned to his exhibition work and was subsequently elected to the Institute of Painters in Water-Colours. Another "inducement" that he rejected in this period was the opportunity to take up where Leech had left off and illustrate a third volume of *The Comic History of England* for Bradbury and Agnew.[26]

A still more compelling reason for Tenniel's cessation of outside work may have been the fragility of his vision. For thirty years he had strained his one functional eye; in 1864 he revealed his fear of going blind from all his close work to his comrades at the *Punch* table.[27] Understandably, he would husband the sight remaining to him.

Fees and Benefits

Some have suggested that Tenniel, and not Carroll, was the more difficult co-worker, taking an inordinate amount of time with his illustrations and requiring a costly reprinting of the first book. But the fact is, from a pecuniary perspective alone, Carroll could hardly have been more fortunate. Tenniel's fee for the forty-two *Wonderland* pictures was £138, or about £3 5s. 8d. apiece. Had he adhered to his scale of charges for *Once a Week* or for *The Ingoldsby Legends,* his total would have been around £230. This suggests that—as he and Leech had done when illustrating H. Cholmondeley-Pennell's *Puck on Pegasus* three years previously—Tenniel lowered his rates to help a fledgling author. This allowed Carroll, who had initially proposed, via Taylor, "a dozen woodcuts. . . . done in pure outline, or nearly so," the forty-two finished drawings that he got. It may, in fact, have given him the liberty to expand his text. Comparing with the usual charges of Carroll's subsequent and less-experienced illustrators: Frost would have required around £170 for *Wonderland;* E. Gertrude Thomson £176; and Furniss, with rates ranging from five to fifteen guineas per design, almost three times as much as Tenniel.[28]

Furthermore, Tenniel's low figure seems to have included an outright sale of copyright; at least there is no indication that his permission was sought for the reuse of his designs in jigsaw puzzles, playing cards, songbook wrappers, biscuit tins, calendars, wallpaper, posters and book for Savile Clarke's play "Alice in Wonderland," Carroll's "Wonderland" Postage-Stamp Case, *The Nursery Alice,* or lantern slides. Tenniel himself was careless of such things, informing A. W. Mackenzie, in the month after Carroll's death, that Mackenzie's lady friend was "welcome to make a Calendar out of" his "'Alice' designs," but typically responding on receipt of the published calendar in the next year, "I venture to hope that you do not expect me to go into transports of admiration over the 'reproduction'—which might certainly have been better."[29]

Although Carroll did not usually exact payment from others for the use of Tenniel's pictures, he must have been aware that the growing *Alice* industry served to publicize his books. Yet some sort of remuneration to artists when a work was used for purposes additional to the original one was not unknown. For example, Bradbury and Evans's republication of Doyle's *Punch* series "Manners and Customs of ye Englishe" in book form led to a nineteen-year dispute with the artist during which the publishers did not entirely discount Doyle's claim. A similar embroilment in the nineties followed the firm's sale of a drawing by Furniss to Pears' Soap.[30]

Tenniel's reputation alone was a great asset to the little-known Carroll. Review after review included such comments as "No less than (42) pictures by John Tenniel"; "When we add that it is . . . illustrated by Tenniel, the great art-draftsman of Punch, we have said enough"; "Forty-two illustrations due to the practic'd pencil of John Tenniel, and that fact itself should be a strong recommendation"; and "Forty-two illustrations by Tenniel! why there needs nothing else to sell this book, one would think." Finally, the *Illustrated Times* (one of the few papers to pan Carroll's story) considered that its best hope of success lay in Tenniel's drawings.[31]

Additionally, being conversant with book production, Tenniel could relieve Carroll of such responsibilities as would later plague him with his other illustrators. The advantage of this was soon apparent when Henry Holiday, a designer of stained glass and a painter, failed to mark the proofs of *The Hunting of the Snark* for the printers. When confusion ensued as to the order and placement of the pictures, Macmillan wrote to Carroll, "I suppose that in the former books you worked with Tenniel who is familiar with these things." Whereas Tenniel worked directly with his engravers, this chore fell to Carroll in the case of Frost's pictures. It seems from Carroll's correspondence that it was also his responsibility to work with Swain on the *Sylvie and Bruno* blocks. Unforeseen problems arose. Lacking the feedback from Frost that he would have received from Tenniel, Carroll allowed the poem "The Three Voices" to become "overpictured"; even more worrisome, he discovered that Thomson and later Furniss had both drawn their illustrations too large to reduce favorably to the sizes planned.[32]

Pictures and Conversations

However, it is the illustrations themselves that are Tenniel's special contribution, for never have pictures so comple-
mented and developed an author's text.
Alice's question, "What is the use of a book
without pictures or conversations?" is especially appropriate here, for Carroll's texts
are practically all conversation (Alice's with
others and those she has with herself), with
just sufficient narration to carry the story
line and next to no description. Consider
Wonderland. Aside from some color designations (the White Rabbit's pink eyes, the
Blue Caterpillar) and various anthropomor-
phisms (the finger that the Dodo presses
upon its forehead, the Caterpillar's folded
arms), little is set forth. We are told that the
Rabbit wears a waistcoat, the Footmen are
in livery with curled and powdered wigs, the
grinning Cat has very long claws and a great
many teeth, and the King wears his crown

Fig. 64. Tenniel, "Sheep in
Shop," illustration for Lewis
Carroll, *Through the Looking-
Glass,* 1872

over his judge's wig. That is all, except for the tardy disclosure, three chapters after she is first introduced, that the Duchess is very ugly and has a sharp
chin (perhaps by this time Carroll had seen the drawings for chapter 6). Similarly, the Hatter's hat is first revealed in the court scene when he is told to
take it off, and in *Looking-Glass* the allusion to the White Queen's "broad,
good-natured face" first occurs when it is about to disappear into the soup
tureen. Clearly, the *Alices* were meant to function in some middle ground
between independent texts and picture books. Carroll himself says, "If you want
to know what a Gryphon is, look at the picture," and later he tells us to "look
at the frontispiece" to see how the King wears his crown over the wig. In *The
Nursery Alice* (1890), which is more of a picture book, he does this frequently.

As we are always discovering, Carroll's texts abound in hidden references
to the Victorian world, its institutions and its games. In a discerning article, Janis Lull has shown that Tenniel created a Carrollian-type "brain teaser"
by loading the White Knight's horse with a number of props (more than twice
those named by Carroll) belonging to future or preceding scenes, thus requiring the reader's memory—like the White Queen's—to "work both ways."[33]
But this game of "hidden pictures" may well have begun in the earlier chapter "Wool and Water." Soon after the White Queen offers her "Twopence a week

and jam every other day," Tenniel pictures Alice standing in the little shop facing the old Sheep—into which the Queen has changed (fig. 64). On the counter between them, next to the basket of eggs from which will emerge Humpty Dumpty, are three jars of the jam that Alice has just declined. Also, the shop contains candles (for the feast later), a purse similar to the one Alice held in the railway carriage, and a gyroscope ("To '*gyre*' is to go round and round like a gyroscope," Humpty Dumpty will shortly tell her). Like the texts, the pictures fairly bristle with meaning. It will require several chapters to explore Tenniel's elaboration of things only hinted at by Carroll.

My Hopes Are Now Postponed

As confided in his journal, Carroll suffered agonies of impatience while the pictures were in progress. On 20 June 1864 he recorded calling on Tenniel, who had "not begun the pictures yet." This turned out to be most fortunate, for on the day following, Carroll would be persuaded by Macmillan to have the book done in octavo rather than in the quarto size originally planned. Any designs existing at that time, if not requiring modification due to the considerable change in scale, would at the least have to be reduced, either by redrawing or by photographing, before being transferred onto the wood. In fact, Tenniel, who had been through a change in page size when working on Tupper's illustrations a decade before—and knowing Carroll's inexperience—may have been in no hurry to begin. On 12 October he showed Carroll one drawing on wood—"the only thing he had." But as Carroll received Tenniel's three final proofs eight months later, the forty-two pictures were not unreasonably timed.[34]

Carroll's letters show that his agitation had little to do with the marketing of his books and everything to do with his eagerness to send off his gift copies. Before the first printing he wrote to Macmillan, "My present idea is to send you 50 copies to be bound first, for me to give away to friends, and the rest of the 2000 you can bind at your leisure and publish at whatever time of the year you think best." With *Looking-Glass,* Carroll's cries of impatience became pathetic indeed. In January 1871, having finally completed his manuscript, he wrote, "It all now depends on him [Tenniel], whether we get the book out by Easter or not." But, as only twenty-two blocks had been electrotyped by the previous October (and may have been the only blocks done), was this a reasonable expectation? In the following months Carroll would mourn, "My hopes are now postponed to midsummer"; "*Through the Looking-Glass* lingers on"; and "Wrote to Tenniel, accepting the melancholy but unalterable fact, that we cannot get *Through the Looking-Glass* out by Michaelmas." Apparently all this agonizing had the same cause as formerly. So eager was he to present his book, first to Alice Liddell and then to others on his gift list, that on 8 December 1871, having obtained 103 copies from Macmillan (three bound in morocco for Alice, Florence Terry, and Tennyson),

Carroll inscribed and sent out all but one copy in little more than a day, although he was confined to his rooms with an illness that would keep him a "prisoner" for two weeks.[35]

He advised subsequent illustrators, "*Please don't hurry. . . . it does not the least matter to me at what time of year the book appears,*" and "*Never hurry yourself in the least over my work, I beg.*" It was only when the lapse threatened to become years that he would remind the artist that life was short and uncertain.[36]

We Shall Have to Do It All Again

Although Alice Liddell received a copy of *Wonderland* exactly three years after Carroll told the story, she and other readers were to wait sixteen weeks longer for the approved edition. By 20 July 1865 Tenniel had objected to the printing done by Oxford's Clarendon Press, thus preventing what would have been a serious mistake.[37] Although Carroll wrote that day in his diary, "I suppose we shall have to do it all again," he does not seem to have been overly perturbed, devoting the rest of that entry to a discussion of his current project in portrait photography.

Tenniel must have indeed received a shock when he saw the original printing with all his carefully wrought dark and light, or value, contrasts undone. It was Tenniel's frequent injunction to his engravers to "preserve plenty of colour," to abstain from overcutting in the darker areas in order to maintain that all-important richness of tonal diversity. It was the practice of fine engravers and printers to follow an artist's specifications as to color and to employ "lowering" and "overlays" to control press pressure on certain portions of the block (see chap. 10). The point was (rather than printing every line of a drawing sharply and distinctly) to convey depth and atmosphere by decreasing the pressure on the finer background lines, even partially losing them so that they might appear in places as dots or dashes. Thus one preserved the softness of fur or hair, the delicate modeling of a face, and suggested the translucency of water or smoke. This was needed, too, to ensure the proper fading out of the vignettes. Tenniel may have followed the procedure he would later use for *Looking-Glass,* making separate value studies for his darker scenes to plan the distribution of the darks and lights.[38] The touched proofs for both books show how closely he monitored the color in the engraving of his blocks. Of course, he could not allow all these nuances to be lost in an insensitive printing.

By juxtaposing the British Library's 1865 and 1866 *Wonderlands,* the difference is clearly seen, a prime example being the first illustration. In the first printing (and in many twentieth-century impressions) the White Rabbit looking at his pocket watch is merely an anthropomorphic figure, whereas the 1866 Rabbit, his soft fur contrasting with the more darkly printed eye, jacket, waistcoat, umbrella, is also a silky and lovable little animal that a child would cherish—one of Alice's own pets playing a role in her dream. In the picture of Alice swimming past the Mouse, see the greater transparency of the water in the 1866 printing; or, in later chapters, see the greater smokiness of the smoke coming from the Caterpillar's hookah or filling the Duchess's kitchen. Beside flattening Tenniel's contrasty effects and placing edges around vignettes, the excessive pressure in the 1865 edition had placed ugly shadows under Alice's eyes, unpleasant lines around her nose and mouth, and far too much eyelash in several pictures. In "Curiouser and Curiouser" she almost looks bearded, and in the Rabbit's house she appears to have two black eyes. To this, add paper that is wavy at the edges, whole pages printed lighter than others, type that actually comes through some of the sheets, and the necessity of the reprinting should be apparent.[39]

Partly because he was an amateur, but also due to his great eagerness to see the book come out, Carroll did not see the faults in the Oxford printing until Tenniel pointed them out to him. Then the edition of two thousand was withheld, and the job of reprinting given to the London firm of Richard Clay—the same press that had printed the Tenniel-illustrated *Lalla Rookh*. In November, receiving his copy of the new impression, Carroll rejoiced, "very far superior to the old, and in fact a perfect piece of artistic printing." Once aware of how much the "brilliance of effect" hinged on presswork, Carroll had specimen sheets of successive *Alice* impressions sent for Tenniel's approval. He himself monitored printings of the books, ensuring that they did "justice to Tenniel" and declaring that "all the copies that *are* sold" must be "artistically first-rate."[40]

Carroll's loss on the rejected 1865 printing was one-hundred pounds (the Clarendon Press setting aside a balance due of twenty-seven pounds and one shilling), which he later recovered in the sale of the rejected edition to the New York firm of D. Appleton and Co.[41] The drawing and engraving costs would, of course, not have had to be repeated as the blocks were still perfectly good.

But had the immediate loss been greater, this would have been no time for Carroll to be pound foolish with respect to his "*table*-book." Victorians were unusually attentive to the artistic quality of their gift books, with publishers proudly announcing such features of their elegantly printed products as "toned paper, strong bindings," and "splendid typography." Books for the young, too, were well put out. An 1866 article in the *Daily News,* "Children's Christmas Literature," speaks of the excellence of pictures and of covers "such as to make the happy young possessors think they have got hold of so many jewelled caskets."[42] At precisely this time, too, an increase of "toy books" with splendid full-color illustrations had come on the market, providing another source of competition. While these were generally for younger readers, there would have been some overlap with buyers of *Wonderland.*

The close scrutiny of printing and paper can be seen in *Wonderland*'s reviews: "we add that it is beautifully printed on fine paper"; "externally and internally it is well suited for the season"; "Few books for Christmas are more attractive to the eye"; "The book is printed and issued in a style which fully sustains the reputation that Macmillan & Co. have justly obtained"; "In external beauty these volumes are models"; and "'Alice's Adventures' are further, exquisitely printed and illustrated."[43] These things could not have been said of the 1865 edition.

The Continued Association

After *Looking-Glass,* the association of the two collaborators did not cease. There was the overseeing of subsequent *Alice* editions and their work on *The Nursery Alice.* By August 1881 Tenniel had colored a frontispiece for Carroll, taken from a regular *Wonderland* edition, and was preparing "to make some changes in the figure of 'Alice.'" With a view to altering Alice's dress, in 1883 he arranged for enlargements with the color printer Edmund Evans, and in July 1885 Carroll (who would not finish his text until early 1889) recorded that Tenniel had completed coloring the twenty enlarged pictures. Tenniel's part on *The Nursery Alice* did not end until December 1889 when he approved the color proofs and thanked Evans for the trouble he had taken.[44]

Then, in September 1896, Tenniel consented to "supervise the pictures" for a "new venture" of Carroll's. Four days later—probably due more to his failing vision than he admitted—he changed his mind, acknowledging that he had been "over hasty . . . simply with a view to helping" Carroll, and that he had "a deal of work," outside of his ordinary work, "on hand." To this he added (which seems to indicate that his overseeing of the *Alice* editions may well have been done gratis over the years), "As to making it a 'matter of business,' that (with much thanks) is equally impossible. The idea of remuneration never entered my head for a moment."[45]

Their last contact was over the fourth edition of *Wonderland* in October 1897 when Carroll reported to Macmillan that Tenniel was "well pleased with the new Alice books." Not long after, Tenniel would be writing of his "very intimate association with poor Mr. Dodgson for so many years—even to within a few months of his death."[46]

Their relationship had never been entirely confined to the *Alice*s. Tenniel provided a link to the world of comic journalism, identifying for Carroll such *Punch* artists as George du Maurier, Captain H. R. Howard ("Trident"), and Georgina Bowers, as well as W. S. Gilbert ("Bab") of *Fun*. He put him in touch with Richard Doyle and later with Linley Sambourne. It was through Tenniel that Carroll learned of *Punch*'s acceptance of his poem "Atalanta in Camden Town," and to Tenniel that the publicity-shunning Carroll applied when Shirley Brooks's "Essence of Parliament" playfully credited the parliamentary chairman of committees, Mr. W. Dodson, with authoring the *Alice* books.[47]

Moving in the same social stratum, they met by chance at the Arthur Lewises' parties at Moray Lodge or on holiday at Bognor. The cordiality between them was demonstrated by Carroll's series of gifts to Tenniel: *Phantasmagoria* in 1868, an illustrated *Midsummer Night's Dream* in 1869 and, over the years, seven of Carroll's post-*Alice* works, all inscribed with the author's "sincere regards."[48]

The word "friend" comes up always: Brooks writes that "A friend of Tenniel's, a scholar and a gent" objected to a piece in *Punch*, only to learn that the "censor" is the author of *Alice's Adventures*, "a delightful book"; in 1878 Carroll tells Frost, "I sent the book [*Hurly-Burly*, which Frost had illustrated] to my friend Mr. Tenniel for an opinion"; and Tenniel responds to Carroll's good wishes on his knighthood, "It is always delightful to receive the congratulations of old friends." After Carroll's death (although actively serving on the committee to raise funds for the Lewis Carroll memorial cot at the Ormond Street Children's Hospital) he would not provide a letter for publication for fear that he might appear to be publicizing himself "over the grave—so to speak" of his "poor dead friend."[49]

Theirs had been the gentlemanly association of men matched in social class, tastes, and exactingness in their respective fields. Money was never the first consideration. Their work together tells of things they most delighted in; their private lives were their own. Tenniel followed his usual course of choosing subjects and sizes, advising on the layout, and monitoring the engraving (all in conjunction with Carroll), and Carroll relied on Tenniel's judgment—even, once or twice, on matters pertaining to the text. Each accommodated the other's wishes, and although neither of them could meet Carroll's perennially optimistic schedules, the books came out in timely fashion to capture their Christmas markets.

13

Harlequin Alice

Comes swift to comfort me, the Pantomime—
Stupendous Phenomenon! . . . when Everything is capable,
with the greatest ease, of being changed into Anything.
—DICKENS, "A Christmas Tree"

The Setting

For "Great and Small Children" the Victorian Christmas culminated yearly in that glittering fairyland spectacle the Christmas pantomime.[1] The hold of this institution on the English imagination can hardly be overstated. Theater managers felt called upon to produce new pantomimes each season, and beginning on December 26 (Boxing Night) and lasting sometimes as late as February, pantomimes could be seen all over England. For the remainder of the year children could relive their joys with toy theaters and figures cut from juvenile drama sheets "penny plain and twopence coloured." Brought up on pantomime, his earlier readers might have seen nothing remarkable in it if Lewis Carroll's two *Alice* books recalled scenes from past holiday seasons with their animated card suits and games of living chess.

One can hardly imagine a greater lover of pantomime than Carroll. A year-round devotee of theater, during the Christmas season he sometimes saw as many as four or five different pantomimes, or, in order to take child friends to his favorite performances, he might see the same pantomime on four separate occasions. In 1877 he would advise one small girl, "I wonder if you have ever seen a pantomime at all? If not, your education is *quite* incomplete, and you had better tell your parents that they mustn't put your lessons in the wrong order! The next lesson ought to be "Pantomime"; then "French"; then "German"; and so on."[2]

Oddly enough, considering the absence of fairies, elves, or similar sprites in either story, Carroll consistently referred to his *Alice* books as "fairy tales." There may a clue here to the pantomime sources of *Alice,* for legends and nursery rhymes, regardless of their original content, automatically became fairy tales once they were staged as pantomimes. This occurred through the intercession of a benevolent fairy queen who, in a stunning "transformation scene," changed the principals of the "opening," or the part containing the main story line, into the characters of the fantastical harlequinade (a comic chase involving many scenes) and then back again for a triumphant denouement. In fact, so fond was Carroll of this form that in 1867 he considered staging *Wonderland* as a pantomime but was advised against it.[3]

Tenniel's taste for this peculiarly British institution (for the Christmas pantomime had strayed a long way from its Italian antecedents) he affirmed in cartoons in which statesmen played Harlequin, Clown, and Pantaloon and in title pages, almanac cuts, and initial letters. Shortly before Carroll broached the *Wonderland* project, Tenniel had illustrated *Punch's Pocket Book* for 1864. Each year this combined almanac, memorandum book, and storybook adopted a different theme. In 1862 the influence was chivalric, in 1863 Japanese, and the 1864 *Pocket Book* celebrated the nation's pantomimes. The section called "Britishlion the Bagdificent; or, Harlequin Happy Hunchback and the Paragon Pocket Book" showed Parliament, the court, and figures denoting various departments of government cavorting onstage in pictures representing the pantomime opening, "dark" scene, grand transformation scene, and harlequinade.[4] In 1864 pantomime was very much "in the air."

Wonderland

Cards, Pantomime Animals, and Outsize Objects

Nothing could have been more natural than for Carroll to look to pantomime for inspiration, as he had first intended to complete the story as a Christmas gift for Alice Liddell. And few motifs were more popular in pantomime than personified playing cards. From the titles of at least seven pantomimes between 1805 and 1862 we may surmise that games of cards and the royalty of various suits figured in their plots. There were probably more, as card characters cannot be discovered by title alone. For example, in *Harlequin Jack of All Trades* (1825) the Jack of the title was a knave in a deck of playing cards. Extravaganzas, which were closely related to pantomimes, might include card people, too. The first play to be so designated—J. R. Planché's *High, Low, Jack and the Game; or, the Card Party* (1833)—featured the celebrated Mme Vestris as the Queen of Hearts, supported by an entire cast dressed as playing cards.[5] Alice's encounters with a pack of cards surely had a familiar ring to contemporary readers.

Fig. 65. "Our Courts of Law. No. 1—The Palace Court," illustration, *Punch*, 20 Jan. 1849, 31

Carroll's interest in card games began at the start of 1858 when, having equipped himself with a copy of *Hoyle's Games*, he set about "learning cards." Before January was out he had invented a card game with the punning title of "Court Circular" after the journal of that title. He would also have seen cards personified in *Punch;* Robert Peel and the Marquis of Londonderry had both been depicted as court cards in the paper's early issues. Perhaps he noted the 1849 *Punch* article "Our Courts of Law," with its little picture of a suit king kicking a knave (fig. 65), and possibly he knew the child's game "Trial by Jury" (c. 1850) in which the court cards were caricatures of courtroom personnel.[6]

There is little sense of pantomime in the first five chapters of *Wonderland.* Despite its bizarre happenings, there lingers something of the idyllic mood—of cottages in the wood, shimmering gardens, and the animal companions of a child's summer. But between Carroll's first writing and the published text, new sections were added and a new mood enters.[7] It is the heady atmosphere of pantomime.

In "Pig and Pepper" Alice straightway encounters beings quite different from any she has met. They are not animals with little human hands, but men—footmen in fact. Yet one has the face of a fish, another a frog—figures occurring frequently in pantomime where actors often wore masks that concealed the entire head (fig. 66). Alfred Crowquill's collage-like drawings for the Christmas supplements of the *Illustrated London News,* celebrating the world of pantomime, show both fish and frog-headed human figures (fig. 67). Doubtless the soldiers of the Queen of the Ocean Waves in one 1865 pantomime—impersonating salmon, dolphin, carp, sharks, pike, roach, alligators, and lobsters, "all in uniform" and marching in detachments—were similarly costumed.[8]

A giveaway to the pantomime nature of the scene is the "great letter, nearly as large

Fig. 66. Tenniel, "The Two Footmen," illustration for Lewis Carroll, *Alice's Adventures in Wonderland,* 1866

Fig. 67. Alfred Crowquill, "What I Saw in the Fire," *Illustrated London News,* 21 Dec. 1861, 635 (detail)

as himself," that the Fish Footman produces. Outsize objects were a pantomime standby, going back to the commedia dell'arte performances in which barbers shaved their clients with razors as large as scythes.[9] In *Looking-Glass* there will be more gigantism: the White King's "enormous memorandum-book"; flowers "something like cottages with the roofs taken off"; and railway tickets "about the same size as the people" that "quite seemed to fill the carriage."

Fig. 68. Tenniel, "Duchess's Kitchen," illustration for Lewis Carroll, *Alice's Adventures in Wonderland,* 1866

Big-Heads and Other Masks, and Rough Nursing in Wonderland

The "howling and sneezing," the crashing, and the large plate that comes skimming out the door give warning, for once Alice goes through the door that, oddly enough, leads into a large kitchen the scene is pure panto (fig. 68). Kitchen scenes were standard in this form of entertainment. In this one, Alice finds the Duchess and cook (both unpleasant), a howling baby, and a large and rather unnatural-looking cat. The ill-natured cook is a stock pantomime type; one, a Dame Dorothy Drippington, appeared in an 1852 production of *Whittington and His Cat.* The cook is a "dame part"—that is, performed by a man. Although the Duchess is not described by Carroll until a later chapter, her "hoarse growl" suggests that she, too, is a dame part.[10] Tenniel drew her with features that he commonly ascribed to his "roughs" or ruffians, garroters, and Irish dissidents as seen in the cartoon "*Odd*-Handed Justice" (fig. 69).

Although Duchess and cook are shown with bodies proportionate to Alice's, both have heads that are considerably larger than hers. They are, in fact, "big-heads"; they wear the huge, often grotesque, papier-mâché masks that covered the heads of actors during the pantomime opening and that were caricature versions of the characters portrayed. Similarly, Prince Bulbo appears as a big-head in Thackeray's "Fireside Pantomime" *The Rose and the Ring* (1855). Following his London visit in 1856, Frenchman Francis Wey described the masks: "Enormous cardboard heads

Fig. 69. Tenniel, "*Odd*-Handed Justice," cartoon, *Punch,* 27 Apr. 1872 (detail)

conceal the actors, who wear historical costumes cleverly exaggerated. No
words can give a correct idea of the
cunning hideosity of these masks, sci-
entifically moulded, as the management proclaims, with the aid of a
phrenologist. The melancholy of
Hastings, the brutality of Tyrrel, the
sufferings of Jane Shore, the sensu-
ality of the Archbishop of Canterbury
are wonderfully imprinted on those
pasteboard countenances." An engraving of a pantomime workshop of
1870 gives a further idea of their size
and character (fig. 70). Tenniel had

Fig. 70. "Preparing for the
Pantomime," *Illustrated London News,*
17 Dec. 1870, 625

drawn big-head halberdiers and standard-bearers for the title page of *Punch*'s
thirty-ninth volume in 1860, and in the 1864 *Pocket Book* the royal cooks and
other servants are likewise shown as big-heads. A side view of a big-head
mask, worn by Bismarck in Tenniel's "Turkey and Grease" (a cartoon in which
the "cooks" of several nations attempt to extinguish the Greco-Turkish crisis of 1869) shows its construction (fig. 71).[11]

What follows next in *Wonderland*'s kitchen suggests the time-honored
routine called "nursing the baby," something that belongs to the unre-

Fig. 71. Tenniel, "Turkey and Grease," cartoon, *Punch,* 2 Jan. 1869

strainedly savage climate of the harlequinade. It was performed by the greedy and amoral Clown, who secreted into his capacious pockets food, drink, dogs, and even babies. A Tenniel cartoon of 1865 shows the statesman John Bright in this character, attempting to steal the reform baby from Lord John Russell. Behind them are, in the usual outsize pantomime proportions, a bottle of the shoe blacking and a bowl of "Democratic Pap"—delicacies that he plans to feed to the infant. One early fan of pantomime, writing rapturously of Clown's "tender nursing" of stolen babies, chortled, "With what grace does he feed the little innocents, venting his impatience with sundry whacks and thumps." The routine, which has strong echoes of the Punch and Judy shows (fig. 72), lived on until late in the century, as shown by these 1882 directions for pantomime clowns:

Fig. 72. Robert Cruikshank, "Doings of Punch and Judy," illustration for G. Smeeton, *Doings in London*, 1828 (detail)

> Toss the baby to Pantaloon, crying 'Catchee, catchee!' Snatch it away from him, and hit him with it over the shins, knocking him down. Squat upon the ground with the baby in your lap and begin feeding it out of a large pan with a great dripping ladle. Ram the ladle into the mouth of the baby, and scrape the lips with the edge of it, then lick them clean. Now wash the baby by putting it in a tub, pouring hot water on it from the kettle, and swabbing its face with a mop. Comb its hair with a rake; then put the baby into a mangle and roll it out flat. Set the baby in its cradle, and tread it well down. Make the baby cry; then take it out of the bed to quiet it, and give it to Pantaloon to hold whilst you administer poppy syrup. Smear the syrup over its face. Take it away again, catch hold of its ankles, and swinging it round your head by its legs, thrash Pantaloon off the stage with the baby, and throw it after him.

Tenniel's first cartoon for 1875 shows some "rough nursing" along these general lines, administered by Clown Bismarck to the New Year baby (fig. 73).[12]

Carroll's Duchess is also abusive. She gives her baby "a violent shake" with each line of her song, she keeps tossing it "violently up and down," and finally, saying "Here! You may nurse it a bit, if you like!" she flings it at Alice and leaves to prepare for the Queen's croquet party. Meanwhile the cook has steadily been throwing fire irons, pans, and dishes at both Duchess and infant. Alice may well ask herself as she carries the creature outdoors, "Wouldn't it be murder to leave it behind?"

Fig. 73. Tenniel, "Rough Nursing for the New Year," cartoon, *Punch*, 2 Jan. 1875

One surmises the theatrical source of the new chapters in Tenniel's portraits of the Cheshire Cat and March Hare—both in sharp contrast to the more or less realistic animals in the rest of the book. If we compare the Duchess's cat with Tenniel's drawing of Dinah and her kitten in the sequel, the difference is evident (fig. 68 and fig. 74). Tenniel, who could draw Gryphons and Mock Turtles persuasively, has, in the Cheshire Cat, fashioned a contrivance.

In pantomime, a small animal such as a cat might be played by a child either concealed inside a papier-mâché form or, if mobility was required, wearing a head mask and a "skin." An example of the latter is shown in Laslett J. Pott's painting *Puss in Boots—behind the Scenes, 1863* in which a father holds a large head mask of a cat over the head of his small boy.[13] The Cheshire Cat, on the other hand, has little movement; it simply appears and fades out, its pose on the branch being essentially the same as in the Duchess's kitchen. All that has moved are its eyes and tail, and this might be ac-

Fig. 74. Tenniel, "Alice and Two Kittens," illustration for Lewis Carroll, *Through the Looking-Glass*, 1872

Fig. 75. Tenniel, "Tea-Party," illustration for Lewis Carroll,
Alice's Adventures in Wonderland, 1866

complished mechanically by a child hidden inside its shell. The March Hare,
too, contrasts with the cuddlesome White Rabbit or the real Dormouse beside him. He is plainly a stiffly staring head mask perched on a small man's
(or a boy's) body, as is the Hatter (fig. 75).

Looking-Glass

Chessmen, Mirror Passages, and the Fireplace Connection

Like cards, chessmen appeared early in pantomime. In 1823 the Boxing
Night offering at the Surrey Theatre was *Fox and Geese; or, Harlequin, the
White King of Chess.* Forty-two years later to the day, the Surrey, just rebuilt
after having been destroyed by fire, presented for its grand opening a new
pantomime written by "Three Jolly Dogs" and entitled *Harlequin King Chess;
or Tom the Piper's Son and See-saw Margery Daw.* So enticing was the prospect
of enjoying both a new theater and a new pantomime on the same night,
that, as the *Times* reported, the route to the theater (Blackfriars Road) was
blocked by hundreds, possibly thousands, of admission seekers hours before
the performance. The opening followed the usual formula with its mixing
of characters from various nursery rhymes. The powerful and sinister King
Chess assumed the guise of Simple Simon in order to woo Margery Daw,
who much preferred Tom the Piper's Son. But what the reviewers were
agreed upon was the novelty of the final scene where, in the palace of King
Chess, the King and Tom played an actual game of chess with living pieces
in a manner that, the writer of the *Athenaeum* predicted, would be "long
talked of."[14]

It is with some surprise, then, that we read about the play at the Standard Theatre, *Pat-a-Cake, Pat-a-Cake, Baker's Man; or, Harlequin Bah! Bah! Black Sheep* (reviewed at the same time): "Here again, we have a magic chessboard, with living chessmen who play for the title of the pantomime." The next Christmas season, animated chess pieces appeared once again on the Surrey's stage; they are pictured in the *Illustrated London News* along with living archery targets, drums, shuttlecocks, kites, and ninepins.[15]

As an ardent follower of pantomime, Carroll would surely have read the detailed reviews that came out directly following the Boxing Night openings of 1865. He probably saw the engraving "'King Chess'—Giving Check to the Queen" published in the *Illustrated London News* on 30 December 1865 with its living chessmen (fig. 76).[16] So might Tenniel have, since *Punch* editor Mark Lemon had authored the first piece on the Surrey's bill that night, a drama called *Honesty Is the Best Policy*.

The summer of 1866 provided another and more direct stimulus for *Looking-Glass*. That August Carroll was at Croft (the family home), where he recorded on the 10th of August, "Spent good deal of the day watching the 'Chess Tournament.'" "Chess," he subsequently noted, "is the family occupation at present." It must have been at this time that Carroll hit upon the concept of the chess framework, for by 24 August he wrote from Croft to Macmillan that he had a "floating idea of writing a sort of sequel to *Alice*."[17]

It is in *Looking-Glass* that pantomime truly holds sway. Alice's passage

Fig. 76. "'King Chess'—Giving Check to Queen," *Illustrated London News*, 30 Dec. 1865, 657

through the large mirror over her fireplace mantel combines elements of both transformation scene and harlequinade. In the transformation scene, fairyland (the "Realms of Bliss") was gradually revealed, to appropriately dramatic strains from the orchestra, by the slow lifting of successive veils of gauze. For little Alice, the fairyland vision of all delights is represented by Looking-glass House: "Let's pretend there's a way of getting through it, somehow, Kitty. Let's pretend the glass has got all soft like gauze, so that we can get through. Why, it's turning into a sort of mist now, I declare!"[18]

When the transformation was completed (stagehands having snatched away the big-head masks and loosely tied costumes worn by the actors for the opening to reveal them as Harlequin, Columbine, Pantaloon, and Clown), there began the harlequinade, or comic chase. Often Harlequin, pursued by Clown, would dive headlong through concealed traps in the scenery that closed after their passage to present an unbroken surface. This might be a hinged trap of simple construction like one shown in a Tenniel initial of 1852 in *Punch,* or the more elaborate star trap. Harlequin and Clown frequently seemed to leap through glass panes such as shop windows, clock faces, and mirrors. In a juvenile drama sheet of 1812 the famous Harlequin Tom Ellar makes a graceful mirror exit.[19] Thus, Alice's mirror passage was not without pantomimic precedents.

Once through the glass, Alice does not hasten to explore the looking-glass world but lingers at the hearth before the blazing fire, where she soon discovers a little landscape of cinders populated by moving chessmen. Comparisons between the forms one might visualize among the glowing coals of a fireplace and the fanciful figures of pantomime were common. Tenniel's title illustration for *Punch*'s twenty-third volume (late 1852) shows Mr. Punch standing before a fireplace opening where, among a host of fairies and elves, Harlequin and his cohorts swarm round the blazing Yule log. Three years later, Thackeray would draw for the title illustration of his "Fireside Pantomime" (which came out as a Christmas book) the little figures of the story silhouetted in the glow of a brilliant fire under the "proscenium" of a fireplace mantel. And Alfred Crowquill's medley of pantomime figures in the 1861 *Illustrated London News* accompanies a poem by "A. C-rambo" (probably another pseudonym for the artist as well as an allusion to the popular Victorian game Dumbo Crambo), "What I Saw in the Fire," that said,

> When all at once amidst the glowing coal
> I saw strange faces—stern, fantastic, droll;
> Bright fairies, gnomes, and witches of the night;
> Kings, ladies, sprites, all marshalled in the light;
> Next frowning rocks, with castles on the top,
> That blazed, and fumed, and spat, but did not stop.[20]

With its fumes of red, blue, and green "fire" rising from the wings as the transformation scene changed into the harlequinade, the pantomime stage was very much like a fireplace fantasy. Appropriately, Alice does not go through any looking glass, but through the looking glass of a chimneypiece.

Harlequinade Devices, Rallies, Masks, and Skins

As Alice moves from square to square the devices of the harlequinade apply. The scene changes from a wood to a railway carriage to a wood again. The Red Queen vanishes, the goat's beard melts away, the shop becomes a boat and then reverts to a shop again, and knitting needles change to oars. So would one shop change into another or one article into another at the slap of Harlequin's magic bat. A scene from *Harlequin Pepin* (1843) is described as follows: "The interior of a confectioner's shop, all the contents of which—cakes, soups, bon-bons and all—are set in motion by a touch of Harlequin's wand." Alice has difficulty getting things to stand still in the little shop:

> "Things flow about so here!" she said at last in a plaintive tone, after she had spent a minute or so in vainly pursuing a large bright thing, that looked sometimes like a doll and sometimes like a work-box, and was always in the shelf next above the one she was looking at. "And this one is the most provoking of all—but I'll tell you what—" she added, as a sudden thought struck her, "I'll follow it up to the very top shelf of all. It'll puzzle it to go through the ceiling, I expect!" But even this plan failed: the "thing" went through the ceiling as quietly as possible, as if it were quite used to it.[21]

The immateriality of walls and of shelves recalls a harlequinade of 1840 in which the whirling fire irons and candles evoke still other Carrollian scenes—"Clown and Pantaloon take refuge in furnished lodgings, which progresses to bare walls at the touch of Harlequin's bat to the bewilderment of the two lodgers. Chair after chair slips through the wall or the floor, fire irons take their way by the chimney, candles whirl round when wanted to light a cigar, window curtains dissolve to nothing, sofas and tables take their departure, chimney ornaments fling themselves at Clown, and the huge looking-glass falls on his head with a fearful smash, leaving him standing in melancholy astonishment in the empty frame."[22]

In crude imitation of the enchantment wrought by Harlequin were Clown's tricks of construction—absurd figures improvised from fruits and vegetables, or armies synthesized from barrels of ale, pots, and various odds and ends, all of which Harlequin animated on the sly to Clown's amazement.[23] Alice encounters some of Carroll's tricks of construction when she meets the looking-glass insects: the Snap-dragon-fly with a plum-pudding body, holly-leaf wings, and a burning raisin for its head; and the Bread-and-butter fly of equally whimsical composition. Finally, in the most grotesque scene of all—Queen Alice's dinner party—the bottles assume forks for legs and go fluttering about with dinner-plate wings.

Fig. 77. Tenniel, "Law," illustration, *Punch's Pocket Book*, 1864

Fig. 78. Tenniel, "Alice Introduced to Lion," illustration for Lewis Carroll, *Through the Looking-Glass*, 1872

Other scenes of pantomimic havoc are recalled by the dinner. In a haunted-kitchen episode of 1825 the cook appears in the dripping pan, a copper lid flies off the stove, a leg of mutton dances up, and six lighted candlesticks pass by.[24] Would the scene of Alice's dinner party with all its hurly-burly, its candles like shooting stars, its fearful confusion between the dinner guests and dinner, have been written at all if Carroll had never seen a harlequinade?

Indeed, the rout that terminates each of Alice's dreams suggests a pantomime "rally," the general melee at the end of the harlequinade that usually involved the throwing about of vegetables and various objects. In *Punch's Pocket Book for 1864* Tenniel had pictured the law courts as such a scene of pantomimic chaos, the air filled with turnips, carrots, fish, and bills of cost (fig. 77).

As in *Wonderland,* Tenniel again mixed his real creatures with grotesques,

Fig. 79. Tenniel, "The Lancashire Lions," cartoon, *Punch,* 13 Apr. 1872

actors in theatrical costume with creatures of fantasy in *Looking-Glass.* The chess kings and queens equivocate between the two groups, though mainly they are humans cleverly costumed as Staunton chess pieces. The Unicorn is an actor in a head mask. The Lion, however, is clearly a "skin part"—a masked actor with a little potbelly in a "skin" that bags slightly above his too-large paws (fig. 78). Those are a man's knees where the animal's ankles would be. In 1872 Tenniel drew Disraeli as another bogus lion in a skin, orating, to the disgust of the real lion Gladstone (fig. 79).[25]

Humpty Dumpty and the mutton are both drawn as children wearing large papier-mâché forms that mask everything except their limbs. This was done frequently in pantomime, small boys being cast as anything from dominos to animated sticks of celery. The artificiality of Humpty Dumpty, a favorite character of pantomime, is apparent in the scene where he shouts into the Messenger's ear (fig. 80). Here, the cloth below his cravat is gathered around the bottom of the body mask, then flounced out to conceal the transition to his living limbs just as the sleeves mask his arm openings. Although his face is necessarily mobile, the contrast between the organic and inorganic is evident when Tenniel's drawing of him is compared with most illustra-

Fig. 80. (*Left*) Tenniel, "Sending Message to Fish," illustration for Lewis Carroll, *Through the Looking-Glass*, 1872. Fig. 81. *(Right)* Tenniel, "Mutton," illustration for Lewis Carroll, *Through the Looking-Glass*, 1872

Fig. 82. Tenniel, "The Gigantic Gooseberry," cartoon, *Punch*, 15 July 1871

tions to the nursery rhyme, which integrate body and limb. The mutton in chapter 9 wears a body mask, too, that conceals a still smaller child (fig. 81). Such a mask is worn by Tenniel's "Gigantic Gooseberry" in an 1871 cartoon (fig. 82).[26] But the frog of that cartoon, like the old Frog in *Looking-Glass,* is no actor in costume since he lacks a human pelvis.

The Reign of King Panto

Pantomime, with its tricks and transformations, pervaded several aspects of the culture. Many were the toys and devices that pictured, or were named for, transformation scenes or characters of the harlequinade. Itinerant or "galantee" showmen projected "magic lantern" scenes from the harlequinade on "Christmas walls"; publishers of toy theaters displayed pictures of Harlequin and Columbine on their shop signs and sold trick sheets and drama sheets for the most loved pantomimes. Columbine and Harlequin were depicted in an optical toy called the thaumatrope in which a disk was spun rapidly so that the pictures on its opposite sides seemed to combine. There were pantomime toy books, "movable" books of "transformation pictures," greeting cards that opened out to reveal transformation scenes, and "harlequin" or "transformation" playing cards in which the pips might be cleverly "transformed" or incorporated into pictures of Harlequin and Clown.[27]

One wonders if the *Alices* with their animated cards and chess pieces, their transformations, hints of violence, giant objects, and rallies, inspired their first readers to make the pantomime connection. Or were these things so integrally part of the scene that no one, not even the reviewer who pronounced *Wonderland* "as tickling as a pantomime," gave their appearance a second thought?[28]

Between 1860 and 1870 pantomime was at the peak of its popularity, and its magic colored the dreams of many a Victorian child. Steeped in the ambience of Carroll's time, the *Alice* books abound in multiple levels of meaning. At one level is the Christmas pantomime. Its presence was not lost on Tenniel, who cleverly drew the habitants of Alice's dreams as actors in big-head and other masks, contrivances, and skins.

14

Alice in the Land of Toys

The only point I really care for in the whole matter
(and it is a source of very real pleasure to me) is that the book should
be enjoyed by children—and the more in number, the better.
—CARROLL, in a letter to Alexander Macmillan, 15 February 1869

Games and Toys

Childhood's Summer Day

In 1848 a *Punch* article, "Why Not Write Children's Books for Children?" suggested that history books might best appeal to the childish imagination if instead of kings, battles, and plagues, they treated of the games and pastimes popular in various historic times. In William Newman's charming little vignettes that accompany the text, the child Romulus flies a kite, a medieval boy spurs his rocking horse, and a small bewigged Samuel Johnson plays at the hoop. Although light, the piece shows the growing interest taken by Victorians in the pleasures of childhood. This trend was reflected in pantomime, which, increasingly oriented toward the young, personified toys that paraded in their hundreds in castles, palaces, islands, and worlds of toys and games.[1]

Although the period following the article has been called a "golden age of childhood" and a "golden age of toys," this heyday of delights for children in the affluent classes might have its bleaker side. Well-to-do youngsters were confined to the care of servants and often lived under restrictive rules of conduct.[2] Carroll's heroine might have no parents for all we learn of them in the *Alice* books. She has an old nurse who calls her for her walks and into whose ear she shouts, "Do let's pretend," and a governess who teaches her French, geography, sums, music, and cooking. She is sometimes punished, but "only for her faults," by going without dinner. In her real world, as in her dreamworld, she is surrounded by cooks, workmen, gardeners, footmen. Thus, in her dreams the queens are like governesses, and even the creatures "order one about, and make one repeat lessons."

There is something essentially lonely about Alice—at the drawing-room window watching boys gathering sticks for a bonfire, talking to her cats, and pretending to be two people at once. And indeed, Alice cries from lone-liness on two occasions in *Wonderland* and once in *Looking-Glass*. Still, she is better off than Mabel, who lives in a "poky little house." While she, like Mabel, "is always having lessons to learn," Alice does not have "next to no toys to play with." Quite the contrary; there is hardly a one that is not in-troduced in the two books.

Carroll was fascinated with childhood. A poem he wrote in his twenties ends on a note of longing: "To be once more a little child / For one bright summer day." In his early years he loved to entertain his younger brothers and sisters—making toys, inventing games, editing and largely writing a series of family magazines; it is probable that Alice's railway journey in *Look-ing-Glass* harks back to his railway game of that time with its precise set of rules providing for ticketless passengers and lost luggage. This he continued into adulthood, devising outings and games for his child friends and fill-ing his cupboards at Christ Church with treasure—"mechanical bears, danc-ing dolls, toys and puzzles of every description"—to delight young visitors.[3] It should come as no surprise, then, that the two *Alices*, like Carroll's cup-boards, are a veritable museum of childhood. As with the pantomime in-fluence, Tenniel's drawings join forces with this aspect of the texts, elabo-rating on their hidden meanings.

A Museum of Childhood

The games and toys begin at once when Alice considers making a daisy chain. Soon she will find herself swimming, running a race, having a "game of play" with a puppy, reciting nursery rhymes, playing croquet, interact-ing with a deck of cards and, in the second book, with chess pieces. Other pastimes and toys are simply named. Alice recollects children digging in the sand with wooden spades; something comes at Bill the Lizard "like a Jack in the box," and up he goes "like a sky-rocket!" *Looking-Glass* adds to the list of diversions begun in Wonderland (snapdragon, rowing, chess), and to toys (rocking horse, rattle, teetotum, doll), and, now that Alice is slightly older, things that a child might be taken to see (bonfires, waxworks, fireworks, Punch and Judy, and conjuring tricks).[4]

Adults play like children: Father William stands on his head, turns a back somersault, and balances an eel on his nose; the Hatter bickers like a child; and jurors write on slates. In *Looking-Glass* the White Knight uses the poker as a slide, and the two fat men, "Tweedledum and Tweedledee, dance "Here we go around the mulberry bush" with Alice, fight over a rat-tle like children, and then prepare for a play sword fight.

Various word games surface, not to mention a liberal sprinkling of puns. It begins with Alice's question as she descends the rabbit hole—"'Do cats eat bats?' . . . 'Do bats eat cats?'"—a transposition of letters that by the twenti-eth century would be termed a "spoonerism." This is followed by several

Fig. 83. Tenniel, "Rocking-Horse-Fly," illustration for Lewis Carroll, *Through the Looking-Glass*, 1872

inversions of words: "a cat without a grin . . . a grin without a cat," "say what I mean. . . . mean what I say," and so on. In *Looking-Glass* when Alice wants to transpose the words "lightning" and "thunder" in the statement she has just made, the Red Queen bars her, just as if they were players in a game: "It's too late to correct it . . . when you've once said a thing, that fixes it, and you must take the consequences." The Dormouse plays traveler's alphabet. The sisters in his story draw things that all begin with an M—"mousetraps, and the moon, and memory, and muchness." There will be more of this from the Aged Man, who says "I hunt for haddock's eyes / Among the heather bright." The riddles begin with the Hatter's question about the raven and the writing desk. In *Looking-Glass* Humpty Dumpty takes two of Alice's questions to be riddles. He then declares that it's his turn to choose a subject—"just as if it was a game!" The examination given Alice by the chess queens includes conundrums, or riddles involving puns. Finally, there is the riddle posed at Alice's dinner party by the White Queen, whose "First, the fish must be caught" sounds somewhat like the well-known injunction "First catch your hare" attributed to cookbook writer Hannah Glasse. A remark of the White King starts Alice on a game of "twenty questions" or "animal, vegetable, or mineral," a pursuit first suggested in *Wonderland* when Alice tries to decide whether mustard is mineral or vegetable.[5]

Tenniel's drawings expand the list of playthings, for he has given the man in white paper the sort of hat that children fold, the White Rabbit a toy trumpet, Tweedledum a child's wooden sword, and the old Frog a toy rake. Furthermore, he has cunningly incorporated a die into the body of the Rocking-horse-fly—which might be used in a number of board games in which counters and dice were required (fig. 83). Inside the little shop there are hoops, a kite, a doll, and displayed in its window are a Noah's ark, jumping jack, and barrel-shaped horse on four pegs.

But most fascinating are the toys we might infer, the ones that are merely suggested. When Alice unlocks the little door behind the curtain she finds that it leads into a small passage, "not much larger than a rat-hole," beyond which she sees "the loveliest garden you ever saw." She longs passionately "to get out of that dark hall, and wander about among those beds of bright flowers and those cool fountains." This sounds very much as if Alice is looking through the aperture of a peep-show box. The gardens of baroque palaces with fountains, formal beds, and topiary arches, such as the one Tenniel drew for chapter 8, where Alice attains her wish, were popular in these nursery toys in which brightly lit flats, scaled to give a sense of perspective and set into successive slots, created a striking illusion of space. One easily imagines a child wishing to somehow squeeze through the peephole, perhaps by "shutting up like a telescope," to enter this radiant and perfect world. In Tenniel's illustration the scenic elements—fountains, shrubbery, conservatory—have the flat and layered look of pieces of stage scenery, and the Queen's pointing finger, almost dead center in the picture, would be the first thing one would see through an aperture (fig. 84). Tenniel may have had this part in mind when choosing the theme for *Punch*'s late 1864 title page in which the political figures of the time cluster round showman Punch's peep-show box.[6]

Fig. 84. Tenniel, "Queen of Hearts (Off with her head)," illustration for Lewis Carroll, *Alice's Adventures in Wonderland*, 1866

For a little girl's nursery the dollhouse would be a central feature. Even a boy might be entranced, as was Dickens, who wrote, "Ah! the Doll's house!—of which I was not the proprietor, but where I visited. I don't admire the Houses of Parliament half so much as that stone-fronted mansion with real glass windows, and door-steps, and a real balcony." In England, dollhouses ranged from quite small to three or four feet high and might be so well appointed that one could take up imaginary residence straightway.[7] Would not a child wonder whether she might actually fit inside those walls, perhaps by lying down, like Alice, with "one arm out the window, and one foot up the chimney," and consider, once inside, how she would ever get out.

Or, we might see the *Wonderland* tea party with its rotating company as a doll's tea with all of a child's miniature dishes set out. As the "milk" tipped out of the tiny jug, or places became soggy, crumb-covered, or otherwise "used up," would she not move her dolls around the table?[8]

The Magic Lantern
Growing, Shrinking, and Going Out Just Like a Candle

Concealed, too, within the *Alices* is that unfailing source of wonder, the magic lantern. With its aptness to create sudden transformations, lanterns could produce effects similar to some found in pantomime. Linkages between the two are found in the "movable" books, cards, and toys that used the words "pantomime," "transformation," and "Harlequin" in their titles but worked in ways similar to movable slides. All these things display the Victorian love of visual surprises. The "movables" were part of a centuries-long effort to reproduce living movement—something that had accelerated in the eighteenth century with the movable-picture boxes of Philippe de Loutherbourg and Gainsborough, and that would culminate in the first motion pictures by the 1890s.

While living cards and chessmen, outsize objects, and big-heads point unmistakably to the Christmas pantomime, magic-lantern comparisons (aside from the scene identified in Carroll's pagination guide as "Dissolving view") are a bit more speculative.[9] Often things in the *Alice* books that can be associated with pantomime may be linked with lantern shows without contradiction. Thus, the proposal in the last chapter that the Cheshire Cat is an artificial pantomime animal does not conflict with the observation that the Cat's appearances and disappearances simulate a slide show.

Around midcentury a simple version of the two-hundred-year-old device the magic lantern—long used for "wizardry" and the projecting of comic pictures—was marketed for nursery use. But it would have been best known to children through the exhibitions of the galantee showmen who made their rounds at Christmas time. For the nursery toy a tin box was fitted with a chimney, candleholder, condenser, channel for the passage of glass slides or "sliders" on which images were painted in transparent oil or watercolors, and focusing lens. Larger and more elaborate machines in mahogany and brass, some comprising two or three lanterns in one ("biunial" and "triunial") for special effects, were made for clergymen who used them for instructional purposes and to entertain the children of their parishes.[10]

Inveterate showman, conjurer, and inventor of visual surprises, by 1856 (the year in which he acquired that other picture-making box, his camera) Carroll conceived a "sort of Marionette performance"—a play reading for children, accompanied by figures painted on lantern slides. By November, the opportunity to test this idea came when Carroll's sister Elizabeth wrote from Croft soliciting his suggestions for the Sunday school Christmas treat. The "exhibition of the Magic-Lantern" was a huge success, playing for two nights to some eighty children plus a large gathering of adults. His interest in this form of entertainment continued, and in the sixties Carroll's annual treat for two young friends, the children of writer George MacDonald, would be a visit to the Polytechnic in Regent Street to see fairy tales done with dissolving views, effects produced with superimposed views from two or more lanterns. In later years, his tellings of the *Alice* stories to children would be accompanied by lantern slides of his own devising—a practice that carried over into his writing of *The Nursery Alice,* about which Carrollian Denis Crutch observed, "It is all very like a lantern show; he points to the pictures, one after another, and talks to the child about them."[11]

Tenniel was intrigued by visual phenomena, as the chronophotographic character of his 1875 drawing of a dancer would show (see chap. 6). As a theater buff, he would be familiar with effects achieved with magic lanterns in various stage productions. For example, in the Christmas 1862 performance of Dickens's *Haunted Man* lanterns and mirrors were used to project the forms of the actors hidden below stage so that they seemed to move wraithlike among the actors onstage.[12]

The growing-shrinking phenomena of *Wonderland* might conceivably have been influenced by phantasmagoric effects with lanterns. Phantasmagoria, first demonstrated to Londoners at the start of the century, required

Fig. 85. Tenniel, calendar page, "Punch's Almanack for 1864"

a special lantern mounted on wheels and equipped with an automatic focusing device. When withdrawn from or advanced toward the semi-transparent screen between it and the audience, the reflected images grew and diminished, advanced and retreated, with alarming rapidity. The fact that lantern images increase in size as the machine is moved back from the screen, and diminish when it is moved forward, agrees with some of the inverse effects encountered in the looking-glass world: the "reverse perspective" that one writer noted in the third square, or Alice's discovery that "the egg seems to get further away" the more she walks toward it.[13]

Spectral effects were produced by the "nebulous magic lantern" which beamed figures upon a cloud of smoke ascending from a chafing dish. This method is shown in Tenniel's 1864 almanac drawing in which Mr. Punch, conjurer, points to the images of the coming year projected onto smoke (fig. 85).[14] If the lantern is concealed beneath the dish (as in Tenniel's picture), the image would need to be reflected upwards by an inclined mirror. Consequently the smoke would not cut the cone of reflected light at right angles, and a figure would have to be drawn contracted on the glass slide— as if it had been "shut up like a telescope"—to prevent an elongated figure, resulting on the smoke. Alice's size changes as she grows and shrinks, strikes her chin against her foot, and then opens out "like the largest telescope that ever was," may have been suggested by phantasmagoria and images projected onto smoke, just as the possibility (raised in both *Alice* books) that one might go out "just like a candle," hints at images projected by means of the candles used in nursery lanterns, which probably went out fairly often. In *The Nursery Alice,* the Cat also vanishes "just like a candle when it goes out."

Movable Slides, Dissolves, and Magic Theater

Comic changes were effected with movable slides. The simplest way to suggest movement in a book is given by Carroll in *The Nursery Alice.* Referring to the White Rabbit's fear of incurring the Duchess's anger, Carroll asks his readers. "Don't you see how he's trembling?" He then suggests, "Just shake the book a little from side to side, and you'll soon see him tremble." Similarly, one might manually jiggle a glass slide portraying a seascape to show the motion of the agitated sea and, by superimposing a second slide on which some ships were painted, show them tossing as well.

Slipping or uncovering slides required (in a single frame) a fixed glass plus one or more supplementary pieces or "slippers" that could be gradually or suddenly shifted, thus relying on persistence of vision to create the illusion of movement. Such slides showed moving limbs, eyes, mouths, the sudden appearance of a head on a dish, a lengthening nose, the unfolding of a flower bud, or a vanishing. The Cheshire Cat's abrupt materializations and disappearances might conceivably be done with a slipping slide. Tenniel's Cat, fitting neatly between two branches of the tree, with no visible

Fig. 86. *(Left)* Tenniel, "Cat in Tree," illustration for Lewis Carroll, *Alice's Adventures in Wonderland*, 1866. Fig. 87. *(Right)* Tenniel, "Cat's Grin," illustration for Lewis Carroll, *Alice's Adventures in Wonderland*, 1866

paws (although the text specifies its "*very* long claws"), would function well on a slipper that could be swiftly slipped in place over the fixed slide depicting the tree and as deftly withdrawn, leaving only the grin (fig. 86 and fig. 87). Or it might work like a slide set manufactured in this period that showed in one position an oak "with foliage [like Tenniel's] rendered in the light elegant manner reminiscent of Gainsborough."[15] As the slipper (which would carry landscape elements) was moved to one side, one saw Prince Charles perching among the leaves and Cromwell's men passing below. To make them disappear one returned the slipper to its original position.

By 1856 the effects created by slipping or uncovering slides were duplicated in the movable books put out by Dean and Sons. Although incorrectly called "dissolving views" (which at least reveals their debt to the magic lantern), these were in reality tab books.[16] One pulled on a flap, tape, or length of copper wire to rotate the movable parts.

Carroll used the same principle in his "Wonderland" postage stamp case (1890). The viewer steadily regarded the Cheshire Cat on the case, meanwhile swiftly withdrawing the case to reveal Tenniel's second picture on the stamp book beneath. Thus the Cat would seem to fade away to its grin. On the other side of the case was Alice holding the Duchess's baby, which could similarly be transformed into a pig. So delighted was Carroll with these two "Pictorial Surprises" that he concluded his instructions with: "If *that* doesn't surprise you, why, I suppose you wouldn't be surprised if your own Mother-in-Law suddenly turned into a Gyroscope!"[17]

Dissolving views required at least two lanterns, equidistant from the screen and turned so that the images registered precisely. Similarly, Tenniel's two pictures of the Cat in the tree register on pages ninety-one and ninety-three of the original editions. The dissolve was effected in one of two ways—either by the use of metal shutters with comblike teeth that were connected in a way that, while one shutter was gradually drawn across one of the lantern nozzles, covering it, the other was slowly uncovered; or by "dissolving taps" that turned down the gas for one lamp while increasing the flow to the other. After Alice complained that its sudden appearances and departures "make one quite giddy," the Cat next "vanished quite slowly, beginning with the end of the tail, and ending with the grin." This suggests a dissolve with the shutters moving laterally.

How were Tenniel's two pictures, which registered on successive recto sheets, meant to function in the book? If we rapidly flutter the first sheet, which pictures Alice with the Cat, to alternately cover and uncover the second drawing, the Cat seems to materialize and dematerialize before our eyes. Or the two pictures might function as in *The Nursery Alice*. By turning down the upper corner of the first sheet, the reader would simply see Alice "looking at the Grin."[18]

Perils of Projecting, and Pictures in Sets

In 1860, after attending a series of dissolving views, Carroll wrote to his sister, "The pictures dissolved rather suddenly into each other, and one of the gentlest of the dissolutions rather lost its effect by coming back by mistake in the same picture. Such little incidents, interspersed with periods of total darkness, when everything seemed to have gone out at once, and periods of bright light, where the doors of the lantern were thrown open, and the gas lights in the room turned on to enable the lecturer to see what to do next, left nothing to complain of on the score of variety."[19] While not quite as erratic as the performance Carroll witnessed, some of the moves in *Looking-Glass* seem like the mishaps—the jerky transitions and dissolves—that might occur in a magic lantern show.

For example, the simplest movable slide was the extra-long "panoramic" slide that could be gradually drawn across the slide stage. When superimposed panoramic slides were taken through the channel at different speeds, a landscape might be animated with moving clouds, ships, and figures. Alice's run with the Red Queen suggests two slides that had somehow gotten caught together and were being drawn through at the same speed. This seems to accord with Tenniel's drawing in which the sharply delineated pair appear to float like cutouts before the hazy wood (fig. 88). Alice may well have wondered if "all the things" moved along with them.

Fig. 88. Tenniel, "Running," illustration for Lewis Carroll, *Through the Looking-Glass*, 1872

The rising of Alice's railway carriage—"straight up in the air" as she moves on to square four—suggests the effect called "magic theatre," which required a lantern with multiple grooves so that slides could also be inserted from below or above (thus showing the raising and lowering of the curtain).[20] But when Alice catches at the Goat's beard and it seems to melt away, this is more in the nature of a dissolve. In the fifth square Alice moves from one dissolving view to another—from shop to river and then back to the shop, only to find that in its dark recesses chairs sprout branches, and a little brook flows. Most often things appear and vanish as if by slipping slides. The Red Queen comes to her last peg and is instantly gone, a crown appears on Alice's head, she is unaccountably flanked by the two queens, and then the "two great heads" of her dozing companions abruptly vanish from her lap.

It does not seem accidental that so many of Tenniel's *Alice* pictures occur, not only in sets, but in sets that register in the same positions on their respective pages. This is something that will be missed in editions that fail to preserve the original placements. *Wonderland* has, besides the Cat pictures, the frontispiece and the L-shaped illustration in which the Knave and counsels are repeated (both on verso pages). Presumably there was no need to again show the Queen as she would have the same murderous glare as in the frontispiece.

Looking-Glass has five sets. Alice's mirror passage—in which the sheet for pages 11 and 12 is treated as the looking glass itself—has been noted by more than one writer.[21] The Walrus and seated Carpenter pictures, both on verso sheets, have the same background. If the reader looks fixedly at the first cut, with its eager little Oysters, and then flips quickly to the second sheet, the two cronies may seem to shift and the Oysters turn to piles of shells. The shop-river scenes, again on verso sheets (but a few pages removed), show a dissolve that does not quite come off; Carroll called the second picture in

this set "Dissolving View (fig. 89). The fourth set, Alice between the two queens (on verso sheets), is the most successful in creating the illusion of movement (fig. 90 and fig. 91). If one holds the sheet showing the queens asleep, together with the three intervening sheets, and flips them rapidly over the first picture, Alice appears to raise her eyelids and rotate her scepter from the viewer's left to right. Beside flip books, the effect might have been achieved with slipping slides or tab books.

Finally, there is the question of the "Shaking"-"Waking" pictures (fig. 92 and fig. 93). In Carroll's pagination guide these were originally planned to be another mirror passage (pages 213 and 214). This plan was discarded, probably because consistency with the earlier mirror set would have required showing either the Queen or kitten in

Fig. 89. Tenniel, "Dissolving View," illustration for Lewis Carroll, *Through the Looking-Glass,* 1872

back view, along with a different view of Alice's hands, as Alice herself did not become a mirror image when she went through the glass. The viewpoint selected, which is Alice's own, makes for a better picture. The final placement on pages 214 and 217 might perhaps be compared with a dissolve, with the intermediate sheet (pages 215–16) simulating the metal shade or shutter that passes before first one and then the other nozzle of a dissolving view lantern. But, more likely, the arrangement was adopted simply because it worked best with the text.

Summation

The toys and pastimes of the *Alice* books were those familiar to children of the more or less affluent Victorian classes. Although Carroll repeatedly urged Macmillan to produce cheaper editions, it was the book's availability to children of the middle classes that he wished to expand. As late as 1887 he said, regarding a cheap *Alice,* "My own idea is, that it isn't a book *poor* children would much care for. But we'll see."[22] Writing for the child whose lessons, servants, toys, amusements, and pet animals commingle with every part of the story, Carroll might understandably question its fitness for those who had never owned a dollhouse, seen a lantern show, been taken to a pantomime. Fortunately, his fears were unwarranted.

The *Alice*s were designed to bring happiness to children. Consequently, Carroll stocked his stories, like his cupboards at Christ Church, with games, toys, and other diversions to delight his young visitors. This was congenial to Tenniel, who supplemented the toys and drew pictures that suggest or function as peepshows, mirrors, and magic lantern slides.[23]

Fig. 90. *(Left)* Tenniel, "Catechism," illustration for Lewis Carroll, *Through the Looking-Glass,* 1872. Fig. 91. *(Right)* Tenniel, "Queens Asleep," illustration for Lewis Carroll, *Through the Looking-Glass,* 1872

Fig. 92. *(Left)* Tenniel, "Shaking Queen," illustration for Lewis Carroll, *Through the Looking-Glass,* 1872. Fig. 93. *(Right)* Tenniel, "It Was a Kitten," illustration for Lewis Carroll, *Through the Looking-Glass,* 1872

15

The Grotesque Alice

*My drawings are sometimes grotesque, but that is from
a sense of fun and humour.*
—TENNIEL, in an interview with M. H. Spielmann, 1889

The Question of the Grotesque

Today's newcomer to the *Alice* books, particularly those with the Tenniel engravings, enters an atmosphere of prodigious strangeness—an environment filled with the things and entertainments, the modes and preferences, of another age. For some readers there is an ambience, a miasma almost, that both repels and attracts. This is because they are in the presence of the grotesque.

The word "grotesque" is employed here to mean, not merely the fantastic (a synonym suggested in most dictionaries), but the definition given by its mid-twentieth-century theorists: an "unresolved clash of incompatibles," or any abnormality that imparts the disturbing sense that the real world may have ceased to be reliable.[1] We can identify many of the grotesque's components in the *Alice* texts and pictures: objects brought to life and human beings deprived of lifelike attributes, the merging of beings and things, deformities of and violence to the human body (which the subject often experiences with cool indifference), a proclivity to deal with the ordinary things of this world while exhibiting such phenomena—all of these occurring within a structured framework that appears to have its own inner logic.

The striking similarity of these ingredients to those proposed by students of nonsense writing (and, to a lesser extent, comedy) leads one to wonder where the nonsensical, comical, and the grotesque diverge, for they are not necessarily one. Here, theorists seem to agree that there is a "safeguarding distance" that the writer of nonsense or comedy must somehow maintain. If he can do this, and not exceed the "human measure," then the reader will experience security, freedom from stress, pleasure. But this is where the argument breaks down, for, of course, readers react differently. One theorist does not at all doubt the grotesque character of Edward Lear's and Carroll's nonsense, whereas another finds in the *Alices* only security and mental delight.[2]

How did children themselves perceive the books? An early reviewer of *Looking-Glass* reported, "We have had it read aloud to a number of little folk and have heard a dismal outcry raised as the nurse, like a returning wave on a rising tide, kept sweeping them ruthlessly off one by one." By 1898 the *Pall Mall Gazette*'s direct polling of children found *Looking-Glass* in eleventh place with *Wonderland* still ranking first among favorites. And a recent study of *Alice*-inspired literature takes the continued reissuance of Carroll's stories (including picture book versions) as proof that "they have lost none of their appeal."[3]

But have we, at least since the end of the nineteenth century, really loved *Alice* as much as is supposed? In 1939 Virginia Woolf wrote, "Down, down we fall into that terrifying, wildly inconsequent, yet perfectly logical world. . . . the two Alices are not books for children; they are the only books in which we become children." The journalist and former *Punch* editor Malcolm Muggeridge declared in 1966, "*Alice* has never, in my experience, been a favourite with children. I myself as a child disliked it intensely, and my own children, as I recall, did not much care for its being read aloud. From a child's point of view the story is full of an indefinable and incomprehensible horror. . . . *Alice* is a very sick book indeed." Writer Flannery O'Connor owned, "Peculiar but I could never stand *Alice in Wonderland*. It was a terrifying book." And more recently, a writer on children's books confessed that as a child her terror of *Wonderland* was so great that she defaced her volume in retaliation. Indeed, two of the most touted reillustrations of *Alice* are not directed toward children at all. One is a sophisticated exposé of contemporary society, the other an exercise in the horrific (a mode that is distinct from the grotesque).[4]

Certainly Carroll had no intention of giving his young readers nightmares, although an occasional frisson would not have been unacceptable. "Grotesque" was a word he used often; he searched for an artist with "any turn for the grotesque," and he was delighted that an actor's "grotesque monster" had exactly caught what he "meant for the Hatter to be."[5] But this was the playful grotesque, the droll, for which the nineteenth century seems to have had a peculiar affinity. Might the slipping of Carroll's fairy tales into a more ominous form of the grotesque be an unintended consequence of nonsense itself, intensified by the fact that we today are unattuned to the Victorian world?

New illustrators have grafted modern perceptions and modern eccentricities onto these peculiarly nineteenth-century stories. They have tried to adapt the books to current sensibilities. But we are still infatuated with the *Alice*'s first pictures—with their insidious grotesqueries and extratextual elements.[6] We acknowledge these subliminally, and it is perhaps in their very mystery that the fascination lies. Looking first at the Victorian fondness for drolleries, let us see how the full-blown grotesque evolved and operated in Carroll's and in Tenniel's work.

A Taste for the Grotesque

The Territory

A great breeding ground for the grotesque was the Christmas pantomime. Victorian harlequinades still bore traces of their Regency antecedents in which "man's plight" was "created by the transformations, misbehavior, and relentless hostility of objects and mechanical devices."[7] Steel traps, mailboxes, and other mechanisms contrived to entrap Clown; clock figures came alive, and, conversely, Clown was transformed into the pendulum of a clock. In the pantomimes of the period, everything that could be transformed was.

Children's literature, too, abounded in grotesqueries. From the century's first decade there were the world-upside-down books with animals busily roasting unconcerned cooks, mice feeding on cats, and fish hooking fishermen. As the century progressed, Punch murdered the baby, lost children starved in the wood ("their wasted form the sod receives"), and the severed heads of Bluebeard's wives lay disclosed on the floor. There was little attempt to shield the timid; Carroll's Alice, we recall, "had read several nice little stories about children who had got burned, and eaten up by wild beasts." In Lear's *Book of Nonsense* (1846) individuals calmly contemplate their predicaments as they cut off their own thumbs, lie in basins of broth, and are stoned, roasted, mixed into cakes, or stung by very large bees. Sportingly they tell us, "What of that?" "I don't care," "What matter?" and "Fiddle-de-dee!" Thackeray's *Rose and the Ring*, taking its cues from pantomime, turns a porter into a brass door knocker, and knocks a king flat, bending his nose sideways.[8]

For older readers, George Cruikshank's vignettes cross over into a disturbing world where "spirits of wine" engage with ghostly night watchmen (visible only by their empty cassocks), and where faces grin at us from oysters, fungi, citrus ends, and bottle corks. In Thomas Hood's comic ballads, grisly content (murder, body snatching, people dining on fish that have fed on people) is wedded to light and punning narrative.[9]

Among the period's most winning grotesques were W. S. Gilbert's illustrated verses appearing regularly over the signature "Bab" in the comic journal *Fun*. At one point Carroll had considered inviting Gilbert to do the *Looking-Glass* drawings but quickly dropped the idea upon discovering that he could draw "*only* grotesques." In typical Bab rhymes, a shipwrecked tar has eaten nine of his shipmates, an elderly man fathers a rapidly aging infant, and a sugar broker's attempt to dance off his excess weight turns him into a perfect sphere. For these, and close to 140 other poems, Gilbert drew goblinlike creatures with heads sunk into immense collars and with tubular or bulbous bodies and bizarre topknots. But their greatest affinity with the grotesque is through their lack of human sympathies and the gravity with which they pursue their pseudo-logical premises to absurd conclusions.[10]

Games, too, reflected the grotesque taste. Prior to the Great Exhibition of 1851 a children's game, "Happy Families," with "forty-four cards of grotesque characters," was produced by John Jacques and Son, Ltd. (later, its delightfully crude cuts were unaccountably attributed to Tenniel). In "Happy Families" the limbs and body of Master Chip the Carpenter's Son are a pair of pincers, the head of Master Bun the Baker's Son is made up of two loaves, the brewer and his son have beer cask bodies, while the body of Mrs. Bung the Brewer's Wife is a bottle of Dublin Stout, its stopper serving as her nose.

A Christmas game that may have inspired the grotesque dinner scene in *Looking-Glass* appeared in a December 1857 issue of the *Illustrated London News*. The inventor and illustrator of "The Field of the Cloth of Damask" was Charles H. Bennett, around that time also illustrating Carroll's verses for the *Train*. The game takes the form of a battle, with armies of foodstuffs (there is a Plum Pudding and a Major O'Mutton) and tableware—perhaps recalling the living foods and utensils of recent pantomimes. In Bennett's

Fig. 94. Charles H. Bennett, "Field of Cloth of Damask," *Illustrated London News*, 19 Dec. 1857, 626

illustration fish and roasts engage with bottles and corkscrews (fig. 94). A pair of tongs astride a coal scuttle lances a pig, and an animated knife and fork join in cutting a large slice from a Christmas pudding. The name of a field marshal, "Sir Loin," may well have caught the attention of Carroll, who was connected through his great-grandmother Lutwidge to the Sir Richard Hoghton at whose table James the First was said to have knighted a loin of beef.[11]

Grotesques in Punch

Had Carroll had no other exposure to the grotesque, he would have found sufficient inspiration through his study of *Punch*. Much of *Punch*'s humor was based on puns (the paper itself had very nearly been named "Funny Dogs with Comic Tales"), and illustrated puns may easily cross over into the grotesque. Thus, an announcement that the admiralty would in the future ban scales (metal epaulettes) was accompanied by the picture of a naval officer, his body covered with fishlike scales; a fish standing before a dressing table (in a drawing that reminds us of Tenniel's *Wonderland* lobster) illustrates a "fish out of water"; and a picture of a "Little Dinner at Greenwich" with its anthropomorphized creatures displays in the background the names "John Dorey" (a type of food fish) and "Ann Chovey."[12]

Although humanized animals are not necessarily grotesque, certain human and beast composites, as in some of "Punch's Fancy Portraits" and initial letters, verged on this element. A fishmonger might be portrayed as a fish-headed man, and bird and fox hunters as amalgams of the sportsmen and their prey. Portraits might pun on names; in one example, Sir Drummond Wolff, MP, was depicted as a drum-playing wolfman.[13]

Fashions were mocked. Drawings exaggerated the cut and ornamentation of ladies' gowns, turning them into crustaceans and insects. Two women are shown conversing at a ship's rail; one's hat resembles a hedgehog, the other's a lobster. A guardsman's busby is, on second glance, a sweep's brush.[14]

Satires on advertising provided accidental grotesques by depicting people who were hired to parade London's streets disguised as various goods. Thus, pictures of animated loaves of bread, warming pans, patent medicines, hats, hair dyes, and other commercial products infused a certain drollery into *Punch*'s pages.[15]

Drawings of living objects were often whimsies. One, Frank Bellew's 1861 picture of a Christmas pudding confronting a diner (which has been named as a possible source for Carroll), was preempted by the plum pudding that made its bow to Mr. Punch in Tenniel's almanac page for 1860. Truly grotesque is Bellew's 1861 drawing of Mr. Punch at his toilet, sans cap so that we see the top of his head as a sawed-off log encrusted with nails. Captain H. R. Howard, his monogram a trident, was another contributor with a leaning toward the grotesque. While most of his drawings were animal cuts (Carroll in his diary refers to him as "the bird and beast man"), others cropped up. A man's sharp nose pierces his shaving mirror; another uses his lancelike nose to unseat an opponent in the lists; a humanized chair regards a wastepaper basket with its dumped writer; and a door knocker thumbs its nose at two ragged street boys. After Trident's departure, Bennett enlivened *Punch* with innumerable clever drawings teeming with animated things and humanoid machines, some resembling the early-twentieth-century inventions of Rube Goldberg.[16]

While political cuts were not often grotesque, mainly because we see their odd juxtapositions as metaphorical, Tenniel's cartoon "The Turf Spider and the Flies" (1868), which attacked corrupt bookmaking practices, tends that way (fig. 95).[17] The spider that menaces its human flies is (like the looking-glass insects) entirely made of objects with the exception of its six insect legs. This construction, comprising saddle,

Fig. 95. Tenniel, "The Turf Spider and the Flies," cartoon, *Punch*, 4 July 1868

jockey cap, horseshoes, reins, bit, and saddle bag, manages to suggest—all at once—a spider, a horse, and a skeletal jockey.

How Queer Everything Is Today!

Carroll's early aptitude for the grotesque surfaced in "The Tale of a Tail," which he composed at twelve. The poem tells of a drunken gardener who, having chopped off a dog's monstrous tail with which he has become entangled, proceeds to laugh himself "black and blue." In other early verses, a farmer makes holes in his own face with a needle, a boy asks the cook for a pan in which to stew his sister, and another runs a fishhook through his brother and dangles him off a pier as bait. The narrator in Carroll's poem "Upon the Lonely Moor" (later adapted for the White Knight's song) kicks the old man calm, punches him on the arm, boxes his ear, tweaks his hair, and "puts him into pain."[18]

Knowing the delight that children often take in outrageous and even daunting statements, well into his later years Carroll sent letters to child friends with such fearful schemes and threats as advice on how to inflict pain on others with tiny penknives and pins; proposals to make a little girl's railway trip "really exciting" by firing a pistol through her carriage window, giving her a rattlesnake disguised as a Banbury cake, and arranging for her to arrive in London without her ticket; and suggestions to enliven another's trip to the zoo by feeding her to the big cats, beating her with a thick stick, and confining her in a coal hole.[19]

Thus, we are not surprised to find the *Alices* filled with threats and acts of cruelty. The Dormouse has hot tea poured on his nose, is punched awake, and is forced into a teapot; the guinea pigs are tied into a bag and sat upon; and the Lizard has an inkstand thrown at him. Alice herself snatches at the Rabbit, kicks the Lizard, threatens to silence the daisies by picking them, shakes the Red Queen into a kitten, and so on. We also find monsters—some innocuous, some not; transformations—baby to pig, queen to sheep; equanimity in the face of horrors; and a crossing, and recrossing, of the borderline between sensate beings and things. Cards become soldiers who become croquet arches, while flamingoes and hedgehogs serve as mallets and balls. A clock grins at Alice from a mantel, chess pieces live, trees rub their branches to make music, slices of plum cake perversely join together after being cut, toys and foods form insects, and forks and dishes assemble to fly about like birds. Everything lives. The Hatter assures Alice, "If you knew Time as well as I do, you wouldn't talk about wasting *it*. It's *him*"; the White Queen complains of her shawl, "It's out of temper. . . . there's no pleasing it!"; and the gardener frog inquires, "To answer the door? What's it been asking of?"

Our sense of strangeness is compounded by the cessation of physical laws. Rather than falling at a normal speed, Alice descends the rabbit hole slowly. She glides airborne down the stairway of Looking-Glass House and must catch at the doorpost to avoid simply floating away. She must take an opposite direction to arrive at her chosen destination, things move along with her when she runs, and perspective seems reversed.

But most fearful is the unreliability of the self. First there are the physical uncertainties—size changes and the opposing dangers of spreading uncontrollably inside a limited space or going out entirely, just "like a candle." Next, Alice's mind plays alarming tricks. Lessons and poems come out all wrong, often with cruel content that is lacking in the originals: hungry crocodiles and sharks, kickings downstairs, and the implication that a panther will eat his fellow diner. In the *Looking-Glass* journey she will lose her grasp of names.

Starting with her plunge into the rabbit hole (her return from which is in no way assured), Alice is threatened with constant menace. She might drown in her own tears, be trampled by a puppy, have her head removed. She is showered with pebbles, rushed at by the White Rabbit's workmen, beaten violently in the face by a pigeon's wings, and attacked by a card pack. The looking-glass world is no less menacing—more by its instability than in any direct physical sense. Here, Alice's feast, with its erosion of boundaries between creatures and things, eaters and eaten, is the ultimate nightmare.

Bizarre as all these events are, they are neither unconnected nor arbitrary; this is not simply fantasy. Carroll's method of imparting cohesiveness, and thus reality, to his worlds is through the offhand remarks of his characters. The Cheshire Cat's assurance, "you'll see me there," refers to the garden that Alice had longingly glimpsed five chapters earlier and will attain two chapters later. The Red Queen tells Alice that she can be the White Queen's pawn since Lily (who, we recall, had rolled over and begun screaming in chapter 1) was "too young to play." The White Queen speaks of the punishment of the King's messenger, who will appear, newly released, two chapters later (and whom we recognize as *Wonderland*'s Hatter, thanks to Tenniel's drawing). Later, the Queen relates that Humpty Dumpty came to the door "with a corkscrew in his hand," referring to verses sung by him three chapters earlier. And the flowers that show up as dinner guests in the eighth square are very possibly the ones Alice met in square two.

For the grotesque to operate, "It is our world which has to be transformed" and not some fantasy realm.[20] We are constantly reminded of the real world by Carroll's references to such specifics as cucumber frames and roofing slates, bolsters and coal scuttles, blotting paper and sealing wax, telescopes and steam engines, and Thomas Telford's great suspension bridge across the Menai Straits. It is, of course, the nineteenth-century world, with its footmen in livery, quadrilles, hansom cabs, macassar oil, and night caps. In this explicitness he is matched by Tenniel.

The Estranged World in Tenniel's Pictures

Realism versus Naturalism

It is often said that Tenniel's matter-of-fact manner is the perfect accompaniment to Carroll's writing. Let us take this idea further and state that Tenniel's realism is crucial in preserving the flavor of the texts and in conveying the sensation that the ground beneath our feet has imperceptibly shifted. This Tenniel accomplished, not by mere naturalism or photographic surfaces—although his carefully hatched drawings do have a greater appearance of truth than many reillustrations. Still, several artists working with paints or silkscreen have achieved results beyond the reach of wood engraving—effects that seem caught by the camera lens. Somehow, their finished surfaces serve to block rather than enhance our sense of actuality.[21] Perhaps we become too conscious of the means.

Realism, however, is something else; it is the validity of setting, type, gesture. It is a subtle thing, Tenniel's realism. His settings might be taken from the vicinity of Oxford itself—gleanings from his pulls along the river: a field of hayricks, eel bucks along the stream, the portico of a Georgian house, a medieval town, a wattle fence. But see how closely he follows the texts, catching the sense of open and sunny country in *Wonderland* and the darker mood of *Looking-Glass,* half of which takes place in a wood (a wood that is, moreover, "full of enemies").[22] Details are not merely real; they are ultra real. Note the nicety of the Victorian fireplace, the dim shop with its notice of two-shilling tea, the clear detailing of Alice's dress—a pattern maker might use it as a model.

Intensifying our immediate sense of reality is the snapshot insouciance with which things that should be present are indeed there. So casually are they inserted that we see them only peripherally: the glimpse of the White Rabbit's checked jacket and legs behind the Knave in the garden scene, the Lobster's bootjack, the White Queen's discarded hairbrush, the broken rattle (fig. 84, fig. 125, and fig. 97). The *London Review*'s comment seems appropriate here: "All these things are illustrated by Mr. Tenniel as if he had gone down the rabbit hole with Alice."[23] Props also, are used with the straightforward practicability of a child at play. To raise Humpty Dumpty to a level with the messenger's ear, Tenniel placed him on a stool; and for Alice to sit prim and ladylike between her two royal interrogators (and on a comfortable level with them) he simply brought in a rustic bench.

But most convincing are the habitants of these strange worlds, performing their roles unselfconsciously—neither playing up to the audience nor pretending to be a party of amiable eccentrics romping through her travels with Alice—they are simply themselves. Carroll had prescribed the stage portrayal of his three queens: "Each, of course, had to preserve, through all her eccentricities, a certain queenly *dignity*. That was essential."[24] Who has observed this more truly than Tenniel? See, too, the stateliness with which the Mock Turtle and Gryphon dance around Alice, and the solemnity of the Knight, even as he is about to tumble over his horse's head.

Monstrosities, and Objects Brought to Life

What of the actual grotesques? Theorist Wolfgang Kayser listed first among these "all monsters." There is no lack of "fabulous monsters" in the *Alice*s. Some, like the Mock Turtle, are more comic than alarming. Several come from the *Looking-Glass* poem "Jabberwocky." But are the toves, borogoves, and mome raths really grotesque? One finds something almost elegiac in Tenniel's illustration of them. This is the balmy word of fantasy rather than our own world turned against us. The same is true of the Jabberwock himself, fearful though he may be with his reptilian head, spectrally glowing eyes, and "claws that catch."[25] This is the world of the epic and not our own. It is in the *Alice* narrative and not in its poetry that the grotesque resides.

More in the category of the monstrous are some disturbing deformities—the impossibly spindly legs of Father William's son (although a cartoon convention for the farm laborer Hodge), and Tweedledum's face—hideously

Fig. 96. Tenniel, first verse of "Father William," illustration for Lewis Carroll, *Alice's Adventures in Wonderland,* 1866

Fig. 97. Tenniel, "Discovery of Rattle," illustration for Lewis Carroll, *Through the Looking-Glass,* 1872

Fig. 98. Tenniel, "Effect of Drink Me," illustration for Lewis Carroll, *Alice's Adventures in Wonderland,* 1866

puffed and distended with rage upon his discovery of his broken rattle (fig. 96 and fig. 97). In the text Alice too suffers distortions of "natural size and shape." Unlike Carroll, in *Alice's Adventures Under Ground,* and some of the book's later illustrators, Tenniel rejected two unpleasant possibilities—Alice with her chin pressed against her foot, or with an immense length of neck "rising like a stalk" above the trees. Still, his "Effect of Drink Me" cut is a true grotesque (fig. 98). Unlike some interpretations in which Alice is evenly lengthened, here her neck is monstrously long. And still more disquieting, to accommodate this growth Tenniel has caused the bit of dress above her pinafore to likewise stretch in a most elastic manner. Clothing will also exhibit organic life in Tenniel's Caterpillar and Jabberwock.[26]

Fig. 99. Tenniel, "Chessmen in Hearth," illustration for Lewis Carroll, *Through the Looking-Glass,* 1872

This introduces one of the eerier motifs of the grotesque—insensate things that seem to exhibit "a dangerous life of their own."[27] *Looking-Glass* is remarkable for this. Alice observes, following her mirror passage, that the pictures on the wall seem alive and that the clock on the chimney-piece "had got the face of a little old man, and grinned at her." Besides the squat-bodied clock with a clown's nose and cap, Tenniel has slyly added a face to the nearby vase; is it sticking its tongue out?

Next, we see among the cinders the chessmen "walking about, two and two" (fig. 99). Are these mechanical objects brought to life or that other motif of the grotesque—human beings deprived of it? The chessmen are equivocal. Whereas the Red King and Queen, the Pawn, and the Bishop (whose head is nothing but a miter) are fixed to pedestals, two Castles walk about on little feet. We note that a deserted pedestal lies on the ground behind the King. Then, in the next drawing, two lively feet dangle beneath the skirt of the panicked little White King in Alice's hand. Will this humanization be progressively increased? It seems not, for after the larkspur hears her approaching footsteps—"thump, thump, along the gravel-walk!" Tenniel's Red Queen, with no feet at all, her skirts resting directly on a substantial wooden base, stands lecturing Alice (fig. 100). But shortly after we see them running, the pedestal gone and the Queen's sandaled feet splaying out from the rigid wooden rings of her skirt (fig. 88). Such incompatibles—the very stuff of the grotesque—had to a lesser extent occurred in *Wonderland.* There the card people equivocate between pasteboard flatness and three-dimensionality (compare

Fig. 100. Tenniel, "Meeting Red Queen," illustration for Lewis Carroll, *Through the Looking-Glass,* 1872

the mask-faced King of Hearts in the frontispiece with his living presence in the illustration in which he gestures toward the tarts). By the "Wool and Water" chapter of *Looking-Glass* Tenniel dispensed entirely with pedestals in favor of human feet, which continue to contrast oddly with the rigid rings of the wooden skirts.

Living and nonliving parts merge as well to form the looking-glass insects. Here, Tenniel affixes real insect legs to the objects specified in Carroll's text. Onto the Rocking-horse-fly he has added a pair of living wings. In the final third of the book, drumsticks wielded by unattached human hands will drum the Lion and the Unicorn out of town; the facelike imposts of a Norman doorway stare in astonishment at the confrontation of Alice and the old Frog (fig. 101), and finally (as per text) bottles assume plate wings and fork legs to flutter about like birds.[28]

Fig. 101. Tenniel, "Frog Gardener," illustration for Lewis Carroll, *Through the Looking-Glass*, 1872

The Human Being Deprived of Life

Equally ominous is the aspect of persons (or humanized animals) reduced to "puppets, marionettes, and automata . . . their faces frozen into masks."[29] In Tenniel's *Wonderland* pictures, masks first appear in Carroll's new chapter "Pig and Pepper" and in several of those following. As indicated in chapter 13 above, the Footmen, Duchess, and cook wear head masks, while the Cheshire Cat is a contrivance (probably worked by a child hidden within its shell). Notice how, in the first picture of the Cat in the tree, Tenniel has given the animal spectrally whitened eyes, as if to emphasize its irreality (fig. 86). When the creature vanishes, Alice goes on to the tea party where, seated on either side of the live Dormouse, are the stiffly staring March Hare and Mad Hatter—head masks perched on the shoulders of boys of about Alice's size (fig. 75). For the next picture, Tenniel has unfrozen the face of the Hatter so that he may be shown singing "Twinkle, twinkle," but he has left the Hare (who appears again in the next picture) unchanged.

Other denizens of *Wonderland* are rigid too. Does the Dodo's petrified stare derive from the stuffed remains in the Oxford University Museum? The Queen of Hearts, whom Carroll identified as a grotesque in a letter to the painter Luke Fildes, is likewise inflexible.[30] But this is because she is possessed by an idée fixe, so that her constant glare is merely comic.

In *Looking-Glass* it is the body masks worn by Humpty Dumpty and the leg of mutton that are grotesque (fig. 80 and fig. 81). This results from the incompatibility of their rigid papier-mâché shells with the characters' mobility of expression. One thinks of Kayser's description: "The mask, instead of covering a living and breathing face, has taken over the role of the face itself."[31] On the one hand, these obvious costumes—the lively arms and legs emerging from stiff body masks and the Lion's "skin" bagging around his ankles—connect us with the real world, and on the other the living masks tell us that this is a world gone berserk.

Here, too, is a form of lifelessness known as "the cold grotesque," in which individuals show an incomprehensible indifference in the face of appalling circumstances. For example, Alice calmly wonders about latitude, longitude, the antipodes, and whether her cat will be fed, while she is falling down a very deep hole.[32] Similar contradictions occur in Tenniel's cuts where such potentially frightening experiences as swimming alongside a mouse of one's own dimensions, expanding to fill a finite space, or meeting with any number of alarming beings, rarely disturbs Alice's equanimity. Similarly, the King's men tumble to the ground as calmly as if they were riding or marching upright (fig. 102) as does the Knight, and finally (as per text) the White Queen's "broad, good-natured face" sinks smiling into the soup.

Fig. 102. Tenniel, "King's Horses and Men," illustration for Lewis Carroll, *Through the Looking-Glass*, 1872

The Waning

By the time *Wonderland* was published, nineteenth-century grotesquerie had abated considerably. Pantomime was far tamer than its 1830s prototypes; the once twelve-scene harlequinade had dwindled to three or four scenes and would soon fade out entirely. In book illustration, the "sixties" men turned to live models and to nature for their inspiration, and the pensive mood usurped the playful grotesque in their new productions. In this period, Dickens turned from the drollery of Phiz's cuts to the naturalism of Marcus Stone and Fildes; and on *Punch,* after the death of Bennett in 1867, the tone was more or less set by du Maurier and Keene. By 1895 Joseph Pennell would assess the works of Phiz, Cruikshank, Doyle, and "even Leech" as "simply rubbish." And while a gentle grotesquerie survived in the light operas of Gilbert and Sullivan, when Gilbert republished his Bab ballads in 1898 he replaced some of his original illustrations, which he decided had "erred in the direction of unnecessary extravagance," with drawings that were less piquant.[33]

In this changing climate how did reviewers react to the grotesque aspects of the *Alice*s, or were they even cognizant of them? Although three writers used the word "grotesque," it is not at all certain that their meaning agrees with ours. Closer to the mark was the *Times* critic who found that "now and then perhaps, something disturbing almost wakes us from our dream." Closer yet was the writer H. A. Page, who in an 1869 article in the *Contemporary Review* stated that Carroll's "spécialité is that he carries a breath of the real world with him wherever he goes, so that a whiff of it ever and anon passes over what is most strange . . . the real and the grotesque, suddenly paired, rub cheeks together."[34]

Then as now, the grotesque was not for everyone. The *Athenaeum*'s critic, who found Tenniel's *Wonderland* pictures "square, grim, and uncouth," imagined that "any child might be more puzzled than enchanted by this stiff, overwrought story." Perhaps a different writer reviewed *Looking-Glass,* for he asserted, regarding Tenniel's Jabberwock, "Many a little head will puzzle itself—children like to be puzzled. . . . much young blood will run cold with fright—children dearly love to be frightened."[35] Yet, by the eighties, grotesquerie in children's literature had more or less vanished, the new mood being characterized by the illustrations of Walter Crane, Randolph Caldecott, and Kate Greenaway.

Fresh Costumiers

In references to the *Alice* books, one finds the designation "grotesque" most often used to denote the unreal—for example, to describe Tenniel's fanciful animal caricatures or his horrific Jabberwock. Or it is equated with fantasy and dreams, both of which theorists of the grotesque (and of nonsense) consider inimical to their subjects. Kayser maintained that while the world of fairy tale may be alien, it is not alienated—"It is our world which has to be transformed." Similarly, Philip Thomson's monograph on the grotesque insists, "If a literary text 'takes place' in a fantasy-world created by the author, with no pretensions to a connection with reality, the grotesque is almost out of the question." And Elizabeth Sewell, in her book on Carroll's and Lear's nonsense, writes that nonsense is "far from being ambiguous, shifting and dreamlike." It is, in fact, "hostile to the dream.[36]

In the fantasy stories that followed the first *Alice* book, the grotesque is seldom evoked despite their heavy reliance on anthropomorphism, transformations, and the cessation of physical laws. Although a recent study judges the *Alices* to have in common with fantasy literature "an episodic structure often centering on encounters with nonhuman fantasy characters," can Carroll's books be considered truly episodic? Alice's quest to attain the "lovely garden" glimpsed through a little door early in her adventures runs through the first seven chapters of *Wonderland,* and the events in *Looking-Glass* relate to Alice's progress from pawn to queen in a game of chess, with conversations in the text providing the occasional cross-reference from part to part (see above). As in a novel by Dickens, there is a "network of interconnections."[37]

Nor are Carroll's creations fantasy characters. Let us compare them with a character called Gloogumpehst in Tom Hood's *From Nowhere to the North Pole* (1875), a being made up of, or resembling, a collection of such things as a gum bottle, tin helmet, gallipot, and sealing wax, and exhibiting little in the way of personality.[38] In contrast, the one thing possessed by each of Alice's new acquaintances—whether cards, flowers, animals, persons, or masks—is a very human temperament. Even among the minor characters: the Lory settles an argument with Alice by claiming to be older than she is, the Dodo is put down by the Eaglet for his pretentiousness, and the fresh young crab tells its mother, "Hold your tongue." Alice herself will observe in chapter 6 "the way all the creatures argue. It's enough to drive one crazy!" Fractious, fidgety, selfish, sentimental, lazy, weak—we know them from our own experiences in the real world. They are as familiar to us as Tenniel's types.

Frequent in the fantasy stories of the late nineteenth century are the benevolent mentors who guide the child protagonist through their domains.[39] By contrast, the individuals whom Alice meets in her journeys are more often her antagonists. When they do offer their counsel it is worthless. The Duchess's words are "a cheap sort of present," the Red Queen's are "nonsense," the White Queen, whose pawn Alice is, is ineffectual, and the White Knight, likeable though he may be, is more dependent on Alice than she on him as they make their unsteady way through the seventh square.

We miss the grotesque in the reillustrations, as most lack Tenniel's realism. Some use the books' eccentric elements as a springboard for extravagant styles and details—things that tend to obtrude between us and the texts. For Tenniel's well-observed characterizations, many substitute a new element—twentieth-century "cuteness." As early as 1901, in Peter Newell's first American reillustration, the mouse tells his tale with joined paws and pathetically turned up eyes, Alice walks behind the piglet admiringly—hands clasped, a "soft-sculpturized" Gryphon runs with Alice along the beach, and a round-eyed guinea pig tilts its head fetchingly before being "suppressed." This is the world of the cuddly toy and the strip cartoon.[40]

The Tenniel-illustrated *Alices*, with their casual realism, unselfconscious performers, odd nineteenth-century conventions, and melding of the animate and inanimate, belong firmly in the grotesque. This is how we should first know these books. Assuredly, some will be put off by their strangeness. But others will have the capacity to incorporate, to be seduced by, and to ultimately be enriched by the fascinating grotesque.

16

Alice and the Gothic Taste

He is ever a knightly adversary. He understands the spirit
of chivalry whose external panoply and pageantry
he presents so ably and vividly in his art.
—E. J. MILLIKEN, prefatory note to Tenniel exhibition,
Fine Art Society, 1895

The Medievalists

In the summer of 1866, his imagination fired by his family's newfound interest in chess, Carroll conceived the idea of a sequel to *Alice.* As the plot would emulate a game of chess, Alice could expect to meet with the chess knights in her progress, a circumstance that coincided with the century-old Gothic revival.

In the previous decade interest in things chivalric, already much intensified since the 1819 publication of Scott's *Ivanhoe,* had gained new impetus through the appearance of Tennyson's *Idylls of the King* (1859). This produced a marked increase in knightly and Arthurian themes in both literature and painting. Tenniel, adept at chivalric subjects, was a fit choice to illustrate Carroll's new book. He at first declined, and Carroll approached two other medievalists, Richard Doyle (on Tenniel's advice) and Noël Paton, before gaining Tenniel's consent.[1] With its acknowledged (and unacknowledged) knights, its veiled allusions to the lore and practices of chivalry, its echoes of medieval knight errantry (and of nineteenth-century attempts at its resuscitation), *Through the Looking-Glass* was in many respects a product of the Gothic revival.

Carroll was acquainted with several of the revival's prominent figures: Tennyson, and the painters Arthur Hughes, Dante Gabriel Rossetti, John Everett Millais, James Archer, and George Frederic Watts. Although opposed to the High Church aspect of revivalism, he was thoroughly caught up with the romance of the movement. His library held many of its key, as well as lesser, works: a large collection of Scott and Tennyson, Spenser's *Faerie Queen,* Percy's *Reliques of Ancient English Poetry* and *Manuscripts, Ballads, and Romances,* William Morris's *Defence of Guenevere,* and various books on English and Scottish minstrelsy. He also had the works of Chaucer, both in the original and modernized versions. His passion for the period first surfaced in the mock medieval poetry of Carroll's early years: "Ye Fattale Cheyse" (1850–53), "Lays of Sorrow, No 2" (1850–53); and "Ye Carpette Knyghte" (1855). He enjoyed medieval parodies in *Punch* and queried Tenniel as to the author (du Maurier) of "A Tale of Camelot" that ran in several issues of 1866.[2]

From an early age, Tenniel was a devotee of all things chivalrous. He was probably acquainted with several of the artists who had attended or illustrated the chief revival event of his youth, the Eglinton Tournament (see chap. 2). Attendees Edward Henry Corbould, John Franklin, and Noël Paton would later, like Tenniel, be among the artists engaged by S. C. Hall for his *Book of British Ballads* (1844). Also, the costumes worn at the other great revival spectacle of the period, the queen's costume ball of 1842, had been delineated by Tenniel's old companions and later kinsmen Leopold and Charles Martin. With his work for Hall and his designs for an 1845 edition of La Motte Fouqué's *Undine,* Tenniel was firmly in what has been called "the Eglinton school of illustrators" and was ideally suited to take over from Doyle his quasi-medieval drawings in *Punch.* In that paper, Tenniel's medieval figures proliferated in initials, title pages (three of his first four title pages showed armored knights), illustrations, and decorative borders. This output drew the admiration of painter Henry Stacy Marks, himself a medievalist, who as "Drypoint" declared in an 1861 issue of the *Spectator,* "And who has drawn armour so well as Mr. Tenniel? Not a joint or rivet escapes his watchful eye. He loves to accompany the steel-clad knight when 'pricking o'er the plain,' encountering the scaly dragon, rescuing beauty in distress, or challenging all comers to a trial of skill. He revives the sports of hunting and hawking, tilting at the ring or quantain, and the joust and tournament, when the 'queen of beauty and love' sits smiling amid the clash of arms and the fanfare of trumpets, ready to award the victor with a laurel wreath." In the same year, Tenniel's illustrations to *Lalla Rookh* would impart chivalric overtones to Moore's Middle Eastern subjects. Men in armor appeared, too, in Tenniel's gift drawings for friends: an 1861 drawing pictured a knight blowing foam from his tankard; in 1866 he drew an "Elritch Knight" for a Captain Letts; and in 1879, for a Miss Alice White, he would depict Linley Sambourne as a crusader.[3]

While Carroll wrote his *Alice* sequel, the revival was at its peak. At this time, there appeared the Doré-illustrated *Idylls* (1867–68); a modern English edition of Sir Thomas Mallory's *Morte Darthur* (1868); and Tennyson's second book of idylls, *The Holy Grail and Other Poems* (1869). In painting, Watts's *Una and the Red Cross Knight* (1869) was shown at the Royal Academy where Millais's *Knight Errant* would cause something of a stir in the year following. In 1870, too, Hughes completed his *Sir Galahad.* Tenniel's contribution in this period was his two successive double-spread tournament cartoons for the 1868 elections—Gladstone and Disraeli in the lists, with "Dizzy" unhorsed in the second cut.[4]

The "Knighte's Tale" and Looking-Glass Knights

As in a game of chess, we should expect the story to have four knights. Alice soon spies the White Knight in Looking-glass House, balancing badly as he slides down a poker. She will meet him again in chapter 8 and also his red double. Directly afterward we see Tenniel's Jabberwock and its diminutive slayer. No knight this, but a page or knight trainee. Then, in the fourth square, Alice comes upon two "fat little men"—hardly the heroes of a medieval romance. But these, too, suggest knights, for once Tweedledum discovers his broken rattle, his dispute with Tweedledee reads like a parody of the "Knighte's Tale" from Chaucer's *Canterbury Tales*—specifically the meeting in the grove.[5]

In Chaucer's story the knights Arcite and Palamon have been taken into captivity after a great battle and incarcerated for life. Sisters' sons, clad in similar armor, bound by knightly vows of brotherhood, both smitten by the sight of the lady Emelye (whom they see at almost the same moment from the window of their "perpetual" prison), they are indeed as alike as Tweedledum and Tweedledee. The object of their quarrel—the sole privilege of cherishing feelings of affection for the lady—seems, considering their circumstances, as trifling as a broken rattle.

Having separately escaped their prison, after some years they accidentally meet in a grove and straightway agree to return there on the following day to battle to the death for the right to worship their inamorata. When they meet at the appointed time, Arcite bearing a load of armor for both, then

> change came o'er the colour of each face,
> E'en as the hunter, in the realm of Thrace
> . . . .
> Thinks—'Here comes my mortal enemy.'

The Tweedle brothers change color too, or at least suspect that they do: "'Do I look very pale?' said Tweedledum, coming up to have his helmet tied on. . . . 'I'm very brave generally . . . only today I happen to have a headache.' 'And *I've* got a toothache!' said Tweedledee."

Despite the bitter enmity of Arcite and Palamon, they follow the brotherly conventions prescribed for medieval tournaments: "Each helped with all his care to arm the other / As friendly as he had been born his brother." With similar amicability Tweedledum and Tweedledee go off "hand-in-hand into the wood" to get their equipment for the coming battle.

Once engaged, Arcite's and Palamon's circling swords

> flashed brightly to and fro
> So forcefully, that with the lightest stroke
> They seemed as they would fell a sturdy oak."[6]

To prepare Alice for their conflict, the brothers warn her against coming too close as they generally hit everything they can see or reach. "You must hit the *trees* pretty often," she replies. Tweedledum looks around him "with a satisfied smile." "I don't suppose," he says, "there'll be a tree left standing, for ever so far round, by the time we've finished!"

Fig. 103. Tenniel, "Preparing for Fight," illustration for Lewis Carroll, *Through the Looking-Glass*, 1872

The odd collection of bolsters, blankets, dish covers, coal scuttles, and so on that the brothers insist they must wear are, of course, a child's version of quilted doublets, cuirasses, gorgets, and helmets. Caricaturists frequently showed combatants in makeshift armor—saucepan and pot lid helmets, and the like. When the brass founders marched in support of Queen Caroline in 1821, some in proper armor, they were pictured by one artist as wearing teakettle and coal-scuttle helmets. An 1839 cartoon by H. B. (John Doyle) shows a kettle-cover shield and a saucepan helmet worn by the tilting Lords Brougham and Durham respectively. Leech used similar imagery for the Chartists in 1848, as did Tenniel for the Irish in 1852 and also for a depiction of a working-class tournament for *Punch*'s 1871 *Pocket Book*. Tenniel's portrayal of the Tweedles preparation more or less follows the text (fig. 103). As Carroll did not describe Tweedledum's sword, Tenniel drew a makeshift one of wood that, like their schoolboy suits, accords with the childishness of the pair.[7]

Fig. 104. Initial letter *T*, "Essence of Parliament," *Punch*, 16 Apr. 1859, 153

The Tournament

A useful prop in this chapter is the large umbrella that Tweedledum spreads over himself and his brother to the exclusion of Alice. Besides showing their selfishness, it will provide a hiding place for Tweedledee (fig. 97) and serve as his weapon. For some, who still recalled how the great tournament at Eglinton Park in 1839 had fizzled out in a great deluge, armored knights and umbrellas held comic associations. Satirists had drawn umbrella-bearing knights for the next two decades (fig. 104, fig. 105, and fig. 106). Did the Tweedle "knights" and their umbrella hint at this theme?[8]

Fig. 105. *(Left)* Charles H. Bennett, initial letter *A*, in William Sangster, *Umbrellas and Their History* (London, before 1867). Fig. 106. *(Right)* William S. Gilbert (Bab), "Sir Guy the Crusader," illustration, *Fun*, 8 June 1867, 139

Carroll would certainly have heard of the fiasco at Eglinton and also of the mock tournament enacted at Wormsley Park, the estate of Colonel John Fane, in the following year. Held some fifteen miles from Oxford, it drew five thousand or more spectators and was a great success, the colonel himself impersonating the "Queen of Beauty." In 1871 Carroll recorded photographing the children of a Captain Fane of Wormsley—probably Colonel Fane's son (who had been the "Knight of the Gridiron") or his grandson.[9]

Chapter 8 of *Looking-Glass* shows that Carroll was well informed on the practices of knights, their observance of the rules of battle, and the war cries by which they identified themselves.[10] The chess knights being near doubles, like the Tweedles, they have the same cry. In fact, the pair seem to take up where Tweedledum and Tweedledee left off. They stare at one another for some time like waxworks and then bicker over Alice like a pair of schoolboys: "'She's *my* prisoner, you know!' . . . 'Yes, but then I came and rescued her!' . . . 'Well, we must fight for her, then.'" It is not until the battle ends, and she helps the White Knight out of his helmet that Alice's gentle companion of the Seventh Square emerges.

As the knight is such a poor rider, Alice jokes, "You ought to have a wooden horse on wheels, that you ought." As Carroll may have recalled, sixteenth-century (and also Eglinton) knights practiced jousting against dummy knights mounted on wooden horses on wheels so that they could be rolled down toward them along grooves. Such a device appears in Richard Doyle's illustrations for *The Tournament* [1840] and another in Tenniel's 1851 cut

Fig. 107. Tenniel, "The Exhibition As It Might Have Been in the Days of Yore," border, *Punch,* Jan.–June 1851, 208 (detail)

showing the great exhibition "as it Might Have Been in the Days of Yore" (fig. 107).[11]

The White Knight's experience of being stuck fast in his helmet is bizarre; he is enveloped by it entirely, and the other White Knight mistakenly puts it on with the first knight inside it. However, in medieval times the head-pieces sometimes did become stuck, and their wearers might consequently be suffocated. During the Eglinton rehearsals Lord Waterford was imprisoned in his armor for some twenty minutes before his squires managed to extricate him, and in 1857 when lack of models made it necessary for the painters of the Oxford Union murals to pose for one another, William Morris became locked in a helmet that had been improperly jointed.[12]

The helmet in which the White Knight had been stuck was of his own design and shaped like a sugar loaf. This item Carroll may have taken from Henry Silver's comic series "Punch's Book of British Costumes," which informs us that at the time of Henry II the headpieces "assumed almost the shape of a sugar-loaf; so when the armourers used to advertise 'a sweet thing in helmets,' there really seemed some reason for their sugary remarks."[13]

For all its fooling, chapter 7 of *Looking-Glass* calls up the essential revival mood with its romantic yearning for a golden past. Before the White Knight's song, Carroll paused in his narrative to evoke the recollections of the future Alice: "Years afterward she could bring the whole scene back again, as if it had been only yesterday—the mild blue eyes and kindly smile of the Knight—the setting sun gleaming through his hair, and shining on his armour in a blaze of light that quite dazzled her—the horse quietly moving about, with the reins hanging loose on his neck, cropping the grass at her feet—and the black shadows of the forest behind—all this she took in like a picture, as with one hand shading her eyes, she leant against a tree, watch-

Fig. 108. Tenniel, "Knight in Ditch," illustration for Lewis Carroll, *Through the Looking-Glass*, 1872

ing the strange pair, and listening, in a half dream, to the melancholy music of the song." In fact, the scene is like several pictures, but most like that revival icon, George Frederic Watts's *Sir Galahad,* with the pure young knight's brilliantly lit armor, the downward curve of the horse's neck behind him, and the dark, almost black, wood.[14] At the conclusion of his song, and before leaving Alice, the Knight asks her to wait and wave her handkerchief when he gets to the turn in the road—"I think it'll encourage me, you see"—perhaps a final echo of days when knights rode forth with their ladies' favors tied to their lances.

The chapter's several references to wind and water invite speculation. The White Knight carries his deal box upside down "so the rain can't get in." He hopes that Alice's hair is well fastened on because "the wind is so *very* strong here." He was stuck in his helmet "as fast as—as lightning, you know." One wonders if knights who shout "Ahoy!" like sailors, and horses fitted with anklets against the bites of sharks, hark back to the dripping mounts that slithered in the flooded lists at Eglinton Park.

Do Tenniel's drawings support this conjecture? As Janice Lull points out (see chapter 12 above) the White Knight's horse carries a number of props belonging to other chapters of *Looking-Glass*. The umbrella, then, which ap-

Fig. 109. Tenniel, initial letter *W, Punch*, July–Dec. 1851, 149

Fig. 110. *(Left)* Tenniel, initial letter *T, Punch*, July–Dec. 1853, 211. Fig. 111. *(Right)* Tenniel, initial letter *T, Punch*, 26 Nov. 1859, 216

Fig. 112. Tenniel, preliminary drawing for frontispiece,
Lewis Carroll, *Through the Looking-Glass,* 1872. (By permission of the Houghton Library, Harvard University)

pears (partly hidden) in three of the White Knight pictures, is explained by
its previous use in chapter 4 (fig. 108). At the same time, it repeats the Eglinton theme of a knight with an umbrella, a motif that Tenniel had incorporated into his bouts rimés, decorated initials, illustrations, and gift drawings at least twenty times (figs. 109, 110, 111). Finally, in a preliminary sketch
for the frontispiece, the White Knight holds a large umbrella, furled and
slanted over his right shoulder (fig. 112).[15] Did it seem too obvious a clue
to be retained?

The winds that livened the looking-glass world blew partly from the nineteenth century's Gothic revival—with a sprinkling of showers from the great
tournament at Eglinton. Carroll's knights—acknowledged and concealed—
his gentle parodies of chivalric practices, and his hints of late-revival romanticism found an answering spirit in Tenniel.

17
◆✕◆

Alice and Social Caricature

You may call it "nonsense" if you like.
—The Red Queen

Caricatures, Political and Social

From text and picture, as profuse as the ornaments of a Victorian draw-ing room, the *Alice* images come to entice us with their hidden messages. Those commenting on contemporary society did not go unnoticed. One early critic of *Wonderland* reproached Carroll for his "direct and earnest social caricatures, as, for instance, in the matter of the jurors."[1] In fact, the texts provide many social portraits, as Tenniel was quick to recognize.

If Tenniel mined his *Punch* work for the *Alice* books, this was not un-warranted. His caricatures were, for the most part, based on types that Car-roll had adopted from *Punch* and similar sources in the popular culture. Still, one descries, or infers, two actual persons, both extraneous to the text. It has long been noted that the man in white paper in Alice's railway carriage resembles the statesman Benjamin Disraeli. His inexplicable presence there seems to accord with the Tory leader's reputation as an enigma. It is also obvious that the ineffectual White Queen displays certain characteristics as well as items of dress taken from Tenniel's *Punch* caricatures of Pope Pius IX. Both of these jokes would have been appreciated by Carroll, who con-sidered Disraeli "the greatest statesman" of his time and mistrusted the pope. The conjecture that Tenniel's Lion and Unicorn in *Looking-Glass* are carica-tures of Gladstone and Disraeli is not borne out by comparison with his cartoon portraits of the statesmen.[2] Nor does it seem likely that Carroll and Tenniel, Conservatives both, would have cast the Liberal party leader in the role of the British Lion.

A devotee of *Punch* from his teens, Carroll would come to agree with many of the paper's positions. For example, he welcomed the arrest of the Irish leader Charles Parnell in 1881, opposed extension of the franchise in 1884, and considered that the defeat of Gladstone's Irish Home Rule Bill had averted "a gigantic catastrophe." His social inclinations are evident in the family magazine "The Rectory Umbrella," which he authored at an early age. Following the sentencing of several working-class leaders of the Chartist agitation of 1848, Carroll wrote of one William Cuffey, "Chartism, or democracy, has always had its little men. It is intrinsically a little ambition which inspires its followers. They would have all men level: all equally little: little as themselves. Their national representative is Cuffey. The little Cuffey was born in humble life: so are all little men: it is a remarkable and peculiar trait of little men: in body he was little, in mind less. . . . His little seditious attempts had little effect: he and his littleness were transported. Ah! little, little man!"[3]

Still, in 1856, after reading Charles Kingsley's *Alton Locke* (1850), a novel sympathetic to the sufferings of the poor although opposed to working-class activism, Carroll was moved to write, "If the book were but a little more definite, it might stir up many fellow-workers in the same good field of social improvement. . . . I would then thankfully spend and be spent so long as I were sure of really effecting something by the sacrifice, and not merely lying down under the wheels of some irresistible Juggernaut." He was charitable, in 1867 proposing a system to more efficiently organize the giving of contributions, and in the late eighties joining his brother Edwin in a campaign to relocate the starving inhabitants of the South Atlantic island of Tristan da Cunha. But, like most of his compeers, he placed people in a ranked system, believing that class determined both character and physical characteristics. Perhaps the clearest expression of Carroll's social philosophy comes through in the conversation between Arthur Forester and the narrator in the third chapter of *Sylvie and Bruno Concluded* (1893).[4] It is the classic justification for inequality of wealth: that affluence initially derives from some contribution to society and is thus justly inheritable, that it provides employment for the lower classes whereas giving money to the poor merely pauperizes them, and so on.

Not all of Carroll's types were engendered by class. Among others, he satirized members of the legal profession and bluestockings. These portraits, as well as Tenniel's White Queen, are discussed in turn.

The Working Folk

Carpenters, Cooks, and Footmen

Following the centuries-old tendency to find comedy in the "Representation of humane Life, in inferior Persons, and Low Subjects,"[5] *Punch* and the other comic papers based a large proportion of their jokes upon working men and women, who are often shown as inept, lazy, and disposed to ape their "betters." The ridicule of domestics was a mainstay of *Punch's* humor throughout the century, one late 1845 series—"Punch's Guide to Servants"—being a very manual for thievery and sloppiness.

It was different for workingmen in the skilled trades. Unlike the necessarily dispersed domestics, these were capable of organizing and of disrupting the status quo, of attracting influential advocates, and of one day gaining the franchise.[6] Thus, during the 1859–61 London builder's strike Tenniel depicted carpenters as sober and respectable. The *Looking-Glass* carpenter has the usual attributes—the apron, paper cap, and basket of sawblades on his back suspended from a hammer held close to his chest. But unlike his *Punch* counterparts, he is a caricature.

Cooks came in for regular stereotyping. In the 1930s Mrs. C. S. Peel's article on Victorian homes and habits described the typical cook as red-faced and (like the Duchess's cook) "inclined to be tempersome." An Irish cook who eats the choicest cuts of meat herself, and who blames kitchen accidents on others or on the self-destructive nature of things, appears in Carroll's "Guida Di Bragia," a "Ballad Opera" written around 1850 for his marionette theater. Carroll's scene is reminiscent of a show called "Kitty Biling the Pot" that was presented with shadow puppets by galantee showmen of the period. A quarter of a century later, in a series in *Fun* (later published in book form and acquired by Carroll), J. F. Sullivan would likewise describe British domestics who cannot cook, who accuse objects of self-destructing, and who eat the best food in the house.[7]

Tenniel, like most of his compatriots, joked about lower-class life. In 1893, in facetious answers to a "truth questionnaire" (a word game of about twenty questions), he gave the cockney music-hall song "Knock'd em in the Old Kent Road" as his favorite air, "Sheepshead and Trotters" (a food provided by street sellers to the poor) as his dish of choice, and "Jemimer ann" (a scoffing name for a maidservant, similar to the Jemimer Janes, Betsy Janes, and Ameliar Anns that appeared in the pages of *Punch*) as his favorite name.[8]

Footmen were particular targets of *Punch,* starting in the midforties when Thackeray's "Jeames" enlivened the paper with his pretentious and invariably misspelled diary entries, his inordinate pride in his plush livery and in his well-developed calves. Within a few years Leech took up the theme with the series "Flunkeiana." Certain aspects of the stereotype seem based on fact. The Frenchman Hippolyte Taine (a visitor to England around midcentury) noted that in the hiring of footmen, points were accorded for such things as "fullness of calves, ankles, nobility of bearing, decorative appearance." Their lordly attributes and finery may have been ludicrous indeed (did no one remark upon the absurdity of those who provided the market for these fripperies?). As they were not usually the subjects of political cartoons, most of Tenniel's footmen appeared in 1851, a time when his *Punch* work was mainly illustrative (fig. 113).[9] His particular contribution to the image was his trick of drawing "Jeames's" or "John Thomas's" feet in ballet position (either third or fifth), a device he generally used to show pretentiousness. The Duchess's footmen, aside from their pantomime masks, are typical (fig. 66).

Fig. 113. Tenniel, "Punch's Anniversaries.—No. 5," small cut, *Punch,* July–Dec. 1851, 122

J. F. Sullivan's series showed the British workingman as one eager to lay blame on others for his mistakes, accomplishing no work when not under surveillance, unwilling to do anything that varied, however slightly, from his usual work, and so on.[10] But Carroll had already exploited this brand of humor in his *Alice* workers, most of whom are in some way unsatisfactory. Pat, the Irish gardener, is "digging for apples." The White Rabbit's other workmen foist every job on the Lizard Bill, advise him "don't be particular," and exclaim in chorus, "It was Bill," when things go wrong. The footmen are stupid and unobliging. The Duchess's cook overpeppers the soup and throws the pans and dishes; later she will turn stubborn when asked to give evidence at the trial. The royal gardeners plant white roses instead of red, then squabble over their work as they try to cover up their mistake; one has given the cook "tulip-roots" (poisonous) in place of onions. The executioner argues that besides the difficulty of removing the Cat's bodyless head, "he had never done such a thing before, and he wasn't going to begin at *his* time of life." The messenger hints to Humpty Dumpty that he will not wake the fishes unless he is rewarded, and the frog rustic of the eighth square is imbecilic.

Hodge

Of all workers, farm laborers were disparaged most. The word "clown" originally meant a countryman or boor, and the first pantomime clown or "clodpole" was a dull-witted rustic. Stage rustics were popular throughout the century; we recall that Tenniel had this role in Lytton's *Not So Bad as We Seem.* One is described by Dickens in *Nicholas Nickleby* (1838–39): "with a turned up nose, large mouth, broad face, and staring eyes," and another by Thackeray in *Punch*: "uttering insane ballads with an idiotic grin on his face." Also in *Punch*, Percival Leigh wrote admiringly of a comic actor who, "with his Clodhopping Gait, and Awkwardness, and Independence, and Impudence . . . did make the veriest Lout" he had ever seen.[11]

Fig. 114. Tenniel, initial letter *T, Punch,* 1 Sept. 1860, 88

W. H. Pyne's *World in Miniature* (1827), a work claiming to describe the "character, manners, customs, dress, diversions, and the peculiarities" of Britons, pictured the "English Peasant," as he would often be shown subsequently, with a round foolish face, soft hat, and smock frock, sitting on a gate or stile and eating his bread and cheese. Tenniel, who owned a copy of Pyne's book, gave a good example of the stereotype in an 1860 *Punch* initial (fig. 114). Before the county franchise bill was passed in 1884, the booby Hodge appeared in several Tenniel cartoons (fig. 115).[12]

Fig. 115. Tenniel, "Cobden's Logic," cartoon, *Punch,* 5 Dec. 1863

Punch artists liked to exaggerate the size of the farm laborer's boots; in one small drawing they are as large as the man himself. Then, around 1846, a new peculiarity surfaced in Leech's cuts. The bit of leg between Hodge's breeches and his hobnailed boots showed no calf development at all, a device that Tenniel would later adopt. Was this deformity based on fact, or was it simply a way of emphasizing the great clodhopper boots? Some thought that the farm worker exhibited this abnormality, one 1827 treatise attributing it to the inhibition of foot and ankle movement by the tightly laced boots. In 1830 another writer asked, "What is this defective being, with calfless legs and stooping shoulders, weak in body and mind?" answering, "That is an English peasant or pauper." A *Punch* article of 1847 ascribed the problem to malnutrition, pointing out that the laborer's diet consisted mainly of bread and potatoes; an earlier piece had shown Hodge complaining, "What we lives upon is mostly taters and zalt. We han't had a taste o' bhaacon for I douooant know how long, nor a drap o' beer since last harvust whooam."[13]

Tenniel drew three types of rustics—the basic yokel and two variants. One variation was the swain—the lovesick shepherd of pastoral poetry. He was a slender youth wearing braces and ribbons, but with Hodge's hobnailed boots and, by the late fifties, Hodge's calfless legs (fig. 116). The other was the gaffer, an aging Hodge—bent and with bristly chin and gnarled hands, his soft hat sometimes changed to a stovepipe one (fig. 117).[14]

All of these rustics Tenniel drew for the *Alice*s. The bucolic swain is Father William's son, his spindly shanks a strange distortion to modern eyes (fig. 96). Here, Tenniel's stereotype is an anomaly since the swain's father appears to be a country squire. The Aged, Aged Man in the illustration to Carroll's wicked parody of Wordsworth's *Resolution and Independence* is Tenniel's gaffer, shown in smock frock and stovepipe hat;

Fig. 116. Tenniel, calendar page, "Punch's Almanack for 1859" (detail)

Fig. 117. Tenniel, "Out of the Parish," cartoon, *Punch*, 27 May 1865 (detail)

Fig. 118. Tenniel, "Old Man on Gate," illustration for Lewis Carroll, *Through the Looking-Glass*, 1872

we can just make out his nose and bristly chin beneath the Knight's elbow (fig. 118). Carroll's original version of the poem is explicit about the man's station:

I met an aged, aged man
    Upon the lonely moor:
I knew I was a gentleman,
    And he was but a boor.

In the Knight's song the second line is changed to "A-sitting on a gate," agreeing with the conventional picture of the rustic on a stile. But the doubled-over posture with which Tenniel pictured the man appears to relate back to Wordsworth's original:

Such seemed this Man, not all alive nor dead
Nor all asleep—in his extreme old age:
His body was bent double, feet and head
Coming together in life's pilgrimage.[15]

The quintessential booby is, of course, the old Frog who in square eight hobbles toward Alice with his enormous boots (fig. 101). An 1845 *Punch* article had credited the "agricultural mind" with only "a sort of consciousness," capable of conceiving external objects "by an effort" and perceiving "just what it sees, but not what it does not see."[16] The old Frog, with his "slow drawl," "dull eyes," and literalism—"'Which door?' . . . 'To answer the door?' . . . 'What's it been asking of?'"—is Hodge incarnate, and so he is pictured by Tenniel.

Jurists, Bluestockings, and Pius IX
The Law

Carroll's satires hit high as well as low, and the law was his frequent mark. In an 1855 poem he created a nightmare vision—a "Palace of Humbug" where "No suits can suit, no plea can please"—a system riddled with tangled evidence, red tape, and empty arguments shouted at "him that nodded in a wig." Eight years later, the dismissal of a case against Professor Benjamin Jowett by the Vice Chancellor's Court at Oxford prompted Carroll's sardonic poem "The Majesty of Justice" with its conclusion that Justice's sole majesty resided in the judge's horsehair wig:

Whose countless rows of rigid curls
  Are gazed at with admiring eyes
    By country lads and servant girls.

Carroll's later works mocked the law as well. In *The Hunting of the Snark* (1876) the Barrister pleads a ridiculous case and next dreams that the Snark, "in gown, bands, and wig," defends a pig and then proceeds (like Old Fury in the Mouse's tale) to decide the verdict and pronounce sentence. Too late, the Snark learns that his client has been dead for some years. Finally, in the poem "Peter and Paul," from *Sylvie and Bruno* (1889), Paul, with the aid of a legal friend, manages to ruin Peter by demanding repayment of a loan that has never been made.[17]

Tenniel had occasionally drawn figures in judicial robes and wigs for *Punch;* the paper's mascot himself appeared as Lord Chancellor Punch in several initials and cartoons. In the months when Tenniel pondered the first *Alice* pictures, one of his cartoons commented on a bill to make bankruptcy proceedings less costly.[18] In "Reversing the Proverb" (alluding to La Fontaine's fable "The Oyster and the Litigants" in which the judge swallows the oyster, handing a shell to each of the disputants), the suitor gets the oyster and the lawyers the shells. An oblique reference to the fable is made in *Looking-Glass* when Haigha explains to Alice that Hatta is "only just out of prison, and he hadn't finished his tea when he was sent in . . . and they only give them oyster-shells in there—so you see he's very hungry and thirsty."

Like Carroll's other satires on the law, the *Wonderland* trial is a total travesty. The jurors are in danger of forgetting their own names; the King-judge wants to have the verdict before the facts are known and constantly threatens the witnesses. The lack of evidence against the accused only increases the King's suspicion of him. As Michael Hancher noted in his study of the illustrations, it was Tenniel who added the bird counsels in the courtroom scene—slyly making one of them a parrot. Another counsel is that bird of prey, the eagle.[19]

But well before her meeting with the deck of cards, Alice had encountered another jurist. Like Carroll, Tenniel took delight in a "pictorial surprise," and his Blue

Fig. 119. Tenniel, "Caterpillar," illustration for Lewis Carroll, *Alice's Adventures in Wonderland,* 1866

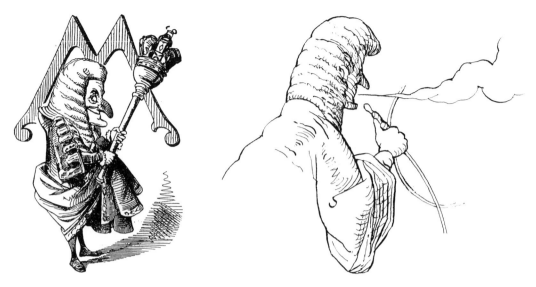

Fig. 120. *(Left)* Tenniel, initial letter *M, Punch,* 28 Mar. 1857, 122. Fig. 121. *(Right)* Author's sketch of upper part of Tenniel's Caterpillar, slightly altered

Caterpillar is a complex of surprises (fig. 119). In *The Nursery Alice* Carroll would chortle, "Do you see its long nose and chin? At least they *look* exactly like a nose and chin, don't they? But they really are two of its legs." However, the trick does not end there. If we view the picture through partly closed lids, the Caterpillar's segmented back seems to separate from the shaded "face" to form the curls of a full-bottomed wig such as Tenniel had frequently drawn for *Punch* (fig. 120). The creature's ample sleeve, falling back to show another sleeve beneath, suggests judicial raiment. In fact, our squint has revealed a veritable robed judge who interrogates Alice from the heights of his mushroom bench—"'Who are *you?*' . . . 'What do you mean by that?' . . . 'Explain yourself'" (fig. 121).[20]

The Amazon

Equally peremptory is Carroll's Red Queen, the stock type of the learning-proud masculine woman or "amazon." Bluestockings had been ridiculed on stage as early as 1730. W. S. Gilbert's *Princess Ida; or, Castle Adamant* of 1884 is a late example of the genre although somewhat lighter in tone than earlier pieces. In 1840 Mark Lemon, soon co-founder and editor of *Punch*, contributed two farces to the London stage—*The Ladies' Club* and *The House of Ladies*—showing the chaos that might accompany feminine clubs or an all-woman parliament. From the start, *Punch*'s staff showed a preference for "domestic angels" over amazons. In an 1848 article by *Punch* writer Ponny Mayhew, the model wife "subscribes to no circulating library, and if she reads a novel, she falls asleep over it. . . . She never talks politics or wishes that she were . . . a man."[21] Dickens provided an amazon type in the strong-minded (but like the Red Queen, not unkind) Betsy Trotwood in *David Cop-perfield* (1849–50). The novel's other amazon, the equally inflexible Miss Murdstone, represents the worst characteristics of the type.

Carroll's 1856 poem "The Three Voices" gives a perfect example of the bluestocking—a formidable maiden who accosts a poor fellow on a lonely beach, pins his hat to the sand with the point of her umbrella, and proceeds to drive him mad with incomprehensible arguments. Thirty-three years later in Carroll's *Sylvie and Bruno* we find another amazon—a forward "young lady in spectacles, the very embodiment of the March of Mind." Still, Carroll was not wholly opposed to women's rights and women's education. He studied the subject, was pleased at the achievement of some measure of suffrage for his sisters, and, while opposing coeducational classes at Oxford, supported the idea of a women's university.[22]

The amazon surfaced in *Punch* during the paper's campaign against the American reformer Amelia Jenks Bloomer (who visited England in 1851) and her followers. Bypassing Bloomer's position on women's education, unjust marriage laws, and other issues of women's rights, the paper focused its at-tack on her outfit (a short skirt over full trousers), which was ridiculed in drawings by Leech and Tenniel. But it wasn't until the midfifties, in one of his "Illustrations to Shakspeare," that Tenniel forecast his rawboned amazon. Here, the sight of three stereotypical spinsters wearing sunshades (floppy wide-brimmed hats also known as "uglies") prompts Macbeth to ask, "What are these? / So wither'd, and so *wild* in their attire?" In *The Ingoldsby Leg-ends* Tenniel's straitlaced spinster who pursues dog Tray in "The Cynotaph" comes still closer to the type.[23]

The fully developed amazon first appeared in Tenniel's cartoons as an American symbol during and immediately following the Civil War. A fine ex-ample is the rawboned Mrs. South who shakes her fist at the Yankee Jonathan in the war's first year. Then, at the war's end, Columbia—a stiff-backed tar-tar personifying the United States—confronts Britannia with reparation claims for the damages caused by British-built ships supplied to the South (fig. 122). Over the years the type would appear in seven more cartoons (sometimes as a woman warrior with helmet and shield) and might repre-sent the effort for women's votes (Miss Sarah Suffrage), political economy (Miss Prudence), and higher education for women. All are tall, thin, straight-backed, plain, and tend to have prominent chins—although the faces are never the same. Sometimes the amazon wears heelless sandals with straps crossed over the instep—a style borrowed from Leech's bloomer girls, which Tenniel likewise used for *Wonderland*'s Duchess.[24] His amazons of the late sixties and early seventies wear hairnets or snoods, a fashion that Tenniel must have deplored.

In the years between the two *Alice*s three of Tenniel's cartoons took on women's issues. By 1865, with franchise reform in the air, the economist

Fig. 122. Tenniel, "The Disputed Account," cartoon, *Punch*,
28 Oct. 1865

John Stuart Mill had advocated suffrage for "all grown persons, both men
and women," who could "read, write, and perform a sum in the rule of three"
(we recall Alice's examination in sums before she becomes a queen). Tenniel's cartoon "Mill's Logic" showed Mill clearing a way at the polls for his
spinsterish clients. Later that year Lemon took advantage of the women's struggle to revise his 1840 play *The House of Ladies,* which was then produced as
The Petticoat Parliament; or Women's Suffrage at the Olympic Theatre. The issue
continued into 1868, when a Tenniel cartoon showed a lady ratepayer denied the franchise she had hoped to receive under the new reform act. Following the defeat of Jacob Bright's bill in 1870 to give votes to women, *Punch*
celebrated with Tenniel's "Ugly Rush"—a crowd of amazons storming the door
against which the smiling John Bull leans his great bulk.[25] Bright's second
women's suffrage bill would be rejected in 1871. Thus, *Looking-Glass* was born
during the height of the period's controversy over women's rights.

To Carroll this queen was a "Fury." He later wrote, "Her passion must
be cold and calm; she must be formal and strict, yet not unkindly; pedantic
to the tenth degree, the concentrated essence of all governesses."[26] She is
proud, saying, "All the ways around here belong to *me*." She is precise. When

Fig. 123. Tenniel, "Mending the Lesson," cartoon, *Punch,* 20 Dec. 1873 (detail)

she questions Alice, she looks at her watch to check the promptness of the reply. Inserting pegs into the ground she measures exact distances to mark the separate stages of her leave-taking with Alice. She is competitive and can better anything Alice cares to mention: she has seen finer gardens and steeper hills and has heard greater nonsense (and probably spoken it, too).

Tenniel's Red Queen is one of the amazon sisterhood—angular, plain-faced, showing by hand gestures her faith in her own mad logic. She is the least human of the chess people, her appearance wavering between that of a carved figure on a pedestal and a creature of flesh and blood (fig. 100 and fig. 90). Even after this equivocation is resolved, she is only marginally human. The folds of her shawl seem nearly as rigid as the turned rings of her chess skirt, in contrast with the softer draperies of the White Queen. Although they both wear snoods, hers is stiffly stylized. She wears the peculiar sandal noted on several of Tenniel's female tartars (fig. 123) and, spurning fashion, does not emulate the crinoline of her fellow queen.

The White Queen and the Pope

The White Queen was regarded by Carroll as "gentle, stupid, fat and pale; helpless as an infant; and with a slow, maundering, bewildered air about her, just *suggesting* imbecility, but never quite passing into it." As Tenniel had for years represented Pope Pius IX ("Pio Nono") as possessing some of these traits, he slyly gave his White Queen a certain resemblance to his caricatures of the pontiff.[27]

It was a Leech cartoon, expressing *Punch*'s displeasure that the 1859 Treaty of Villafranco had left the pope's temporal powers intact, which first showed the pope in the posture of an old woman, knees slightly bent and hands holding his skirts above the ground. From 1860 to 1862, as Victor Emmanuel consolidated his power in Italy, *Punch* derided the papacy as an obstacle to that country's unification. Tenniel's early 1860 title page and his series of some eighteen cartoons on the Italian situation elaborated on Leech's type (fig. 124). It was in this period that Carroll clipped, for the Christ Church common room collection, a small cut by Tenniel in which Mr. Punch, as Shakespeare's Touchstone, warns the pope (who lifts his bedraggled skirts above a muddy brook) "Thou art in a parlous state, Shepherd." Tenniel had first portrayed the pontiff as "Mrs. Pope" in late 1861, transforming the tiara to a cook's cap. In later cartoons the three-tiered crown became a nightcap, a mobcap, and a bonnet supporting a basket of fish. Usually Tenniel's pope wears slippers with large rosettes, the same as had been worn by the famous Joey Grimaldi in the role of Clown, and three cartoons show the pope's skirt pulled out of shape by a skewed crinoline hoop.[28]

In December 1869, a long-heralded ecumenical council convened in Rome, arousing fears that it would embrace the dogma of papal infallibility. That month Tenniel, who had earlier in the year drawn Pio Nono as the Vatican chambermaid, now pictured him, followed by a line of ecclesiastics (all in rosetted slippers), sliding on thin ice toward the dangerous area of "Infallibility."[29] In 1870, as Tenniel began work on his *Looking-Glass* pictures, the dogma was being stormily debated in Rome; it would be affirmed in July. But before the year was out,

Fig. 124. Tenniel, title page, *Punch* vol. 38, Jan.–June 1860 (detail)

the pope, yielding to the troops of Victor Emmanuel, was forced to surrender his temporal power. It was in this climate that Tenniel created his White Queen—pudgy, disoriented, flat-footed in rosette-trimmed slippers, hands clutching ineffectually at her scepter and trailing shawl, and with a crinoline hoop protruding from beneath the rings of her chess piece skirt (fig. 125). Could *Punch*'s readers have failed to make the connection?

Alice

Tenniel's Alice is as much a stereotype as his footmen, farm laborers, and amazons. Readers who look for realism will be disappointed. Although critics wrote, "The sweet figure of little Alice contrasts delightfully . . . with the funny creatures and people she encounters," and, "The very pretty little girl is a charming relief to all the grotesque appearances which surround her," Alice herself is somewhat of a grotesque.[30] That is, we would be surprised to meet a child with her proportions in the real world.

This Tenniel did deliberately, as shown by two of his drawings of Alice discovering the little doorway in *Wonderland.* In the earlier one her proportions are already untrue, with hands and feet a bit small (fig. 126). For the published version, Tenniel appears to have traced portions of the first drawing, bringing the upper part of the figure forward at a slightly greater tilt, sinking the head deeper into the shoulders and shortening the legs so that the entire body is smaller relative to the head (fig. 127). He has also shortened the foot slightly. This is the more striking image. With her sweet face, spreading hair, and bouffant skirts, Alice balances on her tiny feet like a flower on a slender stem. Similarly, Tenniel made Alice's head larger in proportion to her body between the preliminary and final versions of the "Lobster Quadrille" design. Although Carroll might protest that Tenniel had drawn "several pictures of 'Alice' *entirely* out of proportion—head decidedly too large, and feet decidedly too small,"[31] a realistic child would have been incompatible with Tenniel's other inventions and thus an artistic blunder.

The most natural thing about Alice is her unsmilingness, for this is the unselfconscious gravity of the young. Also natural are her movements—never slack, but drawn with an actor's knowledge of gesture.

Fig. 125. Tenniel, "White Queen," illustration for Lewis Carroll, *Through the Looking-Glass*, 1872

Fig. 126. Tenniel, "Little Curtain," preliminary drawing for Lewis Carroll, *Alice's Adventures in Wonderland*, 1872. (By permission of the Houghton Library, Harvard University)

Fig. 127. Tenniel, "Little Curtain," illustration for Lewis Carroll, *Alice's Adventures in Wonderland*, 1866

Even in the simple act of drawing aside the curtain, the slight lifting of the shoulder, the bending of the knee, impart a living tautness to her figure.

In some respects Carroll had envisioned a child more ideal than real. Years later he wrote, "What wert thou, dream-Alice, in the foster-father's eyes? How shall he picture thee? Loving, first, loving and gentle . . . then courteous—courteous to *all*, high and low, grand or grotesque, King or Caterpillar, . . . then trustful, ready to accept the wildest impossibilities with all the utter trust that only dreamers know: and lastly, curious—wildly curious, and with that eager enjoyment of life that comes only in the happy hours of childhood, when all is new and fair."[32] Tenniel's interpretation is in harmony with this. He takes care always to show Alice to advantage, avoiding such un-Victorian choices (found in some of the reillustrations) as a glimpse up her skirts as she falls down the rabbit hole, or a posterior view as she bends to peer through the little door. Unlike Carroll himself, he avoids illustrating grotesqueries best left to the text, such as Alice's chin hitting her shoe as she shuts up "like a telescope," or her head emerging above the trees on a stalklike (or wormlike) neck. Never does she cry brattishly with downturned or open mouth, sit knock-kneed with toes turned in, or let her hands hang awkwardly from upraised elbows. Even after her dunking in the pool of tears, she sits neat as a little doll among the creatures gathered around the mouse.

Contemporary reviewers of *Wonderland* concurred in their praise of Tenniel's Alice, writing, "We are in love with little Alice's face in all its changes," "Alice is a charming little girl," "His representations of sweet little Alice are exquisite," and "The picture representing Alice . . . in the pool of tears, and Alice with the pig in her arms, show her as the perfection of a charming and pretty child." Again, in an 1872 review of *Looking-Glass* we read, "Mr. Tenniel has outdone himself in his illustrations, which preserve the character of the little girl as perfectly as ever." Finally, at the end of the era, there is the affirmation of Monkhouse, "He has drawn for us Wonderland itself, and above all, Alice, that perfect ideal of the English girl, innocent, brave, kind, and full of faith and spirit. Ever on her face, as drawn by Tenniel, is a sweet look of wonder and expectation, but never one of confusion or fear, whether she finds herself swimming with a mouse, playing croquet with a flamingo for a mallet, or carried off at a thousand (or million) miles an hour by the Red Queen. Simply she is a thing of beauty and a joy forever."[33]

This perfect English girl, this "Miss Britannia," as a later writer would call her, belongs, as one might expect, more to Kensington than, say, to Islington. With her short upper lip, strong brow, and abundant hair, she is a sister to the little beauties in annuals, sheet-music covers, advertisements, and also Tenniel's *Punch* drawings of children of the affluent—watching the riders in Rotten Row, wandering the zoological gardens, and lavishing gifts on

Fig. 128. *(Left)* Tenniel, "Strike Home!" cartoon, *Punch,* 5 Oct. 1872
Fig. 129. *(Right)* Tenniel, "Seeing's Believing," cartoon, *Punch,* 1 Dec. 1883

Mr. Punch.[34] As to her tiny feet, they come straight from Victorian fashion plates.

But there is more to these images than the oddities of fashion. There were those who held that the classes were physically different, in fact "two different races." This bias is seen in Carroll's letters. For example, he wrote in 1879 to E. Gertrude Thomson, "Your view as to the diameter of the knee and ankle. . . . is in excess of the truth. Still you *may* have got those dimensions from real life, but in that case I think your model must have been a country-peasant child, descended from generations of labourers: there is a marked difference between them and the upper classes—specially as to the size of the ankle . . . I have come to believe in slender ankles as the normal standard of beauty." Years later he would advise her to make drawings of upper-class children, as hired models were "plebeian and *heavy.*" At the same time he realized that "most artists" drew "children's feet too small," as they had "some conventional ideal of beauty which is *not* nature."[35]

Tenniel was not unaware of natural proportions. In fact, several of his lower-class children tend to err in the opposite direction and have outsized hands and feet.[36] See, for example, the child who carries the workingman's Sunday dinner in an 1872 cartoon, or the slum girl in one of 1883 (fig. 128 and fig. 129). They are all social caricatures—these young proletarians and the dainty Alice.

The Stereotypic Vision

Tenniel's translation of a text into the stereotypical language of social cuts and cartoons was not unique. The birds and beasts in C. H. Bennett's 1857 *Aesop* personate roughs, gulls, and other stock types of the era. And as Martin Gardner's annotations to Carroll's *Snark* point out, Henry Holiday drew the Broker as a Jewish stereotype and the Barrister as Edward Kenealy, the counsel for the notorious claimant to the Tichborne fortune. All along, readers have enjoyed finding social and political analogues to the *Alice* characters, their eccentricities making this a tempting game. Tenniel himself incorporated figures from his *Alice* illustrations into eight political drawings, as have a great number of cartoonists since.[37]

The taste for stereotypes lived on in the early reillustrations to *Wonderland*. Pat, the White Rabbit's Irish gardener, was shown as a typical Paddy in English editions with pictures by W. H. Walker (1907), Harry Rountree (1908), and D. R. Sexton (1937). A. E. Jackson (1915) transferred the Paddy stereotype to the Lizard Bill, and K. M. Roberts (1908) depicted another stock Irish type in the Duchess's cook. Charles Pears (1908) bettered Tenniel by drawing Father William's son as a full-fledged Hodge in a smock frock, and Willy Pogany (1929) gave the Hatter the three hats of the stereotypical Jewish old-clothes peddler and added an American twist by making the Duchess's cook a "black Mammy" or "Aunt Jemima."[38]

Before the *Alices*, Tenniel's pictures in *Punch* had promoted the period's stereotypes of domestics, farm laborers, lawyers, clerics, bluestockings, and representatives of the social classes. Quick to recognize Carroll's stock types, Tenniel followed the author's lead, slyly adding some variations of his own.

THE *PUNCH* CARTOONS

The Pride of Mr. Punch

*Dreamt last night that I saw Tenniel open
Parliament and then we went out snipe shooting.*
—Henry Silver, Diary, 26 February 1862

Keeping Things Straight

For close to half a century, for most Englishmen at home and in such remote places as Melbourne, Toronto, and Bombay, political art was embodied in Tenniel's weekly cartoon in *Punch*. This was the "large cut," the full or double-page engraving that was the central feature of the paper. More limited in application than today, the word "cartoon" was never employed for the humorous half or quarter-page drawings known as "social cuts" or "socials," or to the illustrations, titles, half-titles, and initials that made up the remaining art.

Tenniel's first cartoon appeared in 1851, his last in 1901—over twenty-three hundred in all. Weekly, as the *Daily Telegraph* would recall, "the world awaited the advent of his cartoon at the judgment seat." Its message would be further broadcast by "a mass of newspapers, both in England and in the colonies," describing "this week's cartoon" for countless readers. Tenniel's designs were displayed on kiosks along the Paris boulevards, occasionally blackened by a censor's roller in St. Petersburg or Berlin, and, before a copyright agreement stopped the practice, pirated by *Harper's* and *Leslie's Weekly* in New York.[1]

Before the coming of daily newspapers, which greatly multiplied their numbers, individual cartoons were closely followed. Statesmen might adopt their language in letters and speeches. Reform, a "leap in the dark" (Lord Derby), could be "carried in a canter" (Disraeli); a Liberal might complain of the Conservatives' reform bill, "This offspring is a stolen child. The right honorable gentleman has stolen it" (Bernal Osborne, MP); and a political opponent might be described as an "old painted Pantaloon" (Disraeli) or a "Sicilian bandit" (Lord Salisbury).[2] These all have parallels in Tenniel's cartoons.

Private journals of the era convey the emotions that cartoons might stir.

When news of General Gordon's fate reached England, Lady Balfour noted Tenniel's cartoons in her diary: "'At Last' followed by the tragic 'Too Late'"; and before the home-rule vote of 1886, Mary Gladstone recorded, "Punch came and brought a great lump in my throat with its noble and pathetic cartoon 'Sink or Swim.'"[3]

When Tenniel retired they said, "We have looked to him to help keep things straight for us." His first and last cartoons, along with tributes to his long career, were reproduced in newspapers throughout the country. Thirteen years later he was still recalled as the long-time exponent of "the good sense of the nation."[4]

In Tenniel's cartoons readers found straightforward content, consistent treatment from volume to volume, recognizable portraits of public figures, a host of symbolic beings, and the stock types dear to a theater-loving public. The cartoons were prized for their sense of fun (some 85 percent being humorous), their celebration of the pleasures of Victorian life, and their virtually high-art function in providing symbols for the patriotic sentiments of the day. Most of all, they were loved for an air of truthfulness that seemed to emanate from Tenniel himself.

The Tenniel Cartoon

The Subject

From the start *Punch*'s cartoon subjects had been decided by the literary and artistic staff at their weekly dinner. The rival papers *Fun* and *Tomahawk* attempted a similar system, although, in the case of *Fun* at least, irregular attendance forced a change to the simpler expedient of cartoonist-editor conferences. When holidays or other occasions found the *Punch* men out of town, as frequently occurred, Tenniel met alone with the editor or with his proxy.[5]

How large a role had Tenniel in determining his cartoon subjects? The diaries of colleagues Silver and Brooks record some forty cartoon suggestions or modifications made by him between 1861 and 1871, with over half of his ideas adopted—a record that omits many subjects that were settled in private meetings, changed after staff consensus had been reached, or resolved by Tenniel alone. This says nothing of his veto, which, it was said, could crush any proposal to which he objected. Finally, the scant specifications given him at the table ("the title and legend . . . written on a piece of paper . . . enclosed in an envelope") would seem to leave the interpretation largely in his hands.[6]

Punch's fourth editor, F. C. Burnand, had once remarked that if a cartoon's meaning was not "written in the largest possible letters the British public would exclaim, 'What does it mean? We don't understand it.'" Conciseness was a must. Tenniel rejected superfluities at the *Punch* table with such protests as, "Now you're refining. You'd got quite a good cut and now you want to spoil it."[7]

Fig. 130. Tenniel, "A Lullaby," cartoon, *Punch*, 25 Feb. 1893

Some notes found among the papers of E. J. Milliken, chief cartoon suggestor from 1875 to 1897, outline sixteen ideas for cartoons. Where these correlate with published cartoons, Tenniel is seen to have selected only the essential concepts. For example, one note proposes that Gladstone (as a nursery maid) be shown dressing several parliamentary bills (personified as infants) for the coming session, while warning other small bills, who are tiptoeing into the room, to not disturb the Irish (home-rule) baby. Each of the new arrivals is to hold a card marked "Liberal Party—Autumn Session," and the sleeping Irish bill is to hold a bottle marked "Soothing Syrup." By contrast, Tenniel's charming nursery scene conveys the idea with merely two figures— Nurse Gladstone tenderly lowering the baby home-rule bill into its cradle while musing, "And now I must look after the others" (fig. 130).[8] It is simplicity itself, and it typifies Tenniel's approach.

His directness obviated the speech balloons found in the comic papers *Fun* and *Judy* and the explanatory, and sometimes lengthy, articles that accompanied cartoons in *Tomahawk* and in the Irish journal *Zoz*. While these papers were fond of running oversized cuts week after week, at *Punch* Tenniel held the line to about five double-spreads per year, reserving the large format for times when added emphasis was wanted. No excessive scenic detail or stylistic extravagance diluted the human drama. The touch was light, the message instantly comprehensible, the legend brief and pointed.[9]

The Protean Cartoon

Unlike *Punch*'s other drawings, which could be worked out well in advance, the political cut imposed a tight schedule. Forty-eight hours after the week's subject was settled the boxwood block with its completed drawing went to the engraver. The cartoonist needed to have on tap a precise knowledge of human races and types, animals, costumes, architecture, art, manners, events, and changing fashions. Tenniel—theater buff, sportsman, animalier, medievalist, lover of classics—had all this filed in his photographic memory.

He had the rare ability to be both serious artist and humorist. In 1870, when editor Shirley Brooks wanted an additional staff artist with these qualities he asked "Where to find this double-headed PHOENIX?" and Carroll, who wanted an artist who could draw grotesques and a "pretty child," too, was similarly challenged when Tenniel stopped illustrating.[10]

Fig. 131. Tenniel, "Two Persuasions," cartoon, *Punch,* 11 May 1878

Fig. 132. Tenniel, "Amateur Theatricals. An Othello 'Break-Down,'" small cut, "Punch's Almanac for 1868"

Might this duality in Tenniel's work, which seems often caught between high art and burlesque, be traceable to Tenniel senior? John Baptist was best remembered as a master of dancing and deportment. But he was also an accomplished fencer and horseman. These gentlemanly sports would have fed Tenniel's romantic inclinations, whereas John Baptist's first profession would inspire Tenniel to draw political figures and others suspected of pretentiousness, with the turned out toes and rounded elbows of ballet dancers. The figure of Disraeli in the 1878 cartoon "Two Persuasions" provides a good example (fig. 131).[11]

Tenniel's sense of the absurd might at any time rise to deflate his intense romanticism. This contributes an odd tension to his art. It is like his joke in *Punch*'s 1868 almanac. "Amateur Theatricals. An Othello 'Breakdown'" is one of Tenniel's rare contributions in the social-cut line (fig. 132). The drawing plays on two definitions of the word "breakdown"—a lively, shuffling dance originated by American blacks, and a mental or nervous collapse. It shows a leading man (his costume similar to that worn by the black actor Ira Aldrich in the role of Othello) who, "under the combined influence of sherry and the blackness of the circumstances," finds the blackface minstrel business so "utterly irresistible" that, strumming his sword like a banjo, he executes a spirited dance.[12] Like this player, Tenniel often could not resist inserting bits of comic business into his work, which is, consequently, full of small "breakdowns."

The Cartoon Theatrical

Central to Tenniel's cartoons is the influence of the stage, as this had been one of his lifelong passions. In 180 or more cuts, public figures appear as characters or performers in drama, opera, pantomime, music hall, and the circus, and as street entertainers. The use of stage metaphors, carried over from political prints of the eighteenth century, may be related to the extraordinary number of caricaturists who had trodden the boards as professionals or amateurs and cartoon suggesters who divided their writing efforts between comic journals and the theater.[13]

Journalists, too, liked to couch their political statements in theatrical terms. The *Red Republican* reported the 1850 opening of the Commons as "the annual farce at St. Stephen's theatre"; *Punch* announced that "The next novelty at the Theatre Royal, Westminster, would be a farce called *the budget* to be followed . . . by a pièce de circonstance, entitled the *sack,* in which Mr. DIZZY is said to have a fine exit"; and the *Examiner* dubbed a Tory election in Kent "An Unlucky Burlesque."[14]

Fig. 133. Tenniel, "Victory of the Alma," cartoon, *Punch,* 14 Oct. 1854

What theatrical form did Tenniel's cartoons not embrace? The Crimean War was dramatized in a series of tableaux—noble groupings representing "The United Service," "The Victory of the Alma (fig. 133), "The Harvest of the War." The Franco-Prussian War Tenniel staged as a melodrama with the erotically busty Paris defying the Hun, kneeling with arm flung dramatically over her brow as his dogs attack (fig. 134), and lying trampled beneath his horse's hooves. Remarking on the poignancy with which *Punch*, *Fun*, and *Judy* depicted this struggle, Edmond Duranty of the *Gazette des Beaux-Arts* observed in 1872, "They seem at certain moments to be affected

Fig. 134. Tenniel, "Call Off the Dogs!" cartoon, *Punch,* 4 Feb. 1871 (detail)

by our ills more strongly than we are." Over the years fifty cartoons were based on Shakespeare; if Tenniel's Queen Victoria appeared as a crinoline-gowned Queen Hermione in *The Winter's Tale* so had Ellen Tree on stage.[15]

Tenniel's banditti are stage bandits. His fairies are coryphées from pantomime and ballet, their wands tipped with pasteboard stars. Or else they are burlesque fairies—Abraham Lincoln, his wings patterned with stars and stripes; or Randolph Churchill, a mustached Ariel floating over Charles Bradlaugh's Caliban.[16]

Almanac cartoons, coming out at the year's end, emulated the Christmas pantomimes. The one for December 1893 featured Mother Goose leading a train of politicized nursery favorites: a French Red Riding Hood with the Socialist wolf, a Russian Bluebeard, Jack bearing the (Turkish?) giant's head, a Chinese Aladdin, St. George and the Irish dragon, Puss in Boots, and so on. It is the "Grand Procession of Nursery Stories" (slightly altered) from impresario Augustus Harris's *Cinderella,* which played at the Drury Lane in 1883, with echoes of the fairyland procession from Planché's *Riquet with the Tuft* (1836). Sometimes it seemed as if the stage productions drew upon the cartoons. The Britannia Theatre's 1855 pantomime *Egypt! 3000 Years Ago: A Dream at the Crystal Palace* seems influenced by Tenniel's double spread of the previous year, "A Reverie at the Crystal Palace"; and a Harris procession of beauties from twenty-four nations recalled Tenniel's almanac cut for 1875.[17]

The Cartoon Mimetic

Fashion being generally fair game for satire, it is not surprising that Tenniel mimicked artistic fashions, that is, when he was not using them associatively. Comic pastiches of Flaxman and Hokusai appeared in the fifties and sixties, and in a more serious vein, triumphal progresses of queen, statesmen, and events, with conch-blowing mermen, river gods, sirens, and dancing maenads à la Raphael, Rubens, and Poussin run through his work. Sculpture came in for its share of mimicry. The man-headed *Assyrian Bull* from the British Museum bore the amiable countenance of John Bull in two cartoons, and in another, Matthew Wyatt's *Wellington* looked down anxiously from his plinth.[18]

But it was paintings of modern life that found most correspondence to his cartoons: the crowded scenes at the derby, the seashore, or the London streets, which may in turn have been inspired by the pictures in the magazines. Such scenes were, of course, most prevalent in social cuts, and when Frith first exhibited his modern-life painting *Ramsgate Sands* in 1854, *Punch* hailed him as a "brother illustrator of the life about us," urging "Shake hands MR. *FRITH*. Allow me to introduce you to MR. JOHN LEECH."[19] In the cartoons the street performer, the jockey, the holiday maker was most often a statesman, Mr. Punch, or the British Lion.

Tenniel burlesqued some forty paintings, choosing those that showed the most heroic, tragic, or tragicomic moments. The champion of England nails the flag to the mast (Thomas H. Maguire), an old sailor lays his fist by a map of the Arctic—"It might be done and England should do it" (John Everett Millais), the bride slumps in misery on the waning of the honeymoon (George H. Boughton), and Curtius leaps into the gulf (John Martin). Some are altered cunningly. In "1886," Gladstone and his home-rule followers

Fig. 135. Tenniel, "1886," cartoon, *Punch*, 19 June 1886

emulate the retreating Napoleonic staff of Meissonier's *1814* (fig. 135). But the reduced size of the horses, their necks now lowered and stretched forward, effectively vitiates the pathos of the scene, turning tragedy into farce. With General Boulanger in the title role, David's *Napoleon crossing the Saint-Bernard* suffers a sea change, too (fig. 136). The rider's raised hand, which had pointed onward, is now shown with palm fully open, as if seeking to avert the disaster ahead.[20]

The Cartoon Heroic

From his romantic side came Tenniel's early ambition to be a history painter—a desire known to have infected several caricaturists. This urge found expression in his symbolic maidens: Britannia, Hibernia, Columbia, and other look-alikes who personified states, cities, and such abstractions as Liberty, Peace, and Justice. These incarnations, which

Fig. 136. Tenniel, "Mr. Boulanger as 'General Buonaparte,'" cartoon, *Punch*, 9 Feb. 1889

account for much of the "statuesque conventionalism" that critics found in his cartoons, were loosely based on London's neoclassical monuments. In one cartoon, looking as if she herself had just stepped down from a Flaxman relief in St. Paul's, Britannia exhorts Victoria (portrayed as Hermione as a statue in *The Winter's Tale*), "Descend, be stone no more!"[21]

Other figures might derive from ancient sculptures or from those in Tenniel's own time. The avenging Justice of an Indian Mutiny cartoon of 1857 takes the stance of a Kritios "tyrant slayer" (c. 477 BC). Victims of the Lancashire "cotton famine" of the 1860s resemble Antoine Etex's *Cain and His Race Accursed of God* (1832); and in an 1888 cartoon, Europa, taken straight from Patrick MacDowell's group *Europe* from the *Albert Memorial* confronts the warlike Russian Bear.[22]

Heroic animal subjects in the romantic-sublime tradition of Reinagle, Stubbs, Barye, Delacroix, and Gérome were another Tenniel specialty. Since the paper had always to follow the fortunes of the British Lion, the Tiger of India, the imperial eagles of Austria, Russia, and Germany, these were an obvious source of inspiration. Tenniel's "British Lion's Vengeance on the Bengal Tiger" (1857) is an animal-combat picture of this type (fig. 28).[23]

Unlike sculpture, which continued to flourish in the sphere of public art, patriotic painting languished in Britain. The French writer Hippolyte

Taine, on visiting London's museums in the sixties, declared "Heroic paint-ing" to be "rare and poor," and during the International Exhibition of 1862 a writer for *Blackwood's* imagined that an enlightened Frenchman might say of the English pictures, "Where is your salon of 'Tableaux historiques'— where are the great national deeds which your country naturally expects your artists to record?" The same article conveyed a German critic's surprise "on the absence of allegory and mythology" and of "symbolic figures . . . in-cluding, of course, Neptune and Britannia." This criticism arose in England, too. In the opening article of the new *Fine Arts Quarterly Review* in 1863, Tom Taylor, *Punch* staffer and art critic for the *Times,* called for a state agenda for painting, advocating "history largely conceived, stately commemoration of men and events," and in 1875 Ruskin would demand to know "what tri-umphs in the British Constitution and its present achievements" were cel-ebrated in British art. However, as Taylor and Ruskin acknowledged, the British public was not entirely deprived of such grand conceptions, for they were to be found regularly in Tenniel's cartoons where countries clashed and stately goddesses pointed the way. Dealing as they did in allegory, the car-toons approached the more symbolic paintings of Couture, Delacroix, Meis-sonier, and the English painter Edward Armitage—works that in turn tended to resemble cartoons.[24]

The high-art connection was made by many. Reviewers spoke of "the fa-mous designer," the "great art draftsman of *Punch.*" The writer Charles Kings-ley asserted to editor Shirley Brooks that had *Punch* not "seduced that great genius [Tenniel] from the severe battle of 'high art,' England would have had her Kaulbach, as well as Germany"; and Ruskin attributed to Tenniel "the largeness and symbolic mystery of imagination" of the great leaders of classic art. Art writer Joseph Grego spoke of his "refined and classic ren-derings," and M. H. Spielmann wrote, "High art was his aim, and high art he has maintained ever since in his cartoons." Sensing this, the *Punch* men took pride in seeing their ideas translated into the majesty, the occasional horrificness of Tenniel's grander designs, and readers might congratulate themselves that their feelings of national pride, national indomitability, or righteous indignation were confirmed weekly in the pages of *Punch* by no ordinary cartoonist, but by "that 'great master' Tenniel."[25]

Punch Jingo

A number of Tenniel's cartoons were intended to drum up martial sen-timent. At the time of the Crimean War, those cartoons not designed to ridicule the advocates of peace and the hesitant premier resembled military paintings of the period with their groupings of shoulder-gripping, standard-crossing, canteen-raising Englishmen, Frenchmen, and Zouaves.[26]

Crimea, the volunteer movement, and the colonial wars of the century prompted about fifty patriotic title pages and cartoons, mainly depicting

PUNCH

VOL 119

LONDON:
PUBLISHED AT THE OFFICE, 10, BOUVERIE STREET,
AND SOLD BY ALL BOOKSELLERS.
1900.

Fig. 137. Tenniel, title page, *Punch* vol. 119, July–Dec. 1900

troops—in review, departing for battle, or returning covered in glory. About
one third show the feisty puppet Mr. Punch—by turns recruiting sergeant,
colonel, commander, field marshal—offering his shoulder as a rifle rest for
the queen, inspecting volunteers and regulars, carrying the flag, riding at the
head of columns of troops, and welcoming the returning victors (fig. 137).
Occasionally *Punch* got it wrong. While Britain was experiencing troop shortages in 1899, Tenniel showed the Boer premier staring aghast at an endless column of fighting men; another cartoon reported English defeats as advances.[27]

Punch consistently promoted a strong navy. In 1860 a Tenniel cartoon supported Lord Lyndhurst's effort to boost naval defenses, and in 1889 another applauded Lord Salisbury's efforts in the same direction.[28] Among twelve cartoons of the nineties that urged increased military preparedness, nine specifically targeted the fleet.

The paper invariably threw its support behind England's martial enterprises, its images sometimes taken up by the general public. During the Crimean War, a Leech drawing of a British guard standing back to back with his French counterpart was "reproduced broadcast in many articles of use"; and Tenniel's Indian Mutiny cut "The British Lion's Vengeance" was duplicated almost overnight on banners calling for revenge. In 1882, as a *Punch* supplement of 1900 would boast, Tenniel's "Short Service and Quick Returns" had enabled Mr. Punch to lend "his influence toward ensuring a rousing welcome to the battle-scarred soldiers of the Egyptian campaign." Following the Jameson raid in late 1895, *Punch* again rose to the occasion and, "Owing to the exceptional political circumstances of the time," allowed the Palace Theatre to reproduce Tenniel's "Ready!" as a tableau.[29]

When, in 1900, the City of London officially welcomed its volunteers back from the Transvaal, *Punch* wrote to an applicant who had solicited the use of Tenniel's cartoon "Reporting Himself" (the personified city of London extending a hero's wreath to the City Imperial Guards), "You are probably unaware that we are distributing today to every member of the Volunteer Force an Indian Proof of the Cartoon," and requested that no other copies be "largely circulated." This suggests that the paper had an almost official status.[30]

Fig. 138. Tenniel, "How a Foolish Bird Did Try to Swim across ye British Channel!" small cut, *Punch*, 26 Nov. 1859, 216

The Players

Persons in Real Life and Their Roles

Foremost among Tenniel's cast were actual persons. He was exacting about his likenesses, generally limiting them to those whose faces were known to the public. Thus, during the Eastern crisis of the seventies when *Punch*'s rivals ran cartoons picturing the little-known Russian ambassador, Ignatyev, and the chancellor, Gorchakov, Tenniel adhered to the more familiar image of the czar when not using such symbolic figures as the Russian Bear, Bruin, and the Cossack he had devised during the Crimean War.

However, when the cartoon subject did call for a minor individual to be shown—say, the Prince Imperial of France—Tenniel's was a true portrait-caricature and not a generic type such as appeared in a *Tomahawk* cartoon of the same period. When needed, photographs were

Fig. 139. Tenniel, "What's His Next 'Cry'?" cartoon, *Punch,* 22 Aug. 1885

obtained to acquaint the artist with the subject's features, and Tenniel is recorded to have vehemently protested against being asked to draw a face from description alone.[31]

Perhaps the cleverest of Tenniel's likenesses were his animal caricatures of statesmen. By some trick a half-drowned eagle in the Channel's surf is also Louis Napoleon, and a seemingly valid parrot on its perch is an unmistakable portrait of William Gladstone (fig. 138 and fig. 139).[32]

Attributes might be used to hasten the recognition of statesmen. From Leech, Tenniel adopted the device of showing "Palmerston with the straw he never chewed, Bright with the eye-glass he never wore." Although he informed Spielmann that John Bright had "a weak nose—artistically speaking, no nose at all," in the sixties he had become sufficiently adept at that statesman's features to dispense with the monocle altogether.[33]

Role-playing figures in over half the cartoons. For example, in 116 drawings statesmen are children, in 58 they are women, in 65 they play roles from classical literature, and in 180 or more they play stage parts (see "The Cartoon Theatrical" above). Sporting subjects were popular, with 58 cartoons on racing alone. In derby cartoons statesmen are jockeys, thimble riggers, welshers on bets, drummers, acrobats, blackface minstrels, and gypsy queens. London's streets provided another source, with cabinet ministers as crossing sweepers, navvies, porters, tinkers, newsboys, cats' and dogs' meat sellers, hare- and rabbit-skin sellers, and scrievers (pavement artists).

The casting of public men in a variety of roles was, of course, not new. In James Gillray's prints of the Georgian period an obsessively villainous Charles James Fox was a cook offering William Pitt's roasted head to a French general, an executioner removing the head of George III, and a devil. By the 1830s a lighter treatment had surfaced in Robert Seymour's cuts for *Figaro in London* and in John Doyle's prints. With the early *Punch* artists, satire gradually moved toward the light humor of Tenniel's cartoons where politicians seem as elastic as the acrobats they so often portray. How easily they slip from one role into another. It is like a script by W. S. Gilbert: Ralph becomes the captain and the captain Ralph, pirates change to peers, peers to peris, and the wicked baronet reforms and runs a national school.

Cartoon roles might parallel current stage offerings, particularly burlesques. Tenniel's "Rival Actors" of 1868 in which Gladstone, an actor playing William Tell, gives promise of besting Disraeli's Jeremy Diddler in the general election, closely followed two productions of *William Tell:* a straightforward version and H. J. Byron's *William Tell with a Vengeance! or, the Pet, the Parrott [sic] and the Pippin.* And his "Political Parallel" of the next month, with Disraeli starring as Richard III, was immediately preceded by Burnand's *Rise and Fall of Richard III; or, A New Front to an Old Dicky.* In October 1886 Tenniel's depiction of Randolph Churchill as "The Political Jack Sheppard" followed the production of *Little Jack Sheppard* at the Gaiety Theatre; and a November cartoon, with Churchill as "Little Mephistopheles," came on the heels of the Royalty Theatre's burlesque *Mephisto* and Burnand's *Faust and Loose; or, Brocken Vows* at Toole's Theatre.[34]

The Tricksters

Tenniel liked to depict public figures as tricksters, especially Disraeli and Gladstone. Disraeli, often seen as devious by his contemporaries, shows up in over sixty different roles, most stressing his artfulness: conjurer, tout, sphinx, acrobat, fakir, "Asiatic mystery," gypsy, and wizard. Earlier cast as a fury with snaky hair, by 1868 (the time of his first ministry) Disraeli had become a comic hero in the *Punch* cartoons, gaining his ends with smiling ease and excelling, as had been said of the statesman himself, as "impresario" and "actor manager."[35]

The foil for the mercurial Dizzy was straight-man Gladstone. Tenniel's "Two Augurs" shows them at the start of the 1873 parliamentary session—Gladstone, "stiff and proud" as always, and Disraeli snickering behind his hand, "I always wonder, Brother, how we Chief Augurs can meet on the opening day without laughing" (fig. 140).[36]

Tenniel's cartoons had been critical of Gladstone's first ministry (1868–74), charging it with too passive a stance regarding the abrogation of the Black Sea Clauses, the Alabama claims arbitration, Irish insurgency, strikes, and more. The premier was "The In-'Judicious Bottle-Holder,'" Mrs.

Britannia's unsatisfactory butler, and a too frequent server of humble pie to John Bull. In one 1874 cartoon that seems almost prescient of the Eastern crisis that would erupt in the following year, he stiffly promises theater manager Punch that the coming season will have "something of a very serious and sensational character." Meanwhile, rival dramatist Dizzy characteristically hints at a burlesque. Through the seventies the Gladstone image was as unprepossessing as ever. See, for example, Tenniel's "Colossus of Words," a cartoon commenting on Gladstone's famed verbosity (evidenced during his Midlothian campaign of 1879, in which he was estimated to have spoken 85,840 words).[37]

It was not until early 1883, two years after Disraeli's death, that a new Gladstone emerged in Tenniel's

Fig. 140. Tenniel, "The Two Augurs," cartoon, *Punch*, 8 Feb. 1873

cartoons. Slyly, he shares a joke with Mr. Punch over "a small dose of clôture." With jaunty step the reinvigorated old statesman joins the Liberal oarsmen and, as owner of the parliamentary coconut shy, urges the house members to "Fire Away!!!"[38]

He changes parts frequently; in early 1885, a knight in armor, he makes a fiery speech regarding the Afghan border dispute (fig. 141). The next week, a quick-change artist (his discarded armor lying on the floor), he impersonates the angel of peace (fig. 142).[39] He grants asides to the reader and, enjoying himself, is no longer dull.

But while the vacated post of entertainer-trickster has fallen to Gladstone, this is not the insouciant Dizzy. More accurately, he is the "old, wild and incomprehensible man" of the queen's description, or to cite his colleague Henry Labouchère, he is the leader "whose intelligence seemed to be now limited to a sort of low cunning." As the "Parliamentary 'Ancient Mariner'" with "glittering eye" and "skinny hand," he plucks at the sleeve of the "Session's Business." Proffering a "Franchise" jumping jack, or playing card tricks as the "downy one of Downing Street," he attempts to divert the country's attention from his Egyptian policy. Often he is an old woman sore beset: the "Political 'Mrs. Gummidge,'" the old dame who cannot get her (home-rule) pig over the stile, and Mrs. Nickleby wincing at catcalls. A music-hall

Fig. 141. *(Left)* Tenniel, "The Broken Covenant," cartoon, *Punch,* 9 May 1885
Fig. 142. *(Right)* Tenniel, "Our Protean Premier!" cartoon, *Punch,* 16 May 1885

favorite, he announces his frequent returns to power with "Hope I Don't
Intrude!!!" and "Retire!—What do *You* Think?" Or he is Clown with his home-
rule poker—"Here We Are Again!!!"[40]

But this is not to discount the cartoons that grant a certain nobility to
the aging statesman as he fearlessly and single-mindedly pursues his doomed
goal of Irish home rule. He is a seaman, lifeline in hand, ready to "Sink or
Swim!!" with the yawing ship Hibernia; Pilgrim treading the narrow home-
rule ridge through treacherous sloughs; and the aged knight taking his "For-
lorn Hope" up the unscalable heights of the House of Lords.[41]

The National Players, Persons in Unreal Life, and Other Contrivances

Countries were represented by two or more symbolic figures roughly
equivalent to Britain's John Bull, Britannia, and the British Lion. Enduring
and unchanging, they inspired confidence. Knowing this, Tenniel resisted
his editor's request for a modernized John Bull; Bull's old-fashioned breeches
and top boots are still the conventional dress.[42] To personifications already
in place he added, among others, the myopic Prussian burgher with a meer-
schaum between his drooping mustaches, Madame La République in apron
and sabots, a pudgy Turk, the contending American twins—North and South,
and the Russian Cossack. He produced witty variants for the British symbols: a young Johnny Bull and a plump and homely Mrs. Britannia, her helmet and trident modified to bonnet and umbrella.

Nations were often pictured as wayward children or, in the holiday season when satire gave way to geniality, simply as happy children as in Tenniel's New Year's cut for 1882 (fig. 143).[43] Who can tell from this blithe scene that jolly Africa is troubled by fresh tribal revolts, that the little Turk represents a continual source of territorial conflict, or that pert Miss France behind him has caused some alarm with her recent entry into Tunisia?

Tasteless intimacies between real and imaginary persons were avoided. While personifications might freely mingle with one another (for example, one cartoon showed Britannia snuggled in Neptune's lap), when Punch hobnobs with statesmen, or when Britannia, Bull, or the British Lion converse with them, there are no tender looks or meaningful claspings as appeared in other papers.[44] At most, Britannia might take a minister's arm in ceremonial manner.

Tenniel's best-loved creations were his animals. Always a keen observer at circus and zoo, Tenniel had gained his place on *Punch* owing to his 1848 *Aesop*—appropriately enough, since most cartoons are in themselves fables.[45] Before Tenniel, only one *Punch* cartoon—Doyle's "Modern Orpheus" of 1849—had exploited any of the national beasts, outside of stuffed-toy versions of the British Lion. Tenniel revamped the lion and gradually incorpo-

Fig. 143. Tenniel, "The Latest Arrival," cartoon, *Punch*, 7 Jan. 1882

rated the others, employing the full menagerie by the time of the Eastern crisis in the seventies.

Over the years Tenniel's lion would appear in many aspects. However, as a writer for the *Daily News* observed, "He could show the British Lion in preposterous check trousers and white waistcoat and there would be dig-

Fig. 144. Tenniel, "Disinterested Advisers," cartoon, *Punch*, 20 Nov. 1875

Fig. 145. Tenniel, "The Easter Egg!: What's to Come Out of It?" cartoon, *Punch*, 27 Apr. 1878

nity in it." He would never have shown the national symbol, as was done in the 1876 *Judy*, licking the boot of the Prince of Wales.[46]

He sometimes drew animal-human blends. These are artfully wrought and without the aberrant quality of J. J. Grandville's composites with which Tenniel's animals have been wrongly compared. But it is the wholly animal creations that most delight us: Bruin slavering as he stalks the justly nervous Turkey, or the Russian imperial Eagle, its two heads glumly watchful as it tries to hatch an immense egg—the Treaty of San Stefano (fig. 144 and fig. 145). Here, and in his legendary beasts too, Tenniel insisted on anatomical validity. At *Punch*'s table in 1867 he privately condemned the newly installed Trafalgar Square lions for their disproportionally large hindquarters, and in his cartoon portraying them he cleverly used overlapping and foreshortening to conceal Landseer's error.[47]

All types were amiably portrayed. For example, the roly-poly Bruin, typically pictured in a cartoon of 1877, might be sly, foolish, greedy, but he was never irredeemable (fig. 146). This light treatment gave *Punch* maneuverability between different sides of international questions. By contrast, William Boucher's ably drawn Russian Bear, in a *Judy* issue of the same period, is essentially a predator (fig. 147).[48]

Fig. 146. Tenniel, "What Next?" cartoon, *Punch*, 17 Feb. 1877 (detail)

To round out Tenniel's cast there were easily read stock types from stage and fiction. Blacks derived from minstrel shows. Snapping their fingers, they joked and shuffled their way through Tenniel's Civil War cartoons. Stage Irishmen, stage Jews, and the stage rustic Hodge were *Punch* regulars. Facile with stereotypes, sometimes Tenniel combined them; a pope's tiara resembles the three hats of the stereotypical Jewish old-clothes peddler, and an Irish Paddy performs as a minstrel in blackface.[49]

His ready-made company Tenniel filled out with such inventions as the Duke of Mudford, who presided over "Mud-Salad [Covent Garden] Market"; Sir Giles Overreach, the landowning peer—also appearing as "the Earl of Whatsitsname" and "the Baron" (another stage type); Mr. Bung the publican; Sarah Suffrage; and Bumble the Beadle. These, too, were portrayed amicably. Tenniel's Bumble, taken from *Oliver Twist*, is the epitome of bumbledom with his staff of office, protruding belly, and broad

Fig. 147. William Boucher, "Imperial Neighbors," cartoon, *Judy*, 29 Mar. 1876 (detail)

stupid face (fig. 148). More bumbling than base, more comic than sinister, Tenniel's caricature stands in contrast to Keene's mean-faced beadle in a cartoon of 1866 (fig. 149).[50]

Lastly, humanized constructions were devised to fill special needs. Threatening spigot-headed hydras propelled their water-tank bodies with webbed claws, parliamentary bills and torpedoes sprouted little human limbs, and men bore clock and ballot box heads.[51]

The Readers

Schoolmaster Punch

It was said that *Punch* was not only read, it was studied. As the emphasis was on a classical education, modern history was not taught in the schools, and *Punch* was often a youngster's sole window to world affairs. Furthermore, in "nice" homes, newspapers were forbidden to children and, often, to

Fig. 148. Tenniel, "Move On, Bumble!" cartoon, *Punch*, 19 Jan. 1867

"young persons." Dickens's Mr. Podsnap, whose criterion on many matters was "Would it bring a blush into the cheek of the young person?" had his counterparts in the real world.[52]

Fig. 149. Charles Keene, "The Unrecognised Visitor," cartoon, *Punch,* 21 July 1866

Punch, however, was approved reading for all and might be read aloud on family evenings or be available in bound volumes on the family's bookshelves. Additional volumes, put out at regular intervals by the paper's proprietors, had cartoons only. Thackeray had estimated the number of schoolboys who read *Punch* to be in the "many scores of thousands," and the testimony of others seems to bear him out. Judge Edward Parry recalled that on Sundays he and his brothers were summoned to "a careful examination on our weekly study of the pages of *Punch,* which my father held rightly to be the earliest nursery textbook of history and sociology for the English child"; the historian Cecil Torr urged his sons to "cull wisdom from Mr. Punch's pages"; Burnand, when a schoolboy, found in the issues of *Punch,* sent him by his father, his only source of news on the Crimean War; and *Punch* writer R. C. Lehmann had been "brought up" on the paper, learning history from Tenniel's cartoons. One reads of the daughters of Martin Tupper busily pasting into their scrapbooks "Tenniel's cartoons and anything else they could get hold of about Garibaldi," and of the little son of Edward Corbould (tutor in art to the royal family) borrowing threepence from Princess Alice for the new number of *Punch* he had spotted in a stationer's window. Years later, Winston Churchill would comment that "the responsibility of Sir John Tenniel and other famous cartoonists must be very great. Many is the youthful eye that has rested upon their designs and many is the lifelong impression formed thereby." His own introduction to *Punch* had been at school in Brighton, where on Sundays he was "allowed to study" three or four volumes of reprinted cartoons—"a very good way of learning history, or at any rate of learning something."[53]

On Tenniel's death the *Times* considered his drawings "if not the principal, at any rate the most attractive text-book of modern history known to many of the younger generation," and the *North American Review* said, "From its [*Punch*'s] pages juvenile patriots glean the history of latter-day England, much as Marlborough confessed that he owed what little knowledge of the past he had to Shakespeare."[54] Mr. Punch had no reservations about proclaiming himself the schoolmaster of the nation. Tenniel's title page for late 1870 showed the beaming puppet in cap and gown, distributing his fifty-ninth volume to a cluster of young readers.

The Mythmaking Cartoon

Before news photographs, illustrations in the magazines substituted for reality. Some reified them. Winston Churchill recalled that as a schoolboy he thought of Gladstone as an idealized Caesar and France as a beautiful woman, "terrific in distress"; and writer Max Beerbohm, when a child, had imagined that politicians wore breastplates and brandished swords. Recognizing this tendency, the art historian Ernst Gombrich would question whether all who applauded Tenniel's "British Lion's Vengeance on the Bengal Tiger" were "quite clear in their minds that all that had real existence were Indians—some mutinous, some not—and Englishmen—some revengeful, some not."[55] Tenniel's imagery, authenticated by his consistent style, infiltrated the unconscious thinking of all age groups.

His successors lacked this facility. Sambourne's figures played their roles languidly, and Partridge's stage-lit personifications were like elaborately got-up actors rather than Justice, Peace, or Father Thames incarnate. In time, Mr. Punch himself had seemed a living presence; his sportiveness, impatience, keen conviction of right and wrong, were Tenniel's own. When Tenniel retired, so did Punch, for the Quilpish real-life dwarf drawn by Tenniel's successors was not the vital puppet who had romped through the paper's pages for fifty years. His cartoon role dwindled, and he disappeared entirely from *Punch*'s titles.[56]

Contemporaries recognized in Tenniel's cartoons a "stern and upright" purpose, an intention that was "clear and distinct." Their "moral teaching" was "beyond measure"; they constituted a "school for statesmen" of "morals, manners, discipline, politics, and principles." Few doubted that these purposes and qualities originated in Tenniel himself. An American writer said, "The secret of the power of his cartoons" had "always lain in their inherent truthfulness," and on Tenniel's death the *Athenaeum* spoke of his childlike mind, "uniquely occupied in saying what he had to say as clearly as possible, without any display of cleverness." Finally, to Burnand, Tenniel's hand was "ever the servant of his head and heart. What he most deeply felt he most strongly drew."[57]

After Tenniel's death, some writers on satire would dismiss his work as well-bred and approbatory—a verdict that would have come as a surprise to mutinous sepoys, Northerners in the American Civil War, Fenians and Land Leaguers, trade unionists, suffragists, pacifists, socialists, and republicans. More accurately, the cartoons had resilience. Moving from stern censure to the lightest humor, they lent *Punch* an air of impartiality.

Tenniel's cartoons were a national institution, constituting (for *Punch*'s mainly middle-class readers) a history school for the young, a guide for their elders, and a source of patriotic imagery. Artfully staged, with an instantly recognizable company of statesmen, stock types, and symbolic figures; sweeping in scope; bouncing easily from burlesque to lofty dignity and back again, they were deservedly "the pride of Mr. Punch"[58] and the delight of his loyal public.

19

As for Political Opinions

As for political opinions, I have none; at least,
if I have my own little politics, I keep them to myself
and profess only those of my paper.
—TENNIEL, in an interview with M. H. Spielmann, 1889

A "Non-Partisan Partisanship"

Tenniel's sole verbal statement on his political sympathies was a non-declaration, serving only to obfuscate the orientation of both himself and his paper. Did *Punch* have a party alignment, as did the Liberal comic paper *Fun* or the Conservative *Judy,* or even a consistent political leaning over time? And is it credible that Tenniel, the foremost political cartoonist of his time, would have been as malleable as he purported to be?

Were *Punch* merely a frivolous journal, like several of the time, these questions would have small significance. But *Punch* was unique, some considering that the designation "comic paper" obscured its true role. One journalist called it "the most serious comic paper in the world"; another described it as a "picture newsbook." None doubted its influence. It was "a power in the state," one prominent statesman declaring it to be "the most dangerous antagonist that a politician can have opposed to him." Cabinet ministers and field marshals alike were known to court the favor of the "chartered libertine."[1]

Politically, *Punch* was believed to take its cue from the *Times,* a paper claiming to be the "embodiment of public opinion." Some linked *Punch* with the Liberals; John Ruskin identified Mr. Punch as a "polite Whig." Spielmann concurred, but his portrayal of a staff balanced between Radicals and Tories hardly bears this out. Like the *Times,* which has been described as having a "non-partisan partisanship," *Punch* claimed to have no political preferences, having boldly declared in its opening number in 1841, "Party must destroy patriotism." While its early volumes poured scorn on the Tory papers the *Morning Post, Morning Herald,* and *Standard* and on the ultra-Tory MP Colonel Sibthorpe, *Punch* often took the Conservative side on issues. One is not surprised, then, that Furniss at the end of the century estimated two-thirds of its readers to be Conservatives.[2] Furthermore, the number of instances when important statesmen changed to the other side of the house, or conservative Liberals sided with the Tories, shows that party differences in this period were not particularly deep. It is indicative of the laissez-faire policy of *Punch* that although proprietor William Agnew was a Liberal MP and a Gladstonian, the paper consistently opposed Gladstone's Irish home-rule bills.

Punch's first editors carefully avoided any taint of partisanship. When in 1867 Shirley Brooks's services were strongly solicited by the *Globe* (a former Whig paper newly purchased for the Conservative side), Lemon warned that Shirley's connection with Toryism might injure *Punch*. The paper's fourth editor, Burnand, described as being "neutral with a bias" by his next in command, Arthur à Beckett (himself a Tory), judiciously claimed to have no political preferences.[3] In view of this, it would be naive to expect that the paper's chief cartoonist would admit to any political bias whatever.

Its putative nonpartisanship permitted *Punch* to gain the support of both parties. The pension awarded to the Whiggish Leech by the Liberals was secured for his family by the Conservative leader Disraeli after Leech's death in 1864, and on Lemon's death in 1870 the Liberal Gladstone awarded a pension to the editor's family. Tenniel's knighthood, originally to have been given by the Salisbury government, was instead awarded by Gladstone as the Conservatives had meanwhile left office.[4] And the organizing committee and attendees for the public dinner honoring Tenniel on his retirement included statesmen and adherents from both sides of the political aisle.

A Staff Divided

Punch's cartoon-by-committee system might draw input from staffers ranging from the radical Tom Taylor to such "hot" Tories as Keene. With the acquisition of the Tory Brooks in 1852, most of Tenniel's cartoon suggestions emanated from him, with Taylor as the next most vocal contributor. But whether the initial proposal came from them or, by 1877, from E. J. Milliken, it was usually "knocked about" and modified by the other staffers.[5] For example, Shirley recorded on 13 February 1867: "A good fight over the cut. T. T. [Tom Taylor] very persistent, but I defeated him and carried mine." A few months later he wrote, "8 May—Combative and Toryish, and I opposed a cut until I got it altered to hit both ways."

Except for du Maurier, who refrained from interjecting his "dilettante Radicalism" into cartoon discussions, the artistic staff was solidly Conservative. Tenniel and Keene were Tories. Sambourne was, in the eighties, a Unionist and no admirer of Gladstone. An obituary identified him as "a Tory of the old school" who had "no hesitation in his politics."[6]

Cartoonists might reject unsympathetic subjects. On 22 February 1860 Silver recorded, "S. B. [Shirley Brooks] Savage . . . at Diz being left out—

J. L. [John Leech] won't do him." Nine years later, Shirley was again foiled by an artist and wrote, "Tenniel found that he could not do my cut and did a 'happy new year' one instead. I think these things twaddle, and that *Punch* should be more incisive." Again, as editor in 1872, Brooks wrote, "Got a cut and thinking of another form of it, when I came home, sent that off to J. T. [Tenniel]. But he stuck to the other."[7]

On Tenniel's latitude in determining his cartoon subjects, staff writer R. C. Lehmann recalled "more than a few occasions when he broke in upon our deadlock with a new and happy suggestion of his own which was eventually adopted *nem. con.* Very often, too, when we thought we had reached the term of our labours and referred the suggested picture to him, he crushed it with the one word 'impossible,' very scornfully delivered. From this judgment there was rarely an appeal." The recollections of Burnand, Tenniel's colleague of thirty-seven years, confirm this: "At 'the Board,' Tenniel's known reluctance to urge his own personal view of a disputable point, and his reasonableness in yielding whenever no question of principle seemed to him to be involved, induced his fellow-councilors around the table to modify the sometimes intemperate expression of their individual opinions on the subject in question, so that, as the result of mutual concession, the council was enabled to arrive at a satisfactory decision. On the other hand, when once convinced of what was the only right course to be pursued, John Tenniel might, indeed, listen to, but he would not favourably entertain, a suggestion of compromise."[8]

Staff writer Henry Lucy recalled how "when the picture came out those who had contributed suggestions to its form perceived how by some subtle touch of humour or fancy Tenniel had improved upon them."[9] Might such touches alter the message of a cartoon? This could be explored by comparing his drawings with the paper's texts at some period when an issue might pit Conservative and Liberal staff members against one another.

In searching for the key divisions of the period, the Crimean War will not serve our purpose as it brought the anti-war radicals into opposition with Liberals as well as with Conservatives. Both Tories and conservative Liberals shifted their sympathies to the South during the American Civil War. Gladstone's bill to disestablish the Anglican Church in Ireland and thus placate revolutionary elements in that country did divide the parties, but *Punch* seemed united. The paper's support of the Liberal's bill was conveyed in Shirley's "Essence of Parliament," which expressed "Mr. Punch's conviction upon the propriety and expediency of removing the Irish Church," and in some sixteen of Tenniel's cartoons. However, we do have Tenniel's wry comment on passage of the bill in his "Disendowment and Disarmament," in which a Fenian (a nationalist insurgent) and a priest study a poster announcing the division in the Commons—the Fenian saying "Be jabers, y're riv'rence, its spilin' our thrade they are, intoirely," and the priest retort-

Fig. 150. Tenniel, "Disendowment and Disarmament,"
cartoon, *Punch,* 3 Apr. 1869

ing, "thrue for you, me boy (fig. 150)."[10] We see here one of Tenniel's subtle touches, for the priest holds his umbrella in the same manner as the
Fenian his rifle.

The next decade saw a series of events that, more than any other, brought
out the philosophic differences between the party leaders Gladstone and Disraeli, despite some intraparty divisions. The crisis would endure for three
years and inspire about ninety Tenniel cartoons.

The Eastern Question

Tom Taylor Speaks His Mind

To briefly summarize its complex history, the "Eastern Question" of
1875–78 began with a rebellion of various Slavic peoples against their re-
pression in Turkey's Eastern provinces. At the end of 1875 the Disraeli government joined Austria, Russia, and Germany in demanding Turkish reforms
but declined to join with these powers in a second protest (Turkey not having complied with the first) early in the next year. Soon after, a large British

fleet was sent to Besika Bay near the Dardanelles as a precaution against developments contrary to British interests.

After reports by June of 1876 of Turkish massacres of the Slavic peoples, Britons were torn between revulsion toward the "Unspeakable Turk" and their own mistrust of the "Russian Bogey," fearing that Russia's support of the Christian populations in Turkish-dominated lands might furnish an excuse for its more active involvement in the region. When in April 1877 the Serbo-Turkish War was succeeded by the Russo-Turkish War, the country divided between "Turks," who supported Disraeli's Conservative government and regarded Turkey as a buffer against Russian ambitions in the East, and "Muscos," who followed Gladstone's lead and thought issues of right and wrong should override England's imperial interests. With the war turning in Russia's favor late in that year there was talk of England entering the conflict. From this period comes the music-hall song "The Dogs of War":

> We don't want to fight, but by Jingo if we do
> We've got the ships, we've got the men, and got the money too.
> We've fought the Bear before, and while we're Britons true,
> The Russians shall not have Constantinople.

It was not until July of 1878 that the crisis was finally resolved, a triumphant Disraeli returning from the Congress of Berlin with the announcement that he had achieved "Peace with honour!"[11]

As luck would have it, Disraeli's second premiership, when these events transpired, coincided closely with the *Punch* editorship of the "Radical, anti-Beaconsfield [anti-Disraeli], anti-Imperialist" Tom Taylor. Taylor was inclined to be heavy-handed in his statements; Burnand once said that his arguments were of the "sledge-hammer order."[12]

Where *Punch* may have previously "set its watch by the clock of the *Times*," that paper now steered a wavering course. After equivocating over the government's early handling of the Balkan situation, the *Times* settled on a position of qualified support for Disraeli's policy of watchful neutrality. Conversely, Taylor, at first uncertain, hardened into a position of unqualified mistrust of the premier. In the early summer of 1876, after the reports of massacres in Bulgaria were first made known, Taylor's "Essence of Parliament " remained Russophobic. "The Dogs of War," he wrote (referring to Tenniel's cartoon of the previous week, which had shown the Russian emperor holding the Balkan dogs in leash), "have been checked." Before news of Serbia's declaration of war against Turkey arrived, another "Essence" expressed satisfaction that the British fleet had been sent to Besika Bay, "should the worst come to *the worst* and the Servian [Serbian] dogs of war slip their couples, or drag their Ruski *piqueur* after them, collars and all."[13] But later that July, after Disraeli had dismissed reports of the Turks employing torture with the seemingly flippant observation that Oriental people "generally terminate their connexion with culprits in a more expeditious manner," and after the premier brushed off pertinent dispatches as "coffee-house babble," Taylor's mistrust shifted to the Conservative government.

By late summer of 1876 the government's skepticism toward dismal reports from the East and its inaction in the matter had sparked protest meetings throughout the country. Gladstone's pamphlet of 6 September, "The Bulgarian Horrors and the Question of the East," would bring him to the forefront of the "atrocity agitation." With the spirit of this movement Taylor was already sympathetic. He charged the British ambassador at Constantinople with painting events with "official milk-and-water colours" and the Commons with agreeing to do nothing "in this most do-nothing of all do-nothing worlds." His next to last "Essence" of that parliamentary session said, "Let *Punch* speak his mind in this matter. . . . if anything will fire JOHN BULL'S blood to feverheat, it is such horrors as have been perpetrated in Bulgaria—and part of his wrath will assuredly be visited on those who have striven to interpose official blinds and buffers between England and the sight or shock of these horrors." Aside from the final "Essence" for the session, which made its concessionary bow to Disraeli's elevation to the House of Lords, Taylor's coverage would continue to criticize the government. Elsewhere in *Punch* a poem protested the government's "chilling power of cool official phrases." Another spoke out, "Can't quite see it, BEN," and one in December, taking its analogy from Tenniel's 15 July 1876 cartoon, "The Sphinx Is Silent," declared "'Tis BULL 'gainst BEACONSFIELD—'tis Lion against Sphinx!"[14]

Still, *Punch's* texts that fall were not entirely of a piece. In September one poem warned, "Let not o'ermastering ire against the Turks / Ourselves unwise, in alien toils engage." Another in the next month would caution, "A Statesman must be free to move; / Be careful how you force his hand." In Tenniel's 23 September cartoon (published during the shooting season) Disraeli and his foreign secretary, Lord Derby, walking behind the dogs "Caution" and "Diplomacy," put up their guns at the approach of a dour Gladstone and his followers (fig. 151). The legend reads: "Lord B. 'Confound that fellow! He'll be putting up all our birds!!'" This seems to have foreseen the speech given by Disraeli's chancellor of the exchequer, Sir Stafford Northcote, in Edinburgh on the 16th (with the usual scheduling, Tenniel's cartoon would have been ready for engraving on the 15th) warning that the agitation weakened the government's hand. It also anticipated the *Times*, which in early October began to swing toward the government and to admonish Gladstone as a troublemaker. Despite Taylor's strong words *Punch* seems restrained in this year as seen against the sensational cartoons in the Liberal *Fun* and the Conservative *Judy*, which specialized in barbarous Turks or Serbians (depending on the paper's orientation) and severed heads.[15]

Late in the following year *Punch's* preface made light of the "Russian Bogey," setting the tone for most of the writing in the two succeeding vol-

Fig. 151. Tenniel, "Disturbing the Game," cartoon, *Punch*, 23 Sept. 1876

Fig. 152. Tenniel, "'The Confidence Trick'!" cartoon,
Punch, 9 Feb. 1878

umes. Victoria's assumption of an imperial title was noted with irony, Disraeli being charged with offering her a cheap substitute crown. Taylor's "Essence" saw in "the strong hand of the Muscovite" the only hope of Turkish reform and declared that Gladstone's resolutions censuring the Porte could, in *Punch*'s view, have been made three months earlier. In May, with Russia and Turkey now at war, Taylor declared, "*Punch* has felt a call to be serious" (he had hardly been anything else for the past year). Blaming the war on "the timidity, shilly-shallying, and half-heartedness of our Rulers—of Her Majesty's Opposition, as well as Her Majesty's Government," he was relieved that the government was still pledged to neutrality. But warlike sentiment in the Conservative press increased throughout 1877, and as the year wound down with the Russian taking of Plevna and Turkish negotiations for peace, a *Punch* article, "Regenerate Russia," was anxious to refute the arguments of the Russophobes. Thus *Punch*'s writers entered 1878 generally anti-jingo and leery of the premier's "*coups de théâtre* and acts of recklessness."[16]

With the Russian advance toward Constantinople, in January 1878 Northcote asked for a vote of credit of six million pounds to be applied to military services in case of need. The *Times,* backing this move, said, "Russia is profoundly distrusted, and not without reason. She is profoundly disliked and not without reason also." As the chancellor had indicated that approval would show the country's confidence in the government, Taylor labeled this a "Confidence Trick," as did Tenniel's cartoon of the week (fig. 152), but the "Essence" would eventually applaud its passage, declaring that *Punch* was "an Englishman first and a Liberal after."[17]

In early March, Britain's denunciation of the peace treaty imposed on Turkey by Russia, and its insistence that the terms of the treaty be deliberated by a European congress before approval, led to some amusing cartoons. In *Judy,* William Boucher, noting Taylor's Liberal bias, drew the Russian Bear up a tree, Gladstone's boat capsized, and the corpse of Mr. Punch's dog, Toby, floating belly up. And in a Tenniel cartoon, the Russian Eagle sat broodingly on its disputed "Easter Egg [the treaty]," the legend asking "What's to come out of it?" (see fig. 145).[18]

With the Congress of Berlin, which resulted in an agreement by mid-July, a lighter tone returned to *Punch*'s texts, although the Anglo-Turkish Convention (signed a month earlier) and the consequent cession of Cyprus (which one *Punch* writer dubbed the "Wapping of the Mediterranean") to England were not much praised. And when the first costs resulting from that possession came in, *Punch* (adopting the persona of John Bull) sang, "'Oh, Ben,' I sigh, 'canst tell me why / I'm bled of all this tin?'"[19]

Punchius Imperator

Imperialism was intrinsic to the Eastern Question, as some considered supporting Turkey essential to England's interests in India. Under Taylor's

Fig. 153. Tenniel, "Punchius Imperator A.D. MDCCCLXXVII," almanac cartoon, *Punch*, 1877

editorship, *Punch*'s texts, as one might expect, had pursued an anti-imperialist line. Although John Bull had generally approved Disraeli's 1876 "Suez Coup," Taylor had sided with its critics. Articles in *Punch* had considered the Imperial Titles Act of May 1876 another trick of the "old Hebrew magician" and deplored the subsequent Delhi ceremony (which coincided with an Indian famine). One piece "disclosed" the premier's plans to recolor the Union Jack the gold, white, and black of the imperial powers; a second adopted the voice of Betsy Prig (*Punch*'s personification for the pro-ministry *Daily Telegraph*) to exult, "English Imperial Interests forever! Hurray! who's afeered?"; and a third derided "penny Patriots" who put empire before principle. Later, Betsy's jubilation over the acquisition of Cyprus will be punctured by the Muse of History's "Imperial? Many-sensed word that makes music in many long ears!" and a poem, "The Jingo Englishman," will want to know to "what charter" the Briton owes his "rights" to "annex on sea or shore."[20]

At the same time, looking at Tenniel's titles and almanac cartoons for this period, one might think that the spirit of Shirley Brooks still occupied the editorial chair. Tenniel's title page for the volume of late 1875 marked Disraeli's purchase of Suez shares with a beaming Mr. Punch being garlanded by a bevy of harem beauties. In early 1876 the happy Punch reclines, shoulder pressed against the proud lion, hand resting on the head of the grateful tiger of India. They are fellows to the imperial beasts behind them—the Russian Bear, the Ottoman Turkey, the brooding two-headed eagles of Germany and Austria. Here, and in subsequent titles, Punch adopts the tunic and sandals favored by the great Isaac Van Amburgh, whose lion-taming feats Londoners might have recalled from the late thirties. At the same time the cuirass and laurel crown suggest imperial Rome.[21]

Tenniel's almanac cartoons were unabashedly imperialistic. A triumphal procession of elephants, mounted Eastern princes, musicians, and dancing houris escorts the Prince of Wales on his 1875–76 Indian visit. The following year "Punchius Imperator A.D. MDCCCLXXVII," with close to eighty figures, is a medley of processions (Lord Mayor's, Guy Fawkes, and pantomime) headed by the chariot-driving Emperor Punch, a vainglorious Disraeli, and the glum Liberal contingent (fig. 153). Atop an elephant sits the queen wearing her newly acquired imperial crown and holding Britannia's trident and shield. "Punch's Dream of Things Egyptian" in December 1877 again celebrated Britain's progress abroad.[22]

The Artists Speak

But Taylor's arguments were counteracted by still subtler means in the cartoons, which cleverly followed the letter of the texts while not their spirit. Tenniel contrived this through his portrayal of the two great rivals. Despite Taylor's support, Gladstone clearly comes off second best. As one might expect, being out of office he appears in relatively few cartoons. But when he does, he generally wears a dour expression with mouth turned down. He is the Gladstone of a current music-hall song:

> I'll tell you how to be one day like our beloved Gladstone.
>
> . . . .
>
> Take a dose of bile and 'colic'
> Let your features be symbolic
> Of what's sage and sinister.

Or, as one cartoon critic of the time commented, "He is not amiable."[23]

Disraeli, whom the paper's texts suspect of being unfeeling, unprincipled, a charlatan, and—due to his Semitic background—not an Englishman at all, is clearly the favorite. Although Tenniel makes use of a detractor's epithets—"Great Wizard," "Great Medicine Man," "Asian Mystery" (a term taken from Disraeli's novels), "showman," "acrobat," "conjurer," "trickster," "farceur," "Sphinx"—the premier's image gains, if anything, by it. A song from the generally Conservative halls is again apt:

> "Great Dizzie, our Premier, knows well his book,
> He's as tricky as here and there one.[24]

The very imperturbability that so enflames his foes is Disraeli's chief pictorial asset. With great good nature he perches on a ladder, painting an imperial crown on the "Queen's Head" pub sign (fig. 154); as the augur Dis-

Fig. 154. Tenniel, "The Queen with Two Heads," cartoon, *Punch,* 1 Apr. 1876

raelius he reads the signs of the birds (canards all); or he stands firm in rough seas as "The Man at the Wheel." Calmly he muses as his "awkward-squad" ministers face every which way, "Ah, they always were slow at their facings!" or, watching the London protocol going up in the flames of war, he reminds the exasperated foreign minister, "Ah, my dear Derby, paper *will* burn, you know!!"[25]

Punch's Lucy, a parliamentary observer for some forty years, provides a portrait of the two ministers: "Gladstone, with his untamable energy, his rich verbosity, his susceptibility to religious and moral influences, rather amused Dizzy. When in fine frenzy rolling, whether championing the rights of nationalities or the privilege of minorities, Dizzy, seated on the other side of the table, regarded him through his eyeglass with the air of one studying some strange animal recently imported." Biographer Robert Blake also describes Disraeli's detachment during Gladstone's speeches: "lolling with his legs crossed, his hat tilted forward, and his eyes half closed." This fits the cool Dizzy of Tenniel's cartoons—catnapping on the parliamentary benches, relaxing before the Commons skeet shoot, or resting in a hammock at his estate, Hughenden: "Dizzily, dizzily, leave me to drowse."[26]

We like him all the more for his little frailties: the vainglory with which he wears his coronet, which, being too large for him, sits on his nose; the admiring interest with which he peers through a lorgnette at a sphinx that has his features precisely; his hesitation outside the conference room at Berlin as he whispers to Bismarck, "Bye the Bye! what's the French for compromise?" (a fitting cartoon since Disraeli's French was notoriously poor). But mainly he is the trickster: unctuously offering a humbug crown to Victoria, snickering behind his hand as his chancellor of the exchequer plays the confidence trick on John Bull, or assuring us that the "happy family" act at Berlin has been *"well rehearsed."* As one paper observed in 1879, "on the testimony of these cartoons . . . the English people have from the beginning suspected, liked, and laughed with Lord Beaconsfield; have respected, disliked, and doubted Mr. Gladstone."[27]

Fig. 155. Tenniel, "Woodman, Spare That Tree!" cartoon, *Punch,* 26 May 1877

Consider the 26 May 1877 issue, appearing twelve days after the Commons rejected Gladstone's resolutions condemning the Turkish government by 131 votes. *Punch*'s poem "Woodman, Spare That Tree!" (possibly influenced by John Proctor's cartoon "the Deadly Upas" in *Funny Folks* the previous September) likens the rottenness of Turkish rule to a upas tree "that blasts where'er this trunk its withering shadow casts." Tenniel's cartoon of that title shows William the Woodman (Gladstone) as a heroic figure hacking away at this vile growth from which hangs the "gibbet-fruit" of the verses (fig. 155).[28] But to the side, Disraeli—to whom Gladstone's back-swung axe points like an arrow—captures our attention. With the tips of his fingers joined, head thrust back, the premier, in his robes and oversized coronet, sings,

> Woodman, spare that tree!
> I love it, every bough;
> The Asian mysterie,
> That it has lived till now!

Thus the resourceful Dizzy, in his newly acquired finery, unruffled by Gladstone's ardor and affectedly singing a sentimental ballad, eclipses his stern rival.

Three successive cartoons that comment on the results of the Berlin Conference reveal none of the doubts expressed in related texts. Taking the texts first, the 20 July "Essence" cynically observes, "Dizzy, with Cyprus, and all

Fig. 156. Tenniel, "'Humpty Dumpty'!" cartoon, *Punch*, 20
July 1878

the Queen's men, / Hopes to set Humpty-Dumpty [Turkey] up again." The
next week there appears an equivocal poem, in which John Bull soliloquizes,
"Doubts, thronging and persistent, will break out"; and in a skit of the week
following, an aside from Lord Salisbury (who is executing a pas de deux
with Disraeli) reads, "Methinks a *pas seul* I should rather more relish." But
what occurs in the cartoons? Flanked by hovering doves, the premier and
Miss Cyprus proudly hoist an egg-shaped Turk onto the top of the Asian
wall (fig. 156); in a brilliant display of crackers—a "Blaze of Triumph"—high-
wire artist Dizzy makes his bow; and Disraeli and Salisbury gracefully put
their best (gartered) legs forward in the "Grand Anglo-Turkish ballet."[29]

　　Curiously enough, while Taylor asserted that "the country, *Punch* is glad
to see . . . is with MR. GLADSTONE, not with LORD BEACONSFIELD,"
the cartoons show Mr. Punch on exceedingly companionable terms with
the minister. In fact, he is Disraeli's sidekick. He converses amiably with
trainer Dizzy about his "Dark Horse's" chances; and, as a putto, he hovers
happily over the garlanded premier "on the road to Berlin." Afterward, as

Fig. 157. Tenniel, "Otium cum Diz!" cartoon, *Punch*, 21 Sept. 1878

an old salt, he takes the tiller on their holiday outing; and, as a vacationer in boater and knickers, Punch joins Diz for their well-earned relaxation at Hughenden (fig. 157). That this occurs during Disraeli's premiership cannot be the main factor as the first signs of camaraderie between Mr. Punch and Gladstone will not emerge until the cartoons of the eighties—well into Gladstone's second administration (1880–85).[30]

Sambourne, too, showed Gladstone unfavorably; his "Essence" drawings of the seventies twice portrayed him as a ranting preacher, and in a separately issued cartoon of 1880, he drew him as a jockey on the losing horse "Verbosity." By contrast, for a July 1878 "Essence," he showed Mr. Punch approvingly patting the shoulder of racehorse Beaconsfield, "Winner of the Cyprus Cup." Like Tenniel, Sambourne portrayed Disraeli as a lighthearted trickster. In various "Essence" drawings he bats the shuttlecock of "popularity" to Mr. Punch, he plays a triumphal march on the parliamentary organ for the queen's pleasure while Gladstone sits wincing with ears covered, and he dazzles the British Lion by using a mirror to deflect the sun's rays into its eyes.[31]

How the Readers Saw It

Taylor, of course, could not have been blind to the differences between the paper's texts and its art. Even had he wished to bring them more in line with each other, there was probably little he could do about it. Furthermore, this divergence may have ensured against alienating readers on either side of the question.

None doubted Tenniel's ability to affect public opinion. In 1914 the *Daily Graphic* recalled: "He had an influence on the political feeling of his time which is hardly measurable. . . . While Tenniel was drawing them we always looked to the 'Punch' cartoon to crystallise the national and international situation, and the popular feeling about it—and never looked in vain."[32]

Statesmen followed their likenesses on the cartoon page. Disraeli is reported to have tried to ingratiate himself with Leech, whose pictures of "Dizzy" were hardly flattering. In later years, one politician was heard to lament that he was caricatured in *Punch,* another that he was not, and a third expressed his pleasure on attaining "the highest ambition which a statesman can reach"—a cartoon "all to himself."[33]

Readers assumed that Tenniel's cartoons represented his personal views, although most would probably not have known of *Punch*'s cartoon conferences. More telling perhaps is the testimony of one who knew that it was Tenniel's business "to make a picture of other people's thoughts" as well as his own. This was the prominent American journalist George W. Smalley. Having been party to conversations between Tenniel and their mutual friend James Russell Lowell when Lowell was American minister in London, Smalley considered Tenniel "one of the greatest intellectual forces of his time," declaring: "He had it in him to be statesman as well as artist. He understood social laws and political energies."[34]

Punch was neither consistent over time nor, occasionally, within a single issue. While generally conservative, it followed no party line—a necessary strategy for a paper that courted both sides. Tenniel's translation of staff suggestions might be critical to their meaning. The playfulness, the occasional passion, the interpretation were his own. Appropriately, *Vanity Fair*'s "Spy," who had variously titled his caricatures of the *Punch* artists "Phil" (Phil May), "Trilby" (du Maurier), and "Sammy" (Sambourne), when he came to Tenniel, simply wrote "Punch."[35]

20

King Demos

I ask, if you want venality, ignorance, drunkenness, and the means
of intimidation, if you want impulsive, unreflecting, violent people,
where would you go to look for them—to the top or the bottom?
—ROBERT LOWE, in the House of Commons, 1866

Se join the union while ye may.
Don't wait till your dyin' day,
For that may not be far away,
Ye dorty blackleg miners!
—"The Blackleg Miners"

The Great Unknown

In 1865, as parliamentarians debated the wisdom of opening the franchise to greater numbers in the working classes, *Punch* considered their arguments and confessed, "We have not arrived at the faintest notion of what
the Working-Man is really like. . . . He is the Great Unknown of the present day." The paper and its middle- to upper-class readers would wrestle
with that question for the remainder of the century. Was he the revolutionary, angel, scholar, or simply the sot depicted in Tenniel's accompanying
cartoon? (fig. 158) One thing was certain. Any combinations he might form,
industrial or political, against the ruling classes, had to be speedily quashed.
This imperative lies behind most of Tenniel's working-class cartoons, the
bulk of which divide between two, for the most part, separate concerns: combinations of workmen against the employers and the workingman as a possible political force. Fear of the lower classes, with their unplumbed potential for usurpation of the reins of power, haunted most of the period. As
Walter Bagehot warned in the pre-reform year of 1866, "If you once permit the ignorant class to begin to rule, you may bid farewell to deference
forever."[1]

Over sixty *Punch* cartoons—twice that if we include such related subjects as charity, drink, Sunday opening of pubs—treat of such themes as labor
unrest, unemployment, extension of the franchise, and working-class radicalism. Their illusory world of stock situations, stock types and personifications, was intended to persuade, to instruct, to inculcate certain social
and political viewpoints. Their strategies are the subject of this chapter.

THE WORKING-MAN, FROM THE ROYAL WESTMINSTER EXHIBITION.

450. THE WORKING-MAN - - - - *John Bright.*	1001. THE WORKING-MAN - - - *Edward Horsman.*
451. THE WORKING-MAN - - - - *W. E. Forster.*	1002. THE WORKING-MAN - - - *R. Lowe.*

Fig. 158. Tenniel, "The Working-Man, from the Royal Westminster Exhibition"
cartoon, *Punch,* 20 May 1865

The Strike Cartoons

The "Dismal Science" and "Mischeevous Strangers"

Dominating mid-nineteenth-century thinking regarding the legitimacy
of strikes and unions were the strictures of classical economy. The "dismal
science" (personified in one of Tenniel's cartoons as Miss Prudence or Political Economy, a rawboned female of the Red Queen type) held that the level

of wages was "naturally" determined by the operation of the free market, which created, at any given time, a fixed wage fund. Thus, if a strike resulted in a temporary increase for some, it would either deplete the earnings of others or reduce profits and, therefore, the wage fund. In either case, the loser would be the worker himself, his employer having amassed sufficient means to weather a protracted work stoppage. Accordingly, in a two-part Leech cartoon of 1852, the capitalist sips wine contentedly before a blazing fire, and the striker stares desperately at a cold grate. This pessimistic view of strikes was put forth by Dickens, Mrs. Gaskell, Kingsley, Engels, and numerous others.[2]

Tempting the worker into this disastrous situation were the injunctions of the trade-union delegate. In Dickens's *Hard Times* (1854) mill hand Stephen Blackpool protests to his employer Bounderby, "Mischeevous strangers! When ha' we not hearn, I am sure, sin ever we can call to mind, o' the mischeevous strangers! 'Tis not by *them* the trouble's made." Here Dickens touches on a ubiquitous anti-union strategy of the time—the charge that labor unrest was artificially created by those who were strangers to the workplace and who raised unrealistic expectations among the men, in conflict with the indefeasible laws of political economy. These "outsiders"— paid union delegates or "agitators"—were believed to have come from the lowest fringe of the lower middle classes. In Gaskell's *Mary Barton* (1848) the outsider or union delegate is "the gentleman from London"; in *Hard Times* he is Slackbridge. Reflecting on the strike of the novel, the heroine of Gaskell's *North and South* reasons: "To be sure, the men were cutting their own throats, as they had done many a time before; but if they would be fools, and put themselves into the hands of a rascally set of paid delegates, they must take the consequence." *Punch* did its part in promulgating the belief that worker discontent was fomented by those who were not themselves from the working ranks. During the builders' strike of 1861 the paper asked about strike-leader George Potter:

> Who's this MR. POTTER?
> . . . .
> Is he some hardworking,
>   Honest artisan,
> Or a labour-shirking,
>   Lazy, talking man?
> Does he earn his living?
>   Is he kept, instead?[3]

The truth was, some of the more prominent labor leaders of the time did come from the working classes.[4] Potter, editor of the influential labor journal the *Beehive,* and Robert Applegarth, secretary of the Amalgamated Carpenters' Union, had begun as carpenters. George Howell of the London

Fig. 159. Tenniel, "The Strike.
—Hitting Him Hard," cartoon,
Punch, 22 June 1861

Trades Council (LTC) had been a brick-layer, William Dronfield a printer, and George Odger of the LTC a shoemaker who still kept to his trade. Others coming from workingmen ranks were Daniel Guile of the Ironfounders Union and William Allen of the Amalgamated Society of Engineers.

Union "Tyranny"

The charge that unions tyrannized over workmen was heard constantly. In Gaskell's *North and South* workman John Boucher exclaims, "Yo' know well, that a worser tyrant than e'er the masters were says, 'Clem [starve] to death, and see 'em [the workman's family] a' clem to death, ere yo' dare go again th' union.'" A letter to the *Times* in 1859 defended the "document" (or declaration of non-affiliation with any union, required by masters as a condition of employment) on the grounds that the individual workman was still at liberty to strike following his own free will. Kingsley, too, in his preface to the 1867 republication of *Alton Locke,* argued that unions were "outraging the first principles of justice and freedom" by dictating to the worker his wages, "or any other condition which interferes with his right as a free agent." And Lord Shaftesbury, the factory reformer, considered all of history's despots "as puffs of wind compared with these tornadoes, the Trade Unions."[5]

An aspect of unionism most vulnerable to attack involved the violence of unionized workers against non-union men or strikebreakers. *Punch* took up the cause of these "knobsticks" (scabs) or "blacklegs," as they were called. Following the failed London builders' strike, *Punch* assumed the voice of an out-of-work mason, mourning:

I joined the Trade Union, and more to my shame,
I bullyragged such as would not do the same,
Waylaid 'em and threatened, abused 'em, and curst,
Pitched into and beat and kicked all as I durst.

Tenniel's accompanying cartoon portrays a smart-looking non-union worker slipping a charitable coin to his former co-worker who stands, ragged and dejected, in a workhouse doorway (fig. 159). *Punch* took up the issue of scabbing once more in 1865 with a complaint against the union pickets who "still waylay and 'ratten' [remove the tools of] / the knob-sticks, who work on their own honest hook." And in an 1879 issue, a "free-born British black-leg" declares, "Tyrant man or tyrant Union— / Neither makes a slave of me."[6]

The most notorious case of work-related violence occurred in Sheffield in late 1866 when a series of attacks on non-union men and their equipment, made by members of the saw grinders' union, culminated in the dynamiting of a worker's house. The next year, while a royal commission of inquiry

Fig. 160. Tenniel, "The Order of the Day; or, Unions and Fenians," cartoon, *Punch*, 12 Oct. 1867

deliberated the entire question of trade unionism, Tenniel portrayed policeman A1 Punch warning two furtive-looking union delegates, "no intimidation here."[7]

But for high drama we look to Tenniel's cartoon of 12 October 1867—"The Order of the Day; or, Unions and Fenians" (fig. 160). Following close upon the "Sheffield outrages" came the Fenians' rescue of their compatriots from a prison van in Manchester. In effecting the rescue, these militant nationalists (members of a society dedicated to achieving Irish independence by force) had killed a police sergeant. Like labor leader George Potter, who, deploring the violence at Sheffield, lamented, "To be a trades' Unionist now was as bad as being a Fenian," *Punch* compared the two incidents. In Tenniel's double-spread cartoon, Murder, who shows a medusa's face beneath her eye mask, stares past the viewer with a fearsome look. Her arm and pointing hand are taken from Tenniel's 1853 painting of the angel expelling Adam and Eve from Paradise. One is reminded, too, of lines from Thomas Carlyle's *French Revolution* (1837): "And Murder's snaky-sparkling head has risen in the murk!"[8] Below this giant figure two pygmy groups of men follow her dictates: the saw grinders, busy with pistol and dynamite, and the rifle-carrying Fenians.

Indictments of unions were likewise made on the grounds that they encouraged leveling. *Punch's* "Dig at the Delegates" accused them of trying to "clap a stop on cleverness," and similar articles of the sixties warned that the rate of wages might be "fixed by law" to the disadvantage of skilled workmen who would be "dragged down" to "the level of the unskilled or idle." Other pieces simply protested that unions forced unlike things into the same mold. In 1891 Tenniel, employing an analogy used forty years before by Gaskell, drew a union "Procrustes" whose plan to chop each man down so he will fit into a legislative eight-hour-day bed fills an assorted group of workers with alarm. Those opposed to the shorter workday regarded the ratio of hours worked to pay as something set by immutable laws. During the 1861 builders' strike, the *Times* derided unions for claiming for their members "the right to leave off after nine hours' labour, having ten hours' pay." Similarly, a *Punch* poem of that year depicted unionists as saying: "But all we ask for nine hours' task / Is only ten hours' wage." Over the years four Tenniel cartoons would oppose any reduction in working hours.[9]

The Formula and "Aw a Muddle"

The formula for several subsequent strike cartoons was introduced in Leech's cartoon "The Strike; a Subject for the Consideration of the Real Working Man" (5 November 1859). Published in the first year of the London builders' strike, it shows a union delegate, well fed and dressed, urging the ragged and despairing workingman, "What I say my boy is—Hold out! Hold out." One suspects that the wretched attic room, with its pitiable family, was taken straight from the domestic melodramas popular in proletarian play-

Fig. 161. Tenniel, "The British Slave," cartoon, *Punch*, 20 Apr. 1861

houses. If we omit the union man, the scene had been more or less described by Leech eight months earlier. In an argument over that week's cartoon subject, Leech wanted to know if writer Ponny Mayhew "would prefer a good old fashioned cut of the starving virtuous British workman, with Death in the background [only implied in the cut], wife and children dying, while the British workman refuses work till he can have his rights."[10]

Both here and in Tenniel's 1861 replay of Leech's cut (for a latter phase of the same strike) we are struck by the rich attire, the silk hat, the general look of affluence of the sleekly corpulent union representative (fig. 161). Because he is a traveler, belonging nowhere but stirring up trouble everywhere, he carries with him a portfolio or sheaves of papers and an umbrella. Physically he tallies with an 1890 description of early union leaders—big men who, with their "good coats, large watch chains, and high hats," looked like "chosen representatives of the 'bourgeoisie.'" In Tenniel's cartoons this "professional meddler" bullies the workman, puts up strike posters, canvasses for votes. Our informant describes, too, the "new" delegates at that year's Trades Union Congress: "Not a single one wore a tall hat. They looked workmen; they were workmen." And certainly the delegates in Tenniel's cartoon "A Gloomy Prospect" (1897) seem a different breed from those in earlier cartoons.[11]

Opposed to the trickery of the union agitator was the voice of reason— Mr. Punch or one of his alternates. These varied with the message. Britannia, John Bull, or Mars appealed to the worker's patriotism, fellow workmen to his sense of fairness. From "Mrs. Workingman" there might come protestations or simply mute entreaty as in Leech's cartoon "The Strike." The device of highlighting the distress of the striker's family was used earlier in the century. A broadside of the forties, falsely purporting to be written by a striking miner, mourned, "Our wives and bains ha nowt to eat / This twenty weeks and mair." In a broadside of 1871, when the engineers were striking for a nine-hour day, a wife asks her husband:

> An' if ye work but nine oors here,
> When uthers work the ten,
> How can yer maisters get a job,
> An' pay thor nine oors men?

When the strikers won, a wife spoke up in a Tenniel cartoon. Still scrubbing floors although it is night, she reproved her sullen spouse, "Joe, dear, if you can't enjoy your supper, now you have lost your grumble about nine hours—grumble for me as I've done fourteen and ain't finished yet." Yet another wife scolded a delegate in Tenniel's cartoon of 18 January 1873 during the ironworkers' and colliers' strike in South Wales: "Eh, mister! You can bawl lustily for the ballot for your politics, but if there was a *ballot for "strikes"* you know well that my man there would be at work, earning a dinner for the children and me, look you" (fig. 162). When the capitulation of the strikers chanced to swiftly follow, the paper crowed, "When *Mr. Punch* considers what he does for the nation, he is tempted to echo, with a variation, the celebrated speech of the great LORD CLIVE, and to declare that he is astonished at Himself."[12]

Caught between divergent counsels, what could the workingman on strike be expected to do? In pictures throughout the century he stares before him blankly as if, like Dickens's Steven Blackpool, he finds his life to be "aw a muddle." The murkiness of his thought processes is shown by the shadow that Tenniel casts over his face. The cartoons usually portray him leaning against a wall or doorjamb, legs crossed, arms folded across his chest or hands sunk deep in his pockets—an image calculated to offend against the nineteenth-century work ethic. A *Punch* poem of 1872 protests, "Strange idlers at corners of busy streets I see / With hands in pockets that busy should be."[13]

Always the striker is shown alone. There are no other strikers, no evidence of solidarity such as one finds in late-century continental prints showing groups of workmen confronting management and the police.[14] *Punch's* cartoons suggest that the union representatives have placed the worker in this predicament only to abandon him. The formula was repeated in Hubert Herkomer's 1891 painting *On Strike,* which would be reproduced in a poster for the 1924 Tory campaign against the first Labour government. The distant stare of the workman standing in the doorway of his home, his lax hand holding a pipe, the anxious wife and family behind him, are all familiar.

Fig. 162. Tenniel, "Mrs. Taffy's Elixir," cartoon, *Punch*, 18 Jan. 1873

Fig. 163. Tenniel, "'Mammon's Rents'!!" cartoon, *Punch*, 10 Nov. 1883

The foreign crisis of the mid-to-late seventies (see chapter 19) effectively drove labor issues from the cartoon page, the last confrontation of workingman, family, and union delegate that was shown being the 1873 strike in South Wales. Then, when Andrew Mearns's 1883 pamphlet, *The Bitter Cry of Outcast London,* revealed the unhealthy housing conditions of the poor, Tenniel found a new use for the formulaic scene. The miserable attic room with its crumbling walls, the despairing workman, his gaunt wife and children, are seen again in "Mammon's Rents!!" (fig. 163).[15] But instead of a strike poster, a sheet over the fireplace says "Match Boxes 2d 1/4 pr gross," revealing this family's meager source of income. And the stout intruder with his silk hat, umbrella, lists, and porcine face is the former strike jobber, now in his new role as rent collector or "house-jobber."

In the Great Depression

The workman cartoons of this final period of the eighties and nineties are taken up with two issues: socialism and the downturn in trade. These are the years of the great depression, exacerbated by increased competition from foreign markets. Several cartoons of the mid-eighties express *Punch's* concern that high unemployment would make socialism increasingly attractive to workers: the socialist wolf drools over a breadwinner Riding Hood; the unemployed riot in Trafalgar Square; Satan sows socialist tares in the "field of labour"; and Anarchy tempts the worker, "Come and enlist with me,—I'll find work for You!!" As the decade ends, a *Punch* text warns, ostensibly in the striker's own voice, "Our sort will yield to Socialist seductions." Again, in the cartoons of the nineties, a "Lying Spirit" in liberty cap leads Englishmen off a cliff; the eagle of trade, its wings representing "Capital" and "Labour," battles "In the Air" with the serpent "Socialism"; and Labor's 1892 demonstration in favor of the international eight-hour day is personified in the "May Day Medusa."[16]

Strikes are blamed for destroying British trade. Already, an anti-union poem of 1879 had declared, "Yankees now and Germans / Do the work we did before." But now culpability is shared by Capital. The employer is new to Tenniel's cartoons. He appears first during the dockers' strike of 1889, when he comes "Face to Face!" with the workman, who rebukes him, "If in a general way, you'd think less of *your luxuries* and more of *my necessities,* it would be better for trade all round." By now, new attitudes toward unions, the gradual abandonment of classical economic theory, and recent revelations of the living conditions of the poor play their part in public sympathy with the dockers.[17]

Capital's fondness for the good life is reflected in his ample middle, his silk hat, boutonniere, and spats. He will figure in five more cartoons, at times displaying a look of great stubbornness. In one cartoon of the dockers' strike

Fig. 164. Tenniel, "Beggar My Neighbor!" cartoon, *Punch*, 12 Oct. 1889

he vindictively plays the card of "lock out" against the workman's "strike" (fig. 164). A poem comments, "Look at Capital's face! / There's a look *Punch* can't like," and reminds us that "This mad game of Beggar my Neighbor / Brings ruin to them—and their land."[18] Next to the workman's chair is his bag of tools; next to the master's is a bottle of champagne cooling in a bucket of ice.

In the nineties, strikes in mining and engineering are charged with jeopardizing the country's naval strength. Britannia asks the master shipbuilder, who carries the keys for a lockout, if she is to rule the waves with a fleet "Made in Germany" (the title of a new and ominous best seller). Two years later she demands to know, "When are you two going to make it up, and let me have my ships?" Meanwhile, a cartoon has shown two foreign artisans (German and French) rejoicing as they read about the "Great 'lock-out' in England!"—"So much the better for *me*!!" And in the last of some forty strike and union cartoons, a British tar threatens the striking miner, "Are you going to give us that coal, or must I fetch it myself?"[19] Familiar is the solitary striker leaning against the wall, a pipe in his mouth and his hands sunk deep in his pockets. He seems, perhaps, less muddled now than mulish. But despite some superficial likenesses, the message has changed. The cartoons before 1889 charged unions with victimization and violence toward workers. These later ones hold capital and labor both culpable for strikes that send trade away and weaken defense.

The Workingman and the Reins of Power

The Parliamentary Working Man

The possibility that the working classes might claim a share, if not all, of political power brought three essential working-class images into play. The first two were the respectable workingman and the disreputable one. The third type, the "rough," will be considered separately. Harriet Beecher Stowe is said to have observed when she visited England in 1853, "*Punch* laughs at everyone but the workpeople." There was some truth in this, assuming the statement was restricted to the skilled industrial workers portrayed in the cartoon page. If we look at Leech's Chartist in an April 1848 drawing, or the workmen in his later cartoons, and in Tenniel's, they are as dignified, earnest, and well favored as those pictured in the blacksmith artist James Sharples's 1851 emblem for the Amalgamated Society of Engineers.[20]

In the late fifties, when *Punch* skeptically noted the proliferation of parliamentarians who had come forward as "Supporters of the 'Working Man'" in anticipation of a bill to extend the franchise, the paper gave its notion of how the politicians' workingman might be represented: "Like the British Lion, the Parliamentary Working Man presents, to the mind's eye, exteriors apparently real. They consist of a human shape in a brown-paper cap, a fustian jacket, a short apron, corduroy trousers, and strong nailed highlows, the figure clothed with these garments, and the face wearing a stern and woeful expression." Did this solemnity reflect the earnest tone found in Chartist poetry and in early union literature, or a notion of what the respectable workingman might look like in contrast to workers less virtuous? Is there some mockery here? So integral was this mournful expression to Tenniel's depictions that an 1867 drawing that casts John Bull in the role of a typical workman exchanges his characteristically bright and open look for a downcast frown.[21]

The second type of parliamentary workingman, the dissolute opposite of this upright if dour figure, emerged in the reform debates of the sixties. He is not the unskilled or casual worker. Yet he falls short of the other's respectability. He is the off-duty sot, first seen in the cartoon that appears at the start of this chapter (see fig. 158). In the four-part drawing, Tenniel had shown how four members of Parliament had pictured the workingman in recent debates over a bill to extend the franchise to householders paying rates on six rather than the ten pounds currently required. Gladstone, then chancellor of the exchequer, was reported to have said that the average annual consumption of beer for every adult male was six hundred quarts. Taking this up in the Commons, Lord Elcho calculated, "The difference between a six and a ten pound house may easily be surmounted by knocking off one quart of beer per day." Soon Robert Lowe added his estimate: "Taking beer at 4d. a pot, that consumption represents an annual outlay of 10£. If therefore, persons who live in 8£ houses would only content themselves with

120 quarts annually they might at once occupy a 10£ house, and acquire the franchise."[22] Thus, the fourth image in Tenniel's cartoon (picture number 1002, "The Working-Man . . . R. Lowe") is a dull-eyed, wobbly-legged drunk seated at a pub table.

The Savings Bank and the Losings Bank

Working-class improvidence, often linked with drinking, comes up frequently in Victorian texts. Engels described the constant round between paycheck, pub, and pawnshop. In Gaskell's *North and South* a visitor to the North remarks on the working class's luxurious tastes in furniture and food. It was common to speak of the worker's self-taxation through his addiction to alcohol. In 1850 the *Red Republican* declared, "*The Leeds Mercury* repeats the canting charge against the working classes that they voluntarily tax themselves to the enormous amount of fifty millions sterling annually in the consumption of intoxicating drinks." When the government came up with a surplus in 1873, Tenniel's cartoon comment (an inebriated workingman reminding Chancellor of the Exchequer Lowe, "We're th' people s'makes th' shurplsh") was entitled "The Great Self-Taxed." Similarly, the poem accompanying Tenniel's illustration, "The Old Drunkard," in S. C. Hall's *Trial of Sir Jasper* (1873) says,

> See him—see many such—whose wretchedness
> Will make the Income Tax a penny less
> and swell the boasted "SURPLUS."[23]

Fig. 165. Tenniel, "Seasonable Advice—'Put By for a Frosty Day,'" cartoon, *Punch*, 23 Feb. 1861

Fig. 166. Tenniel, "The New Stamp Duty," cartoon, *Punch*, 27 Nov. 1880

Another concept that addressed working-class profligacy was that of the "savings bank and the losings bank"—language taken from temperance literature. In 1861, when the Post Office Savings Banks were founded, Tenniel showed Mr. Punch directing the attention of a workingman, who stands pondering before the door of a public house (or losings bank), to the eager depositors crowding the door of the savings bank across the street (fig. 165). The similarity in composition to temperance tract illustrations reproduced in Brian Harrison's study *Drink and the Victorians* (1971) suggests that this was a stock scene. Ten years later the American cartoonist Thomas Nast did a variation on the theme, substituting for the public house a deposit box for trade union dues. Tenniel's 1880 cartoon "The New Stamp Duty," marking Postmaster Henry Fawcett's scheme to encourage small savings by means of savings stamps, is a tricky variation on the savings bank and losings bank idea (fig. 166).[24] One cannot readily tell if two of the individuals pictured are lining up to make their deposits in the savings pillar box in front, or merely stepping out of the pub behind it.

While not directly addressing franchise reform, these themes tie in with arguments made during the reform debates. For example, *Punch* declared that there was little chance that the parliamentarians' "pictures" of the British workman would improve

> While men who earn even more by the week than their curate,
>   Are content in one room of a hovel to pig;
> While shop-drinks and Saint Monday their old rate endure at,
>   and the wife and the young-uns come after the swig.

It was not that *Punch* opposed limited extension of the franchise; perhaps as many as fifty Tenniel cartoons had followed the jockeying of Radicals, Whigs, and Tories on the question without really saying anything at all. But it was dead set against manhood suffrage, as shown by Tenniel's cartoon of that title, in which Mr. Punch asks a sober carpenter if the besotted workman propped against the pub wall behind them is "the sort of manhood" he wishes to be "mixed up with."[25]

The Politicized Working Man

As pubs were often the sole meeting places available to workmen, they had long been the venue for trade clubs, debating clubs, and various radical meetings.[26] Pubs had figured in the reform movement of 1831–32 and, over the years, provided meeting rooms for Chartists, Reform Leaguers, and republicans. Thus, *Punch*'s condemnation of the pub culture may well reflect, along with more humane motives, the suspicion that pubs were centers for revolutionary plots.

Also connected with the public house were working-class newspapers, which were available to be taken to one's table for a small fee. Often these had radical as well as sensational content. Bills prohibiting Sunday papers (that being the day when most working-class newspapers came out) had been introduced in the late eighteenth and early nineteenth centuries. It may be that the derision with which some regarded lower-class papers (one thinks of Thackeray's 1838 article "Half-a-Crown's Worth of Cheap Knowledge" or Leech's 1849 *Punch* cartoon "Useful Sunday Literature for the Masses; or, Murder Made Familiar") was political as well as literary. In a *Punch* poem of 1861 the striker deplores that strikebreakers were "at work, while we our minds improved / In tap or club-room near." When extension of the county franchise was broached in 1879, Tenniel's "Cad and Clod" compared the, as yet, unenfranchised rustic or "Clod" to the enfranchised "Cad," who sits intoxicated at a pub table blearily studying a paper (fig. 167). At the threat

Fig. 167. Tenniel, "Cad and Clod," cartoon, *Punch*, 15 Mar. 1879

of Sunday closing of pubs, Tenniel depicted the toper who has laid in a supply of liquor in advance. He sits in a drunken stupor at home, the newspaper dropping from his hand.[27]

Papers, pubs, and agitators all figured in *Punch*'s campaign against republicanism in 1871–72.[28] Hard times, dissatisfaction with the monarchy,
and the declaration of a republic in France had inspired the growth of many
republican clubs in Britain. In cartoon and text the paper railed against the
movement's leaders and its meeting places.

The political agitator, like his labor counterpart, was a constant target of
Punch's barbs. Its article "The Model Agitator," appearing early in 1848, while
alluding to a particular leader of some protest meetings against the income
tax and poor law in that year, might apply to many of *Punch*'s demagogue
portraits. The agitator may be assumed to be from the middle classes as he
"bullies the servants" as a child. He is eager for notoriety, knows how to
flatter the mob and to get "a good grievance" started, and in time "accumu-
lates a handsome fortune." In poems preceding the 1867 reform bill, a worker
warns "misleaders" to not "agitate me with false eloquence," and a demagogue ironically tell his followers to not break windows or bones.[29]

George Odger, *Punch*'s target in the early seventies, departed somewhat
from the stereotype in that his working-class roots were known. His hammer and leather apron identify him in Tenniel's cartoon "A French Lesson,"
where he is rebuked by a furious Britannia. In texts he is "the cobbler too
lively to stick to his last" and a contributor to the "Donkey-bray and goose-
hiss" at the Hole-in-the-Wall (a pub that was headquarters for the London
republicans and that was attacked by *Punch* repeatedly in these years). In Tenniel's cartoon "The Real Cap of Liberty" the figure whose liberty cap is scornfully flipped off his ass's head by the British Lion wears a leather apron and
clutches a roll of paper announcing a great meeting at the Hole-in-the-Wall.
Although the cartoon "Bottom's Dream" (in which Puck-Punch lifts the ass's
head from the worker's shoulders) identifies him as the generic "Working-
Man," in accompanying verses he is "a cobbler stout." And as he, like the
model agitator, seeks notoriety:

> On weekly papers went his pence—
>   Their wind to him was meat:
> And when of his own froth at last
>   Report in them began,
> He to the wind his apron cast,
>   And started public man.[30]

The Rough

Prominent among stock types representing the lower classes was the
"rough" or ruffian. Although Dickens, in his 1868 essay "The Ruffian," main-

tains that "He never did a day's work out of gaol, he never will do a day's work out of gaol," thus distinguishing him from those who were employed casually or who followed occupations involving independent or unruly life styles, in reality the difference might be impossible to tell.[31]

But the rough of art and fiction is easily identified, his appearance coinciding with the supposed physical traits of the urban poor. The late-Victorian theory of "urban degeneration," as described by historian Gareth Steadman Jones, held that after three or four generations the living conditions of the poor in London's cities caused them to be stunted, narrow chested, and pale, and to have close-set eyes—sometimes coupled with a squint. This might well describe Dickens's Artful Dodger (*Oliver Twist,* 1838): "short for his age: with rather bow-legs and little, sharp, ugly eyes." Helping to fill out the portrait is Henry Mayhew's introduction to his survey of London's street folk in the early fifties which asserted that this class (in which are included pickpockets and other petty thieves) were "all more or less distinguished for their high cheekbones and protruding jaws."[32]

Dickens is a mine of information on the stereotypical rough. The "undersized young man" sighted on the way to Tom-all-alones (*Bleak House,* 1853) with "his sleek hair twisted into one fat curl on each side of his head"; the "shrinking fellow" in his essay "The Ruffian," his "neckerchief like an eel, his complexion like dirty dough, his mangy fur cap pulled low upon his beetle brows to hide the prison cut of his hair"; and others "patched and shabby, too short in the sleeves and too tight in the legs," might all have posed for Tenniel's roughs.[33]

Added to Tenniel's numerous parolees, garroters, footpads, and wife beaters are the roughs whose likenesses were invoked to deny genuine social unrest. It was the rough and not the "real working man" (a cant expression of the times) who showed up on picket lines and formed the crowds at political or unemployment demonstrations. The rough appeared in this role following the Hyde Park riots of July 1866. The incident occurred when a crowd, on finding that an anticipated reform meeting was banned from the park, pressed up against the railings and overturned them. As the Reform League president and his immediate followers had already departed to convene instead at Trafalgar Square, the composition of the remaining crowd was unknown. However, in Tenniel's cartoon an irate workingman grasps a stunted rough by his neckerchief: "Look here, you vagabond! Right or wrong, we won't have *your* help!" (fig. 168), and in verses of that issue, the workman protests:

How erroneous you must be
To confound that Rough with me!
. . . .
'Tis the Rough, half men, half boys,
Flings the stones and makes the noise,

Fig. 168. Tenniel, "No Rough-
ianism," cartoon, *Punch*, 4
Aug. 1866

and hiss, groan, and yell "At the mansions
of the Swells." *Fun's* cartoon in that week
likewise attributed the forcing of the park
rails to roughs. And in the same issue of *Fun*,
an article related how the biases of three papers affected their perception of the crowd,
the *Standard* seeing "only roughs," the *Star*
"only respectable mechanics," and the *Pall
Mall Gazette* (and *Fun*) "a majority of work-
ing-men, with a sprinkling of roughs."[34]

In the next year, the "Sheffield outrages"
introduced the rough into the labor cartoons. The armed member of the saw
grinders' union in Tenniel's "Order of the
Day" (see fig. 160) has the protruding jaw
and close-set eyes, leather-visored cap, and
neckerchief of the stereotype. The figure
suggestive of republicanism in Tenniel's
April 1871 cartoon "A French Lesson" has
certain aspects of the rough as well—the
small stature, the brutish jaws. Shortly after,
following a demonstration of the Interna-
tional Democrats held in Hyde Park to express sympathy with the Commune
in France, the *Times* commented, "A little red riband and a great deal of
smoke, a very few working men and a great many 'roughs.'" But the *Graphic*
dissented and, ridiculing the way in which the affair had been misrepresented
in the press, commented: "The imagination busied itself by turns with pictures of artful demagogues and ignorant dupes, typical British roughs with
cudgels, and typical British innocents in the shape of timid old gentlemen
with money in their purse. The figures came and went; one smeared out
the other; and all that remained at last was a great blotch of red without
outline, symmetry, or likeness to anything but itself." Fitting this pattern is
Tenniel's cartoon of 6 May designed to contrast the republicans with some
young match girls whose own demonstration had been banned from the
park. Holding a banner that reads "Demons / Hyde Park," (part of the word
"Demonstration" being cut off by the limits of the cartoon) is a brutal-look-
ing rough, his fellow rowdies behind him. Soon, upon the Commune's fall,
a mocking poem in *Punch*, addressed to the "Gentlemen of the Pavement,"
boasted "No, Roughs, the Powers that be are wide awake."[35]

The remainder of the era, troubled by strike and depression, produced
several cartoons set against backdrops of riot and disorder. Marching with
strikers in 1872, and filling the ranks of demonstrators in 1887, is the rough
with his leather-visored or fur cap, his knee breeches, and his monkey face.[36]

Fig. 169. Tenniel, "Punch's 'Walpurgis Night,'" almanac cartoon, *Punch*, 1895 (detail)

Doubtless the crowds were heterogeneous; following the "Black Monday" riot of 1886 Engels had observed that there were "a sufficient admixture of roughs and 'Arrys' [low-bred types]." But the *Times* went beyond this in several articles portraying the unemployment protests of 1886–87 as if all whom they represented were "the idlers and loafers of London."[37]

In *Punch*'s almanac cartoon for 1895 we see the last of Tenniel's roughs (fig. 169).[38] Sharing the page with other "Walpurgis Night" visions (mostly representing female emancipation) is a group suggestive of a bacchic procession with a liberty-capped standard bearer and working-girl bacchantes. Seated in a donkey cart is the central figure—a burly rough, his fur hat tipped over one eye, his thyrsus a cudgel. As befits a monarch, he is prosperously dressed, for the triumphant banner proclaims "Demos is King."

Images of Demos

The classes in power imagined still more threatening pictures of workingmen en masse. Dread of an uprising peaked periodically through the century, usually correlating with upheavals on the Continent. Thus, the 1859 *Punch* piece on the parliamentary working man, cited earlier, concludes: "What in their hearts they [parliamentarians] imagine and fear the existence of in the interior of their Working Man, is a strong bias towards Socialism and Communism, and a dogged disposition to abolish Consols, and demand a redistribution of property." In London, reform riots and Chartism had, by turns, prompted the swearing in of special constables in 1831, 1848, and 1867. Fear of insurrections had in 1851 and in 1886–87 inspired such measures as moving troops into London (or confining them to barracks in readiness) and barricading or garrisoning buildings, while the republican scare of 1871–72 had resulted in a huge propaganda campaign to popularize the monarchy.[39]

Often the lower classes were conceived of as a dormant giant, a Frankenstein monster that might wake at any time. In writings of the period one reads: "he [a stranger visiting industrial Manchester] contemplates the fearful strength of the labouring population, which lies like a slumbering giant at their feet" (James Kay [later Kay-Shuttleworth], *Working Class in Man-*

Fig. 170. Tenniel, "The Brummagem Frankenstein,"
cartoon, *Punch*, 8 Sept. 1866

Fig. 171. Matt Morgan, "Vox Populi(?); or, A Bully That *Must* Be Put Down," cartoon, *Tomahawk*, 7 Dec. 1867

chester); "The people rise up to life; they irritate us, they terrify us, and we become their enemies. Then, in the sorrowful moment of our triumphant power, their eyes gaze on us with mute reproach. Why have we made them what they are; a powerful monster, yet without the inner means for peace and happiness" (Gaskell, *Mary Barton*); and "As she [the upper-class Adela Mutimer] disappeared there again arose the mingled uproar of cheers and groans; it came to her like the bellow of a pursuing monster. . . . And in truth Demos was on her track. . . . the voice of Demos, not malevolent at the last, but to Adela none the less something to be fled from, something which excited thoughts of horrible possibilities, in its very good-humour and its praise of her a sound of fear" (George Gissing, *Demos*).[40]

To its credit *Punch* usually treated such nightmare symbols ironically. Jerrold had mocked the reaction of the House of Commons in 1842 to the "ogre Chartism . . . the voice of the monster." In 1865, while rejecting glorified portraits of the British workman, the paper still remained skeptical of the antithesis, protesting that

> a rude, rampant monster, all envy and error,
>   From head to foot dyed in Republican red,
> On some rival parade is poked up for our terror,
>   As the real B. W. branded instead.

The next year, when the reform advocate John Bright declared in a speech in Birmingham that he had "no fear of manhood suffrage," Tenniel mischievously drew him as the "Brummagem Frankenstein" muttering "I have no fe-fe-fear of ma-manhood suffrage!" and trying to tiptoe past a giant and glowering navvy (a laborer employed on excavations and earthworks), one of a breed noted for their independent lifestyle and truculence (fig. 170). Unlike *Tomahawk* cartoonist Matt Morgan, who drew the workman (newly enfranchised by late 1867) as a mindless colossus towering over the populace (fig. 171), *Punch* did not seriously embody all the lower classes in one figure.[41] In word and cartoon it was the paper's strategy to disassociate the skilled worker from the lesser skilled, the drunkard, the rough; the "real working man" from the false. Tenniel's alarmist figures, such as his furies, stood rather for such creeds as socialism, nihilism, anarchy.

The Nostrums

Charity and the Education Question

To disarm all these fearful tendencies in the lower classes, those in power proposed various private and mainly charitable measures. They were motivated, some by self-interest, others by the genuine spirit of philanthropy. To most of these remedies *Punch* heartily subscribed.

In support of charity Tenniel drew over twenty cartoons, exclusive of those dealing with foreign or colonial distress such as occurred during the Franco-Prussian War or the 1873 famine in India. Most often the charitable cartoons came out at Christmastime, although special needs such as relief for the English cotton operatives during the American Civil War or the funding of a hospital might prompt others. In articles, too, the paper supported "judicious works of charity" but might also warn against the "tricks" of the "Mendicant Trade." Social cuts, which generally dared more than the closely observed cartoons, portrayed the deceptions of "clever paupers." In Leech's "Agricultural Distress Dodge" of 1851, a beggar's aside to his child gives instructions for the good dinner to be readied for him at home that night; and in du Maurier's "Incomplete Education" of 1873, two mendicant girls, shivering in mid August, explain "We was only taught 'ow to beg in the *winter* time, Sir!"[42]

Some thought that an educated proletariat was the best safeguard against insurrection. Since the previous century the economists Adam Smith, Jeremy Bentham, Thomas Malthus, and John Stuart Mill had advocated instructing workers in the benefits of capitalism, and in the early 1800s the teachings of religious tracts and mechanics' institutes had attempted to combat radical doctrines. Not only political economy but also virtue was to be imparted to the poor. We read in Gaskell's *Mary Barton:* "The actions of the uneducated seem to me typified in those of Frankenstein, that monster of many human qualities, ungifted with a soul, a knowledge of the difference between good and evil," and Ruskin's *Unto This Last* (1860) argues that education will quell insobriety.[43]

Schooling to persuade the working classes to leave power in the hands of those who wielded it was supported by the educator Sir James Kay-Shuttleworth and, once the 1867 reform bill had passed, by Robert Lowe. On the opposing side were the many who believed that education would both demoralize the poor and support their reading of seditious and irreligious works. *Punch* both early and late advocated working-class education. However, one Tenniel cartoon in which the workman confronts the master, "Bother your 'ologies and 'ometries, let *me* teach him [a small boy] something useful!" seems to disfavor educating the child above his "station."[44]

Temperance and Bar Stereotypes

On the other hand, *Punch*'s sympathy with the cause of temperance was unequivocal. While hardly teetotalers themselves, the Punchites were strongly condemnatory of such drink-related abuses as wife beating and the introduction of infants and children to public houses and alcohol. In 1859 the paper signified its approval of the newly formed Metropolitan Free Drinking Fountain Association with Tenniel's cartoon "The Punch Fountain in Fleet Street"—a construct probably more symbolic than real.[45] About twenty cartoons supportive of moderation in working-class drinking would follow over the years.

The sufferings of women at the hands of brutish inebriate husbands engaged the nation's attention in the early seventies as shown in three Tenniel cartoons. At this time Tenniel contributed an illustration to one of S. C. Hall's temperance books—a sordid scene picturing a seated brute sleeping off the night's drinking, his murdered wife visible in the dim light that enters the attic room at "Break of Day."[46]

Touching on a highly publicized abuse, Tenniel's earlier drawing for another of Hall's temperance tales shows a fatuous young mother, smiling as an "Aged Drunkard" feeds gin to the babe in her arms. Representations of gin being fed to an infant (usually by its mother) go back as far as Hogarth's *Gin Lane* (1751). Victorian bar pictures abound in them.[47]

A still more frequent image, so hackneyed that there is hardly a print or painting of a nineteenth-century drinking establishment that does not show it, is that of a child—most often a girl—who has been sent with a container to fetch home the gin or beer. Anywhere from two to fourteen years of age, sometimes in an adult's bonnet and draggling shawl, the girl stretches to rest her jug or bottle on the counter, which is often higher than she is. A child companion, a boy perhaps, may stand sipping from an already filled pitcher. This girl drink fetcher, sometimes along with the woman and infant stereotype, appears in prints and paintings by the Cruikshanks (George, Isaac Robert, Percy), Kenny Meadows, T. B. Smithies, A. B. Houghton, Charles Green, John Henry Henshall, and Fred Bernard. These stereotypes are found in literature as well. Describing the part of London that is home to Newman Noggs (*Nicholas Nickleby*, 1838–39), Dickens writes: "Every doorway is blocked up, and rendered nearly impassable, by a motley collection of children and porter pots of all sizes, from the baby in arms and the half-pint pot, to the full-grown girl and a half-gallon can," In *Alton Locke* (1850) Sandy Mackay exclaims, "Look at that Irishwoman pouring gin down the babbie's throat," and in Gissing's novel *The Nether World* (1889) the heroine is introduced as "a slight girl, perhaps thirteen years old" who "carried a jug, and at the bar asked for 'a pint of old six.'"[48]

These bar images appear in Leech cartoons of 1845 and in 1860. Tenniel's cartoon "The New Stamp Duty" (see fig. 166) suggests several bar stereotypes. A little boy reaches up on tiptoe, not to proffer a jug but to make his deposit in the Post Office Savings Bank pillar. The young woman holding a baby—does she emerge from the pub door behind her or is she waiting to deposit her stamps? Walking off determinedly on the right a rawboned little girl holds her filled bottle close against her chest—another small errand girl sent to fetch her parent's dinner beer.[49]

The Art-House and the Ale-House

To empty those centers of working-class immorality—the pubs—some in the more comfortable classes proposed the remarkable expedient of providing the poor with art exhibitions. The argument that Sunday opening of museums and galleries would both "elevate and refine" the masses and provide an alternative to the public house emerged as early as the 1820s and survived into the twentieth century. It was made in 1829 by William Lovett (soon a drafter of the People's Charter), and five years later, reformer Edwin Chadwick suggested before a select committee that "rational" Sunday recreation might lessen drunkenness; in 1842 he would put forward museums and zoos as an alternative to Chartist meetings. The question of "Public Gallery v. Public-House" was brought before the Parliament in 1840, 1846, 1855, 1856, 1879, and 1882. Exhibitions for the poor were sponsored by mechanics' institutes with the same end in mind; Sunday opening of museums and galleries found proponents among Quakers in Dublin who considered art a viable substitute for revolutionary meetings; and in England a number of free-Sunday societies were formed.[50]

There were, of course, those who argued for Sunday openings simply on the basis of culture for the masses; among them were Dickens, Kingsley, Tom Taylor, and writer Walter Besant. George Potter, in a letter to the *Times* in 1870, also made a case for a few free evenings at the Royal Academy exhibition, based on the "refining and elevating influence of such a scene" on the working classes.[51]

Besides the opposition of those who did not want to secularize the Lord's day—objections that prevailed until 1896 with respect to the South Kensington (Victoria and Albert) and British museums and the National Gallery and until 1932 generally (when the broader Sunday Entertainments Act was passed)—some thought the lower classes too uneducated, too lacking in poetic associations to respond to art. Others maintained that it was simply not art's business to elevate and refine. In the first group was Gissing, whose Hubert Eldon *(Demos)*, deploring the destruction of his valley by industry, exclaims: "And with nature will perish art. What has a hungry Demos to do with the beautiful"; and the writer of an article appearing a year later (1888) in the *Magazine of Art* that scornfully dismissed the "common people" as

Fig. 172. Tenniel, "The Sunday Question. The Public-House; or, The House for the Public?" cartoon, *Punch*, 17 Apr. 1869

too ignorant to be elevated. In the second and smaller group were Whistler, who wrote that art was not to be "confounded with virtue"; and the Americans Hiram Powers and Nathaniel Hawthorne, who maintained that a taste for art did not necessarily accompany high principles in an individual.[52] Nevertheless, the abundant depictions in art and literature of ungainly workingmen and lumpish rustics gawking openmouthed in awed astonishment at the overladen walls of Victorian galleries, testifies to the self-congratulatory smugness of the wealthier classes.

Punch was a hearty advocate of pictures versus pubs, some years having passed since the "hungry forties" when Jerrold scoffed at the "free day" at Westminster Hall accorded to the starving with the ironic comment: "The poor ask for bread and the philanthropy of the State accords an exhibition." Tenniel supported the movement for moderation in drink; his illustrations for S. C. Hall's temperance books were done without recompense. As his friend Sir Henry Thompson was a founder and president of a society for opening national museums and galleries to the public on Sundays, they were in harmony on this. In 1869, in response to the Lord Shaftesbury–led deputation to the home secretary opposing the Sunday opening of museums, Tenniel's double-spread cartoon presented two pictures. In one, the frowning wife tries to draw her already tipsy husband away from the public bar; in the other the same couple, quite respectable, enjoy the displays at the South Kensington Museum (fig. 172). On the defeat in 1879 of a parliamentary resolution to open museums and galleries on Sunday, Tenniel's "Friends in Deed!!" showed Mr. Bung the publican thanking the resolution's opponent, the archbishop of Canterbury, "We've had a narrow squeak this time, my lord!" Almanac cartoons carried on the campaign. In "A Vision of Utopia" (1880), standing by an urn provided by the Coffee Tavern Association are a navvy, a dustman, and a small boy whose sandwich board advertises "Food for the Mind" and gives the Sunday hours for London's museums and galleries. In the same cut a column of youths with drum, fife, and tuba march beneath the banner of the Band of Hope, a national organization promoting temperance among the young. An almanac cartoon of several years later depicts marchers under a row of banners that announce Sunday museum hours, coffee taverns, music for the people, and so on. But *Punch* characteristically took the skeptical side in small cut and verse. Some workmen spend their philanthropic employer's shillings at a tea garden instead of the art exhibit intended, "Policeman 'A'" reflects that the people "don't half understand" pictures and that art "won't draw the Briton from his beer," and a poem relates the horrors befalling a slum family when they succumb to the aesthetic movement.[53]

Restraining King Demos

Tenniel's workingman cartoons with their stock scenes and fatuous nostrums disclose how divorced the affluent were from the realities of working-class life. This was already manifest in *Punch*'s early years when Leech drew farm laborers, needlewomen, "sweaters" (sweatshop workers), and shoemakers as somewhat less than human—as specimens under glass, prize exhibitions, and waxworks. The paper's stereotypes were fairly consistent with those in other publications catering more or less to the same classes. An 1877 cartoon in the Tory *Judy* shows Father Winter warning the British workman against a pugnacious agitator. In a later *Judy* cut, a typically downcast worker stands between the clamorous demagogue and the benevolent capitalist. *Funny Folks* declared its anti-unionism in a cartoon by John Proctor in which a giant workman—a symbol of strikes and intimidation—sits blocking admission to the work site.[54] In books by Gaskell, Dickens, Charles Reade, and Gissing, wily agitators and tyrannical unions are the norm.

Closest to *Punch* in the varied talents of its contributors was the Liberal journal *Fun. Fun* (geared more to the lower middle and, reportedly, lower classes) favored an enlarged franchise in the sixties, but did not refrain from occasionally picturing working-class types as buffoons. On labor issues it purported to support unions, but it condemned picketing and strikes. *Fun*'s model "union," on the evidence of a piece appearing in 1868, seems to have been along the lines of a cooperative store that, although one means of opposing the competitive system, was no union at all. In the seventies the paper would be more overtly middle class with J. F. Sullivan's series "The British

Working Man by One Who Does Not Believe in Him" and with Gordon Thomson's cartoon "The Sham-British Workman" (1877), which pictured a giant workingman who preys on employers by means of strikes, rattening (sabotaging), picketing, and holding back on the job.[55]

While *Punch* texts might adopt a pseudo working-class voice, or pretend to address the workingman, this hardly jibed with its readership. It spoke to the middle and upper classes. These classes were not without influential members who stood ready to assist working-class leaders with legal and political advice, articles, pamphlets, public lectures, letters sent to papers, and help in parliament.[56] Such assistance had been forthcoming during the engineers' lockout of 1852 and the builders' strike of 1851, and in the royal commission inquiry into unions in 1867. In the fight against King Demos middle-class solidarity could not be taken for granted.

Despite shifts in how the lower classes were perceived, change was slow to come. The mass unemployment, wretched housing, horrors of the workhouse, and addiction to drink observed by Jack London during the summer of 1902, and the pathetically inappropriate measures with which these ills were met, seem to have changed little since the 1840s.[57]

And although Tenniel modified his cartoons over time (as with the introduction of the newly culpable capitalist) essentially the old cast played on. Agitators stirred up ruffianly crowds, honest English workmen disassociated themselves from roughs and demagogues, the medusa of anarchy beckoned, union leaders looked to their own pocketbooks, strikers stood solitary and idle, and, signifying the benevolence of those in power, the goddess Charity offered her palliatives.

21

Paddy and Hibernia

You would not confide free representative institutions to the Hottentots, for instance.
—LORD SALISBURY, on the Irish, 15 May 1886 at St. James's Hall

It was early, early in the Spring,
The birds did whistle and sweetly sing,
Changing their notes from tree to tree,
And the song they sang was old Ireland free.
—"The Croppy Boy"

Punch Is Indicted

In 1882 *Punch* was charged by certain English journals with having racially maligned the Irish people. Named in the indictments along with the paper's texts were its "caricatures," doubtless referring to the more or less ape-faced figure in Tenniel's Irish cartoons. This representation we will call "Paddy" after the stereotype from which he evolved, although he is only identified so in one of the forty or more cartoons in which he appears. In others he is "Erin's Little Difficulty," "The Fenian-Pest," "Caliban," "Anarchy," "Captain Moonlight," and so on.

Ninety years later the accusation was again leveled in L. Perry Curtis Jr.'s 1972 study of the Irish in Victorian caricature. Since neither that book nor subsequent critiques of its thesis nor Curtis's revised edition of 1997 make the crucial distinctions between cartoons and (usually) nonpolitical social cuts, between personifications and stereotypes, the issue must be further clarified. When, if ever, should Tenniel's abstractions be taken to represent "the Irish," "the Irishman," "the Irish people"?[1]

To answer this it may be helpful to ask, How did Tenniel's Paddy figures build on previous images? How was Paddy transformed by events connected with the American Civil War, Fenianism, the land war in Ireland? What is the significance of the symbol Hibernia? At what point does a stereotypical figure become, instead, a personification? a caricature? How do the *Punch* images compare with those in American and Irish journals? And, finally, what were *Punch*'s attitudes, biases, and strategies vis-à-vis Irish questions?

Ape-Faced Paddy

Some Early History

Pre-famine Ireland, ruled from Westminster since the start of the nine-teenth century, had been left behind industrially due to a lack of mineral resources and unprotected competition from British manufactures. With insufficient land for a population largely dependent on agriculture, hold-ings were small, rents high, and over 12 percent of the population was con-sidered to be living in extreme distress. Shocked by conditions in which many of the Irish subsisted, in 1839 essayist Thomas Carlyle wrote that the Irish peasant had "sunk from decent manhood to squalid apehood," and, during an 1841 Irish tour, the historian J. A. Froude commented that "the inhabi-tants seemed more like tribes of squalid apes than human beings."[2] Does the similarity of these observations suggest a preexistent source for the simian imagery that would later surface?

Early prints and drawings support this somewhat. From the late eigh-teenth century, when rack-renting, population growth, and conversion of much arable land to pasture had reduced the Irish peasant class to extreme poverty, it was not unusual for artists to show the peasant as wild in ap-pearance, ragged, and with projecting jaws. By the 1830s such types appeared in *Bell's Life in London* and *Figaro in London,* periodicals immediately pre-ceding *Punch.*[3]

Paddy's other ancestor was a stage type, drawn from the comic Irish ser-vant or workman of seventeenth- and eighteenth-century English plays, known for his volubility, verbal blunders, and fondness for whisky and for breaking heads. The character was sufficiently popular in early-nineteenth-century major, minor, and saloon theaters for several actors to have made their reputations in the role. A description of 1913 conveys the general idea:

> The stage Irishman habitually bears the generic name of Pat, Paddy, or Teague. He has an atrocious Irish brogue, makes perpetual jokes, blun-ders and bulls in speaking, and never fails to utter, by way of Hibernian seasoning, some wild screech or oath of Gaelic origin at every third word; he has an unsurpassable gift of "blarney" and cadges for tips and free drinks. His hair is of a fiery red; he is rosy-cheeked, massive, and whiskey-loving. His face is one of simian bestiality, with an expression of diabolical archness written all over it. He wears a tall felt hat (billicock or wideawake) with a cutty clay pipe stuck in front, an open shirt-collar, a three-caped coat, knee-breeches, worsted stockings and cockaded brogue-shoes. In his right hand he brandishes a stout blackthorn or a sprig of shillelagh, and threatens to belabour therewith the daring person who will "tread on the tails of his coat."[4]   (See fig. 173.)

Fig. 173. John Leech, "Improvement in Irish Affairs," small cut, *Punch*, 5 Aug. 1854, 42

Fig. 174. John Leech, "The English Labourer's Burden; or, the Irish Old Man of the Mountain," cartoon, *Punch*, 24 Feb. 1849

With the appearance of Samuel Lover's book and play *Rory O'More* and Charles Lever's novel *Harry Lorrequer,* both in 1837, Irish stereotypes grew in popularity. Some thirty comic Irish songs are found in the *London Singer's Magazine* (c. 1838–39), interspersed among numbers "most celebrated" at the London theaters, the Grecian Saloon, and Evans's song and supper rooms.[5] These are noway lacking in Paddies and their equally roisterous girlfriends, sows, cows, whiskey, and whacks.

Comic Irishness emerged early in *Punch*'s texts. A local election is replete with flying stones, assaults on the police, and casualties to persons and pigs. A country priest is satirized, and a "Broth of a Boy" sings of his prowess in breaking heads and hearts. Political slurs there were, too. In cartoons, the leader Daniel O'Connell (dubbed the "Great Agitator") is the "Irish Ogre" and "King O'Connell," his repeal association personified as "The Irish Frankenstein." Yet, demonstrating *Punch*'s diversity in these early years, an article urges the disestablishment of the Irish Anglican church, and a cartoon compares England's role in Ireland to Russia's domination of Poland.[6]

With the rise of the nationalist group Young Ireland a new bitterness entered *Punch*'s Irish pieces, largely in the work of Thackeray and Leech. Accompanying a Thackeray piece of June 1845 (a response to inflammatory articles in the movement's organ, the *Nation*) is Leech's "Fancy Portrait of Young Ireland," a frenetic and monkey-like imp in a child's high chair.[7]

Irish famine and the Irish outcry against English rule had *Punch* vacillating between sympathy for the starving and its avidity to put down the nationalists. By late 1846 the latter was ascendant. Thackeray's "Snob Papers" called Young Ireland a "frantic dwarf," boastful and traitorous, and the Irish a "servile race." Already by April of that year Leech had embarked on a series of cartoons that, appearing intermittently over the next three years, simianized an insurgent peasantry. In other Leech cartoons John Mitchel (publisher of the nationalist *United Irishman*) was pictured as an out-and-out monkey. Meanwhile, *Punch* texts jeered at divisions in nationalist ranks and at Young Ireland's failed July rebellion.[8]

With the recurrence of the potato blight in early 1849, parliamentarians heatedly debated a relief measure to ameliorate the famine in the west of Ireland. The *Times,* opposing aid, declared the peasantry of the area to be "one vast crowd of miserable dolemen" and counted the Celt with "the lame, the blind, the sick, the aged, and the insane." Two weeks later came Leech's final apish Paddy of the decade (fig. 174).[9] Grinning broadly, a large bag holding the government's grant of fifty thousand pounds slung over his shoulder, he is the "Irish Old Man of the Mountain" sitting on the back of the English farm laborer.

The American War

On joining *Punch,* Tenniel inherited a company of ready-made stereotypes to which he would have been no stranger: many-hatted Jewish old-clothes men, imbecilely grinning moon-faced rustics, minstrel-show blacks, and stage Irishmen. The Irish type he would have known firsthand, having taken this role in one of his earliest amateur performances. Later, he may have sat at *Punch*'s special table at Evans's song and supper rooms when that quintessential stage Irishman Sam Collins offered his renditions of "Limerick Races" and "The Rocky Road to Dublin."[10] In his portraits Collins wears the tall felt hat, long-tailed coat, neckerchief, and knee breeches familiar from Leech's and Tenniel's Irish drawings.

Events of 1861 accelerated Paddy's simianization. Public interest in the great apes was stimulated by a dispute between the Darwinist Thomas Huxley and the anti-evolutionist Sir Richard Owen over the comparative anatomy of man and the higher apes. It was further excited by the published account by French-American explorer Paul du Chaillu describing his years in West Africa observing gorillas and chimpanzees, and the refutation of du Chaillu's assertions by one Dr. Gray. Both controversies sparked several pieces in *Punch,* two of them over the pen name "Gorilla." In May of that year Leech portrayed the "Gorilla" (which he drew as a giant chimpanzee) as the "Lion of the Season." In the volume's preface Mr. Punch receives a deputation of "gorillas" (drawn by Keene as orangutans). The deputation's spokesman asserts, "we are a great nation, we Gorillas, and we are not understood by travelers." Was Mr. Punch's reply, "I have heard that self-assertion from one or two other nationalities," a covert dig at the Irish, the paper later alluding to "the British variety of Gorilla"? Soon after, an article spoke of an Irish MP as a "dacent boy of a Gorilla." Then in November a small cut, "The New Photographic Looking-glass," showed a somewhat simian gentleman gravely studying a photographic portrait of a gorilla (widely circulated at the time)

Fig. 175. John Leech, "Mr. G-O'Rilla," small cut, *Punch*, 14 Dec. 1861, 244

while one of two excited children says: "Ain't it a jolly sell, MR. O'TOOLE? but don't tell Ma when she comes down, cause she said I mustn't show it to YOU on any account!"[11]

The linkage of the Irish with gorillas might have ended here if not for the war in America. That November, a Union captain's removal of two Confederate diplomats from the British merchant ship the *Trent* brought the two countries close to war. It had been axiomatic among Irish nationalists that England's "difficulty" (war with another power) would be "Ireland's opportunity" (to strike for independence). The next month a public meeting in Dublin's Rotunda was announced for the 5th for the purpose of settling a power struggle between nationalist factions. However, placards posted about the city bore such messages as: "War between America and England—Sympathy with America—Ireland's Opportunity!" The meeting began with resolutions to rally to the nationalist cause, and when the chairman and member of Parliament Daniel O'Donoghue ("the O'Donoghue") declared that in this unprecedented chance for independence Ireland would furnish neither men nor money to England, the great crowd shouted and cheered. Irish papers issued equally jubilant pronouncements, the Dublin *Nation* exhorting its readers to "Lift up" their hearts. *Punch* cited some exuberant lines from that paper: "And what of Ireland in this great time? What will Irishmen do when comes this supreme opportunity, the like of which can only come once in many ages? We can tell what they may do, what they will be able to do, if they act well their part as brave men,—they can, most certainly, establish the independence of Ireland." Accompanying this was Leech's "portrait of the Author," "Mr. G-O'rilla"—an exultant chimpanzee dashing off treasonable texts (fig. 175).[12]

This, *Punch* followed with an article comparing an Irish "B'hoy" to "his superior . . . the Gorilla," and a burlesque of the Dublin Rotunda meeting that identified the speakers as "O'DONOHYAHOO" and "MR. O'RANGOUTANG, MR. G. O'RILLA, MR. FIZCALIBAN, and other eminent yahoos." That January, *Fun* followed suit in its page of crudely drawn "Twelfth-Night Characters," among them "The Irish BL-G-D (O'D-gh-e)," shown as a stage Irishman, and "Mrs. O'D-gh-e," a monkey in bonnet and crinoline (fig. 176).[13]

When, on 21 February 1862, chief secretary for Ireland Sir Robert Peel the Younger declared in Parliament that the participants in the December

Rotunda meeting were "mannikin traitors," he was challenged to a duel by the O'Donoghue. At their weekly dinner the Punchites swiftly dubbed the Irish parliamentarian "The O'Mannikin" and suggested that he be pictured as a gorilla. But Tenniel broke in with "No, as descendant of old Irish King," and in the 8 March cartoon he depicted Peel's challenger in ancient garb, in disparagement of his Celtic heritage (fig. 177).[14] The O'Mannikin's grossly protuberant mustache suggests his simian jaws beneath.

As the American Civil War progressed, Irish enlistment in Union armies further enraged *Punch*. Earlier, a poem had assumed the voice of the "Loyal Irishman in

THE IRISH BL—G—D.
(O'D—GH—E.)

MRS. O'D—GH—E.

Fig. 176. "'Sensation' Twelfth-Night Characters," cartoon, *Fun*, 11 Jan. 1862, 166 (detail)

Fig. 177. Tenniel, "The O' Mannikin," cartoon, *Punch*, 8 Mar. 1862

America," resisting recruitment. Then, when it became known that the Fenians were calling for government proscription of Northern recruiters in Ireland for fear it would reduce their numbers, *Punch* cried, "Take them JONATHAN [the personified Yankee]; take as many as you can get." But in light of Irish anticipation that victorious Federals would seek war with Britain, and of Irish enlistment to gain military experience needed for this or any other conflict with England, the paper changed its tune. Intelligence in early 1864 that Yankee agents were enticing Irishmen to the States with false promises of civilian employment only to conscript them provoked several pieces in *Punch* including Tenniel's cartoon "Something for Paddy" in which Death, lurking behind a smiling Jonathan mask, lures the foolish Irishman.[15]

Fenian Paddy

By 1865, thousands of militarily trained Irish volunteers were returning from America's battlefields, some to join the ranks of Fenianism. In about

Fig. 178. Tenniel, "The Fenian Guy Fawkes," cartoon, *Punch*, 28 Dec. 1867

twenty Tenniel cartoons Fenian Paddy issues threats, engages in violence, is punished, and persists in his intransigence. We know him by the gay military plumage of his headwear (either the high-crowned hat of the stereotype or an army service cap), a reminder of his American adventure. In two cartoons, striped trousers rolled to midcalf in approximation of his knee breeches recall Paddy's past service to the Stars and Stripes. The projection of his jaws varies to meet the situation; in most of the drawings this is within human limits. Shrunken to child size, he is more imp or urchin than monster in three cartoons. Following a police raid on the Fenians' Dublin office, he sits glumly in the stocks; a discontented manikin, he awaits Dr. Bull's

Fig. 179. Thomas Nast, "The Usual Irish Way of Doing Things," cartoon, *Harper's Weekly*, 2 Sept. 1871, 824

prescription; or (in a cartoon suggested by Tenniel) as leader of the failed rebellion in 1867, he stands disoriented wearing a lunatic's crown of straw.[16]

That year Fenian violence in England itself brought a new tone to *Punch*'s cartoons. The sinister conspirators in Tenniel's "Order of the Day" (see fig. 160) refer to the rescue of two Fenians from a prison van in Manchester, with the resulting death of a policeman. That December, in another rescue attempt, this time at Clerkenwell Prison in London, a cask of dynamite was exploded, causing death and injury to residents of the adjacent buildings. *Punch*'s reaction was recorded by diarist Henry Silver at the 17 December 1867 dinner: "The devilish Fenian outrage at Clerkenwell has us all savage. . . . But we revert to P. L.'s [Percival Leigh's] Guy Fawkes, blowing Fenianism to the winds, for all mercy is at an end now. . . . M. L. [Mark Lemon] would like to show the savage recklessness of life as injuring the poor workingman—to set them against sympathizing with the scoundrels." "Fenian Guy Fawkes," whom Tenniel shows straddling a barrel of dynamite, seethes with hatred. Nearby, a working-class mother nurses an infant, a toddler plays with a toy, and other children regard the apparition questioningly (fig. 178). Vicious as this Paddy is, he is still human compared with Thomas Nast's bestial variation on the figure for an 1871 issue of *Harper's Weekly* (fig. 179).[17]

However, by mid-1870 a more animalized Paddy shows up in three Tenniel cartoons: shaking his fist at Britannia, airborne as he is ejected from Canada by John Bull's boot, and (pictured as Caliban following a suggestion by Tenniel) threatening to take possession of Ireland (fig. 180). The

Fig. 180. Tenniel, "The Irish 'Tempest,'" cartoon, *Punch*, 19 Mar. 1870

last is a hideous monster, misshapen and fanged, the only thing Irish about him being the stereotypical high-crowned hat with the small pipe affixed to its brim.[18]

Land-League Paddy

With the launching of the Home Rule movement in the seventies, home-rule Paddy made a brief appearance, breaking heads in celebration of O'Connell's centenary, and obstructing government business at the decade's end. But it is the land question that dominates this period. As Gladstone's 1870 Land Act did not adequately address tenant grievances (it compensated evicted tenants for improvements they had made and for disturbances, but lacked provision for those thousands who were in arrears), it failed to stop the epidemic of agrarian crime that had escalated by 1869. Pictures in the comic papers *Punch and Judy, Judy,* and *Tomahawk* reflect the concerns of this time: a gentleman shoots an Irish peasant from a moving carriage (a reversal of what was occurring); a monstrous Fenian bursts forth from a great bandbox that bears the amiable likeness of a stage Irishman; an Irish

Fig. 181. Tenniel, "The Irish Frankenstein," cartoon, *Punch*, 20 May 1882

vampire is quickened by the light of the moon; a monster looks to his Irish Frankenstein creator; and, in an unduly optimistic cartoon, the aggrieved Paddy of 1869 is changed to the happy landowner of 1870 by Time's magic lantern. As for Tenniel, he portrayed the outraged Mr. Punch rebuking Policeman Gladstone, "Isn't it time for you to interfere?" and demanding, "Where's the (Irish) Police?"[19]

While often upstaged by foreign events, the Irish subjects that now emerge indicate further violence. A skeletal skipper guides a barge heavy with explosives along the Thames at night. In Ireland, skylines are defined by cudgels and flying brickbats. By the decade's end the struggle against landlordism and evictions was consolidated under the National Land League, dedicated to nationalization of the land, and soon *Punch*'s sympathy for the Irish peasants who were suffering in a severe agricultural depression vied with its outrage at the continuing land war. As agrarian crime rapidly mounted, Tenniel's Land League Paddy became a vicious hydra, an "Irish Devilfish," and the ugliest specimen in Time's waxworks.[20]

When Irish leader Charles Stewart Parnell failed to endorse Gladstone's second land bill (a bill that satisfied some demands of the tenantry but still offered no protection for some one hundred thousand peasants whose rents were in arrears), Gladstone had the essentially moderate Irish leader and his lieutenants imprisoned. During the six months of Parnell's incarceration, secret and violent societies were formed in Ireland, and on 6 May 1882 (four days after Parnell's release) the new chief secretary for Ireland, Lord Frederick Cavendish, and his undersecretary, T. H. Burke, were murdered in Dublin's Phoenix Park by one of these groups.

In the outcry in England, Parnell was unfairly blamed. The monster of Tenniel's cartoon "The Irish Frankenstein" is a giant Paddy striding forward obsessively with dripping knife, his animal jaws jutting out beneath his eye mask (fig. 181). Behind this nightmare figure kneels Parnell, hand upraised as if to hold the monster back. The legend, a mishmash seemingly composed of excerpts from Mary Shelley's 1817 novel *Frankenstein,* reads: "the baneful and blood-stained Monster . . . yet was it not my Master to the very extent it was my Creature? . . . Had I not breathed into it my own spirit? . . . (extract from the Works of C. S. P-RN-LL, M.P.)." More perceptive of the damage the event would cause, the Irish paper *Pat* pictured Ireland's symbol Erin, her head resting on the draped coffin of the murdered secretary, as "the Chief Mourner."[21]

Hibernia

Hibernia's Testimony

In opposition to insurrectionary Paddy, and appearing almost as frequently in Tenniel's work, was the national symbol Hibernia. This personification, also called Erin or Ireland, is of ancient origin and derives from the Gaelic goddess Eriu. No stranger to British prints, in eighteenth- and nineteenth-century designs her usual attribute was a harp, frequently stringless or partially strung. It was not until his second portrait of her that Tenniel's Hibernia took form (the first had shown a dark-haired beauty in eighteenth-century milkmaid costume leading a beribboned pig). In classical dress with peplum and a wreath of shamrocks in her light and wavy hair, she then took her place among Tenniel's deities, a smaller and more feminine sister to Britannia (see fig. 180). At first she was both guardian and victim to Paddy—taking a rod to the Fenian manikin, consulting Dr. Bull about the little rebel, but fearfully grasping Britannia's arm when the full-grown "Fenian-Pest" threatened. As Paddy grew in menace Hibernia became more passive—clinging to Gladstone as the Irish "Tempest" raged or cowering in the arms of Britannia. In other papers, *Judy*'s John Proctor drew a dark-haired version of Tenniel's goddess during the sixties; in later cuts in *Judy* and *Fun* Hibernia varied from sturdy peasant to pert colleen. Almost always, in Irish papers she was a proud and lovely goddess. In fact, in *United Ireland* she was sometimes Tenniel's goddess.[22]

When, in 1882, *Punch* felt called upon to rebut charges of undue savagery toward the Irish peasantry, it was Tenniel's Hibernia whom Mr. Punch evoked. While *Punch*'s Irish pieces had not gone uncensured previously, the main objections coming from Irish and American papers, now there were increasing protests from the English press itself. In 1881 the *Pall Mall Gazette* (while not specifically naming *Punch*) declared, "If anyone wonders why the Irish should not love England, let him look at the comic papers just now. Hatred and contempt glisten in every line of these caricatures of the national type," and early the next year the *Graphic* found that "the extravagances of Irish disaffection and the revolts of subject races have more than once been handled by our own *Punch* with greater vigour than generosity." Also in 1882 there appeared in Britain an article in the *Nineteenth Century* by E. L. Godkin (a founder of the American weekly the *Nation* and an editor of the *New York Evening Post*) that stated, "If a collection were made of the Irish engravings of *Punch* during the last forty years, it would form a body of brutal satire such as no community has ever been exposed to. No savages have ever been so mercilessly held up to loathing mockery as the Irish peasants by the one comic paper in Europe which has been most honourably distinguished for its restraint and decorum and good-nature."[23]

In September Mr. Punch replied to this article and to one in the *Spectator* that, in his view, had similarly misrepresented him. Taking his case before the "Lord Justice Public Opinion," Punch argued that "whenever HIBERNIA appeared, it was always in the character of a beautiful and lovable girl." Then Hibernia herself arose to give evidence on behalf of Mr. Punch. Recalling some of the paper's more moderate Irish cartoons by way of contrast, she introduced one of Tenniel's more bestial Paddies, "a brute bearing on the ribbon of his hat the word "Anarchy."[24] "This figure," Hibernia argued, "has invariably done duty for the spirit of lawlessness, Fenianism, and agrarian outrage by which a few of my children have brought disgrace and misery upon us all." Next, citing the example of "The Irish Frankenstein," Hibernia concluded, "This hideous type did not represent the honest, loyal, suffering peasant, but the figure in Mr. TENNIEL'S 'Arrears' cartoon [a cartoon of 3 June 1882 depicting a straight jawed Irish peasant] did so, and here English sympathy was enlisted for the evicted peasant." With this, Mr. Punch triumphantly acquitted himself and closed the hearing.

Some Terms Examined

As Mr. Punch's defense hinged on the argument that simian Paddy represented a disposition to "lawlessness, Fenianism, and agrarian outrage" and not a class of people, we must ask, "What exactly do these cartoon figures signify? Are they stereotypes? personifications? caricatures?" Usually social in origin, stereotypes such as the stage Irishman conform to hackneyed notions about the appearance or behavior of members of certain nationalities,

Fig. 182. Tenniel, "The Irish Treason Shop," cartoon, *Punch*, 4 Dec. 1869

Fig. 183. Tenniel, "Fenians 'in a Fix,'" cartoon, *Punch*, 21 Oct. 1865

races, religions, occupations. But should the likeness of the stage Irishman symbolize a place such as Ireland—which it does in several Tenniel cartoons—or a political movement such as Fenianism, then it becomes a personification.[25] And should an actual person be portrayed as a stage Irishman, this would be a caricature. As all these images have attributes in common, their context is the defining element.

Such figures are employed legitimately by cartoonists, often with considerable leeway. Take, for example, Tenniel's Irish priest, an unsavory type who seems to be a perfect portrait of Father Malachi Brennan in Lever's *Harry Lorrequer*—both possibly derived from the Irish priests in seventeenth-century English plays. Tenniel's priest—fat, balding, beetle browed, with a long upper lip—is a stereotype when he produces religious gewgaws to tempt the young or comments wryly on the disestablishment of the Anglican church in Ireland (see fig. 150). At other times he is a personification of such suspected activities as supplying weapons to Paddy (fig. 182) or using intimidation to discourage electors from voting. In one cartoon he is a caricature, his likeness adopted to portray one Father Daly from Galway. But in 1865, when personifying the Catholic Church's declared opposition to Fenianism, his "riverence" appeared as a handsome young man—a veritable Adonis in gaiters (fig. 183). With similar flexibility, in 1849 when it was needed to show the English laborer burdened by the government loan to Paddy, Leech had depicted an intelligent-looking farm worker instead of the conventional rustic booby, carrying on his back the simian Paddy (see fig. 174). Two years later, the adaptable Leech, eager to show the Catholic Church battening on a starving peasantry, drew a stereotypical priest but made Paddy as refined a type as might be desired.[26]

Provoking as it may have been to the Irish to see the hackneyed image of the stage Irishman—never a favorite with them in any case—hideously distorted in Tenniel's cartoons as the representative of their national aspirations, to say that it was meant to represent the Irish people is inaccurate. Tenniel's simian Paddy was Fenianism, home rule, and the Land League. He was not in the same category, for example, with the stereotyped Irish in Keene's social cuts of the seventies and eighties.[27] This is not to deny the ferocity of the cartoons or to imply that Tenniel did not freely employ stereotypes against other races.

For acrimonious stereotyping we look to the New York papers *Harper's Weekly* and *Puck,* where hostility to the immigrant Irish—to their Catholicism, their ties to Tammany Hall, and their adherence to the Democratic Party—inspired numerous cartoons in which the Irish themselves were bestialized. One thinks of Thomas Nast's drawing of repellent St. Patrick's Day celebrants or of his and Frederick Burr Opper's Paddies, who with loathsome ape faces sit smoking their pipes before sty-like shanties (fig. 184), or of Joseph Kep-

Fig. 184. Frederick Burr Opper, "The King of A-Shantee," social cut, *Puck*, 15 Feb. 1882

pler's drawing of Paddy as the only apeman in a line of immigrants boarding the "U S Ark of Refuge" or as the single rowdy in "Uncle Sam's Lodging House."[28]

Of course, Tenniel was not entirely averse to lampooning the Irish. When someone suggested a cartoon implying that Ireland had an extraordinary need for lunatic asylums he concurred: "Let's offend somebody!" In the 1876 cartoon "The (Home-) 'Ruler of the Spirits!'" based on an elaborate pun, he pictured an Irish "Biddy" (a female type popular on stages throughout the century and beyond) who sits grumbling about an MP's proposal to close off-license liquor establishments on Sundays (fig. 185). Vulgar, inebriated, and traditionally played by a man, Biddy was in 1889 described as "the most atrocious calumny on this country" by the Dublin *Jarvey*. In Tenniel's drawing, the face surrounded by Biddy's ragged shawl is Paddy's own, so that we have here a composite stage stereotype—a witty concept that was probably irresistible to the usually diplomatic artist.[29]

Predictably, retaliatory devices were employed by Irish cartoonists. For example, *Zozimus* artist John Fergus O'Hea liked to give an apish face to England's John Bull. As English plays and social cuts often showed the Irish peasant as a fool of a Paddy, what was more natural than for the Irish to avail themselves of that most malignant stereotype in the English repertory— the rustic Hodge with his imbecilely grinning moon face, smock frock, and clodhopper boots? In *Zozimus* a small cut by WM shows two English laborers pointing at the backs of a pair of good-looking Irishmen. They converse in typical Hodge dialect: "*1st Intelligent Native:*—Hey, vather! Theare be tha Hoirishmen as az coom'd over vor 'arvest. Beant thea queer, untoidy lookin' chaps? *2nd Intelligent Native:*—Yoy, John, but tha be: a wuld not like them to cut corn vor huz. Zumhow thea doan't look smart for work; they baint Christian-loike or toidy, loike we!" And we are also not surprised to see England personified as Hodge in the Irish paper *Pat*, as had been done earlier in the American journal *Vanity Fair*.[30]

The Two Irelands—The Rationale

Punch's contention that simian Paddy represented only abstract tendencies might be thought sophistical since Tenniel's adaptation was, after all,

Fig. 185. Tenniel, "The (Home-) 'Ruler of the Spirits!'" cartoon, *Punch*, 27 May 1876

based on a figure that had for some decades served as a social stereotype. But this fails to take the political ramifications into account.

In his 1978 article on English attitudes toward the Irish, Sheridan Gilley suggested that the Englishman's animus toward Irish insurgency was exacerbated by the affront to his sense of imperial unity—that he could not imagine a people so perverse as to reject the benefits of union with England. This is supported by numerous Tenniel cartoons designed to appeal to imperialist sentiment: expressions of love and friendship between the countries; visions of a royal residence in Ireland; Hibernia extending "Céad Míle Fáilte" (a hundred thousand welcomes) to various royals, kissing the queen's hand and beseeching her to come visit. From Tenniel's Britannia and John Bull came famine relief, subsidies in Ireland's Christmas stocking, and aid to peasants whose rents were in arrears. In one of Tenniel's loveliest drawings, Hibernia shades her eyes while searching the sea for the "good ship *Land Act*" (fig. 186).[31]

The Hibernia-Paddy dichotomy was an article of faith with England's representatives in Ireland. In the same speech in which Peel called the na-

Fig. 186. Tenniel, "Suspense!" cartoon, *Punch*, 30 July 1881

tionalists "mannikin traitors," he claimed that "not a single man of respectability in the country" had "answered the appeal" to act against England.
Twenty years later another chief secretary for Ireland would declare, "There
are two Irelands—the Ireland of men of all parties, and creeds, and ranks,
and callings, who, whatever else they differ upon, unite in wishing to preserve law and order and the right of every citizen to go about his business
in peace and safety; and there is the other Ireland—the smaller Ireland, as
I firmly believe—of the men who foment and condone and sympathize with
crime." Similarly, *Punch* reasoned in a bogus draft of the queen's speech to
Parliament in 1882, "The murders and the mutilations which disgrace one
of the fairest parts of my kingdom are the result, not of a popular movement,
but, of the action of those 'village tyrants' and 'dissolute ruffians' whom the
secretary to the Lord Lieutenant once denounced."[32]

The Ireland personified dually but unequally by Hibernia and Paddy has
elements of self-persuasion. It would have been impossible to justify the
union as a benevolent arrangement if most of the country were seen to be
up in arms against it. As was explicated by historian Patrick O'Farrell, to have
associated revolutionary violence with the peasantry en masse would have

suggested a situation out of control, with England as an oppressor nation.[33] The last thing *Punch* might wish would be for revolutionary Paddy to be taken for the national symbol.

The Two Irelands—The Devices

In pieces discrediting the nationalists, *Punch*'s writers often affected a pseudo-Irish voice. After the nationalists made plain their hope for an Anglo-American war to provide "Ireland's opportunity," this device was commonly used. Frequently the "Irish" voice, with its defiance and braggadocio, had a demagogic tone. The strategy is familiar. To disassociate the mass of Irish from the insurgents the paper once more called up those "mischeevous strangers," the agitators by whose presence all discontent might be explained. As pointed out in an Irish memoir of the time, it was the fashion to credit the "invective of those 'agitators' . . . with the exclusive manufacture of Irish sedition." In 1862 Peel blamed "American emissaries" for stirring up Irish nationalism. In three cartoons, Tenniel showed rabble-rousers declaiming to unruly Irish crowds. In one, Pat (a straight-jawed Paddy) stands dazed, hands in pockets, ignoring both the wife who tugs at his arm (offering a sickle for him to return to his work), and Mr. Punch, who advises that he not heed the demagogue inflaming a crowd in the next field (fig. 187). It is the working-man formula translated to an Irish farm. Three years later a Tenniel car-

Fig. 187. Tenniel, "Friend and Foe," cartoon, *Punch*, 4 Sept. 1880

toon pictured a "hired assassin" reaching a bag of gold to an armed and masked Paddy, again playing on the theme of outside instigators.[34]

Supposed Irish loyalty likewise found a voice in *Punch*. In 1862 a "Loyal Irishman in America" boasts to a Union recruiter, "Go, SERGEANT SNAP, don't talk to PADDY CAREY, / Of bloodshed, barrin for me QUEEN, I'm chary." Not many years after, a bogus Irish voice scoffs at the Fenian's dream of an Irish republic; a so-called Fenian confined to Kilmainham jail has bitter thoughts about the promises made to him by agitators; and another "Irishman" declares that those who said that Ireland would "un-crown" the monarchy and set up a republic had underestimated the kinship between the two countries. In Tenniel's cartoons John Bull arms the "loyal Irish" with staves against the Fenian threat, broadly grinning peasants accompany the Prince and Princess of Wales on a shooting expedition, and others cheer various visiting royals. *Judy*, too, embraced this strategy, dedicating a Proctor cartoon (St. Patrick driving out the Fenians) to "all loyal Irishmen." When Tenniel depicted Hibernia welcoming the royals to Ireland, he changed her goddesslike draperies to peasant dress, thus identifying her with the people. In *Judy*, Proctor did the same. Tenniel stressed the two-Ireland dichotomy. Rejecting Paddy and his warlike offerings, Hibernia accepts a land bill bouquet from suitor Gladstone. In other scenes, the snarling Paddy sends her to Britannia's side or to Gladstone's.[35]

How Punch Saw It

Ungrateful Paddy

Punch's resentment at perceived Irish ingratitude for famine relief and other benefits believed to accrue from the union with England flared up in the forties. It still smoldered thirty years later when a poem complained, "We gave,—it was naught: we withheld,—'twas a crime." The Punchites' sense of injury was always exacerbated by physical force directed against British rule; it had been the direct provocation for the rise of bestial Paddy. Thus, in the forties drawing after drawing showed Young Ireland inseparable from his blunderbuss. The instinctive condemnation of lower-class violence would in 1880 be expressed by the Radical statesman Joseph Chamberlain when he said of the government's coercion bill, "For my part I hate coercion. I hate the name, I hate the thing . . . But I hate disorder more."[36]

There was always the threat of an Irish coalition with Radical forces in England. From the 1830s the Irish had figured in England's labor struggles and as writers for radical journals; the Irish MP Feargus O'Connor is said to have proposed an alliance between the Irish peasantry and the English working classes. It has been argued that the immigrant Irish were generally too caught up in basic survival to be a serious political threat. But still, some Irish in 1848 allied themselves with English Chartism, although the actual number of Irish Chartists at Kennington Common on 10 April is unknown. Certainly Irish involvement was strongly suspected, for on that day the *Times* called the movement "a ramification of the Irish conspiracy," and, on the next day, the Chartist procession having failed to achieve its object, the paper crowed, "We congratulate them on their booty, which we hope they will divide with their partners in Dublin." Later, Marx considered a partnership with the Irish nationalists necessary to a class-conscious British labor movement, and, in the months before the 1867 Reform Bill passed, the ruling classes dreaded the possibility of a partnership between the Irish, the reformers, and the trade unions.[37]

Such fears were reflected in Tenniel's 1867 "Order of the Day" (fig. 160), a cartoon that explicitly compared Fenians to trade unionists, and in "Fenian Guy Fawkes" (fig. 178), with its dynamiter deliberately placed in a plebeian setting to discourage working-class sympathy. The feared coalition is personified in Tenniel's cartoon of 30 November 1867, "Check to King Mob," in which the linkage of the Irish terrorist in Britannia's deadly grip to the British worker is implied by the word "League" on his sash (referring to the Reform League and the agitation of the previous summer). The poem "King Mob" (a takeoff on Barry Cornwall's song "King Death") appearing in the next month would clump labor leaders, the Reform League president, Fenians, pickpockets, and garroters into one clamoring mob.[38]

The Race Question

In the face of nationalist expectations rashly proclaimed at the start of the American Civil War, *Punch* spared little vitriol in its Irish pieces. One wonders at times if its writers could clearly distinguish in their own minds the politicized Irish from the Irish of the lower classes. In the year following the Rotunda meeting a particularly nasty piece, Percival Leigh's "Missing Link," held that the "Irish Yahoo" represented an intermediate stage between men and gorillas. Although the word "Yahoo" had represented nationalists (particularly journalists) in *Punch*'s previous articles—"The Irish Yahoos" and "The Yahoos of the Yankee Press"—here it seems to take in the immigrant poor as well. The idea was first put forth as a cartoon suggestion, but the staff, fearing that a cartoon "might get the Punch windows broken," persuaded Leigh to "write his notion" instead.[39]

In one 1863 article the paper incontinently cried, "The rowdies and the Irish are the scum of the earth." When reprimanded by the London *Morning Star, Punch* accused the *Star* of pretending that *Punch* had confounded "The loyal people of 'Ireland as it is' with the exported vagabonds [Irish enlistees] who take the Yankee blood-money," and that he had called "as they [the *Star*] affect to suppose . . . Irishmen in general the scum of the earth." In a later article it asked, "Would *Punch* call the DUKE OF WELLINGTON scum of the earth, SWIFT scum of the earth, BURKE scum of the earth, GOLDSMITH, SHERIDAN, TOM MOORE scum of the earth?" However, this disclaimer could be thought disingenuous as most of those named were Anglo Irish.[40]

One might get the impression, at least from reading the comic journals, that the issue of race emanated from the Irish themselves. References to the Saxon or Sassenach (a name given by Gaelic-speaking peoples to the English) began in the forties, possibly in opposition to the romantic revivalism of the Young Irelanders with its stress on the uniqueness of Ireland's history and language, such cultural separatism being anathema to imperially minded Englishmen. In one *Punch* article the "Irishman" rants against the "oppressor, tyrant, rascal, liar, blood-thirsty murderer—Saxon" who would impugn an Irish journalist; in another he fumes over the "pickpocket Saxon." When, in 1852, a letter to the *Times* from a Mr. MacElheran of Belfast charged that paper with racism and lauded the Celt as compared with the "flaxen-haired, bullet-headed, pig-eyed, huge-faced, long-backed, potbellied, bad-legged, stupid, slavish, lumbering, sulky boor of a Saxon," *Punch* straightway published a bogus letter from "An Ill-Made Saxon," accompanied by Leech's drawing of a handsome "Anglo-Saxon" navvy and a prognathous "Tipperary Man." It soon followed this with an ironic piece in the "Irish" voice on Celt and Saxon attributes. Fenianism brought more of *Punch*'s pseudo-Irish ravings against the Saxon while, in a *Fun* article of the period, a Hibernian crowed, "Halloa, boys, here's another victory over the Saxon!"[41]

The Role of Class

Some have suggested that English prejudice against the Irish peasantry was largely a matter of class. This seems most probable, especially since loyalty to the Union was chiefly found, not among the Irish poor, but among those in the middle to upper classes. Class bigotry is well substantiated by drawings and texts in *Punch* that, from the first, stressed the rags and impoverishment of the "Wild Irish." Class bias is similarly evident toward other nationalities. While the faces of Tenniel's English roughs and garroters, and his French Communards, are distinguishable from his Paddies, they too tend toward prognathism. And when the midcentury social investigator Henry Mayhew suggested that the itinerate poor of London (of which the Irish made up only a portion) were "distinguished by their high cheekbones and protruding jaws," this was a class observation.[42]

In *Punch*'s texts, contempt for the lower-class Irish is ever present. Ireland is said to abound in "the sons and daughters of beggary." Many a native is observed to lack "a decent coat on his back." The Irish "Yahoo" is a "climbing animal" often "seen ascending a ladder laden with a hod of bricks." He colonizes the slums of England and America. To distinguish him from members of the more affluent classes, a text will specify that a journalist is "an Irishman of a peculiar class" or of "the baser sort."[43] As with those English who wielded little political power—domestic servants, farm laborers, paupers—*Punch* showed its disdain.

Class, and not race, seems to have determined qualification for *Punch's* inner circle. Although still in his teens, artist Richard Doyle, a Roman Catholic of Irish descent, was taken on as a staff member. When he resigned in 1850, despite the pleadings of Jerrold and Thackeray, this was in protest against the paper's anti-popery stance and not due to ill treatment at the hands of his colleagues. But Doyle's parents had come from wealthy landowning families, in contrast with the English artist William Newman, who contributed many delightful drawings to *Punch* in those years, but who was shabbily treated.[44] Newman however, a very poor man, was thought to lack the breeding expected of *Punch* staffers.

Despite Tenniel's readiness to bait the insurgent peasantry, this in no way applied to Irishmen of the higher classes. His first sale of a painting had been to the Irish actor Tyrone Power. Tenniel's proudest artistic achievement had always been his set of designs for the *Lalla Rookh* of Ireland's "national lyrist" Thomas Moore (a book suspected of "cloaking Irish patriotic aspirations under the garb of oriental romance").[45]

Du Maurier, too, could be savage toward politicized Irishmen of the lower classes. In 1862, after attending a lecture in which the naturalist Sir Richard Owen argued against a link between man and ape, du Maurier boasted to his fiancée, "I politely interrupted him and said that if he would take the trouble to make a post mortem on the Irish roughs I intend to kill next Sunday in the Park, he might convince himself that the 'missing link' had been found." Still, the exquisite heroine of du Maurier's novel *Trilby* is the daughter of Dubliner Patrick Michael O'Ferrall.[46] Of course, she has the virtue of being the granddaughter of a famous Dublin physician and is thus no plebeian.

Aftermath and Summation

It would be hard to say if the reprimands of the early eighties affected Tenniel's later cartoons. Already by the end of 1881 Paddy's face was frequently modified by an eye or face mask—an allusion to those worn in the "Captain Moonlight" raids occurring in Ireland at the time. Or the face might be masked by Paddy's raised arm or by intervening figures. Still, the animal jaws protrude below Paddy's eye mask in three cartoons, and the few revealed faces include those of the bestial "O'Caliban."[47] After 1882 Tenniel drew only twelve more Paddies, the Irish cartoons of this period being mainly taken up with Gladstone's two home-rule bills and with Parnell.

There had been little change in simian Paddy since he emerged in Leech's drawings in the forties. Unlike Tenniel's Paddy, Leech's figure appeared at times to denote the Irish themselves. Early on, the personification would have represented but a small fraction of the population. The Young Irelanders who had first incited Leech's ire started no mass movement. Their leaders were intellectuals, divorced from agricultural concerns in a country in which some two-thirds of the population were dependent upon agriculture, and their 1848 uprising was thought to have involved less than six hundred persons. Fenianism, too, inspired no popular movement, drawing a large part of its followers from the lower middle classes.[48] It did not attract sufficient numbers to stage a successful rebellion, largely because the Catholic Church, with its sway over the peasantry, condemned the organization. It was not until the Land League and the land wars of 1879–82 that one could speak of a mass movement in Ireland. But such a possibility, neither *Punch* nor its readers were ready to admit.

For close to fifty years Tenniel personified Irish resistance to British rule by various mutations of the stage Irishman Paddy. In 1865 he introduced Hibernia, Britannia's goddesslike sister. The concept of two Irelands, one faithful to England, the other a fractious and demagogue-driven minority, helped to justify the union between the countries. While one might question the validity of this construct, Tenniel's cartoons are consistent with the defense offered *Punch*'s critics in 1882. His "hideous type" was never meant to be taken as a national stereotype, for *Punch*'s whole strategy rested on dissociating the putative "loyal majority" (Hibernia) from simian Paddy, an aberration that needed to be put down.

The Dis-United States

O JONATHAN and JEFFERSON,
Come listen to my song;
I can't decide, my word upon,
Which of you is most wrong.
—PUNCH, 25 May 1861

A Verdict Revisited

When Tenniel died, just months before the First World War, Americans were reminded of his coverage of another great conflict. The *New York Evening Post* recalled that "around the days of the Civil War his American cartoons in *Punch* were as gall and wormwood to the North," and that "at the time of the Mason-Slidell affair Tenniel's drawings did much to tighten the strain between the two countries." Under the headline "The Famous Cartoons . . . the Sneer and the Apology" his cuts were reproduced in the *Boston Evening Transcript,* and comments on his "merciless caricatures" appeared nationwide in otherwise eulogistic notices.[1]

The cartoons in question are about sixty in number, or 30 percent of Tenniel's output for the period. For four years Britons had followed America's war with intense interest, with many in the dominant classes torn between their antislavery principles and self-interest or social biases. Various factors— economic, jingoistic, and ideological—led a number of Englishmen to move from an initial pro-North position to one sympathetic to Southern nationhood and antagonistic to Lincoln.

While Oscar Maurer's 1957 article on *Punch* and the American Civil War has points of agreement with what is said here, his study deals more fully with the paper's texts than with its pictures.[2] A rereading of Tenniel's Civil War cartoons in the context of the events, prejudices, visual language, and rival cartoons of the period will help to determine if they were as vitriolic as reputed.

The Dramatis Personae

Of the stock types familiar to theatergoers, key players in this series were the stage Yankee Jonathan, representing the American North (and his look-alike Southern twin); and Sambo, a comic black derived from the minstrel shows of the time. An alternate black stereotype was the "patient suffering slave," by 1853 a stage character thanks to the dramatization of Harriet Beecher Stowe's novel *Uncle Tom's Cabin*. A theatrical bent is seen, too, in such minor parts as Mrs. South, an amazon breed of female, and the stage Irishman Paddy.[3] Statesmen and personifications, who might be cast in roles ranging from pantomime to Shakespeare, filled out the company.

Brother Jonathan

The folk character Brother Jonathan was born during America's revolutionary period.[4] He first trod the stage in New York City in 1787, originally appearing as a country lad of deceptive simplicity. Later, he would exemplify a lean and crafty New England trader. By 1830 certain aspects of the still-beardless Yankee's appearance—his swallowtail coat, striped trousers, and the tall hat atop his flaring long hair—anticipated Uncle Sam.

Nineteenth-century stage versions of Jonathan owed much to the work of Charles Mathews Sr. The English comedian traveled in the United States in the early 1820s, observing and learning to mimic various American types. He presented his one-man show, *Trip to America,* there before taking it to the London stage in 1824. One sequence in Mathews's medley of monologue, comic song, and dance portrayed Jonathan, "a country fellow, unpolished and a hard bargainer," who proclaimed that as America was "a land of liberty and freedom . . . every man has a right to buy a Nigger."[5] The skit was soon expanded into Mathews's play *Jonathan in England* in which the slave-owning Yankee was an unmannerly boor, dishonest and a braggart.

Jonathan portraits range from amusing to sinister. The hero of Tom Taylor's play *Our American Cousin* (1861) is a boaster and introduces himself as "the tallest gunner, the slickest dancer, and generally the loudest critter in the State." Another braggart is Tenniel's Jonathan, who in a cartoon of 1862 warns the French emperor Louis Napoleon, "If you come meddlin' with any o' your mediation sarce; soon as ever I've whipped the rebels and walked into Canada—and chaw'd up John Bull—darned if I don't put that thar young man [Le Comte de Paris] in your location!!!" The Yankee had been unflatteringly portrayed in *Punch* during the forties, a time when "Yankee" was used in its broader sense for "American." An 1844 article described him as lank, sallow, and gimlet-eyed, and with a mouth like a steel purse. Most often he wore a wide-brimmed straw hat (a legacy from the Mathews costume) and carried a cat-o'-nine tails. By the midfifties the scourge identified Jonathan's Southern variant. Then, by late 1861, when *Punch* changed sides and made the wizened Yankee type a Northern symbol, it was dropped entirely.[6]

Our other principal type, the comic black, was also impersonated by Mathews. Actors in blackface had been performing song and dance routines in America since colonial days, anticipating the later minstrel shows. From the 1830s on blackface minstrelsy would be the rage in London as troupe after troupe came over from the United States. In *Trip to America* Mathews's parody of a black actor's soliloquy from Hamlet, which had degenerated into a rendition of "Opossum up a Gum Tree," would have delighted his English audiences, for Shakespearean travesties had been popular since the late eighteenth century. As a youth, Tenniel had seen Maurice Dowling's *Othello Travestie* in which the Moor addressed the Senate: "Potent, grave and rev'rend sir, / Very noble massa," to the tune of "Yankee Doodle." Similarly, in Tenniel's Civil War cartoons Shakespeare's Othello, Caliban, and Caesar's ghost speak in comic darktown dialect, while the servant Lucius, in Tenniel's "Brutus and Caesar," is a full-fledged minstrel nodding over his banjo.[7]

In his study of nineteenth-century race and class prejudices, Douglas A. Lorimer found that Victorians had three essential images of blacks: the "comic minstrel," the "patient suffering slave," and the "cruel, lustful savage." Tenniel drew on the second of these types as well for his Civil War drama, variations of the suffering slave figuring in four of his cartoons. The image derived from the seal of the Society for the Abolition of the Slave Trade, founded in Britain in 1787, which pictured a kneeling black, his manacled hands raised in supplication, with the motto, "Am I Not a Man and a Brother?" This question had historical significance; in a court case of 1772 it was only by virtue of being considered a man that the Negro could come under the protection of English law. In Victorian times the seal's design was reproduced on letterheads, broadsides, dishes, and various trinkets.[8] Its motto turns up frequently in Civil War cartoons from both sides of the Atlantic, often in ludicrous contexts.

Punch Tacks Southward

King Cotton

In a Tenniel small cut of 1860, Sambo thrusts some sheets of newsprint at the slaveholder Jonathan, its giant headline an-

Fig. 188. Tenniel, "Monkey Uncommon Up, Massa!" small cut, *Punch*, 1 Dec. 1860, 220

nouncing "Lincoln President" (fig. 188). The black asks, "Hab you seen de papar Sar?" and some accompanying text divulges that South Carolina, "in an ecstasy of slave-owner's rage," has threatened secession. Issued in New York on the same day, a cartoon in *Harper's Weekly* depicts "The Tyrants of the Old World," including Britain's queen and premier, scarcely trying to conceal their delight at America's predicament. But *Punch* rejoiced for more altruistic reasons. Anticipating the "Beginning of Slavery's End," the paper had exclaimed, "Bravo, hurray, O my brothers!" and soon advised:

> If any talk of separation,
>   Hang all such traitors if you please.
> Break up the Union? Brothers, never!
> No; the United States for ever,
>   Pure Freedom's home beyond the seas![9]

Through early spring *Punch* favored the Union. In a January cartoon, Tenniel's handsome, beardless North places a protecting hand on a little black boy and confronts Mrs. Carolina—a virago armed with pistol and scourge (fig. 189). This personification of North we have seen before. In a Tenniel cartoon of 1856, "The American Twins; or, North and South," he had grappled in a life or death struggle with South (a gaunt Jonathan) over the admission of new territories to the Union. Tenniel's first cartoon of the war occurred in May 1861. In it North and South engage as gladiators before black spectators. It would be the last appearance of North as a noble young man.[10]

At this juncture *Punch* seemed unaware of Lincoln's denial that he had any intention "directly or indirectly, to interfere with the institution of slavery" in the states where it already existed. It was not until November that doubts concerning the North's motives as to slavery began to surface.[11]

Punch's first parting with the Federals, which occurred that May, had been over the North's protectionist policies, its "Ode to the North and South" admitting

Fig. 189. Tenniel, "Divorce à Vinculo," cartoon, *Punch*, 19 Jan. 1861

> I do declare I am afraid
>   To say which worse behaves,

The North, imposing bonds on Trade,
Or South, that Man enslaves.

Before Lincoln took office the Republicans had passed the Morrill tariff, a move that angered Englishmen, then firmly committed to free trade. An April cartoon in *Harper's* had pictured the British Lion championing the black, "Before the Morrill Tariff," but advising Jonathan, "After the Morrill Tariff," to "drive 'em [the blacks]; drive 'em Sir! with the lash, Sir!" From that time forward, *Punch* would repeatedly weigh the evils of slavery against the benefits of free trade, identifying protection as the North's casus belli as late as 1864. In this it followed the lead of the London *Times,* which pursued a vigorously anti-North policy throughout the war.[12]

Fig. 190. Henry Louis Stephens, "The Idol of England," cartoon, *Vanity Fair* (New York), 22 June 1861

The Federal blockade of Southern ports likewise became an issue since American raw cotton accounted for four-fifths of Britain's supply. The Confederacy curtailed shipment as well, banking on a cotton-starved Europe's support and intervention. By June, Henry Louis Stephens, owner and cartoonist of the New York journal *Vanity Fair,* pictured John Bull, Mr. Punch, and Lords Derby, Russell, and Palmerston worshipping at the feet of "The Idol of England," a humanized cotton bale shown feeding on blacks (fig. 190). In other *Vanity Fair* cartoons the cotton-hungry John Bull swallows Granny Jeff Davis's dose of slavery, weighs a cotton bale against a black, and is a rat tempted toward the cotton "cheese" in South's trap. Similarly, in *Harper's,* John Bull falls between two stools—"cotton interest" and "principle"—and leaps in terror at the shout of a blackface jack-in-the-box, "No more cotton!"[13]

The South had claimed "Cotton is King," a boast that was personified in Tenniel's gladiatorial cartoon in which the contest was being waged before a black emperor elevated on a throne of cotton bales. That year, a drawing in *Fun* showed the British mill owner imploring the enthroned cotton king, "Am I not a man and a brother?" Then, in November, Tenniel pictured King Cotton as the "Modern Prometheus" bound to the rock by the steel band of the blockade, his vitals rent by the American Eagle. The eagle's wings are differently starred—one with the linear arrangement of the Union, the other with the Confederacy's circular design—thus assigning blame to both sides. Soon Tenniel would show Britain's intention of taking its busi-

Fig. 191. Tenniel, "Look Out for
Squalls," cartoon, *Punch*, 7 Dec. 1861

ness to the Indian cotton shop "Over the Way." Indeed, as the mill owners had large surpluses in raw cotton and in cotton goods from the bumper crops of three preceding years, the chief sufferers were the mill operatives, who by 1862 were laid off in large numbers.[14]

Punch *Is Pugnacious*

Punch's growing antagonism to the North was provoked further by articles in Yankee papers. The Northern press had reacted angrily to the queen's proclamation of 13 May, which had affirmed Britain's neutrality and granted belligerent status to the Confederacy (thus recognizing its sovereignty). In July Tenniel portrayed "Naughty Jonathan" in a fit of temper over this policy. For the first time North displayed the pinched and displeasing countenance that had earlier typified the Southern slaveholder.

Responding to a piece in the *New York Herald* that had proposed that the United States "possess itself of Canada" in retaliation for Britain's neutrality, Tenniel portrayed troops of gaunt-faced Yankees rushing to the Canadian border while John Bull smilingly inquires, "Hello Brother Jonathan, where are you all running to?"[15]

English chauvinistic ire was substantially aroused by the Trent affair—the North's forced removal of two Confederate agents from a British merchant ship, an action that threatened to precipitate an Anglo-American war. Tenniel drew seven successive cartoons on the crisis, the first suggested by himself. In "Look Out for Squalls," honest sailor Jack Bull warns the wizened Yankee runt, "You do what's right, my son, or I'll blow you out of the water" (fig. 191).[16] The bellicose sentiments of this time were reflected at the *Punch* dinner as recorded by Silver in the following week: "4 Dec. 1861—War talk predominates. P. L. [Percival Leigh] throwing cold water on the fire of indignation. Thinks people too prone to fight. M. L. [Mark Lemon] and all dissent. Thackeray—"British ships are British soil—I, Makepeace, declare for war." To this Silver later appended: "fighting cuts always send the sale up. This week 2000 above average."

Early in the next year *Vanity Fair* ridiculed Britain's saber rattling, at the same time playing on the gorilla craze of the time. Picturing John Bull as "Gorilla Britannicus," Stephens quoted from du Chaillu: "He stood there and beat his breast with his huge fists, till it sounded like an immense bass drum, meantime giving vent to roar after roar." But Tenniel's six subsequent cartoons, even at the height of the crisis, were relatively mild. Britannia calmly waits "For an Answer" that Columbia, "In a Fix," deliberates. The trickster Jonathan tells "A Likely Story" (fig. 192); as Pantaloon he starts with alarm at Clown-Punch's red-hot poker; and, finally, after Lincoln (the "'Yankee' Coon") submits to Colonel Bull's ultimatum, as the contrite young Master Jonathan he is forgiven (fig. 193). The last is typical; Tenniel would portray Jonathan as a naughty child in one-third of his Civil War appearances.[17]

An Irish element entered the crisis when the nationalists foresaw in all this an "opportunity" to strike for independence. The call was taken up by pro-Irish papers in America; in early 1862 *Punch* scornfully quoted from the *New York Herald:* "There are five millions of Irish ready to throw off the British yoke, and to aid the American republic when she gives the signal for the retribution of British wrongs, never to be forgiven till they are redressed and avenged." *Punch* had taken a shot at the *Herald* in 1861 over the blockade issue. Now, suspecting the author of this piece to be "an Irishman of a peculiar class," the paper began a campaign against the Northern press in general, and the *Herald* and its editor in particular.[18]

Tenniel contributed to this warfare by slyly inserting sheets of the paper

Fig. 192. Tenniel, "A Likely Story," cartoon, *Punch,* 21 Dec. 1861

Fig. 193. Tenniel, "Naughty Jonathan," cartoon, *Punch*, 18 Jan. 1862

Fig. 194. Tenniel, "Retrogression (A Very Sad Picture): War-Dance of the I. O. U. Indian," cartoon, *Punch*, 1 Feb. 1862

320   THE *PUNCH* CARTOONS

into two cartoons. An issue of the *Herald* flutters from the lance of Jonathan, an Indian painted for war in stars and stripes who executes a savage dance at Charleston Harbor in 1862, his "Retrogression" owing to a "vast infusion of Convict Irish" (fig. 194). And sheets of the *Herald* lie on the counter where wily bartender Lincoln concocts a New York "Eye-Duster"—a mixture of "Bunkum," "Bosh," and "Brag."[19]

Lincoln's "Difficulties"

From the war's first year some at *Punch* thought the Federal's cause hopeless. In this they were continuously misled by the London *Times,* which favored the South's propaganda over the North's. In the months following the Union defeat at the first Bull Run, *Punch* published these doom-filled lines:

> You will never
> More for ever,
> North and South together pull.

To this prediction Stephens of *Vanity Fair* responded with a "Grand Death Dance of the English War Chiefs" in which Lords Palmerston, Derby, and Russell—in feathers and buckskin—encircle the perishing Columbia while dancing to the drum rhythms of Mr. Punch.[20]

The three subthemes of defeat were "no men," "no money," "no victories," the first two being epitomized in "Lincoln's Two Difficulties" (1862) in which Tenniel showed the president standing nonplussed between his financial and military advisers (fig. 195). In other cartoons, short-of-funds Jonathan calculates his war costs, or falls, still grappling with his Southern twin, into the crevasse of bankruptcy. Then, close to the war's end, both Lincoln and Davis are shown entrapped in the coils of debt—"How will they get out of it?" The shortage of recruits drives Lincoln to entreat Sambo, "Lend us a hand, Old Hoss, du!" or, in a takeoff on the farcical black brigades of wartime minstrel shows, to spoon the bitter dose of conscription to comically grimacing blacks.[21]

Punch commented wryly on Irish enlistment—sneering at the "remarkable exodus" of Paddy from "The Dis-United States" at the commencement

Fig. 195. Tenniel, "Lincoln's Two Difficulties," cartoon, *Punch,* 23 Aug. 1862

of the war, then condemning him for enlisting in the North's armies. Paddy was also the butt of the anti-Irish *Harper's*. When the militia act of 1862 made all able-bodied male citizens from eighteen to forty-five liable to the draft, *Harper's* pictured the Irishmen of New York's Sixth Ward brawling while rigged out in the sober suits and broad-brimmed hats of peace-loving Quakers.[22]

While constituting a substantial percentage of the foreign-born enlistees, the Irish were also to be found in large numbers among the immigrant working poor in the North's cities. They opposed abolition, fearing competition from an influx of Southern blacks. Anti-black sentiment in the North was utilized by Southern propagandists. For example, in 1863 the Richmond-based *Southern Punch* pictured Pat, whip in hand, inquiring of the Yankee boss, "What am I to do with the Nagers?"[23]

By the summer of 1862 there had been anti-Negro riots with heavy Irish involvement in several Northern cities. But the worst violence accompanied New York City's implementation in July 1863 of the conscription act of the previous March. The act's escape clause, which allowed those who could afford it to buy their way out of service, infuriated workers already inflamed by the use of contrabands (escaped slaves) to break a stevedore's strike. Soldiers and police were brought in to quell the four-day riot, the casualties of which are estimated to run anywhere from seventy-four dead to fifteen hundred. The event was marked by Tenniel's "'Rowdy' Notions of Emancipation" in which a "suffering slave" black at the mercy of the mob stretches a sup-

Fig. 196. Tenniel, "'Rowdy' Notions of Emancipation," cartoon, *Punch*, 8 Aug. 1863

Fig. 197. Tenniel, "The Great 'Cannon Game,'" cartoon, *Punch*, 9 May 1863

plicating hand toward the preoccupied Lincoln (fig. 196). Prominent in the lynching party is Paddy, his newly acquired Americanism highlighted by his striped pants and star-spangled shirt.[24]

The third subtheme, "no victories," was a constant. By mid-1862 Shirley's "Essence" thought it exceedingly probable that "the beginning of the end" had come. Although in July 1863 the battles of Vicksburg and Gettysburg marked the turning of the war in the North's favor, cartoons still forecast defeat: Lincoln mixes a cocktail of bogus victories; he is presented with an "Overdue Bill"—the promise to subdue the South in ninety days; and he watches gloomily as Jefferson Davis scores in the "Great 'Cannon Game'" (fig. 197). In a Tenniel cartoon of 1864, just days before the fall of Atlanta, the British premier confides that he may have to recognize the Confederacy "some of these days." This was followed in the next week by Tenniel's "American Juggernaut" in which a giant cannon propelled by the furies of war rolls over Union troops. *Fun* lagged still further behind; as late as January 1865 a cartoon showed South as a knight in armor receiving the accolade (the crown of "Independent Statehood") from the goddess Liberty.[25]

Meanwhile, cartoons in *Harper's* rebutted the doomsayers. Jonathan retorts to France and England, "Why you foreign Jackasses, I haven't BEGUN to fight yet!"; John Bull rages because the Union won't quit; and the Yankee warns the British premier (a smithy hammering out a sword for the Confederate president), "Wal, look out it don't fly up and hit yer in the eye." In

Vanity Fair the "Simple Rustic" John Bull (pictured as the English stereotype Hodge) swallows Southern lies, forgeries, and bogus Northern defeats; and, in the New York paper *Mr. Merryman's Monthly,* John Bull complains to Yankee Jonathan: "You go to war without consulting me, you continue fighting against my expressed wish, you persist in being victorious when I tell you that you are certain to be defeated, you continue to be prosperous when I tell you you are ruined."[26]

Black and White Slavery

Throughout the war *Punch* wavered between its anti-slavery principles and its sympathy with the South's push for independence. Slavery presented a real dilemma, the paper having long denounced the American Eagle as a carrion bird that fed on human flesh. The shadow cast by "English Liberty in America" in Doyle's 1850 drawing formed the silhouette of a black woman in chains, and Tenniel's parody of Hiram Powers's *Greek Slave* in "dead stone" was the "Virginian Slave" in "living ebony," her pedestal embellished with chains and scourges.[27]

But its abstract principles did not obscure the paper's essential bigotry. In text and picture not a black speaks except in minstrel-show dialect. Sambo wonders why that "lubly gal" the *Greek Slave* has no mark "ob de cow-hide" on her back; a darktown comic sings of how Lincoln will "libbelate de black"; a black Caesar's ghost informs Brutus-Lincoln, "I am dy ebil genus, massa LINKING"; and a black envoy tells the Grand Duke Punch, "Iss Ighness, you berry good King, you outrageous good King, you dam good King." By suggesting a likeness to blacks as a way of deriding Paddy, the paper implicitly denigrated blacks as well. "You to SAMBO I compare," Mr. Punch cried in 1852. Ten years later he made an offer to the South—"give us the niggers in exchange for the Irish peasantry"—and proposed to the scientific community that Paddy was the missing link between apes and blacks.[28]

The temptation to merge the comic-black and suffering-slave types was irresistible. In Tenniel cartoons a finger-snapping native compliments the French emperor for advocating the cause of liberty: "Now you am a man and a broder"; and in the text accompanying "Brutus and Caesar," the black Caesar's ghost reminds Lincoln that he once called him "man and brudder." *Harper's* used the motto, too. The black whom John Bull kicks out of Exeter Hall (London's venue for abolitionist meetings) is a comic minstrel carrying a sign that asks, "Am I Not a Man and a Brother?"[29]

But black stereotyping in *Punch* in no way indicated an about-face on the slavery issue. A poem in early 1862 addressed the South (said to be using bell metal for the casting of cannon):

> For all your daring against odds,
>   Still in your cannon's roar

We hear the dreary ringing of the
    Vile plantation Bell.[30]

However, the paper's anti-slavery comments had appreciably dwindled by then.

In conflict with this issue, *Punch* raised the concept of "white slavery"—the North's subjugation of a South yearning for independence and, consequently, for the right to hold slaves. By late 1861 the paper challenged the North: "Is the South, a conquered nation, / To be held and ruled by you!" The vehemence with which *Punch* writer Percival Leigh opposed the North's actions is seen in his cartoon suggestion in the following year (not taken up): "The Yankee reign of terror, a bigger guillotining than the world has ever seen."[31]

There were inevitable comparisons with the colonists' revolt against Britain. In late 1860 the *New York Tribune* had argued that if the Declaration of Independence "justified secession from the British Empire of three million of colonists in 1776," they did not see why it should not "justify the secession of five million of Southerners from the Federal Union in 1861." Along the same lines, the London *Times* asserted that "the spirit of George III had entered the Northern people." The theme arose at the *Punch* table in late 1862 when Thackeray, reported by Silver to have been "brimming with bad jokes all dinner time," suggested "George Washington as Peacemaker 'I was called a Rebel.'" The connection took form in Tenniel's 10 January 1863 cartoon, devised in the wake of the Federal defeat at Fredericksburg. The spirit of George III is shown nudging the ghost of Washington: "What do you think of your fine republic now, eh?—What d'ye think? What d'ye think, eh?" That month at the *Punch* dinner Leech's denunciation of the Confederacy was rebuffed by the other Punchites: "But what right had the States to secede from England, eh Jonathan? And *Punch* can't cry bravo to a Bully—or sympathise with an Invader. South fighting for hearth and home and therefore successful."[32]

By 1863 *Punch* had evolved a further argument against the North. In an article condemning the war, it reasoned: "Surely the white man has as much right to liberty as the black man. The South only asks to be let alone, and this is not an outrageous demand on the part of those who complain that hordes of Irish, Germans, and the ruffianism of New York are hired to cut the throats of native Americans [Southerners] merely for interpreting the Constitution differently from certain attorneys in the North." Here *Punch* revealed its class biases, as German and Irish immigrants comprised the largest segments of the North's laboring poor. This "mongrel" population the paper contrasted with the landed classes in the South. As early as May 1861 the London *Times* declared, "The inhabitants of the North and those of the South are two distinct peoples, as opposed as the Austrians to the Italians, or the Muscovites to the Poles." That December, *Punch* suggested that

Fig. 198. Tenniel, "The Overdue Bill," cartoon, *Punch,* 27 Sept. 1862

America send to the International Exhibition "a model of the model repub-lic" with the Irish element shown by "spots of mingled green and blood-red," and the Germans by "patches of whity-brown." And in the next year it in-quired, "Who is an American?" concluding that the country was composed of "aliens and immigrants," "roughs and rowdies," "partly Irish, partly any-thing you please." The class element emerges, too, in a text of 1863 that de-clared that the pro-North *Morning Star* (the "London New York Herald") was "an American organ, and being written for the uneducated class, of course abuses the South." Soon *Punch* would consider its prejudices justi-fied by the New York riots of 1863.[33]

The South was much romanticized. Precedents were close to home, *Punch*'s own Thackeray having painted an idealized picture of its landed society in his 1859 novel *The Virginian.* Ascribing to the South all that might be considered cultivated in America, a *Punch* poem in pseudo-Southern voice spoke of Britain's policy of non-involvement with bitter irony:

Let Arts decay, let millions fall, for aye let freedom perish,
With all that in the Western world men fain would love and cherish,
Let Universal Ruin there become a sad reality,
We cannot swerve, we must preserve our rigorous neutrality.

Meanwhile, in New York, Stephens's *Vanity Fair*—always ready to satirize the foibles of the English press—had shown "Old Marm Britannia," a pipe-smoking vendor of penny ballads, singing "Dixie—the Land of the Free" and "Bold Beauregard."[34]

Tenniel's portrayal of the South as a dashing military man, a cavalier, makes clear his paper's sentiments. Compare, for example, the sway-backed, red-nosed officer in "Lincoln's Two Difficulties" with his Southern counterpart in the "Overdue Bill" of the month following (fig. 195 and fig. 198). Also, compare him with the gentleman officer in a Morgan cartoon in the 1863 *Fun* (fig. 199). That paper was more explicitly pro-South than *Punch,* in 1864 eulogizing General Jeb Stuart as a leader of "dauntless cavaliers. . . . A soldier of the Right."[35]

Similarly, affluent Southerners felt a sense of kinship with Britain, adopting much of its culture. This is evident in the many references to British books, plays, and journals in Confederate papers. It is not surprising then that the *Southern Punch,* flourishing in Richmond, featured a column entitled "sips from Punch," and that the *Southern Illustrated News* published Tenniel's cartoons crudely reengraved.[36]

The Lincoln Image

Punch *Makes Merry*

For five or six months following the election of 1860 *Punch* had continued to favor the American president. It hoped its "esteemed friend, ABRAHAM LINCOLN," would "at his earliest convenience smash the Morrill and immoral Tariff," and it ran Tenniel's not unhandsome first portrait of the president. Once it became clear that the "American Difficulty," and the consequent blockade of Southern ports, would create English difficulties, then the increase in the injudicious articles in Northern papers, the rout at Bull Run, and the Trent affair swiftly took their toll. Most disappointing was Lincoln's stance on slavery. Having done an about-face on the president, *Punch* derided his scheme for compensated emancipation,

Fig. 199. Matt Morgan, "Tricks v. Honours," cartoon, *Fun,* 18 July 1863

Fig. 200. Tenniel, "Abe Lincoln's Last Card; or, Rouge-et-Noir," cartoon, *Punch*, 18 Oct. 1862

Tenniel picturing him as a wily Oberon with starred and striped wings attempting to secure a "little nigger boy" from the proud Titania (Miss Virginia).[37]

With Europe deliberating whether to recognize the Confederacy, Lincoln was persuaded to abandon compensated emancipation for something more forceful. By July of 1862 he had alerted his cabinet that he would soon issue a proclamation of emancipation. Recognizing that the current state of the war might make such an announcement seem "a last shriek on the retreat," he waited for a more favorable turn of events.[38] Five days after the 17 September repulse of Lee's offensive at Antietam, the proclamation was delivered.

It was a compromise, Lincoln having pointed out earlier that month that total emancipation could drive fifty thousand Union soldiers from the border states over to the South. Thus, its terms applied to blacks in rebel-held territory only, leaving slavery intact in the loyal states and in areas within Union lines. In the short run, as Lincoln admitted, the proclamation was inoperative.

The move was regarded with skepticism by many, not least by *Punch*. The 18 October 1862 issue ridiculed it in drawing and verse. In Tenniel's cartoon the desperate president, in a game of rouge-et-noir with the unruffled South, flings down his last card (fig. 200). Punning on the slang word for

Negro, it is an ace of spades, the single pip formed by the head of a comic black. In the same issue, a black minstrel's "Serenade to Lincoln" pointed out the fallacies in the proclamation, ending each verse with the refrain: "Ole ABE LINCOLN, him berry cute and clebber [repeated thrice] / Ole ABE LINCOLN, de President for ebber!"[39]

Some suspected the measure of trying to stir up a slave insurrection in the South, which might in turn provoke the desertion of soldiers fearful for the safety of their families. The London *Times*, which had previously warned that the war was intended to lead to a series of Cawnpores (recalling the massacre of white women and children during the Indian mutiny), now declared: "He [Lincoln] will seek out the places which are left but slightly guarded, and where women and children have been trusted to the fidelity of coloured domestics. He will appeal to the black blood of the African. He will whisper the pleasures of slaughter, and the gratification of yet fiercer instincts, and when blood begins to flow and shrieks come piercing through the darkness, MR. LINCOLN will wait till the rising flames tell that all is consummated, and then he will rub his hands and think that revenge is sweet." *Punch* was not quite so alarmist. Although the poem "Abe's Last Card; or, Rouge-et-Noir" hints at such an insurrection,[40] this is balanced in the same issue by the "Serenade to Lincoln," which maintained:

> Ole ABE'S subjicks may hab deir slaves as well,
> Whiles agin de rebel master de black nigger may rebel;
> But dere's so many ob um as prefers to wear de collar,
> Dat de risin' ob de niggers ain't no certainty to foller.

When the proclamation went into effect the next January, Tenniel drew a "Scene from the American 'Tempest'" in which a black Caliban accepts the proclamation from Lincoln and, pointing to Davis, says: "*You* beat him 'nough, Massa! Berry little time, I'll *beat him too*." But this Caliban is no grotesque monster, no "cruel lustful savage." He is our old friend Sambo, the comic black. In the same issue, *Punch* acknowledged the "fix" into which the slavery question had forced the president. Lincoln is shown reflecting:

> Then there's Loyal States, and Rebel States, and harf way 'twixt sound
>   and errin','
> There's Border States, that's neither flesh nor fish, nor good red-herrin.'
> Which side, at last, *they'll* go for, you ain't certain till you axes
> (And Greenbacks can't last for ever) their citizens for taxes.
> Now in them Rebel States folk count about three million niggers,
> And a million in the Harf-an-harf—guess them's about the figgers—
> And here's my hitch, ef I proclaim hull-hog emancipation,
> The Harf-and-harfs they'll cut up rough, go out on confiscation.[41]

Fig. 201. Tenniel, "Brutus and Caesar," cartoon, *Punch,* 15 Aug. 1863

Punch's final word on the proclamation came in Tenniel's Shakespearean travesty of that August. In it Brutus-Lincoln is beset by a black Caesar's ghost who comes to tell him that "Dis child am awful Inimpressional" (fig. 201).[42]

Punch *Is Perplexed*

In the spring of 1864 Shirley's "Essence of Parliament," while cleverly paraphrasing words spoken in the Commons by the attorney general, gave a fair idea of the dilemma that faced *Punch*: "If we only knew which way the war was going! If we were certain that the glorious and almighty bird of freedom that waves its alabaster wings in Washington would triumph over those savage, disloyal, ferocious rebels, those stealers and floggers of men and women . . . we should know what to do. But if that resolute and gallant band of Confederate gentlemen, who have . . . maintained so noble a resistance against the loafers, jobbers, miscreants, scum and spawn of the North—if these Southern patriots should establish their independence—why—."[43]

By fall the paper, believing the Union's defeat to be imminent, brought the goddess Columbia (absent since 1861) back to the cartoon page. The American symbol recalled ideals attendant on the nation's founding, ideals that had once inspired a *Punch* writer to praise the soundness of the "'great Republic'. . . . Her own foundation; holy ground!" Now, as Mrs. North, Columbia comes in mourning veils to warn Lincoln of his impending dismissal (fig. 202). The next month, holding her torn American map, she listens to the sympathetic words of Britannia. Her reemergence seems to forecast a new era, one in which North and South will amicably agree to go their separate ways and end this terrible war.[44]

Soon after these auguries of defeat, events moved quickly: Lincoln's re-election, Sherman's march to the sea and capture of Savannah, the passage of the Thirteenth Amendment. In Shirley's "Essence" of 18 February 1865 fear of Yankee designs on Canada mingled with rejoicing over abolition. Tenniel's cartoon of that date shows Lincoln sternly cautioning the Congress (personified by a blend of Jonathan and the American Eagle) against abrogating its Canadian treaties. It is the first time since the early months of the war that the president is not pictured as a buffoon.[45]

Successive "Essence"'s show that Parliament, too, is conciliatory. An "American debate" reveals that the federal government has been "well-disposed" toward England, its actions marked by "amity and discretion." Still, *Punch* hangs back, uncertain of America's intentions. In a Tenniel cartoon

Fig. 202. Tenniel, "Mrs. North and Her Attorney," cartoon, *Punch*, 24 Sept. 1864

that March Britannia exhorts Vulcan (the striking ironworkers) to help arm against Jonathan, seen strutting as Mars in the distance.[46]

The war was drawing to a close. As it took up to twelve days for American news to reach Londoners, ten days had elapsed since Lee's surrender when Silver recorded, "The report of the taking of Richmond in Saturday's *Times* makes the gladiator subject a good one we think, but we don't agree that the time to ask the "Habet? [he is hit] question is come yet?" However, news of the war's end did come in time for the word "habet" to be added to the cartoon. Tenniel closed the series as he had opened it—with the gladiatorial contest of North and South.[47] At this time, unknown to *Punch*, Lincoln was dead.

The next week, when word of the assassination had arrived, Taylor, who five months before had helped devise Tenniel's most damning Lincoln portrait, "The Federal Phoenix" (fig. 203), burst into the *Punch* dining room exclaiming, "This is terrible news!" Soon he would declare that *Punch* had been too "hasty" in its condemnation and that his own pen had been "lamed" by the later acts of Lincoln.[48]

Fig. 203. Tenniel, "The Federal Phoenix," cartoon, *Punch*, 3 Dec. 1864

Fig. 204. Tenniel, "Britannia Sympathises with Columbia," cartoon, *Punch*, 6 May 1865

On 6 May there appeared Tenniel's tribute to the dead leader—a contrite Britannia laying a wreath on Lincoln's draped body (fig. 204). Grieving at the president's head is Columbia; at his feet is the suffering slave, his severed chains beside him. The accompanying verses by Taylor spoke first to the cartoonist:

> You lay a wreath on the murdered LINCOLN'S bier,
>   You, who with mocking pencil wont to trace,
> Broad for the self-complacent British sneer,
>   His length of shambling limb, his furrowed face,
> His gaunt, gnarled hands, his unkempt, bristling hair,
>   His garb uncouth, his bearing ill at ease,
> His lack of all we prize as debonair,
>   Of power or will to shine, of art to please.

The writer, too, is chastised: "Beside this corpse . . . say, scurril-jester, is there room for *you*?"[49]

The Summing Up

Taylor had come down a bit hard on himself and *Punch*. While *Punch* had, on two or three occasions, been sufficiently roused by Lincoln's usurpation of extralegal powers to call him a dictator and a despot, for the most part

Fig. 205. F. Wilfred Lawson, "You Have Swollen the Earth with the Blood of My Children," cartoon, *Fun*, 3 Dec. 1864

the paper's texts treated the American president facetiously. He was pictured as inept and childishly devious, a bungler given to tasteless joking. Tenniel, it is true, had villainized Lincoln in three cartoons. We see the president deaf to the pleas of a doomed black; grasping hands with the repressive Russian czar; and, after the election of 1864, reborn from the ashes of commerce and constitution as the "Federal Phoenix" (see fig. 203). But mainly he was a trickster manqué with ruffled hair and high-water pants: serving up false victories, sidling up to Sambo, and fuddled by shortages and defeats. This was not unlike the treatment Tenniel accorded to other heads of state. For example, in this period he pictured the emperor of the French as a Mephistopheles with designs on Italy, and the Prussian and Austrian emperors as brigands "Dividing the Spoil" of Schleswig Holstein. After 1862, Lincoln more or less replaced Jonathan as the comic figure in Tenniel's American cartoons.[50]

Compared, for example, with the London *Fun,* a paper that had suggested that some might want to string Lincoln up "to the nearest lamp-post to the White House," *Punch* had been moderate. In *Fun*'s cartoons the president was a skeletal apparition urging his grotesquely maimed troops to "have another round"; a mangy dog with cans (an ill-performing American fleet) tied to his tail; the Yankee Guy Fawkes setting fire to the Constitution; a war-painted Indian, his waist ringed with scalps; the goblin-like nightmare who sits on Columbia's writhing form; and the murderer to whom she cries, "You Have Swollen the Earth with the Blood of My Children" (fig. 205).[51]

Soon after Tenniel's death, the American cartoon historian Frank Weitenkampf rebutted the charge that Tenniel had unmercifully scourged the American president, arguing: "Tenniel's cartoons against Lincoln have been referred to repeatedly, but there can be no doubt of the good faith that animated them. And be it said now that for the height of bitterness in attacks on the War President one must turn over the caricatures produced at the time in our own land." The New York *Cartoons Magazine* took this view, too, for it stated in the following year that Tenniel's cartoons "were not nearly so malicious as they might have been." Still, a half century later, Oscar Maurer's study of *Punch*'s Civil War coverage observed that "Lincoln the humanitarian, the statesman, the preserver of the Union and the Great Emancipator, was nowhere evident" in its pages.[52] But neither were these qualities evident in the columns of major Northern papers, for Lincoln was hardly the most popular of presidents. His party barely retained control of Congress in the 1862 elections, his own state falling to the Democrats; prominent Republicans considered forcing his withdrawal after nominating him in 1864; and for a time Lincoln himself doubted that he would be returned to office.

The copperhead press (Northern papers sympathetic to the South) saw Lincoln as a compound of cunning, heartlessness, and folly. Even the pro-North *Harper's* interspersed its pro-Lincoln cartoons with others in which Lincoln was the "Presidential Merryman": joking with his cronies while the hearse-borne Constitution passes; responding to Columbia's "Where are my 15,000 sons murdered at Fredericksburg?" with "This reminds me of a little joke"; and, as a theater manager, unctuously announcing the withdrawal of the night's tragedy, "The Army of the Potomac," and the substitution of three new farces devised by his secretary of the navy. In separately issued prints, Currier and Ives put out as many anti-Lincoln lithographs as pro-Lincoln ones, while in the border state of Maryland, Adalbert J. Volck created a series of exquisitely done etchings of the president that were filled with symbols of death and diablerie.[53]

His bid for reelection prompted a spate of prints that coarsely disparaged Lincoln. He stands with his colleagues at the "Grave of the Union"; the caskets hold "Constitution," "Habeas Corpus," "Free Speech & Free Press," and "Union." He promenades with his black paramour. Visiting the dead and wounded on the battlefield at Antietam, he requests his marshal to sing a ribald song.[54] By contrast, the copy of *Joe Miller's Joke Book* that Lincoln holds in the cartoon "Brutus and Caesar" is Tenniel's only reference to the president's taste for jokes.

Punch had explained its quarrel with Lincoln in 1862:

You say, ole ABE, now you libbelate de black;
What a pity dat you didn't do it long time back,
Cause al de world would den have stood wid old ABE LINCOLN,
Old ABE LINCOLN, dis am bery sad to think on!

This was explicated further in the next year:

First ABE LINCOLN gave out
That he'd fain bring about
The Re-union with slavery too, or without.[55]

Unable to espouse either cause, although leaning toward the South, *Punch* backed the government's neutral policy. In late 1863 both cartoon and poem acclaimed Foreign Secretary Russell as the "Modern Ulysses," guiding the ship "Neutrality" between the "Yankee Scylla" and the "Slave Charybdis."[56]

One might expect that the passage of the Thirteenth Amendment abolishing slavery in early 1865 would have given pause to the *Punch* staff. That February the expatriate artist and former *Punch* contributor William Newman drew a apotheosis of Lincoln for the New York *Budget of Fun*. Behind Lincoln, who is shown presenting the amended Constitution to the goddess Liberty, a tiny figure kneels in the dirt. It is Mr. Punch. But this was not the reality. On 15 February Shirley wrote in his diary that although he had "stood up for the Federals" at the *Punch* dinner that day, "the current of feeling in society, just now, is all against them, even to the point of unfairness."[57] Only with the South's final defeat and Lincoln's death would *Punch* say that it had been mistaken.

Swayed by the North's rejection of free trade, pugnacious articles in Yankee papers, early Federal defeats, mistrust of Lincoln's cautious approach to emancipation, a romanticized view of life in the South, and the Confederate propaganda purveyed by the London *Times*, *Punch* had misread the American war. What was Tenniel's own view? This might perhaps be deduced from his cartoon "The Great 'Cannon Game'" in which Mr. Punch, billiard marker, eyes Lincoln with a comic look of bored disgust (fig. 197).[58]

Still, *Punch*'s stance was not fixed; it wavered between its pro-Confederacy biases and a policy of nonalignment. In the end, the South's cotton diplomacy failed due to economic factors, Union victories, and the foresight of Britain's ministers. Meanwhile, recording the key issues and avoiding the more immoderate images that his subjects might suggest, Tenniel melded black minstrelsy, Yankee theater, tragedy, farce, melodrama, and Shakespearean travesty into a Civil War extravaganza.

Appendix
A Guide to Tenniel's Unidentified Punch *Work*

Over the space of fifty years Tenniel did more than thirty-nine hundred draw-ings for *Punch,* excluding his work for *Punch's Pocket Book.* About fifteen hun-dred of these, all falling within his first twelve years on the paper, do not display his oriental-looking monogram—a large *T* crossed with a smaller *J*—that can be seen on many of the figures in this book. These cuts, the most lighthearted that Tenniel designed, need to be brought into the recognized body of his work.

Among the hallmarks of Tenniel designs are the clean precise line with which he explicates his forms so that there is scant need for shading, and the sure figural draftsmanship, expressive body language, and perfect hands and feet of his little figures. His line alone would be enough to certify his cartoons, for Leech (with a far sketchier technique) was the only other *Punch* cartoonist in this period. A portion of the small cuts and initial letters were done by outside contributors, most being indifferent draftsmen whose work is easily distinguished from Tenniel's.

Other salient features of Tenniel's cuts are his types, his engaging humor, his excellent knowledge of the costumes and customs of divers times and places. One cannot mistake, for example, his calendar pages, their borders teeming with as many as fifty or sixty figures—swains, knights, workmen, schoolboys. There is a certain type of lady's head, a certain kind of mustached dandy, an unmistakable way that his people turn out their toes, lift their noses in pride, bow ceremoniously, play pranks, register surprise, that is sheer Ten-niel. Frith had said of his style, "Nothing like it has ever been seen before . . . nothing so quaint, so humorous, so completely appreciative of the sub-ject suggested, will be seen again" (*Victorian Canvas,* 2:228–29). Like the yearly calendar, the other decorative pages—the title pages, half titles, pref-ace and index headings and tailpieces—are also hard to mistake, for Tenniel's fun-loving Mr. Punch and his alert Dog Toby are not at all like Keene's and Leech's.

Distinct, too, is Tenniel's strong sense of design, undoubtedly gained from his study of German book illustration. This gives his pieces a unity and a def-inition that contrasts with the more diffuse drawings of others. As a corol-lary of this (and something that seems to have gone quite unrecognized),

Tenniel was a superb creator of letterforms. All of the hand lettering for his titles, prefaces, indexes, and calendars was designed and executed by him. For some fine examples see the half title of volume 21 or the prefaces to volumes 25 and 28. The striking characters of his decorated initials, too, whether rustic or black letter, help us recognize these as his.

The following list identifies Tenniel's unmonogrammed work by type and page number. Since Tenniel used his monogram intermittently until sometime in early 1853, the list does not represent his entire output for the period. The cuts listed as illustrations range from border designs that take up most of a page to small vignettes. His initials for "Punch's Book of British Costumes" are included with the illustrations for that series. When more than one Tenniel cut appears on a page, the total is shown in parentheses, and where the attribution was uncertain, a question mark in parentheses follows the entry. Readers should be aware that some pages also have designs by other hands.

VOLUME 19, July–Dec. 1850, title page, preface heading and tailpiece, index heading and tailpiece
Initials: 224, 229, 230, 234, 235, 241, 244, 250, 251, 253, 254, 264, 265

VOLUME 20, Jan.–June 1851, calendar page
Cartoons: 46
Illustrations: 1, 18, 56, 122, 132, 133, 197(?), 218
Initials: 7, 11, 20, 21, 23 (2), 32, 33, 37, 49, 51, 52, 55, 61, 64, 65, 71, 75, 91, 103, 106, 121, 141, 147, 153, 157, 173, 235, 239, 245(?), 250

VOLUME 21, July–Dec. 1851, index heading
Cartoons: 193
Illustrations: 213
Initials: 9, 10, 24, 33, 44, 51, 52, 81, 83, 117, 124, 136, 158, 159, 165, 175, 179, 196, 199, 207, 219, 228, 237, 239

VOLUME 22, Jan.–June 1852, title page, preface tailpiece, half title
Illustrations: 71, 96, 238 (5), 244, 254
Initials: 60, 70, 97, 111, 156, 249

VOLUME 23, July–Dec. 1852, title page
Cartoons: 27, 37
Illustrations: 18, 55, 76(?), 126(?), 191, 235, 243
Initials: 3, 12, 17, 21, 24(?), 45, 50, 51, 53, 64, 77, 101, 105, 106, 122, 127, 133, 137, 146, 167, 171, 177, 181, 187, 192, 195, 213, 217, 223, 237, 239, 245, 253, 264, 268

VOLUME 24, Jan.–June 1853, title page, preface heading and tailpiece, index heading and tailpiece
Cartoons: 45, 145, 165, 205, 215, 225
Illustrations: 12, 28, 42–43 (7)(?), 83, 92, 109, 210 (2), 240
Initials: 9, 17, 41, 49, 57, 63, 84, 97, 103, 112(?), 119(?), 123, 129, 133, 139, 151, 153(?), 158, 159(?), 162, 171, 173(?), 177, 179, 188, 197, 203, 217, 219, 222, 227, 243, 252

VOLUME 25, July–Dec. 1853, title page, half title, preface heading and tailpiece, index tailpiece

Cartoons: 25, 35, 45, 55, 65, 75, 86–87, 169, 179, 219, 229, 239, 259

Illustrations: 9, 12, 28, 58, 63, 64, 71, 80, 84, 102, 114, 176, 182, 186, 204, 222, 232, 238, 253, 255, 258

Initials: 7, 13, 17, 19, 22, 29, 39, 49, 52, 53, 73, 92, 93, 95, 101, 114, 131, 133, 157, 161, 167, 171, 172, 173, 175, 177, 187, 193, 194, 195, 197, 201, 207, 211, 216, 218, 233, 237, 243, 246, 247, 252, 261

VOLUME 26, Jan.–June 1854, title page, half title, preface heading and tailpiece, index tailpiece

Cartoons: 67, 89, 101, 111, 131, 143, 155, 185, 238, 250–51, 261

Illustrations: 22, 50, 64, 73, 75, 93, 114, 117, 162, 178, 194, 204, 213, 219, 220, 234, 267

Initials: 3, 8, 13, 19, 23, 27, 29, 33, 37, 39, 41, 50, 52, 54, 59, 60, 61, 62, 64, 72, 74, 75, 82, 91, 93, 98, 103, 105, 109, 115, 117, 123, 124, 125, 127, 133, 135, 136, 145, 147, 149, 153, 157, 169, 172, 173, 177, 179, 191, 193, 197, 200, 201, 202, 209, 212, 226, 231, 236, 241, 242, 244, 265, 267

VOLUME 27, July–Dec. 1854, title page, half title, preface heading and tailpiece, index heading and tailpiece

Cartoons: 5, 25, 35, 37, 45, 55, 66, 77, 87, 137, 148, 160, 171, 223, 233, 253

Illustrations: 8 (2), 13, 17 (2), 28, 57 (3), 61, 80 (3), 94, 125, 143, 151, 164, 168 (2)(?), 179, 184, 190, 198, 204, 208, 226, 240, 242

Initials: 8, 9, 14, 32, 47, 49, 50, 51, 64, 72, 79, 89, 93, 103, 104, 105, 115 (2), 119, 120, 121, 130, 131, 132, 133, 141, 158, 173(?), 193, 197, 198, 199, 203, 205, 207, 210, 218, 221, 227, 237, 240, 241, 245, 247, 251

VOLUME 28, Jan.–June 1855, title page, half title, preface heading and tailpiece, calendar page

Cartoons: 25, 105, 135, 187, 227, 237

Illustrations: 11, 47, 111, 124, 139, 142, 163, 169, 174, 202, 220, 233, 235

Initials: 2, 9, 17, 18, 21, 23, 27, 32, 33, 37, 39, 40, 42, 44, 49, 53, 54, 57, 63, 67, 73, 77, 82, 87, 91, 93, 97, 99, 101, 113, 121, 132, 133, 137, 147, 149, 152, 159, 161, 177, 179, 182, 184, 193, 195, 199, 201, 205, 214, 219, 220, 221, 223, 231, 245, 254

VOLUME 29, July–Dec. 1855, title page, half title, preface heading and tailpiece, index tailpiece

Cartoons: 86, 117, 147, 167, 178, 199, 229, 239

Illustrations: "Punch's Illustrations to Shakspeare," 2, 20, 32, 42, 50, 60, 63, 82, 90, 93, 112, 120, 123, 140, 150, 162, 172, 175, 192, 204, 212, 222, 225, 242, 254, 255. Other illustrations: 99, 165, 196, 227

Initials: 14, 19, 24, 32, 34, 44, 45, 51, 59, 65, 80, 89, 104, 115, 125, 131, 142, 144, 151, 155, 161, 165, 171, 173, 181, 184, 185, 187, 198, 201, 211, 213, 218, 221, 233, 243, 246, 251, 255, 256, 258

VOLUME 30, Jan.–June 1856, title page, half title, preface heading and tailpiece, calendar page, index heading and tailpiece

Cartoons: 105, 125, 155, 175

Illustrations: "Punch's Illustrations to Shakspeare," 11, 90, 100, 108, 130, 131, 148, 164, 178, 188, 222, 234, 244, 254. Other illustrations: 3, 17, 142, 161, 211

Initials: 1, 2, 23, 27, 28, 29, 33, 37, 39, 43, 81, 83, 87, 102, 112, 113(?), 122, 129, 133,

137, 139, 147, 159, 167, 173, 179, 183, 191, 204, 217, 224, 226, 231, 232, 235, 241, 243, 252, 256

VOLUME 31, July–Dec. 1856, title page, half title, preface heading and tailpiece, index heading and tailpiece
Cartoons: 5, 64, 85, 95, 105, 115, 124, 135, 145, 155, 225, 235
Illustrations: 29, 32, 39(?), 50, 61 (4), 71 (3), 72, 91–92 (3), 149, 161, 171, 180, 202, 209 (3), 210(?), 243, 248
Initials: 1, 11, 13, 19, 21, 27, 31, 37, 39, 41, 49, 51 (2), 57, 59, 61, 62, 70, 87, 90, 92, 107, 113, 129, 132, 153(?), 163, 167, 183, 189, 193, 197, 207, 219, 233, 237, 241

VOLUME 32, Jan.–June 1857, title page, half title, preface heading and tailpiece, calendar page, index tailpiece
Cartoons: 5, 35, 75, 85, 125, 175, 216, 227, 237
Illustrations: 7, 11, 12–13 (4), 42, 60, 93, 97, 101, 132, 137, 138, 141, 142, 148, 151 (2), 157, 161, 179(?), 180, 184, 187, 202, 219, 220, 221, 252
Initials: 18, 32, 38, 47, 52, 61, 62, 63, 68, 69, 72, 73, 77, 79, 82, 87, 89, 99, 103, 108, 109(?), 118, 122, 123, 128, 129, 133, 139, 143, 149, 150, 152, 154, 159, 161, 163, 168 (2), 169, 173, 177, 189, 193, 199, 209, 214, 222, 230, 231, 234, 239, 254

VOLUME 33, July–Dec. 1857, title page, half title, preface heading and tailpiece
Cartoons: 15, 25, 45, 76–77, 88–89, 99, 109, 119, 151, 231, 241
Illustrations: 11, 12, 97, 101, 103, 126, 132, 134, 137 (2), 180, 189, 205, 207, 234, 237, 246, 247, 257
Initials: 9, 13, 19, 20, 22, 28, 29 (2), 33, 39, 47, 48, 49, 55, 60, 62, 80, 83, 96, 107, 111, 121, 127, 135, 136, 150, 155, 157, 159, 163 (2), 169, 179, 193, 203, 205, 208, 209, 215, 219, 227, 239, 250, 258

VOLUME 34, Jan.–June 1858, title page, preface heading and tailpiece, calendar page
Cartoons: 15, 45, 127, 137, 147, 157, 173, 179, 185, 197, 237, 247
Illustrations: 20, 24, 58, 89, 90, 93, 102, 113–14 (7), 130, 184
Initials: 2, 11, 17, 19, 28, 29, 32, 39, 42, 44, 47, 48, 52, 61, 62, 63, 71, 73, 78, 82, 92, 109, 111, 119, 122, 123, 139, 149, 155, 164, 165, 166, 171, 183, 199, 200, 204, 205, 211, 221, 224, 225, 229, 231, 232, 233, 249

VOLUME 35, July–Dec. 1858, title page
Cartoons: 15, 45, 56–57, 67, 77, 87, 97, 107, 117, 137, 147, 157, 217, 227, 247
Illustrations: 22, 41, 48, 64, 112, 203, 212(?), 235, 239
Initials: 3, 19, 21, 23, 27, 29, 33 (2), 34, 62, 63, 69, 71, 74, 89, 93, 101, 109, 114, 121, 125, 131, 139, 142, 149, 154, 159, 172, 173, 175, 181, 185, 189, 191, 195, 199, 200, 201, 203, 211, 229, 241, 245, 251

VOLUME 36, Jan.–June 1859, title page, half title, preface heading, calendar page
Cartoons: 25, 55, 65, 85, 105, 115, 125, 145, 155, 165, 175, 205, 217, 229, 239, 249
Illustrations: 11, 12–13 (2), 22, 38, 57–58 (3), 151, 163, 182, 183, 191
Initials: 19, 34, 62, 72, 79, 82, 92, 97, 99, 103, 112, 122, 132, 142, 147, 153(?), 157, 159, 169, 179, 192, 197, 199, 208, 214, 234, 236, 246, 257

VOLUME 37, July–Dec. 1859, title page, half title, preface heading and tailpiece
Cartoons: 5, 16–17, 27, 37, 47, 57, 87, 97, 107, 117, 127, 135, 137, 147, 177, 194, 237, 267
Illustrations: 100, 202, 216, 255

Initials: 11(?), 22, 25, 49, 74, 75, 81, 89, 99, 101, 106, 121(?), 124, 129(?), 134, 136, 145, 155, 165(?), 186, 191, 195, 205, 211, 215(?), 216, 225, 229, 234, 235, 241, 264, 265

VOLUME 38. Jan.–June 1860, title page, half title, calendar page
Cartoons: 7, 17, 27, 37, 48, 69, 89, 100, 111, 121, 131, 141, 163, 173, 183, 193, 213, 223, 233, 243, 253, 263
Illustrations: "Punch's Book of British Costumes," 62–63 (4), 72 (2), 82–83 (4), 86–87 (3), 105–6 (2), 110–12 (2), 119 (3), 128–29 (4), 144–45 (3), 156–57 (4), 165 (2), 170–71 (3), 185 (3), 191 (3), 206–7 (4), 219 (3), 236–37 (4), 240 (2), 257 (3)
Initials: 19, 46, 57, 58, 66

VOLUME 39, July–Dec. 1860, title page, half title, preface heading and tailpiece
Cartoons: 5, 25, 35, 45, 55, 65, 75, 85, 95, 105, 115, 125, 135, 195, 205, 215, 225, 235, 245
Illustrations: "Punch's Book of British Costumes," 9 (2), 18–19 (5), 28–29 (3), 38–39 (3), 48 (2), 58 (2), 68 (4), 97 (3), 108–9 (4), 128–29 (4), 138 (3), 148–49 (4), 152–53 (3), 168 (3), 178–79 (3), 198–99 (3), 208 (3), 212–13 (2), 228 (2), 238 (2), 248 (3), 252 (2). Other illustrations: 20, 92, 220
Initials: 52(?), 87, 88

VOLUME 40, Jan.–June 1861, title page
Cartoons: 4, 27, 37, 59, 79, 91, 101, 111, 121, 131, 141, 152, 163, 173, 183, 193, 203, 223, 233, 243, 253
Illustrations: 14(?), 20, 25, 46, 147 (2), 208, 209
Initials: 11(?), 57, 66, 76, 83(?), 109, 150, 201, 227(?)

VOLUME 41, July–Dec. 1861, title page
Cartoons: 5, 16–17, 27, 37, 47, 67, 77, 87, 97, 107, 117, 127, 137, 147, 177, 187, 197, 219, 229, 249, 259
Illustrations: 62, 83

VOLUME 42, Jan.–June 1862, title page, calendar page
Cartoons: 5, 15, 25, 35, 45, 55, 65, 75, 85, 95, 105, 115, 125, 137, 147, 157, 167, 177, 187, 197, 207, 217, 227, 237, 247, 257
Initials: 215(?), 225(?), 239(?), 241(?)
Illustrations: 215(?)

VOLUME 43, July–Dec. 1862
Cartoons: 5, 15, 25, 35, 45, 77, 101, 121, 131. Beginning with the cartoon of 4 October 1862, p. 141, all of Tenniel's *Punch* work is monogrammed.

Notes

London is the city of publication for all daily newspapers unless otherwise stated. As all of Tenniel's cartoons (full-page political drawings) were published in *Punch* and appeared singly each week, they are identified by their date alone, as are other cartoons in *Punch*. For cartoons in *Fun*, *Judy*, and *Tomahawk*, periodicals that followed the same system, the paper's name and date are given. The following are abbreviated: *Dictionary of National Biography (DNB);* and *Illustrated London News (ILN)*.

Introduction

1. "Banquet to Sir John Tenniel," *Times*, 13 June 1901; and M[arion]. H. Spielmann, "Sir John Tenniel: An Appreciation," *Daily Graphic*, 5 Jan. 1901.

2. Richard D. Altick, *Punch: The Lively Youth of a British Institution, 1841–1851* (Columbus: Ohio Univ. Press, 1997).

3. Joseph Hatton, *Journalistic London* (Samson Low, Marston, Searle, & Rivington, 1882), 10; and Robert Walker, "John Tenniel and Punch," in *Toilers in Art*, ed. H. C. Eward (London: Isbister, [between 1884–1889]), 24.

4. Scott Nelson, introduction to *Art of the Eye: An Exhibition on Vision* (Minneapolis: Forecast Public Artspace Productions, 1986), 9, 11; M. H. Spielmann, *The History of "Punch"* (London: Cassell, 1895), 463; and Margaret Livingstone, *Vision and Art: The Biology of Seeing* (New York: Harry N. Abrams, 2002), 201.

5. Semir Zeki, *Inner Vision: An Exploration of Art and the Brain* (Oxford: Oxford Univ. Press, 1999), 40–41; and Spielmann, *History of "Punch,"* 466.

6. Hippolyte Taine, *Notes on England* (London: Strahan, 1872), 207–8; *New York World*, 1914; and *Truth*, 1914.

7. Taylor Stoehr, *Dickens: The Dreamer's Stance* (Ithaca, N.Y.: Cornell Univ. Press, 1965), 276; and Tenniel, cartoons, 26 May 1860 and 25 Nov. 1865.

8. Mark Girouard, *Return to Camelot: Chivalry and the English Gentleman* (New Haven, Conn.: Yale Univ. Press, 1981), 64.

9. William Makepeace Thackeray, *The Newcomes* (1855); Tenniel to George C. Pulford, 20 Oct. 1903, Houghton Library, Cambridge, Mass.; Tenniel to A. W. Mackenzie, 12 Nov. 1899, Harry Ransom Humanities Research Center, Austin, Texas; "Fine Art Gossip," *Athenaeum*, 7 Mar. 1914, 349; and Tenniel, cartoons, 2 Mar. 1872 and 25 Oct. 1879.

10. "Death of Sir John Tenniel," *Times*, 27 Feb. 1914; "Sir John Tenniel," *Supplement to "Punch," or the London Charivari*, 4 Mar. 1914 (hereafter cited as "Tenniel," *Supp. "Punch"*), 15; Girouard, *Return to Camelot*, 269; and John T. Jost, Jack Glaser, Arie W. Kruglanski, et al., "Political Conservatism as Motivated Social Cognition," *Psychological Bulletin* 129 (May 2003): 339–69.

11. "Minor Exhibitions," *Athenaeum*, 6 Apr. 1895, 449.

12. David Low, *British Cartoonists, Caricaturists and Comic Artists* (London: William Collins, 1942), 19.

13. Anstey Guthrie to Bernard Partridge, 24 Feb. 1914, Anstey Papers, British Library, London.

14. Tenniel, cartoons, 22 Feb. 1879, 26 May 1888, 22 Aug. 1857, and 20 Sept. 1879.

15. Tenniel, cartoon, 31 Dec. 1859; and John Ruskin, "Lecture 5. the Fireside. John Leech and John Tenniel," in *The Art of England* (Sunnyside, UK: George Allen, [1884?]), 193.

16. Tenniel, cartoons, 17 Feb. 1877 and 4 Mar. 1882.

17. Spielmann, *History of "Punch,"* 471; and *Journal de Genève*, 1914.

18. William Powell Frith, *A Victorian Canvas: The Memoirs of W. P. Frith, R. A.*, 2 vols., ed. Nevile Wallis (London: Geoffrey Bles, 1887), 2:228–29; and Tenniel, cartoons, 18 Nov. 1865 and 15 Apr. 1876.

19. F. Anstey [Thomas Anstey Guthrie], *A Long Retrospect* (London: Oxford Univ. Press, 1936), 160.

20. "Fine Art Gossip," *Athenaeum*, 7 Mar. 1914, 349.

1. Toast of the Evening

1. Harold P. Clunn, *The Face of London* (London: Spring Books, n.d.), 125, on the Hôtel Métropole; "Banquet to Sir John Tenniel," *Times*, 13 June 1901; and program, "Public Banquet to Sir John Tenniel," Bradbury and Evans albums, Bodleian Library, Oxford.

2. Linley Sambourne diary, 12 Dec. 1900 and 2 Jan. 1901, Linley Sambourne House, London.

3. "Sir John Tenniel," unidentified and undated newspaper clipping, Sambourne diary, 14 Mar. 1901; "The Dinner to Sir John Tenniel," *Times*, 18 Apr. 1901; and, on Tenniel's speech, G. W. Smalley, "Sir John Tenniel," *New York Tribune*, 5 Apr. 1914; and "Tenniel," *Supp. "Punch,"* 7.

4. Sambourne diary, 12 June 1901; and F. Anstey diary, 12 June 1901, Anstey Diaries, British Library.

5. Anstey diary, 12 June 1901.

6. Tenniel, cartoons, 7 Nov. 1891, 20 Feb. 1892, and 8 Mar. 1899.

7. Henry W. Lucy, *Sixty Years in the Wilderness: Some Passages by the Way* (London: Smith, Elder, 1909), 380.

8. Bernard Partridge, cartoon, *Punch*, 12 June 1901; Henry Dickens, *The Recollections of Sir Henry Dickens, K. C.* (London: William Heinemann, 1934), 330; and, for the toastmaster, Anstey diary, 12 June 1901.

9. Tenniel, cartoons, 6 Feb. 1875, 20 May 1882, 12 June 1886, and 9 Sept. 1893.

10. George Calkin and Emily Mary Riviere, marriage, 22 Jan. 1857, St. Pancras Old Church, in International Genealogical Index, p. 126,342 (hereafter cited as the IGI).

11. Sambourne diary, 3 Jan. 1893, on Reed's support.

12. Tenniel, cartoon, 26 Aug. 1893.

13. "Tenniel," *Supp. "Punch,"* 7, for other ladies present.

14. Hector H. Munro [Saki, pseud.], *The Westminster Alice,* illustrated by F. Carruthers Gould (London: Westminster Gazette Office, [1903?]). Frederick Macmillan was the nephew of Alexander Macmillan, original publisher of Lewis Carroll's *Alice's Adventures in Wonderland* (London: Macmillan, 1866), hereafter cited as *Wonderland,* and *Through the Looking-Glass, and What Alice Found There* (London: Macmillan, 1872), hereafter cited as *Looking-Glass.*

2. A Pretty Place

1. *A View of St. Mary le Bone from the Bason,* engraving, in W. H. Manchée, "Marylebone, and Its Huguenot Associations," in *Proceedings of the Huguenot Society of London,* vol. 11, no. 1 (London: Spottiswoode, 1915), 83. On early Marylebone see Gordon Mackenzie, *Marylebone: Great City North of Oxford Street* (London: Macmillan, 1972); Sigrid Baer, *Marylebone* (n.p., 1961); Samuel Lewis, *A Topographical Dictionary of England* (London: Samuel Lewis, 1831), s.v. "Mary le Bone (St.); and Mary L. Pendered, *John Martin, Painter: His Life and Times* (London: Hurst & Blackett, 1923), 66–76. Marylebone Library, London, is the prime depository for histories, maps, and photographs.

2. *Extant Monumental Inscriptions of St. Marylebone Paddington Street Cemetery* and *The Monumental Inscriptions of St. Marylebone Parish Chapel and Churchyard and Parish Church,* Marylebone Library.

3. Pictured in Michael Leapman, ed., *The Book of London: The Evolution of a Great City* (New York: Weidenfield & Nicolson, 1989), 270. The gardens were closed in 1778.

4. Mackenzie, *Marylebone,* pl. 12, and William Hogarth, "The Rake's Marriage," pl. 5 of *A Rake's Progress,* 1735, for early parish churches of Marylebone; Manchée, "Marylebone Huguenot Associations," 74, on the 1740 church; Noel Tenniel and Margaret Parker, 31 Oct. 1776, "Register of Marriages, St. Marylebone, Middlesex," 141, no. 422 (microfilm 0584222); Noé Tenielle [*sic*], 6 Apr. 1777, *Baptisms,* vol. 23 of *The Publications of the Huguenot Society of London* (1916), 314m; and Louisa Tenniel, 2 Dec. 1790, "Baptisms 1786–1812," in vol. 6, "St. James Picadilly Parish Registers" (microfilm 1042309). Microfilm copies of public records pertaining to marriages, births, baptisms, census returns, and microfiche copies of the IGI are available at Mormon family history libraries in the United States and United Kingdom and at public record offices and local history libraries in the UK.

5. On Westminster, see Robin D. Gwynn, *Huguenot Heritage: The History and Contribution of the Huguenots in Britain* (London: Routledge & Kegan Paul, 1985), 71. Baptismal dates of children of Noel and Margaret Tenniel, in "The Register of Births and Baptisms in the Parish of St. James in Westminster," vols. 5 and 6 (microfilms 1042308 and 1042309), are Mary Frances, 24 Mar. 1776; Mary, 8 Jan. 1780; Margaret, 5 May 1783; Sarah, 22 Feb. 1786; Victoire, 6 Feb. 1788; Louise, 2 Dec. 1790; and John Baptist, 25 Aug. 1792 (under "Baptisms in August Omitted by the Curate").

6. On the back of the miniature is written "Noel Tenniel, born 30 May 1745 died 11 June 1811." Dancing masters in the Calkin branch of the family include James Calkin, 1767–1836; James Ellis Calkin, 1803–1849; James C. Calkin, 1811–1874; and Joseph George Calkin, 1818–1875. The son of Noel Tenniel's daughter Mary, Dennis Etienne Victor Gouriet (married to Juliana Calkin), was likewise a professor of dancing. Information is from the family tree compiled by Maurice Calkin; the *Staffordshire Examiner*, 24 Nov. 1849; and "Individual Entry" 7122201, no. 93, Family History Library, Salt Lake City. On Huguenots among the petty nobility see G. A. Rothrock, *The Huguenots: A Biography of a Minority* (Chicago: Nelson-Hall, 1979), 154.

7. Mrs. C. H. Smith (née Fanny Riviere, 1813–?) wrote of the "pleasant walk" through the fields from Portland Place to Primrose Hill (*Wanderings of My Memory over My Life* [1890], 2, collection of Robert Riviere Calkin).

8. John Babtist [*sic*] Tenniel and Eliza Foster, 18 Apr. 1816, "Register of Marriages in the Parish of Portsea in the County of Southhampton," 47 (microfilm 919748). The census record for John Babtist's household in 1851 (microfilm 0087817) gives Eliza Maria's birthplace as Haddington, Scotland. Her engagement ring is described in the will of John Tenniel's sister Victoire.

9. Baptismal dates for Tenniel and his siblings are: Bernard, 7 Apr. 1817; Eliza Margaret, 29 July 1818; John, 24 Mar. 1820; William Rickards, 24 Sept. 1821; and Lydia Victoire, 7 Jan. 1824 (IGI p. 147,634); James d'Egrille Tenniel, 14 June 1826, and Caroline Tenniel, 23 Apr. 1834, recorded in the parish registers of Christ Church, Cosway Street (*Paddington Society Newsletter* 36, Jan. 1963, Marylebone Library); and Adolphus, born c. 1828; Mary, born c. 1830; George E., born c. 1836; Frederick Henry, born c. 1838; and Charles, born c. 1841, who appear in census records for John Babtist's household. There is no record of a Reginald, named in "Tenniel," *Supp. "Punch,"* 9, the writer probably meaning William Rickards, who assisted John Baptist in all his vocations. Adolphus, according to census records—John Baptist's in 1851 and his own in 1871 (microfilm 824712)—lived in London and was a collector, first for a water company and then for a public comptroller. His will ("Calendar of Grants of Probate—1883," fol. 265) gives his occupation as accountant.

10. Clunn, *Face of London*, 206.

11. S. C. Hall, *Retrospect of a Long Life: From 1815 to 1883* (New York: D. Appleton, 1883), 2, 78, 6, 25; and Henry Vizetelly, *Glances Back through Seventy Years*, 2 vols. (London: Kegan Paul, Trench, Trübner, 1893), 1:27.

12. *Topographical Dictionary of England*, s.v. "Mary le Bone (St.)"; Mackenzie, *Marylebone*, 116–19; and Robert Harling, ed., *A London Miscellany: A Nineteenth Century Scrapbook* (New York: Oxford Univ. Press, 1938), 47–48. John Glover's painting of the view from York Gate is described in Manchée, "Marylebone Huguenot Associations," 60.

13. *Topographical Dictionary of England*, s.v. "Mary le Bone (St.)"; *An Encyclopaedia of London*, ed. William Kent (London: J. M. Dent & Sons, 1951), s.v. "St. Marylebone"; and personal observation.

14. The census return for 1821 for the parish of St. Marylebone (microfilm 0566918) shows the Tenniels at 25 Alsops [*sic*] Buildings, there being three male occupants, two of them under five, and four female occupants, one under five. See Hermione Hobhouse, *History of Regent Street* (London: Macdonald & James, 1975), 15, for a map of 1792 showing Allsop's Buildings already in place. On Allsop's Buildings see Mackenzie, *Marylebone*, 198–99.

15. The 1821 census return (microfilm 0566918) shows the Martins at 30 Alsops [*sic*] Buildings; their location relative to the Tenniels is shown on a map of 1846, Marylebone Library. See Pendered, *John Martin, Painter*, 80–81; Leopold Charles Martin, "Reminiscences of John Martin, K. L.," part 7, *Newcastle Weekly Chronicle*, 16 Feb. 1889; and Thomas Balston, *John Martin, 1789–1854: His Life and Works* (London: Gerald Duckworth, 1947), 44, on the rental. Similarly, in 1839 when Dickens took 1 Devonshire Terrace (a few blocks to the east on the New Road) he described it as "a house of great promise (and great premium), undeniable situation, and excessive splendour." He is quoted in Frederic G. Kitton, *The Dickens Country* (London: Adam & Charles Black, 1905), 57. The rents are shown in rate book E61 for 1830–31, Marylebone Library.

16. Balston, *John Martin*, 44, on the demolition of the homes; Mackenzie, *Marylebone*, 282, on the setback requirement; Pendered, *John Martin, Painter*, 81, on Martin's painting room; and rate book E61, on the stable.

17. In 1841 John Baptist was living at 22 Gloucester Place, New Road, with a rental of eighty-seven pounds and a ratable value of seventy pounds—an increase over what he paid at Allsop's Terrace. The rate book H16 for 1834 shows that 25 Allsop's Terrace (formerly Allsop's Buildings) was empty by the Christmas rent day. According to *The Boarding School and London Masters' Direc-*

tory (1828), some professors were employed "from morning till night" at the rate of one guinea for forty minutes while others were "pining in obscurity" (copy at British Library). See Dickens, *Bleak House* (1853), chap. 38, on the Turveydrop Academy; and Smith, *My Life*, 31, on the drawing master Riviere.

18. Incomplete sets of the *Royal Blue Book, Fashionable Directory, Containing the Town and Country Residences of the Nobility and Gentry* at various depositories show that John Baptist was listed in 1828, 1831, 1841, 1845, 1850, and 1859. He also appears in *Boyle's Fashionable Court and Country Guide* for 1831, 1841, and 1856.

19. For John Baptist's various professions see census returns for 1841–71 (microfilms 438793, 0087817, 0542670, and 0838752); and for his students' recollections of his teaching see Herbert Harlakenden Gilchrist, ed., *Anne Gilchrist, Her Life and Writing*, 3rd ed. (London: T. Fisher Unwin, 1887), 20–21; and John Callcott Horsley, *Recollections of a Royal Academician*, ed. Mrs. Edmund Helps (London: John Murray, 1903), 11. Apparently John Baptist followed the pattern set by the French immigrants in this district who were "drawing and fencing masters . . . and masters (or otherwise) of many other avocations" (Mackenzie, *Marylebone*, 228–29).

20. Victoire Tenniel and James Calkin, marriage, 30 Apr. 1808 (IGI, p. 147,634). For composers, singers, musicians, and professors of music in the Calkin family, see *A Dictionary of Music and Musicians (AD 1450–1880) by Eminent Writers, English and Foreign*, 4 vols., ed. George Grove (London: Macmillan, 1879) 2:659, 3:544, and 4:449; and *The Musical Directory, Register and Almanack and Royal Academy of Music Calendar for the Year 1853*, 56, 57, 64 65, 90, 123. On the marriage of Emily Mary Riviere and George Calkin, see chap. 1 n. 10 above. Fanny Riviere Smith, who describes herself as a painter of miniatures, writes of her father's pleasure in playing the flute (Smith, *My Life*, 2–4, 32). See also *DNB*, s.v. "Riviere, Henry Parsons (1811–1888)"—painter; "Riviere, Robert (1808–1882)"—bookbinder; "Riviere, William (1806–1876)"—painter; and *The New Grove Dictionary of Music and Musicians* (London: Macmillan, 1980), s.v. "Bishop (née Riviere), Anna" (singer). On the Gianis, the *London Masters' Directory* for 1828 lists on p. 55, "Mr. Julius Gioni [*sic*], Dancing Master, 66, Norton Street, Fitzroy Square"; and *Boyle's Court Guide* for 1811 lists on p. 31, "Lorenzo Giani, art." Lorenzo's daughter, Maria Angela Georgina (IGI, p. 83,114), is listed in the parish of Islington census for 1861 (reference no. RG9/128) as Georgina A. Giani, professor of music, and in the *Musical Directory* for 1853, p. 126. The Corbould-Keene connection is through John Martin's wife, whose niece, Ann Middleton Wilson, was the second wife of the painter Edward Henry Corbould. Corbould's brother married Charles Keene's sister Mary Grace Keene (Balston, *John Martin*, 229–30).

21. L. C. Martin, "Reminiscences of John Martin," part 6, 9 Feb. 1889, and part 8, 23 Feb. 1889; Pendered, *John Martin, Painter*, 20–21; and Balston, *John Martin*, 13–15, 159.

22. Stella Margetson, *Regency London* (New York: Praeger, 1971), 23; and William Feaver, *The Art of John Martin* (Oxford: Clarendon Press, 1975), 46, 47, figs. 28, 29.

23. "Night Noises" in Hugh Massingham and Pauline Massingham, *The London Anthology* (London: Phoenix House, 1950), 217; Smith, *My Life*, 35; and Dickens, *Dombey and Son* (1844–46), chap. 3.

24. Smith, *My Life*, 4, on the funerals of Byron and Queen Caroline; and Alvin Redman, *The House of Hanover* (New York: Coward-McCann, 1960), 256, on George IV.

25. Vizetelly, *Through Seventy Years*, 1:33, on children's dress; and, on the Diorama, Miss Weeton (Ellen), *Journal of a Governess*, ed. Edward Hall, 2 vols. (London: Oxford Univ. Press, 1936), 2:29; and Feaver, *Art of John Martin*, 68.

26. Mackenzie, *Marylebone*, 119, on the development of Regent's Park; Percival Leigh, "A Prospect of ye Zoological Societye its Gardens. Feeding ye Beasts," in *Manners and Customs of ye Englyshe* [1849], no. 35; and on the Colosseum, *London Miscellany*, 37.

27. Marion Lochhead, *The Victorian Household* (London: John Murray, 1964), 162–63; Gustave Doré and Blanchard Jerrold, *London: A Pilgrimage* (1872; reprint, New York: Benjamin Blom, 1968); Benjamin Haydon's painting *Punch or May Day* (1829); Tenniel, illustration to "The Cinderella of 1851," *Punch*, 20 Sept. 1851, 130; and "A Short Account of the St. Marylebone Charity School for Girls" (1887), Marylebone Library.

28. Horsley, *Recollections*, 11–13, on the school in Kensington; and Henry W. Lucy's article in the *DNB*, s.v. "Tenniel, Sir John (1820–1914)." The school's location may have led Lucy and others to conclude that Tenniel had been born there. I am indebted to Michael Hancher, *The Tenniel Illustrations to the "Alice" Books* (Columbus: Ohio State Univ. Press, 1985), 4, for identifying the suits worn by the Tweedles as skeleton suits.

29. Dickens, "Our School," in *Household Words*, 11 Oct. 1851, 51. Vizetelly, *Through Seventy Years*, 1:116, speaks of cab fares of a shilling or more per mile. This may be why the drawing master Riviere rose early each day to walk, his heavy portfolio under his arm, to a school in Kensington that may have been further from his home near Fitzroy Square than John Baptist's was from Allsop's Buildings (Smith, *My Life*, 31).

30. Balston, *John Martin*, 173.

31. The *London Masters' Directory* of 1828 gives James Calkin's address as 13 Edward Street, Hampstead Road. The children of James and Victoire Calkin appear in the family tree compiled by Maurice Calkin. Joseph "Tennielli" Calkin's son, John William Archibold Calkin (c. 1850–1924), was Tenniel's solicitor, one of his beneficiaries, and an executor of his estate, and John William Archibold's children, Edith Lily Calkin and Stanley J. P. Calkin, witnessed Tenniel's will. The Italianized version of the name may have been adopted by Joseph Calkin when he studied voice in Milan under Lamperti. See *Grove's Dictionary of Music and Musicians* (1955 ed.), s.v. "Calkin (no. 5) Joseph Calkin—called Tennielli—(1816–1874)."

32. Mackenzie, *Marylebone*, 55; *Topographical Dictionary of England*, s.v. "Mary le Bone (St.)"; and Vizetelly, *Through Seventy Years*, 1:117, on ladies costumes of the period.

33. L. C. Martin, "Reminiscences of John Martin," part 6, 9 Feb. 1889; Cosmo Monkhouse, *The Life and Work of Sir John Tenniel, R.I.* (London: Art Journal, 1901), 31; J. D. Aylward, *The English Master of Arms: From the Twelfth to the Twentieth Century* (London: Routledge & Kegan Paul, 1956), 232–34, on protective masks; and Smith, *My Life*, 33, on the "distant deference" with which fathers were addressed.

34. L. C. Martin, "Reminiscences of John Martin," part 6, 9 Feb. 1889. According to Spielmann, *History of "Punch,"* 498, Tenniel also studied at the National Gallery with Charles Martin and T. Harrison Wilson (later a special correspondent for the *ILN*—was he related to John Martin's brother-in-law Thomas Wilson?). At the Townley Gallery, Tenniel would probably have seen Henry Corbould at his thirty-year task of executing finished drawings of the marbles (*DNB*, s.v. "Corbould, Henry [1787–1844]"). See Feaver, *Art of John Martin*, 231 n. 8, for Martin's letter to Smith; *DNB*, s.v. "Martin, Leopold, (1817–89)"; Edward Miller, *That Noble Cabinet: A History of the British Museum* (London: André Deutsch, 1973), 120, on Smith; *DNB*, s.v. "Smith, John Thomas (1766–1833)"; and *DNB*, s.v. "Tenniel." The Madden Diaries, British Museum, contain about five of Madden's sketches.

35. J. Mordaunt Crook, *The British Museum* (London: Allen Lane, 1972), 67; Arundell Esdaile, *The British Museum Library* (London: George Allen & Unwin, 1948), 327; P. R. Harris, *The Reading Room* (London: British Library, 1979), 3, 6–7; Smith, *My Life*, 29–30; and Vizetelly, *Through Seventy Years*, 1:255, on Charles Martin.

36. Scrapbook no. 2, in family possession. The title of Chery's book as given by Tenniel is "Recherches sur les Costumes et sur les Theatres de toutes les nations."

37. Tenniel, "Pencillings in the Pit," Harvard Theater Collection, Harvard College Library, Cambridge, Mass. (a 6 1/4 × 10 1/4–inch album with about three tiny drawings affixed to each of its fifty-six pages); and Jacqueline Knight, "The Theatre of John Tenniel," *Theatre Arts Monthly* 12 (1928): 111–18. See also *Actors by Daylight and Pencilings in the Pit* 1, 14 Apr. 1838, Huntington Library, San Marino, Calif.

38. V. C. Clinton-Baddely, *All Right on the Night* (London: Putnam, 1954); Charles Rice, *The London Theatre in the Eighteen-Thirties*, ed. Arthur Colby Sprague and Bertram Shuttleworth (London: Society for Theatre Research, 1950); and Ernest Bradlee Watson, *Sheridan to Robertson: A Study of the Nineteenth Century London Stage* (1926; reprint, New York: Benjamin Blom, 1963), particularly chaps. 4 and 5; and Vizetelly, *Through Seventy Years*, 1:99–101. Hablôt K. Browne's illustration, "Mr. Guppy's Desolation," in *Bleak House*, provides a good picture of the audience in the pit.

39. Taine, *Notes on England*, 267; Watson, *Sheridan to Robertson*, 301, on Macready; and Vizetelly, *Through Seventy Years*, 1:99–101.

40. Harley Granville-Barker, "Exit Planché—Enter Gilbert," in *The Eighteen-Sixties: Essays by Fellows of the Royal Society of Literature* (New York: Macmillan, 1932), 107; and Rice, *London Theatre*, 31.

41. Stanley Weintraub, *Victoria: An Intimate Biography* (New York: Truman Talley, 1987), 117.

42. It was probably for this purpose that Tenniel made several small watercolors after Van Dyke, Rubens, Velasquez, and Rembrandt (in family possession) besides studies after Rubens, Holbein, and Hogarth, in the large scrapbook no. 2.

43. Balston, *John Martin*, 77–78; and *Works Exhibited at the Royal Society of British Artists 1824–1893*, comp. Jane Johnson, 2 vols. ([Woodbridge? UK]: Antique Collector's Club, 1975), s.v. "Tenniel, John."

Of sixteen works eleven are identified as watercolors, with five based on Scott. Unless it was prior to 28 Feb. 1837, Tenniel would have been seventeen when he exhibited and sold *The Stirrup Cup*. For other exhibited work of this period see Algernon Graves, *The Royal Academy of Arts: A Complete Dictionary of Contributors and Their Work from Its Foundation in 1769 to 1904* (New York: Burt Franklin, 1972), s.v. "Tenniel, Sir John, R.I." "The Old and Young Courtier" is in *The Percy Reliques of Ancient English Poetry*, 2 vols. (London: J. M. Dent, n.d.), 2:128–30.

44. Balston, *John Martin*, 163, 166, 168; Pendered, *John Martin, Painter*, 115, 117, 120, 124–27; and L. C. Martin, "Recollections of John Martin," part 2, 12 Jan. 1889.

45. Balston, *John Martin* 191–93; Feaver, *Art of John Martin*, 124–26, 130, 150; and Pendered, *John Martin, Painter*, 216.

46. Balston, *John Martin*, 199–202, on Martin's *Coronation of Queen Victoria*.

47. Ibid., 200, on Martin "going on in glory"; and Ian Anstruther's definitive account, *The Knight and the Umbrella: An Account of the Eglinton Tournament, 1839* (London: Geoffrey Bles, 1963).

48. Anstruther, *Knight and Umbrella*, 153–63; Robert Bernard Martin, "Plum'd Like Estridges," in *Enter Rumour* (London: Faber & Faber, 1962), 92–96; Mackenzie, *Marylebone*, 158–59; Pendered, *John Martin, Painter*, 70; and materials on the Eyre Arms Tavern at the Marylebone Library.

49. Ticket of admission, Marylebone Library; *Guide to the Tournament at Eglinton Castle* (1839), 25, for the quotation from a passerby; and Feaver, *Art of John Martin*, 156.

50. Girouard, *Return to Camelot*, 107, naming also at the event: Daniel Maclise, Noël Paton, William Bewick, John Franklin, and William Allan; and *Allgemeines Lexicon der Bildenden Künstler*, s.v. "Nixon, James Henry." The five volumes of letters applying for tickets (collection of the eighteenth Earl of Eglinton) contain no Tenniel letters.

51. *Times*, 13 Aug. 1839; Girouard, *Return to Camelot*, 101; and Jeanie D. Boswell to Patrick Boswell, 8 Sept. 1839, typescript, p. 2, collection of the Earl of Eglinton.

52. "The Eglinton Tomfooleryment," drawing, *Cleave's Penny Gazette*, 1834, in Anstruther, *Knight and Umbrella*, 239; Richard Doyle, *The Tournament; or, The Days of Chivalry Revived* (London: J. Dickinson, [1839?]); Charles H. Bennett, initial letter in William Sangster, *Umbrellas and Their History* (London: Cassell, Peter & Galpin, n.d.), 33; and Bab [William S. Gilbert], "Sir Guy the Crusader," illustration, *Fun*, 8 June 1867, 139.

3. "Jan"

1. Tenniel, "To Henry Hemming Junr. on breaking an engagement. A.D. 1840"; and "The Broken Tryst—to Henry Hemming Jr. somewhere about A.D. *1840*," in Tenniel et al., "*Bouts Rimés* (and other *nonsense*)," Tenniel, J / Works, Harry Ransom Humanities Research Center.

2. R. J. Cruikshank, *Charles Dickens and Early Victorian England* (New York: Chanticleer Press, 1949), 141–42, on London streets.

3. Ruth Manning-Sanders, *Seaside England* (London: B. T. Batsford, 1951), 34–35, which quotes a young lady on holiday at Scarborough (c. 1860): "Pictures, living pictures in the Albanian style, are on view from morning to night, not, as in London on the banks of the *Serpentine*, veiled by the pearly mists of the early hours or partly concealed by twilight shades, but in the full glare of day and sunshine."

4. Balston, *John Martin*, 121; R. H. Mottram, "Town Life" in *Early Victorian England, 1830–1865*, 2 vols. (London: Oxford Univ. Press, 1934), 1:171; and "The State of the Serpentine," *Punch*, 19 Oct. 1850, 163.

5. *Julius Caesar*, act 1, sc. 2, lines 101–18; and *King Henry the Fifth*, act 4, sc. 3, lines 64–67.

6. Henry Hemming to Winifred and Cecil, 14 Feb. 1901, Hemming family papers. In *Hamlet*, act 1, sc. 3, lines 62–63, Polonius advises Laertes, "The friends thou hast, and their adoption tried, / Grapple them to thy soul with hoops of steel."

7. Edith Hemming (granddaughter of Henry Keene and Sophia Wirgman Hemming), note, Sept. 1916, describing Tenniel's friendship with the family; "Interesting Weddings," 20 Sept. 1904, unidentified newspaper relating that present at the wedding of Margaret Marian Keene, niece of artist Charles Keene, were the following cousins of the bride: "the Misses Corbould; Mr. and Mrs. Walter Corbould; Mr. George [Wirgman] Hemming, K.C.; Miss Hemming; and Miss E. Hemming"; and scrapbook in which Tenniel's paintings of the Hemmings are listed in notes extracted from the letters of Edith Hemming (all of the above in Hemming papers). See also Tenniel to Shirley Brooks, 17 Jan. 1872, in which he writes: "My very old friend Geo. Hemming—not the original 'Glaucus,' but Senior wrangler, Chancery barrister, and Saturday reviewer, is coming to dinner *next Saturday—en garçon*." (Brooks Album, Harkness Collection, New York Public Library).

8. Henry Hemming to Kit (Christopher Hemming), 16 June 1892, Hemming papers.

9. Playbill (8 × 12 1/4 inches), Hemming papers; Charles Dance, *Naval Engagements; A Comedy in Two Acts,* in *Acting National Drama,* ed. Benjamin Webster, vol. 4 (London: Chapman & Hall, 1838), 5, act 1, sc. 1; J. M. Morton, *Chaos Is Come Again; or, The Race-Ball! A Farce in One Act,* in *Acting National Drama,* vol. 6 (London: Chapman & Hall, n.d.); and *DNB,* s.v. "Vining, George J. (1824–1875)." Other Vining roles played by Tenniel were Don Leon in Charles Kemble's *Plot and Counterplot* and Gustavus de Mervelt in J. R. Planché's *Charles the XII.*

10. Characters return "from the dead" in Thomas Morton, *The School of Reform;* George Coleman, *The Heir at Law;* and Tom Taylor, *A Sheep in Wolf's Clothing.*

11. Cover, Charles Kemble, *Plot and Counterplot; or, The Portrait of Cervantes,* French's Acting Edition (London: Samuel French, 1895), for the scenery advertisement.

12. *Society of British Artists,* vols. 1 and 2; and Helene E. Roberts, "Exhibition and Review: The Periodical Press and the Victorian Art Exhibition System," in *The Victorian Periodical Press: Samplings and Soundings,* ed. Joanne Shattock and Michael Wolff ([Leicester] UK: Leicester Univ. Press, 1982), 92, 99.

13. William Sandby, *The History of the Royal Academy of Arts: From Its Foundation in 1768 to the Present Time,* 2 vols. (London: Longman, Green, Longman, Roberts & Green, 1862), 2:364; Sidney C. Hutchinson, *The History of the Royal Academy, 1768–1968* (New York: Taplinger, 1968), 104; and *DNB,* s.v. "Landseer, Edwin Henry (1802–73)."

14. Henry Holiday, *Reminiscences of My Life* (London: William Heinemann, 1914), 31, in which he recalled that in 1855 he was required to submit several drawings of antique statues and one of a skeleton. Tenniel's "ivory ticket" is in family possession.

15. "Tenniel," Supp. *"Punch,"* 1; and Anne Gilchrist, 21. The initials F.S.A. that John Baptist sometimes used after his name may have denoted membership in the Society of Arts as he was not a fellow of the Society of Antiquaries.

16. George Cockburn Hyde, "A Night Alarm" (yacht *Amethyst,* Portsmouth Harbour, 1842), in Tenniel et al., *"Bouts-Rimés."*

17. Holiday, *Reminiscences of My Life,* 46, 71; and Tenniel, quoted in Spielmann, *History of "Punch,"* 461.

18. Monkhouse, "Sir John Tenniel," 10; Smith, *My Life,* 8–9; Lenore Van Der Vere, "The Artists' Society and the Langham Sketching Club," *Studio* 32 (Sept. 1904): 279–98; and Henry Stacy Marks, *Pen and Pencil Sketches,* 2 vols. (London: Chatto & Windus, 1894), 1:61, 89. Tenniel may have known Smith, who was a close friend of Martin's son-in-law Joseph Bonomi.

19. George Somes Layard, *The Life and Letters of Charles Samuel Keene* (London: Samson Low, Marston, 1892); Marks, *Pen and Pencil Sketches,* 1:89; and Simon Houfe, "Charles Keene, Draughtsman and Illustrator, 1823–1891," in *Charles Keene "the Artist's Artist," 1823–1891* (London: Christie's & *Punch,* n.d.), 14.

20. Vizetelly, *Through Seventy Years,* 1:164; and Holiday, *Reminiscences of My Life,* 40.

21. Derek Hudson, *Charles Keene* (London: Pleiades Books, 1947), 18.

22. Tenniel, "Punch's Illustrations to Shakspeare [sic]," illustration, *Punch,* 21 July 1855, 32.

23. Balston, *John Martin,* 213, 215; "The Art Exhibition in Westminster Hall," *New Monthly Magazine,* Aug. 1844, 551, which commented, "The human figure was always a terrible stumbling block to Mr. Martin; but he never before produced such a huddle of humanity as the man in this cartoon with his head on his arm"; and on Haydon, Massingham, *London Anthology,* 167; and *DNB,* s.v. "Haydon, Benjamin Robert (1786–1846)."

24. John Leech, cartoon, *Punch,* 15 July 1843; and Tenniel, "Chivalry—Parmilientary [sic] Cartoon," a drawing in colored chalks, 8 3/4 × 11 1/4 inches.

25. "The Art-Union of London," *Era* 6 (7 Jan. 1844): 5; and S. C. Hall, ed., *The Book of British Ballads,* 2nd series (London: Jeremiah How, 1844). Other Germanists were J. Franklin, F. R. Pickersgill, and Noël Paton.

26. Hall, *Retrospect,* 188–91.

27. The term "shaded outlines" was clarified for me by Stephen Calloway, Victoria and Albert Museum, London.

28. Hall, *Retrospect,* 191; and William Powell Frith, *John Leech: His Life and Work,* 2 vols. (London: Richard Bentley, 1891), 1:104.

29. F. Knight Hunt, ed., *The Book of Art: Cartoons, Frescoes, Sculpture, and Decorative Art as Applied to the New Houses of Parliament* (London: Jeremiah How, 1846), 169; and John Charlton, introduction to *Works of Art in the House of Lords,* ed. Maurice Bond (London: Her Majesty's Stationary Office, 1980), 30.

30. George Cruikshank, "Guy Fawkes Treated Classically," reproduced in *George Cruikshank: A Revaluation*, ed. Robert L. Patten (1974; reprint, Princeton, N.J.: Princeton Univ. Press, 1992), fig. 43b; "Punch's Dream of the House of Lords, *Punch*, 8 May 1847, 193; "Punch's Own Picture," *Punch*, 17 July 1847, 19, illustrated by Richard Doyle; and Tenniel, quoted in Spielmann, *History of "Punch,"* 461.

31. Ford M. Hueffer, *Ford Madox Brown: A Record of His Life and Work* (London: Longmans, Green, 1896), 38, 82. Others at Tudor Lodge to win premiums were Edward Armitage and John Cross.

32. Tenniel to Charles Eastlake, before 30 June 1845, National Art Library, London; William Vaughan, *German Romanticism and English Art* (New Haven, Conn.: Yale Univ. Press, 1979), 202, on the 1842 notice; and "Westminster-Hall," *Times*, 30 June 1845.

33. "Cartoons in Westminster Hall," *ILN*, 12 June 1845, 25; and for a reproduction of the lithograph, Monkhouse, *Sir John Tenniel*, 13.

34. Tenniel's other "Last Judgments" are the frontispiece border for *The Haunted Man* (London: Chapman & Hall, 1848) and the title page for *Punch* 19 (July–Dec. 1850). The "terrified boy" motif surfaces in the illustration to "The Countryman and the Snake," in Rev. Thomas James, *Aesop's Fables: A New Version, Chiefly from Original Sources* (London: John Murray, 1848, and rev. ed., 1858); and the fourth illustration to Dickens, *The Haunted Man*. On Knights Templar see Hyginus Eugene Cardinale, *Orders of Knighthood, Awards and the Holy See*, ed. Peter Bender Van Duren (Gerrards Cross, UK: Van Duren, 1985), 178, 20; and Richard Horchler, *The Fighting Monks* (New York: Walker, 1961), 38.

35. "Exhibition of Cartoons, Sketches, and Frescoes, in Westminster Hall," *ILN*, 5 July 1845, 10; "Westminster Hall: The Cartoon Exhibition and New Houses of Parliament," *Art-Union Monthly Journal of the Fine Arts* 7 (July 1845): 255; "Exhibition at Westminster Hall," *Builder* 3 (1845): 316; and "Fine Arts—the Cartoon and Fresco Exhibition, Westminster Hall," *Athenaeum*, 12 July 1845, 693. In future circular compositions—Tenniel's title pages for the "Great Exhibition Catalog" and for several *Punch* volumes—the central space would be occupied by type. In November, in a strange departure for a journal that had usually praised Tenniel extravagantly, the *Art-Union Monthly Journal* article "The Orders of the Royal Commission" (Nov. 1845): 319, suggested that the commission's selection savored of partiality.

36. "Westminster Hall," *Times*, 30 June 1845; and "Fine Arts—Fresco Exhibition," *Literary Gazette and Journal of Belles Lettres*, no. 1487 (19 July 1845): 482.

37. *Parliamentary Papers*, "Fifth Report of the Commissioners on the Fine Arts, 7 Aug. 1845," 259; "The Frescoes for the New Palace," *Art-Union Monthly Journal* 7 (Nov. 1845): 349, reporting that Dyce, Horsley, and Tenniel were "at present on the continent"; and "Frescoes, in Westminster Hall," *ILN*, 5 July 1845, 10.

38. Besides theatrical sources cited in chap. 2 n. 38, see Clement Scott and Cecil Howard, *The Life and Reminiscences of E. L. Blanchard*, 2 vols. (New York: Hutchinson, 1891); and Harold Simpson and Mrs. Charles Braun, *A Century of Famous Actresses* (New York: Benjamin Blom, 1971), 314. Macready's profile from Tenniel's "Pencillings in the Pit" resurfaces in "Punch's Illustrations to Shakspeare," *Punch*, 20 Oct. 1855, 162.

39. Vizetelly, *Through Seventy Years*, 141, on T. P. Cooke; "Theatrical Examiner—No. 390," *Examiner*, 27 Feb. 1820, 139–40, on Vestris; and Tenniel, initial letter, *Punch*, Jan.–June 1851, 223.

40. "Amateur Artists' Play," *Art-Union Monthly Journal* 8 (1 Mar. 1846); 92. On the Institution see Martin Hardie, "The Artists' General Benevolent Institution," *Studio* 132 (May 1946): 137; Balston, *John Martin*, 65; and Tenniel to Sir James D. Linton, 3 Apr. 1907, National Art Library.

41. Thomas Morton, *The School of Reform; or, How to Rule a Husband, A Comedy in Five Acts* (London: Longman, Hurst, Rees, & Orme, 1805); "Amateur Artists' Play," 92; "Tenniel," Supp. *"Punch,"* 15, and Anstey, *Long Retrospect*, 159, on Tenniel's diction; and Blanchard Jerrold, *The Life of George Cruikshank: In Two Epochs*, 2 vols. (London: Chatto & Windus, 1882), 2:53.

42. Charles Greville, *The Greville Diary*, 2 vols. (London: William Heinemann, 1927), 2:287–92; and Vizetelly, *Through Seventy Years*, 1:332–34.

43. "Tenniel," Supp. *"Punch,"* 16; Zachary Cope, *The Versatile Victorian: Being the Life of Sir Henry Thompson, Bt. 1820–1904* (London: Harvey & Blythe, 1951), 20; and Frith, *John Leech*, 1:237.

44. "St. James's Theatre—Amateur Artists' Performance," *ILN*, 6 May 1848, 299; and George Coleman, *The Heir at Law—A Comedy in Five Acts* (Dublin: P. Byrne, 1800).

45. Kemble, *Plot and Counterplot*; and "St. James's Theatre," *ILN*, 6 May 1848, 299.

46. Dickens, *The Haunted Man; The Book of Nursery Tales, a Keepsake for the Young* (London: James Burns, 1845), vol. 3; F. H. C. de la Motte Fouqué, *Undine* (London: James Burns, 1845); *Poems and*

Pictures (London: James Burns, 1846), which counted among its contributors Westminster Hall competitors H. C. Selous, E. Corbould, J. C. Horsley, W. C. Thomas, W. Dyce, F. R. Pickersgill, and C. W. Cope; and "St. Michael's Eve," 7 Feb. 1846, and "Griseldis, the Peasant-Bride," 27 Mar. 1847, *Sharpe's London Magazine.*

47. Tenniel to Mr. Bishop, postmarked 5 Mar. 1847, bound into vol. 2, after p. 124, expanded version of *The Brothers Dalziel: A Record of Fifty Years' Work, 1840–1890* (London: Methuen, 1901), Huntington Library. By the 1851 census (microfilm 087812) Tenniel was at 23 Newman Street, just east of his Berners Street address. The composition of John Baptist's household varied from census to census. See I. [*sic*] B. Tenniel, *On the Importance of Including Personal Exercise in a Scheme of General Education* (London: Caleb Turner, Hackney Press, 1845), copy at British Library. The 1851 census lists John Baptist and his sons William and James as teachers of personal exercise. Elsewhere John Baptist advertised to "the nobility, gentry, and his friends" a course of instruction that included "Dancing, Deportment and modified Calisthenics" (quoted in Ronald Pearsall, *Victorian Popular Music* [Newton Abbot: David & Charles, 1973], 183). The combining of dance and exercise was not unusual. See treatises mentioned in Cyril W. Beaumont, *A Bibliography of Dancing* (New York: Benjamin Blom, 1963), 56, 124. John Baptist's treatise impresses one with his dedication to the principles he advances and with his scholarship. It contrasts favorably, for example, with Francis Mason, *A Treatise on the Use and Peculiar Advantages of Dancing and Exercises* (London, 1854), which is little more than a sales pitch for the writer's academy.

48. Because *Aesop's Fables* came out early in 1848, Tenniel may have started on the 108 illustrations as early as 1846. See L. C. Martin, "Reminiscences of John Martin," part 6, 9 Feb. 1889, on the introduction to Murray; and "Aesops Fables," *Art-Union Monthly Journal* 10 (1848): 153. Leopold was engaged in various printmaking ventures in the forties and early fifties. Frederic G. Kitton, *Dickens and His Illustrators* (London: George Redway, 1889), 173, relates that Tenniel's frontispiece to *The Haunted Man* was "admirably engraved on wood by Martin and Corbould." Edward Corbould's father-in-law was the engraver Charles Heath.

49. Dickens to John Leech, 30 Oct. 1848, in *The Letters of Charles Dickens*, ed. Walter Dexter, 3 vols. (Bloomsbury: Nonesuch Press, 1938), 2:125; and John Forster, *The Life of Charles Dickens*, ed. J. W. T. Ley (New York: Doubleday, Doran, n.d.), 527, which lists Tenniel among those familiar to Devonshire Terrace. At Dickens's Tenniel might have met future *Punch* colleagues William Makepeace Thackeray, Douglas Jerrold, and Tom Taylor, such old friends as the Landseers and the S. C. Halls; and Robert Keeley, Samuel Phelps, Helen Faucit, Benjamin Webster, John Pritt Harley—actors he had sketched from the pits of London's theaters.

50. *Parliamentary Papers*, "Eighth Report of the Commissioners of the Fine Arts, 5 Sept. 1848," 358; "Seventh Report of the Commissioners of the Fine Arts, 9 July 1847," 277, specifying that the choice of subject (from a given list of English poets) would be left to the artists, subject to approval by the commissioners; and *DNB*, s.v. Calkin, James (1786–1862), and s.v. "Calkin, John Baptiste (1827–1905)"; and *Grove's Dictionary of Music*, s.v. "Calkin (No. 3) William Calkin."

51. Charlton, introduction to *Works of Art*, 134, on the painting schedule; Spielmann, *History of "Punch,"* 461, on the change in subject; and "Exhibition of Modern British Art," *Spectator*, 7 Dec. 1850, 1171, which pans Tenniel's study for his first subject. The change in Horsley's subject was mentioned to me by Malcolm Hay, curator of works of art at the Palace of Westminster.

52. T. J. Gullick, *A Descriptive Handbook for the National Pictures in the Westminster Palace* (London: Bradbury, Evans, 1865), 105, which identifies the stanza illustrated by Tenniel; and John Dryden, "A Song for St. Cecilia's Day," (1687). The line beginning "What passion" is the opening one for stanza two.

53. Charlton, introduction to *Works of Art*, 29, on fresco requirements; and MS, "Collection of Writing and articles by William Dyce, Compiled by his son" (Office of the Curator of Works of Art, Palace of Westminster), on difficulties encountered.

54. Abstract of letters of William Dyce (who had endorsed fresco for the project and received the first commission) to Eastlake (Office of the Curator of Works of Art), detailing such problems as trapped moisture and contaminants in the air from 17 Feb. 1846 on.

55. J. B. Groves, "The Rambling Recollections and Modern Thoughts by an Old Engraver" (1916), 39, unpublished MS, *Punch* archives; R. H. Horne, "Father Thames," *Household Words*, 1 Feb. 1851, 446; and in *Punch*: "Dirty City!" 10 July 1847, 3; William Newman, cartoon, 7 Oct 1848; and Richard Doyle, "Sanitary and Insanitary Matters," almanac design (Jan.–June 1850). For the artists' testimonies see Charlton, introduction to *Works of Art*, 34; abstract of Dyce's letters to Eastlake; and Charles Henry Cope, *Reminiscences of Charles West Cope, R.A.* (London: Richard Bentley & Son, 1891), 157.

56. "The Art Decorations in the New Houses of Parliament," *Art Journal*, n.s., 4 (1852): 349; and M. H. Port, *The Houses of Parliament* (New Haven, Conn.: Yale Univ. Press, 1976), 273, on Tenniel's fluid washes.

57. Both *Justice* and *Saint Cecilia* were publicized by lithographic copies, possibly commissioned by the *Art Journal*, which twice referred to the print of *Saint Cecilia* ("The Frescoes of the New Houses of Parliament," *Art Journal* 12 [Jan. 1850]: 16, and "Art Decorations in Parliament," 349).

58. On Haydon, see Balston, *John Martin*, 192–94; Pendered, *John Martin, Painter*, 216; and William Bell Scott, quoted in Feaver, *Art of John Martin*, 181. Haydon took his own life on 22 June 1846. Tenniel would depict him in two illustrations to W. Haigh Miller's book *The Mirage of Life* (London: Religious Tract Society, 1867), in one sourly watching as the "connoisseurs" appraise his work, in the other seated despairingly before his easel.

4. "Jackides"

1. Spielmann, *History of "Punch,"* 461–63, for Tenniel's account of his engagement.

2. Smalley, "Sir John Tenniel," *New York Tribune*, 5 Apr. 1914; and F. M. Evans (draft of letter) to Richard Doyle, 15 Nov. 1850, Bradbury and Evans albums, Bodleian Library. *Punch*'s almanac generally went to press in mid-December. On the almanac dinners see "Nights at ye Round Table," Henry Silver's diary of the *Punch* dinners (4 Aug. 1858–23 Mar. 1870), 14 Dec. 1864 and 15 Dec. 1869. Tenniel's first initial appeared on 30 Nov. 1850, p. 224. Following the schedule for cartoons, the block with its drawing would have had to be in the engraver's hands by Friday, 22 Nov., in order for it to be in the printer's forms on the 23rd in time for the foreign edition on Monday the 25th. The paper would actually have come out on Wednesday the 27th although dated 30 Nov.

3. Spielmann, *History of "Punch,"* 463, on Jerrold's advocacy; and Hueffer, *Ford Madox Brown*, 38, for his visits to Tudor Lodge. Bradbury and Evans had printed the 1848 *Aesop*.

4. Amy Evans, quoted in "Tenniel," *Supp. "Punch,"* 9. In 1861 George du Maurier wrote that Tenniel received five hundred pounds for doing the cartoons (nine pounds fifteen shillings each). *Fun* paid four pounds for its cartoon (proprietor's copies, Huntington Library). See Daphne du Maurier, ed., *The Young George du Maurier* (Garden City, N.Y.: Doubleday, 1952), 13, 50, 57. Tenniel is quoted in Spielmann, *History of "Punch,"* 466.

5. Spielmann, *History of "Punch,"* 187–88, dates the earliest use of "cartoon" in this meaning to 1863. The first use of "cartoonist" that I have seen is in the review of the staff benefit performance in Manchester (*ILN*, 3 Aug. 1867). For "cartooner" see "Mark Lemon's Triumphal Car," *Mask*, Apr. 1868.

6. Preface to Susan Briggs and Asa Briggs, eds., *Cap and Bell* (London: Macdonald, 1972), xxii. For the unidentified drawings, see xi, xiv, xxxi.

7. Tenniel, initials A, K, and H, *Punch*, July–Dec. 1851, 138, 196; and Jan.–June 1851, 141. See also Jan.–June 1851, 123, 147; July–Dec. 1851, 149; July–Dec. 1852, 253; July–Dec. 1853, 211; Jan.–June 1856, 241; and July–Dec. 1859, 216.

8. Tenniel, cartoon, 3 May 1851; and "Sketch for a large picture in progress, representing allegorically the great Industrial Meeting of all nations, A.D. 1851," listed in Graves, *Royal Academy of Arts*, s.v. "Tenniel, Sir John, R.I."

9. Tenniel to Frederic Mullet Evans, 24 Dec. 1850, Bradbury album, and 26 Dec. 1850, *Punch* letter boxes; Tenniel to Evans (before Sept. 1853, as it was mailed from 23 Newman Street), *Punch* letter boxes, on *Household Words* (all in *Punch* archives). See Tenniel to Evans, 9 Feb. 1856, *Punch* letter boxes; *Young George du Maurier*, 50; Tenniel to Bradbury, 15 May 1875, *Punch* letter boxes; and A. M. W. Stirling, *Victorian Sidelights: From the Papers of Mrs. Adams-Acton* (London: Ernest Benn, 1954), 266, on Tenniel's annual *Punch* earnings, which were about £360 in 1856, £500 in 1861, £900 in 1875, and £1200 at the close of his career. By comparison, in 1879 du Maurier realized £1491, and in 1883 Sambourne was already earning about £1200 (du Maurier to Bradbury, 4 Jan. 1880, Bradbury and Evans albums, Bodleian Library; and Sambourne file, *Punch* letter boxes). For requests from various *Punch* artists for increased payments, and for disputes over money, see Doyle to Evans, dated 1848 [1858?], Bradbury album; Keene to Bradbury, Evans & Co., 11 July 1871, *Punch* letter boxes; Philip Agnew and W. Lawrence Bradbury to Harry Furniss, 2 Mar. 1894, and letters 19, 69, and 100 in "'Punch' Letter Book for 1 Jan. 1894–6 Dec. 1895," *Punch* archives; du Maurier to Bradbury, Agnew & Co., 1 and 4 Jan. 1880, Bradbury and Evans albums; and Brooks diaries, 5 June 1871, and 4 and 8 Nov. 1871, and 28 Sept. 1873, London Library. The Shirley Brooks diaries are at the following locations: 1867 and 1872, *Punch* archives; 1864, Houghton Library; and 1869, 1871, and 1873, London Library.

10. Evans, quoted in the Silver diary, 1 Nov. 1865. See Vizetelly, *Through Seventy Years*, 1:426; Arthur Adrian, *Mark Lemon: First Editor of "Punch"* (London: Oxford Univ. Press, 1966), 36, 59; Spielmann, *History of "Punch,"* 254; and George Somes Layard, *A Great "Punch" Editor: Being the Life, Letters, and Diaries of Shirley Brooks* (London: Sir Isaac Pitman & Sons, 1907), 389, on Lemon; Silver diary, 23 July 1862, on *Punch* sociability; "Statistics of the Chartist Petition," *Punch*, vol. 2, Jan.–June 1842, 206, which derided the intelligence and motives of the signatories; and, in the same issue, Douglas Jerrold, "The Charter:—The House of Commons 'Hushed and Still,'" 210–13, which argued that Chartism was the natural outcome of a reform bill that had failed a large portion of the population; and Frith, *John Leech*, 2:33, on Lemon's Thursday morning visits.

11. See the Silver diary and Brooks diaries.

12. Tenniel, cartoon, 29 May 1852; "Ode on the Derby," 223, same issue; half-title to vol. 27, July–Dec. 1854; and on Leech's horsemanship, Spielmann, *History of "Punch,"* 427.

13. *Guild of Literature and Art* [1854?], British Library.

14. *Not So Bad as We Seem; or, Many Sides to a Character*, in *Dramatic Works by the Right Hon. Lord Lytton*, 2 vols. (London: Routledge & Sons, 1876), vol. 1; J. B. Amerongen, *The Actor in Dickens* (New York: Appleton, 1926), 17–23; Forster, *Life of Charles Dickens*, 516–20; R. H. Horne, "Bygone Celebrities," *Gentleman's Magazine*, Feb. 1871, 248–49; and, on the program design, Mrs. E. M. Ward, *Memories of Ninety Years*, ed. Isabel G. McAllister (London: Hutchinson, n.d.), 235.

15. Horne, "Bygone Celebrities," 257; Tenniel to George N. Rogers, 13 Oct. 1903, Harry Ransom Humanities Research Center; and, for the 21 July 1821 playbill, "Tenniel an Actor," *Daily Sketch*, 2 Mar. 1914.

16. Horne, "Bygone Celebrities," 249, on Tenniel's work on the scenery; and Tenniel to Rogers, 13 Oct. 1903, on his "important role."

17. Forster, *Life of Charles Dickens*, 520; Dion Bourcicault [sic], *Used Up: A Petit Comedy in Two Acts* (London: National Acting Drama Office, n.d.); and J. R. Planché, *Charles the XII: An Historical Drama in Two Acts*, in *Cumberland's British Theatre*, vol. 25 (London: John Cumberland, n.d.), 46.

18. *Manchester Courier*, 28 Feb. 1914.

19. Tony Augarde, *The Oxford Guide to Word Games* (Oxford: Oxford Univ. Press, 1984), 137, on bouts-rimés; Tenniel, initials, *Punch*, July–Dec. 1850, 234, 241, 250, 253; Jan.–June 1851, 7, 23, 55, 123, 157; and July–Dec. 1851, 67, 86, 149, based on the bouts-rimés, as are his illustrations to "Punch's Anniversaries," 82; "Where Is Mazeppa?" 201; and "The Wonderful Whalers," 242–43, July–Dec. 1851 volume.

20. Tenniel's drawing of Widdicomez has some resemblance to a drawing of Henry Widdicomb that appeared earlier in *Punch* ("Widdicomb the Fox-Hunter," July–Dec. 1844, 252). The Saracen's daughter in "Count Robert" resembles George Cruikshank's drawing of Sophia in *The Loving Ballad of Lord Bateman*, 3rd ed., notes by Charles Dickens (London: David Bogue, 1851).

21. Julia, "A Romaunt of ye Crusades," in Tenniel et al., "*Bouts-Rimés*; IGI p. 83,112, on the Gianis; *Marriages Solemnized in the Parish of St. Mary-le-Bone, in the County of Middlesex, 1821*, nos. 886 and 887, p. 296, Greater London Record Office; and *Times*, 29 Dec. 1821, on the marriage of Eve Berry and Julius Giani, 26 Dec. 1821; IGI p. 12,651, which shows that Eve Berry, child of Henry and Ann Berry, was christened on 2 Feb. 1803 at the parish church of St. Marylebone, St. Mary; and *Boyle's Court and Country Guide* (1811), 230, which lists "Giani, Lorenzo. Esq" at 28 Charles Street, Middlesex Hospital.

22. "Marriages," *Gentleman's Magazine* (Jan.–June 1818), 637; *Baptisms in the Parish of St. Mary-le-Bone*, county: Middx. 1824, church—St. Mary-le-Bone, no. 1966, which gives Julia's date of birth as 1 July; IGI p. 83,114, for her baptism; and *London Masters' Directory* (1828), 55.

23. Rate book for 1834, showing rents of eighty pounds for 66 Norton Street (now Bolsover Street) as compared with sixty pounds for Allsop's Terrace; and reference Engl. 5. 1314 St. Marylebone, London census returns 1831, p. 377. On the houses in Cirencester Place (in the upper part of Great Titchfield Street), see Smith, *My Life*, 1. Rents were due on four Quarter Days: Lady Day (25 Mar.), Midsummer Day (24 June), Michaelmas (29 Sept.), and Christmas. The rate book for 66 Norton Street shows no payment for Midsummer Day 1834. For Julius's death see "Died," *Times*, 20 Feb. 1834; and for his will see "Giani, Julius," 1834, fol. 105, Middx. Mch 148, PROB 11 (film 1828), Rolls Room, Public Record Office, London. The attestation was accomplished on 28 Feb. 1834 (fol. 390). Eve's will identifies Ann Berry as her sister (vol. 1879, fol. 133, Probate Registry, Somerset House, London).

24. *Royal Blue Book, Fashionable Directory*, 1841, 387; and *Boyle's Fashionable Court and Country Guide* for 1843, 421; and census returns for 28 Oxford Terrace, Hyde Park in 1851 (reference no.

HO 107 / 1467), fol. 476 for the parish of Paddington, listing only William James Giani, his wife, two daughters, and three servants.

25. Tenniel and Julia Giani, marriage, 1 Sept. 1853, recorded in the *Register of Marriages No. 2, 1853,* no. 436, Greater London Record Office. Tenniel's Newman Street neighbors were typical for this neighborhood; in *Bleak House,* chap. 14, the Turveydrop Academy shared its Newman Street premises with a drawing master, a coal merchant, and a lithographic artist.

26. Eve Giani, will, 25 Aug. 1877, which bequeathed the property to Tenniel (Calendar of the Grants of Probate, 1879, fol. 133, "Giani, Eve," Probate Registry, Somerset House); 1834 wall map, Marylebone Library, showing Maida Vale to have been all open country; and C. R. Elrington, ed., *The Victoria History of the Counties of England* (London: Univ. of London Institute of Historical Research, 1989), 9:212–13, which indicates that by 1851 only the Edgeware, Blomfield, and Warwick Roads had buildings.

27. Frank Danby, *Dr. Phillips: A Maida Vale Idyll* (London: Vizetelly, 1887), 334.

28. Anstey, quoted in "Tenniel," *Supp. "Punch,"* 15, on Tenniel's studio; Tenniel to William Bradbury [1868], in which he appends to his dinner invitation, "and we will have a game of billiards on the wee table" (Bradbury album); and Brooks diary, 20 Jan. 1872.

29. On 7 Feb. 1879 the administration of Eve Giani's estate was granted to Ann Berry of 10 Portsdown Road (Probate Registry, 1879, fol. 133).

30. Francis C. Burnand, quoted in "Tenniel," *Supp. "Punch,"* 10; and Alice Julia Tenniel Evans (grandniece of Tenniel) to Frances Sarzano, 20 Mar. 1946, collection of Charles Press, which says of Julia, "She had an illness which only gave her a year—Sir John married her." For the death and burial of Julia Tenniel, see registration district Kensington, subdistrict St. Mary Paddington, entry 320, General Register Office, London; the General Cemetery Co., Kensal Green Cemetery re. grave no. 12957 / 54 / 7; and *Burials in the Year 1856 in All Soul's Cemetery,* General Cemetery Co. Transcript Register 1856, no. 25301, Greater London Record Office. The *Daily Telegraph,* 28 Feb. 1914, describing Tenniel's death, said, "By his wish the portrait of his young bride—taken away from him sixty years ago—is placed above his head. This drawing of a beautiful face and form was made by Tenniel just after her death."

31. Tenniel, no. 13683—*Queen Victoria Visiting Fort Pitt Military Hospital, Chatham. 3rd April 1855,* watercolor 9 3/4 × 13 1/4 inches; no. 13684—*Queen Victoria in a Ward of the Military Hospital, Chatham;* watercolor 9 3/4 × 13 1/4 inches; no. 16783—*Distribution of Crimean Medals on the Horse Guards Parade. May 18th 1855,* watercolor 12 1/2 × 18 1/2 inches; and no. 16788—*Unveiling of the Scutari Monument & a Peace Trophy. 9 May 1856,* watercolor 13 1/4 × 18 3/4 inches, Royal Library, Windsor Castle (the last two in a volume entitled "Military Drawings 5B," pp. 75 and 78). Tenniel may have been recommended to the queen by his friend Edward Corbould, then instructor of historical painting to the royal family. See Tenniel, cartoon, 6 May 1854. In this period Tenniel tended to model his Britannia on the queen.

32. Tenniel to M. H. Spielmann, 24 Aug. 1900, *Punch* archives. The other design in the Westminster mode illustrates "Of Estimating Character," and the copy after Maclise is in the large scrapbook no. 1, in family possession.

33. Leech was art supervisor of *Once a Week* for its first two years, and Shirley Brooks was on its staff. The most highly paid of its artists were Tenniel, whose first contribution began with the first number in July 1859, and Leech's friend John Everett Millais. See William E. Buckler, "Once a Week under Samuel Lucas, 1859–65," *Publications of the Modern Language Association of America* 67 (1952): 929, 937–38. On Brooks, see Spielmann, *History of "Punch,"* 356–59; *DNB,* s.v. "Brooks, Charles William Shirley (1816–1874)"; Layard, *Great "Punch" Editor,* 69, 16, 428; and Frances C. Burnand, *Records and Reminiscences: Personal and General* (London: Methuen, 1905), 442; and on gifts from women friends, Brooks diaries, 16 Apr. 1867, 4 Feb. 1869, 4 May 1871, 2 Sept. 1872; and Brooks to Torie Matthews, 7 Nov. 1870, in Layard, *Great "Punch" Editor,* 428. Brooks's concern for his family can be gathered from the six diaries that survive. On 19 Jan. 1867 he recorded, "Today I accomplished the important purpose of my life, the making of a provision [a substantial life insurance policy] for Emily and the children." For his comment on holidays see Brooks diary, 20 Aug. 1873.

34. "Agreement as to a serial novel 'The Gordian Knot,'" 4 Sept. 1857, Dexter Collection, British Library; Tenniel to R. Young, n.d., collection of Michael Hancher, preparing him to receive one of the plates the next day for "biting" and signed "with perish'd fingers"; and Tenniel to Brooks [1858?], Dexter Collection.

35. Shirley Brooks, *The Gordian Knot: A Story of Good and Evil* (London: Richard Bentley, 1860), 40–43, 60, 190–94, 74.

36. Spielmann, *History of "Punch,"* 473; and Brooks, *Gordian Knot*, 59.

37. Thomas Moore, *Lalla Rookh: An Oriental Romance* (London: Longman, Green, Longman, & Roberts, 1861); Samuel Lucas, "Mr. Tenniel's Lalla Rookh," *Times*, 31 Oct. 1860; and "Lalla Rookh," *Art Journal*, n.s., 6 (1860): 379–80.

38. Balston, *John Martin*, 201–2; and "Martin's Picture of the Coronation of Queen Victoria," *Art-Union Monthly Journal* 6 (1844): 148.

39. Tenniel, "There on that throne, to which the blind belief / Of millions rais'd him, sat the Prophet-Chief," illustration, Moore, *Lalla Rookh*, 11.

40. Except for Thackeray's cuts, which were less significant than his texts and ceased with his resignation in 1854, the rest of *Punch's* art depended on outside contributors.

41. Tupper, quoted in Derek Hudson, *Martin Tupper: His Rise and Fall* (London: Constable, 1949), 158; Spielmann, *History of "Punch,"* 430, for "Handsome Jack"; Simon Houfe, *John Leech and the Victorian Scene* ([Suffolk, UK]: Antique Collectors' Club, 1984), pl. 29; and 65–66, on Leech as a storyteller and mimic; and Barry Cornwall [B. W. Procter], "King Death," stanza 1.

42. Frith, *John Leech*; Houfe, *John Leech*; and *DNB*, s.v. "Leech, John (1817–1864)."

43. Ponny Mayhew, quoted in the Silver diary, 2 Mar. 1859; and Leech in Frith, *John Leech*, 2:18.

44. E. V. Lucas, for Keene on Leech; "Thackeray's Punch-Table Talk," *Outlook*, 28 Sept. 1912, 189; and on Leech's generosity, Frith, *John Leech*, 2:289–90; and George Hodder, *Memories of My Time* (1870), 81.

45. Frith, *John Leech*, 1:235.

46. Anstey, *Long Retrospect*, 267, for Tenniel's hunts with Leech and Trollope; Tenniel, "The First of October, a 'Warm Corner' for Jones," social cut in "Punch's Almanack for 1870"; and Anthony Trollope, ed., *British Sport and Pastimes, 1868* (London: Virtue, 1868), chap. 2.

47. Spielmann, *History of "Punch,"* 173–74, on their Saturday hunts; and Leech, quoted in the Silver diary, 2 Mar. 1859.

48. "Sir John Tenniel: Ninetieth Birthday," *Daily Telegraph*, 26 Feb. 1910; and Tenniel, social cut, *Punch*, Jan.–June 1851, 218.

49. Tenniel, "Persecution and Punch in 1851," 81; "The Ballad of John Bull, and the Loathly Thing That Sat on His Shoulders," 102; and "The Virginian Slave, " 236, illustrations, *Punch*, Jan.–June 1851; and initials, *Punch*, 27 Mar. 1852, 131; Jan.–June 1853, 41, 97; and Jan.–June 1855, 21.

50. Tenniel, caricatures of actors in "Punch's Illustrations to Shakspeare": 8 Sept. 1855, 93 (Kean); 20 Oct. 1855, 162 (Macready); and 12 Jan. 1856, 11 (the introduction to the *Times* reprint of vol. 30 says of this illustration, "Trunculo is an excellent portrait of the late MR. HARLEY, comedian"); and political illustrations in this series: 29 Sept. 1855, 123; 1 Mar. 1856, 90; 12 Apr. 1856, 148; and 3 May 1856, 178; and Tenniel sketchbook no. 70.58, Huntington Gallery, San Marino, Calif.

51. Tenniel, cartoons, 9 Apr. 1853, 16 July 1853, 3 Nov. 1855, and 15 Mar. 1856, for his animal cuts; and 10 June 1854, 26 Aug. 1854, 28 Oct. 1854, and 2 Dec. 1854.

52. Tenniel, cartoon, 22 Aug. 1857; Winston Churchill, "Cartoons and Cartoonists," *Strand Magazine*, June 1931, 583, on the tiger being "ill-placed"; Tenniel, cartoon, 29 Aug. 1857; Spielmann, *History of "Punch,"* 177; "Standard," *Times*, 28 Dec. 1857; and "Literature," *ILN*, Jan.–June 1858, 70.

53. Silver diary, 17 Feb. 1859. Since Silver's diary covers only a fraction of the large-cut discussions, the twenty cartoon suggestions made by Leech in four to five years may be more than it seems. See Houfe, *John Leech*, 85–86, on Leech's difficulty with likenesses.

54. "Punch's Book of British Costumes" ran from 4 Feb. through 29 Dec. 1860. See "Tenniel," *Supp. "Punch,"* 3, on Tenniel's accession to cartoonist-in-chief.

5. On Gen'l Punch's "Staff"

1. Silver diary, 2 Feb. 1859.

2. From 1851 through 1859 Tenniel drew political figures as women and children in five cartoons. In the next four years—in which he drew a like number of cartoons—there were twenty-one. See cartoons, 13 Sept. 1862, 26 Sept. 1863, and 19 Nov. 1864, for comic blacks; and Tenniel, quoted in Spielmann, *History of "Punch,"* 463.

3. Silver diary, 17 Dec. 1866, and 25 Mar. 1868; and Tenniel, "The Royal Blankshire Hussars (Yeomanry). 'Inspection Parade,'" social cut, "Punch's Almanack for 1871."

4. Francis C. Burnand, "The 'Punch' Pocket-Books," *Pall Mall Magazine*, July–Dec. 1905, 190–97, 327–32. The books measured about 3 1/4 × 4 7/8 inches.

5. Tenniel, illustration to "The Adventures of Prince Lulu," *Once a Week*, 26 Apr. 1862, 490; and "Current Literature," *ILN*, 31 Oct. 1863, 43.

6. Marks, *Pen and Pencil Sketches*, 1:61, 184, on Lewis and the etching club. The club produced *Passages from the Poems of Thomas Hood* (London: E. Gambart, 1858) and *Passages from Modern English Poets* (London: Day & Son, 1861).

7. Marks, *Pen and Pencil Sketches*, 1:184–190; *Young George du Maurier*, 283, 297; Sheila Birkenhead, *Illustrious Friends* (London: Hamish Hamilton, 1965), 144–45; and the Silver diary, 16 Oct. 1867, on the Minstrels; and Francis C. Burnand, "Personal Recollections," *Daily Telegraph*, 27 Feb. 1914; and Hesketh Hubbard, *A Hundred Years of British Painting, 1851–1951* (London: Longmans, Green, 1951), 70, on the Arts Club.

8. Burnand, "Personal Recollections," *Daily Telegraph*, 27 Feb. 1914.

9. H. W. Lucy, *Sixty Years*, 380, and *The Diary of a Journalist*, 3 vols. (London: J. Murray, 1920–23), 2:261; Gladys Storey, "The Late Sir John Tenniel," *Graphic*, 7 Mar. 1914, 396; Brooks diaries, 15 July 1870 (quoted in Layard, *Great "Punch" Editor*, 417); and Gladys Storey, *All Sorts of People* (London: Methuen, 1929), 9. Tenniel's ranting about his cartoon subject follows the overblown style of pantomime advertisements. For example, in 1856 the Drury Lane announced "an entirely new and original, symbolical, hyperbolical, parabolical, and extra-physiognomical, grotesque, and picturesque, grand comic Christmas pantomime." See A. E. Wilson, *King Panto: The Story of Pantomime* (New York: E. P. Dutton, 1935), 152.

10. Carroll, 11 June 1869, in *The Diaries of Lewis Carroll*, 2 vols., ed. Roger Lancelyn Green (New York: Oxford Univ. Press, 1954), 2:281 (hereafter cited as *Carroll Diaries*); Carroll to Margaret Gatty, 2 Feb. 1870, in *The Letters of Lewis Carroll*, 2 vols., ed. Morton N. Cohen (New York: Oxford Univ. Press, 1979), 1:149 (hereafter cited as *Carroll Letters*), on *Looking-Glass*; Carroll, 12 Mar. 1870, *Carroll Diaries*, 2:287, on the game of billiards; and Marks, *Pen and Pencil Sketches*, 190, on Lewis's billiard room.

11. Sotheby, Wilkinson & Hodge Sales Catalogue for 3 Dec. 1915.

12. Silver diary, 12 Sept. 1865, 8 Aug. 1866, and 1 Sept. 1867; Carroll, 3 Oct. 1872, *Carroll Diaries*, 2:314; and Kenneth Stanley Green, "The Story of T. G. Green Limited," 27 Jan. 1972, later appearing as "The History of TG Green Pottery," parts 1 and 2, *Antiques Magazine*, no. 871 (7–13 Apr. 2001) and no. 872 (14–20 Apr. 2001), with a postscript by Derek Stanley Green. See Silver diary, 11 Aug. 1869, which notes: "Tenniel to Ashby de la Zouch"; and Tenniel to William H. Bradbury, n.d., in which he writes that he will be in Leicestershire for several days (*Punch* letter boxes).

13. George Tenniel (age twenty-four), burial 1860, recorded at Kensal Green Cemetery; Bernard Tenniel (age forty-four), Calendar of Wills 1860, fol. 722, Probate Registry, Somerset House; Frith, *John Leech*, 303, on Leech's burial at Kensal Green on 8 Nov. 1864 (with Tenniel serving as pallbearer); Tenniel to R. T. "Bob" Pritchett (occasional *Punch* artist and future producer of the Pritchett or Enfield rifle), 22 Sept. 1864, saying, "Poor Mummie has been very ill, but is quite better now" (collection of Sandor Burstein); backing of her 1819 portrait on which is written, "Eliza Maria Tenniel (mother of John Tenniel), Born June 11th 1797, Died December 16th 1864"; and, for Tenniel's position on suicide, Silver diary, 17 May 1865. These discussions (there was one in the previous week) show how radically attitudes had changed since 1820 when the law still required the midnight burial of suicides at crossroads with a stake driven through the body (see Hall, *Retrospect*, 26).

14. Silver diary, 1 Nov. 1865; James Kinsley, ed., *The Oxford Book of Ballads* (Oxford: Clarendon Press, 1969), 245, for "The Three Ravens"; and *The Spanish Lady, a Musical Entertainment* (London, 1769).

15. Brooks diary, 3 Apr.–11 May 1867; and Spielmann, *History of "Punch,"* 132–34.

16. Lucy, quoted in "Tenniel," *Supp. "Punch,"* 13; Tom Taylor, *A Sheep in Wolf's Clothing: A Domestic Drama in One Act* (New York: Robert M DeWitt, n.d.); Burnand, "Personal Recollections," *Daily Telegraph*, 27 Feb. 1914; *ILN*, 3 Aug. 1867; and Spielmann, *History of "Punch,"* 134.

17. Brooks diary, 16, 23, 25 Apr. 1873; G. A. Storey, *Sketches from Memory* (London: Chatto & Windus, 1899), 314; and Gladys Storey, *All Sorts of People*, 7–8, and "Late Sir John Tenniel," 396 (see n. 9 above). For an earlier visit to the Agnews, the participants in the Bennett benefit in Manchester were put up at the three Agnew homes there in 1867. Silver's diary notation on 20 July 1869— "Tenniel at Manchester with Prince of Wales"—probably refers to another visit.

18. In 1865 Pater Evans relinquished his place in favor of his son Fred. Aside from their New Year's Eve dinners, Mrs. Brooks seems not to have joined the group. See Brooks diary, 14 Aug. 1872, on Laura Vigers, and 11 May 1869; 27 Feb. 1872, 13 May 1872, 14 Aug. 1872; and 28 May 1873, on the Vigers family; and 31 Dec. 1867 for the Brookses' "Eve." See also Layard, *Great "Punch" Editor*, 306.

19. Brooks diary for 1867, 1 Apr., 12 Aug., 24 and 31 Dec.; Augarde, *Guide to Word Games*, 25, on charades; and Carroll, "Phantasmagoria" (1869), canto 3, for a similar word play on "inspector."

20. Brooks diaries, 9 and 10 Oct. 1871.

21. Tenniel, "From Oxford to Henley (Tune—The 'Bold Gensdarmes [sic]),'" in Tenniel et al., *Bouts-Rimés;* Silver diary, 29–31 July 1865, 2 Aug. 1865; and 29 Aug. 1866, for other "pulls"; and Theo Bergstrom, *A Picture Book: The Thames* (London: Bergstrom & Boyle Books, 1975); George D. Leslie, *Our River* (London: Bradbury, Agnew, 1881); and David Periott, ed., *The Ordnance Survey Guide to the River Thames and River Wey* (London: Robert Nicholson, 1984).

22. Brooks diary for 1872, 9 Mar., 15 and 29 June, 31 July, 14 Aug., 16, 22, 23, and 26 Oct., 6, 13, and 28 Nov. The excision from this diary of pages for 9 Sept.–15 Oct. may have something to do with this affair.

23. Tenniel to Brooks, 17 Jan. and 18 May 1872, Brooks Album, pp. 40–41, Harkness Collection; Brooks diary for 1873, 9 and 12 Apr. and 3 May; the "Candidates Book May 1873–Apr. 1878, no. 6," Garrick Club, London, showing that Millais proposed Tenniel on 12 Apr. and bearing the signatures of thirty-seven added seconders, many of them well known in their fields.

24. Brooks diary for 1873, 31 Oct., 6 and 13 Dec.; and Arthur William à Beckett, *Recollections of a Humourist: Grave and Gay* (London: Sir Isaac Pitman, 1907), 387, on the number of figures.

25. Cope, *Versatile Victorian,* 26, 92–97.

26. Brooks diary, 9 May 1867.

27. Cremation Society of Great Britain, *The History of Modern Cremation in Great Britain from 1874* (Maidstone, Kent: Cremation Society of Great Britain, n.d.), 65–69; Brooks diary, 20 Dec. 1873; Hall, *Retrospect,* 52–53; Dickens, *Bleak House* (1853), chap. 16; "The Spa-Fields Burial Ground," *Times,* 5 Mar. 1845; W. H. Wills and George Hogarth, "Heathen and Christian Burial," *Household Words,* 6 Apr. 1850, 43–48; and Tenniel, initial letter to "The Graveyards of London," *Punch,* 23 Apr. 1853, 169, on London's graveyards. See also in *Punch,* "Hamlet in the London Churchyard," 13 Oct. 1849, 145, and Doyle's cartoon of the same title and date; "London Graveyards," 2 Oct. 1847, 128; and "The Battle for Intramural Churchyards," 25 May 1850, 207. On the 7 Jan. 1874 meeting, see Brooks to Leigh, n.d., in Layard, *Great "Punch" Editor,* 580–81; and [Percival Leigh?], "Cremation," *Punch,* 10 Jan 1874, 12.

28. Cremation Society of Great Britain, "The Declaration of 1874," 13 Jan. 1874.

29. Brooks to Leigh, n.d., in Layard, *Great "Punch" Editor,* 580–81; and Brooks diary, 31 Dec. 1873.

6. Good Sir John!

1. Burnand, *Records and Reminiscences,* 280. See also *Young George du Maurier,* 207; and Vizetelly, *Seventy Years,* 287–88.

2. Silver diary, 25 Apr. 1865; Dennis Farr, *English Art, 1870–1940* (Oxford: Clarendon Press, 1978), 14–15, on the Whistler-Ruskin trial; and Tom Taylor, "English Painting in 1862," *Fine Arts Quarterly Review* 1 (May 1863): 26.

3. Tenniel to George Bentley, 6 Nov. 1871, Berg Collection, New York Public Library; and census returns for Paddington: 1861 (microfilm RG 9/5–45), 1871 (microfilm 0838752), 1881 (microfilm 1341002), 1891 (microfiche 6095114).

4. Tenniel's watercolors in the years 1854–73 include works for the queen (1855–56); the portrait of Julia Tenniel (1856); *Britannia Defending Her Realm* (1867), 7 1/2 × 4 1/2 inches, Fine Art Society, London, based on cartoon, 14 Dec. 1861; *The British Lion's Vengeance on the Bengal Tiger,* 1870, based on cartoon, 22 Aug. 1857, collection of Draper Hill; and *Leonardo da Vinci,* 1866, gouache, 36 1/2 × 26 1/4 inches, Victoria and Albert Museum. See *Royal Academy of Arts,* s.v. "Tenniel, Sir John, R.I."; "Art Notes and Minor Topics," *Art Journal* 13 (1874): 158, on his election; and Roberts, "Exhibition and Review," 95, on the watercolor societies. See, too, Charles Holme, ed., *The Royal Institute of Painters in Water Colours* (London: Offices of the 'Studio,' 1906). Early members of the institute related to Tenniel were Henry Parsons Riviere (1834), John Martin (1836), and Edward Henry Corbould (1838).

5. Tom Taylor, "Exhibition in Black and White at the Dudley Gallery," *Graphic,* 17 June 1876, 598; and "The Institute of Painters in Water Colours, *Graphic,* 1 May 1877, 4.

6. "Exhibition of the Royal Academy," n.s., 12 (1873): 236–41; "The Royal Academy—Concluding Notice," n.s., 13 (1874): 228; "Institute of Painters in Water-Colours," n.s., 14 (1875): 58–59; "Exhibition of the Institute of Painters in Water Colours," n.s., 15 (1876): 221; "The Royal Academy Exhibition" (two reviews under this title), n.s., 17 (1878): 56, 179; "The Institute of Painters in Water Colours," n.s., 18 (1879): 34; and "The Institute of Painters in Water Colours" (1883): 307, for *Art Journal* reviews; and Silver diary, 23 Oct. 1861, 5 May 1869.

7. [F. G. Stephens?], "Fine Arts—the Institute of Painters in Water Colours, *Athenaeum*, 24 Apr. 1875, 558. There are two versions of the watercolor—one, 14 1/2 × 7 7/8 inches, was the Royal Institute's jubilee gift of 1887, Royal Library, Windsor Castle; the other, 25 1/2 × 15 1/4 inches, is in the collection of the Walker Art Gallery, Liverpool.

8. "Royal Academy," *Times*, 4 May 1878, for Armitage's *Pygmalion and Galatea;* and "Institute of Painters in Water Colours, *Art Journal*, n.s., 17 (1878): 154, "The Institute of Painters in Water Colours," *Athenaeum*, 20 Apr. 1878, 513–14; and *Times*, 18 Apr. 1878, on Tenniel's *Pygmalion*.

9. Tenniel, *A Sheep in Wolf's Clothing* (also called *The Misfits*), 1876 (from *Old Mortality*), and *Doleful Dumps*, 1888 (from *The Fortunes of Nigel*), for works based on Scott; and *Don Quixote Making Ready His Armour* (review in *Graphic*, 5 May 1883, 454. Tenniel had exhibited a work of this title in 1838—see *Society of British Artists*, s.v. "Tenniel, John"); and *Sir Rupert the Fearless*, 1873 (from *Ingoldsby Legends*), and *An Idyll*, 1884 (from *The Course of Time*), for works based on his illustrations. Six are based on *Punch* cartoons.

10. Christopher Hibbert, *The Horizon Book of Daily Life in Victorian England* (New York: American Heritage, 1975), 22.

11. Brooks diaries, 10 Sept. 1873, on Eve's illness. For 10 Portsdown Road as Ann Berry's address see Calendar of the Grants of Probate, 1879, fol. 388, "Tenniel John Baptist," in which she witnessed the signing of the second codicil, 17 Sept. 1877; and fol. 133, "Giani Eve," in which she is named administrator of Eve's estate, 7 Feb. 1879, Probate Registry, Somerset House.

12. Census return for 1871, Paddington (microfilm 0838752); and "Births, Marriages and Deaths—Died," *Ashby-de-la-Zouch Gazette*, 15 Mar. 1879.

13. Burnand, *Records and Reminiscences*, 370; and Allardyce Nicoll, *Late Nineteenth Century Drama, 1850–1900*, vol. 5 of *A History of English Drama, 1660–1900* (1962), 287–92.

14. Silver diary, 27 June 1866, on Tenniel and Burnand as friends; Burnand, *The Latest Edition of Black-Eyed Susan; or, The Little Bill That Was Taken Up*, which first played at the Royalty Theatre in 1866 (Nicoll, *Late Nineteenth Century Drama*), 289; Tenniel, drawing of E. Danvers, 15 Dec. 1875, Francis Burnand's estate; David Kunzle, *History of the Comic Strip: The Nineteenth Century* (Berkeley: Univ. of California Press, 1990), 349, on Busch; Francis C. Burnand, "Mr. Punch's Table: Another Vacant Seat," 8 Aug. 1910, and "Personal Recollections," *Daily Telegraph*, 27 Feb. 1914.

15. Spielmann, *History of "Punch,"* 378; and Tenniel to John Everett Millais, 2 Feb. 1883, Millais Papers, Pierpont Morgan Library, New York City.

16. See, for example, Tenniel, "Punch's Almanack for 1886."

17. Tenniel, cartoons, 29 Oct. 1887 and 20 Feb. 1886.

18. Tenniel, cartoons, 13 Feb. 1875, 17 Jan. 1885, and 12 Feb. 1887; and John Martin, *Marcus Curtius* (in Feaver, *Art of John Martin*, 98, fig. 69).

19. Tenniel, cartoons, 15 Sept. 1888, 7 Nov. 1885, 26 Feb. 1887, 7 Feb. 1891, and 6 Aug. 1892.

20. Tenniel, quoted by Lucy in "Tenniel," *Supp. "Punch,"* 12. On the staff visit to Paris, see Burnand, *Records and Reminiscences*, 257; and *Mr. Punch in Paris* (London: Bradbury, Agnew, 1889), 4.

21. Spielmann, *History of "Punch,"* 463; L. C. Martin, "Reminiscences of John Martin," part 6, 9 Feb. 1889; Burnand, quoted in *Pall Mall Gazette*, 27 Feb. 1914; and Harry Furniss, *The Two Pins Club* (London: John Murray, 1925), 9–10.

22. Burnand, *Records and Reminiscences*, 308–12; Layard, *Great "Punch" Editor*, 327, on Levy-Lawson; and Lucy, *Sixty Years*, 278.

23. Tenniel to James Russell Lowell, 23 Nov. 1884, 22 May 1886, Houghton Library; Smalley, "Sir John Tenniel," *New York Tribune*, 5 Apr. 1914; and H. Fletcher Moulton, *The Life of Lord Moulton* (London: Nisbet, 1922), 147. Tenniel could have met Moulton through his friends Robert Romer, Sambourne, or Guthrie.

24. Arthur à Beckett, "Our Caricaturists—John Tenniel," *Art Journal* (1882): 13, on the ovation given Tenniel; and Tenniel's speech, quoted in Joseph Hatton, "The True Story of 'Punch,'" *London Society*, July 1876, 59.

25. Spy [Leslie Ward], "Punch," caricature, *Vanity Fair* (London), 26 Oct. 1878; Tenniel to William Powell Frith, 19 Feb. 1882, in Frith, *Victorian Canvas*, 2:229; "The Institute of Painters in Water Colours: Touching Day," *Graphic*, 28 Apr. 1883, 422; "Exhibitions," *Magazine of Art* 6 (1883): 352; R. C. Lehmann, quoted in "Tenniel," *Supp. "Punch,"* 14, on Tenniel's appearance; Allen Fea, *Recollections of Sixty Years* (London: Richards Press, 1927), 160; and Mary Gladstone to Lavinia Lyttelton, 7 Mar. 1884, in *Mary Gladstone (Mrs. Drew): Her Diaries and Letters*, ed. Lucy Masterson (London: Methuen, 1930).

26. Ruskin, "Lecture 5. The Fireside," 161–97; Walker, "John Tenniel and *Punch*," 19–38; Frith,

Victorian Canvas, 2:228–29; Graham Everitt, *English Caricaturists and Graphic Humourists of the Nineteenth Century* (London: Swan Sonnenschein, le Bas & Lowry, 1886), 394–400; and "People in the Front Rank—XXII.—Mr. John Tenniel," *Wit and Wisdom,* 8 Oct. 1892, 373.

27. Lucy, *Sixty Years,* 382–84; Frank Lockwood to his daughter Lucy, 29 Apr. 1893 and 6 May 1893, quoted in Augustine Birrell, *Sir Frank Lockwood: A Biographical Sketch,* 2nd ed. (London: Smith, Elder, 1898), 162–63, 164; and Lucy, *Sixty Years,* 300, for Gladstone on *Punch's* cartoons. Gilbert was knighted in 1872, Millais was created a baronet in 1885, and Boëhm was made a baronet in 1889.

28. Anstey, *Long Retrospect,* 160–61; and Sambourne diary, 2, 3, and 4 Jan. 1893.

29. Spielmann, *History of "Punch,"* 473; Tenniel to Lewis Carroll, 4 July 1893, Fales Library, New York City; and Tenniel to William Agnew, 2 Dec. 1893, *Punch* letter boxes.

30. John Richard Robinson's recollections of the events of 11 Aug. 1893 are given in the *Westminster Gazette,* 27 Feb. 1914.

31. "Good Sir John!" *Punch,* 24 June 1893, 292; Spielmann, *History of "Punch,"* 89, 474; and *Cartoons from "Punch" by Sir John Tenniel,* 2 vols. (London: Bradbury, Agnew, 1895).

7. Exeunt

1. Spielmann, *History of "Punch,"* 539, on Riviere; Paul Hogarth, *Arthur Boyd Houghton* (London: Victoria & Albert Museum, 1975); E. V. Lucas, "George du Maurier at Thirty-Three," *Cornhill Magazine,* Oct. 1934, 387–90, 405–6; and Brooks diary, 4 Jan. 1872.

2. Nelson, introduction to *Art of the Eye,* 8–11.

3. Tenniel, cartoons, 29 Mar. 1890, 25 Jan. 1899, and 8 Feb. 1899.

4. Burnand, "Personal Recollections," *Daily Telegraph,* 27 Feb. 1914, on Tenniel's riding; and Bernard Partridge, quoted in "Tenniel," *Supp. "Punch,"* 15, on his walking.

5. Anstey, *Long Retrospect,* 268.

6. Tenniel, "Punch's Almanack for 1879"; Punch's Almanack for 1882"; Tenniel to Elspeth Thomson, 25 Jan. 1898, Elspeth Grahame correspondence, Bodleian Library; Tenniel, title illustration for vol. 95, late 1888 (see also cartoon, 11 Aug. 1888); Beril Becker, *Dreams and Realities of the Conquest of the Skies* (New York: Atheneum, 1967), 136–44; and "Notes" for the *Times* reprint of *Punch,* vol. 95, n. 66; and for vol. 96, n. 293.

7. Edith L. Calkin to Frances Sarzano, 16 Feb. 1946, referring to Tenniel as "Uncle John," collection of Charles Press; and photograph of Tenniel, signed "With Uncle John's love," in family possession.

8. Paula Ashton King (great-granddaughter of Tenniel's sister Eliza Margaret) to author, 15 July 1980; W. Tenniel Evans to author, 15 Jan. 1980; and Alice Julia Tenniel Evans to Frances Sarzano, 20 Mar. 1946, collection of Charles Press.

9. Anstey, *Long Retrospect,* 160; Marion Sambourne diary, 8 Mar. 1909, Linley Sambourne House; Shirley Nicholson, "Marion Sambourne, 1851–1914: Her Life and Times" (1987); and prayer book and miniature, in family possession (on the back of the miniature is written, "This portrait was presented to T. Stanley Green of Hartshorne Burton on Trent by his Aunt Victoire L. Tenniel—August 26th 1887"); Thomas Stanley Green to Sarzano, 26 Feb. 1946, collection of Charles Press; and Gladys Storey, *All Sorts of People,* 7.

10. See 1866 *Wonderland,* Durning-Lawrence Library, London; Tenniel to Thomas Agnew, "Darbyday" 1879, collection of Selwyn H. Goodacre; and Tenniel to Alice White, n.d., listed in Sotheby & Co. Catalog, 3 Apr. 1926, items 343 and 344.

11. Tenniel to Mrs. Furniss, 14 Nov. 1892, on the widows' and orphans' fund, Tenniel papers, University Research Library, UCLA, Los Angeles; and on his support of children's hospitals, *Manchester Guardian,* 27 Feb. 1914; "Sir John Tenniel," *Daily Telegraph,* 26 Feb. 1910; and "The Classics of the Nursery," *St. James's Gazette,* 15 Feb. 1898; Tenniel to A. W. Mackenzie, 22 Feb. 1898, Harry Ransom Humanities Research Center, and 3 Jan. 1877 (copy provided to me by John Wilson Autographs, Oxford). See also Tenniel, "The Pied Piper Up-to-Date," drawing from "Mr. Punch's Souvenir Book," reproduced in the *Lady's Pictorial,* 12 May 1900; and *Pelican,* 12 May 1900, *Punch* archives, on Irene Rickards.

12. Dicksee, portrait of Elspeth Thomson, reproduced in Patrick R. Chalmers, *Kenneth Grahame: Life, Letters and Unpublished Work* (London: Methuen, 1933), facing p. 96. See Elspeth Grahame correspondence, Bodleian Library.

13. Tenniel to Elspeth Grahame, 22 Mar. 1900, Elspeth Grahame correspondence, Bodleian Library; and verses in Thomas Stanley Green's scrapbook, collection of Derek Stanley Green.

14. Tenniel to M. H. Spielmann, 20 Dec. 1894 and 7 Jan. 1901, *Punch* letter boxes.

15. "Good Sir John! The "Black-and-White Knight," *Punch,* 24 June 1893, 292; F. C. Burnand, "Jackides," *Punch,* 2 Jan. 1901, deploring that "preux chevalier et sans reproche" he "hangs up his pencil-sword"; Spielmann, "Sir John Tenniel," *Daily Graphic,* 5 Jan. 1901, on his "high chivalry"; "The Cartoons of Sir Jackides the Inimitable," *Punch,* 27 Mar. 1901, 238, calling him "the knight that has conquered the Chinese Dragon"; and Owen Seamon, "In Memoriam," *Punch,* 4 Mar. 1914, 162, recalling him as a "chivalrous true knight in deed and thought" (the *Westminster Gazette,* 27 Feb. 1914, and the *Daily Telegraph,* 28 Feb. 1914, call him "the old warrior"); Girouard, *Return to Camelot,* 271, on fellowship knights and knights-errant; and Tenniel, "Our Enthusiastic Artist Is Quite Prepared for the French Invasion," small cut, *Punch,* Jan.–June 1852, 83.

16. Arthur William à Beckett, *The à Becketts of "Punch"* (New York: E. P. Dutton, 1903), 85, on Tenniel and the proprietors; Tenniel's letters to William Bradbury (William H. Bradbury?), Bradbury album and *Punch* letter boxes; Tenniel to "Will" Agnew, 2 Dec. 1893, calling him "my old friend of 40 years standing!!!" *Punch* letter boxes; Layard, *Great "Punch" Editor,* 397; à Beckett, *à Becketts of "Punch,"* 215, on the selection of editors; and Brooks diary, 1 Jan. 1872.

17. Tenniel to Philip Agnew, 28 May 1900, *Punch* letter boxes.

18. Sambourne diary, 21 Mar., 26 Sept., and 3 Oct. 1900; Bradbury and Agnew to the *Punch* staff, 7 Nov. 1900, "'Punch' Letter Book, 11 July 1900 to 30 June 1903"; Smalley, "Sir John Tenniel," *New York Tribune,* 5 Apr. 1914, on the design, fashioning, and presentation of the box; *Punch* to Frederick Hollingshed of Messrs Garrard & Co., 7 Dec. 1900, "'Punch' letter books"; and Anstey diary, 5 Dec. 1900.

19. Sambourne diary, 28 Nov. 1900.

20. Sambourne diary, 17 Dec. 1900. Tenniel's 1895 and 1900 exhibitions at the Fine Art Society were doubtless for the purpose of augmenting his retirement funds. Sales of his *Punch* drawings in Mar. 1895 (exhibition no. 132 of 177 pieces) brought in £1746.1.0 before commission (presumably, his 1900 exhibition, which had over 150 pieces, was similarly successful). Sambourne's exhibition in 1893 realized £1249.18.0, and Furniss's in 1894 made £901.11.0 ("Sale Book 1892–1895," Fine Art Society, London). See Tenniel's jingo cartoons of the Boer War, 11 Oct. 1899 and 18 Oct. 1899; and Monkhouse, *Sir John Tenniel,* 6, and Burnand, "Jackides," 2, on his last cartoon.

21. Anstey diary, 2 Jan. 1901; and Anstey, *Long Retrospect,* 254.

22. "'Punch' Letter Book, 8 Dec. 1900 through 3 Apr. 1901"; F. Carruthers Gould, cartoon, *Fun,* 19 Jan. 1901; Tenniel to Elspeth Grahame, 28 Jan. 1901, Bodleian Library; and "Sir John Tenniel," 14 Mar. 1901, newspaper clipping in Sambourne diary, paper unidentified.

23. Sambourne diary, 17 Apr., 29 May, and 5 June 1901.

24. "Banquet to Sir John Tenniel," *Times,* 13 June 1901; Anstey diary, 12 June 1901; Lucy, *Sixty Years,* 380; and Anstey, *Long Retrospect,* 161.

8. Out of the *"Show"* Altogether

1. Calkin was a noted portraitist and a member of the Royal Society of British Artists and the Royal Institute of Portrait Painters. See Simon Houfe, *The Dictionary of British Book Illustrators and Caricaturists, 1800–1914,* rev. ed. (Woodbridge, UK: Antique Collectors' Club, 1981), s.v. "Calkin, Lance (1859–1936)." The portrait (commissioned or acquired by *Punch*) was shown in the Royal Academy Summer Exhibition of 1902.

2. Anstey, *Long Retrospect,* 267–68, 287, 293–94, 300, 319, 327–28, 330, 336, 340–41, on Tenniel's retirement years; and Tenniel, quoted in "Sir John Tenniel's 88th Birthday," unidentified and undated newspaper clipping, family possession.

3. Tenniel to Marion H. Spielmann, 7 Nov. 1902, Spielmann Correspondence, John Rylands Library, Manchester; to Isidore Spielmann, 9 Mar. 1908, Bodleian Library; and to Phil Agnew, 11 Apr. 1902, *Punch* letter boxes, for his demurrals; and Anstey, *Long Retrospect,* 327, on the 1911 show. As one of Tenniel's objections in 1902 was that Leech and du Maurier were not represented, presumably their work was shown in 1911.

4. Anstey, *Long Retrospect,* 294; U.S. ambassador J. H. Choate, who said that Tenniel "had appealed to their hearts more effectively than if he had spoken at learned length"; Augustine Birrell, K.C., who commented that "they had had from Sir John Tenniel a speech which made one in love with silence" (both quoted in "Banquet to Sir John Tenniel," *Times,* 13 June 1901); Lucy, who wrote that it was agreed that "no speech, however pointed and well ordered, could have exceeded the eloquence of this ungovernable flood of emotion" (*Sixty Years,* 381); Henry Dickens, *Recollections,* 330; Balston, *John Martin,* 65; and Ward, *Memories of Ninety Years,* 317. The term "appallingly respectable assembly" is borrowed from Lucy's description of the early House of Commons, *Sixty Years,* 427.

5. Tenniel to Mr. Stonehouse, 8 July 1910, tipped into the original sketch copy of *Lalla Rookh*, Pierpont Morgan Library, New York City; and to Arthur Edward Calkin, 6 Oct. 1905, collection of Robert Riviere Calkin, on the mounting of his *Ingoldsby* tracings by the Riviere firm of bookbinders; Tenniel, *"Bouts-Rimés,"* which includes some post-retirement verses and "Pencillings in the Pit." Gift drawings of this period include one around 1902 to Arthur William à Beckett—"a speaking likeness" of Burnand, who had declared Tenniel "too old" to catch likenesses (Harry Ransom Humanities Research Center); a 1903 watercolor sketch of an "elderly beau" of about 1666 (Gladys Storey, "Late Sir John Tenniel," 396); one of his *"Latest* Cartoons" for Anstey Guthrie (Tenniel to Guthrie, 31 Dec. 1904, Anstey Papers); and a sketch "in loving remembrance!!!" for Winnie Burnand (Tenniel to Winnie Burnand, 24 Mar. 1908, Francis Burnand's estate). On the Royal Drawing Society see "A Wonderful Career," *Daily Telegraph,* 27 Feb. 1914; and the large file of this society's papers at the British Library.

6. Ronald Pearsall, *Edwardian Life and Leisure* (New York: St. Martin's Press, 1973), 128–39.

7. Tenniel to Lucy, 25 Mar. and 12 June 1907, in Lucy, *Sixty Years,* 381, 385.

8. The move was to 52 Fitzgeorge Ave., a still-imposing block of flats opened by the lord mayor just days before the queen's death, with turrets, balconies, dormered upper stories done in red brick with buff trim. A stone drive creates an entrance courtyard leading to the ground-floor flat. Doubtless Tenniel suffered from insufficient stimulation in his retirement years. By 1904 his calls to various friends had tapered off, and by 1907 visitors were less frequent. Besides Guthrie, there was William Agnew (increasingly deaf), who came regularly until his death in 1910 ("Sir John Tenniel," *Daily Telegraph,* 26 Feb. 1910). The art dealer Ernest Brown, who had managed Tenniel's two exhibitions at the Fine Art Society, called on Tenniel's birthdays (Oliver Brown, *Exhibition: The Memoirs of Oliver Brown* [London: Evelyn Adams & Mackay, 1968], 5). Others were Phil Agnew, E. V. Lucas, Laurence Bradbury, and Burnand (Tenniel to Phil Agnew, 12 May 1906, *Punch* letter boxes; and "Illness of Sir John Tenniel: His Eighty-Ninth Birthday," 27 Feb. 1909, paper unidentified, clipping at the Witt Library, London). For Tenniel's comments to reporters see "Sir John Tenniel's 88th Birthday"; "Death of Tenniel," *Daily Telegraph,* 27 Feb. 1914; and *Globe,* 26 Feb. 1914. On his deathbed Tenniel asked his companion, Inez Juster, if she thought the "Daily Telegraph gentleman" would remember to call again (*Daily Telegraph,* 28 Feb. 1914).

9. Quoted in "Death of Tenniel," *Daily Telegraph,* 27 Feb. 1914.

10. Tenniel, cartoons, 31 July 1897 and 2 Aug. 1899.

11. Anstey diary, 24 Dec. 1911; and R. C. Lehmann, quoted in "Tenniel," *Supp. "Punch,"* 14, on his military appearance.

12. Anstey, *Long Retrospect,* 336 (the quotation is from *Julius Caesar,* act 5, sc. 1, lines 121–22), 340. See also "Death of Tenniel," *Daily Telegraph,* 27 Feb. 1914; and Anstey diary, 15 Feb. 1914.

13. Guthrie to Partridge, 24 Feb. 1914, Anstey Papers.

14. "Death of Tenniel," *Daily Telegraph,* 27 Feb. 1914.

9. Postscript

1. "'Punch' Letter Book, 1 Dec. 1913–31 March 1914," including Proprietors of "Punch" to General Birdwood, 2 Mar. 1914; and *Daily Telegraph,* 28 Feb. 1914, on the burial instructions. Tenniel's grave, in which are also interred Julia Tenniel, Eve Giani, Victoire Tenniel, and Julia V. Martin (died 1940) is no. 12957/54/7. Nearby, marked by a stone, is no. 15841/54/7, the grave of Tenniel's parents, Eliza Maria and John Baptist, in which are also interred George, Bernard, Frederick H., and Adolphus Tenniel. William Rickards Tenniel (died 1876) is in grave 25680/54/6 (records of the General Cemetery Company, Kensal Green Cemetery).

2. "Wonderful Career," *Daily Telegraph,* 27 Feb. 1914; and "Death of Tenniel," *Daily Telegraph,* 27 Feb. 1914.

3. "Sir John Tenneil [sic] et Le 'Punch,'" *L'Est Republicain* (Nancy), 4 Mar. 1914 (see also Tenniel, cartoon, 23 Oct. 1886); *L'Eclair* (Paris) 28 Feb. 1914; *Journal de Genève,* 11 Mar. 1914; and *Kölnische Zeitung,* 28 Feb. 1914.

4. *New York World,* 28 Feb. 1914.

5. "A Lifetime of Art," *Evening News,* 26 Feb. 1914 (repeated in an American paper, unidentified). Furniss had left *Punch* under a cloud in 1894. His series, "Round the 'Punch' Table: 'Punch' Humorists and 'Punch' Artists as I Remember Them," appeared in *Tit-Bits* on 30 May 1914, 362–63; 6 June 1914, 394–95; 13 June 1914, 426; and 20 June 1914, 458–59. Furniss generally prefaced his attacks with compliments. Thus the May installment is fairly mild. By installment two he had disparaged Sambourne and du Maurier, and in the third installment Keene. In the last article, typi-

cally, he moved from flattery to condemnation, writing, "Sir John was a wonderful man, a supreme artist; the greatest cartoonist. . . . But . . . he had no ideas, not a very extensive knowledge of current politics, and absolutely no initiative."

6. Burnand to Spielmann, 20 Dec. 1897, *Punch* archives.

7. Quoted in "Tenniel," *Supp. "Punch,"* are Lucy, 12; Partridge, 15; Lehmann, 13; Anstey, 16; and Sambourne, 12.

8. Poynter, quoted in "The Academy Banquet," *Times*, 4 May 1914 (the Royal Academy and the Royal Institute sent wreaths); and *Pall Mall Gazette*, 6 Apr. 1914.

9. Sotheby Catalog for 3 Dec. 1915. Thibault's book is item 229. On its history see Egerton Castle, *Schools and Masters of Fence: From the Middle Ages to the Eighteenth Century*, 3rd ed. (London: Arms & Armour Press, 1969), 122–28; and John Harthan, *The History of the Illustrated Book: The Western Tradition* (London: Thames & Hudson, 1981), 130.

10. The *Paddington Society Newsletter* 36, Jan. 1963, Marylebone Library, with a drawing of the plaque that was affixed on 12 Mar. 1930; and Clunn, *Face of London*, 447, on Portsdown Road (now Randolph Avenue).

11. Tenniel's portrait of Lemon, *ILN*, 17 Oct. 1868, 384, was reproduced in a poster for the Kent Opera Co.

12. "Wonderful Career," *Daily Telegraph*, 27 Feb. 1914; and Port, *Houses of Parliament*, 273.

13. E. T. Reed, cartoon, *Punch*, 4 Dec. 1907.

14. See *Bandersnatch: The Newsletter of the Lewis Carroll Society*, published quarterly in the UK, for examples.

15. Tenniel, title page, *Punch* vol. 46, Jan.–June 1864; cartoons, 1 Feb. 1868, 30 Oct. 1880, "Punch's Almanack for 1884," 15 July 1893, "Punch's Almanack for 1897," and 8 Mar. 1899. See also cartoon, 5 Aug. 1871, in which the voter's protective "armor" of pillows reminds one of the bolsters, blankets, etc., of the Tweedles in "preparing for a fight"—drawn to my attention by Draper Hill, who also urged the inclusion here of the cartoon of 16 Mar. 1872 in which the Tichborne Claimant (or "*Wagga*-wock") has the bat's wings, vest, and gaiters of Tenniel's Jabberwock. This cartoon was probably suggested by Shirley Brooks, who frequently quoted from "Jabberwocky," reportedly his favorite poem (Layard, *Great "Punch" Editor*, 85). See also F. Carruthers Gould, *Westminster Gazette*, Nov. 1904–Nov. 1905, in *Political Caricatures 1906* (London: Edward Arnold, 1905), and also *Political Caricatures 1906*; and Munro, *Westminster Alice* (London: Westminster Gazette Office, [1903?]). See also Horace Wyatt, "Malice in Kulturland," illustrated by W. Tell, *Cartoons Magazine* 7 (Feb. 1915): 202–6, and (Mar. 1915): 441–44.

16. Ezra Bowen, *Knights of the Air* (Alexandria, Va.: Time-Life Books, 1980), 18–28.

17. See wartime supplements "The New Rake's Progress," 16 Sept. 1914; "The Prussian Bully," 14 Oct. 1914; "The Unspeakable Turk," 16 Dec. 1914; and "Our Volunteer Army," 3 May 1915; and memorial supplement for the queen, 30 Jan. 1901, with ten Tenniel cartoons; and for Edward VII, 18 May 1910, with eight Tenniel cartoons.

18. "'Punch' letter book, 1 Dec. 1913–31 March 1914"; Tenniel, cartoon, 29 Mar. 1890; *Cartoons Magazine* 7 (June 1915), 828, on the Hippodrome review; David Low, "Dropping the Pirate," cartoon, *Sidney Bulletin*, in *Cartoons Magazine* 7 (Feb. 1915): 182; "The Haunted Ship," cartoon, *Punch*, and Robert Carter, "Dropping the Pilot," cartoon, *New York Evening Sun*, in *Cartoons Magazine* (June 1915): 818, 828; Hugh Hagnis, "Dropping the Pilot," *Louisville Courier Journal* (196?); and *Punch* cover, 26 Mar. 1986.

19. Pseudo-*Punch* issue published in New York in 1915 and reproduced by the American Truth Society, New York (*Punch* archives).

20. Balfour, quoted in "Banquet to Sir John Tenniel," *Times*, 13 June 1901. See also "Mr. Punch's Victorian Era," *Athenaeum*, 15 Dec. 1888, 818. Quoted are "Wonderful Career," *Daily Telegraph*, 27 Feb. 1914; "Sir John Tenniel," *Daily Graphic*, 27 Feb. 1914; and "Obituaries," *La Chronique des Arts et de la Curiosité* 11 (14 Mar. 1914): 86.

21. For Tenniel's cartoons reproduced in school texts see *Punch* to McDougall's Educational Co., Edinburgh, 8 Dec. 1900, "'Punch' Letter Book, 11 July 1900–30 June 1903"; Denis Richards, *An Illustrated History of Modern Europe, 1789–1938* (1938); and Denis Richards and J. W. Hunt, *An Illustrated History of Modern Britain* (1950).

22. "Wonderful Career," *Daily Telegraph*, 27 Feb. 1914, on his influence; and à Beckett, *Recollections of a Humourist*, 372, on the waning power of the cartoon. In addition to its articles, *History Today* used Tenniel's cuts for its pullout cartoon in vol. 33, Dec. 1983, and vol. 34, Apr., May, and June 1984. His cartoon of 16 July 1892 appeared on the cover of the *Journal of Newspaper and Periodical*

History 3 (Winter 1986–87 and Spring 1987 issues); that of 18 Nov. 1871 on the jacket of Douglas Woodruff, *The Tichborne Claimant: A Victorian Mystery* (New York: Farrar, Straus & Cudahy, 1957); and Britannia from the cartoon of 14 Feb. 1885 is on the jacket of Bernard Porter, *Britannia's Burden: The Political Evolution of Modern Britain, 1851–1990* (London: Routledge, Chapman & Hall, 1994). Tenniel's work is often credited to Leech as in the following: "John Leech and His Cartoons of the Crimean War," *Cartoons Magazine* 7 (Jan. 1915): 8, five cartoons; Adrian, *Mark Lemon*, 65, two cartoons; Michael Wynn Jones, *The Cartoon History of Britain* (1971), 161, 163–64, 166, seven cartoons; and Peter Mellini and Roy T. Matthews, "John Bull's Family Arises," *History Today* 37 (May 1987): 19, 22, two cartoons.

10. Drawing on Wood

1. Forrest Reid, *Illustrators of the Sixties* (London: Faber & Gwyer, 1928), 21, indicates that Gilbert made some thirty thousand cuts for the *ILN;* and Eric de Mare, *Victorian Woodblock Illustrators* (New York: Sandstone Press, 1981), 35, reports that William Harvey drew over three thousand illustrations in eleven years.

2. Henry Holiday, "Wood-Engraving.—V," *Magazine of Art* 2 (1879): 284.

3. Du Maurier, "The Illustrating of Books. From the Serious Artist's Point of View.—I," *Magazine of Art* 13 (1890): 352. See also W. J. Linton, *Wood-Engraving: A Manual of Instruction* (London: George Bell & Sons, 1884), 35. So slavishly did the engraver follow the artist's lines that in the 1890s, when Tenniel's failing vision caused him at times to draw his hatching lines too closely (resulting in unsightly splotches), these were not corrected.

4. Geoffrey Wakeman, *Victorian Book Illustration: The Technical Revolution* (Detroit: Gale Research, 1973), 73; and du Maurier, "The Illustrating of Books," 352.

5. Silver diary, 7 Nov. 1864, and 27 Feb. 1867. Although Leech may have designed the relatively simple "French Porcupine" on the block as he was eager to be off hunting with Tenniel, ordinarily he traced his designs onto the wood from his sketch on paper (Frith, *John Leech,* 2:279; "John Leech," unidentified typescript, Bradbury and Evans albums; and Spielmann, *History of "Punch,"* 430). See Vizetelly, *Through Seventy Years,* 1:232, on Gilbert's speed; *DNB,* s.v. "Gilbert, John (1817–1897)," on his ability to draw on one section of a block while another was being engraved; Tenniel to George Hodder, n.d., Berg Collection, and Tenniel sketchbooks, Huntington Gallery.

6. Hogarth, *Arthur Boyd Houghton,* 11; and, on Millais, Houfe, *British Illustrators and Caricaturists,* 100.

7. Spielmann, *History of "Punch,"* 78, 475, 520.

8. William A. Chatto, *Gems of Wood Engraving from the "Illustrated London News"* (London: W. Little, 1849), 27; and John Jackson, *A Treatise on Wood Engraving. Historical Portion by William A. Chatto,* 2nd ed. (London: Henry G. Bohn, 1861), 603; ibid., 565, on early methods of joining blocks; Mason Jackson, *The Pictorial Press* (London: Hurst & Blackett, 1885), 317, on bolted blocks; typescript on Joseph Swain, p. 7a, Hartley Collection, Boston Museum of Fine Arts; and Spielmann, *History of "Punch,"* 249. On *Punch*'s blocks see "Obituary [Joseph Swain]," *Bookseller,* 12 Mar. 1909, 396.

9. William Feaver, introduction to *George Cruikshank* (London: Arts Council of Great Britain, 1974), 7; and Daria Hambourg, *Richard Doyle* (London: Art & Technics, 1948), 12–13. Examples of Tenniel's calendar designs in pencil are in the two large scrapbooks in family possession.

10. John Ruskin, *Ariadne Florentina: Six Lectures on Wood and Metal Engraving Given before the University of Oxford, 1872* (London: George Allen, 1890), 91; Tenniel, cartoon, 2 Nov. 1872; Holiday, "Wood Engraving," 284; and W. J. Linton, *The Masters of Wood-Engraving* (New Haven, Conn., 1889), 205.

11. S. C. Hall, *Retrospect,* 188; W. J. Linton, *Some Practical Hints on Wood Engraving: For the Instruction of Reviewers and the Public* (Boston: Lee & Shepard, 1879), 78; Vizetelly, *Through Seventy Years,* 1:160; and *Brothers Dalziel,* 56.

12. Houfe, *British Illustrators and Caricaturists,* 125; Vizetelly, *Through Seventy Years,* 1:283; and Thackeray to Tenniel, n.d., Berg Collection.

13. Uncut woodblocks by various artists in a variety of techniques, Hartley Collection; Walter Crane, *An Artist's Reminiscences* (1907), 49, on his pencils; Amanda-Jane Doran, "The Development of the Full-Page Wood Engraving in *Punch,*" *Journal of Newspaper and Periodical History* 7 (1991): 54, on Doyle's pencils; *Brothers Dalziel,* 58, 59, 64, on Doyle's problems with rubbing; Tenniel to Joseph Swain, 20 Oct. n.d., Houghton Library; and du Maurier to Tom Armstrong, Jan. 1862, in *Young George du Maurier,* 100. For engineering drawing, commercial drafting and design, and scientific drawing, leads may go up to 9H.

14. John Jackson, *Treatise on Wood Engraving*, 572; Chatto, *Gems of Wood Engraving*, 27; and Spielmann, "Our Graphic Humourists: Sir John Tenniel," *Magazine of Art* 18 (1895): 204.

15. Furniss, *The Confessions of a Caricaturist*, 2 vols. (London: T. Fisher Unwin, 1901), 1:18, on his having taught himself to engrave his own work with the help of an engraver. He and Spielmann jointly hatched the idea of a *Punch* history. Writing to Spielmann one year before the paper's fifty-year anniversary and referring to an earlier conversation, Furniss suggested a series of three or four articles that he himself would illustrate "in a most unique and elaborate style" and that he would also write. Conspiratorially, he warned Spielmann "on no account to mention this to anyone because if this subject is noised about or F. C. B. [Burnand] get a hint, parties will completely dry up" (Furniss to Spielmann, 21 May 1890, *Punch* archives). The final work was Spielmann's 575-page *History of "Punch."* See Furniss to Burnand, 28 Feb. 1894, *Punch* archives, for his resignation; Furniss to Milliken, 28 Feb. 1894, complaining about the subjects given him by Burnand, "I positively could not draw for *Punch*" (collection of Simon Houfe); and his later statement about the "good terms on which the editor [Burnand]" and he "worked so pleasantly and for so long" (*Confessions of a Caricaturist*, 1:233). See J. B. Groves, "Moving Pictures: A Memory Film by an Old Engraver—2," *Farmer's Advocate*, 23 Dec. 1915; Furniss, "Round the 'Punch' Table—IV," 458; and Burnand to Spielmann, 8 Jan. 1895, *Punch* archives.

16. Spielmann, *History of "Punch,"* 461–74; Tenniel to Spielmann, 5 May 1895, *Punch* letter boxes (typically, Tenniel had been more concerned with the reproduction—asking to see the "rough pulls"—than he was with the text). See Tenniel to Spielmann, 19 and 21 Mar. 1895, *Punch* letter boxes); and Monkhouse, *Sir John Tenniel*, 8.

17. Furniss, "Round the 'Punch' Table—IV," 458. Although Groves, a former Swain engraver, concurred with Furniss's contention that "Poor Swain" had been misrepresented and that he had actually improved Tenniel's work ("Moving Pictures"), Groves claimed in his unpublished memoir ("Rambling Recollections," 16) that Swain "had no artistic capability and was but a poor engraver." The largest of the uncut blocks that I examined is for a *Punch* cartoon with six bolted sections, explained by two entries in the Brooks diary: "12 July 1870—On Peace or War . . . we actually made three cuts to do [for the 23 July issue], in case there should be on Thursday, War, Peace, or Nothing Final"; and "14 July 1870—The *Times* declaring peace, as indeed we had a right to expect it, had not war [the Franco-Prussian War] been resolved on. . . . I went to Tenniel, and settled that we should have our Peace Cut, Napoleon as Bombastes [from W. B. Rhodes's 1810 play *Bombastes Furioso*]. Which was drawn. But before it could be cut came war news" (Layard, *Great "Punch" Editor*, 416–17). Tenniel reused most of the drawing in his 4 Aug. 1877 cartoon "Benjamin Bombastes," in which Disraeli replaced Louis Napoleon, and the figure's right arm, instead of reaching forward, is raised in defiance. See Rodney Searight Collection, National Art Library, for drawings on prepared paper; E. J. Milliken, prefatory note to *Catalogue of a Collection of Drawings for Punch Cartoons &c. by Sir John Tenniel, Fine Art Society Exhibition 132, March 1895*, 6; and Gilbert Dalziel, "Sir John Tenniel," letter to editor, 6 Mar. 1914, unidentified newspaper clipping, Hartley Collection, which states, "In all his lovely designs Tenniel seems to have attained the high-water mark of pencil manipulation."

18. Although an incompletely cut block cannot be proofed, as inking would destroy the remaining drawing, a pencil rubbing of the cut portion can be taken. On proof taking see Gilbert Dalziel to Harold Hartley, 15 Aug. 1928; and J. B. Swain to Hartley, 28 Mar. 1923, Hartley collection. Sir Algernon West, *Recollections: 1832 to 1886* (London: Harper & Brothers, 1900), 353, relates that Tenniel said he "saw no [cartoon] proof and had no opportunity of correcting his original sketch." See Groves, "Moving Pictures"; and on the differences between the published cut and proofs taken on India paper, John Jackson, *Treatise on Wood Engraving*, 603.

19. J. Swain [probably J. B. Swain, Joseph Swain's son and successor] to Spielmann, 15 May 1895, *Punch* letter boxes; and Spielmann, *History of "Punch,"* 250, on *Punch* scheduling; National Art Library, for Tenniel's touched proofs; Groves, "Moving Pictures," which states that all Tenniel's drawings on paper had "preserve plenty of color" written in the corner; and John Jackson, *Treatise on Wood Engraving*, 613–15, and Chatto, *Gems of Wood Engraving*, 27, on overlays and lowering.

20. Chatto, *Gems of Wood Engraving*, 26; J. F. Sullivan, "The Comic Paper," *Magazine of Art* 14 (1891): 419; Spielmann, *History of "Punch,"* 252; Houfe, *John Leech*, 134; *Young George du Maurier*, 17, 56, 62; Sambourne to Spielmann, 10 Jan. 1901, *Punch* letter boxes; and Tenniel to Bradbury and Evans, 13 Feb. and 16 Feb. 1868.

21. Tenniel to Swain, [188–?], and 20 Oct. [?], Houghton Library; J. B. Swain to Hartley, n.d., Hartley Collection; *Brothers Dalziel*, 130, 132; and Tenniel's proofs, National Art Library.

22. Wakeman, *Victorian Book Illustration*, 76–78, on early attempts; and for differing accounts

of when the method was adopted, typescript on Joseph Swain (p. 16a) in the Hartley Collection; Joseph Pennell, *Modern Illustration*, ed. Gleeson White (London: George Bell & Sons, 1895), 35–36; *Brothers Dalziel*, 42; Layard (*Life of Charles Keene*, 140–41; R. G. G. Price, *A History of Punch* (London: Collins, 1957), 338–39; and on his conversion to the method, Sambourne diary, 13 Dec. 1889.

23. Linton, *Practical Hints*, 80; Wakeman, *Victorian Book Illustration*, 79; Tenniel to Edmund Evans, 9 Aug. 1883, Rosenbach Library, Philadelphia; and Carroll to A. B. Frost, 24 Feb. 1885.

24. Partridge, quoted in "Tenniel," *Supp. "Punch,"* 15; Tenniel to J. B. Swain, 18 Feb. 1891, Houghton Library; Spielmann, *History of "Punch,"* 464; and Tenniel, pencil drawings for cartoons on prepared paper, 27 Jan. 1894 and 27 Feb. 1897, Searight collection.

25. Sambourne, drawing, "The Fight for the Standard," 3 Dec. 1892, 254, the first process cut in *Punch* according to a grangerized copy of Spielmann, *History of "Punch,"* 253, *Punch* archives; Wakeman, *Victorian Book Illustration*, 131; and Edward Hodnett, *Five Centuries of English Book Illustration* (Aldershot, UK: Scolar Press, 1988), 187.

26. Pennell, *Modern Illustration*, 43; Spielmann, *History of "Punch,"* 251; Sambourne, "How I Do My 'Punch' Pictures: An Interview with Mr. Linley Sambourne," *Pall Mall Gazette*, 8 Nov. 1889; "Mr. Punch: His Cartoonist-in-Chief," *Sketch*, 16 Jan. 1901, 511; Sambourne diary, 1889, which indicates that he might finish his cartoon as late as 10:30 Saturday morning; and Sambourne, "Political Cartoons: Part II," *Magazine of Art* 15 (1892): 46.

27. Pennell denied that wood gave a richer impression, maintaining that in almost all cases the wood engravings were printed from electrotypes made from the same metal as the process block. But this would not apply to Tenniel's cartoons for the woodblocks were put directly into the forms, and the electrotypes were taken only after the press run (Pennell, *Modern Illustration*, 42; and Spielmann, *History of "Punch,"* 250–51). Speaking against process were M. H. Spielmann, prefatory note to *Catalogue of a Collection of Drawings Political, Social & Fanciful by Linley Sambourne, Fine Art Society Exhibition 108, June 1893*, 8–9, and *History of "Punch,"* 253; and J. Comyns Carr, "Book Illustration, Old and New, Lecture II—delivered 22 May 1882," *Journal of the Society of Arts* 30 (27 Oct. 1882): 1055, 1059–60.

28. As Pennell admitted, it was still necessary for the process blocks to be finished by an engraver (*Modern Illustration*, 42). For the two methods see Carl Hentschel, "Process Engraving," *Journal of the Society of Arts* 48 (20 Apr. 1900): 464; and on bad process, see Pennell, *Modern Illustration*, 96; and Partridge, quoted in Price, *History of Punch*, 60.

29. *Punch* to Joseph Swain, 22 Apr. 1893, "'Punch' Letter Book, 18 Nov. 1892–30 Dec. 1893."

30. Tenniel to Phil Agnew, 28 May 1900, *Punch* letter boxes.

31. Cf. Carr, "Book Illustration": 1059–60, on the weaknesses in early process work.

32. Vizetelly, *Through Seventy Years*, 1:118–21, on Linton; Linton, *Practical Hints*, 35; *Brothers Dalziel*, 124–25; Gilbert Dalziel, "Sir John Tenniel"; Edward Dalziel to Hartley, 30 Nov. 1902, Hartley Collection; *Brothers Dalziel*, 260–62; and Sotheby Catalog for 3 Dec. 1915, items 162 and 204.

33. J. B. Swain. "Sir John Tenniel," in handwritten notes commenting on various artists, Hartley Collection; and "Late Sir John Tenniel," unidentified and undated newspaper clipping at Sambourne House.

11. Before Alice

1. Gleeson White, *English Illustration 'The Sixties'; 1855–70* (London: Archibald Constable, 1897) and Reid, *Illustrators of the Sixties*. These are annotated catalogs rather than studies in art history and doubtless have much useful information for collectors. Their artistic judgments and strong advocacy of adherence to nature seem to contain an element of defensiveness toward the upheavals occurring in the art world at the time they were written. White may have shared the sentiments of his friend Joseph Pennell, whose diatribes against Postimpressionism appear in *Pen Drawing and Pen Draughtsmen: Their Work and Their Methods* (New York: Macmillan, 1889), 337–48. Later, at the request of White, editor of the Ex-Libris series, Pennell wrote *Modern Illustration*.

2. Du Maurier, "Illustrating of Books," 351; Charles Baudelaire, "Some French Caricaturists," in *Mirror of Art* (Garden City, N.Y.: Doubleday, 1956); Graham Everitt, *English Caricaturists and Graphic Humourists of the Nineteenth Century* (London: Swan Sonnenschein, le Bas & Lowrey, 1886), 381, on Doyle; and du Maurier to his mother, Nov. 1862, in *Young George du Maurier*, 180.

3. Nicoll, *Late Nineteenth Century Drama*, 120–31.

4. Once illustration ceased to augment the meaning of the text, there was nothing for it to do but disappear, which it has more or less done (children's books excepted). See Tenniel to the Dalziels [1857?], in *Brothers Dalziel*, 130.

5. White said he could not help but feel that all of Tenniel's illustrations had "some satirical motive underlying their apparent purpose" (*English Illustration 'The Sixties,'* 22). Did White sense a satirical motive in Tenniel's illustration "The Norse Princess" (*Good Words,* Mar. 1863, 201), reproduced in his book? Reid claimed that Tenniel was "essentially a humorous draughtsman" (*Illustrators of the Sixties,* 27); and Paul Goldman, *Victorian Illustrated Books, 1850–1870: The Heyday of Wood-Engraving* (Boston: David R. Godine, 1994), 96, maintained that Tenniel's "heart lay more with *Punch* and with *Alice in Wonderland* [than with 'serious' illustration?]." More accurately, Monkhouse wrote of Tenniel's "ideal creations" as well as his "dramatic and humorous conceptions" (*Sir John Tenniel,* 28). See Tenniel to the Dalziels, 11 Jan. 1870, and two letters, [1857?], in *Brothers Dalziel,* 128, 130, 132; Tenniel to Edward Dalziel, 1852 or 1853, University Research Library, Los Angeles; to H. Cholmondeley-Pennell, 9 Jan. 1861, Berg Collection; to George Bentley, 1 May 1862, Berg Collection; and to Tupper, [1852?], in Hudson, *Martin Tupper,* 159.

6. Reid, *Illustrators of the Sixties,* 26.

7. Monkhouse, *Sir John Tenniel,* 12; Harthan, *Illustrated Book,* 188–89, on the German school; and in *Punch,* "The Classical German Mania," 10 Jan. 1846, 31–32; "The German School," 28 Mar. 1846, 145; and "Mr. Dyce's Designs," 23 Jan. 1847, 42. For Tenniel's fantastic border designs see Fouqué, *Undine;* and "The Children in the Wood," in *The Book of Nursery Tales,* vol. 3.

8. Reviews of Fouqué's *Undine* in vol. 7 (Oct. 1845): 324, and of *Aesop's Fables* in vol. 10 (1848): 153, *Art-Union Monthly Journal.* See Sir Joshua Reynolds, "Discourse IV," in *Discourses on Art,* ed. Robert R. Wark (New Haven, Conn.: Yale Univ. Press, 1975), 57–73, esp. 72.

9. *Aesop's Fables* (1848), 49, 85, 17, and 201.

10. Tenniel, cartoons, 1 Feb. 1851, "Welcome to Kossuth!" July–Dec. 1851, 6 Aug. 1853, 14 Oct. 1854, and 23 Dec. 1854. Tenniel is quoted in Spielmann, *History of "Punch,"* 470.

11. Tenniel, illustrations to *Aesop's Fables* (1858), 33, 55, 13, 99. On the last, cf. Monkhouse, *Sir John Tenniel,* 16, who wrote, "The artist has given for once a strong effect of light and shade, the woman shedding the light of a candle on the pretty faces of her sleeping servants."

12. Cf. Monkhouse, *Sir John Tenniel,* 15. See *Wonderland,* chap. 3 (titles used for the *Alice* illustrations are Carroll's own).

13. Tenniel, illustrations to *Aesop's Fables* (1858), 33, 55, 99, 24; and *Aesop's Fables* (1848), 43.

14. Tenniel, quoted in Monkhouse, *Sir John Tenniel,* 1; John Everett Millais, "The Sweet Story of Old," illustration to Henry Leslie, *Little Songs for Me to Sing* (London: Cassell, Petter & Gilpin, [1865]); and Tenniel, "Alice in arm-chair," illustration to *Looking-Glass,* chap. 1.

15. Tenniel, quoted in Kitton, *Dickens and His Illustrators,* 173.

16. Frank Rahill, *The World of Melodrama* (University Park: Pennsylvania State Univ. Press, 1967), 208; and E. L. Blanchard, quoted in Scott and Howard, *Life of E. L. Blanchard,* 129, on O. Smith; and "The Drama," *Bell's New Weekly Messenger,* 24 Dec. 1848, p. 5. See also "Adelphi Theatre: The Haunted Man and the Ghost's Bargain," *Morning Post,* 21 Dec. 1848, which called Smith's phantom "an unreal mockery."

17. *Examiner,* 23 Dec. 1848, pp. 819–20; *Morning Post,* 21 Dec. 1848; and *Bell's New Weekly Messenger,* 24 Dec. 1848, p. 6.

18. Tenniel to Tupper, 1852, in Hudson, *Martin Tupper,* 159. Tupper's suggestion to Martin (presumably after Tenniel's letter) that he contribute to this edition came to nothing (Balston, *John Martin,* 228–29). For the despairing man pose see third illustration to Robert Blair, *The Grave: A Poem* (Edinburgh: Adam & Charles Black, 1858), 16; first illustration to Shirley Brooks, *Silver Cord,* in *Once a Week,* 10 Nov. 1860, 533; and second illustration to "The Artist" in Miller, *Mirage of Life.*

19. Tenniel, illustrations to Barry Cornwall [Bryan Waller Procter], *Dramatic Scenes* (London: Chapman & Hall, 1857); *The Poetical Works of Edgar Allan Poe* (London: Sampson, Low, Son, 1858); and Blair, *The Grave.*

20. Tenniel, illustrations to Byron, *Childe Harold* (London: Art-Union of London, 1855); Pollok, *Course of Time* (Edinburgh: William Blackwood & Sons, 1857); *Poets of the Nineteenth Century,* ed. Robert Aris Willmott (London: George Routledge, 1857); William Cullen Bryant, *Poems* (London: Sampson Low, [1857?]); *The Home Affections Portrayed by the Poets* (London: George Routledge, 1858); and *Lays of the Holy Land: From Ancient and Modern Poets* (London: James Nisbet, 1858).

21. Buckler, "Once a Week," 926, 929. See Tenniel, illustrations to George Meredith, "The Song of Courtesy," 9 July 1859, 30; Goethe, "Eckhart the Trusty," 30 July 1859, 90; "A Railway Journey," 8 Oct. 1859, 285; A. Stewart Harrison, "The Pythagorean," 28 Jan. 1860, 103; and Alfred B. Richards, "The Negro's Revenge," 7 July 1860, 52. Buckler (p. 929) notes that Lucas strongly held that pictures should illustrate the author's text.

22. Tenniel, "Attention," illustration to *Gordian Knot*, chap. 6, facing p. 192; and to *Silver Cord*, in *Once a Week*, 2 Feb. 1861, 141. For Shirley's aside see *Gordian Knot*, 369.

23. Tenniel to Spielmann, 27 Aug. 1900, *Punch* archives, on his *Gordian Knot* pictures. For his social types see "Modern Druids," facing p. 119; "Duke's Grandfather," facing p. 242; and "The Little Star," facing p. 347. See "Love in Idleness," facing p. 99, for the seaside scene; and "Alban," facing p. 293; and "A Willing Witness," facing p. 234, for weaknesses in drawing. This book, aside from his two plates for the Junior Etching Club (1858 and 1861) and two frontispieces in 1862, was Tenniel's sole departure from wood engraving.

24. Those who count *Gordian Knot* among Tenniel's best works include Reid, *Illustrators of the Sixties*, 26–27; Frances Sarzano, *Sir John Tenniel* (London: Art & Technics, 1948), 14; Hodnett, *English Book Illustration*, 172; and Rodney Engen, *Sir John Tenniel: Alice's White Knight* (Aldershot, UK: Scolar Press, 1991), 41, 166. Regarding seriousness, White, *English Illustration 'The Sixties,'* 149, noted (approvingly?) that "not a few" men of the sixties, who "took themselves quite seriously," had "committed suicide, or died from over-work."

25. "Literature," review of *Gordian Knot*, in *ILN*, Jan.–June 1858, 70. The *ILN* went to the added expense of producing a wood-engraved version of one of the etched plates to accompany the review.

26. Reid, *Illustrators of the Sixties*, 26. Brooks is quoted in Layard, *Great "Punch" Editor*, 171, 172. The *Silver Cord* ran weekly in *Once a Week* from 10 Nov. 1860 through 31 Aug. 1861. It was published (pirated?) in book form in New York by Harper and Brothers in 1861 and 1871 with some of the Tenniel illustrations (recut).

27. For Shirley's asides in *Silver Cord* see chaps. 81 and 97.

28. Tenniel, illustrations to Brooks, *Silver Cord*, in *Once a Week*, 19 Jan. 1861, 85; 18 May 1861, 561; and 26 Jan. 1861, 113; and for acting instructions, Dick's *Actor's Handbook*, quoted in Allardyce Nicoll, *Early Nineteenth Century Drama, 1800–1850*, vol. 4 of *A History of English Drama, 1660–1900*, 2nd ed. (Cambridge: Cambridge Univ. Press, 1963), 22. Reid, *Illustrators of the Sixties*, 26, particularly objected to the last cited drawing.

29. Cf. struggling figures in Tenniel, illustration to Brooks, *Silver Cord*, in *Once a Week*, 13 July 1861, 57; and cartoon, 16 Nov. 1861.

30. Thomas Moore, *Lalla Rookh: An Oriental Romance* (London: Longman, Orme, Brown, 1817) with three metal engravings after Richard Westall; 19th ed. (1838) with thirteen metal engravings after Edward Henry Corbould, Kenny Meadows, and T. P. Stephanoff; and *Pearls of the East; or, Beauties from Lalla Rookh*, designed by Fanny Corbeaux and drawn on the stone by Louisa Corbeaux (London: Charles Tilt, 1837).

31. *Scenes from the Fire Worshippers* (London: Henry Vernon, 1857) with six illustrations by O. S. T. D.; *Lalla Rookh* (London: T. J. Allman, 1859) with five metal engravings; *Paradise and the Peri* (London: Day, 1860) with chromolithographs by Owen Jones and Henry Warren; *Lalla Rookh: An Oriental Romance* (London: Routledge, Warne, & Routledge, 1860) with forty-one engravings on wood after eleven artists; and *Lalla Rookh: An Oriental Romance* (London: Longman, Green, Longman, & Roberts, 1861) with sixty-nine illustrations by Tenniel engraved on wood. See Lucas, "Mr. Tenniel's Lalla Rookh," *Times*, 31 Oct. 1860 (the introductory pages mentioned have Persian designs by T. Sulman Jr.); and, on gift book prices, see Ruari McLean, *Victorian Book Design and Colour Printing* (Berkeley: Univ. of California Press, 1972), 160.

32. Moore, *Lalla Rookh* (1861), 180; Dickens, *Old Curiosity Shop* (1840–41), chap. 56; and Lewis Carroll, "The Dear Gazelle," *Comic Times*, 18 Aug. 1855.

33. The stories, in order, are "The Veiled Prophet of Khorassan," "Paradise and the Peri," "The Fire-Worshippers," and "The Light of the Haram [*sic*]."

34. Two of the thirteen cuts in Longman's 1838 edition are of the keepsake-beauty type, and out of the forty-one illustrations in Routledge's 1860 edition there are ten landscapes and two interiors. For Tenniel's melodrama see pp. 25, 68, 94, 151, 152, 197, 248, 315, and cf. the text on pp. 150, 249, 314. On Celeste see Watson, *Sheridan to Robertson*, 257–59; and Mark Lemon, "Madame Celeste," *ILN*, 23 Feb. 1856, 205 (this star and directress of the Adelphi from 1844 to 1858 appeared in such pieces as "The Maid of Cashmere" and "The Revolt of the Harem"). No less contrived than Tenniel's Zelica was Edward Henry Corbould's illustration for "Thy oath! Thy oath!" in Longman's 1838 edition. The artificiality of Mokanna's hand play, Zelica's "disordered air" as she presses her hand to her head are sheer melodrama. See Tenniel, cartoon, 14 Feb. 1885 (also cartoon, 4 Feb. 1871); and "Mr. Punch's Victorian Era," *Athenaeum*, 15 Dec. 1888, 819.

35. See illustrations pp. 47 and 109 for the main action placed downstage, pp. 8 and 236 for

symbolic vignettes, pp. 14 and 50 for harem scenes, and pp. 192 and 238 for landscapes. See "The Lay of St. Thomas à Becket," in vol. 3, *Ingoldsby Legends*, for another of Tenniel's landscapes.

36. *DNB*, s.v. "Moore, Thomas (1779–1852)." The "Fire-Worshippers" would have been the applicable story. For scenes that recall Arthurian legends or knightly themes see illustrations pp. 113, 117, 205, 256. See also pp. 96, 104, 233, 263, 269.

37. Thomas Ingoldsby, Esq. [R. H. Barham], *The Ingoldsby Legends; or, Mirth and Marvels*, 3 vols. (London: Richard Bentley & Son, 1864). Tenniel's earlier lighthearted cuts illustrated H. Cholmondeley-Pennell, *Puck on Pegasus*, rev. ed. (London: J. C. Hotten, 1869); and "The Adventures of Prince Lulu," *Once a Week*, 26 Apr. 1862, 490.

38. Tenniel to George Bentley, 1 M[ar. or May] 1862, Berg Collection.

39. Francis Talfourd, *Sir Rupert the Fearless*, Strand Theatre, 1848 (Nicoll, *Early Nineteenth Century Drama*, 410); and H. J. Byron, *The Nymph of the Lurleyberg; or, the Knight and the Naiads*, Adelphi Theatre, 1859 (Scott and Howard, *Reminiscences of E. L. Blanchard*, 232); Barham, *Ingoldsby Legends*, vol. 3, on Widdicomb; and Tenniel, "Widdicomez," in "*Bouts Rimés*." Tenniel's stage devil appears in the third illustration to "The Hand of Glory," vol. 1.

40. Tenniel, third illustration to "The Ingoldsby Penance," vol. 2; first illustration to "The Lord of Thoulouse," vol. 3; and Tenniel's chalk drawings based on the designs for "The Smuggler's Leap," vol. 1, in family possession.

41. Tenniel, second illustration to "Sir Rupert the Fearless," vol. 2; and first illustration to "The Tragedy," vol. 3.

42. Tenniel, third illustration to "Sir Rupert the Fearless" and fourth illustration to "The Ingoldsby Penance," vol. 2; fourth illustration to "The Tragedy" and third illustration to "A Lay of St. Romwold," vol. 3; third illustration to "A Lay of St. Odile," vol. 2, for Saint Ermengarde; and, for *Punch* stereotypes, third illustration to "The Hand of Glory" and third illustration to "The Cynotaph," vol. 1; and third illustration to "A Lay of St. Thomas à Becket," vol. 3.

43. "Current Literature," *ILN*, 31 Oct. 1863.

12. The Draftsman and the Don

1. Carroll had published some mathematical books, poems in *College Rhymes*, and occasional pieces in the *Comic Times* and the *Train*. See Carroll to Tom Taylor, 20 Dec. 1863, *Carroll Letters*, 1:62.

2. Carroll, *The Rectory Umbrella and Mischmasch* (London: Cassell, 1932), 43, 48, 49, for his early admiration for *Punch*; "Senior Common Room Papers of C. L. Dodgson," Christ Church archives, Oxford; Carroll diary no. 5, 24 Feb. 1857, British Museum; and *Lewis Carroll's Library*, ed. Jeffrey Stern (Silver Spring, Md.: Lewis Carroll Society of North America, 1981), Brooks Catalogue, lot nos. 665, 848, and 873. Tenniel's later book illustrations are in lot nos. 281, 730, 838, and 863, and his cartoons are in lot nos. 293, 371, and 533. Robinson Duckworth's recollection of strongly encouraging Carroll to send the manuscript to Tenniel (*The Lewis Carroll Picture Book*, ed. Stuart Dodgson Collingwood [London: T. Fisher Unwin, 1899], 360) does not necessarily mean that the suggestion originated with him.

3. Duckworth, quoted in Carroll, *Picture Book*, 360.

4. Grangerized copy of Spielmann, *History of "Punch,"* *Punch* archives, for drawing of Lord Palmerston beneath which is written in mirror writing, "Drawn with the left hand. J Tenniel"; and Silver diary, 25 Jan. 1865. He would, of course, have had to draw any letters on his woodblocks in reverse. See Carroll's plan for an expurgated Shakespeare for girls (preface to *Sylvie and Bruno* [London: Macmillan, 1889]); Shakespearean quotations in *Sylvie and Bruno Concluded* (London: Macmillan, 1893), chaps. 6 and 18; Jean Gattégno, *Lewis Carroll: Fragments of a Looking-Glass* (New York: Thomas Y. Crowell, 1974), 115; and, for five cuttings from Tenniel's 1856 series "Punch's Illustrations to Shakspeare," "Common Room Papers Dodgson."

5. Tenniel to George Evans, 24 Oct. 1882, Houghton Library; and Charles Keene to George Evans, [1883?], microfilm in collection of Simon Houfe, for rebuffs to a would-be biographer of John Leech. Eighteen years earlier Dickens informed another Leech biographer that "shocked by the misuse of the private letters of public men," he had "destroyed a very large and very rare mass of correspondence" (quoted in Houfe, *John Leech*, 211). See Derek Hudson, *Lewis Carroll: An Illustrated Biography* (London: Constable, 1976), 233; and Tenniel to Frederick Dolman, 6 Sept. 1891, and to A. W. Mackenzie, 12 Nov. 1899, both at Harry Ransom Humanities Research Center, for their dislike of publicity; "Lewis Carroll Dead," *Daily Chronicle*, 15 Jan. 1898; and Harry Furniss, *Confessions of a Caricaturist*, 1:134–35, for his openness to interviews.

6. Carroll to Furniss, 11 Nov. 1886, 29 Nov. 1886, 26 Aug. 1889, 8 Sept. 1893, and 21 Oct. 1893, *Carroll Letters*, 2:649, 651–53, 753–54, 987 n. 2, and 987–88; Furniss, "Recollections of 'Lewis Carroll,'" *Strand Magazine*, Jan.–June 1908, 50; and *Confessions of a Caricaturist*, 1:103, 179–80. See also *Carroll Diaries*, 2:474.

7. Stuart Dodgson Collingwood, *The Life and Letters of Lewis Carroll* (London: T. Fisher Unwin, 1899), 130; Carroll to Macmillan, 10 Dec. 1896, in *Lewis Carroll and the House of Macmillan*, ed. Morton N. Cohen and Anita Gandolfo (Cambridge: Cambridge Univ. Press, 1987), 349 (hereafter cited as *Carroll and Macmillan*), mentioning the précis (these consist of one or two sentences only); "Lewis Carroll: An Interview with His Biographer," *Westminster Budget*, 9 Dec. 1898, 23, quoted in *Lewis Carroll: Interviews and Recollections*, ed. Morton N. Cohen (Iowa City: Univ. of Iowa Press, 1998), 11; "Wood Engravings by the Brothers Dalziel," vol. 28, proofs no. 669–78, Print Room, British Museum; Carroll to Furniss, 29 Nov. 1886, in *Carroll Letters*, 2:653; and Carroll to Furniss, 1 Sept. 1887, in Collingwood, *Life of Lewis Carroll*, 260. To my knowledge, only one letter from Carroll to Tenniel survives, and that only because it was passed on to Shirley Brooks. Brooks had mischievously, in his series "Punch's Essence of Parliament" (hereafter cited as "Essence"), credited W. Dodson, M.P., with fathering *Wonderland*, and Carroll had written to Tenniel in protest. See Carroll to Tenniel, 18 Apr. 1872, Brooks Album, Harkness Collection.

8. Carroll, 16 and 20 July 1863, *Carroll Diaries* 1:199, 200; and Carroll to Taylor, 20 Dec. 1863, *Carroll Letters*, 1:62.

9. Carroll, 5 Apr., 13 Sept., and 12 Oct. 1864, *Carroll Diaries*, 1:212 and 1:222. Only twenty-seven of Tenniel's forty-two pictures apply to scenes in *Alice's Adventures Under Ground* (Carroll's first version of *Wonderland*), the other fifteen resulting from such additions as the caucus race, the new chapters "Pig and Pepper" and "A Mad Tea-Party" (with the consequent reappearance of the Cheshire Cat, Duchess, and Hatter in succeeding chapters), the poem "'Tis the voice of the lobster," and Alice upsetting the jury box. Out of these twenty-seven, only twenty parallel Carroll's choices—roughly the same correlation (about 75 percent) as in Arthur Rackham's 1907 reillustration of the book.

10. Chap. 11 n. 5 above, on Tenniel's autonomy; and Tenniel to Carroll, 8 Mar. 1865, Bodleian Library. See also Tenniel to Carroll, 1 June 1870, in which Tenniel states that he cannot see his "way to a picture" in the "wasp" chapter (Collingwood, *Life of Lewis Carroll*, 148). This procedure was not unusual. For other artists choosing their subjects see Carroll, 18 Mar. 1875, *Carroll Diaries*, 2:338, on Sambourne; Carroll to Holiday, 15 Jan. 1876, *Carroll Letters*, 1:239; and Carroll to Arthur Burdett Frost, 25 Apr. 1878, *Carroll Letters*, 1:309–10.

11. Tenniel to Dalziel, 27 Dec. 1870, in Flora V. Livingston, *The Harcourt Amory Collection of Lewis Carroll in the Harvard Library* (Cambridge, Mass.: privately printed, 1932), 30, on the chessboard landscape. Two of the *Alice* blocks were entirely redone—the White Rabbit as herald and Hatta in prison—and five others needed some plugging (removal of that portion of the block that required change and insertion of a piece of wood of the same dimensions) and recutting to alter the style of Alice's skirt ("Engravings by Dalziel," vol. 20, proofs no. 361–62; vol. 28, proofs no. 648–49, 669–78).

12. Tenniel to Dalziel, 11 Jan. 1870 (*Brothers Dalziel*, 128); proofs for *Looking-Glass*, National Art Library; and Tenniel to Dalziel, 27 Dec. 1870, instructing Dalziel not to send the block for the chessboard landscape to Macmillan until hearing from him (Livingston, *Amory Collection of Carroll*, 30).

13. *Brothers Dalziel*, 126; Carroll to Frost, 5 Apr. 1881, *Carroll Letters*, 1:413; and Carroll to Dalziel, 31 Mar. 1881, Huntington Library.

14. Carroll, 28 Oct. 1864, *Carroll Diaries*, 1:223; and Wakeman, *Victorian Book Illustration*, 76, on the adoption of electrotyping. The book was printed from electrotypes.

15. *Carroll and Macmillan*, for their transactions; *Wonderland* pagination guide, in Sidney Herbert Williams et al., *The Lewis Carroll Handbook* (Folkestone, Kent, UK: Dawson Archon Books, 1979), 197; guide for *Looking-Glass* in Edward Wakeling, "The Illustration Plan for *Through the Looking-Glass*," in *Jabberwocky* 21 (Spring 1992): 36–37; and Tenniel to Carroll, 4 Apr. [1870], Fales Library.

16. Carroll to Holiday, 15 Jan. 1876 (1:239); and to Frost, 25 Apr. 1878 (1:309), *Carroll Letters*; Carroll to Frost, 25 Apr. 1881 (shared with me by Edward Wakeling); and to E. Gertrude Thomson, 16 July 1885, *Carroll Letters*, 1:591; *The Selected Letters of Charles Dickens*, ed. F. W. Dupee (New York: Farrar, Straus & Cudahy, 1960), 142, 148–49; and *The Letters of Charles Dickens*, ed. Kathleen Tillotson (Oxford: Clarendon Press, 1977), 4:140, 5:35–36.

17. Carroll to Holiday, 15 Jan. 1876 (1:238); to Frost, 9 Dec. 1880 (1:399); to Furniss, 29 Nov. 1886 (2:653) and 30 Sept. 1893 (2:987 n. 2), *Carroll Letters*, for his praise; Carroll to Furniss, 30 Sept. 1893 (2:987 n. 2); to Frost, 5 Apr. 1881 (1:413); and to Furniss, 29 Nov. 1886 (2:651) and 26

Aug. 1889 (2:754), *Carroll Letters,* for his criticisms. Tenniel, too, could be honest to the point of bluntness. One correspondent, approaching him on behalf of a friend, received this reply: "If your friend really desires it—and will send me a few *examples* of his 'work'—he may rely on my giving a perfectly honest and straightforward opinion of its 'quality,' more or less a *thankless* duty in my experience" (Tenniel to George C. Pulford, 20 Oct. 1903, Houghton Library).

18. Macmillan's comments would have reinforced Carroll's regard for his illustrator. He advised Carroll that "Mr. Tenniel's drawings in the book need no such meretricious help" as ornamental type in the title page, and wrote, "I do think with Tenniel's pictures that *Alice* at 7s 6d is a cheap enough book" (Macmillan to Carroll, 19 Sept. 1864 and 4 Oct. 1866, in *Carroll and Macmillan,* 11, 45).

19. Carroll to Furniss, 26 Aug. 1889, *Carroll Letters,* 2:754, on the change in Alice's face; and Canon Duckworth, quoted in *Lewis Carroll Picture Book,* 360; *Carroll Letters,* 508 n. 2; and Livingston, *Amory Collection of Carroll,* 33, on Carroll's delight in Tenniel's work. On his eagerness to procure Tenniel's services for *Looking-Glass* see Carroll, 24 Jan. 1867, 8 Apr. 1868, 19 May 1868, 21 June 1868, 25 June 1870, and 3 July 1871, *Carroll Diaries,* 1:249, 2:267, 269, 270, 288, 301; and Carroll to Mrs. G. MacDonald, 19 May 1868, *Carroll Letters,* 1:119–20. In his 24 Jan. 1867 diary entry Carroll noted that he had approached Richard Doyle. But this was on the suggestion of Tenniel, whom he had tried first (Lucy, *Sixty Years,* 384–85). See also Carroll to G. L. Craik (of Macmillan), 25 Nov. 1876, in Hudson, *Lewis Carroll,* 237, asking him to "Please keep a look-out among illustrated books, and let me know if you see any artist at all worthy of succeeding to Tenniel's place"; and Carroll to Fildes, 2 July 1877, in *L. V. Fildes, R.A.: A Victorian Painter* (London: Michael Joseph, 1968), 44, on his long-time discouragement "from going on with it [*Sylvie and Bruno*], by the apparent hopelessness of finding an artist worthy to succeed Mr. Tenniel." See Carroll, *The Nursery Alice* (London: Michael Joseph, 1890), 21, 53 for Carroll's asides; and Mrs. E. M. Ward, *Memories of Ninety Years,* ed. Isabel G. McAllister (London: Hutchinson, [1924]), 58 for Carroll's comment on the success of *Alice.* On 18 Feb. 1946, David Williamson, editor of the *Daily Mail Year-Book,* wrote to Frances Sarzano that his neighbor (Tenniel's niece) recalled that "Tenniel looked back with satisfaction to his illustrations to 'Alice' and found Lewis Carroll an appreciator who encouraged him" (collection of Charles Press).

20. Carroll, 16 Jan. 1874, *Carroll's Diaries,* 2:326 (on Holiday); Carroll to Frost, 7 Jan. 1878 (*Carroll Letters,* 1:298); Carroll to Frost, 25 Apr. 1881 and 24 Feb. 1885 (shared with me by Edward Wakeling); *Carroll Diaries,* 2:474, on Furniss; and Furniss, "Recollections of Lewis Carroll," 48–52.

21. Holiday did the ninth and final picture for *The Hunting of the Snark* (London: Macmillan, 1876) when Carroll had but three stanzas (*Carroll Diaries,* 2:335); and Carroll was still "getting on" with *Sylvie and Bruno* in Mar. 1889, although he had considered publication by 1886 to be "possible" and by 1887 to be "probable" (Carroll, 9 Mar. 1885 and 18 Mar. 1889, *Carroll Diaries,* 2:432, 468). His projection for the sequel was off by three years. See Carroll to Maude Standen, 1 Sept. 1873, on his writing (*Sotheby and Co. Catalogue—28 Feb. 1933*).

22. Carroll, 2 July 1863, *Carroll Diaries,* 1:199, noting his receipt of a second trial page (at this date Carroll had found neither publisher nor artist); Williams et al., *Lewis Carroll Handbook,* 31, for his receipt of another specimen sheet on 13 May 1864; and on the book's progress, Carroll, 2 and 6 May 1864 and 2 Aug. 1864, *Carroll Diaries,* 1:215, 221; Carroll to Macmillan, 16 Dec. 1864, *Carroll and Macmillan,* 36; and Carroll, calendar of events *September 1864, Carroll Letters,* 1:72. For word counts see Justin G. Schiller, *Alice's Adventures in Wonderland: An 1865 Printing Re-described* (Kingston, N.Y.: privately printed for the Jabberwock, 1990), 55.

23. Carroll, 4 Jan. 1871, *Carroll Diaries,* 2:294. On the letter of 4 Apr. 1870 see n. 15 above.

24. Tenniel to Carroll, 4 Apr. [1870], Fales Library.

25. Tenniel, quoted in Collingwood, *Life of Lewis Carroll,* 146; and Carroll, 1 Mar. 1875, *Carroll Diaries,* 2:337.

26. Tenniel did twenty-nine illustrations for Miller's *Mirage of Life* (1867), a frontispiece for Dinah Mulock's book *A Noble Life* (London: Hurst & Blackett, 1868), and one design for Adelaide Ann Procter's *Legends and Lyrics* (London: Bell & Daldy, 1866). See Carroll, 1 Nov. 1871, *Carroll Diaries,* 2:305, on the "printing off" of *Looking-Glass;* Tenniel to George Bentley, 6 Nov. 1871, Berg Collection; Silver diary, 1 Apr. 1863, and chap. 6 above on his resumption of painting; and on the *Comic History of England,* see à Beckett, *à Becketts of "Punch,"* 109. Tenniel also began, but abandoned, work on an illustrated Shakespeare for Bradbury and Agnew in 1878 (*Brothers Dalziel,* 127).

27. Silver diary, 14 Dec. 1864.

28. Carroll, 2 Aug. 1865, *Carroll Diaries,* 1:234, for Tenniel's charges; "Bradbury and Evans Account Book," *Punch* archives, showing an average of five pounds per design for *Once a Week;* Royal A. Gettmann, *A Victorian Publisher: A Study of the Bentley Papers* (Cambridge: Cambridge Univ. Press,

1960), 81, showing that his thirty-one illustrations for *Ingoldsby Legends* came to £180 4s. 4d., or about £5 16s. 3d. each; and du Maurier to Pem, 1862, *Young George du Maurier*, 174, stating that Tenniel charged £215, or £5 each, for his forty-three relatively simple vignettes for "Punch's Book of British Costumes." H. Cholmondeley-Pennell wrote to Frith that when they were illustrating his *Puck on Pegasus* (1861), "Seeing that I was a débutant in literature, he [Leech] only let me pay him about half his usual price—a generosity in which he was equalled by my friend Mr. John Tenniel" (quoted in Frith, *John Leech*, 2:289–90). See, too, Tenniel to Cholmondeley-Pennell, 9 Jan. 1861, Berg Collection, in which he charges him seven guineas for the four illustrations to "Lord Jollygreen's Courtship," or about £1 16s. 9d. apiece. Carroll must have realized how low Tenniel's charges to him were. See Carroll to Craik, 12 May 1876, *Carroll and Macmillan*, 129, in which he estimated that one hundred pounds to the artist alone (for *Rhyme? and Reason?*) might purchase "perhaps a dozen pictures." Frost, at the start of his career, charged six guineas for a large and three for a small picture (Carroll, 8 Sept 1884, *Carroll Diaries*, 2:428); and Thomson charged £50 8s. for twelve draw-ings, or £4 4s. apiece (Carroll to Thomson, 4 Mar. 1895, *Carroll Letters*, 2:1054). Using the scale of charges cited in Carroll to Furniss, 21 Nov. 1887, in *Lewis Carroll and His Illustrators: Collaborations and Correspondence, 1865–1898*, ed. Morton N. Cohen and Edward Wakeling (Ithaca, N.Y.: Cornell Univ. Press, 2003), 153, Furniss's charge for *Wonderland* would have been £389 14s.

29. As Carroll had asked Thomson, "What am I to do with the copyright, for which I have paid you a total of £50. 8. 0," (see n. 27 above) it may have been his practice to purchase the copyright outright. Susan E. Meyer, *A Treasury of Great Children's Book Illustrators* (New York: Harry N. Abrams, 1983), 35, comments that royalties were awarded to artists only in the latter nineteenth century. See *American Art Association Catalog* (n.d.), which lists some *Alice* jigsaw puzzles, c. 1870, and an *Alice* clockwork toy based on Tenniel's designs, in Misc. Dodgson. New York Public Library; forty-eight *Alice* playing cards (n.d.), Christ Church Library; *Lewis Carroll at Texas—Carroll Studies No. 8* (Lewis Carroll Society), items 353, 355, 468, 490; Collingwood, *Life of Lewis Carroll*, 107, 237; Car-roll to Macmillan, 17 May 1896, *Carroll and Macmillan*, 337; and Tenniel to Mackenzie, 22 Feb. 1898 and 12 Nov. 1899, Harry Ransom Humanities Research Center.

30. Carroll did expect remuneration for publication of Tenniel's pictures as slides (Carroll to Macmillan, 1 Mar. 1876, *Carroll and Macmillan*, 122). On disputes over royalties see Doyle to Evans, 15 Feb. 1848 [1858?], Bradbury Album; Evans to Doyle, 6 Nov. 1849; Doyle to Evans, n.d. (no. 132), 16 Apr. 1859 (no. 133), and canceled check of 31 May 1868, Bradbury and Evans Albums; Price, *History of Punch*, 166; and Philip Agnew and W. Laurence Bradbury to Harry Furniss, 2 Mar. 1894, "'Punch' Letter Book, 1 Jan. 1894–6 Dec. 1895."

31. *Publisher's Circular*, 8 Dec. 1865, 686; *Bookseller*, 12 Dec. 1865; *ILN*, 16 Dec. 1865; *Aunt Judy's Magazine*, 1 June 1866, 123; and *Illustrated Times*, 16 Dec. 1865.

32. Macmillan to Carroll, 15 Mar. 1876, *Carroll and Macmillan*, 125 n. 2; Carroll to Furniss, 1 Nov. 1889, to Frost, 9 Dec. 1880, and to Thomson, 4 Mar. 1895, *Carroll Letters*, 2:760–61, 1:398, 2:1053; and Carroll to Macmillan, 25 Nov. 1889, *Carroll and Macmillan*, 270.

33. Janis Lull, "The Appliances of Art: The Carroll-Tenniel Collaboration in *Through the Look-ing-Glass*," in Edward Guiliano, *Lewis Carroll: A Celebration* (New York: Clarkson N. Potter, 1982), 101–11.

34. Carroll, 20 and 21 June 1864, *Carroll Diaries*, 1:216, 217. On 17 Apr. 1865 (1:229) Carroll wrote, "Settled with Macmillan the size of the book 7" by 5". On the size change for Tupper's book see Tenniel to Edward Dalziel, [1852?], bound into Forster, *Life of Charles Dickens*, 372, Special Collec-tions, University Research Library, UCLA, Los Angeles. On the timing of Tenniel's pictures see Carroll, 12 Oct. 1864, *Carroll Diaries*, 1:222, and calendar of events *September 1864*, *Carroll Letters*, 1:72 (noting that on 18 June 1865 Carroll received the final proofs). Since Oct. 1864 Tenniel had produced about five *Alice* pictures per month besides his regular *Punch* work.

35. Carroll to Macmillan, 24 May 1865, *Carroll and Macmillan*, 37; and Carroll, 15 Jan. 1871, *Car-roll Diaries*, 2:295. There were twenty-two blocks done before 11 Oct., 1870, the day when Carroll's diary shows the change from black to violet ink, as his pagination guide shows blocks "ordered to be electrotyped" in violet after that. See Carroll, 11 Mar., 25 Apr., and 29 Aug. 1871, *Carroll Diaries*, 2:295, 297, 303, for other mournful entries; and 7, 8, and 18 Dec. 1871, 2:306–7, on the gift copies.

36. Carroll to Frost, 9 Dec. 1880; to Furniss, 6 May 1885, 11 Nov. 1886, 1 Nov. 1889, *Carroll Let-ters*, 1:399, 574, 2:649, 760.

37. Carroll, 20 July 1865, *Carroll Diaries*, 1:234; and Tenniel to Dalziel, 1865, in 1865 edition of *Wonderland*, Huntington Library.

38. The 250 sets put out by the Rocket Press in 1988 may in fact have erred on the side of clar-

ity. The three value studies tipped into the Harold Hartley 1872 copy of *Looking-Glass* that I examined at Christie's in 1987 were for the scenes Carroll called "sheep in shop," "King's horses and men," and "Frog gardener."

39. The 1865 *Alice* that I examined at the Pierpont Morgan Library, New York City, is similarly faulty in type and in the reproduction of the illustrations—too gray for the most part, but with uneven pressure from page to page.

40. Carroll, 9 Nov. 1865, *Carroll Diaries*, 1:236; Carroll to Macmillan, 30 Aug. 1866, 28 Sept. 1866, 17 Dec. 1871, and 7 Oct. 1897, *Carroll and Macmillan*, 44, 45, 97, 357, on proofs sent to Tenniel; and Carroll to Macmillan, 17 Apr. 1867 and 17 Dec. 1871, pp. 51, 97, on his own monitoring. Carroll suppressed the first ten thousand copies of *The Nursery Alice* (Carroll to Macmillan, 23 June 1889, p. 257); and the first 1893 printing of *Looking-Glass* (Hudson, *Lewis Carroll*, 181, 196).

41. Harry Morgan Ayres, *Carroll's Alice* (New York: Columbia Univ. Press, 1936), 93, for the Clarendon Press charges; and Percy Muir, *English Children's Books, 1600 to 1900* (New York: Frederick A. Praeger, 1969), 140, on Carroll's receipt of £120 from Appleton. Carroll's diary entry of 2 Aug. 1865, *Carroll Diaries*, 1:234, says "total cost" and not "total reprinting cost," a point that was missed by Ayres, pp. 89–90, and by Morton N. Cohen, *Lewis Carroll: A Biography* (New York: Alfred A. Knopf, 1995), 129.

42. Carroll to Macmillan, 24 May 1865, in *Carroll and Macmillan*, 36–37, stating that he wanted *Wonderland* "to be a *table*-book"; and on the value Victorians placed on fine books, see *Carroll and Macmillan*, 161 n. 3; Goldman, *Victorian Illustrated Books*, 66; and "Children's Christmas Literature," *Daily News*, 19 Dec. 1866.

43. *Bookseller*, 12 Dec. 1865; *ILN*, 16 Dec. 1865; *Monthly Packet*, 1 Jan. 1866; *Sutherland Herald*, 25 May 1866; and *Scotsman*, 22 Dec. 1866. A *Looking-Glass* review would similarly remark that "with its big print, good paper, and capital illustrations by Tenniel," it was "a very attractive book for children" (*Globe*, 15 Dec. 1871).

44. Carroll to Macmillan, 17 Aug. 1881, in *Carroll and Macmillan*, 162; Tenniel to Edmund Evans, 9 Aug. 1883, Rosenbach Museum and Library, Philadelphia; Carroll, 10 July 1885, *Carroll Diaries*, 2:437; 20 Feb. 1889, 2:468–69, when Carroll recorded finishing his MS; and Tenniel to Edmund Evans, 18 Dec. 1889, Rosenbach Museum and Library.

45. Tenniel to Carroll, 5 Sept. 1896, Montague Collection, New York Public Library; and Tenniel to Carroll, 9 Sept. 1896, Fales Library.

46. Carroll to Macmillan, 7 Oct. 1897, in *Carroll and Macmillan*, 357. Tenniel's involvement may not have ended here; his letter to Macmillan, 13 Dec. 1906, begins, "*Certainly*. I shall sign the 'document'" (in Myers & Co., booksellers, to Frances Sarzano, 18 Feb. 1946, collection of Charles Press). On their "intimate association," see Tenniel, quoted in Hudson, *Lewis Carroll*, 23.

47. Carroll, 9 Apr. 1866 and 8 Apr. 1868, *Carroll Diaries*, 1:241–42, 2:267; Lucy, *Sixty Years*, 384–85; and Carroll, 22 June 1874, *Carroll Diaries*, 2:329; and n. 7 above.

48. Carroll, 11 June 1869, 12 Mar. 1870, and 3 Oct. 1872, *Carroll Diaries*, 2:281, 287, 314, for their social meetings; and *Sotheby Catalogue, 3 Dec. 1915*, lots no. 180–187 and 219; and Tenniel to Carroll, 22 July 1890 and 9 Sept. 1896, Fales Library; and 29 Jan. 1894, Houghton Library, on gifts to Tenniel.

49. Brooks diary, 11 Apr. 1871, in Layard, *Great "Punch" Editor*, 449; Carroll to Frost, 7 Feb. 1878, shared with me by Edward Wakeling; Tenniel to Carroll, 4 July 1893, Fales Library; and Hudson, *Lewis Carroll*, 23.

13. Harlequin Alice

1. William Makepeace Thackeray [M. A. Titmarsh, pseud.], *The Rose and the Ring; or, The History of Prince Giglio and Prince Bulbo: A Fire-Side Pantomime for Great and Small Children* (London: Puffin Books, 1855), for "Great and Small Children."

2. Carroll, 31 Dec. 1877, and 4, 8, 10, and 15 Jan. 1878, *Carroll Diaries*, 2:368–69, for his attendance during this season. On four of these occasions he saw *Robin Hood*. On 17 Jan. 1856 Carroll recorded enjoying the pantomime at the Haymarket, *The Butterfly's Ball and the Grasshopper's Feast; or, Harlequin and the Genius of Spring* (*Carroll Diaries*, 1:74 (see also *Times*, 22 Dec. 1855) based on the poem by William Roscoe, which is believed to have influenced Carroll's verses "I passed by his garden" (chap. 10, *Wonderland*) and "O Looking-Glass creatures" (chap. 9, *Looking-Glass*). See *The Parodies of Lewis Carroll and Their Originals*, ed. John Mackay Shaw, catalogue of an exhibition at the Florida State University Library, 1960; and F. J. Harvey Darton, *Children's Books in England: Five Centuries of Social Life*, 3rd ed. (Cambridge: Cambridge Univ. Press, 1982), 199. The Wasp of this

play, later transformed to Clown in the harlequinade, may have inspired the discarded "Wasp in the Wig" chapter of *Looking-Glass*. See Carroll to Gertrude Chataway, 11 Feb. 1877, *Carroll Letters*, 1:270–71, on pantomime.

3. Carroll to Taylor, 10 June 1864, *Carroll Letters*, 65, suggesting such titles for his book as "Alice among the Elves," "Alice among the Goblins," and "Alice in Elf-Land." In the "opening" (played by actors in big-head masks) a pair of lovers are threatened with separation by the girl's grim father. Their rescuer is a benevolent fairy who, in a grand transformation scene, changes them to Harlequin and Columbine. The father and his servant, now Pantaloon and Clown, chase the pair through the riotous scenes of the harlequinade until, in a "dark scene," Clown captures the magic bat with which Harlequin has until now managed to escape. Again interceding, the fairy restores all to their original selves, uniting the lovers. Apparently Carroll had queried the entertainer Mr. Coe on the advisability of staging *Wonderland* as a pantomime (Carroll, 11 May 1867, *Carroll Diaries*, 1:259).

4. Tenniel, illustrations to "Britishlion the Bagdificent; or Harlequin Happy Hunchback and the Paragon Pocket Book." The "State," the "Royal Household," the "Ambassadors," and the "Legislature" are shown as scenes from the opening; the "House of Commons" and "Taxes" as dark scenes, and "Commerce," "Army and Navy," "Law," "Amusements," and "Population" as scenes from the harlequinade.

5. Carroll, 13 Nov. 1862, *Carroll Diaries*, 1:188, on the book as a Christmas gift. Titles naming court cards or card games are *Laugh and Lay Down; or, Harlequin King of Spades* (Royal Amphitheatre, 15 Apr. 1805); *The Cassowar; or, Harlequin's Rouge et Noir* (Sadler's Wells, 3 Aug. 1807); *The Card Party; or, Harlequin King of Spades* (Olympic, 28 Feb. 1808); *Harlequin and the King of Clubs; or, The Knave Who Stole the Syllabubs* (Adelphi, 26 Dec. 1832); *Harlequin the Queen of Spades, and the Fairy the Fawn* (Grecian, 27 Dec. 1852); *Plum Pudding and Roast Beef; or, Harlequin Nine Pins and the Card King of the Island of Games* (Standard, Dec. 1853); and *Harlequin Old Mother Goose; or, The Queen of Hearts and the Wonderful Tarts* (Surrey, 26 Dec. 1862). The last-named title was brought to my notice by Canon Ivor Davies upon reading my article that made the pantomime connection: "Alice and King Chess," *Jabberwocky* 12 (Autumn 1983). See "The Theatres, Drury-Lane Theatre," *Times*, 27 Dec. 1825; and David Mayer III, *Harlequin in His Element: The English Pantomime, 1806–1836* (Cambridge, Mass.: Harvard Univ. Press, 1969), 233, on W. Barrymore, *Harlequin Jack of All Trades* (Drury Lane, 26 Dec. 1825); "The Theatres," *ILN*, 30 Dec. 1865, 655, for a review of the 1865 pantomime at Astley's entitled *Harlequin Tom, Tom, the Piper's Son, Pope Joan, and Bo Peep; or, Old Daddy Longlegs, and the Pig Who Went to Market, and the Pig Who Stopped at Home*, describing a scene at the Palace of Diamonds as a "grand jeu de cartes vivant"; and *Pantomimes, Extravaganzas and Burlesques*, vol. 5 of *English Plays of the Nineteenth Century*, ed. Michael R. Booth (Oxford: Clarendon Press, 1969), 10, on J. R. Planché and Charles Dance, *High, Low, Jack and the Game; or, The Card Party* (Olympic, 30 Dec. 1833).

6. Carroll, 16 and 25 Jan. 1858, *Carroll Diaries*, 1:138, 139; M. Dorothy George, *English Political Caricature to 1792: A Study of Opinion and Propaganda* (Oxford: Clarendon Press, 1959), 48, 108, 190–91, and *English Political Caricature, 1793–1832* (Oxford: Clarendon Press, 1959), 212, for political figures as playing cards in prints dating back to at least the seventeenth century; "Our Courts of Law. No. 1.—The Palace Court," illustration, *Punch*, 20 Jan. 1849, 31; and Catherine Perry Hargrave, *A History of Playing Cards* (New York: Dover Publications, 1966), 212, for court cards as courtroom personnel.

7. The interjection of "Pig and Pepper" with its strong flavor of the Christmas pantomime may have been owing to Carroll's original intention—to get the book out by Dec. 1864. Failing this, he next considered Apr. 1865 (Carroll to Macmillan, 20 Nov. 1864, in *Carroll Letters*, 1:74).

8. Alfred Crowquill [Alfred Henry Forrester], illustrations, *ILN*, "What I Saw in the Fire," 21 Dec. 1861, 635; and "Gathering for the Pantomime: A Dream of Chancifancia," 24 Dec. 1870, 661. Forrester himself wrote two pantomimes for the Surrey Theatre, one playing in 1853, the other in 1871 (Nicoll, *Late Nineteenth Century Drama*, 371). See also "The Christmas Pantomimes, Burlesques, &c.: Surrey," *Times*, 27 Dec. 1865.

9. V. C. Clinton-Baddeley, *All Right on the Night* (London: Putnam, 1954), 227.

10. *Pantomimes, Extravaganzas and Burlesques*, 44; and Clinton-Baddeley, *Right on the Night*, 223, on kitchen scenes; and Gerald Frow, *"Oh, Yes It Is!" A History of Pantomime* (London: BBC, 1985), 133, on *Whittington and His Cat*, in which the Cook of the opening was transformed into Clown in the harlequinade. The comparison first made in W. A. Baillie-Grohman, "A Portrait of the Ugliest Princess in History," *Burlington Magazine* 38 (Apr. 1921): 172–78, between Tenniel's Duchess and Quentin Matsys's picture of a grotesque woman (National Gallery, London), is not accepted here

as it relies overmuch on both having coarse features (although dissimilar) and both wearing fifteenth-century high headdresses such as Tenniel had already drawn for "Punch's Book of British Costumes—Chap. 35," (*Punch*, 3 Nov. 1860, 178).

11. *Carroll's Library*, Brooks Catalogue, item 660, for his copy of Thackeray's book; Francis Wey, *A Frenchman among the Victorians*, trans. Valerie Pirie (New Haven, Conn.: Yale Univ. Press, 1936); "Preparing for the Pantomimes," illustration, *ILN*, 17 Dec. 1870, 625. Tenniel portrayed big-heads in "Britishlion the Bagdificent" and also in his cartoon of 2 Jan. 1869.

12. Tenniel, cartoon, 30 Dec. 1865; and A. E. Wilson, *King Panto*, 107, on Clown's "tender nursing." It is this part of the entertainment that reveals pantomime's connection with the Punch and Judy show, likewise originating in the sixteenth-century Italian commedia dell'arte, and the relationship of Policinello (Punchello, Pulcinalla), later Punch, to Clown. For example, in the early-nineteenth-century *Harlequin Amulet* the famous Clown Joey Grimaldi played Punch in the opening and was later transformed to Clown for the harlequinade. The pugnacious puppet of the Punch and Judy show, like Clown, plays "Catchee, catchee" with the baby, tossing it up in the air, the play getting progressively more violent. Finally he flings the little corpse out of the window with cries of "Get away, nasty baby!" See Robert Leech, *The Punch and Judy Show: History, Tradition and Meaning* (London: Batsford Academic & Educational, 1985), 11, 90, 156. Similarly, in an Adelphi pantomime of 1827 Clown flung a lifelike effigy of a baby toward the audience in the pit. See Frow, *"Oh, Yes It Is!"* 84, and for directions for pantomime clowns, p. 86; and Tenniel, cartoon, 2 Jan. 1875.

13. Frow, *"Oh, Yes It Is!"* 175; and for Pott's painting, Susan P. Casteras, *Victorian Childhood* (1986), 36.

14. Nicoll, *Early Nineteenth Century Drama*, 464, on *Fox and Geese*; and on *Harlequin King Chess*, see "The Christmas Pantomimes, Burlesques, &c.: Surrey," *Times*, 27 Dec. 1865; "The Theatres: Pantomimes, Burlesques, and Christmas Entertainments," *ILN*, 30 Dec. 1865, 655; and "Pantomimes," *Athenaeum*, 30 Dec. 1865, 932.

15. "The Theatres," *ILN*, 30 Dec. 1865, 655; and engraving, *ILN*, 29 Dec. 1866, 637. The play was *A, Apple-Pie; or, Harlequin Jack-in-the-Box and the Little Boy Blue*.

16. "Surrey Theatre: 'King Chess'—Giving Check to the Queen," engraving, *ILN*, 30 Dec. 1865, 657.

17. Carroll, 10 Aug. and 3 Sept. 1866, *Carroll Diaries*, 1:246; and Carroll to Macmillan, 24 Aug. 1866, in *Carroll and Macmillan*, 44.

18. Chap. 1, *Looking-Glass*.

19. Tenniel, initial, *Punch*, 7 Feb. 1852, 53; and Mayer, *Harlequin in His Element*, 117, for the re-production from a juvenile drama sheet. These had characters that could be colored, cut out, and used with toy theaters.

20. A. C-rambo, "What I Saw in the Fire," illustration, *ILN*, 21 Dec. 1861, 637; and Hudson, *Lewis Carroll*, 147, on Carroll's fascination with fireplaces.

21. A. E. Wilson, *Pantomime Pageant*, 36; and chap. 5, *Looking-Glass*.

22. A. E. Wilson, *Story of Pantomime*, 37–38. The theme of haunted lodgings was used by Tenniel in his illustration for "Taxes" in "Britishlion the Bagdificent."

23. Mayer, *Harlequin in His Element*, 48–49.

24. Ibid., 81–82.

25. Tenniel, cartoon, 13 Apr. 1872.

26. Frow, *"Oh, Yes It Is!"* 171, on children in pantomime; George W. B. Shannon, *Humpty Dumpty* (La Jolla, Calif.: Green Tiger Press, 1980) for depictions by about fifty artists; Tenniel, cartoon, 15 July 1871; and A. E. Wilson, *King Panto*, 101, describing an 1840 pantomime at Drury Lane: "Clown is crammed into a giant gooseberry and Pantaloon into a great raspberry which are respectively labelled 'Gooseberry fool' and 'Raspberry jam.'"

27. Colin Gordon, *By Gaslight in Winter: A Victorian Family History through the Magic Lantern* (London: Elm Tree Books, 1980), 13, on galantee showmen; Leslie Gordon, *Peepshow into Paradise* (London: George G. Harrap, 1953), 67, 212, 204, 24, on various toys and devices; and Harcourt Amory Collection, Houghton Library, for a copy of *Changing Pictures: A Book of Transformation Pictures* (London: Ernest Nister, n.d.) that belonged to Carroll; Victoria and Albert Museum, collection of Victorian moveable and pop-up greeting cards; Hargrave, *History of Playing Cards*, 214–19, indicating (p. 214) that transformation cards of 1808 pictured the favorite pantomimes of the day; Sylvia Mann, *Collecting English Playing-Cards* (London: Stanley Gibbons, 1978), 21; and Roger Tilley, *Play-*

ing Cards (London: Weidenfeld & Nicolson, 1967), 106. See, also, transformation cards in the print section of the Guildhall Library, London.

28. Carroll drew on other traditions of pantomime for the *Alice*s. The Mock Turtle's song "Beautiful Soup" recalls such popular food songs such as "Hot Codlins." The White Knight's pudding recipe (blotting paper, gunpowder, and sealing wax) or the ingredients given in the chorus to Queen Alice ("Then fill up the glasses with treacle and ink," and so on) are like the recipe that Clown used for ice cream in one play—paste and boot blacking poured over ice (see Frow, *"Oh, Yes It Is!"* 83). The popular "awkward squads" of soldiers (Mayer, *Harlequin in His Element,* 276) recall the inept soldiery in chapter 7 of *Looking-Glass:* "She thought that in all her life she had never seen soldiers so uncertain on their feet. They were always tripping over something or other, and whenever one went down, several more always fell over him, so that the ground was soon covered with little heaps of men." The Drury Lane offering for 1862, *Little Goody Two-Shoes; or, Harlequin and Cock Robin,* had live flowers ("Pantomimes and Other Christmas Pieces," *ILN,* 27 Dec. 1862; and "Drury Lane," *Times,* 27 Dec. 1862). See review of *Wonderland," John Bull,* 20 Jan. 1866, in *Jabberwocky* 9 (Winter 1979/80): 36, for "tickling as a pantomime."

14. Alice in the Land of Toys

1. "Why Not Write Children's Books for Children?" *Punch,* 16 Sept. 1848, 117. Pantomimes naming toys include *Battledore and Shuttlecock; or, Harlequin Trap, Bat, and Ball,* Surrey, UK, 1847 ("The Christmas Pantomimes and Burlesques," *Times,* 28 Dec. 1847); *King Humming Top; or, Harlequin and the Land of Toys,* Drury Lane, 1853 ("Christmas Pantomimes, &c.," *Times,* 27 Dec. 1853,); *Plum Pudding and Roast Beef; or, Harlequin Nine Pins and the Card King of the Island of Games,* Standard, 1853, and *Harlequin and King Nutcracker; or, The World of Toys,* Strand, 1853 ("The Theatres," *ILN,* 31 Dec. 1853); and *Hush-a-by, Baby, on the Tree Top; or, Harlequin Fortunio, Prince Heydiddle, Princess Olivebranch, King Frog of Frog Island, and the Magic Toys of Lowther Arcadia,* Astleys, 1866, and *A, Apple Pie; or, Harlequin Jack-in-the-Box and the Little Boy Blue,* Surrey, UK, 1866 (*ILN,* 29 Dec. 1866, 638). Reviews spoke of animated kites, archery targets, drums, shuttlecocks, ninepins, dice, dominoes, peg tops, toy soldiers, and marbles, as well as cards and chesspieces. See Casteras, *Victorian Childhood,* 4, for "golden age of childhood"; and Jac Remise and Jean Fondin, *The Golden Age of Toys* (Lausanne, Switzerland: Edith Lausanne, 1967).

2. Hibbert, *Horizon Book of Daily Life,* 41–45; Lochhead, *Victorian Household,* 6; Mr. Serjeant Ballantine, *Some Experiences of a Barrister's Life* (New York: Henry Holt, 1882), 3; and Burnand, *Records and Reminiscences,* 4.

3. Hudson, *Lewis Carroll,* 66 (for lines from "Solitude" [c. 1853]), 43; and Leslie Gordon, *Peepshow into Paradise,* 88, on Carroll's railway games; Livingston, *Amory Collection of Carroll,* between 128–29, for Carroll's "Railway Rules" and his "Love's Railway Guide"; and *Carroll Letters,* 1:209 n. 1, on his cupboards.

4. Possibly influential for *Wonderland*'s final chapters was a children's game, "Trial by Jury" (c. 1850), with eleven court cards to each suit that caricatured the personnel of English courts of the time (Hargrave, *History of Playing Cards,* 212). The Snap-dragon and Rocking-horse flies appear in chap. 3; the Old Sheep asks Alice if she is "a child or a teetotum"; Alice "pursues" a doll in the little shop (later the Red Queen will dwindle "to the size of a little doll"); she recalls watching boys "getting in sticks for a bonfire"; Tweedledum tells Alice, "If you think we're wax-works you ought to pay, you know"; at the dinner the pudding reappears "like a conjuring trick," and the candles resemble fireworks; the Knights hold their clubs with their arms "as if they were Punch and Judy"; and Haigha takes a dish, carving knife, and large cake out of a bag, "just like a conjuring trick."

5. Augarde, *Guide to Word Games;* and *Cassell's Book of In-door Amusements, Card Games, and Fireside Fun* (London: Cassell, c. 1885), 48. The gnat's "You *would* if you could," which is also a pun on *wood* (the wood to which Alice wishes to return), suggests spoonerisms. Alice's remark to the King of Hearts, "That's not a regular rule; you invented it just now," hints of games. The White Queen's riddle recalls the instructions in Hannah Glasse, *The Art of Cookery made Plain & Easy; Which far exceeds any THING of the kind ever yet Published* (London, 1796), for example, on p. 19. The White Queen's "Let it lie in a dish!" may have come from Glasse's recipe for carp in an earlier edition (London: printed for the author, 1747), 61, which advises, "FIRST, knock the Carp on the Head. . . . Lay the fish in the Dish."

6. Richard D. Altick, *The Shows of London* (Cambridge, Mass.: Belknap Press of Harvard Univ. Press, 1978), 56; and Olive Cook, *Movement in Two Dimensions* (London: Hutchinson, 1963), 26,

on formal gardens in peep shows. Examples at the Bethnal Green Museum of Childhood, London, include sets representing the Tuileries Gardens, produced in Paris (c. 1835); and an earlier Rococo set by Martin Engelbrecht of Augsburg (c. 1721) with fountains and topiary arches. Tenniel's title page, *Punch* vol. 47 (Jul.–Dec. 1864), has a peep-show theme; the title for vol. 46 (Jan.–June 1864) had a proto Alice.

7. Dickens, "A Christmas Tree," *Household Words*, 31 Dec. 1850, 290; and *Children's Toys of Yesterday*, ed. C. Geoffrey Holme (London: Studio, 1932), 59.

8. In *Alice in Wonderland* (New York: Clarkson N. Potter, 1973), 100–101, Ralph Steadman made the connection with play by drawing the jury box as a toy box on wheels and the jurors as stuffed toys.

9. Carroll's illustration plan calls no. 28 "Dissolving view." See the *Encyclopaedia Britannica*, 6th ed. (1823), s.v. "Dioptrics," and 11th ed. (1910–1911), s.v. "Lantern," for a general discussion of magic lanterns.

10. Carroll, 12 Jan. 1870, *Carroll Diaries*, 2:286, in which he notes his attendance at a lantern show for children at the vicar's.

11. Alexander Taylor, *The White Knight: A Study of C. L. Dodgson* (Edinburgh: Oliver & Boyd, 1952), 2, on Carroll as amateur conjurer. His acquaintance with conjuring tricks is apparent in Carroll's prescription for a haunting: "Blue lights to burn (say) two an hour, / Condensing lens of extra power, / And set of chains complete" (*Phantasmagoria*, 1869). See Carroll, 29 Jan., 31 Dec. 1856, and 1 Jan. 1857, *Carroll Diaries* 1:75, 99, 100; and Carroll, 21 Nov. 1856, Carroll diary no. 4, British Library; *Carroll Diary*, 1:155, for visits to the Regent Street Polytechnic; *DNB*, s.v. "Dodgson, Charles Lutwidge (1832–1898)," on his slides; and Denis Crutch, "Alice for the Little Ones," Jabberwocky 4 (Autumn 1975): 87. By 1876 Carroll saw *Wonderland* done at the Polytechnic as an entertainment using dissolving views (Carroll, 18 Apr. 1876, *Carroll Diaries*, 2:352).

12. Terry Castle, "Phantasmagoria: Spectral Technology and the Metaphorics of Modern Reverie," *Critical Inquiry* 15 (Autumn 1988): 39.

13. Alexander Taylor, *White Knight*, 138. Surveying the country from her hill, Alice sees distant elephants that she first mistakes as bees because of the enormous flowers from which they feed.

14. Tenniel, "Punch's Almanack for 1864," calendar page.

15. Cook, *Movement in Two Dimensions*, 87.

16. Peter Haining, *Moveable Books: An Illustrated History* (London: New English Library, 1979); and Iona Opie and Peter Opie, "Books That Come to Life," *Times Literary Supplement*, 19 Sept. 1975, 1055. True "dissolving" picture books were created in Germany around 1890 by Ernest Nister and consisted of pictures printed on slats that slid over each other to create wholly new scenes.

17. Carroll, "Eight or Nine Wise Words about Letter-Writing" (1890).

18. As flicker books were not invented until 1868 (Martin Quigley Jr., *Magic Shadows: The Story of the Origin of Motion Pictures* [Washington, D.C.: Georgetown Univ. Press, 1948], 172) it is more likely that one would turn down the corner of the first sheet. Since "Cat in tree" and "Cat's grin" were printed on successive verso sheets in *The Nursery Alice*, Carroll instructed his readers to turn up the corner of the second picture to see Alice "looking at the Grin."

19. Carroll to his sister Mary, 11 Apr. 1860, in *Carroll Letters*, 1:40–41.

20. Thus, by lowering the glass that pictured the stage curtains (since slides are inserted upside down), the curtains would appear to rise.

21. For example, *The Illustrators of "Alice in Wonderland" and "Through the Looking-Glass,"* ed. Graham Ovenden (1979), 8.

22. Carroll to Macmillan, 28 Sept. 1866, in *Carroll and Macmillan*, 45; Carroll to Macmillan, 1869, in which he wrote that the book as priced was "entirely out of reach of many thousands of children of the middle classes . . . (below that I don't think it would be appreciated)," quoted in Hudson, *Lewis Carroll*, 129; and Carroll to Edith Nash, 4 Mar. 1887, in *Carroll Letters*, 2:667.

23. The mechanical movements implied by the texts appear to be recognized by the number of moveable books and toys based on the *Alices*.

15. The Grotesque Alice

1. Philip Thomson, *The Grotesque* (London: Methuen, 1972), 27. See also Wolfgang Kayser, *The Grotesque in Art and Literature,* trans. Ulrich Weisstein (Bloomington: Indiana Univ. Press, 1963), 179–89; and Michael Steig, "Defining the Grotesque: An Attempt at Synthesis," *Journal of Aesthetics and Criticism* 29 (Winter 1970): 253–260.

2. Elizabeth Sewell, *The Field of Nonsense* (London: Chatto & Windus, 1952). On the equivocal

relationship between the comic and the grotesque see Charles Baudelaire, "On the Essense of Laughter," in *The Painter of Modern Life and Other Essays,* trans. and ed. Jonathan Mayne (London: Phaidon Press, 1964), 157, which refers to the grotesque as "the absolute comic"; Ernst Kris and Ernst Gombrich, "The Principles of Caricature," *British Journal of Medical Psychology* 17 (1938): 334, on the "double-edged character" of the comic in that it is "always on the verge of falling down" to "the uncanny or embarrassing"; Steig, "Defining the Grotesque," 256, 259–60; and Thomson, *Grotesque,* 5, 21. In Henri Bergson, "Laughter," in *Comedy* (Garden City, N.Y.: Doubleday Anchor Books, 1956), 96, the central ingredient of the comic is "something mechanical encrusted on something living." This is essentially the same as "the human being . . . deprived" of life in Kayser, *Grotesque,* 183. See Sewell, *Field of Nonsense,* 149; and Kayser, *Grotesque,* 118, 122, on the differences between and responses to the grotesque and the comic.

3. *Saturday Review,* 30 Dec. 1871, 860; "What the Children Like," *Pall Mall Gazette,* 1 July 1898; and Carolyn Sigler, introduction to *Alternative Alices: Visions and Revisions of Lewis Carroll's "Alice" Books* (Lexington: Univ. Press of Kentucky, 1997), xi.

4. Virginia Woolf, "Lewis Carroll," in *The Moment and Other Essays* (New York: Harcourt, Brace, 1948), 82; Malcolm Muggeridge, "Alice, Where Art Thou?" *New Statesman,* 23 Dec. 1966, 933; Flannery O'Connor, *The Habit of Being,* ed. Sally Fitzgerald (New York: Farrar, Straus & Giroux, 1979), 288; and Michele Landsberg, introduction to *The World of Children's Books* (New York: Simon & Schuster, 1988), paraphrased in *Bandersnatch: The Newsletter of the Lewis Carroll Society* 78 (Jan. 1993): 12. While I was drawn to the grotesque aspects of the *Alice*s as a child, my younger sister found the books terrifying. Versions that seem to be produced for adults rather than for children are *Alice in Wonderland* (1973), illustrated by Ralph Steadman; and *Alice's Adventures in Wonderland* (New York: Harcourt, Brace, Jovanovich, 1982), illustrated by Barry Moser.

5. Carroll to Mrs. G. MacDonald, 19 May 1868, in *Carroll Letters,* 1:120; and Carroll to Macmillan, 2 and 7 June 1868, in *Carroll and Macmillan,* 63, 65. See also Carroll, "'Alice' on the Stage," *Theatre* (1 Apr. 1887), quoted in Charles C. Lovett, *Alice on Stage* (Westport, Conn.: Meckler, 1990), 212.

6. Still, Tenniel omitted some of Carroll's more grotesque episodes—Alice falling down the rabbit hole, Alice's chin striking her foot, Alice's head raised above the treetops on "an immense length of neck."

7. *Pantomimes, Extravaganzas and Burlesques,* 7.

8. Ronald Reichertz, *The Making of the Alice Books: Lewis Carroll's Uses of Earlier Children's Literature* (Montreal & Kingston: McGill-Queen's Univ. Press, 1997), 141–45, 155–56; Philip James, *Children's Books of Yesterday,* ed. C. Geoffrey Holme (1933; reprint, Detroit: Gale Research, 1976), 71, 82, 103; Edward Lear, *A Book of Nonsense* (1846; reprint, New York: Metropolitan Museum of Art & Viking Press, 1980); and Thackeray, *Rose and the Ring,* 18, 56, for examples.

9. John Buchanan Brown, *The Book Illustrations of George Cruikshank* (Newton Abbot, UK: David & Charles, 1980), figs. 48, 61–64; Max Keith Sutton, "'Inverse Sublimity' in Victorian Humor," *Victorian Studies* (Dec. 1966): 181, on Cruikshank's faces on the corks of rum bottles; and Thomas Hood, "Pathetic Ballads": "Tim Turpin," "Mary's Ghost," and "The Supper Superstition."

10. Carroll to Macmillan, 2 and 7 June 1868, in *Carroll and Macmillan,* 63, 65; W. S. Gilbert, "The Yarn of the Nancy Bell," "The Precocious Baby," and "A Discontented Sugar Broker," in *The Bab Ballads,* ed. James Ellis (Cambridge, Mass.: Belknap Press of Harvard Univ. Press, 1980), 76–78, 129–31, 133–34. Cf. Deems Taylor, preface to *Plays and Poems of W. S. Gilbert* (New York: Random House, 1932), xxv, lviii–lx, on Gilbert's people.

11. Charles H. Bennett, "The Field of the Cloth of Damask," *ILN,* 19 Dec. 1857, 626–27; "The Theatres," *ILN,* 31 Dec. 1853, for the Standard's *Plum Pudding and Roast Beef; or, Harlequin Nine Pins, and the Card King of the Island of Games;* "Christmas Pantomimes, &c.," *Times,* 27 Dec. 1854, for the Drury Lane's *Jack and Jill; Harlequin King Mustard;* and Hudson, *Lewis Carroll,* 22, on "Sir Loin."

12. "Naval Intelligence," July–Dec. 1847, 219; Captain H. R. Howard, "A Fish out of Water," July–Dec. 1854, 110; and Leech, "Little Dinner at Greenwich," "Almanack for 1858," drawings, *Punch.* See also Tenniel's uncharacteristic illustration to his own article, "Pigeons," *Punch,* 8 Feb. 1851, 56.

13. "Fancy Portrait," July–Dec. 1846, 248; and drawings, Jan.–June 1847, 42; and July–Dec. 1847, 23; and Sambourne, "Punch's Fancy Portraits—No. 102—Sir Drumming Wolff, M.P.," 23 Sept. 1882, 142.

14. Drawing, 10 Jan. 1863, 17; and initial, July–Dec. 1874, 167, *Punch.*

15. Frankie Morris, "Smiles and Soap: Lewis Carroll and the 'Blast of Puffery,'" *Jabberwocky* 24 (Spring 1997): 38–48, for *Punch* on advertising.

16. Frank Bellew, "A Christmas Visitor," *Punch*, 19 Jan. 1861, 30, cited by Hancher, *Tenniel Illustrations to "Alice,"* 15, as a likely inspiration for the pudding in *Looking-Glass;* Bellew, initial, *Punch*, 16 Mar. 1861, 115; Carroll, 9 Apr. 1866, Carroll diary no. 9, British Library; Captain H. R. Howard, initials, *Punch*, 1 June 1861, 220; 6 June 1863, 238; 13 June 1863, 247; and 6 May 1865, 185; and C. H. Bennett, "Mechanism for the Million," initial, *Punch*, 29 Apr. 1865, 169.

17. Tenniel's emblematic figures with clock or ballot-box heads and animated parliamentary bills are merely playful. More grotesque are some of Leech's anti-papal cuts of 1851—for example, his "Episcopus Vastator," *Punch*, 6 Sept. 1851, 112, which portrays a cross between a priest and a bloated larva. Tenniel's " Turf Spider" of 4 July 1868 resembles George Cruikshank's "Judicium Astrologicum," *Comic Almanac*, 1850, in which the spider's body is a liquor bottle. See Blanchard Jerrold, *The Life of George Cruikshank: In two Epochs*, 2 vols. (London: Chatto & Windus, 1882), 2:2.

18. Carroll, "The Tale of a Tail," "Melodies I," and "Brother and Sister," in *Useful and Instructive Poetry* (New York: Macmillan, 1954), 23–24, 22, 28–29; and "The Two Brothers" ("The Rectory Umbrella," 1853) and "Upon the Lonely Moor" (*Train*, 1856), in *The Humorous Verse of Lewis Carroll* (1933; reprint, New York: Dover, 1960), 27–32, 44–46.

19. Carroll to Kathleen Tidy, 30 Mar. 1861; to Edith Blakemore, 7 Nov. 1882; to Isabel Seymour, 29 May 1869; and to Enid Stevens, 7 Apr. 1891, in *Carroll Letters* 1:49–50, 468, 131–32, 2:830.

20. Kayser, *Grotesque*, 184.

21. Monkhouse, *Sir John Tenniel*, 29; Sarzano, *Sir John Tenniel*, 18; Michael Patrick Hearn, "*Alice's* Other Parent: John Tenniel as Lewis Carroll's Illustrator," *American Book Collector* 4 (May/June 1983): 17; Hancher, *Tenniel Illustrations to "Alice,"* 15; and Jane Doonan, "Realism and Surrealism in Wonderland: John Tenniel and Anthony Browne," *Signal* (Jan. 1980), 15, on Tenniel's seeming factualness; and, for a naturalistic treatment, Peter Blake's 1970 reillustration of *Looking-Glass.*

22. The fourth through seventh squares of *Looking-Glass* are in a wood.

23. Review of *Wonderland* in *London Review*, 29 Dec. 1866.

24. Carroll, "'Alice' on the Stage," 182.

25. Kayser, *Grotesque*, 181, on monsters as grotesques.

26. Ibid., 183, on distortions. The Jabberwock's waistcoat was probably borrowed from that pantomime favorite the Dragon of Wantley. Tenniel's "Pencillings in the Pit," 53, has a drawing of Paul Bedford as the Dragon, wearing a scaly jacket and a waistcoat.

27. Kayser, *Grotesque*, 183.

28. Imposts are also humanized in Tenniel, third illustration to "Sir Rupert the Fearless," in Barham, *Ingoldsby Legends*, book 2.

29. Kayser, *Grotesque*, 183.

30. Carroll to Fildes, 2 July 1877, in Fildes, *Luke Fildes*, 44; Kayser, *Grotesque*, 128, on the idée fixe and the grotesque. The Queen's expression in Tenniel's frontispiece was compared by Hearn, "'*Alice's* Other Parent," 13, with that of the Lion-judge in C. H. Bennett's frontispiece for *The Fables of Aesop and Others Translated into Human Nature* (New York: Viking Press, 1857). Both may derive from King Noble the Lion, who holds court among the beasts in Wilhelm von Kaulbach's illustration to Johann Wolfgang von Goethe's *Reineke Fuchs*, Stuttgart, 1846, and London, 1860.

31. Kayser, *Grotesque*, 184.

32. Ibid., 148–49. Compare Alice's indifference with Gregor Samsa's prosaic reflections upon waking to find that he has been transformed into a giant insect in Kafka's "Metamorphosis."

33. *Pantomimes, Extravaganzas and Burlesques*, 42; Pennell, *Modern Illustration*, 82; White, *English Illustration 'The Sixties,'* 18, which scorned those "exaggerators . . . who aimed at the grotesque"; Forrest Reid, *Illustrators of the Sixties*, 27, which found "more charm" in Tenniel's lifelike drawing of Alice's black kitten than in any of his "grotesque comedy"; and Ellis, introduction to *Bab Ballads*, 28.

34. *Illustrated Times*, 16 Dec. 1865, which considered Tenniel's animals "clothed in human guise" to be grotesque; *John Bull*, 20 Jan. 1866; *Literary Churchman*, 15 May 1866, 206; *Times*, 13 Aug. 1868 (quoted in Sigler, introduction to *Alternative Alices*, xii); and H. A. Page (pseud. for Alexander Japp), "Children and Children's Books," *Contemporary Review* 11 (May–Aug. 1869): 24. Page declared (p. 7), "The only humour which children can comprehend is the humour of the simple grotesque."

35. *Athenaeum*, 16 Dec. 1865 (was this the same critic who, four years later, panned Gilbert's Bab ballads because they lacked "a real human heart"? See *Athenaeum*, 10 Apr. 1869, 502, quoted in Ellis, introduction to *Bab Ballads*, 16); and "Through the Looking-Glass and What Alice Found There," *Athenaeum*, 16 Dec. 1871, 787.

36. In Monkhouse, *Sir John Tenniel*, 30, and Hearn, "*Alice*'s Other Parent," 19, the word "grotesque" is used only with regard to Tenniel's Jabberwock; Doonan, "Realism and Surrealism," 15, 21, 27, uses it in reference to Tenniel's animals. See Kayser, *Grotesque*, 184; Thomson, *Grotesque*, 23 (also 8, 17); and Sewell, *Field of Nonsense*, 23, 37.

37. Sigler, introduction to *Alternative Alices*, xviii; and, for the phrase "network of communications" (used with reference to Dickens), Stoehr, *Dickens: The Dreamer's Stance*, 25.

38. Tom Hood, *From Nowhere to the North Pole: A Noah's Ark-Aelogical Narrative*, chap. 5, reproduced in *Alternative Alices*, 208–15, for the character Gloogumpehst.

39. Eleven of the eighteen "Alice-type" books (I do not include political parodies) reproduced in part in Sigler, *Alternative Alices*, and in Reichertz, *Making of Alice Books*, employ mentors, and four include a Man-in-the-Moon.

40. Some reillustrations failed to note that the only animal attributes Carroll gives to the footmen are their fish and frog heads, and that the Tweedles are described as "fat little men," not boys. In *Illustrators of "Alice*," aside from Tenniel's, only Philip Gough's illustrations (c. 1940), maintain some period consciousness, in fact predating Carroll's time by several decades. For a brilliant exposé of the trend toward cuteness see Daniel Harris, "Cuteness," in *Best American Essays, 1993*, ed. Joseph Epstein (Boston: Houghton Mifflin, 1993), 131–40. Newell's Gryphon fits Harris's description of cute toys (pp. 134–35). Similarly, we reillustrate Lear, thereby losing the charm of his own preposterous drawings, and we allow our Gilbert and Sullivan performers to dance and sway through their grotesque roles in ways unimagined by the plays' creators.

16. Alice and the Gothic Taste

1. Carroll, 24 Jan. 1867, 19 May 1868, and 1 Nov. 1868, *Carroll Diaries*, 1:249, 2:269, 275.

2. Carroll, 22 Sept. 1857, 21 July 1863, 30 Sept. 1863, 7 Apr. 1864, 14 July 1864, and 8 Apr. 1867, *Carroll Diaries*, 1:125, 200, 201, 213, 220, 254; Carroll to Mrs. G. MacDonald, 3 Oct. 1863, and to E. Gertrude Thomson, 24 Jan. 1879, in *Carroll Letters*, 1:61, 326; and *Carroll's Library*, Brooks Catalogue, items 282, 322, 352, 364, 378, 380, 390, 396, 466, 480, 481, 486, 834, 842, 856 (*Chaucer Modernized*); Blackwell's Catalogue, items 943, 977 (*British Poets*, 48 vols. incl. Chaucer), 1044; and Parker's Catalogue, Chaucer G., *The Poems Modernized* (1841); Carroll, *The Collected Verse of Lewis Carroll* (Boston: Houghton Mifflin, 1932), 15, 20–26, 162; Carroll, 9 Apr. 1866, *Carroll Diaries*, 1:241–42; and du Maurier, "A Legend of Camelot," *Punch*, 3, 10, 17, 24, 31 Mar. 1866, 94, 97, 109, 128, 131.

3. Rev. John Richardson, *The Eglinton Tournament* (London: Colnachi & Puckle, 1843), illus. James Henry Nixon; *The Eglinton Tournament* (London: Hodgson & Graves, 1840), illus. Edward Henry Corbould; Girouard, *Return to Camelot*, 107, for "Eglinton school of illustrators"; Tenniel, *Punch* vols. 19 (July–Dec. 1850), 21 (July–Dec. 1851), and 22 (Jan.–June 1852); and Drypoint [Henry Stacy Marks], "The Art of 'Punch.' Second Notice," *Spectator*, 21 Sept. 1861, 1035. Tenniel's gift drawing of a knight with a tankard accompanies Tenniel's letter to John Eliot Hodgkins, 20 Apr. 1861, National Art Library. The "Elritch Knight" was presented to a Captain Letts in 1866 (information from the backing of the framed drawing examined at Christie's, South Kensington, in 1987). This wild-eyed knight with a reddish bulbous nose (signifying a fondness for drink), mounted on a spectral horse, is not a self-portrait of Tenniel as claimed in Engen, *Alice's White Knight*, 96. Tenniel had an aquiline nose and would not have presented himself as a tippler. The verse on the bottom of the drawing, in the joking style of Tenniel's bouts rimés, reads:

And, Oh he hath don'd the Elritch suit,
Y'wrought by glamour's art;
And as he bestrode his demon brute
The hue of his nose was the hue of the fruit
That's put into raspb'ry tart.
　　　　　—Old ballad.

On the drawing of Sambourne see Sotheby catalog, 2–4 Apr. 1928, 344.

4. Tenniel, cartoons, 21 Nov. 1868 and 28 Nov. 1868.

5. Geoffrey Chaucer, "The Knighte's Tale," in *The Canterbury Tales* (c. 1386–1400).

6. Quotations from Chaucer are from the modernized version of *The Knighte's Tale*, ed. R. J. Cunliffe (Glasgow: Blackie & Son, 1915), lines 779–80, 793–94, 843–44.

7. For depictions of makeshift armor see Girouard, *Return to Camelot*, 67; H. B. [John Doyle], "The Rival Quixotes," separately issued print, 12 Feb. 1839; Leech, cartoon, *Punch*, 2 Sept. 1848;

Tenniel, "Donnybrook Fair under the New Lord Lieutenant," small cut, *Punch,* Jan.–June 1852, 134; and Tenniel, illustration to Tom Taylor, "A Donkey Tournament," *Punch's Pocket Book, 1871,* 170. See Tenniel, illustration for "Book of British Costumes" (chap. 18, 9 June 1860, 237), which points out the lantern, saucepan, and oyster-keg shapes of twelfth-century helmets. Tweedledee's wooden sword might also suggest the sword of wood held by a quintain (a dummy opponent mounted on a pole against which knights practiced riding). See Sir Walter Scott, *Essays on Chivalry, Romance, and the Drama* (London: Frederick Warne, n.d.), 26.

8. Anstruther, *Knight and Umbrella;* and Roger Simpson, "A Triumph of Common Sense: The Work of Sir John Tenniel (1820–1914)," PhD diss., University of Essex, UK, 1987, 368 (published as *Sir John Tenniel: Aspects of His Work* [Rutherford, N.J.: Fairleigh Dickinson Univ. Press, 1994]). This was a parallel research. My talk "Alice and the Eglinton Tournament" was presented to the Lewis Carroll Society, London, on 4 Sept. 1987. For knights with umbrellas see Alfred Crowquill, "Birds Eye View of the Grand Procession by a High Witness," in *The Tournament: A Mock-Heroic Ballad* (London: Thomas McLean, 1839), 15; "Aristocratic Sense; Or, The Eglintoun [*sic*] Tomfooleryment," drawing, *Cleave's Gazette of Variety,* 14 Sept. 1839; Bennett, initial, in Sangster, *Umbrellas and Their History,* 33; initial to "Essence," 16 Apr. 1859, 153; and W. S. Gilbert [Bab, pseud.], illustration to "Sir Guy the Crusader," *Fun,* 8 June 1867, 139.

9. Anstruther, *Knight and Umbrella,* 230–31; "The Wormsley Tournament," *Oxford University City, and County Herald,* 15 Aug. 1840; and Carroll, 14 June 1871, *Carroll Diaries,* 2:299.

10. Scott, *Essays on Chivalry,* 23, 40.

11. Anstruther, *Knight and Umbrella,* 154; Doyle, illustration to *The Tournament;* and Tenniel, "The Exhibition as It Might Have Been in the Days of Yore," illustration, *Punch,* Jan.–June, 1851, 208.

12. Anstruther, *Knight and Umbrella,* 135; and Debra N. Mancoff, *The Arthurian Revival in Victorian Art* (New York: Garland, 1990), 158.

13. Henry Silver, "Punch's Book of British Costumes," chap. 8, *Punch,* 9 June 1860, 236. Silver's speculation (chap. 5, 3 Mar. 1860, 87) that long-haired Anglo-Saxons, when "taking a hairing" on a windy day, might have looked "as mad as a March hare or a hatter" is turned around in the return of the Hare and Hatter as Anglo-Saxons in *Looking-Glass.* Heigha's and Hatta's costumes are more or less taken from Tenniel's drawings for Silver, including the elbow to wrist accordion-wrinkled sleeves emulating the manuscript drawings of the time. The "Anglo-Saxon attitudes" are Carroll's joking allusion to Lady Hamilton's "attitudes" or *tableaux vivants,* much celebrated in the 1780s (*Carroll's Library,* Brooks Catalogue, lists, item 272, *Lady Hamilton's Attitudes,* illustrated by Rehberg).

14. Watts, *Sir Galahad,* exhibited at the Royal Academy in 1862 and, according to Girouard, *Return to Camelot,* 150, "probably his best-known painting." Carroll's pagination guide shows that page 179 was first planned to be illustrated with "Knight singing." This would have detracted from the poetry of the quoted passage, and "Old man on gate" was substituted.

15. Lull, "Appliances of Art," 101–11. For Tenniel's knights with umbrellas see initials, *Punch,* July–Dec. 1850, 251; Jan.–June 1851, 123, 147; July–Dec. 1851, 149; July–Dec. 1852, 253; July–Dec. 1853, 211; 14 June 1856, 241; and 26 Nov. 1859, 216; "Punch's Anniversaries—No. 3. Henry, Earl of Richmond, Landed at Milford Haven, in His Enterprise against Richard the Third, August 7th, 1485," July–Dec. 1851, 82; "Donnybrook Fair under the New Lord Lieutenant," Jan.–June 1852, 134; "A Banquet of Civic Shades," July–Dec. 1852, 215; "Punch's Almanack" for 1851, 1859, and 1865; second illustration to "The Cynotaph" in Barham, *Ingoldsby Legends,* 1:61; and his preliminary drawing for the frontispiece for *Looking-Glass,* Harcourt Amory Collection.

17. Alice and Social Caricature

1. Page, "Children and Children's Books," 25. "Jurors" should probably be understood in its broader sense, referring to all the legal personnel in the *Wonderland* trial.

2. Carroll, 25 Apr. 1881, to Mrs. V. Blakemore, in *Carroll Letters,* 1:423, on Disraeli; and Senior Common Room Papers of C. L. Dodgson, cuttings from *Punch,* which include a small cut by Tenniel in which Mr. Punch as Shakespeare's Touchstone informs the pope, "Thou art in a parlous state, Shepherd" (25 May 1861, 209). Contemporaries did not seem to equate Gladstone and Disraeli with Tenniel's Lion and Unicorn. *Punch* writer E. J. Milliken's cartoon suggestions based on *Looking-Glass* include "Lion and Unicorn—England and America . . .(Unicorn with Chin-Tuft would make a good *Yank*)" (collection of Simon Houfe).

3. Carroll, 14 Oct. 1881 and 7 June 1886, *Carroll Diaries,* 2:400, 442; Carroll to Lord Salisbury, 10 July 1884, in *Carroll Letters,* 1:544–45; and Carroll, "Representative Men—Lecture 2nd: Cuffey,

or the Chartist," in *Rectory Umbrella and Mischmasch,* 55. Cuffey was a particular butt of *Punch* (see, for example, "To Cuffey in Misfortune," *Punch,* 7 Oct. 1848, 154).

4. Carroll, 7 Jan. 1856, 24 Jan 1867, *Carroll Diaries,* 1:71, 250; *Lewis Carroll and Hatfield House* ([London]: Lewis Carroll Society, 1975), 12ff; and Carroll, *Sylvie and Bruno Concluded* in *The Complete Works of Lewis Carroll* (London: Nonesuch Press, 1939), 490–96.

5. John Dryden, preface to his translation of Charles-Alphonse du Fresnoy, *De Arte Graphica* (1695).

6. While some workmen might effectively go on strike, around midcentury in London alone an estimated fifteen thousand servants were out of work at any given time (Hibbert, *Life in Victorian England,* 22).

7. Mrs. C. S. Peel, "II. Homes and Habits" in *Early Victorian England, 1830–1865* (London: Oxford Univ. Press, 1934), 123; Granville-Barker, "Exit Planché—Enter Gilbert," 138, which quotes the burlesque lines from a travesty of *Lucia di Lammermoor,* "May Mudie never send you a new book!! / And may you never get a sober cook!!!"; Silver diary, 22 June 1864, on Tenniel's drunken cooks; Carroll, "La Guida Di Bragia," act 3, sc. 2 (c. 1850), excerpts of which were provided by the Lewis Carroll Society at their program "The Drama of Lewis Carroll," London, 27 Mar. 1987; Cook, *Movement in Two Dimensions,* 79, on "Kitty Biling the Pot"; and J. F. Sullivan, *The British Working Man by One Who Does Not Believe in Him* (London: "Fun" Office, 1878). See *Lewis Carroll's Library,* Brooks Catalogue, item 542, for Sullivan's book.

8. The list of nineteen questions with responses in Tenniel's hand is dated 16 Aug. 1893 (collection of John Lindseth). In the word game "Truth Questionnaire" each player gets about twenty questions, and the answers, to be read aloud, are expected to be truthful. See Clement Wood and Gloria Goddard, *The Complete Book of Games,* 3rd ed. (New York: Halcyon House, 1940), 452. The only truthful answer given by Tenniel was on his "greatest dislike," to which he responded, "Being 'Interviewed'!!!" See Leech, "Jemimer Harris's Last Sweet Thing in Head-dresses!" drawing, *Punch,* 2 Nov. 1861, 182; and "Jemimer Jane on Jimcracks," 31 Jan. 1880, 37.

9. Taine, *Notes on England,* 40–42; Spielmann, *History of "Punch,"* 316, on Thackeray's series "Jeames's Diary," which began in *Punch* vol. 9 (July–Dec. 1845). To this Leech added the series "Servantgalism" in 1853. For Tenniel's footmen see "The Crusaders of St. Ignatius.—A Romaunt of the Period," and "The Lay of the London Wanderer," illustrations, Jan.–June 1851, 1, 158; "Punch's Anniversaries.—No. 5. Tea First Introduced into England, Sept 2nd, 1666," drawing, July–Dec. 1851, 122; and cartoon, 15 Mar. 1884, *Punch.*

10. Brooks's diary entries for 1873 reflect the tendency to mock working people: 10 Nov., "We have the infernal British workman again, by reason of the fall of plaster in the conservatory"; 11 Nov., "British workman battering"; 14 Nov., "House still infested with the workmen, and likely to be"; and 18 Nov., "The British workman finally cleared out."

11. Thackeray, "Travels in London: A Night's Pleasure," *Punch,* Jan.–June 1848, 65; and Percival Leigh, "Mr. Pips His Diary," *Punch,* 3 Nov. 1849, 182. This brand of humor survived in such late-century music-hall songs as "E Can't Take a Roise Out of Oi!" and "Her Showed Oi the Way."

12. *The World in Miniature: England, Scotland, and Ireland,* 4 vols., ed. W. H. Pyne (London: R. Ackermann, 1827), 3:176 (item 196 in the Sotheby sales catalog of Tenniel's library); Tenniel, initial, 1 Sept. 1860, 88; and cartoons, 5 Dec. 1863, 9 Aug. 1873, and 15 Mar. 1879.

13. "The Agricultural Mind," initial, *Punch,* July–Dec. 1845, 97; Tenniel, "Punch's Illustrations to Shakspeare," 21 June 1856, 254 (in Carroll's Common-Room cuttings); I. [*sic*]. B. Tenniel, *Importance of Personal Exercise,* 9, on the treatise of 1827; Friedrich Engels, *Condition of the Working Classes in England,* trans. and ed. W. O. Henderson and W. H. Chaloner (Stanford, Calif.: Stanford Univ. Press, 1958), 298, for lines beginning "What is this defective being"; "Guide to Country Gentlemen," *Punch,* 1 May 1847, 183; Hibbert, *Life in Victorian England,* 64; P. E. Razzell and R. W. Wainwright, *The Victorian Working Class* (London: Frank Cass, 1973), 5; and "Slaves in Smock Frocks," *Punch,* 1 Aug. 1846, 44.

14. Calendar page, "Punch's Almanack for 1859," for Tenniel's swain; and cartoons, 27 May 1865 and 2 Aug. 1899, for his gaffer.

15. See Simpson, *Sir John Tenniel,* 132, for his comment that the depiction of Father William as a squire and his son as a rustic confuses the relationship; Carroll, "Upon the Lonely Moor," *Train,* 1856; and William Wordsworth, "Resolution and Independence," 1802, stanza 10.

16. Similarly, in Charles Kingsley, *Alton Locke: Tailor and Poet* [1850], chap. 11, Locke observes of a countryman: "I was surprised at the difficulty with which I got into conversation with the man; at his stupidity, feigned or real . . . at the dogged, suspicious reserve with which he eyed me . . . before he seemed to think it safe to answer a single question."

17. Carroll, "Lays of Mystery, Imagination, and Humour. No. 1.—The Palace of Humbug," and "The Majesty of Justice: An Oxford Idyll," in *Complete Works of Carroll*, 810–12, 905; *The Hunting of the Snark*, "Fit the Fourth" and "Fit the Sixth"; and "Peter and Paul" in *Sylvie and Bruno*, chap. 11.

18. Tenniel, "Reversing the Proverb," cartoon, 4 June 1864.

19. Hancher, *Tenniel Illustrations to "Alice,"* 37.

20. Carroll, *The Nursery Alice* (London: Macmillan, 1890), 27. American ambassador Joseph Hodges Choate may have spoken more truly than he realized when he said at the Tenniel banquet, "The gentlemen of England loved to sit upon benches great and small. What lessons did they not learn from the Caterpillar?" (*Times*, 13 June 1901).

21. Jacqueline Pearson, *The Prostituted Muse: Images of Women and Women Dramatists, 1642–1737* (New York: St. Martin's Press, 1988), 84; Leona W. Fisher, "Mark Lemon's Farces on the 'Woman Question,'" *Studies in English Literature, 1500–1900* 28 (Autumn 1988): 649–70; Horace ("Ponny") Mayhew, "The Model Wife," *Punch*, Jan.–June 1848, 187; and, on *Punch*'s "vulgarizing" of married women in the mid-nineteenth century, Alice Maynell, "Victorian Caricature," in *Essays* (London: Burns Oates & Washbourne, 1923).

22. Carroll, "The Three Voices," *Train*, 1856; and *Sylvie and Bruno*, in *Complete Works of Carroll*, 416; Carroll's library, for about ten volumes on higher education, employment, degrees, and civil rights as they pertained to women; Carroll to Richard Harrington, 29 Jan. 1883, in *Carroll Letters*, 1:480; and "Resident Women Students," 7 Mar. 1896, in *Complete Works of Carroll*, 1185–88.

23. Charles Neilson Gatty, *The Bloomer Girls* (London: Femina Books, 1967); James Laver, *Manners and Morals in the Age of Optimism, 1848–1914* (New York: Harper & Row, 1966), 183–84; Tenniel, "Punch's Illustrations to Shakspeare," 20 Oct. 1855, 162; and third illustration to "The Cynotaph," *Ingoldsby Legends*, vol. 1.

24. Tenniel, cartoons, 28 Sept. 1861, 28 Oct. 1865, 30 Mar. 1867, 26 Sept. 1868, 28 May 1870, 20 Dec. 1873, "Punch's Almanack for 1879," 5 Dec. 1891, 14 May 1892; and Leech, cartoon, *Punch*, July–Dec. 1851.

25. Tenniel, cartoon, 30 Mar. 1867; Fisher, "Mark Lemon's Farces," 652, 663; and Tenniel, cartoons, 26 Sept. 1868 and 28 May 1870.

26. Carroll, "'Alice' on the Stage," 182.

27. Ibid., on Carroll's view of the White Queen. Hancher, *Tenniel Illustrations to "Alice,"* 11, notes a likeness in "general posture" between Tenniel's portrayals of Pius IX and the White Queen, and the crinolines in which both are shown.

28. Leech, cartoon, *Punch*, 3 Dec. 1859; Francis Hitchman, *Pius the Ninth: A Biography* (London: Houlston & Sons, 1878); *Times* introductions to the relevant *Punch* volumes; Tenniel, title page, vol. 38 (Jan.–June 1860); and cartoons, 7 Jan. 1860, 7 and 21 Apr. 1860, 18 Aug. 1860, 29 Sept. 1869, 8 Dec. 1860, 13 Apr. 1861, 24 Aug. 1861, 14 and 21 Sept. 1861, 15 and 26 Mar. 1862, 17 May 1862, 28 June 1862, 30 Aug. 1862, 20 Sept. 1862, 4 and 11 Oct. 1862; and Tenniel, "Thou art in a parlous state, Shepherd," *Punch*, 25 May 1861, 209. On Grimaldi's slippers see A. E. Wilson, *King Panto*, 111.

29. Tenniel, cartoon, 18 Dec. 1869.

30. For readers who would have preferred a more realistic Alice, see du Maurier, "Illustrating of Books," 351; Reid, *Illustrators of the Sixties*, 27; Sarzano, *Sir John Tenniel*, 19; and Hearn, "*Alice*'s Other Parent," 19; and for comments contrasting Alice to her companions, see *Spectator*, 22 Dec. 1866, and *Literary Churchman*, 5 May 1866.

31. Tenniel, preliminary drawings, "little curtain," and "Lobster Quadrille," Houghton Library (the latter is in a collection of *Wonderland* drawings, some by Tenniel and others traced by different hands); and Carroll to E. Gertrude Thomson, n.d., Huntington Library.

32. Carroll, "'Alice' on the Stage," 181.

33. *Aunt Judy's Magazine*, June 1866; *Spectator*, 22 Dec. 1866; *Court Circular*, 22 Dec. 1866; *Sunderland Herald*, 25 May 1866; *Aunt Judy's Christmas Volume for 1872*, ed. Mrs. Alfred Gatty (1872), 249; and Monkhouse, *Sir John Tenniel*, 30. The American artist Peter Newell, who reillustrated the *Alice*s in 1901, wrote that the childish sweetness of Alice is a characteristic that Tenniel "has caught and fixed in a way none may rival" ("Books and Men: Sir John Tenniel," *Nation*, 19 Mar. 1914, 294).

34. Doonan, "Realism and Surrealism," 13, for the designation "Miss Britannia"; Tenniel, *Punch* titles for vols. 51 (July–Dec. 1866) and 54 (Jan.–June 1868); and "How Captain Bettington Binks Won His Wajah, by Jove," social cut, "Punch's Almanack for 1868."

35. George Gissing, *Demos: A Story of English Socialism* (New York: E. P. Dutton, n.d.), 97, for

"two different races"; Carroll to E. Gertrude Thomson, 24 Jan. 1879, Houghton Library; and *Carroll Letters*, 2:980–81 n. 2.

36. Tenniel, cartoons, 8 July 1871, 5 Oct. 1872, 1 Dec. 1883, and 27 Nov. 1888.

37. Bennett, *Fables of Aesop;* and *The Annotated Snark*, ed. Martin Gardner (New York: Bramhall House, 1962), 39 n. 9 and 76 n. 48; J. B. Priestley, "The Walrus and the Carpenter," *New Statesman*, 10 Aug. 1957, 168, for political analogies to the *Alice* texts; and chap. 9 n. 15 above, for Tenniel's Alician takeoffs.

38. See *Illustrators of Alice*. Pogany's use of the "Black Mammy" type instead of Robert's Irish Cook follows stage precedents. Robert C. Toll, *Blacking Up: The Minstrel Show in Nineteenth-Century America* (New York: Oxford Univ. Press, 1974), 28, states, "In American drama, Negroes assumed the comic relief role that the ignorant Irish played in England." Among the social types pictured by Ralph Steadman are the proletarian gardeners of the Queen of Hearts, their bodies composed of union cards (*Alice's Adventures in Wonderland*, 69).

18. The Pride of Mr. Punch

1. For the total of Tenniel's cartoons—about 2,314—I added the 310 cartoons counted in volumes 20–43 (Jan 1851–Dec. 1862) to 1,976 cartoons (26 cartoons per half-yearly volume for volumes 44–119) plus 27 almanac cartoons from 1874 to 1900, plus one cartoon for volume 120. See "Wonderful Career," *Daily Telegraph*, 27 Feb. 1914; Spielmann, *History of "Punch,"* 207–8 and, for *Punch*'s cartoons banned in other countries, 190–94; Henry Blackburn, *The Art of Illustration* (London: W. H. Allen, 1894), 36; and "A Journalistic Amenity—Puck's Compliments to 'Punch,'" *Puck*, 8 Feb. 1882, 361. For cartoons pirated by *Harper's Weekly* see Frankie Morris, *John Tenniel, Cartoonist* (Ann Arbor, Mich.: University Microfilms, 1986), 319–20, and for those plagiarized in British and colonial papers, 291–98. See *Frank Leslie's Illustrated Newspaper*, 17 Dec. 1870, 240; 18 Mar. 1871, 16; 29 Apr. 1871, 112; and 1 July 1871, 264, for pirated cartoons, and 4 Feb. 1871, 356, for one co-opted in part. Copyright was established by the Chase Act of 1891. But Hilary Guise, *Great Victorian Engravings* (London: Astragal Books, 1980), 12, indicates that a convention of copyright had been concluded between the United States and England in 1879.

2. "Essence," 17 Aug. 1867, 65, on Lord Derby's speech of 6 Aug. in which he described the reform bill "(by the kind permission of CARTOON PUNCH, ESQ.)" as a "Leap in the Dark" (title of Tenniel's 3 Aug. cartoon); Asa Briggs, *Victorian People* (London: Oldhams Press, 1954), 294, 279 (cf. the last quotation with Tenniel's cartoon, 16 Feb. 1867), and rev. ed. (1872), 69; and Robert Rhodes James, *The British Revolution, 1880–1939* (New York: Alfred A. Knopf, 1977), 87–88.

3. Lady Balfour, quoted in Amy Cruse, *The Victorians and Their Reading* (Boston: Houghton Mifflin, 1936), 395; Mary Gladstone, quoted in Peter Stansky, *Gladstone: A Progress in Politics* (Boston: Little, Brown, 1979), 158; and Tenniel, cartoons, 7 Feb. 1885, 14 Feb. 1885, and 10 Apr. 1886.

4. Spielmann, "Sir John Tenniel," *Daily Graphic*, 5 Jan. 1901; and "Fine Art Gossip," *Athenaeum*, 7 Mar. 1914, 349.

5. On *Fun* and *Tomahawk* see Burnand, *Records and Reminiscences*, 263; Sullivan, "Comic Paper," 418; Hogarth, *Arthur Boyd Houghton*, 45; à Beckett, *à Becketts of "Punch,"* 159, 161, and, on settling subjects away from the *Punch* table, 13, 169; Brooks diary, 28 Feb. 1871, 25 May 1871, 21 July 1871, and 27 Feb. 1873; and Layard, *Great "Punch" Editor*, 399.

6. Silver's diary, which records twenty-seven of Tenniel's suggestions; Brooks diaries, 2 Jan. 1869, 14 and 21 July 1871, and 27 Feb. 1873; Layard, *Great "Punch" Editor*, 399, 560; à Beckett, *à Becketts of "Punch,"* 13, 169; and "Tenniel," *Supp. "Punch,"* 14. See Spielmann, *History of "Punch,"* 170, stating that Leech, while chief cartoonist in the forties, proposed eleven subjects in three years; and Spielmann, "The *Punch* Dinner—the Diners and Their Labours," *Magazine of Art* 18 (1895): 93, on the specifications given Tenniel.

7. Burnand, quoted in à Beckett, *Recollections of a Humourist*, 385; and Tenniel, quoted in Anstey, *Long Retrospect*, 160. See also, Partridge, quoted in "Tenniel," *Supp. "Punch,"* 15.

8. Milliken, cartoon suggestions, collection of Simon Houfe; and Tenniel, cartoon, 25 Feb. 1893. The suggestions correlate with three of Tenniel's cartoons.

9. Silver diary, 10 Apr. 1867, for Tenniel's reluctance to draw double spreads; and on the instant intelligibility of the cartoons, see "The Hanover Gallery," *Standard*, 16 Nov. 1880, and "The Cartoonist," *Times*, 27 Feb. 1914.

10. Brooks, quoted in Layard, *Great "Punch" Editor*, 425; Carroll to Mrs. MacDonald, 19 May 1868, in *Carroll Letters*, 1:119–20; and Carroll, 17 Aug. 1883, *Carroll Diaries*, 2:419.

11. Tenniel, cartoon, 11 May 1878.

12. Tenniel, "Amateur Theatricals. An Othello 'Break-Down,'" social cut, "Punch's Almanack for 1868." For Aldrich's costume see James Laver, *Costume in the Theatre* (New York: Hill & Wang, 1965), pl. 92. Tenniel's friend Lewis Strange Wingfield had played Roderigo to Aldrich's Othello at the Haymarket Theatre, 21 Aug. 1865 (*DNB*, s.v. "Wingfield, Lewis Strange [1842–1891]).

13. Caricaturists who acted in the eighteenth century include John Boyne, Robert Dighton, and James Gillray, and, in the nineteenth, George and Isaac Robert Cruikshank, Leech, Tenniel, Sambourne, Partridge, Furniss, George Baxter, Phil May, the Frenchman Henri Monnier, and the American Joseph Keppler. Writers contributing to both the stage and comic journals include Gilbert Abbot à Beckett, Douglas Jerrold, Robert and William Brough, John Hollingshead, H. J. Byron, W. S. Gilbert, and, of course, *Punch*'s Lemon, Brooks, Taylor, and Burnand. The number of nineteenth-century plays by *Punch* writers was estimated to be over five hundred (Spielmann, *History of "Punch,"* 128).

14. *Red Republican*, 24 Aug. 1850; "Theatre Royal, Westminster," *Punch*, 20 Nov. 1852, 219; and "An Unlucky Burlesque," *Examiner*, 10 Jan. 1863, 19.

15. Tenniel, cartoons, 4 Mar. 1854, 14 Oct. 1854, and 22 Sept. 1855; Nicoll, *Early Nineteenth Century Drama*, 47, on tableaux in melodrama; Tenniel, cartoons, 17 Dec. 1870, 4 Feb. 1871, and 11 Mar. 1871; and Edmond Duranty, "Caricature and Imagery in Europe during the War of 1870–1871," *Gazette des Beaux-Arts* 6 (1872): 393–408. On Queen Hermione's crinoline see Tenniel, cartoon, 23 Sept. 1865; and George Rowell, *The Victorian Theatre: A Survey* (London: Oxford Univ. Press, 1956), 17.

16. Tenniel, cartoons, 5 Apr. 1862 and 12 May 1883.

17. Tenniel, "Punch's Almanack for 1894"; and "Punch's Almanack for 1897," in which some of the nursery characters assume new roles—Policeman Jack kills the Giant "Lawlessness," the forty thieves are personified jars of explosives, Aladdin holds an electric lamp, and St. George accosts the Dragon Anarchy; Mayer, *Harlequin in His Element*, 324–26; and Frow, *"Oh, Yes It Is!"* 96. On the Egyptian theme see Tenniel, cartoon, 17 Jan. 1854; and Alan Delgado, *Victorian Entertainment* (New York: American Heritage Press, 1971), 96; and for the procession of beauties see Tenniel, "Punch's Almanack for 1875," and A. E. Wilson, *King Panto*, 184. Burnand, who authored four pantomimes between 1868 and 1885 (Nicoll, *Late Nineteenth Century Drama*, 289, 291) may have had some influence here.

18. Tenniel, illustrations to "The Rime of the Ancient Ministere," *Punch*, 13 Mar. 1852, 106–7; *Punch's Pocket Book for 1863*, "Punch's Almanack for 1887," and, for sculptural burlesques, cartoons, 7 Apr. 1855, 6 Nov. 1869, and 8 Apr. 1882. The last are based on the man-headed winged bull from the palace of Assur-Naser-Pal II (BC 883–859), and Matthew Cotes Wyatt, *Wellington* (1846).

19. "Punch among the Painters—No. 3," *Punch*, 1954, 222. Leech and Frith were, in fact, friends.

20. Tenniel, cartoons, 16 Mar. 1889, 5 Dec. 1874, 25 Jan. 1896, and 12 Feb. 1887, *Punch*, based on Thomas H. Maguire, *Champion of England* (engraved 1860); John Everett Millais, *North West Passage* (1874); George G. Boughton, *Waning of the Honeymoon* (1878); and, possibly, John Martin, *Marcus Curtius* (1827). See also Morris, *John Tenniel, Cartoonist*, 317–18. Compared are Tenniel's cartoon, 19 June 1886, with Jean Louis Meissonier, *1814* (1864); and his cartoon, 9 Feb. 1889, with Jacques Louis David, *Napoleon Crossing the St. Bernard* (1800). For book illustrations mined for *Punch* see Tenniel, illustration for Aesop's "Countryman and the Snake," and cartoon, 3 Jan. 1857; the camel and rider from *The Mirage of Life* and "Punch's Almanack for 1878"; and his illustrations to *Lalla Rookh* and cartoons, 3 June 1871 and 28 Feb. 1874. See chap. 9, n. 15 for his burlesques on his *Alice* cuts.

21. Caricaturists who aspired to be history painters include Hogarth, Gillray, George Cruikshank, Matt Morgan, and the American Thomas Nast. Compare Britannia in Tenniel's cartoon, 23 Sept. 1865, with John Flaxman, *Monument to Capt. Ralph Willet Miller* (1801–4), St Paul's Cathedral.

22. Cf. Tenniel, cartoons, 12 Sept. 1857, with Kritios, *Tyrant Slayers* (c. 477 BC); 15 Nov. 1862, with Antoine Etex, *Cain and His Race Accursed of God* (Paris Salon, 1832); and 21 Jan. 1888, with Patrick MacDowell, *Europe, Albert Memorial*, Hyde Park, London.

23. Tenniel, cartoon, 22 Aug. 1857. The prone body of a mother with the supine infant lying in the crook of her arm may be a conventional motif as it appears in Ary Scheffer's painting *The Suliot Women* (Paris Salon, 1827) and again in Edward Armitage's *Retribution* (1858). Tenniel's cartoon of 9 July 1859 is a fine example in the heroic animal tradition.

24. Taine, *Notes on England*, 258; "Exhibitions, Great and Small," *Blackwood's Edinburgh Magazine*, July 1862, 65, 66; Tom Taylor, "English Painting in 1862," *Fine Arts Quarterly Review* 1 (May 1863): 18; and John Ruskin, *Academy Notes*, ed. E. T. Cook and Alexander Wedderburn (London: George Allen, 1904), 265, 306–7. Armitage would have come under continental influences from 1837 to 1843 when he studied in Paris with Paul Delaroche. See *DNB*, s.v. "Armitage, Edward (1817–1896)."

25. "Minor Exhibitions," *Athenaeum*, 6 Apr. 1895, 449; *Bookseller*, 12 Dec. 1865; Charles Kingsley to Shirley Brooks, 31 Dec. 1872, Harkness Collection; Ruskin, "Lecture 5. The Fireside," 195; Joseph Grego, "The Exhibition of Humourists in Art," *Magazine of Art* 12 (1889): 334; and Spielmann, "Sir John Tenniel," *Daily Graphic*, 5 Jan. 1901.

26. For comparable images in France see Armand Dayot, *Le second empire (2 Décembre 1851–4 Septembre 1870)*, (Paris: Flammarion, n.d.), 45ff., esp. those by Hippolyte Bellangé.

27. Tenniel, cartoons, 25 Oct. 1899 and 6 Dec. 1899.

28. Tenniel, cartoons, 12 May 1860 and 16 Mar. 1889.

29. Spielmann, *History of "Punch,"* 176–77, wrongly identifying the design as Tenniel's cartoon of 4 Mar. 1854 while describing a small cut by Leech entitled "The French Cent Guards and the British Life Guards," *Punch*, July–Dec. 1854, 106. See Tenniel, cartoon, 21 Oct. 1882; "Field-Marshal *Punch*," *Supp. "Punch,"* 25 Apr. 1900; Tenniel, cartoon, 18 Jan. 1896; and *Punch* to Manager Palace Theatre, 18 Jan. 1896, "'Punch' Letter Book, 7 Dec. 1895–8 May 1897," *Punch* archives.

30. *Punch* to Hy Pritchard, 27 Oct. 1900, "'Punch' Letter Book, 11 July 1900–3 June 1903"; and Tenniel, cartoon, 24 Oct. 1900 (the date of this cartoon was mistakenly printed as 24 Sept. 1900). Anstey, *Long Retrospect*, 244, describes the City Imperial Volunteer procession with its "tremendous crowds" and "immense wave of people" that came surging in its wake. See chap. 19 above on government pensions awarded to the families of Leech and Lemon.

31. Tenniel, cartoon, 28 Aug. 1869; cartoon, *Tomahawk*, vol. 6–7, 1870; and Brooks diary, 10 May 1871.

32. Tenniel, "How a Foolish Bird Did Try to Swim across Ye British Channel!" small cut, *Punch*, 26 Nov. 1859, 216; and cartoon, 22 Aug. 1885.

33. "Art Exhibitions," *Times*, 1 Apr. 1895; and Tenniel, quoted in Spielmann, *History of "Punch,"* 466.

34. Tenniel, cartoon, 31 Oct. 1868; and William Davenport Adams, *A Book of Burlesque: Sketches of English Stage Travestie and Parody* (London: Henry, 1891), 156–57, for various productions of *William Tell*; Tenniel, cartoon, 7 Nov. 1868, for his burlesque on *Richard III*, and Nicoll, *Late Nineteenth Century Drama*, 289; and Tenniel, cartoons, 16 Oct. 1886 and 6 Nov. 1886, on Randolph Churchill, and Adams, *Book of Burlesque*, 190.

35. Robert Blake, *Disraeli* (New York: St. Martin's Press, 1967), 764.

36. Tenniel, cartoon, 8 Feb. 1873.

37. Tenniel, cartoons, 25 Feb. 1871 (here Gladstone's foreign policy is contrasted to that of Palmerston, the "Judicious Bottle-Holder" of Leech's 1851 cartoon), 26 Aug. 1871, 4 May 1872, and 9 Nov. 1872. His cartoon of 3 Jan. 1874 seems to foretell the Eastern crisis that came later in the decade. On Gladstone's wordiness see cartoon, 13 Dec. 1879, and D. C. Somervell, *Disraeli and Gladstone: A Duo-Biographical Sketch* (Garden City, N.Y.: Garden City Publishing, 1926), 221.

38. Tenniel, cartoons, 20 Jan, 1883, 10 Mar. 1883, and 26 May 1883.

39. Tenniel, cartoons, 9 May 1885 and 16 May 1885.

40. The queen, quoted in Robert Rhodes James, *British Revolution*, 136; and Labouchere, quoted in Peter Fraser, *Joseph Chamberlain, Radicalism and Empire, 1868–1914* (London: Cassell, 1966), 97. See Tenniel, cartoons, 29 Nov. 1890, 8 Mar. 1884, 5 July 1884, 2 May 1885, 18 Feb. 1893, 22 July 1893, 26 Feb. 1887, 7 Feb. 1891, and 6 Feb. 1886.

41. Tenniel, cartoons, 10 Apr. 1886, 15 Apr. 1893, and 30 Sept. 1893.

42. Silver diary, 20 Feb. 1867 and 16 Dec. 1868.

43. Tenniel, cartoon, 7 Jan. 1882.

44. Tenniel, cartoon, 30 Oct. 1875; Fred Bernard, cartoon, *Fun*, 1869, reproduced in *Brothers Dalziel*, 275; and William Boucher, cartoon, *Judy*, 16 Feb. 1870.

45. Silver diary, 30 Oct. 1861 and 13 Mar. 1867.

46. *Daily News*, quoted in "Tenniel," *Supp. "Punch,"* 8; and almanac cartoon for 1876, *Judy*, vol. 18, 8–9.

47. Morris, *John Tenniel, Cartoonist*, 160–63, for a refutation of the claim in Margaret Mespoulet, *Creators of Wonderland* (New York: Arrow Editions, 1934), 60–63, that Tenniel's animal caricatures were influenced by the work of J. J. Grandville. More correctly identified as followers of Grandville are Henry Heath and Ernest Griset. See Tenniel, cartoons, 20 Nov. 1875 and 27 Apr. 1878; Silver diary, 13 Feb. 1867; and Tenniel, cartoon, 9 Feb. 1867.

48. Tenniel, cartoon, 17 Feb. 1877; and Boucher, cartoon, *Judy*, 29 Mar. 1876. For political animal dramas in painting at this time, see engravings after paintings by Samuel E. Waller: "The European Happy Family," 4 Nov. 1876, 448–49 (text on 446); and "The European Happy Family, No. II," 9 June 1877, 535, *Graphic*; and Morris, *John Tenniel, Cartoonist*, 172–80.

49. Tenniel, "Punch's Almanack for 1860," calendar page; and cartoon, 8 Sept. 1894.

50. For wicked barons and baronets in melodrama see *Dramas, 1800–1850*, vol. 1 of *English Plays of the Nineteenth Century*, ed. Michael R. Booth (Oxford: Clarendon Press, 1969), 203; Clinton-Baddeley, *Right on the Night*, 229ff.; and Rahill, *World of Melodrama*, 155. See Tenniel, cartoon, 19 Jan. 1867; and Keene, cartoon, 21 July 1866.

51. Tenniel, cartoons, 8 Mar. 1873 and 21 July 1888.

52. John M. MacKenzie, *Propaganda and Empire: The Manipulation of British Public Opinion, 1880–1960* (Manchester: Manchester Univ. Press, 1984), 175–76; and Hibbert, *Life in Victorian England*, 46, on the lack of history instruction in English preparatory, public, and state schools; Kennedy Jones, *Fleet Street and Downing Street* (London: Hutchinson, 1919), 86, on reading for the young; and Dickens, *Our Mutual Friend*, (1865), chap. 11, "Podsnappery."

53. Diana Dixon, "Children and the Press, 1866–1914," in *The Press in English Society from the Seventeenth to Nineteenth Centuries*, ed. Michael Harris and Alan Lee (Rutherford, N.J.: Fairleigh Dickinson Univ. Press, 1986), 144; Parry and Torr, quoted in Cruse, *Victorians and Their Reading*, 406, 393–94; Burnand, *Records and Reminiscences*, 1:55; R. C. Lehmann, quoted in "Tenniel," Supp. "Punch," 13; Hudson, *Martin Tupper*, 221; A. M. W. Sterling, *Victorian Sidelights* (London: Ernest Benn, 1954), 210; and Winston Churchill, "Cartoons and Cartoonists," *Strand Magazine*, June 1931, 582.

54. "The Cartoonist," *Times*, 27 Feb. 1914; and "Tenniel and 'Punch,'" *North American Review* 199 (1914): 506.

55. Churchill, "Cartoons and Cartoonists," 583–84; R. F. Foster, *Lord Randolph Churchill: A Political Life* (Oxford: Clarendon Press, 1981), 2–3; and Ernst H. Gombrich, "Cartoons and Progress," in *The Public's Progress: A Contact Book* (London: Contact Publications, 1947), 78. The reification of Tenniel's work was further facilitated by Tenniel's copyists (see Morris, *John Tenniel, Cartoonist*, 291–98).

56. "Mr. Linley Sambourne," *Manchester Guardian*, 4 Aug. 1910, which maintained that Tenniel's pencil was a weapon, carrying "the seeds of persuasion and scorn. . . . Mr. SAMBOURNE's was simply a pencil"; Tenniel, title page for vol. 119 (July–Dec. 1900)—Mr. Punch leading the CIV troops, for Mr. Punch's last title-page appearance; and Frank Weitenkampf, "Sir John Tenniel—Cartoonist," *Scribner's*, 1914, 796, which pointed out that Tenniel gave Punch's dog Toby a personality, too. See Toby mimicking Punch's horse as well as Punch himself in titles for vols. 19, 32, 75, and 80, and aping the British Lion in Tenniel's almanac cut for 1886.

57. "Minor Exhibitions," *Athenaeum*, 6 Apr. 1895, 449; Spielmann, "Sir John Tenniel," *Daily Graphic*, 5 Jan. 1901; *Brothers Dalziel*, 130; "Banquet to Sir John Tenniel," *Times*, 13 June 1901; Weitenkampf, "Sir John Tenniel—Cartoonist," 794; "Fine Art Gossip," *Athenaeum*, 7 Mar. 1914, 349; and Burnand, quoted in "Tenniel," Supp. "Punch," 11.

58. E. J. Milliken, quoted in Spielmann, *History of "Punch,"* 474.

19. As for Political Opinions

1. David Anderson, "The Rise of the Comic Paper," *Magazine of Art* 14 (1891): 154; Kennedy Jones, *Fleet Street*, 236; Hatton, *Journalistic London*, 10; A. J. Mundella, quoted in Spielmann, *History of "Punch,"* 189; and Price, *History of Punch*, 159. On *Punch* as a chartered libertine see Spielmann, *History of "Punch,"* 234; and "Mr. Punch among the Pictures," *Punch*, Jan.–June 1853, 198.

2. Ruskin, "Lecture 5. The Fireside," 180; Spielmann, *History of "Punch,"* 99, 169; Mark Lemon, "The Moral of Punch," *Punch*, July 1841, 1; and Furniss, *Confessions of a Caricaturist*, 1:254. The term "non-partisan partisanship" is used with reference to the London *Times* in Stephen Koss, *The Rise and Fall of the Political Press in Britain*, 2 vols. (Chapel Hill: Univ. of North Carolina Press, 1981), 1:454.

3. Brooks diary, 14 Jan. 1867; and à Beckett, *Recollections of a Humourist*, 384.

4. Spielmann, *History of "Punch,"* 199, 267, 473.

5. À Beckett, *Recollections of a Humourist*, 385; and Spielmann, "*Punch* Dinner," 92.

6. À Beckett, *Recollections of a Humourist*, 384; Spielmann, "*Punch* Dinner," 92; and "A Public Loss," *Huddersfield Examiner*, 4 Aug. 1910.

7. Silver diary, 15 Feb. 1860; and Brooks diaries, 2 Jan. 1869 and 26 June 1872.

8. Lehmann, quoted in "Tenniel," Supp. "Punch," 14; and Burnand, "Personal Recollections," *Daily Telegraph*, 27 Feb. 1914. See also Spielmann, "*Punch* Dinner," 93.

9. Lucy, quoted in "Tenniel," Supp. "Punch," 12.

10. Brooks, "Essence," 11 Apr. 1868, 151 (see also "Essence," 3 Apr. 1869, 137); and Tenniel, cartoon, 3 Apr. 1869.

11. "The Dogs of War" (or "By Jingo"), a music-hall song of around 1878, was written by G. W. Hunt and popularized by singer G. H. Macdermott. Tenniel's cartoon of that title appeared on 17 June 1876.

12. Taylor's editorship ran from late Feb. 1874 until his death on 12 July 1880; and Disraeli's premiership went from 17 Feb. 1874 to late Apr. 1880. See Spielmann, *History of "Punch,"* 99, on Taylor's politics; and Burnand, *Records and Reminiscences,* 280, on his manner. Disraeli became Earl of Beaconsfield in Aug. 1876.

13. Douglas Jerrold, quoted in Adrian, *Mark Lemon,* 58, on *Punch* following the *Times;* Taylor, "Essence," 24 June 1876, 254, and 8 July 1876, 3.

14. Taylor, "Essence," 29 July 1876, 37; 12 Aug. 1876, 58; 19 Aug. 1876, 71; and 26 Aug. 1876, 79; "A Word in Season," 12 Aug. 1876, 62; "British Interests—and Principles," 30 Sept. 1876, 135; and "Our Home Conference," 16 Dec. 1876, 264, *Punch.* Tenniel's 15 July 1876 cartoon may have been inspired by "Mr. Disraeli and the Foreign Crisis," *Spectator,* 10 June 1876, 729–30, condemning a government directed by a "sphinx." For similar depictions of Disraeli see Tenniel, cartoons, 25 Nov. 1876; and "Punch's Almanack for 1878."

15. "England Aroused," 16 Sept. 1876, 114; "Talk about Turks," 7 Oct. 1876, 152; Tenniel, cartoon, 23 Sept. 1876; David Harris, *Britain and Bulgarian Horrors,* 293, 356, for anti-agitation statements of Northcote and the *Times;* Boucher, cartoon, *Judy,* 23 June 1876; and Gordon Thomson, cartoons, *Fun,* 6 Sept. 1876 and 4 Oct. 1876.

16. Preface to vol. 72, Jan.–June 1877, iii–iv; "Kaiser-I-Hind," 13 Jan. 1877, 2; Taylor, "Essence," 3 Mar. 1877, 88; 12 May 1877, 206; and 19 May 1877, 220; "Regenerate Russia," 29 Dec. 1877, 300; and Taylor, "Essence," 9 Feb. 1878, 52.

17. *Times,* quoted in Richard Millman, *Britain and the Eastern Question, 1875–1878* (Oxford: Clarendon Press, 1979), 382; Taylor, "Essence," 9 Feb. 1878, 51; and 16 Feb. 1878, 63; and Tenniel, cartoon, 9 Feb. 1878.

18. Boucher, cartoon, *Judy,* 10 Apr. 1878; and Tenniel, cartoon, 27 Apr. 1878.

19. "Riddles for the Recess," 3 Aug. 1878, 48; and "When the Bill Comes In," 24 Aug. 1878, 73, *Punch.*

20. "Asian Mysteries," 15 Apr. 1876, 146; "Kaiser-I-Hind," 13 Jan. 1877, 2; "The Premier's Portfolio," 22 Apr. 1876, 161; "Betsy Prig's Soliloquy," 23 Dec. 1876, 271; "Un-English," 4 Aug. 1877, 42; "Betsy Prig and the Muse of History," 17 Aug. 1878, 61; and "The Jingo-Englishman," 9 Nov. 1878, 215, *Punch.* Thus, Spielmann's assertion, "From first to last *Punch* has always been an Imperialist" (*History of "Punch,"* 120), while presenting the overriding trend, is not strictly correct.

21. Tenniel, title page, vol. 69, July–Dec. 1875; cartoon, 11 Dec. 1875; and title pages, vol. 70, Jan.–June 1876; vol. 71, July–Dec. 1876; and vol. 72, Jan.–June 1877. The American lion tamer Isaac Van Amburgh made his London debut in 1838 and was greatly admired by the queen.

22. Tenniel, "Punch's Almanack for 1876," "Punch's Almanack for 1877," and "Punch's Almanack for 1878."

23. Laurence Senelick, "Politics as Entertainment: Victorian Music-Hall Songs," *Victorian Studies* 19 (Dec. 1975): 161; and "The Beaconsfield, Bright, and Gladstone Cartoons," *Saturday Review,* 18 Jan. 1879, 78.

24. See, for example, "The Sphinx's Soliloquy," *Punch,* 28 July 1877, 30. See Disraeli, *Coningsby* (1844), and *Tancred* (1846), for the term "Asian mystery"; and Senelick, "Politics as Entertainment," 160.

25. Tenniel, cartoons, 1 Apr. 1876, 12 Aug. 1876, 19 May 1877, 24 Feb. 1877, and 28 Apr. 1877.

26. Lucy, *Sixty Years,* 408; Blake, *Disraeli,* 568; and Tenniel, cartoons, 15 May 1875, 24 July 1875, and 11 Sept. 1875.

27. Tenniel, cartoons, "Punch's Almanack for 1878" and 22 June 1878; R. W. Seton-Watson, *Disraeli, Gladstone and the Eastern Question* (New York: W. W. Norton, 1972), 438, on Disraeli's French; Tenniel, cartoons, 15 Apr. 1876, 9 Feb. 1878, and 29 June 1878; and "Beaconsfield, Bright, and Gladstone Cartoons," 78.

28. "'Woodman, Spare That Tree!'" *Punch,* 26 May 1877, 234, and Tenniel's cartoon of that date and title; and John Proctor, "The Deadly Upas," cartoon, *Funny Folks,* 23 Sept. 1876.

29. Tenniel, cartoons, 20 July 1878, 27 July 1878, and 3 Aug. 1878; Taylor, "Essence," 20 July 1878, 14; "A Blaze of Triumph!" 27 July 1878, 30, and Taylor's "Essence" of that date, p. 27 (in which he grudgingly admits that it is the paper's task to record the public mood); and "The 'Pas de Deux,'" 3 Aug. 1878, 42.

30. Contrast Taylor, "Essence," 19 May 1877, 208, with Tenniel, cartoons, 8 June 1878, 15 June

1878, 31 Aug. 1878, and 21 Sept. 1878. See Tenniel, cartoon, 19 Aug. 1882, for an early sign of a softening toward Gladstone.

31. Sambourne's "Essence" drawings, 18 Mar. 1871, 106; and 19 May 1877, 219; and no. 108 in *Collection of Political and Other Broadsides, vol. 1* (before 9 Apr. 1880), British Library, for the separately issued cartoon. Sambourne reused parts of this drawing in his *Punch* cartoon of 29 May 1880, which was more favorable to Gladstone. See also Sambourne's "Essence" drawings, 20 July 1878, 14; 8 July 1876, 3; 26 Jan. 1878, 26; and 24 Aug. 1878, 74.

32. "Sir John Tenniel: History in Pencil," *Daily Graphic,* 27 Feb. 1914.

33. Vizetelly, *Through Seventy Years,* 1:302–4, on Disraeli's wooing of Leech; Koss, *Political Press in Britain,* 316; and Spielmann, *History of "Punch,"* 200, for how politicians felt about being caricatured in *Punch,* and 180, 182, 199, on politicians acquiring cartoons in which they figured. See also "Chamberlain and the Cartoonists," *Cartoons Magazine* 6 (Sept. 1914).

34. Smalley, "Sir John Tenniel," *New York Tribune,* 5 Apr. 1914.

35. Spy, "Punch," caricature, *Vanity Fair* (London), 26 Oct. 1878.

20. King Demos

1. "Pictures of the Working-Man," 20 May 1865, 202; Tenniel's cartoon of the same date; and Walter Bagehot, *The English Constitution,* 2nd ed., ed. Forrest Morgan (Hartford, Conn.: Traveller's Insurance, 1889), 271.

2. Tenniel, cartoon, 20 Dec. 1873, for his Political Economy; Leech, cartoon, *Punch,* 17 Jan. 1852; Mrs. Gaskell, *North and South* (1855), chap. 17; Engels, *Condition of Working Class,* 246; and, for the strictures of classical political economy imbued with God-given sanction, Mrs. Gaskell's *Mary Barton* (1848), chap. 37; and Kingsley's 1867 preface to *Alton Locke.* Cf. Patrick Brantlinger, "The Case against Trade Unions in Early Victorian Fiction," *Victorian Studies* 13 (Sept. 1969): 50.

3. Dickens, *Hard Times* (1854), bk. 1, chap. 14; Brantlinger, "Case against Trade Unions," 41; Gaskell, *North and South,* chap. 20; and "Who Is Mr. Potter?" *Punch,* 20 Apr. 1861, 162.

4. Sidney Webb and Beatrice Webb, *The History of Trade Unionism* (1894; reprint, New York: Augustus M. Kelley, 1965), 233–39; Briggs, *Victorian People* (Chicago: Univ. of Chicago Press, 1972), 170; Henry Pelling, *A History of British Trade Unionism,* 3rd ed. (London: Macmillan, 1976), 52, 53, 55; and *DNB,* s.v. "Potter, George (1832–93)."

5. Gaskell, *North and South,* chap. 19; "Strike, But Hear," letter to the editor, *Times,* 13 Dec. 1859; and Shaftesbury, quoted in Webb, *History of Trade Unionism,* 293 n. 1.

6. "The End of the Strike," 22 June 1861, 252; Tenniel, cartoon, 22 June 1861 (note the play on the word "Union," inscribed over the workhouse door and also denoting a body that administered the workhouses for several parishes); "The British Workman and His Pictures," 28 Oct. 1865, 166; and "Blacklegs or Blackguards?" 26 Apr. 1879, 181, *Punch.*

7. Tenniel, cartoon, 6 July 1867.

8. Potter, quoted in the *Times,* 29 June 1867; Tenniel, painting, *Expulsion from Eden,* exhibited at the Royal Academy in 1853; and Thomas Carlyle, *The French Revolution: A History* (1837), vol. 1, bk. 1, chap. 4.

9. "A Dig at the Delegates," 27 Apr. 1861, 176; "A Bright View of Reform," 30 Nov. 1861, 222; "The Aristocracy of Labour," 26 Jan. 1867, 32; Tenniel, cartoon, 19 Sept. 1891; Gaskell, *Mary Barton,* chap. 15, for "But they had no right to tyrannize over others, and tie them down to their own Procrustean bed"; *Times,* 3 May 1892, in which a letter protested that the proposal for the eight-hour day "runs so much upon lines generally accepted as innocent, or even laudable, that few people have so much as realized the cast-iron uniformity which it is sought to establish"; *Times,* 28 Mar. 1861, on the ratio between hours and pay; "Potter's Last Push," *Punch,* 4 May 1861, 186; and Tenniel, cartoons, 14 Oct. 1871, 19 Sept. 1891, 30 Apr. 1892, and 20 Jan. 1894.

10. See *Dramas, 1800–1850,* 27–28, 204–5; and Leech, quoted in the Silver diary, 2 Mar. 1859.

11. Tenniel, cartoon, 20 Apr. 1861; E. H. Hunt, *British Labour History, 1815–1914* (Atlantic Highlands, N.J.: Humanities Press, 1981), 306; Briggs, *Victorian People* (1972), 181; and Tenniel, cartoon, 6 Nov. 1897.

12. "Mrs. Jane Gimlet on 'Strikes,'" *Punch,* 3 Dec. 1853, 234, for the workingman's wife used propagandistically; and "A New Song" and "The Greet Strike; or the Nine Oors Movement," in Martha Vicinus, *Broadsides of the Industrial North* (Newcastle, UK: Frank Graham, 1975), 51, 58–59. An article in the *Times,* 28 Mar. 1861, said of the builders' strike for a nine-hour day: "The demands of the men are so utterly unreasonable. . . . Most of the wives of these very men work from twelve to fourteen to sixteen hours daily, at washing or as charwomen, and their children, as errand boys or

in factories, work from ten to twelve hours" (cf. Tenniel's cartoon, 14 Oct. 1871). See Tenniel's cartoon, 18 Jan. 1873, for another wife as the voice of reason. In "Bless Thee, Thou Art Translated," 25 Jan. 1873, 35, Mr. Punch assumes credit for ending a strike.

13. Dickens, *Hard Times*, chap. 10, for "Aw a muddle"; Tenniel, cartoons, 25 Mar. 1865, 12 Mar. 1892, 7 Dec. 1895, and 2 July 1898; and "Strike, But Hear!" *Punch*, 29 June 1872, 266.

14. Jean Louis Forain, *Scene de Grêve* (n.d.), and Théophile Steinlen, *En Grêve* (1898), reproduced in Gabriel P. Weisberg, *Social Concern and the Worker: French Prints from 1830–1910* (Cleveland: Cleveland Museum of Art, 1980), catalog nos. 12, 77, pp. 63, 122.

15. Tenniel, cartoon, 10 Nov. 1883.

16. Tenniel, cartoons, 26 Jan. 1884, 20 Feb. 1886, 27 Feb. 1886, and 27 Nov. 1886; and "Face to Face!" *Punch*, 7 Sept. 1889, 114. See also Tenniel, cartoons, 19 July 1890, 13 Sept. 1890, and 30 Apr. 1892.

17. "Blacklegs or Blackguards?" 26 Apr. 1879, 181; Tenniel, cartoon, 7 Sept. 1889; and, on late-nineteenth-century shifts in perception, Gareth Stedman Jones, *Outcast London* (Oxford: Clarendon Press, 1971), 1–10, 316–20; and Hunt, *British Labour History*, 120–21.

18. Tenniel, cartoon, 12 Oct. 1889; and accompanying text, "Beggar My Neighbor!" 174.

19. Tenniel, cartoons, 7 Dec. 1895, 9 Oct. 1897, 24 July 1897, and 2 July 1898. On the book *Made in Germany* see R. K. Webb, *Modern England: From the Eighteenth Century to the Present* (New York: Dodd, Mead, 1968), 374.

20. Stowe, quoted in Cruse, *Victorians and Their Reading*, 391; Leech, cartoon, *Punch*, 15 Apr. 1848; and for Sharple's design, Pelling, *British Trade Unionism*, pl. 3.

21. "The Representation of the Smith," *Punch*, 16 Apr. 1859, 159; and Tenniel, cartoon, 16 Mar. 1867.

22. Lord Elcho and Robert Lowe, quoted in "The Borough Franchise Extension Bill," *Times*, 4 May 1865.

23. Engels, *Condition of Working Class*, 143; Gaskell, *North and South*, chap. 20; *The Red Republican and the Friend of the People*, 2 vols. (New York: Barnes & Noble, 1966), 1:122; Tenniel, cartoon, 12 Apr. 1873; and S. C. Hall, *The Trial of Sir Jasper: A Temperance Tale in Verse* (London: Virtue, 1873), 8.

24. Tenniel, cartoon, 23 Feb. 1861; and, on "losings banks," Brian Harrison, *Drink and the Victorians: The Temperance Question in England, 1815–1872* (Pittsburgh: Univ. of Pittsburgh Press, 1971), 338, and figs. 12, 13. Might the "losings bank" concept have been a sly reference to the earlier role of public houses as savings depositories for the funds of workmen's clubs and friendly societies? See also Tenniel, cartoon, 27 Nov. 1880 (cf. the figure of the boy with one in Thomas Nast's cartoon "The Workingman's Mite," *Harper's Weekly*, 20 May 1871).

25. "British Workman and Pictures," 28 Oct. 1865, 166 ("Saint Monday" refers to the day taken off from work after imbibing too freely on Sunday); and Tenniel, cartoon, 15 Dec. 1866.

26. Brian Harrison, "Pubs," in H. F. Dyos and Michael Wolff, *The Victorian City*, 2 vols. (London: Routledge & Kegan Paul, 1973), 1:179–80.

27. William Makepeace Thackeray, "Half-a-Crown's Worth of Cheap Knowledge," *Fraser's Magazine*, Mar. 1838, 274–90; Leech, cartoon, *Punch*, July–Dec. 1849; "Potter's Last Push," *Punch*, 4 May 1861, 186; and Tenniel, cartoons, 15 Mar. 1879 and 13 Apr. 1889. For bills introduced in 1787, 1799, and 1820 to prohibit Sunday papers, see John Wigley, *The Rise and Fall of the Victorian Sunday* (Manchester, UK: Manchester Univ. Press, 1980) 27, 29.

28. For the campaign of the illustrated press against republicanism in these years, see Frankie Morris, "The Illustrated Press and the Republican Crisis of 1871–72," *Victorian Periodicals Review* 25 (1992): 114–26.

29. "The Model Agitator," Jan.–June, 1848, 130; "Memento to Misleaders," 15 Dec. 1866, 242; and "The Demagogue's Ditty," 4 May 1867, 178, *Punch*.

30. Tenniel, cartoon, 8 Apr. 1871; "When * * * * * Fall Out," *Punch*, 16 Dec. 1871, 258; Tenniel, cartoons, 30 Dec. 1871 and 9 Mar. 1872; and "Peter Quince His Ballad of Bottom's Dream," *Punch*, 9 Mar. 1872, 102.

31. Dickens, "The Ruffian," in *All the Year Round*, 10 Oct. 1868. Gareth Stedman Jones, *Outcast London*, 12, cites the speculation of the 1855 *Quarterly Review* that "very many workers" had, "besides their acknowledged calling, another in the background in direct violation of the eighth commandment."

32. Gareth Stedman Jones, *Outcast London*, 127; Dickens, *Oliver Twist* (1838), chap. 8; and Henry Mayhew, *London Street Folk* (London: Charles Griffith, n.d.), 3–5.

33. Dickens, *Bleak House*, chap 22.

34. Such designations as "the real working man," the real British workman," and "the real unemployed" occur frequently. In *Punch* see Leech, cartoon, 5 Nov. 1859 (entitled "The Strike, a Subject for the Consideration of the Real Working Man"); "Representation of the Smith," 16 Apr. 1859, 159; "British Workman and His Pictures," 28 Oct. 1865, 166; and Tenniel, cartoon, 29 Oct. 1887. In *Fun* see "Another Working Man's Views on Reform," 25 June 1864, 143; "Town Talk," 9 July 1864, 166; "Something Like a Trades' Union," 14 Mar. 1868, 12; and Gordon Thomson, cartoon, 7 Nov. 1877. See also the *Times*, 27 Oct. 1887, on a demonstration organized "in the name of the unemployed." On the Hyde Park Riots see Tenniel, cartoon, 4 Aug. 1866, and accompanying text, "The Wright and the Rough," 50; and [W. J. Weigand?], cartoon, and "Town Talk," 207, *Fun*, 4 Aug. 1866.

35. Tenniel, cartoons, 12 Oct. 1867 and 8 Apr. 1871; *Times*, 18 Apr. 1871; "International Democrats," *Graphic*, 29 Apr. 1871, 390 (E. Buckman's accompanying cut, "A Republican Procession in London—Sunday Morning," 388, shows no roughs); Tenniel, cartoon, 6 May 1871; and "The London Commune," *Punch*, 10 June 1871, 241. On the purported demise of English republicanism the paper crowed, "Cobblers have not assumed the Crown, / Nor roughs smashed *all* the rails" ("Peter Quince His Ballad," 102).

36. Tenniel, cartoons, 14 Dec. 1872 and 29 Oct. 1887.

37. Engels, quoted in Gareth Stedman Jones, *Outcast London*, 344; and *Times*, 18 Oct. 1887 (see also 22 Feb. 1886, 19 and 27 Oct. 1887, and 14 Nov., 1887).

38. Tenniel, "The Christmas Number of Punch and Almanack for 1895."

39. "Representation of the Smith," 16 Apr. 1859, 159; Walter Houghton, *The Victorian Frame of Mind, 1830–1870* (New Haven, Conn.: Yale Univ. Press, 1957), 54–58 (cf. on the fear of revolution); and for panics of the century, David Goodway, *London Chartism, 1838–1848* (Cambridge: Cambridge Univ. Press, 1982), 72, 87, 278; Royden Harrison, "The 10th April of Spencer Walpole: The Problem of Revolution in Relation to Reform, 1865–1867," *International Review of Social History* 7 (1962): 351–99; Gareth Stedman Jones, *Outcast London*, 291–97; Morris, "Illustrated Press," 114–26; *Times*, 10 Apr. 1851 and 25 Mar. 1859; Vizetelly, *Seventy Years*, 1:57–58; and Webb, *History of Trade Unionism*, 387.

40. J. Kay (later Sir James Kay-Shuttleworth), *The Moral and Physical Condition of the Working Class in Manchester in 1832*, quoted in Brian Simon, *The Two Nations and the Educational Structure, 1780–1870* (London: Lawrence & Wishart, 1974), 166; Gaskell, *Mary Barton*, chap. 15; and George Gissing, *Demos: A Story of English Socialism* (1886), chap. 34. Cf. Chris Baldick, *In Frankenstein's Shadow: Myth, Monstrosity, and Nineteenth-Century Writing* (Oxford: Clarendon Press, 1987), 84–91.

41. Douglas Jerrold, "The Charter.—The House of Commons 'Hushed and Still,'" Jan.–June 1842, 210; "British Workman and Pictures," 28 Oct. 1865, 166; and Tenniel, cartoon, 8 Sept. 1866, *Punch*. By contrast see Matt Morgan, cartoon, *Tomahawk*, 7 Dec. 1867.

42. "Ladies' Labour and the Poor," 8 Sept. 1866, 108; "Revival of the Mendicant Trade," July–Dec. 1849, 227; Leech, "The Agricultural Distress Dodge," small cut, Jan.–June 1851, 206; and du Maurier, "An Incomplete Education," small cut, 1873, *Punch*.

43. Simon, *Educational Structure*, 126–27, 139–40, 154, 168–69, 355–57; Gaskell, *Mary Barton*, chap. 15; and John Ruskin, *Unto This Last: Four Essays on the First Principles of Political Economy* (1860), essay 4, "Ad Valorem."

44. Simon, *Educational Structure*, 169, 355–57, on those who believed widespread education would support the status quo; and Tenniel, cartoons, 26 Mar. 1870 and 19 Nov. 1887.

45. Tenniel, cartoon, 10 Sept. 1859.

46. Tenniel, cartoons, 27 Apr. 1872, 30 May 1874, and 3 Oct. 1874, and "At Break of Day," illustration to S. C. Hall, *An Old Story: A Temperance Tale in Verse* (London: Virtue, 1874).

47. Tenniel, "The Old Drunkard," illustration to Hall, *Trial of Sir Jasper*; Robert Cruikshank and George Cruikshank, "Tom and Jerry Taking Blue Ruin after the Spell Is Broke Up," illustration to Pierce Egan, *Life in London* (1821); George Cruikshank, "The Gin Shop," etching from *Scraps and Sketches* (London: Published by the artist, 1829); Leech, cartoon, 14 Apr. 1860; and John Henry Henshall, *The Public Bar* (c. 1882), painting, reproduced in Christopher Wood, *The Dictionary of Victorian Painters*, 2nd ed. (Woodbridge, UK: Antique Collectors' Club, 1978), 620.

48. Vizetelly, *Seventy Years*, 122–23, describes a second and lower counter in one gin palace to accommodate children and juvenile thieves. For child drink-fetchers in art see n. 47 above and Kenny Meadows, "The Dram Drinker," *ILN*, 1848; T. B. Smithies, "A London Ginshop," *Working Man's Friend* (1852); Percy Cruikshank, "Sunday Evening at the Red Cross Gin Shop, Barbican," 1854; and Charles Green, "Sunday Afternoon in a Gin Palace," *Graphic*, 8 Feb. 1879. In literature see Dickens, *Nicholas Nickleby* (1838–39), chap. 14; Kingsley, *Alton Locke*, chap. 8; and George Gissing, *The Nether World* (1889), chap. 1.

49. Leech, cartoons, 11 Jan. 1845 and 14 Apr. 1860; and Tenniel, cartoon, 27 Nov. 1880 (see also cartoon, 13 Apr. 1889). Despite the prolonged condemnation of children in bars, during his stay in the East End in 1902 Jack London observed in *The People of the Abyss* (1963), chap. 26, "Children are to be found in it [the public house] as well, waiting till their fathers and mothers are ready to go home, sipping from the glasses of their elders."

50. On Sunday openings as an alternative to drink or to revolutionary activities, see Norris Pope, *Dickens and Charity* (New York: Columbia Univ. Press, 1978), 57; Peter Bailey, *Leisure and Class in Victorian England* (London: Routledge & Kegan Paul, 1978), 36; Wigley, *Victorian Sunday*, 53, 69, 180; Taylor, "Essence," 17 May 1879, 219; "Exhibitions of Mechanics' Institutes," *Penny Magazine*, 20 Mar. 1841, 108; and Elizabeth Malcolm, *Ireland Sober, Ireland Free: Drink and Temperance in Nineteenth-Century Ireland* (Syracuse, N.Y.: Syracuse Univ. Press, 1986), 179, 326. London commented wryly in 1902 (*People of the Abyss*, chap. 26), "I have gone through an exhibition of Japanese art, got up for the poor of Whitechapel with the idea of elevating them, of begetting in them yearnings for the Beautiful and True and Good."

51. Dickens, "Sunday under Three Heads—III. As It Might Be Made" (1836), in *The Uncommercial Traveller and Reprinted Pieces;* Kingsley, "The Worker in the National Gallery—The National Gallery—No. 1," in *Politics for the People* (1848); Winton Tolles, *Tom Taylor and Victorian Drama* (New York: Columbia Univ. Press, 1940), 259; Walter Besant, *All Sorts and Conditions of Men* (London: Chatto & Windus, 1882), 18; and George Potter, "To the Editor of the Times," *Times*, 22 July 1870.

52. Denying the capability of the poor to respond to art were Gissing, *Demos*, chap. 21; and David Anderson, "Art and the Common People," *Magazine of Art* 11 (1888), 103–4. On the function of art see James McNeill Whistler, lecture, "The Ten O'Clock," 20 Feb. 1885; and Neil Harris, *The Artist in American Society: The Formative Years, 1790–1860* (New York: George Braziller, 1966), 141.

53. Jerrold, "Cartoon No. I. Substance and Shadow," *Punch*, July 1843, 23; Brooks diary for 31 Aug. 1873 in which he grumbled that Hall had written "some rubbish which he has got a lot of the best artists to illustrate gratis"; Cope, *Versatile Victorian*, 6–7, 126, on Thompson; Tenniel, cartoons, 17 Apr. 1869, 17 May 1879, "Punch's Almanack for 1881" and "Punch's Almanack for 1885; Keene, "Culture for the Working Classes," small cut, 25 Aug. 1877, 75; and texts: "Policeman 'A' on Popular Art," 24 May 1879, 234, and "A Kyrley Tale," 19 Feb. 1881, 84, *Punch*.

54. Leech, "The Great Moral Lesson at Madame Tussaud's," small cut, Jan.–June 1846, 210, and cartoons, "The Rivals," July–Dec. 1846, "Specimens from Mr. Punch's Industrial Exhibition of 1850," Jan.–June 1850, and "Lord Palmerston's Prize (Agricultural) Baby," small cut, Jan.–June 1854, *Punch* (see also Taine, *Notes on England*, 209); Boucher, cartoon, *Judy*, 2 Oct. 1872; "Between His Best Friend and His Worst Foe," cartoon, *Judy*, 1886 (in the same year the workingman faced a similar choice in Thomas Nast's "Between Two Fires," cartoon, *Harper's Weekly*, 22 May 1886); and Proctor, "Blunderbore the Dog-in-the-Manger Giant, who wouldn't work himself nor let the work be done by anybody else," cartoon, *Funny Folks*, 3 Nov. 1877.

55. Alvar Ellegård, "The Readership of the Periodical Press in Mid-Victorian Britain," *Göteborgs Universitets Årsskrift* 63 (1957): 37; and in *Fun*, "Another Working Man's Views on Reform," 25 June 1864, 143; "Mrs. Brown Attends the Reform Meeting," 4 Aug. 1866, 210; "Town Talk," 13 July 1867, 186; "How Does It Strike You?" cartoon, 22 Dec. 1866; and "Something Like a Trades' Union," 14 Mar. 1868, 12. Sullivan's *Fun* series, starting in 1875, was put out in book form in 1878 (see chap. 17 n. 7). On its character see Morris, *John Tenniel, Cartoonist*, 283 n. 156; and Kunzle, *History of Comic Strip*, 324–28. See also Thomson, cartoon, *Fun*, 7 Nov. 1877.

56. Webb, *History of Trade Unionism*, esp. chap. 5; and Pelling, *British Trade Unionism*, 55, 61.

57. On conditions for the lower classes in the Edwardian period see London, *People of the Abyss;* and Robert Tressell, *The Ragged Trousered Philanthropists* (1914).

21. Paddy and Hibernia

1. L. Perry Curtis Jr., *Apes and Angels: The Irishman in Victorian Caricature* (Washington, D.C.: Smithsonian Institution Press, 1971, and rev. ed., 1997). Citations are to the rev. ed. Taking issue with Curtis's thesis are Sheridan Gilley, "English Attitudes to the Irish in England, 1780–1900," in *Immigrants and Minorities in British Society*, ed. Colin Holmes (London: George Allen & Unwin, 1978), 85–102; and, to a lesser extent, R. F. Foster, "Paddy and Mr. Punch," *Journal of Newspaper and Periodical History* 7 (1991): 45–46.

2. Carlyle and Froude, quoted in Patrick O'Farrell, *England and Ireland since 1800* (London: Oxford Press, 1975), 69, 80.

3. Prints in the British Museum, reel 20, BMC 15721 (2 Apr. 1829); BMC 15996 (1830); and

BMC 16493; Thomas Rowlandson, watercolor, *A Tub Thumper*, 1811, showing a simian pipe-smoking Irish Biddy, in *The Drawings of Thomas Rowlandson in the Paul Mellon Collection*, comp. John Baskett and Dudley Snelgrove (New York: Brandywine Press, 1978), catalog no. 186; "Studies from Lavater," *Gallery of Comicalities—Part I*, a collection of caricatures from *Bell's Life in London* (n.d.), 2; "The Irish Tithe Bill," political cut, *Figaro in London*, 23 Aug. 1834, 133; and C. J. Grant, "Old Grill among the Paddies," in *The Political Drama* (London: G. Drake, 1834–35), no. 61.

4. There were two types of stage Irishmen: the eighteenth-century gentleman of fortune and the servant (the precursor of Paddy). On the evolution of the stage Irishman see J. O. Bartley, *Teague, Shenkin and Sawney* (Cork, Ireland: Cork Univ. Press, 1954); Max Caulfield, *The Irish Mystique* (Englewood Cliffs, N.J.: Prentice-Hall, 1973); G. C. Duggan, *The Stage Irishman* (New York: Benjamin Blom, 1969); and W. J. Lawrence, "Irish Types in Old-Time English Drama," *Anglia* 35 (1912): 347–56. Nineteenth-century actors achieving fame as stage Irishmen include Charles Conner, Jack Johnstone, Tom Hudson, Tyrone Power, and Sam Collins. See Maurice Bourgeois, *John Millington Synge and the Irish Theatre* (London: Constable, 1913), 109–10, for the description given; and Leech, "Improvement in Irish Affairs," small cut, *Punch*, 5 Aug. 1854, 42.

5. *London Singer's Magazine* (London: John Duncombe, 1838–39), copy at the British Library. See, for example, nos. 24 and 52.

6. "The Election of Ballinafad," 24 July 1841, 21; "Father O'Flynn and His Congregation," 25 Sept. 1841, 125; and "The Broth of a Boy," 18 Dec. 1841, 269, *Punch*. See, too, "The O'Connell Papers," 13 Nov. 1841, 208; and *Punch* cartoons, 8 July 1843, 26 Aug 1843, and 4 Nov. 1843. For a more conciliatory tone see "Punch's Labours of Hercules," 8 July 1843, 18–19; and cartoon, 15 June 1844.

7. Leech, "Fancy Portrait of Young Ireland," illustration to Thackeray, "Young Ireland," *Punch*, 14 June 1845, 262–63.

8. Thackeray, "Radical Snobs," 8 Aug. 1846, 59, and "Irish Snobs," 15 Aug. 1846, 63; and Leech, cartoons, 22 Aug. 1846, 12 Dec. 1846, 2 Jan. 1847, 25 Dec. 1848, 8 July 1848, 16 Sept. 1848, 8 Apr. 1848, and 13 May 1848; and texts, "Our Irish Prize Bull," 5 Feb. 1848, 51; "The Battle of Limerick," 6 May 1848, 195; and "The Limerick Tragedy," 13 May 1848, 198, *Punch*. Young Ireland appears as a small monkey-like manikin clinging to the leg of Smith O'Brien, one of the movement's leaders, in "The Convalescent from Limerick," cartoon, *Puppet Show*, 1848, 69.

9. "Parliamentary Intelligence," *Times*, 8 Feb. 1849; and Leech, cartoon, 24 Feb. 1849.

10. W. Willson Disher, *Music Hall Parade* (New York: Charles Scribner's Sons, 1938), 12–13; and Charles Douglas Stuart and A. J. Park, *The Variety Stage: A History of the Music Halls from the Earliest Period to the Present Time* (London: T. Fisher Unwin, 1895), 99, on Sam Collins and Evans's; and Burnand, *Records and Reminiscences*, 1:244–46, and Vizetelly, *Through Seventy Years*, 2:45–46, on the *Punch* staff and Evans's.

11. "Monkeyana," 18 May 1861, 206; "The Gorilla's Dilemma," 18 Oct. 1862, 164; Leech, cartoon, 25 May 1861; "Preface," vol. 40, 29 June 1861, iii–iv; "A Neat Kind of Lord," 15 June 1861, 245; and "The New Photographic Looking-Glass," small cut, 23 Nov. 1861, 204, *Punch*.

12. Joseph M. Hernon Jr., *Celts, Catholics and Copperheads: Ireland Views the American Civil War* (London: T. Fisher Unwin, 1968), chap. 3, 48, 49; *Times*, 7 Dec. 1861; and Leech, "Mr. GO'Rilla," illustration to "A Great Time for Ireland!" *Punch*, 14 Dec. 1861, 244.

13. "The Irish Yahoos," *Punch*, 21 Dec. 1861, 245; and cartoon, *Fun*, 11 Jan. 1862, 166. See, too, *Fun*'s article of the previous week, "Another Irish Victory," 4 Jan. 1862, 159.

14. Hernon, *Celts, Catholics and Copperheads*, 51, "Notes" in *Times* introduction to *Punch*, vol. 42, Jan.–June 1862; Silver diary, 26 Feb. 1862; and Tenniel, cartoon, 8 Mar. 1862.

15. "The Loyal Irishman in America," 30 Aug. 1862, 91; "Soldiers to Spare for the Union," 11 Apr. 1863, 156; "Food for Confederate Powder," 29 Oct. 1864, 184; and Tenniel, cartoon, 20 Aug. 1864.

16. Tenniel, cartoons, 3 Mar. 1866 and 11 June 1870, for Fenian Paddy's dress, and 30 Sept. 1865, 16 Dec. 1865, and 8 Dec. 1866, for child-size Fenian Paddy, and 21 Oct. 1865, 8 Dec. 1866, and 8 June 1867; and Silver diary, 29 May 1867, on the creation of the 8 June 1867 cartoon.

17. Proctor, cartoon, *Judy*, 9 Oct. 1867, for another comment on the rescue at Manchester. Cf. Tenniel, cartoon, 28 Dec. 1867, with Thomas Nast, "The Usual Irish Way of Doing Things," cartoon, *Harper's Weekly*, 2 Sept. 1871, 824.

18. Tenniel, cartoons, 23 Oct. 1869, 11 June 1870, and 19 Mar. 1870. In the last the legend identifies Caliban as "Rory of the Hills," the name adopted by a secret society in Ireland.

19. For Tenniel's early comments on home rule see cartoons, 28 Aug. 1875 and 31 May 1879. *Punch*'s continued opposition to home rule is shown in Tenniel, cartoons, 9 Jan. 1886, 24 Apr. 1886,

and 4 July 1991. For the views of various journals as the land war escalated see "Justice to Ireland," cartoon, *Punch and Judy,* 16 Oct. 1869; Boucher, cartoon, *Judy,* 26 Dec. 1869; Morgan, cartoons, *Tomahawk,* 7 Aug. 1869 and 15 Jan. 1870; and Tenniel, cartoons, 4 Dec. 1869 and 12 Mar. 1870.

20. Tenniel, cartoons, 17 Oct. 1874, 12 Mar. 1870, 9 Apr. 1870, 31 Aug. 1872, 5 Feb. 1881, 18 June 1881, and 31 Dec. 1881. On the increase in agrarian crime see Joseph Lee, "The Land War," in *Milestones in Irish History,* ed. Liam de Paor (Cork: Mercier Press, 1986), 111.

21. On the Phoenix Park murders the *Times,* 8 May 1882, commented, "Mr. Gladstone's prospect of keeping the peace in Ireland by the aid of Mr. Parnell has endured just four days with what results we see," quoted in J. L. Hammond, *Gladstone and the Irish Nation* (Cork, Ireland: Mercier Press, 1964), 285. See Tenniel, cartoon, 20 May 1882; and "The Chief Mourner," cartoon, *Pat,* 13 May 1882.

22. British Museum prints: BMC 5653, "Suiters [*sic*] to Hibernia on her having a Free Trade" (1780); BMC 14163, George Cruikshank, "The Bloodhound" (1821); and BMC 16754, "Natural History of Two Species of Irish Vampire" (1831); "Tithes for Irish Parsons," cartoon, *Figaro in London,* 6 Oct. 1832; Tenniel, cartoons, 31 Aug. 1861, 3 Mar. 1866, 8 Dec. 1866, 19 Mar. 1870, and 29 Oct. 1881; Thomson, cartoon, *Fun,* 24 Mar. 1886; Proctor, cartoon, *Judy,* 1 Apr. 1868; J. R. [John D. Reigh?], "Irish America Offers Her 'Resources,'" cartoon, *United Ireland,* 12 Nov. 1881, in which the figure of Hibernia is a reversed copy of Tenniel's 25 Nov. 1871 cartoon, the only change being that the goddess's arm has been lowered, and "The New Recruit," 3 Feb. 1883, which uses parts from other Tenniel drawings such as the 7 Jan. 1871 cartoon. In the Irish journal *Pat,* "Spex" devised his own Erin, a pretty girl quite unlike Tenniel's.

23. The *Irish Quarterly Review,* 1853, 182, had complained about Thackeray's "Irish caricatures." In 1862 the *New York Herald* alluded to *Punch*'s "shabby wit, low sarcasm, and serious caricatures [of the Irish]" ("Yahoos of the Yankee Press," *Punch,* 18 Jan. 1862, 21); and in its Oct. 1871 announcement of its new series (p. 423) the Dublin journal *Zozimus* stated that the paper was started "to amend the deliberate and scornful hostility to the Irish in English comic papers." Charles L. Graves, *Mr. Punch's History of Modern England,* 4 vols. (London: Waverly, n.d.), 3:28–29, quotes the following from *Punch*'s response (undated) to objections to Tenniel's cartoons: "The ogreish character is the embodiment of the spirit of Lawlessness, of Anarchy, and of that Communism which, by its recent No Rent manifesto, has now drawn upon itself the just condemnation of such men as the Archbishop of Dublin and Cashel. Houghing and mutilating dumb animals, maiming men and women, and shooting defenceless victims, are ugly crimes, and the embodiment of them in a single figure cannot be made too hideous or too repulsive. On the other hand, *Punch* has constantly and persistently kept before the public his ideal classic figure of Hibernia, graceful, gentle, tender, loving but 'distressful,' as being more or less in fear of that Ogre, her evil genius, from whose bondage may she soon be free." For English journals see "Occasional Notes," *Pall Mall Gazette,* 16 June 1881; "Art Caricature in Germany," *Graphic,* 4 Feb. 1882, 118; and E. L. Godkin, "An American View of Ireland," *Nineteenth Century* (July–Dec. 1882), 175.

24. "Justice to Punch and Ireland!" *Punch,* 23 Sept. 1882, 142–43. Tenniel's cartoon of 29 Oct. 1881 shows Paddy as "Anarchy."

25. Tenniel, cartoons, 7 Jan. 1882, 25 Mar. 1882, 27 Dec. 1884, 3 Jan. 1891, and "Punch's Almanack for 1890."

26. Charles Lever, *Harry Lorrequer* (1837), chap. 6; Bartley, *Teague, Shenkin and Sawney,* 100–101; Edward D. Snyder, "The Wild Irish, etc.," *Modern Philology* 17 (1920): 169; Tenniel, cartoons, 30 June 1860, 3 Apr. 1869, 4 Dec. 1869, 8 June 1872, 15 June 1861, and 21 Oct. 1865; and Leech, cartoons, 24 Feb. 1849, and 20 Sept. 1851.

27. Keene, "Waiting for the Landlord!" 27 July 1787, 27; "Had Him There!" 19 July 1879, 14; "One of the Family," 11 Oct. 1879, 166; "'In Extremis,'" 29 Nov. 1879, 243; "'De Profundis,'" 17 Jan. 1880, 15, and so on, social cuts, *Punch.*

28. Thomas Nast, "The Day We Celebrate," 6 Apr. 1867, and "All the Difference in the World," 26 Sept. 1868, cartoons, *Harper's Weekly;* Frederick Burr Opper, "The King of A-Shantee," social cut, *Puck,* 15 Feb. 1882; and Joseph Keppler, "Welcome to All," 28 Apr. 1880, and "Uncle Sam's Lodging-House," 7 June 1882, cartoons, *Puck.*

29. Silver diary, 2 Mar. 1869, on Tenniel's cartoon, 13 Mar. 1869; Tenniel, cartoon, 27 May 1876 (the title, "The [Home-] 'Ruler of the Spirits!'" is a play on the subtitle of Weber's opera *Euryanthe* and on "home rule"); and "Persons in Unreal Life—1. 'The Stage Irish,'" *Jarvey,* 20 July 1889, 456. A twentieth-century survival was "Old Mother Riley," a stage character devised by Arthur Lucan and played by him on English stage and television until his death in 1954.

30. John Fergus O'Hea, "Benevolent Neutrality," 26 Oct. 1870, 259; and "Jumped through It!" 7 Dec. 1870, 319, cartoons, *Zozimus*; WM, "Aboriginal Criticisms," social cut, *Zozimus*, 29 June 1870, 84; and "Ball Practice," cartoon, *Pat*, 1 Oct. 1881.

31. Gilley, "Attitudes to the Irish," 95. See also O'Farrell, *England and Ireland*, 28, 33, 40; and Lawrence J. McCaffrey, *The Irish Question: Two Centuries of Conflict*, 2nd ed. (Lexington: Univ. Press of Kentucky, 1995), 92. For support of the union see Tenniel, cartoons, 31 Aug. 1861, 18 Apr. 1868, 2 May 1868, 13 June 1874, 11 Apr. 1885, 31 Aug. 1889, 21 Aug. 1897, and 4 Apr. 1900, and for relief and subsidies for Ireland, 17 Jan. 1880, 24 Dec. 1881, 3 June 1882, and 30 Aug. 1890.

32. Sir Robert Peel the younger, quoted in Hernon, *Celts, Catholics, and Copperheads*, 51; G. O. Trevelyan, quoted in O'Farrell, *England and Ireland*, 157; and "The Queen's Speech," *Punch*, 4 Feb. 1882, 57.

33. O'Farrell, *England and Ireland*, 39, 158.

34. The pseudo-Irish voice was adopted in about half of *Punch's* Irish pieces of the 1860s. See Hernon, *Celts, Catholics and Copperheads*, 50–51; Alexander Martin Sullivan, *New Ireland: Political Sketches and Personal Reminiscences of Irish Public Life* (New York: P. J. Kenedy, Excelsior, 1884), 9; and O'Farrell, *England and Ireland*, 52, 157–58, on blame ascribed to outsiders; and Tenniel, cartoons, 28 Aug. 1875, 4 Sept. 1880, 20 Nov. 1880, and 3 Mar. 1883.

35. "Loyal Irishman in America," 91; "The Irish Republic," 7 Oct. 1865, 142; and "The Missing Link Found," 4 Aug. 1866, 55; Tenniel, cartoon, 4 Jan. 1868; Proctor, cartoons *Judy*, 23 Oct. 1867 and 1 Apr. 1868; and stressing the concept of the two Irelands, Tenniel, cartoons, 13 Aug. 1881, 3 Mar. 1866, 19 Mar. 1870, and 29 Oct. 1871.

36. "Paddy Stops the Way," *Punch*, 14 Apr. 1877, 165; and Joseph Chamberlain, quoted in Nicholas Mansergh, *The Irish Question, 1840–1921* (Toronto: Univ. of Toronto Press, 1965), 156. *Punch* deplored the recourse to violence by the protestant Irish as well (see "How to Tame Ireland," 22 Apr. 1848, 166; "The Irish Orange Flower," 20 Oct. 1849, 161; and "Gavazzi Kilt at Galway," 16 Apr. 1859, 159).

37. See Dorothy Thompson, "Ireland and the Irish in English Radicalism before 1850," in *The Chartist Experience: Studies in Working-Class Radicalism and Culture, 1830–60*, ed. James Epstein and Dorothy Thompson (London: Macmillan, 1982), 120–51; John W. Boyle, *The Irish Labor Movement in the Nineteenth Century* (Washington, D.C.: Catholic Univ. of America Press, 1988), 43; Gilley, "Attitudes to the Irish," 103; and *Times*, 10 and 11 Apr. 1848 (quoted in Goodway, *London Chartism*, 68; and Royden Harrison, "10th April," 351). On the possibility of a coalition between the Irish and English working classes see Royden Harrison, *Before the Socialists: Studies in Labour and Politics, 1861–1881* (London: Routledge & Kegan Paul, 1965), 221, and "10th April," 356; and Gareth Stedman Jones, *Outcast London*, 241–42.

38. "King Mob," *Punch*, 21 Dec. 1867, 257.

39. Percival Leigh, "The Missing Link," 18 Oct. 1862, 165; "Irish Yahoos," 21 Dec. 1861, 245; and "Yahoos of Yankee Press," 18 Jan. 1862, 21, *Punch*. The windows mentioned were those at *Punch's* publishing office at 85 Fleet Street, which wrapped around the curved corner from Fleet Street to St. Bride's Avenue.

40. "A Good Riddance," 6 June 1863, 238; and "Specimen of an Irish Howl," 26 Sept. 1863, 134, *Punch*. Only Moore seems to have had a purely Irish background.

41. Thackeray, "Young Ireland," 262; "Half a Word about a Bit of Ireland," 21 July 1849, 26; "An Elegant Extract," 16 Oct. 1852, 165 (the captions for Leech's accompanying illustrations were accidentally reversed); "What the Celt Does, and What the Saxon Does," 30 Oct. 1852, 194; "The Fenian Drill-Book," 7 Oct. 1865, 136; and "Fenian Figures and Fenian Facts," 11 Nov. 1865, 191, *Punch*. For the same strategy see "Another Irish Victory," *Fun*, 4 Jan. 1862, 159.

42. O'Farrell, *England and Ireland*, 125; Roger Swift and Sheridan Gilley, introduction to *The Irish in the Victorian City* (London: Croom Helm, 1985), 5; Sheridan Gilley, "The Irish," *History Today* 35 (June 1985): 20; and Henry Mayhew, *London Labour and the London Poor*, 4 vols. (London: Griffin, Bohn, 1861), 1:4. Mayhew's use of the word "race" is fairly unscientific, as are other references to "race" in this chapter. For example, he writes of costermongers (4:6), "They appear to be a distinct race—perhaps originally of Irish extraction."

43. "Sweets from Ireland," 15 May 1852, 202; "Yahoos of Yankee Press," 18 Jan. 1862, 21; "The Yahoo in Yankee Land," 13 Dec. 1862, 245; "What the Celt Does," 30 Oct 1852, 194; "Missing Link," 18 Oct. 1862, 165; and "Men and Monkeys," 10 Jan. 1863, 19, *Punch*.

44. Daria Hambourg, *Richard Doyle: His Life and Work* (London: Art & Technics, 1948), 10, 15, 21; and, on Newman, Spielmann, *History of "Punch,"* 413–17.

45. Thomas Moore, preface to the 1841 edition of *Lalla Rookh*; *DNB*, s.v. "Moore, Thomas

(1779–1852)"; and Brooks, "Essence," 18 May 1861, 207, in which he comments, "When THOMAS, in *Lalla Rookh*, sang of the wrongs of Iran, he meant Erin," and "Al Hassan with his 'bloody, bold, and countless crowd,' was a delicate figurement of JOHN BULL."

46. Du Maurier, quoted in *Young George du Maurier*, 178; and *Trilby* (1894), part 1.

47. Tenniel, cartoons, 31 Dec. 1881, 20 May 1882, 3 Mar. 1883, 10 Oct. 1885, 18 Aug. 1888, and 4 July 1891. For a hideous revealed face see Tenniel's cartoon, "Crowning the O'Caliban," 22 Dec. 1883.

48. See Giovanni Costigan, *A History of Modern Ireland* (New York: Pegasus, 1970), 211.

22. The Dis-United States

1. *New York Evening Post,* 26 Feb. 1914; and "The Passing of Sir John Tenniel . . . Recent Deaths," *Boston Evening Transcript,* 26 Feb. 1914. See also "Noted Cartoonist Dies," *Birmingham Ledger,* 26 Feb. 1914; "Sir John Tenniel. British Artist Dead," *Charlotte (N.C.) Daily Observer,* 27 Feb. 1914; and unidentified New York City newspaper, 28 Feb. 1914, in "Tenniel Scrapbooks," New York Public Library.

2. Oscar Maurer, "'Punch' on Slavery and Civil War in America, 1841–1865," *Victorian Studies* 1 (Sept. 1957).

3. Douglas A. Lorimer, *Colour, Class and the Victorians* (Leicester, UK: Holmes & Meier, 1978), 90, on the "patient suffering slave"; and chap. 17 of this book, on amazons.

4. See Francis Hodge, *Yankee Theatre: The Image of America on the Stage, 1825–1850* (Austin: Univ. of Texas Press, 1964); and Winifred Morgan, *An American Icon: Brother Jonathan and American Identity* (Newark: Univ. of Delaware Press, 1988).

5. Hodge, *Yankee Theatre,* 69.

6. Tenniel, cartoon, 21 June 1862. For early *Punch* portrayals of Jonathan see "A Yankee Notion," July–Dec. 1844, 56; "The Eyes of America," July–Dec. 1842, 69; Richard Doyle, cartoon, 4 Dec. 1847; and for the scourge as an attribute, see illustration to "America in Crystal," 24 May 1851, 209; Tenniel, cartoon, 27 Sept. 1856, and "Monkey Uncommon Up, Massa!" small cut, 1 Dec. 1860, 220, *Punch.*

7. Robert C. Toll, *Blacking Up: The Minstrel Show in Nineteenth-Century America* (New York: Oxford Univ. Press, 1974); Hodge, *Yankee Theatre,* 68, for Mathews's parody of a black actor; R. Farquharson Sharp, "Travesties of Shakespeare's Plays," *Library,* 1 June 1920, 9–10, 12, for *Othello* and *Hamlet* travesties with comic black dialect; Toll, *Blacking Up,* 56, for a "new serio-comico-tragicomelodramatical" Negro version of *Macbeth,* one of the farces or parodies commonly terminating minstrel shows of the 1850s; and Tenniel, cartoons, 9 Nov. 1861, 24 Jan. 1863, and 15 Aug. 1863.

8. Lorimer, *Colour, Class and Victorians,* 90; Tenniel, cartoons, 19 Jan. 1861, 5 Apr. 1862, 8 Aug. 1863, and 6 May 1865, for his suffering slave, and 4 Mar. 1876, for his most conventional depiction of the type. Tenniel first portrayed the "cruel, lustful savage" for the Zulu War in 1879. See Daniel P. Mannix, *Black Cargoes: A History of the Atlantic Slave Trade, 1518–1865* (New York: Viking Press, 1962), 177, 176, on the seal and the court case of 1772; and Lorimer, *Colour, Class and Victorians,* 70, on the popularity of the seal's design.

9. Tenniel, "Monkey Uncommon Up, Massa!" 220; "What the Tyrants of the Old World Think of Secession," cartoon, *Harper's Weekly,* 1 Dec. 1860, 768; and "The Beginning of Slavery's End," *Punch,* 8 Dec. 1860, 221.

10. Tenniel, cartoons, 19 Jan. 1861, 27 Sept. 1856, and 18 May 1861.

11. See J. G. Randall and David Donald, *The Civil War and Reconstruction,* 2nd ed. (Boston: Little, Brown, 1969), 165; and "The Orleans Boy," *Punch,* 2 Nov. 1861, 182.

12. "Ode to the North and South," *Punch,* 25 May 1861, 209; "Before the Morrill Tariff / After the Morrill Tariff," cartoon, *Harper's Weekly,* 20 Apr. 1861, 256; "Paddy before Richmond," *Punch,* 20 Aug. 1864, 74; and Leslie Stephen, *The "Times" on the American War: A Historical Study* (1865; reprint, New York: William Abbatt, 1915), 80.

13. Henry Louis Stephens, "The Idol of England," 22 June 1861; "Open Your Mouth and Shut Your Eyes," 30 Mar. 1861; "Not the Cheese," 8 June 1861; "Design for a Statue of English Justice," 15 June 1861; and "No Go!" 21 Dec. 1861, cartoons, *Vanity Fair* (New York); and "John Bull between Two Stools," 29 June 1861, 416; and "A Mild Shock for Our Virtuous Friend, Mr. John Bull," 3 Aug. 1861, 496, cartoons, *Harper's Weekly.*

14. Tenniel, cartoon, 18 May 1861; cartoon *Fun,* 16 Nov. 1861; Tenniel, cartoons, 2 and 16 Nov. 1861 (see accompanying text, "How We'll Break the Blockade," 196); and J. R. Pole, *Abraham Lincoln and the Working Classes of Britain* (n.p.: Commonwealth American Affairs Unit of the English Speaking Union, 1959), 27–28; and Thomas Boaz, *Guns for Cotton: England Arms the Confederacy*

(Shippensburg, Penn.: Burd Street Press, 1996), 3, on the effects of the war on British workers. Boaz writes that layoffs began almost immediately in 1861.

15. Tenniel, cartoons, 6 July 1861 (the first of two cartoons entitled "Naughty Jonathan") and 17 Aug. 1861 (and the text of the same date, "The Run from Manassas Junction," 66).

16. Silver diary, 27 Nov. 1861; and Tenniel, cartoon, 7 Dec. 1861.

17. Stephens, "Gorilla Britannicus," cartoon, *Vanity Fair* (New York), 8 Feb. 1862; and Tenniel, cartoons, 14, 21, and 28 Dec. 1861, and 4, 11, and 18 Jan. 1862, on the Trent affair; and 6 July 1861, 8 Feb. 1862, 2 May 1863, and 3 Oct. 1863, for other cartoons representing Jonathan as a child.

18. *New York Herald,* quoted in "Yahoos of Yankee Press," 18 Jan. 1862, 21; "How We'll Break the Blockade," *Punch,* 16 Nov. 1861, 196; and for other pieces against the Northern press, "Vengeance and Repudiation," 25 Jan. 1862, 33; "Yahoo in Yankee Land," 13 Dec. 1862, 245; "'Fighting Joe' at Fredericksburg," 6 June 1863, 237; "A Poke at President Lincoln," 22 Aug. 1863, 81; "Specimen of Irish Howl," 134; "The Yankee Hercules," 19 Dec. 1863, 247; and "To the Yankee Braggarts," 21 Jan. 1865, 25, *Punch.*

19. Tenniel, cartoon, 1 Feb. 1862; and accompanying text, "The I. O. U. Indian," 44 (cf. Morgan's cartoon, *Fun,* 12 Sept. 1863, in which Indian Jonathan wears sheets of the *New York Herald* and *New York Times*); and Tenniel, cartoon, 26 July 1862 (possibly influenced by Morgan's cartoon, *Fun,* 5 Apr. 1862). Morgan's cartoon of the same date showed General McClellan in retreat, claiming "Another Great Victory!!!"

20. See Stephen, *"Times" on American War,* 11–12; Arnold Whitridge, "British Liberals and the American Civil War," *History Today* 10 (Oct. 1962): 695; Randall and Donald, *Civil War and Reconstruction,* 499–500; "To Pot and Kettle," 28 Sept. 1861, 126; and, for more *Punch* predictions, "Run from Manassas Junction," 17 Aug. 1861, 66; and "Mr. John Bull to the United States," 7 Sept. 1861, 100. On this, see Stephens, "Columbia at the Stake," cartoon, *Vanity Fair,* 19 Oct. 1861.

21. Tenniel, cartoons, 23 Aug. 1862 (*Fun* on the same day published Morgan's portrayal of Lincoln and Treasury Secretary Chase vainly "Angling for Recruits"), 8 Feb. 1862, 7 June 1862, 5 Nov. 1864, 9 Aug. 1862, and 19 Nov. 1864; and Toll, *Blacking Up,* 120–24. The portrayals of Negro troops in wartime minstrel shows seems an extension of the "awkward squads" of pantomime.

22. "Emigrants and Remigrants," 25 May 1861, 218; "A Word on a Demonstration," 7 Feb. 1863, 51; and "Soldiers to Spare for the Union," 11 Apr. 1863, 156, *Punch;* and "Strange Effect of the Draft," cartoon, *Harper's Weekly,* 30 Aug. 1862, 560.

23. Hernon, *Celts, Catholics and Copperheads,* 11, 19–23; James I. Robertson Jr., *Soldiers Blue and Grey* (Columbia: Univ. of South Carolina Press, 1988); and "Fate of Contrabands," cartoon, *Southern Punch,* 26 Dec. 1863, 8.

24. Cf. casualty figures in Hernon, *Celts, Catholics and Copperheads,* 19, with Randall and Donald, *Civil War and Reconstruction,* 317. See Tenniel, cartoon, 8 Aug. 1863, and Morgan's cartoon of that date in *Fun* showing Paddy as "King Mob upon His Throne," his feet resting upon a frightened black.

25. Brooks, "Essence," 26 July 1862, 32; Tenniel, cartoons, 26 July 1862, 27 Sept. 1862, 9 May 1863, 27 Aug. 1864 (an anonymous *Fun* drawing of this date [p. 283] showed "Yankee Doodle's Three Deliverers"—General Butler, Paddy, and Sambo in retreat from Richmond), and 3 Sept. 1864 (later adopted by M. Woolf in "The Social Juggernaut," cartoon, *Harper's Weekly,* 21 Mar. 1874, 257); and F. Wilfred Lawson, cartoon, *Fun,* 7 Jan. 1865.

26. Cartoons, *Harper's Weekly* from 10 Aug. 1861, 510, to Nov. 1861, 720; and 2 May 1863, 288; "The Simple Rustic, John Bull," drawing, *Vanity Fair,* 16 Aug. 1862, 79; and cartoon, *Mr. Merryman's Monthly,* 2 Jan. 1864. See Winifred Morgan, *American Icon,* 76, for print, "A Kean [sic] Shave between John Bull and Brother Jonathan," c. 1836, in which John Bull resembles Hodge. See also Stephens, "Guarding the Trout Pond," cartoon, *Vanity Fair* (New York), 16 Nov. 1861.

27. "American Liberty.—American Eggs," 23 Oct. 1847, 154; Richard Doyle, "The Shadow of English Liberty in America," small cut, 11 May 1850, 190; Tenniel, "The Virginian Slave: Intended as a Companion to Power's 'Greek Slave,'" small cut, 7 June 1851, 236, *Punch* (suggested by "America in Crystal," 209).

28. "Sambo to the Greek Slave," 16 Sept. 1851, 105; "Serenade to Lincoln," 18 Oct. 1862, 158; "Brutus and Caesar," 15 Aug. 1863, 71; and "Preface," vol. 46, Jan.–June 1864, iii–iv, *Punch.* William Fletcher Thomson Jr., "Pictorial Propaganda and the Civil War," *Wisconsin Magazine of History* 46 (Autumn 1962): 30, notes similar bigotry in Northern cartoons. For comparisons between the Irish and blacks see, in *Punch,* "Ode on the Irish Election," 14 Aug. 1852, 82; "An Offer to the South," 12 July 1862, 18; and Leigh, "Missing Link," 18 Oct. 1862, 165.

29. Tenniel, cartoon, 20 July 1861; "Brutus and Caesar," 71; and cartoon, *Harper's Weekly*, 28 Sept. 1861, 624.

30. "The Gifts of the South," *Punch*, 26 Apr. 1862, 171.

31. "Word on a Demonstration," 7 Feb. 1863, 51; "An Appeal to the North," 9 Nov. 1861, 186, *Punch*; and Percival Leigh, quoted in the Silver diary, 18 Sept. 1862.

32. *New York Tribune*, 10 Nov. 1860, quoted in Robert S. Harper, *Lincoln and the Press* (New York: McGraw-Hill, 1951), 102; Stephen, *"Times" on American War*, 30; Silver diary, 18 Sept. 1862; Tenniel, cartoon, 10 Jan. 1863; and Silver diary, 14 Jan 1863.

33. "Appeal to the North," 186, for *Punch*'s class biases; Sheldon Vanauken, *The Glittering Illusion: English Sympathy for the Southern Confederacy* (Washington, D.C.: Regnery Gateway, 1989), 59–71; *Times*, 30 May 1861, quoted in Stephen, *"Times" on American War*, 33; "Model of the Disunited States," 14 Dec. 1861, 242; "Who Is an American?" 11 Jan. 1862, 12; and "The London New York Herald," 13 June 1863, 247, *Punch*.

34. Vanauken, *Glittering Illusion*, 26–27, on Thackeray's *The Virginian*; "England's Neutrality," *Punch*, 5 Sept. 1863, 97; and Stephens, "Old Marm Britannia and Her Penny Ballads," cartoon, *Vanity Fair* (New York), 25 Oct. 1862, 199.

35. Tenniel, cartoons, 23 Aug. 1862 and 27 Sept. 1862; Morgan, cartoon, 18 July 1863, and "The Death of General Stuart," 2 July 1864, 163, *Fun*.

36. Tenniel, cartoons, 9 Aug. 1862 and 15 Aug. 1863, republished as "One Good Turn Deserves Another," 14 Mar. 1863, 8; and "Brutus and Caesar," 31 Oct. 1863, 136, *Southern Illustrated News*; Herbert Mitgang, "The Art of Lincoln," *American Art Journal* 2 (1970): 8, which reports that the *Southern Illustrated News* also reproduced Tenniel's cartoons, 18 Oct. 1862 and 9 May 1863; and Rufus Rockwell Wilson, *Lincoln in Caricature* (New York: Horizon Press, 1953), pls. 76, 88, 119, 124, 149, 154, and 157, for seven of Tenniel's cartoons, obviously reengraved, probably for other papers.

37. Brooks, "Essence," 11 May 1861, 189; Tenniel, cartoon, 11 May 1861; and for *Punch*'s change of heart, Brooks, "Essence," 18 May 1861, 206; and Tenniel, cartoon, 5 Apr. 1862.

38. These words are attributed to Secretary of State William H. Seward (S. E. Morrison, *The Oxford History of the United States, 1783–1917*, 2 vols. [London: Oxford Univ. Press, 1927], 2:237).

39. Tenniel, cartoon, 18 Oct. 1862; and "Serenade to Lincoln," 18 Oct. 1862, 158. See Vanauken, *Glittering Illusion*, 68, on leader writers in English papers who referred to the proclamation as "Lincoln's Last Card." The South's secretary of state, seeing that the proclamation had forestalled European recognition of the Confederacy, conceded that "spades were trumps" (Randall and Donald, *Civil War and Reconstruction*, 391). See also Morgan, cartoon, *Fun*, 18 July 1863.

40. *Times*, quoted in Stephen, *"Times" on American War*, 80, 44. *Punch* hints at a black insurrection in the line "at white let slip darky" in "Abe's Last Card; or, Rouge-et-Noir," 18 Oct. 1862, 160.

41. "Old Abe in a Fix," *Punch*, 24 Jan. 1863, 34.

42. Tenniel, cartoon, 15 Aug. 1863, and accompanying text, "Brutus and Caesar," p. 71. Cf. Stephens, "The Modern Brutus," cartoon, *Vanity Fair*, 28 July 1860, in which a black Caesar's ghost warns Douglas-Brutus that he is his "evil spirit."

43. Brooks, "Essence," 21 May 1864, 208.

44. "Beginning of Slavery's End," 8 Dec. 1860, 221; "The Star-Spangled Banner," 15 Dec. 1860, 234; and "Ink, Blood, and Tears," 11 May 1861, 192, for *Punch*'s early glorification of the republic; and Tenniel, cartoons, 24 Sept. 1864 and 1 Oct. 1864.

45. Brooks, "Essence," 18 Feb. 1865, 64; and Tenniel, "The Threatening Notice," cartoon, 18 Feb. 1865.

46. Brooks, "Essence," 4 Mar. 1865, 85; 25 Mar. 1865, 716; and 1 Apr. 1865, 125; and Tenniel, cartoon, 25 Mar. 1865.

47. Silver diary, 19 Apr. 1865; and Tenniel, cartoon, 29 Apr. 1865.

48. Tenniel, cartoon, 3 Dec. 1864; and Silver diary, 26 Apr. 1865. To Leigh's initial suggestion Taylor had added the damning modification, "riding out of the ashes of Free Press—State Rights etc." (Silver diary, 23 Nov. 1864 and 10 May 1865).

49. Tenniel, cartoon, 6 May 1865, and Taylor, "Abraham Lincoln, Foully Assassinated, April 14, 1865," *Punch*, 6 May 1865, 182.

50. Randall and Donald, *Civil War and Reconstruction*, 307, for Lincoln's seizure of wartime powers; Tenniel, cartoons, 8 Aug. 1863, 24 Oct. 1863, and 3 Dec. 1864, and for his treatment of other heads of state, 4 Oct. 1862 and 13 Aug. 1864. Jonathan appears in six cartoons in 1861, seven in 1862, two in 1863, and one in 1864, whereas the Lincoln images increase from one in 1861 to eight in 1862, decreasing only slightly afterward.

51. "Town Talk," 31 Dec. 1864, 152; Morgan, cartoons, 9 May 1863, 7 Nov. 1863, 5 Dec. 1863, and 10 Sept. 1864; and F. Wilfred Lawson, cartoon, 3 Dec. 1864, *Fun*.

52. Weitenkampf, "Sir John Tenniel—Cartoonist," 794; "Abraham Lincoln in Caricature," *Cartoons Magazine* 7 (Feb. 1915): 258; and Maurer, "'Punch' on Civil War," 19, 20.

53. Harper, *Lincoln and the Press*, 117; Randall and Donald, *Civil War and Reconstruction*, 457; "Our Presidential Merryman," 2 Mar. 1861; "Columbia Confronts the President," 3 Jan. 1863; and "Manager Lincoln," 31 Jan. 1863, cartoons, *Harper's Weekly*; and examples in Rufus Wilson, *Lincoln in Caricature*.

54. Zeke, "The Grave of the Union, or Major Jack Downing's Dream," cartoon, Sept. 1864, in Rufus Wilson, *Lincoln in Caricature*, 277, pl. 138; Thompson, "Pictorial Propaganda," 31, which describes a cartoon of Lincoln with a black lover; and "The Commander-in-Chief Conciliates the Soldiers' Vote on the Battlefield," cartoon, Oct. 1864, in Wilson, p. 293, pl. 146.

55. "Serenade to Lincoln," 18 Oct. 1862, 158; and "Britisher to Beecher," 31 Oct. 1863, 184, *Punch*. Silver's diary, 3 May 1865, comments on *Punch*'s anti-Lincoln biases: "Our principle mistrust in Lincoln arose from his saying he would throw over the slave question if he thereby could maintain the Union: And then afterwards declaring it was Slavery alone that caused the War and alone could finish it. But he was an honest man."

56. Tenniel, cartoon, 10 Oct. 1863, and the accompanying poem "Ulysses," 148.

57. William Newman, "Lincoln Triumphs in Act to Amend the Constitution," *Budget of Fun*, Feb. 1865, in Rufus Wilson, *Lincoln in Caricature*, 317, pl. 158; and Brooks, quoted in Maurer, "'Punch' on Civil War," 27.

58. Tenniel, cartoon, 9 May 1863.

Index

Illustration Credits